Foundations of Logic

Completeness, Incompleteness, Computability

Dag Westerståhl

CSLI
PUBLICATIONS
Center for the Study of
Language and Information
Stanford, California

Center for the Study of Language and Information
Leland Stanford Junior University
Printed in the United States
27 26 25 24 23 1 2 3 4 5

Names: Westerståhl, Dag, 1946– author.

Title: Foundations of logic: completeness, incompleteness, computability / by Dag Westerståhl.

Description: Beijing: CSLI Publications & Tsinghua University, [2023] | Includes bibliographical references and index. | Summary: "This book covers completeness of first-order logic, some model theory, Gödel's incompleteness theorems and related results, and a smattering of computability theory. The text is self-contained and provides full proofs of the main facts. Ideally, the reader of this work has already taken at least one introductory logic course; however, everything needed to understand the syntax and semantics of first-order logic is presented herein. Students from philosophy, linguistics, computer science, physics, and other related subjects will find this work useful and enlightening" — Provided by publisher.

Identifiers: LCCN 2022026704 (print) | LCCN 2022026705 (ebook) | ISBN 9781684000005 (paperback; acid-free paper) | ISBN 9781684000784 (ebook)

Subjects: LCSH: First-order logic—Textbooks. | AMS: Mathematical logic and foundations — Instructional exposition (textbooks, tutorial papers, etc.). | Mathematical logic and foundations — General logic — Classical first-order logic. | Mathematical logic and foundations — General logic — Other applications of logic.

Classification: LCC BC128 .W47 2022 (print) | LCC BC128 (ebook) | DDC 160—dc23/eng/20220720

LC record available at https://lccn.loc.gov/2022026704
LC ebook record available at https://lccn.loc.gov/2022026705

CIP

∞ The acid-free paper used in this book meets the minimum requirements of the American National Standard for Information Sciences—Permanence of Paper for Printed Library Materials, ANSI Z39.48-1984.

CSLI Publications is located on the campus of Stanford University.

Visit our web site at
`http://cslipublications.stanford.edu/`
for comments on this and other titles, as well as for changes and corrections by the author and publisher.

Contents

Foreword

Since its birth in the 19th century, modern logic has evolved into a rich and wide-ranging discipline. Its themes, methods and insights have made contact with a range of fields today, including mathematics, philosophy, computer science, linguistics, and even the cognitive and behavioral sciences. But in all this outreach, there is a classical mathematical core, based on the great discoveries of the 1930s by Gödel, Turing, and others, which is indispensable to any in-depth understanding of the field. This book presents the fundamental results from that period to a student audience, in a modern setting, and including important insights that have been added over time.

The course on which the book is based has been taught and honed over years of teaching at Tsinghua University, as a part of a broader undergraduate honor's curriculum. The latter also includes a first introduction to logic, language and philosophy, a course in modal logics with their philosophical and linguistic applications, and a course in logic, computation and games reaching out to computer science, mathematics and game theory. Textbooks for all four courses are in the making, and together they will present a broad-range picture of logic today based on the proven methods of the field. All books in this series will appear in both English and Chinese versions.

Johan van Benthem
Professor of Philosophy, Stanford University
Founding director, Institute for Logic, Language & Computation (ILLC), Amsterdam.
First chair and honorary member, European Association for Logic, Language and Information

Fenrong Liu
Changjiang Distinguished Professor
Tsinghua University, Beijing, 100084
Amsterdam-China Logic Chair, ILLC, University of Amsterdam

Preface

This book derives from lecture notes for logic courses I have taught in recent years at Stockholm University and Tsinghua University in Beijing. Since there never is a textbook that covers exactly what you would like it to cover, or in exactly the way you think is the right way, the temptation to write your own book is strong. Thanks to the encouragment of Fenrong Liu at the Tsinghua Philosophy Department, and of my three co-holders of the Jin Yuelin Chair in Logic—Johan van Benthem, Jerry Seligman, and Martin Stokhof—I yielded to that temptation.

The book treats completeness of first-order logic, some model theory, Gödel's incompleteness theorems and related results, and a smattering of computability theory. Inevitably, it overlaps with many other textbooks, but its choice of topics doesn't exactly coincide with any of them. One ambition has been to make the text self-contained, and to provide full proofs of the main facts. With a few exceptions, I hope this goal is attained, although some details are relegated to exercises.

Another goal has been to make the text readable to a wide variety of students. Ideally, the reader has already taken an introductory logic course; however, everything needed about the syntax and semantics of first-order logic is presented in Part I. The main prerequisite is a willingness to engage in exact reasoning, where claims are not just made plausible but *proved* to follow from precise definitions by standard methods, such as mathematical induction. (The technical terminology and the methods used are presented in the Appendix.) Some readers may already have experience with this kind if reasoning, others will perhaps acquire it as they read on. In my experience, not only mathematics students but also students from philosophy, linguistics, computer science, physics, and other subjects satisfy the prerequisite, and the book is intended for all of them.

As a result, the text is somewhat long, but in can be read and taught in several ways. A course covering the whole book from beginning to end would require at least a full semester, but selections for shorter courses are easily made. For example, a course on FOL, the completeness theorem and its consequences would use Parts I and II. Focusing on incompleteness instead one might replace most of Part II with Part III, but here again there are various choices. The background, content, and proof ideas for the incompleteness theorems, and an overview of what is needed in order to implement those ideas, are given in Chapter 7. One can then go to Chapter 12 for full statements and proofs, referring back to the intervening chapters (primitive recursive functions, arithmetization, etc.) to the extent desired. Similarly, to cover undecidability, a quick perusal of Chapter 13.1 followed by Chapter 14.1 – 14.3 would suffice. The final Chapter 15 on recursively enumerable sets is in one sense free-standing, but on the other hand, by framing the incompleteness phenomena in an abstract computational setting, it provides an illuminating perspective on them, and thus an appropriate ending of the book.

Chapter sections that digress from the main flow, or contain technical details that may be skipped, are marked with an *. There are numerous exercises: some serve as practice for the student and could be used as homework, others significantly extend the text. Somewhat harder exercises are marked with *. Many have hints; the * usually applies to the problem without the hints.

In presenting basic material from logic, it is impossible not to be influenced by other similar textbooks. I am particularly indebted to G. S. Boolos, Burgess, and Jeffrey 2007, and have found Franzén 2004 and Smith 2007 very helpful. Occasionally I have relied on classics such as Rogers 1967, Shoenfield 1967, and advanced texts like Lindström 2003, G. Boolos 1993, Odifreddi 1999, Soare 2016, Hájek and Pudlák 1993, and Smoryński 1991.

Several TAs, inquisitive students, and colleagues have helped shape this book, discovered errors, and improved the presentation in various ways. I am most grateful to all of them, and in particular to Sama Agahi, Qian Chen, Huanfang Dong, Sebastian Enqvist, Eric Johannesson, Dazhu Li, Lei Li, Anders Lundstedt, Jialiang Yan, and Tianwei Zhang. Special thanks go to Johan van Benthem and Larry Moss, who offered excellent advice and suggestions, and to Lingyuan Ye, who read the final manuscript very carefully, spotting errors of various kinds and offering suggestions. I have tried to follow most of the suggestions I got, in ways for which I am of course solely responsible. Last but not least, I thank Fenrong Liu, who is the prime mover behind the whole project.

Stockholm, May 2023
Dag Westerståhl

1 Introduction

This book is about properties of first-order logic (FOL)—also called predicate logic—and of theories expressible in it. There is by now a vast number of logical languages, with various uses, but it is fair to say that FOL (sometimes only the propositional part) forms the basis of almost all of them. That is one reason to study it. Another is that its properties are particularly nice, and not shared by more expressive formalisms. Still, the first-order language can express standard set theory, and in this way practically all of mathematics can be developed in it. Familiarity with FOL and first-order theories is basic for anyone who wants to study logic beyond an introductory course.

1.1. Completeness

We start with completeness. This is a property of *inference systems* for the first-order language—two such systems are presented in some detail. Such a system is *complete* if, whenever a conclusion follows logically from certain premises, that conclusion can be *derived* from the premises by the rules of the system. This entails that every fact about 'what follows from what' (expressed in FOL) can in principle be *known*, since there is a finite configuration of sentences constituting a *proof* of the conclusion. Moreover, it can be mechanically checked (e.g. by a computer) that this configuration has the desired properties. The intuitive, semantic, notion of logical consequence—as necessary truth preservation—says nothing about proofs, so the completeness theorem, first proved by the Austrian logician Kurt Gödel in his doctoral thesis in 1930, is an important and characteristic fact about FOL.

Furthermore, this result, and the methods developed to prove it, turn out to provide extremely fruitful tools for logic. One immediate consequence is the so-called *compactness theorem*, a recipe for proving the existence of models with various properties. Together with the Löwenheim-Skolem Theorem, also stemming from the completeness proof, it forms the basis of the branch of mathematical logic called *model theory*; we give a glimpse in Chapter 6. But the technique for proving completeness that we present (Chapters 4 and 5), using maximal consistent sets of sentences, is now a staple ware in all branches of modern logic.

1.2. Incompleteness

One year later, in 1931, Gödel upset the world of logic with two new theorems, the first and second Incompleteness Theorems. Incompleteness in this sense concerns not the logic itself, but *theories* expressed in a formal language such as FOL. Typical examples are number theory and set theory. Consider well-formed sentences in a basic arithmetical language: each such sentence is either *true* or *false*. For example, Goldbach's Conjecture, that every even number bigger than 2 is the sum of two prime numbers, is readily expressed by a first-order sentence. If some large even number happens not to be the sum of two primes, that sentence is simply false. Otherwise it is true. At present we don't know which: it is an open mathematical question.

Now, the first incompleteness theorem says that in any such theory T, if it is consistent (free from contradiction) and contains a minimum of arithmetic, there will always exist *true but unprovable* sentences. Indeed, Gödel gave an explicit recipe for *constructing* a true sentence such that neither it nor its negation is provable in T. Furthermore, that sentence turns out to be equivalent in T to another sentence which in a precise sense expresses the claim that T is consistent, i.e. that no contradictions are derivable. It follows that the consistency of T is not provable in T itself: this is the second incompleteness theorem.

It should come as no surprise that these results have potentially vast ramifications. An age-old idea in mathematics has been that all mathematical questions are in principle answerable, and thus that all mathematical truths are in principle provable. As one of the most famous mathematicians of the early 20th century, David Hilbert, said in his retirement address in 1930: In mathematics, there is no *ignorabimus*: "We must know. We shall know." But if knowing, say, number-theoretic truths means proving them in a fixed theory about numbers, Gödel's first theorem shows that this is an impossible dream. Moreover, for a theory to have any use, it must at a minimum be consistent. But if we are not sure about that—indeed, some proposed theories have turned out to be inconsistent, and had to be abandoned—the second incompleteness theorem appears to severely restrict our possibilities of attaining this knowledge.

We will present the background in logic and mathematics against which Gödel's two theorems appeared, and explain why they had such a profound impact. Again, not only the results themselves, but the methods used to prove them, have become cornerstones of modern logic. For example, as Alfred Tarski observed, it follows almost immediately from the diagonalization technique used in Gödel's proof that *truth is not definable*—this would lead to paradox—in this kind of theories. We shall discuss the role of the incompleteness theorems in the philosophy of logic and mathematics, but our main focus is on their proofs. Amazingly, the idea behind the construction of the true but unprovable sentence, although ingenious, is quite easy to explain. Carrying through the details requires some work. But this work is rewarding in itself, and yields tools and techniques that can be used in a variety of contexts. Part III lays out the road to incompleteness, from beginning to end.

1.3. Computability

A byproduct of the discovery of incompleteness was an effort to find a a precise notion of a *computable* function, or a *decidable* problem. Roughly, this means that there is a mechanical or effective procedure, an algorithm given in advance by a finite description, which calculates the function value for each argument, or answers each query about the problem. Gödel had assumed, for the theories to which his result applied, that the problem of *recognizing the axioms* was primitive recursive, which means that the corresponding (characteristic) function is computable in a particularly simple way (see Chapter 8). But certain intuitively computable functions were known not to be primitive recursive, so for maximum generality in the incompleteness theorems one would need a precise notion of computability.

Furthermore, there was the more intriguing problem of *recognizing the theorems* of a theory. Even if the property of being an axiom of a theory T, and therefore the property of being a *proof* in T, is decidable, deciding if *there exists* a proof, or not, of any given sentence seems much harder. There are infinitely many proofs, but one can (in principle) do a systematic search. If a proof of the sentence in question does exist, it will eventually be found, but if it doesn't, how can the search terminate? Indeed, one might suspect that in many cases there is no effective method to verify theoremhood. But to even formulate this conjecture, one needs a precise notion of computability.

Many scholars worked on this issue in the early 1930s, but it was the definition suggested by the British mathematician Alan Turing that most directly formalized from first principles an intuitive notion of computability, in terms of what was soon called *Turing machines*. Amazingly, all known intuitively computable functions turned out to be Turing computable. Moreover, several other proposed definitions of the class of computable functions, based on seemingly very different ideas, all turned out to yield exactly the class of Turing computable functions. This soon led to a general acceptance of the *Church-Turing*

Thesis, that the intuitive idea of computability is *exactly* captured by the notion of Turing computability (or any of the other equivalent definitions).

The most remarkable aspect of this development was the availability, for the first time in history, of a mathematically precise notion of an *unsolvable* problem, or an *undecidable* theory. It soon became clear that all theories to which the incompleteness theorems apply are undecidable (i.e. the problem of recognizing their theorems is undecidable). And as was shown by Alonzo Church and Turing, even FOL is undecidable: there is no effective method to decide if a sentence follows logically or not from other given sentences, or if it is logically true. In other words, it is not only the case that no one has been able to come up with such a method: one can prove that no such method exists!

These facts are dealt with in Part IV. We present Turing machines as well as another useful characterization of computability, in terms of so-called recursive (or μ-recursive) functions, and show that they are equivalent. Then we establish the undecidability facts just mentioned, as well as other undecidable problems, and we also take the opportunity to significantly generalize the incompleteness theorems.

But the appearance of undecidable theories is just the tip of a large iceberg. On the one hand, Turing's work can be seen to lay the foundations of modern computer science (long before there were any modern computers). Here, not just decidability but *tractability* is a desirable feature, i.e. that the best algorithm for the problem uses a 'reasonable' amount of time (or space). The theory of *computational complexity*, although it has strong ties to logic, is not dealt with in this book. But on the other hand, even unsolvable problems can be classified according how difficult their decision problem is. For example, although the set of (code numbers of) theorems is often not decidable, it is *semi-decidable* in the sense just indicated: *positive* answers to the query "Is φ a theorem of T?" can be found effectively.

In fact, semi-decidable (or recursively enumerable) sets have been intensely studied in what used to be called *recursion theory*, but now is most often referred to as *computability theory* (although a more appropriate name would perhaps be 'non-computability theory'). We end the book with a brief introduction to this fascinating area of logic, which also serves to put the incompleteness phenomena in a broader computational perspective.

1.4. Plan

Here is an overview of the following chapters. Part I presents the syntax and semantics of first-order logic (FOL) in Chapter 2, and two inference systems, a natural deduction system and a Hilbert style system, in Chapter 3. Ideally, the reader is already somewhat familiar with FOL—although not strictly necessary, this will certainly facilitate reading these chapters, which serve to lay down notation and terminology, and to make the book self-contained.

Part II treats completeness with the machinery of maximal consistent sets, first in the simplest case of propositional logic (Chapter 4) and then the slightly more involved case of FOL (Chapter 5). Chapter 6 builds on these tools to introduce the reader to the model-theoretic perspective on logic, with the basic relations of isomorphism and elementary equivalence between models. In particular, the notion of expressive power of a logic is discussed, and the Compactness and Löwenheim-Skolem Theorems are proved and given some first applications. We outline how the addition of generalized quantifiers to FOL can increase expressive power, and how such quantifiers are also relevant to the semantics of natural languages. The chapter ends with stating the Ehrenfeucht-Fraïssé characterization of elementary equivalence, and sketching the proof of Lindström's theorem, showing that Compactness and Löwenheim-Skolem characterize FOL.

Part III on incompleteness starts with a rather comprehensive overview (Chapter 7), which gives the background to Gödel's theorems and maps out the idea of their proofs, as well as what needs to be done to implement these ideas. The reader who wishes to avoid nitty-gritty details, at least on a first reading, can then go directly to Chapter 12, where the actual proofs of the incompleteness theorems and many other related results are given. In between, we present primitive recursive functions and relations (Chapter 8), and the first-order theory of arithmetic *PA* (Peano Arithmetic, Chapter 9). Chapter 10 shows that all primitive recursive functions and relations are representable (in a precise sense) in *PA*, and Chapter 11 presents a coding, or *Gödel numbering*, of syntactic objects such as terms, formulas, and proofs, and goes on to show that the corresponding number-theoretic relations are all primitive recursive. The stage is now set to reap the fruits of all this labor in Chapter 12, which ends with a general discussion of the import of the incompleteness phenomena.

In Part IV, finally, Chapter 13 introduces Turing machines and (partial) recursive functions, and shows that the latter coincide with the Turing computable functions. Specifically, Kleene's Normal Form Theorem is proved here, and used repeatedly from then on. The first part of the chapter presents the ideas, which are simple and easy to understand, and the second part fills in details. Chapter 14 starts by establishing the undecidability of the theories earlier shown to be incomplete, as well as that of FOL. We then present Robinson Arithmetic, a theory very much weaker than *PA* which, remarkably, still has the property (as we proceed to show) that all recursive functions are representable in it, indeed by formulas of a particularly simple kind (Σ_1 formulas). This motivates a brief survey of weak systems of arithmetic, an active area of research in logic. The chapter ends by showing how diagonalization immediately yields the undecidability of the halting problem, i.e. the problem of deciding, for any Turing machine and any input, whether the machine halts or not in a finite number of steps when started on that input.

The final Chapter 15 presents the semi-decidable or recursively enumerable sets under several different guises, all shown to be equivalent (eventually we obtain 10 different characterizations). As indicated above, the chapter presents a quick overview of basic computability theory, including the arithmetical hierarchy, the so-called enumeration, s-m-n, and fixed point theorems, m-reducibility, and creative and simple sets. At the end we close the circle by showing how these computational notions and results provide a new perspective on the incompleteness phenomena in logic.

The Appendix (Chapter 16) reviews basic facts about sets, relations, and functions that are used throughout the book. In particular, it presents ordered sets, equivalence relations and partitions, countable and uncountable sets, and the method of proof by mathematical induction.

All chapters have exercises, and some of these, in particular the exercises to Chapters 2, 6, 12, 14, and 15, significantly extend the treatment in the text.

Part I

Background

2 First-order logic

This chapter presents syntax and semantics for classical first-order logic.[1] The presentation is somewhat compact, since the reader is supposed to have encountered (some version of) this formalism before. But everything needed is here—in the text or occasionally in the exercises—and the notation, terminology, and basic facts about first-order logic will be used throughout the book. We start with propositional logic, but first a methodological digression.

2.1. Object language and metalanguage

Reasoning, arguing, proving, expressing and communicating thoughts are at the center of logic's domain of study. These activities, as well as the logical study of them, take place in a *language*. In the 1930s, Alfred Tarski coined the useful terms *object language* and *metalanguage*. The object language is the language studied, the language in which the reasoning, arguing, etc. takes place. It could be a natural language like English or Chinese, or a formal language designed by us. The metalanguage is the language in which the study is carried out, the language in which we *talk about* the object language.

One could argue that natural languages are their own metalanguages: surely we can talk *about* English *in* English! But Tarski pointed out—and this was the point of his distinction—that if the language contains the word "true", it doesn't take much to formulate the well-known Liar Paradox in it: a sufficiently rich language containing its own metalanguage becomes contradictory. As we will see later, the Liar Paradox plays a surprisingly large role in the foundations of logic. The point for now is just that in logic, the object/metalanguage distinction makes good sense and is usually crystal clear.

[1] The label "classical" is often used to distinguish classical from *intuitionistic* logic, which has the same syntax but a different semantics, and where some classical validities, such as the Law of Excluded Middle, do not hold. Unless otherwise stated, we deal with classical logic in this book. The label "first-order" signifies that the quantifiers range over individuals of the domain, not, for example, also over relations on the domain, as in second-order logic.

For example, in propositional logic, the object language consists of an exactly specified set of sentences, such as

$$p_0, \quad (\neg p_1 \vee p_2), \quad (p_1 \rightarrow (p_3 \rightarrow p_1)), \ldots$$

There is a notion *true in an interpretation* for these sentences, but this notion has no correspondent in the object language. Using it, other fundamental concepts like *logical truth* and *logical consequence* are defined, all belonging to the metalanguage but not the object language. Thus,

$$(p_1 \rightarrow (p_3 \rightarrow p_1))$$

is an object language sentence, but

$$\models (p_1 \rightarrow (p_3 \rightarrow p_1))$$

or, put differently,

(1) $(p_1 \rightarrow (p_3 \rightarrow p_1))$ is a logical truth.

is a (true) claim in the metalanguage. The metalanguage here seems to be English equipped with some technical terms. Indeed, this is the informal metalanguage we will be using.

Sometimes one wants to be more specific about the *metatheory*, i.e. the theory in which metalinguistic claims can be *proved*. This theory is often taken to be some version of set theory. Then our informal metalanguage has to be translated into the language of set theory. Most of the time, however, we can stay informal. But we will at times reflect on the methods used to prove metalinguistic claims, in particular the method of mathematical induction. And later on we will see that, via a *coding of syntax*, the arithmetical theory *PA* can be seen as a metatheory, in which many—though not all—true claims about the relevant object language can be proved.

Strictly speaking, a metalanguage needs *names* of object language expressions to be able to talk about them. A standard method is to use quotation marks. We should then, instead of (1), write

"$(p_1 \rightarrow (p_3 \rightarrow p_1))$" is a logical truth.

But this gets awkward after a while. Instead, we use a general *convention* to the effect that object language expressions, and more generally, all formal expressions, can be used as *names of themselves*. This is how we understand (1) and similar claims in what follows.

2.2. Propositional logic (PL)

2.2.1. PL syntax

The syntax of a language specifies its *well-formed expressions*. In a natural language like English, well-formed expressions are usually grouped into *categories*, such as proper names, nouns, noun phrases, intransitive and transitive verbs, adjectives, prepositions, declarative sentences, questions, etc. The language of propositional logic can make do with only one syntactic category: *sentences* or *formulas*.[2] And in contrast with natural languages, we can give a simple and exact definition of the set of well-formed formulas—hardly surprising, since formal languages but not natural languages are designed by us.

The well-formed expressions of the PL language are certain *finite strings of symbols*. The symbols are as follows:[3]

(2) a. sentential letters: $p_0, p_1, p_2, \ldots$
 b. connectives: $\neg,\ \wedge,\ \vee,\ \rightarrow,\ \leftrightarrow$
 c. parentheses: $(\,,\,)$

Here is $\neg$ is a *unary* connective, and the others are *binary*. Some remarks:

- Clause (2b) lists five *primitive* connectives. Sometimes it is convenient to have a smaller set of primitives, and treat the others as *defined*. For example, if $\neg$ and $\vee$ are taken as primitives, we treat $\wedge$ and $\rightarrow$ as defined, in the sense that a formula $\varphi \rightarrow \psi$ is taken as an *abbreviation* of $\neg\varphi \vee \psi$, and $\varphi \wedge \psi$ as an abbreviation of $\neg(\neg\varphi \vee \neg\psi)$, and $\varphi \leftrightarrow \psi$ as an abbreviation of $(\varphi \rightarrow \psi) \wedge (\psi \rightarrow \varphi)$. Other common choices of primitive connectives are $\neg$ and $\rightarrow$, or $\neg$ and $\wedge$. For more on this matter, see Exercise 2.4.7.

- Occasionally we will use $\bot$ (*falsum*) as a primitive logical sentence symbol, not a sentence letter but a 0-ary connective, standing for a contradiction (a logically false sentence). Then one can take $\bot$ and $\rightarrow$ as the only primitive connectives, and treat $\neg\varphi$ as an abbreviation of $\varphi \rightarrow \bot$.[4]

We just used a convention that will be followed in the rest of the book: *metavariables* for various items that we talk about. In particular, we used φ and ψ to stand for arbitrary formulas. Officially:

---

[2]Alternatively, we could count connectives as expressions too. Then we would have, in addition to the category *formula*, the category *n-ary connective*, for $n \geqslant 0$ (or just for $n = 0, 1, 2$).

[3]Some texts use variants of these symbols, for example, $\sim$ instead of $\neg$, & instead of $\wedge$, $\supset$ instead of $\rightarrow$, or $\equiv$ instead of $\leftrightarrow$.

[4]The label "connective" doesn't fit $\bot$, or $\neg$ for that matter, since these symbols don't connect things. But this is established terminology.

(3) a. $\varphi, \psi, \chi, \theta$ are metavariables for *formulas*.
b. p, q, r are metavariables for *sentential letters*.
c. Γ, Δ, Σ are metavariables for *sets of formulas*.

We also use these same symbols with primes or indices as metavariables. Now we can define the set of formulas in propositional logic. First:

Definition 2.2.1 (atomic formulas)
An *atomic formula* is either a sentential letter or $\bot$, if the latter is used.

Then we define:

Definition 2.2.2 (formulas in propositional logic)

(i) Atomic formulas are *formulas*.

(ii) If φ and ψ are *formulas*, then $\neg\varphi$, $(\varphi \wedge \psi)$, $(\varphi \vee \psi)$, $(\varphi \rightarrow \psi)$, and $(\varphi \leftrightarrow \psi)$ are also *formulas*.

(iii) Nothing is a *formula* except the expressions obtained by (repeated) application of (i) and (ii).

Note the use of metavariables. (ii) is a compact way of saying the following, for example in the case of conjunctions: "If φ and ψ are formulas, then the string of symbols obtained by first writing a left parenthesis, then φ, then the symbol $\wedge$, then ψ, and then a right parenthesis, is a formula". This can of course also be said in plain English, without metavariables, but the formulation becomes more cumbersome.

In (2a), a (countably) infinite number of sentential letters are available. Sometimes it is convenient to indicate precisely which such letters are used. So if L is any non-empty set of sentential letters, we can define the set of *L-formulas* just as in Definitions 2.2.1 and 2.2.2, except that "formula" is replaced by "L-formula".

Definition 2.2.2 is an exact specification of which strings of symbols are (L)-formulas. It is an *inductive* (or *recursive*) definition, building up the well-formed strings from below. Clause (iii) says that the only way to build such strings is by using (i) and (ii). Clauses like this are usually taken for granted, and in what follows we will leave them out. Indeed, definitions like the combination of 2.2.1 and 2.2.2 are often written in a more compact form (the so-called Backus-Naur Form, or BNF):

Definition 2.2.3 (formulas in propositional logic, version 2)
$\varphi := p \mid \neg\varphi \mid (\varphi \wedge \varphi) \mid (\varphi \vee \varphi) \mid (\varphi \rightarrow \varphi) \mid (\varphi \leftrightarrow \varphi)$

Here $:=$ stands for 'equal by definition to'.

The fact that the set of formulas is inductively defined is crucial for verifying facts that hold for *all* formulas. There are infinitely many formulas, even infinitely many L-formulas when L has just one element, say, $L = \{p_0\}$. So one cannot prove general facts about formulas by looking at them one by one. Instead, one uses *induction over formulas*. This technique is used again and again in logic. Here is an informal statement; numerous applications will follow.

Suppose you want to prove that all formulas have a certain property P. Then it is enough to prove the following:

- (*base step*) Atomic formulas have property P.
- (*induction step*) If φ and ψ have property P (*induction hypothesis*), then $\neg\varphi$, $(\varphi \wedge \psi)$, $(\varphi \vee \psi)$, $(\varphi \rightarrow \psi)$, and $(\varphi \leftrightarrow \psi)$ also have property P.

In the induction step, we need to prove *five* things, not infinitely many! But it should be clear that if we manage to prove both the base step and the induction step, we can conclude that *every* formula has property P. Here is a simple example:

Example 2.2.4
Suppose we want to verify the following claim:

(4) Every formula has an even number of parentheses.

This may look trivial, but can we really *know* that in very long formulas, with perhaps millions of propositional letters and connectives, and hence millions of parentheses, there is always an even number of them? Yes—we can argue by induction:

(base step) Atomic formulas have *no* parentheses, and 0 is an even number.

(ind. step) Suppose that φ and ψ each has an even number of parentheses, say that φ has $2k$ parentheses and ψ has $2n$ parentheses. This is the induction hypothesis. Then $\neg\varphi$ also has $2k$ parentheses, an even number. And $(\varphi \wedge \psi)$, $(\varphi \vee \psi)$, $(\varphi \rightarrow \psi)$, and $(\varphi \leftrightarrow \psi)$ each has $2k + 2n + 2 = 2(k + n + 1)$ parentheses, which is also an even number.

So (4) follows. □

Parentheses play an important role in (our) logical syntax: without them we would obtain *ambiguous* formulas, like

(5) $\quad p \vee q \wedge r$

Structural ambiguity of this kind occurs in natural languages, but logical languages are *designed* to be non-ambiguous. Instead of (5), we have, according to Definition 2.2.2, two distinct formulas in propositional logic:

(6) $\quad ((p \vee q) \wedge r) \quad$ and $\quad (p \vee (q \wedge r))$

The two formulas are not only syntactically distinct, they also have distinct meanings (see the next section).[5]

However, always writing all parentheses is cumbersome. So we will employ a couple of common *parentheses conventions*, which increase readability. First, we almost always *leave out the outermost parentheses*—these are not needed for disambiguation anyway. So instead of (6) we write

(7) $\quad (p \vee q) \wedge r \quad$ and $\quad p \vee (q \wedge r)$

A second convention that we sometimes use is that $\wedge$ and $\vee$ *bind stronger than* $\rightarrow$ (and $\leftrightarrow$).[6] This means that we can write, for example,

$$\varphi_1 \wedge \psi_1 \rightarrow \varphi_2 \vee \psi_2$$

instead of

$$(\varphi_1 \wedge \psi_1) \rightarrow (\varphi_2 \vee \psi_2)$$

But observe that these are just writing conventions. Officially, formulas have parentheses according to Definition 2.2.2 (or 2.2.3).

2.2.2. PL semantics

A semantics for a logical language gives *truth conditions* for its sentences, i.e. the conditions under which a sentence is true or false. In PL, the truth value of a sentence, or a formula (which in this case is the same thing), depends on the truth values of the sentential letters occurring in it. There are two *truth values*: 1 (True) and 0 (False). An assignment of truth values to the sentential letters is called an

[5]There is a non-ambiguous PL notation without parentheses, so-called *Polish notation*, in which you write all connectives *before* the arguments. So $(p \vee q)$ becomes $\vee pq$, and $(p \rightarrow (q \vee \neg r))$ becomes $\rightarrow p \vee q \neg r$. It was popular among some logicians in the early 20th century, but is now rarely used.

[6]Compare the corresponding convention for plus (+) and times $(\cdot)$ in elementary arithmetic. We write $3 \cdot 5 + 7 \cdot 2$ to mean $(3 \cdot 5) + (7 \cdot 2)$, i.e. 29, and not $3 \cdot (5 + 7) \cdot 2$ (which would be 72). That is, $\cdot$ binds stronger than +.

interpretation, or a *valuation*. Thus, an interpretation is a function V from $\{p_0, p_1, p_2, \ldots\}$ to $\{0, 1\}$. More generally, if L is a set of sentential letters, and *L-interpretation* is a function from L to $\{0, 1\}$.

Given a valuation V, the truth value of a complex sentence is usually calculated via *truth tables* for the connectives. Rather than writing down these tables explicitly, we express them in the form of an inductive *truth definition*, following Definition 2.2.2. That is, we define the relation

$$V \models \varphi,$$

which is read

$$\varphi \text{ is true in } V,$$

for any formula φ and any interpretation V, as follows:[7]

Definition 2.2.5 (truth definition for PL)

(i) $V \models p$ iff $V(p) = 1$, for any sentence letter $p \in L$

(ii) $V \models \neg\varphi$ iff $V \not\models \varphi$ (i.e. not $V \models \varphi$)

(iii) $V \models (\varphi \wedge \psi)$ iff $V \models \varphi$ and $V \models \psi$

(iv) $V \models (\varphi \vee \psi)$ iff $V \models \varphi$ or $V \models \psi$ (or both)

(v) $V \models (\varphi \rightarrow \psi)$ iff $V \not\models \varphi$ or $V \models \psi$

(vi) $V \models (\varphi \leftrightarrow \psi)$ iff either $V \models \varphi$ and $V \models \psi$, or $V \not\models \varphi$ and $V \not\models \psi$

It should be clear that each of the clauses (ii) – (vi) could be expressed as a truth table for the corresponding connective. For example, clause (v) expresses the table for implication:

φ	ψ	$\varphi \rightarrow \psi$
1	1	1
1	0	0
0	1	1
0	0	1

According to this table, an implication is false iff the antecedent is true and the consequent false. In other words, it is true iff either the antecedent is false (the last two rows) or the consequent is true (the first row), which is what clause (v) says. Similarly, an equivalence $\varphi \leftrightarrow \psi$ is true iff φ and ψ have the same truth value, as clause (vi) states.

[7] "Iff" abbreviates "if and only if". Sometimes, instead of "A iff B", we write $A \Leftrightarrow B$, and similarly $A \Rightarrow B$ for "A implies B". So $\Rightarrow$ and $\Leftrightarrow$ are symbols in our informal metalanguage, not to be confused with $\rightarrow$ and $\leftrightarrow$ in the logical object language.

Another way to view Definition 2.2.5 is that it *extends* the valuation V from sentence letters to all formulas: if we stipulate

(8) $V(\varphi) = 1$ iff $V \models \varphi$

we see how the definition inductively assigns a (truth) value $V(\varphi)$ to every formula φ.

In each formula, only a finite number of sentence letters occur. It is intuitively clear that the truth value of this formula only depends on what the interpretation assigns to these sentence letters. This property is called *locality*: the truth value of a formula is local to the interpretation of the sentence letters in it. The next simple but important lemma formulates this in a precise way.

Lemma 2.2.6 (Locality Lemma for PL)
If V and V' are interpretations that agree on the sentence letters occurring in φ (that is, for all such letters p, $V(p) = V'(p)$), then $V \models \varphi$ iff $V' \models \varphi$.

Proof. We give the proof as another simple illustration of an argument by induction over formulas. In the *base case*, φ is a sentential letter, say, q, and the asssumption is that $V(q) = V'(q)$. Thus, $V(q) = 1$ iff $V'(q) = 1$, which, by the truth definition, clause (i), means that $V \models q$ iff $V' \models q$. Now consider the *inductive cases*. Suppose φ is a conjunction $\psi_1 \wedge \psi_2$. The assumption is that V and V' agree on all sentence letters occurring in φ. But then they must agree on all sentence letters occurring in ψ_1, and on all sentence letters occurring in ψ_2. Then the *induction hypothesis* entails that $V \models \psi_1$ iff $V' \models \psi_1$, and $V \models \psi_2$ iff $V' \models \psi_2$. By the truth definition, clause (iii), we have: $V \models \psi_1 \wedge \psi_2$ iff ($V \models \psi_1$ and $V \models \psi_2$) iff ($V' \models \psi_1$ and $V' \models \psi_2$) iff $V' \models \psi_1 \wedge \psi_2$, which is what we wanted to prove in this case. The other inductive cases are similar. □

We have now seen two examples of proofs by *induction over (the complexity of) formulas*; many more will follow. Such arguments can be reduced to ordinary induction over numbers. Let the *degree* of a formula φ be the number of occurrences of connectives (and later quantifiers) in φ. So atomic formulas have degree 0. Suppose you want to prove by induction:

(9) Every formula has property P.

This can be done by proving by induction over n:

(10) For all n, every formula of degree at most n has property P.

For more on mathematical induction, and on proofs by induction in logic, see Appendix 16.6.

2.2.3. Logical consequence

After these preliminaries we can proceed to define logical consequence, logical truth, and other fundamental concepts. Intuitively, the semantic notion of logical consequence is *necessary truth preservation*: the truth of the premises should guarantee the truth of the conclusion. Truth preservation is in itself obviously a good thing: if the conclusion of an argument is the grounds for a decision or an action, we had better have true premises lead to true conclusions. But mere truth is not enough. If the premises and the conclusion just happen to be true, 'by accident', we are not helped by the argument. What we want is that if the premises are true, the conclusion *must* be true.

"Must" is a *modal* notion. But in logic, we cash it out as "under all circumstances". And in propositional logic, circumstances are interpretations. So we define a relation

$$\Gamma \models \varphi$$

which is read "φ is a logical consequence of Γ", for all sentences φ (the *conclusion*) and all sets Γ of sentences (the *premises*), to mean that every interpretation making every premise in Γ true also makes φ true.

Here is the official definition of logical consequence (in a slightly reformulated but equivalent version), and some related notions.

Definition 2.2.7 (logical consequence etc. in PL)

(i) φ is a *logical consequence* of Γ, in symbols,

$$\Gamma \models \varphi$$

if there is *no* interpretation in which all sentences in Γ are true and φ is false.

(ii) φ is *logically true*, or a *tautology*, or *valid*, in symbols,

$$\models \varphi$$

if φ is true in *all* interpretations.

(iii) φ and ψ are *logically equivalent*, in symbols,

$$\varphi \equiv \psi$$

if they are true in the *same* interpretations.

(iv) Γ is *satisfiable* if *there is* an interpretation in which all sentences in Γ are true.

Note that the intuitive explication of logical consequence only refers to truth of sentences in interpretations. It doesn't matter, for example, in which *order* the premises are taken. That is why we are taking a *set* of premises as the first argument of the consequence relation, rather than, say, an ordered sequence of sentences.[8]

Definition 2.2.7(i) allows Γ to be an infinite set of sentences. Does this matter? The answer is No: if $\Gamma \models \varphi$ there is always a finite subset Γ_0 of Γ such that $\Gamma_0 \models \varphi$. But this fact is not trivial: we will obtain it as a consequence of the completeness theorem for propositional logic (Chapter 4).

When Γ is finite, say $\Gamma = \{\varphi_1, \ldots, \varphi_n\}$, we usually write

$$\varphi_1, \ldots, \varphi_n \models \psi$$

instead of $\{\varphi_1, \ldots, \varphi_n\} \models \psi$. Similarly, we often write

$$\Gamma, \varphi \models \psi$$

instead of $\Gamma \cup \{\varphi\} \models \psi$.

Definition 2.2.7(i) also allows $\Gamma = \varnothing$. In this case, the claim that there is no interpretation making all sentences in Γ true and φ false is equivalent to the claim that there is no interpretation making φ false. In other words:

(11) $\varnothing \models \varphi$ iff $\models \varphi$

This shows that logical truth can be defined in terms of logical consequence. Logical consequence in turn can be defined in terms of satisfiability:

(12) $\Gamma \models \varphi$ iff $\Gamma \cup \{\neg\varphi\}$ is not satisfiable.

(12) is rather useful fact, and it is important to be clear about why it is a direct consequence of Definition 2.2.7.

In fact, each of the four logical concepts in that definition can be defined in terms of each of the others (under one condition); see Exercise 2.4.3. Here is how we can express logical equivalence in terms of logic truth:

(13) $\varphi \equiv \psi$ iff $\models \varphi \leftrightarrow \psi$

A number of 'laws' of propositional logic (mostly equivalences and tautologies) are used all the time. Below we list a few of them. The reader should make sure (s)he understands these laws and the reasons why they hold.

---

[8]WARNING: The symbol $\models$ is used in two ways in logic: for truth in an interpretation, and for logical consequence. This is perhaps unfortunate, but established terminology. In practice, no confusion is possible: when an interpretation stands to the left of $\models$, it means truth or satisfaction. When a set of sentences (or just sentences) stands to the left, it means logical consequence.

(14)
a. $\neg(\varphi \wedge \psi) \equiv \neg\varphi \vee \neg\psi$
b. $\neg(\varphi \vee \psi) \equiv \neg\varphi \wedge \neg\psi$ (de Morgan laws)
c. $\varphi \wedge (\psi \wedge \chi) \equiv (\varphi \wedge \psi) \wedge \chi$
d. $\varphi \vee (\psi \vee \chi) \equiv (\varphi \vee \psi) \vee \chi$ (associativity)
e. $\neg\neg\varphi \equiv \varphi$ (double negation)
f. $\varphi \wedge \psi \equiv \psi \wedge \varphi$
g. $\varphi \vee \psi \equiv \psi \vee \varphi$ (commutativity)
h. $\varphi \wedge (\psi \vee \chi) \equiv (\varphi \wedge \psi) \vee (\varphi \wedge \chi)$
i. $\varphi \vee (\psi \wedge \chi) \equiv (\varphi \vee \psi) \wedge (\varphi \vee \chi)$ (distributive laws)
j. $\varphi \equiv \varphi \wedge \varphi \equiv \varphi \vee \varphi$ (idempotency)
k. $\varphi \rightarrow \psi \equiv \neg\varphi \vee \psi$
l. $\varphi \rightarrow \psi \equiv \neg(\varphi \wedge \neg\psi)$
m. $\varphi \leftrightarrow \psi \equiv (\varphi \rightarrow \psi) \wedge (\psi \rightarrow \varphi)$
n. $\varphi \rightarrow \psi \equiv \neg\psi \rightarrow \neg\varphi$
o. $\models \varphi \vee \neg\varphi$ (Law of Excluded Middle)
p. $\models \neg(\varphi \wedge \neg\varphi)$ (Law of Contradiction)
q. $\models \varphi \rightarrow \varphi$
r. $\models \varphi \rightarrow (\psi \rightarrow \varphi)$
s. $\models (\varphi \rightarrow (\psi \rightarrow \chi)) \rightarrow ((\varphi \rightarrow \psi) \rightarrow (\varphi \rightarrow \chi))$

The associativity laws (14c) and (14d) entail that we can drop parentheses in long conjunctions and disjunctions; writing

$$\varphi \wedge \psi \wedge \chi \wedge \theta$$

instead of, for example, $\varphi \wedge (\psi \wedge (\chi \wedge \theta))$. This is a third *parentheses convention* that we will use.[9]

Using the equivalences in (14) one can write formulas of propositional logic in *normal forms* of various kinds. Here is one example (another useful normal form is given in Exercise 2.4.6). A formula φ is said to be in *negation normal form* (nnf) if (a) the only connectives occurring in it are $\neg$, $\wedge$, and $\vee$, and (b) all occurrences of $\neg$ in φ are in front of atomic symbols. We have:

(15) For every formula φ of propositional logic there is a formula ψ in nnf such that $\varphi \equiv \psi$.

Here is a sketch of how to verify this. First, use (14m) and (14k) to eliminate all occurrences of $\leftrightarrow$ and $\rightarrow$ in φ, leaving only $\neg$, $\wedge$, $\vee$. Then move each negation 'inward' as far as possible, by using de Morgan's laws, and eliminating double negations with (14e). The end result will be a formula in nnf, and since every step leads to a logically equivalent formula, the end result is logically equivalent to φ.

[9]Officially, we can take $\varphi_1 \wedge \varphi_2 \wedge \ldots \wedge \varphi_n$ as an abbreviation of $(\varphi_1 \wedge (\varphi_2 \wedge (\ldots \wedge \varphi_n)\ldots))$, and similarly for disjunction.

An example will make clear how the procedure works. In order to write the formula $\neg(p \rightarrow (q \wedge \neg r))$ in nnf, we can perform the following steps:

a. $\neg(p \rightarrow (q \wedge \neg r))$
b. $\neg(\neg p \vee (q \wedge \neg r))$
c. $\neg\neg p \wedge \neg(q \wedge \neg r)$
d. $p \wedge \neg(q \wedge \neg r)$
e. $p \wedge (\neg q \vee \neg\neg r)$
f. $p \wedge (\neg q \vee r)$

In this argument we implicitly used the fact that if you replace in a formula an occurrence of a subformula ψ with a formula ψ' which is logically equivalent to ψ, then the result is equivalent to the original formula. (For the notion of *subformula*, see Exercise 2.4.9.) This intuitively obvious but important fact is used all the time; we formulate it here as an explicit lemma:

Lemma 2.2.8 (replacement lemma for PL)
If φ' is obtained from φ by replacing one or more occurrences of ψ in φ by a formula ψ' such that $\psi \equiv \psi'$, then we have $\varphi \equiv \varphi'$.

Proof. See Exercise 2.4.4. □

2.3. First-order logic (FOL)

The presentation of the first-order language uses the same format as that of the propositional language, even though first-order formulas have a more sophisticated structure.

2.3.1. FOL syntax

The following *symbols* may occur in a first-order language:

(16) a. (individual) variables: $v_0, v_1, v_2, \ldots$
b. (individual) constants: $c_0, c_1, c_2, \ldots$
c. n-ary predicate symbols ($n \geqslant 1$): $P_0^n, P_1^n, P_2^n, \ldots$
d. n-ary function symbols ($n \geqslant 1$): $f_0^n, f_1^n, f_2^n, \ldots$
e. logical constants: $\neg, \wedge, \vee, \rightarrow, \leftrightarrow, \forall, \exists, =$
f. parentheses: (,)

A few remarks are in order:

- The *logical constants* are as before, plus the quantifier symbols $\forall$ and $\exists$, and the identity symbol $=$. This symbol is a special binary (2-ary) predicate symbol. The individual constants, n-ary predicate symbols (except $=$) and function symbols are *non-logical* symbols or constants. Variables and parentheses are neither logical nor non-logical.

- We could have allowed 0-ary predicate symbols, which can be identified with PL sentence letters. Then PL would be a *syntactic fragment* of FOL: every PL-formula would also be a formula in FOL. But there is not much point in doing this. The presence of the propositional connectives among the logical constants in FOL guarantees that propositional logic is 'built into' FOL.

- (16) makes available an infinite number of non-logical constants of each kind, from which we may choose the ones we need on each occasion. The superscript on predicate and function symbols marks their *arity*, i.e. the number of arguments they take (Definitions 2.3.2 and 2.3.4 below).

However, it is cumbersome, and in fact not really necessary, to state the arity explicitly. Instead, we will almost always use metavariables instead, as follows (with possible primes or indices):

(17)
a. a, b, c, d, e stand for *individual constants*.
b. P, Q, R, S stand for *predicate symbols*. So the arity is not shown, but it will always be clear in formulas what the arity is.
c. f, g, h stand for *function symbols*; same comment about the arity.
d. x, y, z, u, v stand for *individual variables*.
e. s, t stand for *terms* (see Definition 2.3.2).

Definition 2.3.1 (vocabularies)
A *vocabulary* is a set of non-logical symbols. We use L, L', etc. for vocabularies.

We can now define the meaningful (well-formed) expressions of FOL. They are of two kinds: terms and formulas, or, more precisely, for each vocabulary L, *L-terms* and *L-formulas*. We begin with the terms.

Definition 2.3.2 (L-terms)

(i) Variables are *L-terms*.

(ii) Individual constants in L are *L-terms*.

(iii) If f is an n-ary function symbol in L, and $t_1, \dots, t_n$ are *L-terms*, then $ft_1 \dots t_n$ is an *L-term*.

An L-term is *open* if it contains at least one variable, otherwise it is *closed*.

This is an inductive definition. But we shall often consider vocabularies that do not contain function symbols. Then the L-terms are just the individual constants in L and the variables.

Some examples of terms:

$$c_2, \ c_{91}, \ v_{17}, \ f_1^3 c_2 v_{223} c_{120}$$

These are actual well-formed terms in the object language. That is, they are L-terms whenever c_2, c_{91}, c_{120}, and f_1^3 belong to L. However, as noted, usually we do not write the actual terms, but use metavariables instead:

$$c, \ d, \ x, \ fcya$$

The fact that f is followed by three terms shows that it stands for a 3-ary function symbol.

Terms are expressions intended to denote individuals. Formulas are intended to make claims that can be true or false (relative to an interpretation). Next, we define *atomic* formulas. In contrast with the case of propositional logic, atomic formulas in FOL have structure: they say that an individual has a property, or that certain individuals stand in a relation to each other.

Definition 2.3.3 (atomic L-formulas)

If P is an n-ary predicate symbol in L and $t_1, \dots, t_n$ are *L-terms*, then $Pt_1 \dots t_n$ is an *atomic L-formula*.

This is an *explicit*, not an inductive, definition. It specifies the exact shape of atomic L-formulas. $Pt_1 \dots t_n$ says, intuitively, that (the individuals denoted by) $t_1, \dots, t_n$ stand in the relation (denoted by) P to each other.

Note that since = is a binary predicate symbol, we should write

$$= t_1 t_2$$

to say that t_1 is equal to t_2. In practice, however, we almost always use *infix* notation:

$$t_1 = t_2$$

Similarly for other binary predicate symbols; we may write: $x < y$, xRy, $x \in y$. Some common function symbols also use infix notation: one writes $x + y$ rather than $+xy$, etc. Furthermore, we usually write

$$t_1 \neq t_2$$

instead of $\neg\, t_1 = t_2$. Finally, we may sometimes write

$$P(t_1, \ldots, t_n) \quad \text{and} \quad f(t_1, \ldots, t_n)$$

with parentheses and commas, instead of $Pt_1 \ldots t_n$ and $ft_1 \ldots t_n$, respectively, whenever this is easier to read. But these are writing conventions, used to increase readability. Officially, atomic formulas are as described in Definition 2.3.3.

With these preparations, we can define (inductively as before) the set of L-formulas.

Definition 2.3.4 (L-formulas)

(i) Atomic L-formulas are *L-formulas*.

(ii) If φ and ψ are L-formulas, then $\neg\varphi$, $(\varphi \wedge \psi)$, $(\varphi \vee \psi)$, $(\varphi \rightarrow \psi)$, and $(\varphi \leftrightarrow \psi)$ are also *L-formulas*.

(iii) If ψ is an *L-formula* and x is a variable, then $\forall x\psi$ and $\exists x\psi$ are also *L-formulas*.

Again, we could write Definitions 2.3.2 and 2.3.4 more compactly:

Definition 2.3.5 (L-terms and L-formulas)

$t \;:=\; c \mid x \mid ft_1 \ldots t_n$

$\varphi \;:=\; Pt_1 \ldots t_n \mid \neg\varphi \mid (\varphi \wedge \varphi) \mid (\varphi \vee \varphi) \mid (\varphi \rightarrow \varphi) \mid (\varphi \leftrightarrow \varphi) \mid \forall x\varphi \mid \exists x\varphi$

To illustrate the use of vocabularies, here are some examples:

Example 2.3.6 ($L = \varnothing$)
This vocabulary has no non-logical symbols at all. But since $=$ is a predicate symbol, we have atomic formulas of the form $x = y$, and can write sentences like $\exists x\, x = x$, $\exists x \exists y(x \neq y \wedge \forall z(z = x \vee z = y))$.

Example 2.3.7 ($L = \{R\}$)
This vocabulary has just one binary predicate symbol as non-logical constant. It fits, for example, a theory about *order relations*; then we usually write $<$ or $\leqslant$ instead of R. Likewise, it can be used for talking

about *equivalence relations*; we will then use E instead. It also fits *set theory*, formulated in FOL, where the only non-logical symbol is $\in$, and the intended meaning of $x \in y$ is "x is an element of y".

Example 2.3.8 ($L_{PA} = \{0, ', +, \cdot\}$)
This vocabulary is for the language of *arithmetic*, which we will have a lot to say about later in this book. (*PA* stands for Peano Arithmetic.) Here 0 is an individual constant, and $+$ and $\cdot$ are binary function symbols with the obvious intended meanings. $'$ is a unary function symbol, standing for the *successor function* s: for every natural number n, $s(n) = n + 1$.

Apart from the structured atomic formulas, the main feature of the first-order language is obviously the quantifiers $\forall$ and $\exists$. Quantifiers can *bind* variables in formulas. We make this precise as follows. First, in formulas of the form $\forall x\psi$ and $\exists x\psi$, ψ is said to be the *scope* of (these occurrences of) $\forall x$ and $\exists x$. Thus, every occurrence of $\forall x$ or $\exists x$ in a formula φ has a unique scope.

Definition 2.3.9 (free and bound occurrences)
An *occurrence* of a variable x in an L-formula φ is *free*, if it is not within the scope of any quantifier expression $\forall x$ or $\exists x$ in φ. An occurrence of x is *bound* if it is not free.

This definition is concise, but does not say explicitly, when a variable occurrence is bound in a formula, *which* quantifier expression *binds* it. This is because we are allowing formulas like

(18) $\quad \exists x(Px \wedge \forall x Qxy)$

Here the second occurrence of x is within the scope of both $\forall x$ and $\exists x$.[10] We want to say that this occurrence of x is bound by $\forall x$ in this formula, and not by $\exists x$. Each bound variable occurrence should be bound by a *unique* quantifier expression occurrence. We achieve this by stipulating that if an occurrence of a variable x in a formula φ is bound, then it is *bound by* the occurrence of $\forall x$ or $\exists x$ with the *smallest scope* within which this x occurs.

Now it is clear that the first occurrence of x in (18) is bound by $\exists x$, and the second by $\forall x$. But in general we try to avoid formulas like (18). This can always be achieved, by *change of bound variables*. For example, instead of (18) we could use

(19) $\quad \exists x(Px \wedge \forall z Qzy)$

As we will see, (18) is logically equivalent to (19).

[10] The 'x' that appears in $\forall x$ and $\exists x$ does *not* count as an occurrence. Only variable occurrences in atomic formulas count.

Note also that the same variable can occur both free and bound in a formula.[11] For example, in

$$Px \to \exists x Rxy$$

the first occurrence of x is free and the second is bound. This is no problem for the meaning of such formulas, but, as above, we can always avoid them, by selecting bound variables more carefully, e.g:

$$Px \to \exists u Ruy$$

Finally, note that Definition 2.3.4 also allows formulas like

(20) $\forall x Pc,\ \exists x Ryd,\ \forall x \exists x Px$

Here the quantification is *vacuous*: there are no free variables in the scope of the quantifier to bind. Some versions of FOL use special syntactic conditions to rule out such formulas. But this makes the notion of a formula more complicated, and not much is gained. Indeed, the formulas in (20) have a well-defined meaning: it will be easy to see that they are logically equivalent to, respectively,

(21) $Pc,\ Ryd,\ \exists x Px$

We can now draw the important distinction between formulas and sentences. This distinction does not exist in propositional logic, but in first-order logic it is crucial.

Definition 2.3.10 (L-sentences)
An L-*sentence* is an L-formula with no free variables.

Only sentences can be true or false (relative to interpretations). Formulas with free variables (sometimes called *open formulas*) do not make claims that are straightforwardly true or false: not until we know what individuals are *assigned* to the free variables. For example, the formula

$$Px$$

says that x is P. An interpretation will tell us what P is, but as long as we don't know what x refers to, this formula makes no claim. By contrast, the sentence

$$\exists x Px$$

[11]When there is no need to mention the vocabulary, we say "formula" instead of "L-formula". This can happen because we are talking about a particular L, which is understood from context. Also, if we display a formula explicitly, as (18), there is no need to mention a vocabulary. Clearly, (18) and (19) are L-formulas for any L such that $P, Q \in L$.

says that *something* is P, and this is either true or false (depending on what the interpretation says about P).

Substitution

In FOL, and in any language with variable-binding operators, the notion of *substitution* is crucial, but slightly tricky to define in a precise way. The basic syntactic operation is to a replace a free variable x in a formula φ with a term t. This is done all the time. Consider a claim, say, that $\forall x \exists y(x < y \wedge \mathit{prime}(y))$. This should entail, for example, that $\exists y(9 + z < y \wedge \mathit{prime}(y))$. Here we have replaced the free occurrence of x in

(22) $\exists y(x < y \wedge \mathit{prime}(y))$

with the term $9 + z$.

However, not all terms are allowed in replacement. If we were to replace x in (22) with $9 + y$, we obtain $\exists y(9 + y < y \wedge \mathit{prime}(y))$. This means something completely different (indeed the sentence would always be false in the intended interpretation), and should *not* count as a substitution instance of (22). The reason, clearly, is that y in the term $9 + y$ becomes bound by the quantifier $\exists y$ in (22).

So we need to prevent this. It would be too restrictive to require that t is always a closed term (no variables). Variables can occur in t, but we must see to it that they are not 'accidentally bound' after replacement. So we define:

(23) *t is free for x in φ* if no free occurrence of x is within the scope of a quantifier $\forall y$ or $\exists y$ in φ, for any variable y in t.

Only then is replacing such an occurrence of x with t permitted.

In practice, this is never a problem! We can always choose bound variables of quantifiers in φ so that they do not occur in t. And in the next chapter one of the inference systems for FOL will have

$$\forall x \varphi(x) \rightarrow \varphi(t)$$

as an axiom, but then t is required to be a closed term, so the problem doesn't even arise. However, later when we want to formally describe the process of substitution in FOL, and formalize it within an arithmetic theory (Chapter 11), we need a precise description.

Here, and in the rest of the book, we will use the following practical notation. When we write

$$\varphi(x_1, \ldots, x_n)$$

instead of just φ, this indicates that the free variables of φ are *among* $x_1, \ldots, x_n$; we don't require that all of them actually occur in φ. (Note that this is a notation in the metalanguage: there are no formulas in FOL of this shape!) Next, if $t_1, \ldots, t_n$ are terms,

(24) $\varphi(t_1/x_1, \ldots, t_n/x_n)$

stands for the result of *simultaneously replacing all free occurrences* of $x_1, \ldots, x_n$ by $t_1, \ldots, t_n$, respectively, provided each t_i is free for x_i in φ. "Simultaneous" means that we don't first replace x_1 with t_1, then x_2 with t_2, etc.; that could actually give a different result (for example, if t_1 contains the variable x_2).

Whenever it is possible without confusion, and when φ has been given as $\varphi(x_1, \ldots, x_n)$, we write, more simply,

(25) $\varphi(t_1, \ldots, t_n)$

Similarly for terms: we may write a term t as $t(x_1, \ldots, x_n)$, and after substitution, $t(t_1/x_1, \ldots, t_n/x_n)$ or $t(t_1, \ldots, t_n)$.

This is all we need for most of the book about substitution. But for later use in Part III, the next subsection—which can be skipped until we get to Chapter 11—gives inductive definitions of the notions needed for substitution.

*Substitution defined

First, we define the relation 'x occurs free in the expression U'. Here U can be a term or a formula; when U is a term, the word "free" plays no role, but we use it anyway, in order to make do with one definition instead of two.

(26) **the relation 'occurs free in'**

a. x occurs free in x.

b. x occurs free in $Pt_1 \ldots t_n$ (or $ft_1 \ldots t_n$) if x occurs free in some of $t_1, \ldots, t_n$.

c. x occurs free in $\neg\varphi$ if x occurs free in φ.

d. x occurs free in $(\varphi \wedge \psi)$ if x occurs free in φ or in ψ, and similarly for the other connectives.

e. x occurs free in $\forall y\varphi$ (or $\exists y\varphi$) if x occurs free in φ and y is a variable distinct from x.

A couple of things may be noted:

(a) (26) is correct in the sense that it defines a unique relation 'x occurs free in U', where x is a variable and U is a term or a formula, by induction on (the complexity of) U.[12]

[12] In Part III we will make this precise and see that the relation defined by (26) between (code numbers of) variables and expressions is 'primitive recursive'; see Chapter 11.4.

(b) Definition 2.3.9 specified what it means for an *occurrence* of a variable x to be free in a formula φ. (26) does not mention occurrences, but nevertheless gives the same result, since we have:

(27) x occurs free in φ (in the sense of (26)) iff x has at least one free occurrence in φ (in the sense of Definition 2.3.9).

The proof, by induction on the complexity of φ, is left as an exercise. The fact that 'occurs free in' can be defined without talking about occurrences is actually an advantage, since handling distinct occurrences formally can be a bit tricky.

Next, we define substitution in terms. More precisely, we give a definition of the term $s(t/x)$, the result of replacing all occurrences of x in s by t, by induction on the complexity of s:

(28) **substitution in terms**

a. $c(t/x) = c$.

b. $y(t/x) = \begin{cases} y & \text{if } y \neq x \\ t & \text{if } y = x \end{cases}$

c. $(ft_1 \dots t_n)(t/x) = ft_1(t/x) \dots t_n(t/x)$

Here $y \neq x$ means that y is a variable distinct from x, and $y = x$ means that y is the variable x.

Finally, we can define substitution in formulas. To this end it is practical to have a symbol, say †, which is definitely *not* a formula or a term (in any vocabulary); for example, † could be the left parenthesis. Then, for each variable x, each term t, and each formula φ, we define the formula $\varphi(t/x)$ by induction on φ as follows:

(29) **substitution in formulas**

a. $(Pt_1 \dots t_n)(t/x) = Pt_1(t/x) \dots t_n(t/x)$

b. $(\neg\varphi)(t/x) = \neg\varphi(t/x)$

c. $(\varphi \wedge \psi)(t/x) = (\varphi(t/x) \wedge \psi(t/x))$; similarly for other connectives

d. $(\forall y\psi)(t/x) = \begin{cases} \forall y\psi & \text{if } y = x \\ \dagger & \text{if } y \neq x, y \text{ occurs in } t, \text{ and} \\ & x \text{ occurs free in } \psi \\ \forall y\psi(t/x) & \text{otherwise} \end{cases}$

and similarly for $(\exists y\psi)(t/x)$.

About clause d: When y is x, there are no free occurrences of x in $\forall y\psi$, so nothing happens. When y is distinct from x and occurs in t, and x is free in φ, then t is not free for x in $\forall y\psi$, so substitution is not allowed. But when y is distinct from x, and either y doesn't occur in t or x isn't free in ψ, then we can perform the replacement in ψ without problem.[13]

This defines substitution of t for one variable x. It is fairly straightforward to generalize (29) to simultaneous substitution of several variables, that is, to define $\varphi(t_1/x_1, \ldots, t_n/x_n)$.

Again one can verify that our inductive definition agrees with the way we informally defined substitution earlier, in terms of occurrences (see Exercise 2.4.11). In particular, it will be the case that

(30) t is free for x in φ iff $\varphi(t/x) \neq \dagger$.

The technical advantage of this, besides not having to talk about occurrences, is that the substitution operation $\varphi(t/x)$ is now *always defined* (although its value is a formula only when t is free for x in φ).

2.3.2. FOL semantics

Informal semantics

The (admittedly rough) correspondence of $\wedge$ to "and", $\vee$ to "or", $\rightarrow$ to "if – then" or "implies", and $\neg$ to "not", already gives an intuitive understanding of what formulas in propositional logic mean. Similarly for first-order logic, since $\forall x$ corresponds to "for all individuals x", and $\exists x$ to "there is an individual x such that". This kind of informal understanding of the logical language actually goes a long way. Using it, after some amount of instruction and practice, one learns to translate or 'formalize' many English sentences in FOL. Here are a few examples, where we have chosen predicate symbols and individual constants in a way that should make it evident which English names, and which property and relation expressions, they correspond to.

(31) a. Martin sleeps or reads
b. $Sm \vee Rm$

(32) a. Susanna knows a professor
b. $\exists x(Px \wedge Ksx)$

(33) a. Every student knows some teacher
b. $\forall x(Sx \rightarrow \exists y(Ty \wedge Kxy))$

(34) a. No graduate student knows everyone who knows Eve
b. $\neg\exists x(Gx \wedge \forall y(Kye \rightarrow Kxy))$

[13] In the latter case of course, when x isn't free in ψ, again nothing happens at the substitution, but we don't need to state that here; it is taken care of by the other clauses applied to ψ. For example, it follows from clauses a. and d. that $Pzc(t/x) = Pzc$, and $(\forall x Pzx)(t/x) = \forall x Pzx$.

One also learns to handle cases where the translation is less obvious:

(35) a. Every logician dislikes at least two philosophers
b. $\forall x(Lx \rightarrow \exists y \exists z(Py \wedge Pz \wedge y \neq z \wedge \neg LKxy \wedge \neg LKxz))$

(36) a. Some student met at most one supervisor
b. $\exists x(Sx \wedge \forall y \forall z((SPy \wedge SPz \wedge Mxy \wedge Mxz) \rightarrow y = z))$

(37) a. The oldest teacher retired
b. $\exists x(Tx \wedge \forall y((Ty \wedge x \neq y) \rightarrow Oxy) \wedge Rx)$

The intuitive understanding that allows one to correctly make translations of this kind is *indispensable* for learning the language of FOL. The reader should check that (s)he understands how the translations above work, and preferably try some other examples (see the exercises). This ability is presupposed when we talk later about first-order theories and what can be expressed in them.

However, in a logical study of the *properties* of FOL we also need an exact specification of the meaning—that is, the truth conditions—of sentences in this language. Just as for propositional logic, we must specify exactly under which *circumstances* a FOL sentence is true or false. Again, the relevant circumstances are called *interpretations* (or *models*), although interpretations are no longer simple assignments of truth values. Thus, we need a formal semantics for FOL.

Let me emphasize again that the informal understanding is absolutely crucial. In principle, I suppose it would be possible to learn the meaning of FOL sentences, and the ability to make translations as above, directly from the formal truth definition given below. But in practice, one has the informal understanding first, and then one can see that the truth definition in fact is an exact version of it.

Formal semantics

As in PL, a FOL interpretation provides suitable meanings, or *semantic values*, to the non-logical symbols of the vocabulary. Our semantic values are *extensional*: for sentence letters they were simply truth values. Likewise, the value of an individual constant is any *object*, the value of an unary predicate symbol is a *set*; more generally, the value of an n-ary predicate symbol is an *n-ary relation*, and the value of an n-ary function symbol is an *n-ary function*. Also, an interpretation comes with a *domain* or *universe*, in which the values of the non-logical symbols are taken, and over which the quantifiers range.

Here is the precise definition. Specifying interpretations in FOL necessarily involves the use of some basic set-theoretic notions (sets, relations, functions; see the Appendix for this). Let L be a vocabulary.

Definition 2.3.11 (L-interpretations)
An *L-interpretation* is a pair $\mathcal{M} = (M, I)$, where M is any non-empty set (the *domain* or *universe*), and I is a function assigning semantic values to the symbols in L as follows:

(38) a. If c is an individual constant in L, then $I(c) \in M$.

b. If P is an n-ary predicate symbol in L, then $I(P)$ is an n-ary relation over M, i.e. $I(P) \subseteq M^n$.

c. If f is an n-ary function symbol in L, then $I(f)$ is an n-ary function on M, i.e. $I(f)\colon M^n \to M$.

This is the official definition and notation. But we will use other notations too. Very often, in place of $I(c)$, $I(P)$, and $I(f)$ we write $c^{\mathcal{M}}$, $P^{\mathcal{M}}$, and $f^{\mathcal{M}}$. And sometimes we simply list the interpretions of the symbols in L. Then, for example, if $L = \{c, d, P, Q, f\}$ we may write

$$\mathcal{M} = (M, I) = (M, c^{\mathcal{M}}, d^{\mathcal{M}}, P^{\mathcal{M}}, Q^{\mathcal{M}}, f^{\mathcal{M}})$$

Now our task is to define the truth relation, $\mathcal{M} \models \varphi$, or '$\varphi$ is true in $\mathcal{M}$', between L-interpretations and L-sentences. Note that only *sentences* are true or false in interpretations, not formulas with free variables. But precisely this is what complicates the truth definition. We have an inductive definition of L-formulas, not of L-sentences. Indeed, it is impossible to define the set of L-sentences by induction on the complexity of sentences. For example, $\exists x Px$ is a sentence, which is true in $\mathcal{M}$ iff something belongs to $P^{\mathcal{M}}$, i.e. iff $P^{\mathcal{M}}$ is non-empty. But the subformula Px is not a sentence! Thus, we cannot define the truth of $\exists x Px$ in $\mathcal{M}$ in terms of the *truth* of Px in $\mathcal{M}$.

It is, however, fairly obvious what we must do. We need to say that x can be *assigned* a value in the domain M which belongs to $P^{\mathcal{M}}$. Such a value is said to *satisfy* Px in $\mathcal{M}$. That's exactly the truth condition for $\exists x Px$, expressed in terms of a *satisfaction condition* for Px.

In the general case, we must deal with arbitrary formulas of the form $\exists x\psi$ and $\forall x\psi$, where ψ may contain other free variables besides x. When this is the case, it is again satisfaction conditions, rather than truth conditions, that must be stated. The upshot is that we shall define a *3-place* relation,

$$\mathcal{M} \models \varphi\,[\sigma]$$

which is read "σ satisfies φ in $\mathcal{M}$", where σ is an assignment of values in M to the variables, φ is an L-formula, and $\mathcal{M}$ is an L-interpretation. σ assigns values to *all* the variables in the language, although we will see that only the (free) variables actually occurring in φ matter. Thus, an *assignment in* M is a function from $\{v_0, v_1, v_2, \ldots\}$ to M.

We use $\sigma, \tau, \ldots$ for assignments. We shall also need the following notation. If σ is an assignment in M, x is a variable, and $a \in M$, then

$$\sigma(a/x)$$

is the assignment in M which is just like σ, *except* that x is assigned the value a.

Before we can state the definition of $\mathcal{M} \models \varphi[\sigma]$, we must explain how *terms* are interpreted by $\mathcal{M}$. That is, to every L-term t, we must associate an object in the domain M. Clearly, if t is an individual constant c, we associate $I(c)$, or $c^{\mathcal{M}}$, with it. But open terms contain variables, and variables are assigned values by assignments. So it is $\mathcal{M}$ together with an assignment σ that gives an interpretation of each L-term t in M. We write this interpretation

$$t^{\mathcal{M},[\sigma]}$$

If L contains function symbols there are also complex L-terms. The interpretation of these is obtained by applying the interpretation of the function symbols, i.e. the corresponding functions, to the values of the subterms. Thus:

Definition 2.3.12 (interpretation of L-terms)
(i) $c^{\mathcal{M},[\sigma]} = c^{\mathcal{M}}$, for $c \in L$

(ii) $x^{\mathcal{M},[\sigma]} = \sigma(x)$, for each variable x

(iii) $(ft_1 \ldots t_k)^{\mathcal{M},[\sigma]} = f^{\mathcal{M}}(t_1^{\mathcal{M},[\sigma]}, \ldots, t_k^{\mathcal{M},[\sigma]})$, for $f \in L$

Now we are ready for the formal truth definition—it is still often called a truth definition, even though it really is a definition of satisfaction, not truth. But we will soon see that truth is a special case of satisfaction.

It is not hard to see what the truth definition should look like. Consider an atomic formula $Pt_1 \ldots t_k$. It simply says that the individuals that $t_1 \ldots t_k$ denote, that is, $t_1^{\mathcal{M},[\sigma]}, \ldots, t_k^{\mathcal{M},[\sigma]}$, stand in the relation $P^{\mathcal{M}}$ to each other. A k-ary relation is a set of k-tuples of elements of M. So $Pt_1 \ldots t_k$ is satisfied by σ in $\mathcal{M}$ if $\langle t_1^{\mathcal{M},[\sigma]}, \ldots, t_k^{\mathcal{M},[\sigma]}\rangle$ belongs to $P^{\mathcal{M}}$, that is, if $P^{\mathcal{M}}(t_1^{\mathcal{M},[\sigma]}, \ldots, t_k^{\mathcal{M},[\sigma]})$ holds.

Next, the clauses for negation, conjunctions, etc. should be just as in the propositional case. And we have already sketched what the clause for $\exists x\psi$ is. Namely, $\exists x\psi$ is satisfied in $\mathcal{M}$ by an assignment σ iff *there is* some object a in M such that ψ is satisfied by the same assignment, except that a is assigned to x, i.e. by the assignment $\sigma(a/x)$. Similarly, $\forall x\psi$ is satisfied in $\mathcal{M}$ by an assignment σ iff *for all* a in M, ψ is satisfied by $\sigma(a/x)$.

Understanding the satisfaction relation in this way will enable the reader to work out whether the relation $\mathcal{M} \models \varphi[\sigma]$ holds or not in specific examples. Furthermore, recall that a *sentence* has no free variables, which means that assignments play no role. So we can say that a sentence φ is *true* in $\mathcal{M}$, written, as before,

$$\mathcal{M} \models \varphi$$

when φ is satisfied in $\mathcal{M}$ by *some* assignment. This accomplishes the task of defining truth in interpretations for FOL.

However, for later use we should *state* the truth (satisfaction) definition carefully as an inductive definition, and then *prove* that the satisfaction relation has the desired properties. Let us do this.

Truth definition

Recall that we are defining satisfaction relative to a vocabulary L. So strictly speaking, we obtain a relation $\models_L$, one for each L. We will soon see, however, that the dependence on L can be eliminated.

Definition 2.3.13 (truth definition for L-formulas)

(i) $\mathcal{M} \models_L Pt_1 \ldots t_n[\sigma]$ iff $P^{\mathcal{M}}(t_1^{\mathcal{M},[\sigma]}, \ldots, t_k^{\mathcal{M},[\sigma]})$

(ii) $\mathcal{M} \models_L t_1 = t_2[\sigma]$ iff $t_1^{\mathcal{M},[\sigma]}$ is identical to $t_2^{\mathcal{M},[\sigma]}$

(iii) $\mathcal{M} \models_L \neg\varphi[\sigma]$ iff $\mathcal{M} \not\models_L \varphi[\sigma]$

(iv) $\mathcal{M} \models_L (\varphi \wedge \psi)[\sigma]$ iff $\mathcal{M} \models_L \varphi[\sigma]$ and $\mathcal{M} \models_L \psi[\sigma]$, and similarly for $(\varphi \vee \psi)$, $(\varphi \rightarrow \psi)$, and $(\varphi \leftrightarrow \psi)$

(v) $\mathcal{M} \models_L \exists x\psi[\sigma]$ iff for some $a \in M$, $\mathcal{M} \models_L \psi[\sigma(a/x)]$

(vi) $\mathcal{M} \models_L \forall x\psi[\sigma]$ iff for all $a \in M$, $\mathcal{M} \models_L \psi[\sigma(a/x)]$

The next step is to show that only the free variables actually occurring in a formula matter for whether it is satisfied or not by an assignment in an interprtetation. This is one form of *locality* for first-order logic (cf. Lemma 2.2.6):

Lemma 2.3.14 (Locality Lemma for variables)
If σ and τ agree on the free variables in φ, i.e. if $\sigma(x) = \tau(x)$ whenever x is a free variable in φ, then: $\mathcal{M} \models_L \varphi[\sigma]$ iff $\mathcal{M} \models_L \varphi[\tau]$.

The inductive proof is left, with many hints, to Exercise 2.4.18. Now observe that if φ is a sentence, and thus has no free variables, then *any* two assignments trivially agree on the free variables in φ. This leads to the following:

Corollary 2.3.15
A sentence φ is either satisfied in $\mathcal{M}$ by all *assignments in M, or by* no *assignment in M.*

And now we finally see that the following definition makes sense.

Definition 2.3.16 (truth for L-sentences)
An L-sentence φ is *true* in an L-interpretation $\mathcal{M}$, written

$$\mathcal{M} \models_L \varphi$$

if φ is satisfied in $\mathcal{M}$ by some assignment in M (and hence by all assignments in M).

It remains to show that the reference to a particular vocabulary L in the definitions of satisfaction and truth can be eliminated. This depends on another kind of locality: whether an assignment satisfies a formula in an interpretation depends on the non-logical symbols actually occurring in the formula, but not on other symbols. The next lemma gives a precise formulation.

Lemma 2.3.17 (Locality Lemma for vocabularies)
Suppose φ is both an L-formula and an L'-formula, i.e. the non-logical symbols occurring in φ belong to both L and L'. Suppose further that $\mathcal{M}$ is an L-interpretation and $\mathcal{M}'$ an L'-interpretation which both have the same universe M, and which interpret all non-logical symbols in φ in the same way. That is, whenever U is such a symbol (individual constant, predicate symbol, function symbol), $U^{\mathcal{M}} = U^{\mathcal{M}'}$. Then, for all assignments σ in M, we have: $\mathcal{M} \models_L \varphi[\sigma]$ iff $\mathcal{M}' \models_{L'} \varphi[\sigma]$.

The proof is an instructive illustration of what a proof by induction over first-order formulas can look like; most of the details are given in Exercise 2.4.19.

Lemma 2.3.17 entails that we don't need to put a subscript $_L$ on the satisfaction relation, or the truth relation. So we write

$$\mathcal{M} \models \varphi[\sigma]$$

(or $\mathcal{M} \models \varphi$ when φ is a sentence), assuming that some vocabulary L has been specified in the context, or that it is immaterial which L we use, as long as it contains all non-logical symbols occurring in φ.

A simpler notation

Writing $\mathcal{M} \models \varphi\,[\sigma]$ is useful for some purposes (such as proving Lemma 2.3.14), but sometimes a bit clumsy in practice, e.g. when you want to verify that a certain sentence is true or false in an interpretation. So we shall also employ a more intuitive notation. Suppose $\varphi = \varphi(x_1, \ldots, x_n)$, that is, φ has at most the variables $x_1, \ldots, x_n$ free, and that $\mathcal{M}$ is a suitable interpretation (one whose vocabulary contains the non-logical symbols in φ), and that $a_1, \ldots, a_n \in M$. Then we will write

(39) $\quad \mathcal{M} \models \varphi\,[a_1, \ldots, a_n]$

which is read

(the sequence) $a_1, \ldots, a_n$ satisfies φ in $\mathcal{M}$

(39) is taken to mean that an assignment which assigns a_1 to x_1, a_2 to x_2, …, and a_n to x_n, satisfies φ in $\mathcal{M}$. As we know from Lemma 2.3.14, what the assignment does to other variables is immaterial. So the difference between this and the official notation is just that we let the relevant part of the assignment be explicit.

We can extend this notation a bit further when we spell out the truth conditions (v) och (vi) in Definition 2.3.13 for quantified formulas. Supposing that $\psi = \psi(x, x_1, \ldots, x_n)$, these could now be written:

(v′) $\mathcal{M} \models \exists x\psi\,[x, a_1, \ldots, a_n]$ iff for some $a \in M, \mathcal{M} \models \psi\,[a, a_1, \ldots, a_n]$

(vi′) $\mathcal{M} \models \forall x\psi\,[x, a_1, \ldots, a_n]$ iff for all $a \in M$, $\mathcal{M} \models \psi\,[a, a_1, \ldots, a_n]$

The left-hand side uses a kind of hybrid notation. It would be more correct to write (v′) as follows:

$\mathcal{M} \models \exists x\psi(x, x_1, \ldots, x_n)\,[a_1, \ldots, a_n]$ iff
for some $a \in M$, $\mathcal{M} \models \psi(x, x_1, \ldots, x_n)\,[a, a_1, \ldots, a_n]$

and similarly for (vi′). This doesn't mix syntactic variables with elements of the domain in the notation. But (v′) and (vi′) are simpler, easy to understand, and will be used whenever convenient.

FOL stands for the system of first-order logic, with the syntax and semantics spelled out here. Sometimes one leaves out the identity symbol *and* function symbols. This system, *first-order logic without identity*, is weaker as we will see, and will be called FOL^-. Another weaker system is *monadic first-order logic*, $\mathrm{FOL}^{\mathrm{mon}}$, which has no function symbols and only unary (1-ary) predicate symbols (except for =).

Back to informal semantics

Learning how to formalize natural language sentences involving quantification is a good way to test your mastery of the FOL language.

The same holds for checking truth and falsity of FOL sentences in interpretations. Often, such interpretations or models can be *visualized* in ways that make assessing truth and falsity easy. In Chapter 6 we illustrate this with ordered sets and equivalence relations. Also, small models for vocabularies whose predicate symbols are unary or binary can be easy to visualize:

Example 2.3.18
Here is a picture of an interpretation $\mathcal{M} = (M, P^{\mathcal{M}}, Q^{\mathcal{M}}, R^{\mathcal{M}})$, where P, Q are unary and R binary. We draw closed curves around the elements of $P^{\mathcal{M}}$ and $Q^{\mathcal{M}}$, and represent $R^{\mathcal{M}}$ with dotted arrows: an arrow from a to b means that $R^{\mathcal{M}}(a, b)$ holds.

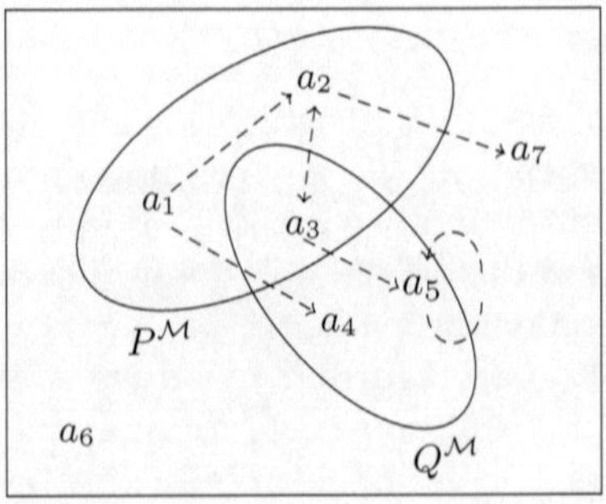

So $M = \{a_1, \ldots, a_7\}$, $P^{\mathcal{M}} = \{a_1, a_2, a_3\}$, $Q^{\mathcal{M}} = \{a_3, a_4, a_5\}$, and

$$R^{\mathcal{M}} = \{(a_1, a_2), (a_1, a_4)(a_2, a_3), (a_3, a_2), (a_3, a_5)(a_2, a_7)(a_5, a_5)\}$$

Now, simply looking at the diagram, we can see that, for example, the following sentences are true in $\mathcal{M}$:

(40) a. $\forall x(Px \to \exists y(Qy \wedge Rxy))$
b. $\exists x(Px \wedge \exists y(Rxy \wedge Ryy))$
c. $\neg\forall y(Qy \to \exists x Rxy)$
d. $\exists x \exists y \exists z(Rxy \wedge Ryz \wedge \neg Pz \wedge \neg Qz)$
e. $\exists x(Px \wedge Qx \wedge \forall z(Pz \wedge Qz \to z = x))$

For example, to verify that (40a) is true, we look at the points in $P^{\mathcal{M}}$, i.e. a_1, a_2, and a_3, and check that for each point there is an arrow to some point in $Q^{\mathcal{M}}$. Similarly, (40e) is true since a_3 is the only point in both $P^{\mathcal{M}}$ and $Q^{\mathcal{M}}$. (See also Exercise 2.4.15.)

2.3.3. Logical consequence (again)

The definition of logical consequence, logical truth, logical equivalence, and satisfiability for FOL has *exactly* the same form as the corresponding definition for PL (except that we don't use the term "tautology" for first-order logical truths). We repeat it here anyway. Note that we take these logical properties and relations to hold between *sentences*, not formulas with free variables. So in the definition below, φ, ψ are first-order sentences, and Γ is a set of first-order sentences.

Definition 2.3.19 (logical consequence etc. in FOL)

(i) φ is a *logical consequence* of Γ, in symbols,

$$\Gamma \vDash \varphi$$

if there is *no* interpretation in which all sentences in Γ are true and φ is false.

(ii) φ is *logically true*, or *valid*, in symbols,

$$\vDash \varphi$$

if φ is true in *all* interpretations.

(iii) φ and ψ are *logically equivalent*, in symbols,

$$\varphi \equiv \psi$$

if they are true in *the same* interpretations.

(iv) Γ is *satisfiable* if *there is* an interpretation in which all sentences in Γ are true.

Logical laws in FOL

Below is a list of some useful logical laws that hold in FOL. Note that all the laws we listed in (14) in Section 2.2.3 hold for FOL as well. This is because PL is a part of first-order logic in the sense that the truth (satisfaction) clauses for the connectives are exactly the same. So the laws in (41) concern the logical behavior of the quantifiers.

These laws are about *sentences*. So when we write, for example, $\forall x\varphi$, or $\forall x\varphi(x)$, we are assuming that φ has at most x as a free variable. Furthermore, in (41c) – (41i), ψ has to be a sentence (no free variables), and in (41o) and (41p), *t* is a *closed* term.

(41)
a. $\forall x\varphi \equiv \neg\exists x\neg\varphi$
b. $\exists x\varphi \equiv \neg\forall x\neg\varphi$
c. $\exists x(\varphi(x) \wedge \psi) \equiv \exists x\varphi(x) \wedge \psi$
d. $\forall x(\varphi(x) \vee \psi) \equiv \forall x\varphi(x) \vee \psi$
e. $\forall x(\varphi(x) \rightarrow \psi) \equiv \exists x\varphi(x) \rightarrow \psi$
f. $\exists x(\varphi(x) \rightarrow \psi) \equiv \forall x\varphi(x) \rightarrow \psi$
g. $\forall x(\psi \rightarrow \varphi(x)) \equiv \psi \rightarrow \forall x\varphi(x)$
h. $\exists x(\psi \rightarrow \varphi(x)) \equiv \psi \rightarrow \exists x\varphi(x)$
i. $\forall x\psi \equiv \psi$ and $\exists x\psi \equiv \psi$ (when x is not free in ψ)

j. $\forall x(\varphi(x) \wedge \psi(x)) \equiv \forall x\varphi(x) \wedge \forall x\psi(x)$
k. $\exists x(\varphi(x) \vee \psi(x)) \equiv \exists x\varphi(x) \vee \exists x\psi(x)$
l. $\models \exists x(\varphi(x) \wedge \psi(x)) \to \exists x\varphi(x) \wedge \exists x\psi(x)$
m. $\models \forall x\varphi(x) \vee \forall x\psi(x) \to \forall x(\varphi(x) \vee \psi(x))$
n. $\models \forall x\varphi(x) \to \exists x\varphi(x)$
o. $\models \forall x\varphi(x) \to \varphi(t)$
p. $\models \varphi(t) \to \exists x\varphi(x)$
q. $\forall x\forall y\varphi \equiv \forall y\forall x\varphi$
r. $\exists x\exists y\varphi \equiv \exists y\exists x\varphi$
s. $\models \exists y\forall x\varphi \to \forall x\exists y\varphi$

The reader will do well to go through these laws, and the reason why they hold (or at least come back to them when they are used later on).

The following two facts are instructive.

(42) Suppose c is an individual constant not occurring in any sentence in Γ, nor in $\psi(x)$ or φ. Then we have:

a. If $\Gamma, \psi(c) \models \varphi$, then $\Gamma, \exists x\psi(x) \models \varphi$.

b. If $\Gamma \models \psi(c)$, then $\Gamma \models \forall x\psi(x)$.

Intuitively, (42b) says that if it follows from the premises in Γ that c has property $\psi(x)$, but neither these premises nor $\psi(x)$ say anything about c, then it follows that an *arbitrary* c has the property, i.e. that $\forall x\psi(x)$. This seems right, and indeed we can verify that it holds, using the truth definition and the definition of logical consequence.

Let's carry out this verification for (42a); the argument for (42b) is similar. So assume that $\Gamma, \psi(c) \models \varphi$, where c is as described, and let $\mathcal{M}$ be any interpretation in which the premises in Γ as well as $\exists x\psi(x)$ are true. We must show that $\mathcal{M} \models \varphi$. According to condition (v′) above, there is an element a of M such that $\mathcal{M} \models \psi\,[a]$. Let L be the set of non-logical constants occurring in (sentences in) Γ, $\psi(x)$, and φ. By the second Locality Lemma (2.3.17), we can assume that $\mathcal{M}$ is an L-interpretation. And by assumption, c is not in L. So let $L' = L \cup \{c\}$, and let $\mathcal{M}'$ be the L'-interpretation which is just like $\mathcal{M}$ on the symbols in L, and interprets c as a. Again by the second Locality Lemma, all sentences in Γ are true in $\mathcal{M}'$. Furthermore, $\mathcal{M}' \models \psi(c)$, since we have $\mathcal{M}' \models \psi\,[a]$, and $c^{\mathcal{M}'} = a$.[14] Since $\Gamma, \psi(c) \models \varphi$, it follows that $\mathcal{M}' \models \varphi$. But c does not occur in φ, so a final application of Locality gives $\mathcal{M} \models \varphi$. □

[14]This looks self-evident, but if we are really picky, we should give a proof; see Exercise 2.4.21.

2.3.4. Equivalent formulas

We defined logical consequence, validity, and equivalence for *sentences*, and the facts in (41) were stated for sentences. But there is a natural way to generalize these notions to formulas with free variables. For example, we would say that a formula $\varphi(x_1, \ldots, x_n)$ is *valid* if the sentence $\forall x_1 \ldots \forall x_n \varphi(x_1, \ldots, x_n)$ (called its *universal closure*) is valid. Let us focus on equivalence, and state the corresponding facts for formulas a little more carefully. The following lemma follows more or less directly from the relevant definitions.

Lemma 2.3.20
Let $\mathcal{M}$ be an L-interpretation, and let $\varphi = \varphi(x_1, \ldots, x_n)$ and $\psi = \psi(x_1, \ldots, x_n)$ be L-formulas. Then (a) *and* (b) *are equivalent:*

(a) *For all* $a_1, \ldots, a_n \in M$, $\mathcal{M} \models \varphi[a_1, \ldots, a_n]$ *iff* $\mathcal{M} \models \psi[a_1, \ldots, a_n]$.

(b) $\mathcal{M} \models \forall x_1 \ldots \forall x_n(\varphi \leftrightarrow \psi)$

When (a) and (b) hold, we say that the formulas φ and ψ are *equivalent in $\mathcal{M}$*. And when this holds for *all* L-interpretations $\mathcal{M}$, we say that φ and ψ are *logically equivalent*, writing $\varphi \equiv \psi$ as before. Now the facts in (41) have obvious extensions to formulas. Take, for example, (41c), and suppose $\varphi = \varphi(y, x_1, \ldots, x_n)$ and $\psi = \psi(x_1, \ldots, x_n)$, where y is *not* among $x_1, \ldots, x_n$. Then, abbreviating $x_1, \ldots, x_n$ as $\overline{x}$, we have

(43) $\quad \exists y(\varphi(y, \overline{x}) \wedge \psi(\overline{x})) \equiv \exists y \varphi(y, \overline{x}) \wedge \psi(\overline{x})$

The other logical equivalences in (41) are similarly generalized. Analogously for the validities; for example, (41o) can be written in the same form,

(44) $\quad \models \forall x \varphi(x) \rightarrow \varphi(t)$

but now we allow φ to have other free variables, $\varphi = \varphi(x, x_1, \ldots, x_n)$, and t can be any term (open or closed). So (44) says that the universal closure of that formula is true in every interpretation.[15]

Similarly, we may write the claims that the identity relation is reflexive, symmetric, and transitive as follows:

(45) a. $\models x = x$
b. $\models x = y \rightarrow y = x$
c. $\models (x = y \wedge y = z) \rightarrow x = z$

So, for example, (45b) says that $\models \forall x \forall y(x = y \rightarrow y = x)$.

[15] Just as for sentences, validity can be seen as a special case of logical equivalence. Let $\top$ be any logical truth without free variables (e.g. $\exists x\, x = x$). Then the claim that $\varphi(x_1, \ldots, x_n)$ is valid is the same as the claim that $\varphi(x_1, \ldots, x_n) \equiv \top$.

Next, here is an intuitively obvious but important fact about substitution. Let t, s_1, s_2 be terms and φ a formula. The terms may contain variables and φ may have free variables, among which could be x.[16]

(46) a. $\models s_1 = s_2 \rightarrow t(s_1/x) = t(s_2/x)$

b. $\models s_1 = s_2 \rightarrow (\varphi(s_1/x) \leftrightarrow \varphi(s_2/x))$

The verification of this is sketched in Exercise 2.4.22.

Finally, we can now state a replacement lemma for first-order logic, generalizing Lemma 2.2.8. This extremely useful fact says that if we replace a subformula of a formula φ with a logically equivalent formula, the result is logically equivalent to φ.

Lemma 2.3.21 (replacement lemma for FOL)
Let φ be a formula containing a subformula $\psi(x_1, \ldots, x_n)$, and suppose that $\psi(x_1, \ldots, x_n) \equiv \psi'(x_1, \ldots, x_n)$, where ψ and ψ' have the same free variables $x_1, \ldots, x_n$. Then, if φ' results from φ by replacing ψ by ψ', we have $\varphi \equiv \varphi'$.[17]

The proof of this and some applications are indicated in the final exercises below.

2.4. Exercises to Chapter 2

Exercise 2.4.1

1. Suppose there is only one sentential letter, say, $L = \{p_0\}$. Show that there are infinitely many different propositional L-formulas. How many *non-equivalent* propositional L-formulas are there? (Reason informally.)
2. How many non-equivalent formulas when L contains two sentential letters?
3. Suppose we use only the connectives $\rightarrow$ and $\perp$, and that there are *no* sentential letters, so $L = \varnothing$. Same questions as in 1.!

Exercise 2.4.2
Given (8), verify that the second and third clauses in the truth definition 2.2.5 can be written

$$V(\neg\varphi) = 1 - V(\varphi)$$
$$V(\varphi \wedge \psi) = V(\varphi) \cdot V(\psi) = min(V(\varphi), V(\psi))$$

[16] As usual, we are assuming that the substitution is allowed, i.e. that s_1 and s_2 are free for x in φ (see the end of Section 2.3.1).

[17] In the definition of (logical) equivalence we didn't assume that φ and ψ have exactly the same free variables,.The Replacement lemma holds without this assumption, which is made here just for simplicity. The present version suffices for most applications.

Write corresponding clauses for $V(\varphi \vee \psi)$ and $V(\varphi \rightarrow \psi)$.[18]

Exercise 2.4.3

(a) Verify that (12) holds.

(b) More generally, check that each of the three notions defined in Definition 2.2.7(i), (ii), and (iv) can be expressed in terms of each of the other two notions, provided Γ is a *finite* set of sentences.

(c) Do the same for the notion defined in (iii).

Exercise 2.4.4 (replacement)

(a) Verify the following:

- If $\psi \equiv \psi'$, then $\varphi \wedge \psi \equiv \varphi \wedge \psi'$, and $\psi \wedge \varphi \equiv \psi' \wedge \varphi$.
- Similarly for $\neg$, $\vee$, $\rightarrow$, and $\leftrightarrow$.

(b) Use (a) to give an inductive proof of Lemma 2.2.8.

Exercise 2.4.5 (truth functions)

An *n-ary truth function* is a function F from $\{0,1\}^n$ to $\{0,1\}$, that is, F takes n truth values as arguments and delivers a truth value. For example, the meaning of $\wedge$ can be identified with the binary truth function $F_\wedge$, defined by $F_\wedge(1,1) = 1$, $F_\wedge(1,0) = F_\wedge(0,1) = F_\wedge(0,0) = 0$.

In this exercise, let an *n-formula* be a formula in propositional logic where exactly the sentence letters $p_1, \ldots, p_n$ occur. We say that an n-formula φ *expresses* the truth function F if, for every interpretation V of $p_1, \ldots, p_n$, we have $F(V(p_1), \ldots, V(p_n)) = 1$ iff $V \models \varphi$.

(a) Explain why there are exactly $2^{(2^n)}$ n-ary truth functions, and why each n-formula φ expresses a unique n-ary truth function.

(b) *Show that each n-ary truth function F is expressed by an n-formula φ whose connectives are $\neg$, $\wedge$, and $\vee$. [Hint: For every sequence $\overline{s} = s_1, \ldots, s_n$ of truth values, let $\psi_{\overline{s}} = p_1^{(s_1)} \wedge \ldots \wedge p_n^{(s_n)}$, where $p_i^{(s_i)} = p_i$ if $s_i = 1$, and $p_i^{(s_i)} = \neg p_i$ if $s_i = 0$. Then let φ be the disjunction of all such $\psi_{\overline{s}}$ for which $F(s_1, \ldots, s_n) = 1$.]

Exercise 2.4.6 (disjunctive normal form)

*A *literal* is a sentence letter or a negated sentence letter. A formula φ is in *disjunctive normal form* (dnf) if it is a disjunction $\psi_1 \vee \ldots \vee \psi_k$ (where k may be 1), where each ψ_i is a conjunction of literals (possibly just one literal). The dnf is *full* if each sentential letter in φ occurs exactly once

[18] These observations, essentially from the British mathematician George Boole in 1847 (though he had a different notion of disjunction), are the very first steps in what is now called *algebraic semantics*. That is, the logical operations are interpreted as arithmetical ones, or, more generally, as the operations of some algebra.

in each ψ_i. Show that every formula in propositional logic is logically equivalent to a formula in (full) disjunctive normal form. [Hint: see Exercise 2.4.5(b).]

Exercise 2.4.7 (functional completeness)
A set X of propositional connectives is said to be *functionally complete* if every truth function can be expressed by a formula in the propositional language based on X.

(a) Show that $\{\neg, \wedge\}$ is functionally complete. [Hint: Use (14l), (14b), and Exercise 2.4.5.]

(b) Show that the same holds for $\{\neg, \vee\}$, $\{\neg, \rightarrow\}$, and $\{\bot, \rightarrow\}$.

(c) Let the binary connective $|$ (the Sheffer stroke, also called 'nand') be defined so that $\varphi|\psi$ is true (has value 1) iff $\neg(\varphi \wedge \psi)$ is true. Show that $\{|\}$ is functionally complete. [Hint: The trick is to express $\neg\varphi$ in terms of $|$.]

(d) Show that $\{\wedge, \vee\}$ and $\{\wedge, \rightarrow\}$ are *not* functionally complete.

(e)* Same thing for $\{\neg, \leftrightarrow\}$.

(f)* Show that $\vee$ is expressible in terms of $\rightarrow$. Conclude that the set $\{\wedge, \vee, \rightarrow\}$ is not functionally complete.

Exercise 2.4.8
Show that no formula in propositional logic with just the connectives $\wedge$ and $\vee$ is a tautology.

Exercise 2.4.9 (subformulas)
The subformulas of a formula φ are, informally speaking, all the formulas used in the build-up of φ, including φ itself. Formally, we define $sub(\varphi)$, the set of subformulas of φ, inductively as follows:

$sub(\varphi) = \{\varphi\}$, if φ is atomic.

$sub(\neg\varphi) = sub(\varphi) \cup \{\neg\varphi\}$

$sub(\varphi \wedge \psi) = sub(\varphi) \cup sub(\psi) \cup \{\varphi \wedge \psi\}$, and similarly for other connectives.

$sub(\forall x\varphi) = sub(\varphi) \cup \{\forall x\varphi\}$, and similarly for $\exists x\varphi$.

So ψ is a *subformula* of φ if $\psi \in sub(\varphi)$, and ψ is called *proper* if it is distinct from φ. Verify the following claims:

1. A formula φ is atomic iff it has no proper subformulas.
2. Every formula is a subformula of itself.
3. The subformula relation is transitive, i.e. subformulas of subformulas of φ are subformulas of φ. (Argue informally.)

Exercise 2.4.10
*Prove the following claim:

(#) If φ is a propositional formula such that each sentence letter that occurs in φ occurs exactly once, then $\not\models \varphi$.

[Hint: Find a more general claim that you can prove by induction.]

Exercise 2.4.11 (substitution)
*The following are instructive exercises in proving facts about formulas by induction on their complexity.

1. Prove (27).
2. Prove that if t is free for x in φ, then $\varphi(t/x)$ (as defined in (29)) is the result of replacing all free occurrences of x in φ by t.
3. Generalize (29) to simultaneous substitution of $t_1, \ldots, t_n$ for $x_1, \ldots, x_n$.
4. Prove (30).

Exercise 2.4.12 (consequence relations)

(a) Show that the relation $\models$ of logical consequence in propositional or first-order logic has the following properties:

(R) If $\varphi \in \Gamma$, then $\Gamma \models \varphi$. ('reflexivity')
(T) If $\Delta \models \varphi$ and for all $\psi \in \Delta$, $\Gamma \models \psi$, then $\Gamma \models \varphi$.('transitivity')

Let us say that an arbitrary relation $\vdash$ between sets of sentences and sentences is a *consequence relation* if (R) and (T) hold for $\vdash$.

(b) Show that every consequence relation $\vdash$ is *monotone*, i.e.:

(M) If $\Gamma \vdash \varphi$ and $\Gamma \subseteq \Delta$, then $\Delta \vdash \varphi$.

(c) Let S be any set of sentences (in some language), and let (in this exercise) a *valuation* be any assignment v of truth values 0 and 1 to the sentences in S. For every set K of valuations, define the relation $\vdash_K$ as follows:

$\Gamma \vdash_K \varphi$ iff for every $v \in K$ we have that if $v(\psi) = 1$ for all $\psi \in \Gamma$, then $v(\varphi) = 1$.

Show that $\vdash_K$ is a consequence relation.

(d) Again let $\models$ be logical consequence in propositional logic. Is there some set K of valuations such that $\models\; = \;\vdash_K$?

(e) Let the relation $\vdash_0$ be defined by $\Gamma \vdash_0 \varphi$ if $\varphi \in \Gamma$. Show that $\vdash_0$ is the *smallest* consequence relation (in a given language), i.e. that (i) $\vdash_0$ is a consequence relation, and (ii) for every consequence relation $\vdash$ it holds that if $\Gamma \vdash_0 \varphi$, then $\Gamma \vdash \varphi$. Is there some set K such that $\vdash_0 \; = \; \vdash_K$?

Exercise 2.4.13
Formalize (as far as possible) in first-order logic:

a. No woman likes every man
b. Harry likes no one except himself
c. Every man likes some woman that he has not met
d. Nina likes Jim only if he likes no one else
e. Every logician who wrote a paper wants to publish it
f. If a logician meets a linguist they start arguing

Exercise 2.4.14
Let $M = \{\text{Sweden}, \text{Norway}, \text{Denmark}\}$, and let $\mathcal{M} = (M, P^{\mathcal{M}}, Q^{\mathcal{M}}, R^{\mathcal{M}})$, where $R^{\mathcal{M}}$ is the relation 'has a larger surface than', $P^{\mathcal{M}}$ the property 'is a NATO member', and $Q^{\mathcal{M}}$ the property 'is an EU member'. (Draw a diagram. Background information: Sweden has a larger surface than Norway, which in turn has a larger surface than Denmark. Norway and Denmark but not Sweden are NATO members, and Sweden and Denmark but not Norway are EU members.)

Determine with the help of Definition 2.3.13 (in the simplified version) if the following holds:

1. $\mathcal{M} \models Rxy \wedge Ryz$ [Sweden,Norway,Denmark]
2. $\mathcal{M} \models \exists x(\neg Rxy \wedge Py)$ [Denmark]
3. $\mathcal{M} \models \forall x \forall y(Rxy \rightarrow (Qx \vee Py))$

Exercise 2.4.15
Draw a diagram of the interpretation $\mathcal{M} = (M, P_1^{\mathcal{M}}, P_2^{\mathcal{M}}, P_3^{\mathcal{M}}, R^{\mathcal{M}})$, where the 1-ary P_1, P_2, P_3 and the 2-ary R are interpreted as follows: $M = \{a_1, \ldots, a_6\}$, $P_1^{\mathcal{M}} = \{a_1, a_2\}$, $P_2^{\mathcal{M}} = \{a_2, a_3, a_4, a_5\}$, $P_3^{\mathcal{M}} = \{a_5, a_6\}$, and $R^{\mathcal{M}} = \{(a_1, a_1), (a_1, a_2), (a_1, a_4), (a_2, a_3), (a_3, a_5), (a_4, a_6)\}$, and use it check which of the following sentences are true in $\mathcal{M}$.

(47) a. $\exists x(P_1 x \wedge P_2 x)$
b. $\forall x(P_1 x \rightarrow \exists y \exists z(P_2 y \wedge P_3 z \wedge Rxy \wedge Ryz))$
c. $\forall x \forall y(P_1 x \wedge Rxy \rightarrow P_2 y)$
d. $\forall x \forall y(P_1 x \wedge \neg Rxx \wedge Rxy \rightarrow P_2 y)$

Exercise 2.4.16
Show that the sentences below are *not* logically true, by giving a *counter-example* (an interpretation where the sentence is false):

a. $Pc \rightarrow \forall x Px$
b. $(\exists x Px \wedge \exists x Qx) \rightarrow \exists x(Px \wedge Qx)$
c. $\forall x \exists y Rxy \rightarrow \exists y \forall x Rxy$
d. $\exists x Px \rightarrow \exists x \exists y((Py \vee \neg Py) \wedge x \neq y)$

Exercise 2.4.17
In propositional logic, the atomic sentences are *independent* of each other, in the sense that neither p nor $\neg p$ is a logical consequence of any set Γ of atomic sentences such that $p \notin \Gamma$.

1. Is this also true for first-order logic with identity?
2. What about first-order logic *without* identity?

Exercise 2.4.18 (proof of Lemma 2.3.14)
First show that for every interpretation $\mathcal{M}$,

(a) If σ and τ agree on the variables in t, then $t^{\mathcal{M},[\sigma]} = t^{\mathcal{M},[\tau]}$

by induction on terms. Then show by induction on formulas that (for every interpretation $\mathcal{M}$):

(b) If σ and τ agree on the free variables in φ, $\mathcal{M} \models \varphi\,[\sigma]$ iff $\mathcal{M} \models \varphi\,[\tau]$.

[Hint: When φ is $Pt_1 \dots t_n$ or $t_1 = t_2$, use the truth definition and (a). The cases when φ is $\neg\psi$, $(\psi \wedge \chi)$, etc. follow easily from the induction hypothesis (i.e. that (b) holds for ψ and χ). When φ is $\exists x\psi$ or $\forall x\psi$, use the induction hypothesis and the fact that if σ and τ agree on the free variables in φ, and $a \in M$, then $\sigma(a/x)$ and $\tau(a/x)$ agree on the free variables in ψ.]

Exercise 2.4.19 (proof of Lemma 2.3.17)
We use the simpler notation $\mathcal{M} \models \varphi\,[a_1, \dots, a_n]$, which we abbreviate further as $\mathcal{M} \models \varphi\,[\overline{a}]$. Also, we let L_φ be the set of non-logical symbols occurring in φ, and similarly for L_t when t is a term. First, show the corresponding claim for terms, which can be formulated as follows:

(a) If $L_t \subseteq L$, $L_t \subseteq L'$, $\mathcal{M}$ is an L-interpretation, and $\mathcal{M}'$ is an L'-interpretation with the same domain M which agrees with $\mathcal{M}$ on the symbols in L_t, then, for all $a_1, \dots, a_n \in M$, $t^{\mathcal{M},[\overline{a}]} = t^{\mathcal{M}',[\overline{a}]}$.

Here it is assumed that $t = t(x_1, \dots, x_n)$, and that a_i is assigned to x_i. Then show by induction on formulas, and with the corresponding assumption about the free variables in φ:

(b) If $L_\varphi \subseteq L$, $L_\varphi \subseteq L'$, $\mathcal{M}$ is an L-interpretation, and $\mathcal{M}'$ is an L'-interpretation with domain M which agrees with $\mathcal{M}$ on the symbols in L_φ, then, for all $a_1, \dots, a_n \in M$, we have $\mathcal{M} \models_L \varphi\,[\overline{a}]$ iff $\mathcal{M}' \models_{L'} \varphi\,[\overline{a}]$.

(b) says that φ has a certain (complex) property, say P, and we want to show that *every* formula φ has the property P. We do one case here.

Suppose that φ is $\exists x\psi$, and that ψ has property P (the induction hypothesis). Reason as follows:

$$\begin{aligned}\mathcal{M} \models_L \exists x\psi\,[x,\overline{a}] \quad &\Leftrightarrow \quad \text{there is } a \in M \text{ s.t. } \mathcal{M} \models_L \psi\,[a,\overline{a}] \quad \text{(truth def.)}\\ &\Leftrightarrow \quad \text{there is } a \in M \text{ s.t. } \mathcal{M}' \models_{L'} \psi\,[a,\overline{a}] \quad \text{(ind. hyp.)}\\ &\Leftrightarrow \quad \mathcal{M}' \models_{L'} \exists x\psi\,[x,\overline{a}] \quad \text{(truth def.)}\end{aligned}$$

Do the other cases in the inductive proof. Exactly how is the induction hypothesis used in the second equivalence above?

Exercise 2.4.20
Verify that (42b) holds.

Exercise 2.4.21
The proof of (42a) used that if $\mathcal{M} \models \varphi(x)\,[a]$ and $c^{\mathcal{M}} = a$, then $\mathcal{M} \models \varphi(c)$. Prove, by induction on φ, the following more general fact, for any terms $t_1, \ldots, t_n$ (with $\overline{t} = t_1, \ldots, t_n$ and $\overline{x} = x_1, \ldots, x_n$):

$$\text{If } \sigma(x_i) = t_i^{\mathcal{M},[\sigma]} \text{ for } 1 \leqslant i \leqslant n, \text{ then } \mathcal{M} \models \varphi(\overline{x})\,[\sigma] \Leftrightarrow \mathcal{M} \models \varphi(\overline{t})\,[\sigma]$$

(At the induction step you will need to use that the substitution t_i/x_i is correct, i.e. that no variables in the t_i get bound by quantifiers in φ.)

Exercise 2.4.22 (sketch of a proof of (46))
*The terms and formulas may contain free variables, say $x_1, \ldots, x_n$ altogether, so we universally quantify over these, and, in an arbitrary interpretation $\mathcal{M}$, choose a corresponding sequence $\overline{a} = a_1, \ldots, a_n$ of elements in M. Then, what we need to show for (46a) is:

(a) if $s_1^{\mathcal{M},[\overline{a}]} = s_2^{\mathcal{M},[\overline{a}]}$, then $t(s_1/x)^{\mathcal{M},[\overline{a}]} = t(s_2/x)^{\mathcal{M},[\overline{a}]}$.

This is done by induction over the term t, following the inductive definition (28) of the operation $s(t/x)$.

Similarly, for (46b) we need to show by induction over φ:

(b) If $s_1^{\mathcal{M},[\overline{a}]} = s_2^{\mathcal{M},[\overline{a}]}$, then $\mathcal{M} \models \varphi(s_1/x)\,[\overline{a}]$ iff $\mathcal{M} \models \varphi(s_2/x)\,[\overline{a}]$.

For this, use definition (29).

Exercise 2.4.23
Verify that Lemma 2.3.20 holds.

Exercise 2.4.24 (proof of replacement lemma for FOL)
Write the claim of Lemma 2.3.21, with $\overline{x} = x_1, \ldots, x_n$, as:

$$\psi(\overline{x}) \equiv \psi'(\overline{x}) \text{ implies } \varphi[\psi(\overline{x})] \equiv \varphi[\psi'(\overline{x})]$$

Prove this by induction on φ.

[Hint: Note that if φ is atomic it has no proper subformulas, so ψ must be φ and the claim is trivial. The propositional cases are essentially as in Exercise 2.4.4. When φ is $\exists y\theta$ or $\forall y\theta$, the interesting case is when y is one of $x_1, \ldots, x_n$, so one may as well assume that y is x_1, and also that the free variables of φ are $x_2, \ldots, x_n$.]

The remaining exercises rely on the Replacement lemma.

Exercise 2.4.25
Show that every FOL-formula is logically equivalent to one in which $\rightarrow$ and $\leftrightarrow$ do not occur.

Exercise 2.4.26 (bound variable change)
Show: If $\forall x\varphi$ is a formula and y is a *fresh* variable—i.e. y doesn't occur at all in φ—then $\forall x\varphi \equiv \forall y\varphi(y/x)$. Similarly for $\exists x\varphi$. [Induction on φ.]

Exercise 2.4.27

1. Find a fomula logically equivalent to the following formula, but in which no variable occurs both free and bound, and all variable-binding is done with distinct variables.

   $$Rxy \wedge \forall x\exists y(Px \rightarrow \exists yQxyz)$$

2. Find a formula which is logically equivalent to the following but contains just two variables.[19]

   $$\forall y\forall z((Rxy \wedge Ryz) \rightarrow Pz)$$

   [Hint: Rewrite the formula with $\rightarrow$ as the only connective, move $\forall z$ inside, and 're-use' the variable x.]

Exercise 2.4.28 (prenex normal form)
A first-order formula is said to be in *prenex normal form* if all quantifiers are at the front, i.e. if it has the form

$$Q_1x_1 \ldots Q_kx_k\psi$$

where each Q_i is either $\forall$ or $\exists$, and ψ is quantifier-free.

[19]For the reader familiar with modal logic: this fact plays a role in showing that basic propositional modal logic can be translated—the so-called *standard translation*—into the *2-variable fragment* of FOL, i.e. the language which is just like FOL except that there are just two variables, say x and y. (See, for example, Blackburn, de Rijke, and Venema 2001, Ch. 2.4.) This fragment is known to be decidable, unlike full FOL (or even 3-variable FOL), and it follows that the same holds for basic modal logic. Decidability, and the undecidability of FOL, is treated in Part IV of this book.

It can be shown that transitivity, i.e. the similar-looking sentence

$$\forall x\forall y\forall z((Rxy \wedge Ryz) \rightarrow Rxz)$$

cannot be expressed in 2-variable FOL.

1. For each of the following formulas, find a logically equivalent formula in prenex normal form.

   (a) $\forall x(Rxy \rightarrow \exists z(Rxz \wedge Rzy))$

   (b) $\forall x P_1 x \rightarrow \forall x P_2 x$

   (c) $\forall x(\exists y Rxy \rightarrow \exists z(Ryz \wedge z \neq y))$

   (d) $Rxy \rightarrow \forall x(Rxx \rightarrow Qxy)$

2. Show informally that every FOL-formula is logically equivalent to a formula in prenex normal form.

   [Hint: Describe a method for successively moving quantifiers *out* of conjunctions, disjunctions, implications, and negations, where at each step a logically equivalent formula results. E.g. a subformula of the form $\neg\forall x\theta$ can be replaced by $\exists x\neg\theta$. And a subformula of the form $(\exists x\varphi \wedge \psi)$ is logically equivalent to $\exists x(\varphi \wedge \psi)$, *provided* x is not free in ψ. And if x is free in ψ, change the bound variable x in the first conjunct appropriately.]

3 Inference

We have presented the semantic version of logical consequence, in terms of the notion of truth in an interpretation. It is the classical idea of consequence as necessary truth preservation, whose modern explication goes back to Bolzano 1837 and Tarski 1936: a conclusion *follows from* a set of premises if it is true in *every* interpretation that makes the premises true.

The other way to define 'follows from' builds on a different idea: that every logically binding argument can be broken down into a small number of simple inference steps, each of which is obviously correct. An argument of this kind allows us in principle to *know* that the final conclusion is true, given that the assumptions are. If knowledge is something like true *justified* belief, then at each small inference step, it is evident that the conclusion is justified if the premises are, and, provided the initial assumptions need no further justification, the chain of inferences, however long, leads to a justification of the end conclusion.

Mathematical proofs are the paradigmatic case. From certain basic assumptions (axioms) mathematicians derive highly non-trivial theorems, with proofs that may take tens of pages to write down. Proofs are the only things that convince the mathematical community that the theorem is true. And proofs usually proceed in small steps, where each step can easily be seen to be correct, even if there is no way to see directly that the theorem follows from the axioms.

Of course, the proofs mathematicians write are still informal, and many small inference steps are usually not attended to or even made explicit. But precisely that was a main impetus of modern logic from Frege onwards: to write the proofs in an exactly specified language, and to clearly state all the logical axioms and rules that are used in them. Even Aristotle's syllogistics had a similar motivation, but, although elegant, the syllogistic language was too weak to be able to formalize any interesting proofs in, say, Euclid's treatises on geometry. Modern logic on the other hand has been remarkably successful in this respect. It appears that, in principle, all known theorems of modern mathematics could be expressed and proved in Zermelo-Fraenkel set theory (*ZF*) plus some extra axioms, and this is a first-order theory.

This is not to say that modern logic is useful only for mathematics. In daily life we reason, we argue, we consider evidence, we run programs, we share information, we acquire and give up beliefs. All of these activities have been studied with logical tools, and there are now a multitude of logical systems developed for these purposes. But first-order logic is still basic.

In the case of FOL, several systems of inference rules have been proposed. They are all extensionally equivalent, as it turns out—what can be proved in one system can also be proved in the others—but they build on quite different ideas, and are useful for different purposes. One purpose could be to construct systems that are easy to implement on computers. Another would be to find rules that correspond as closely as possible to the way we actually reason and argue informally. And yet a third criterion is to have a system whose properties are easy to study. For the purposes of this book, i.e. for presenting results *about* first-order logic and *about* theories expressed in that logic, the third criterion becomes important.

In the abstract, an *inference system* S is a collection of rules. There will be a notion of a *derivation in* S, where a derivation has a set Γ of *assumptions* and a *conclusion* ψ. A derivation is (in the cases discussed here) a *finite* syntactic object, for example, a finite sequence of sentences, or a finite arrangement of sentences in tree form. We write

$$\Gamma \vdash_S \psi$$

for

"There exists a derivation in S of ψ from assumptions in Γ"

or "ψ is *derivable* in S from Γ". Since derivations are finite, only a finite number of assumptions can be used in each. Thus, we may assume that Γ is a finite set, say, $\Gamma = \{\varphi_1, \ldots, \varphi_n\}$, and instead of $\{\varphi_1, \ldots, \varphi_n\} \vdash_S \psi$ we often write

(1) $\varphi_1, \ldots, \varphi_n \vdash_S \psi$

We require of derivations that there is a *mechanical method* for *verifying* whether or not a configuration of sentences is a well-formed derivation in S of the conclusion from the assumptions.[1] Such a verification, even though it may be long and tedious, could in principle be left to a computer. This requires in particular that the rules of S are formulated solely in terms of the *form* of the sentences involved. One

[1]In more technical language: the property of being a derivation in S is required to be *decidable*. We get to decidability in Part IV of the book.

doesn't need to know what these sentences *mean* (in which interpretations they are true, etc.) in order to see if a rule is correctly applied. In this sense, inference systems belong to the *syntactic* part of logic.

We assume that the assumptions and conclusion are *L-sentences*, for some vocabulary L, but we usually leave L implicit. The idea, of course, is that if we have established that $\Gamma \vdash_S \psi$, then we can be sure that ψ really does follow logically from Γ, that is, $\Gamma \models \psi$. An inference system with this property is called *sound*. Clearly, soundness is a necessary property of any good inference system. Checking that a system is sound is usually easy: it is a matter of verifying that all the rules lead from true assumptions to true conclusions (in any interpretation).

A system S where the converse holds, i.e. that $\Gamma \models \psi$ implies $\Gamma \vdash_S \psi$ is called *complete*.[2] It turns out that (each of the usual inference systems for) first-order logic is in fact complete. But this is a remarkable fact, and far from trivial: how can the fact that ψ is true in all interpretations where the assumptions in Γ are true help us construct a derivation of ψ from Γ in S? Chapters 4 and 5 are devoted to this issue.

This chapter presents two of the main inference systems for FOL: a natural deduction system and a Hilbert system. We also show that they are indeed extensionally equivalent. So you can use either one, whichever is more handy for a certain goal. For our purposes in Part III, the Hilbert system is easiest to use. [3]

3.1. Natural deduction

Natural deduction is a format for inference aimed at coming close to actual reasoning.[4] A further idea behind these systems is that they actually give the *meaning* of the logical constants involved, independently of the notion of truth in an interpretation. This is actually part of a philosophical theory of meaning, which some philosophers endorse and other disagree with. We need not take a stand on this dispute here. Our goal is just to make the reader sufficiently familiar with the system and the idea about inference that it implements.

The rules for each logical constant (except one) come in pairs: an *introduction rule* and an *elimination rule*. The most straightforward illustration of the idea is provided by the rules for conjunction: the

[2]This property is often called *strong completeness*; then *weak* completeness is the property that $\models \psi$ implies $\vdash_S \psi$ (ψ is derivable in S without assumptions), for all ψ.

[3]For a detailed and instructive comparison of inference systems for first-order logic, see Sundholm 1983.

[4]The earliest versions of natural deduction systems go back to Jaśkowski in 1929. The system we use here originates with Gerhard Gentzen's dissertation in 1934. A classic study of natural deduction is Prawitz 1965.

rule of $\wedge$-*introduction* infers $\varphi \wedge \psi$ from the two premises φ and ψ, and the two rules for $\wedge$-*elimination* infer φ from $\varphi \wedge \psi$, and similarly ψ from $\varphi \wedge \psi$. Clearly, this closely mirrors the truth table for $\wedge$.[5]

Other rules allow one to *discharge assumptions* that have been made. For example, the rule of $\rightarrow$-*introduction* says that if ψ has been derived from the assumption φ, then one may infer $\varphi \rightarrow \psi$ while discharging φ. This rule is sometimes called *Conditionalization*. The rule for $\rightarrow$-*elimination* is the usual rule of *Modus Ponens*: from φ and $\varphi \rightarrow \psi$, infer ψ.

The system of rules used here will be called *ND*. We gradually present the rules, with illustrations of how they work, beginning with the rules for propositional connectives.

Derivations in natural deduction can be written as *proof trees*, with assumptions at the top (the leaves) and the final conclusion at the bottom (the root). Furthermore, one needs a way to keep track of which assumptions have been discharged and which are still in force: we will put discharged assumptions in square brackets. It is also possible to write natural deduction derivations as linear sequences of sentences with some extra annotations. We illustrate this in (11) and (12) below, but otherwise we shall use the tree format.

3.1.1. Rules for the connectives

As already said, the rules for $\wedge$ are as follows.

$$\wedge\text{I:} \quad \frac{\varphi \qquad \psi}{\varphi \wedge \psi}$$

$$\wedge\text{E:} \quad \frac{\varphi \wedge \psi}{\varphi} \qquad \frac{\varphi \wedge \psi}{\psi}$$

$\wedge$I is to be read in the following way: if there is a proof tree for φ (a tree with φ as its root) and a proof tree for ψ, then these two trees may be combined to a new proof tree with $\varphi \wedge \psi$ as its root. No assumptions are discharged, so the assumptions of the new proof tree are the assumptions of the tree for φ and the assumptions of the tree for ψ. All this could be stated in a much more precise way, but the compact formulation above usually suffices.[6]

We also mentioned the rules for $\rightarrow$:

[5]Indeed, there is a precise sense in which the truth table for $\wedge$, and the introduction and elimination rules for $\wedge$, are equivalent. We explore this further in Exercise 3.1.11.

[6]Without explicit reference to proof trees, one can also present the rule $\wedge$I as follows: if we have $\Gamma \vdash_{ND} \varphi$ and $\Delta \vdash_{ND} \psi$, then $\Gamma \cup \Delta \vdash_{ND} \varphi \wedge \psi$. But we shall continue to write the rules as informal 'tree construction' rules.

$$\to\text{I:}\quad \dfrac{\begin{matrix}[\varphi]\\ \vdots \\ \psi\end{matrix}}{\varphi \to \psi} \qquad\qquad \to\text{E:}\ \dfrac{\varphi \qquad \varphi \to \psi}{\psi}$$

$\to$E is a tree construction rule similar to $\wedge$I. $\to$I says that if you have a proof tree for ψ, where φ may be among the assumptions, you may form a new tree by adding $\varphi \to \psi$ at the bottom, and *discharging* φ. More precisely, to obtain maximum generality, let us stipulate that one may discharge (put brackets around) *as many occurrences of the assumption* φ *as one wants* (perhaps all, perhaps just one, perhaps none).

Officially, we also need an *assumption rule*:

(A) Any sentence may be introduced as an assumption. More formally, the tree consisting of a single sentence occurrence φ is a proof tree (with φ as both assumption/premise and conclusion), which may then be extended using the other rules.

Here is the official notion of *derivability in ND*:

(2) $\Gamma \vdash_{ND} \varphi$ iff there is a proof tree for φ, all of whose undischarged assumptions belong to Γ.

Assumptions play a crucial role in natural deduction. Note that *only assumptions can be discharged* in *ND*: the rules never allow you to put brackets around any sentence occurrences that are not assumptions.

With the rules at hand so far, we can already build some derivations. When writing proof trees, we put an index—a number i—to the right of the rule application line, and the same i as a superscript on the right bracket of the assumptions discharged by that application (if it is a rule that allows discharge). This means that a finished proof tree can always be unambiguously read. We also sometimes write the name of the rule to the right of the application line.

The following proof tree shows that $\vdash_{ND} \varphi \to (\psi \to (\varphi \wedge \psi))$, i.e. that $\varphi \to (\psi \to (\varphi \wedge \psi))$ is derivable in *ND without assumptions* (from the empty set of assumption):

$$\dfrac{\dfrac{\dfrac{[\varphi]^2 \qquad [\psi]^1}{\varphi \wedge \psi}\,\wedge\text{I}}{\psi \to (\varphi \wedge \psi)}\,\to\text{I}_1}{\varphi \to (\psi \to (\varphi \wedge \psi))}\,\to\text{I}_2$$

In words: we start on the top line by introducing φ and ψ as assumptions (rule (A)), and then conclude $\varphi \wedge \psi$ on the next line with $\wedge$I. Then, one application of $\rightarrow$I gives $\psi \rightarrow (\varphi \wedge \psi)$ on the third line, at the same time discharging the one occurrence of ψ, marked by the index 1. Finally, a second application of $\rightarrow$I yields $\varphi \rightarrow (\psi \rightarrow (\varphi \wedge \psi))$, discharging φ. The resulting proof tree has no undischarged assumptions, so it is a derivation of the conclusion without assumptions.

The next tree shows that $\vdash_{ND} \varphi \rightarrow (\psi \rightarrow \varphi)$:

(3)
$$\dfrac{\dfrac{[\varphi]^2}{\psi \rightarrow \varphi}\,{\rightarrow}\mathrm{I}_1}{\varphi \rightarrow (\psi \rightarrow \varphi)}\,{\rightarrow}\mathrm{I}_2$$

The first application of $\rightarrow$I in (3) may seem odd. But recall that, as we formulated the rule, there was no requirement that ψ actually occurs as an assumption in the derivation of φ. In the present case, that derivation consists of φ itself (the assumption rule). So on the second line we get $\psi \rightarrow \varphi$, even though there are no assumptions of ψ to discharge here. Note that this is perfectly truth-preserving (the rule is sound): if φ is true in an interpretation, then so is $\psi \rightarrow \varphi$, for any sentence ψ. On the third line, applying $\rightarrow$I again, the assumption φ is discharged.

This was an illustration of an application of $\rightarrow$I where no assumptions are discharged. In other cases, we may discharge more than one occurrence of an assumption at the same time. The proof tree (5) shows that (4) holds.

(4) $\varphi \rightarrow (\varphi \rightarrow \psi) \vdash_{ND} \varphi \rightarrow \psi$

(5)
$$\dfrac{\dfrac{[\varphi]^1 \qquad \dfrac{[\varphi]^1 \qquad \varphi \rightarrow (\varphi \rightarrow \psi)}{\varphi \rightarrow \psi}\,{\rightarrow}\mathrm{E}}{\psi}\,{\rightarrow}\mathrm{E}}{\varphi \rightarrow \psi}\,{\rightarrow}\mathrm{I}_1$$

Here both occurrences of φ are discharged at the last step.[7]

Next come the rules for disjunction. The introduction rules are obvious, but the elimination rule has to be formulated in an indirect way.

---

[7]There are systems of natural deduction requiring that *at least one* occurrence of the assumption is discharged when applying $\rightarrow$I, and other systems which require that *exactly one* assumption is discharged. In the former type of system, $\varphi \vdash \psi \rightarrow \varphi$ does not hold; this is characteristic of so-called *relevance logic*. In the latter case, (4) will fail: the idea is that every occurrence of an assumption is a 'resource', so using an assumption twice requires more resources that using it once. But this distinction cannot be made in our format here (except as restrictions on dischargement): there is no difference between $\Gamma, \varphi \vdash_{ND} \psi$ and $\Gamma, \varphi, \varphi \vdash_{ND} \psi$, since $\Gamma \cup \{\varphi\}$ and $\Gamma \cup \{\varphi\} \cup \{\varphi\}$ are the same set.

$$\vee\text{I:}\quad \frac{\varphi}{\varphi \vee \psi} \qquad \frac{\psi}{\varphi \vee \psi}$$

$$\vee\text{E:}\quad \frac{\varphi \vee \psi \qquad \begin{matrix}[\varphi] \\ \vdots \\ \theta\end{matrix} \qquad \begin{matrix}[\psi] \\ \vdots \\ \theta\end{matrix}}{\theta}$$

$\vee$I says that if I have a proof of φ (or of ψ), then I can extend it to a proof of $\varphi \vee \psi$. $\vee$E, on the other hand, says that if I have a proof of some sentence θ from φ, and also a proof of the same sentence θ from ψ, then I obtain a proof of θ from $\varphi \vee \psi$, discharging (if I want) both φ and ψ. So here three proof trees are combined into one. This rule expresses a common way of *reasoning by cases*. Suppose I know that $\varphi \vee \psi$ is true, and I want to show that θ follows. Then, if I can show both that θ follows from φ and that θ follows from ψ, my desired conclusion θ follows from $\varphi \vee \psi$ alone.[8]

As an example of the use of $\vee$E, let us derive a distributive law for conjunction over disjunction in *ND*. We can formulate it as follows:

$$\varphi \wedge (\psi \vee \chi) \;\equiv_{ND}\; (\varphi \wedge \psi) \vee (\varphi \wedge \chi)$$

where $\varphi_1 \equiv_{ND} \varphi_2$ means: $\varphi_1 \vdash_{ND} \varphi_2$ and $\varphi_2 \vdash_{ND} \varphi_1$. First:

$$\varphi \wedge (\psi \vee \chi) \vdash_{ND} (\varphi \wedge \psi) \vee (\varphi \wedge \chi)$$

The assumption is a conjunction, so if we can show

$$\varphi, \psi \vee \chi \vdash_{ND} (\varphi \wedge \psi) \vee (\varphi \wedge \chi)$$

we are (using $\wedge$E) in principle done. One of the premises is a disjunction $\psi \vee \chi$, so we apply $\vee$E by first assuming ψ and (together with the other premise φ) try to derive the conclusion, and then do the same thing assuming χ. The following proof tree shows how this is done.

$$\dfrac{\psi \vee \chi \qquad \dfrac{\dfrac{\varphi \qquad [\psi]^1}{\varphi \wedge \psi}}{(\varphi \wedge \psi) \vee (\varphi \wedge \chi)}\,\vee\text{I} \qquad \dfrac{\dfrac{\varphi \qquad [\chi]^1}{\varphi \wedge \chi}}{(\varphi \wedge \psi) \vee (\varphi \wedge \chi)}\,\vee\text{I}}{(\varphi \wedge \psi) \vee (\varphi \wedge \chi)}\,\vee\text{E}_1$$

In this tree and later, we have not written the names of all the rules used, only the less obvious ones. For the other direction, it is enough to show

$$(\varphi \wedge \psi) \vee (\varphi \wedge \chi) \vdash_{ND} \varphi$$

[8] In a sense, I *have to* prove θ is this way: note that $(\varphi \vee \psi) \to \theta$ is logically equivalent to $(\varphi \to \theta) \wedge (\psi \to \theta)$.

and

$$(\varphi \wedge \psi) \vee (\varphi \wedge \chi) \vdash_{ND} \psi \vee \chi$$

because then we can use $\wedge$I to combine these proof trees into a proof tree for $\varphi \wedge (\psi \vee \chi)$. The premise is a disjunction, so again we reason by cases ($\vee$E):

$$\dfrac{(\varphi \wedge \psi) \vee (\varphi \wedge \chi) \qquad \dfrac{[\varphi \wedge \psi]^1}{\varphi} \qquad \dfrac{[\varphi \wedge \chi]^1}{\varphi}}{\varphi} \vee E_1$$

and

$$\dfrac{(\varphi \wedge \psi) \vee (\varphi \wedge \chi) \qquad \dfrac{\dfrac{[\varphi \wedge \psi]^1}{\psi}}{\psi \vee \chi} \qquad \dfrac{\dfrac{[\varphi \wedge \chi]^1}{\chi}}{\psi \vee \chi}}{\psi \vee \chi} \vee E_1$$

It remains to give rules for negation. In *ND* it is often practical to use the primitive logical symbol $\bot$ (*falsum*), which stands for a logically false sentence (see Chapter 2.2.1). Then we *define* negation by

(6) $\quad \neg\varphi := \varphi \to \bot$

This means that the following two rules become *special cases* of $\to$I and $\to$E:

$\neg$I: $\dfrac{\begin{matrix}[\varphi] \\ \vdots \\ \bot\end{matrix}}{\neg\varphi}$ $\qquad$ $\neg$E: $\dfrac{\varphi \qquad \neg\varphi}{\bot}$

These rules are quite useful, but they can tell us nothing *new* about negation, at least not until we have given some rule describing the behavior of $\bot$.[9] The rule *Reductio Ad Absurdum* (RAA) does precisely this. It corresponds to the following common method of reasoning: in order to show that φ holds, assume the contrary, i.e. $\neg\varphi$, and derive a contradiction. Thus:

[9] Let ψ_0 be *any* fixed sentence, and define $\neg\varphi$ as $\varphi \to \psi_0$. Then the rules $\neg$I and $\neg$E are still special cases of $\to$I and $\to$E, but this has nothing to do with negation.

RAA: $$\dfrac{\begin{array}{c}[\neg\varphi]\\ \vdots \\ \bot\end{array}}{\varphi}$$

Observe the difference between $\neg$I and RAA: if a contradiction follows from φ we may conclude $\neg\varphi$ already from $\rightarrow$I and the definition of negation (6). RAA, on the other hand, says that if a contradiction follows from $\neg\varphi$, we may conclude φ. The rules look similar, but whereas one is just an instance of an earlier rule, the other is a significant addition.

One illustration of this is as follows. If we apply $\neg$I to the sentence $\neg\varphi$ we may conclude, provided that $\neg\varphi$ leads to a contradiction, that $\neg\neg\varphi$. Thus, if we had a rule of *double negation elimination*,

DNE: $$\frac{\neg\neg\varphi}{\varphi}$$

RAA would follow; it becomes a *derived rule*. And conversely it holds that RAA (together with $\neg$E) makes DNE a derived rule:

$$\dfrac{\dfrac{\neg\neg\varphi \qquad [\neg\varphi]^1}{\bot}\,\neg\mathrm{E}}{\varphi}\,\mathrm{RAA}_1$$

This is a typical use of RAA: we assume $\neg\varphi$ and derive from it, *and possibly other assumptions*, a contradiction. Then we may conclude φ and discharge the assumption $\neg\varphi$, but of course the other assumptions remain.

The upshot of these observations is that we can add any one of the two rules, RAA and DNE, to handle negation.

An important special case of RAA is that *any* sentence can be derived from a contradiction. This is often called by its Latin name, *Ex Falso Quodlibet* (EFQ), or the *Law of Explosion*:

EFQ: $$\frac{\bot}{\varphi}$$

Because of the way we allow discharging of assumptions, EFQ becomes an instance of RAA. Recall that in a rule like RAA we do not require the discharged assumption to actually occur in the derivation. So assume $\bot$. This assumption is in itself a proof tree, with conclusion $\bot$, so we may conclude φ according to RAA, at the same time discharging any occurrences of $\neg\varphi$, but there aren't any, so nothing more happens.

EFQ is also a rule for how $\bot$ behaves, but it is weaker than RAA. Still, it suffices to derive some well-known laws of negation. To begin, any contradiction (not just $\bot$) implies any sentence:

(7) $\psi, \neg\psi \vdash_{ND} \varphi$

A derivation establishing this is as follows.

$$\dfrac{\dfrac{\psi \qquad \neg\psi}{\bot}\,\neg\text{E}}{\varphi}\,\text{EFQ}$$

And with two applications of $\to$I we obtain

(8)
$$\vdash_{ND} \psi \to (\neg\psi \to \varphi)$$
$$\vdash_{ND} \neg\psi \to (\psi \to \varphi)$$

The next law is called *disjunctive syllogism* (the English translation of its medieval name):

(9) $\varphi \vee \psi, \neg\varphi \vdash_{ND} \psi$

$$\dfrac{\varphi \vee \psi \qquad \dfrac{\dfrac{[\varphi]^1 \qquad \neg\varphi}{\bot}\,\neg\text{E}}{\psi}\,\text{EFQ} \qquad [\psi]^1}{\psi}\,\vee\text{E}_1$$

Note the use of $\vee$E in this derivation. The sentence θ in the formulation of $\vee$E is ψ here, i.e. one of the disjuncts. And the derivation of ψ from ψ is simply ψ itself, by the assumption rule (A).

But for other classical tautologies the full strength of RAA is needed. Here is a derivation of the Law of Excluded Middle (LEM):

(10) $\vdash_{ND} \varphi \vee \neg\varphi$

The proof strategy is as follows: assume the negation of the conclusion, i.e. $\neg(\varphi \vee \neg\varphi)$, and proceed to derive $\bot$. In this derivation we need to make this assumption twice; both are discharged by one application of RAA.

(11)
$$\dfrac{\dfrac{[\neg(\varphi \vee \neg\varphi)]^2 \qquad \dfrac{\dfrac{\dfrac{[\neg(\varphi \vee \neg\varphi)]^2 \qquad \dfrac{[\varphi]^1}{\varphi \vee \neg\varphi}\,\vee\text{I}}{\bot}\,\neg\text{E}}{\neg\varphi}\,\neg\text{I}_1}{\varphi \vee \neg\varphi}\,\vee\text{I}}{\bot}\,\neg\text{E}}{\varphi \vee \neg\varphi}\,\text{RAA}_2$$

The reader will do well to go through how this derivation works. But is such a complicated derivation of such a simple law necessary? An alternative would be to add LEM as an *axiom*—a rule without premises. Then it turns out that if we also assume EFQ, RAA is derivable (Exercise 3.1.2).

To conclude about the rules for negation, we see that these rules differ from the earlier ones in some respects. One can think of RAA as an elimination rule for negation, since $\neg$ occurs above the line (although in a discharged assumption) but not below. But the rule is not *pure*, since another logical constant (namely $\bot$) occurs above the line as well. Similarly if one views $\neg$I as an introduction rule for negation. So in this sense, the rules for negation in natural deduction do not have the simplicity and symmetry of the rules for the other connectives.

Digression 1: a linear format

Writing *ND* derivations as trees is perspicuous once you have the trees. But for finding the derivations, and for formalizing the intuitive reasoning behind it, many prefer a linear format. Here is how the derivation (11) could look in a linear version of natural deduction:

(12)

1	$\neg(\varphi \vee \neg\varphi)$	A
2	φ	A
3	$\varphi \vee \neg\varphi$	$\vee$I 2
4	$\bot$	$\neg$E 1,3
5	$\neg\varphi$	$\neg$I 2,4
6	$\varphi \vee \neg\varphi$	$\vee$I 5
7	$\bot$	$\neg$E 1,6
8	$\varphi \vee \neg\varphi$	RAA 1,7

The left column enumerates the rows, the middle column contains the sentences in the derivation, with explicit marking of how long each assumption is in force (until it is discharged), and the right column says which rule has been used, and on which rows.

Note that in (12) we do not need to write the assumption $\neg(\varphi \vee \neg\varphi)$ twice, even though it is used twice. In this way, the linear format is simpler. Experience shows that this format is easier to learn for beginning logic students. However, when one wants to study the *structure* of proofs, as one does in the logical discipline *proof theory*, the tree format has many advantages.

Digression 2: intuitionistic logic

The Law of Excluded Middle and the double negation law are examples of logical truths in classical logic that do not hold in *intuitionistic* logic. Consequently, the semantics of intuitionistic logic cannot be based on truth in an interpretation as in Chapter 2, and intuitionistic logical consequence is not necessary truth preservation (with respect to that semantics). Instead, these notions are based on an informal explanation of the meaning of the logical constants in terms of, not truth conditions, but *proof conditions*, or *assertibility conditions*.

The idea, for propositional logic, is to explain when you have the right to assert (or when you have a proof of) a negation, a conjunction, a disjunction, or an implication, in terms of when you have the right to assert (when you have a proof of) their parts.[10] Let us choose the formulation in terms of proofs. Then a proof of a conjunction $\varphi \wedge \psi$ consists of a proof of φ and a proof of ψ. And a proof of $\varphi \vee \psi$ consists of either a proof of φ or a proof of ψ.

The proof condition for an implication is the one that differs most from classical reasoning. A proof of $\varphi \rightarrow \psi$ is a *method* or *procedure* which, given any proof of φ produces a proof of ψ. Finally, $\neg\varphi$ is defined as $\varphi \rightarrow \bot$, and there is no proof of $\bot$, so a proof of $\neg\varphi$ is a proof showing that φ leads to contradiction.

These informal explanations already show why LEM cannot be considered valid in intuitionistic logic: it would say that for any sentence φ, we either have a proof of φ or a proof that φ leads to contradiction. But that is certainly not the case. For example, there are many mathematical open problems, statements of which we do not know if they are true or false, and may perhaps never know. So we have no proof one way or the other. Let θ be such a statement. Then the classical logician can still affirm $\theta \vee \neg\theta$; either θ or $\neg\theta$ is true, regardless of what θ 'says'.[11] But the intuitionistic logician cannot assert this.[12]

One natural reaction to this state of affairs is to say that although classicalists and intuitionists use the same logical *symbols*, they *mean* very different things by these symbols, and therefore the seemingly opposed views about LEM, for example, are not *really* in conflict. Be that as it may (it is actually a matter of debate), it is interesting to note that intuitionistic and classical *inference* are quite similar, and easily

[10]This is a rough version of the so-called BHK (Brouwer-Heyting-Kolmogorov) explanation of the meaning of the connectives. For (much) more information about these and about intuitionistic logic, see, for example, Moschovakis 2015.

[11]There are many cases when we do not know if a certain statement θ is true or not, even though we have a *method* that in principle decides the issue, only it (so far) takes too long to make the calculation. For example, θ could say that some very large number n is prime, and the method could be to divide n by smaller numbers; a procedure which ends after a finite number of steps. In this case the intuitionist too accepts $\theta \vee \neg\theta$. The problem, for the intuitionist, arises when infinitely many steps would be required to establish the truth value of θ.

[12]But this doesn't mean that the intuitionist asserts the negation of LEM; (s)he just *refrains* from asserting LEM. Indeed, the negation of LEM, $\neg(\varphi \vee \neg\varphi)$, is a contradiction in intuitionistic logic, as well as in classical logic. Thus, although $\varphi \vee \neg\varphi$ is not intuitionistically valid, $\neg\neg(\varphi \vee \neg\varphi)$ *is* intuitionistically valid! (See Exercise 3.3.12.)

comparable. In fact, *intuitionistic propositional logic* (in the natural deduction format) results from simply replacing RAA in our system of rules by EFQ, but keeping all the other rules.

But *why* would one deprive oneself of the use of RAA, which is obviously a very powerful rule? It boils down to different views of what a correct proof or argument is. This is most clear in the realm of mathematics. We emphasized in the introduction to this chapter that the *only* way for a mathematician to be able to assert the truth of a mathematical claim is to exhibit a proof of it. This holds for classicists and intuitionists alike. But RAA allows certain *non-constructive* proofs. For example, suppose you want to prove that *there is* something, a number, say, with the property P. Assume that there is no such number, and suppose you can derive a contradiction from that assumption. By RAA, you may conclude that some number is P. But you have not told us how to *find* any particular such number.

Intuitionists do not accept this as a proof that some number is P. They require of an existence proof that such a number be *exhibited*, or at least that one specifies a method for finding it.[13] We could now say that these are two different notions of proof, and that there is a real disagreement after all, namely, about which notion of proof is the *right* one. Alternatively, one may find both notions interesting. For example, constructive proofs often give more *information* than non-constructive proofs—we just saw an example in the case of proofs of existence claims. Even a classicist can be interested in finding such proofs, when they exist.

We shall not pursue intuitionistic logic, or the dispute between intuitionists and classicists, in this book. But the issue of what can be proved in PL (as well as in FOL) by means of EFQ, and what really needs the stronger RAA, is a matter of some interest; more information can be found in the exercises at the end of Section 3.1.

3.1.2. Rules for the quantifiers and identity

In the rules below, all premises and conclusions are *sentences* (no free variables), t is a *closed* term, and c is an individual constant.

[13]The BHK condition in this case says that a proof of $\exists x\varphi(x)$ consists of a closed term t and a proof of $\varphi(t)$.

$$\forall\text{I}: \quad \frac{\begin{array}{c}\vdots \\ \varphi(c)\end{array}}{\forall x\varphi(x)} \qquad\qquad \forall\text{E}: \quad \frac{\forall x\varphi(x)}{\varphi(t)}$$

$$\exists\text{I}: \quad \frac{\varphi(t)}{\exists x\varphi(x)} \qquad\qquad \exists\text{E}: \quad \frac{\exists x\varphi(x) \qquad \begin{array}{c}[\varphi(c)] \\ \vdots \\ \psi\end{array}}{\psi}$$

In $\forall$I, the constant c must not occur in $\varphi(x)$, nor in undischarged assumptions in the derivation of $\varphi(c)$. In $\exists$E, c must not occur in $\varphi(x)$, ψ, or in undischarged assumptions in the derivation of ψ, except in the assumption $\varphi(c)$.

Here the conditions on c in $\forall$I and $\exists$E are crucial. In the case of $\forall$I, it is assumed that there is a derivation of $\varphi(c)$ whose (undischarged) assumptions say nothing about c, so c is 'arbitrary', which is why we may conclude $\forall x\varphi(x)$. In the case of $\exists$E, we have a derivation of ψ where the only assumption that says anything about c is $\varphi(c)$. So here too c is 'arbitrary', and it is enough to assume that *there is* an x such that $\varphi(x)$ in order for ψ to follow.

These two rules usually take a little while to master. But note that their correctness, i.e. the fact the conclusion really is a logical consequence of the premises, is an immediate consequence of (42) in Chapter 2.3.3.

Let us look at a few examples. In order to show

(13) $\quad \vdash_{ND} \forall x(Px \vee \neg Px)$

we choose an arbitrary individual constant c and use (11), which gives us a derivation of $Pc \vee \neg Pc$. Note that (11), like our other examples so far, is a *derivation scheme*. If we *instantiate* (11) with Pc, i.e. we let φ be Pc, we obtain a derivation of $Pc \vee \neg Pc$. Then we apply $\forall$I, which is allowed since c does not occur in any undischarged assumption in this derivation of $Pc \vee \neg Pc$ (there are no undischarged assumptions at all), and neither in $Px \vee \neg Px$. So the requirement in $\forall$I is satisfied, and we have a derivation of $\forall x(Px \vee \neg Px)$.

The next derivation shows that

(14) $\quad \vdash_{ND} \forall xPx \rightarrow \exists xPx$

$$\cfrac{\cfrac{\cfrac{[\forall xPx]^1}{Pc}\,\forall\text{E}}{\exists xPx}\,\exists\text{I}}{\forall xPx \rightarrow \exists xPx}\,{\rightarrow}\text{I}_1$$

Here is a slightly more involved derivation, which shows that

(15) $\forall x \neg Px \vdash_{ND} \neg \exists x Px$

Before trying to find a derivation, one should decide on a strategy. When nothing else is obvious, it is often a good idea to try proof by contradiction. So we attempt to derive $\neg\exists x Px$ by assuming the opposite, that is, $\exists x Px$, and derive a contradiction from that. This existentially quantifed assumption is hard to use directly, but we know that if we assume Pc instead, where c is any new constant, and derive a contradiction from that, then we are done, by ∃E. And this is easy, since our premise $\forall x \neg Px$ entails $\neg Pc$ (using ∀E), so we have our contradiction. It only remains to carry through this idea formally:

$$\dfrac{\dfrac{[\exists x Px]^2 \qquad \dfrac{[Pc]^1 \qquad \dfrac{\forall x \neg Px}{\neg Pc}\,\forall\mathrm{E}}{\bot}\,\neg\mathrm{E}}{\bot}\,\exists\mathrm{E}_1}{\neg\exists x Px}\,\neg\mathrm{I}_2$$

As planned, for the application of the rule ∃E, we have derived a contradiction $\bot$ from the assumption Pc (and the assumption $\forall x \neg Px$, which is our premise). The constant c does not occur in Px or in $\bot$, nor in any assumption of the derivation of $\bot$, except of course in Pc. So the conditions for ∃E are satisfied, and we can conclude $\bot$ again, but now from $\exists x Px$; the assumption Pc is discharged. Finally, since $\exists x Px$ (together with $\forall x \neg Px$) leads to contradiction, we conclude $\neg\exists x Px$.

We may note that this proof by contradiction does not use RAA, but only the weaker ¬I, at the last step. This means that (15) holds not only in intuitionistic logic, but in fact without any rules for negation, except that negation is defined by means of $\rightarrow$ and $\bot$.[14]

Here is one more example (see also the exercises).

(16) $\forall x Px \vee \forall x Qx \vdash_{ND} \forall x (Px \vee Qx)$

The strategy this time is rather obvious: derive $Pc \vee Qc$ and use ∀I. Also, since the premise is a disjunction, we will need to use ∨E, thus deriving $Pc \vee Qc$ from both disjuncts.

$$\dfrac{\dfrac{\forall x Px \vee \forall x Qx \qquad \dfrac{\dfrac{[\forall x Px]^1}{Pc}\,\forall\mathrm{E}}{Pc \vee Qc}\,\vee\mathrm{I} \qquad \dfrac{\dfrac{[\forall x Qx]^1}{Qc}\,\forall\mathrm{E}}{Pc \vee Qc}\,\vee\mathrm{I}}{Pc \vee Qc}\,\vee\mathrm{E}_1}{\forall x (Px \vee Qx)}\,\forall\mathrm{I}$$

[14]The inference system consisting of just the rules for $\wedge$, $\vee$, and $\rightarrow$, and with the definition (6), but without RAA or EFQ, is called *minimal propositional logic*.

In this and the previous proof tree, it was obvious that the conditions for application of the rules $\forall$I and $\exists$E were satisfied. This is how it should be, for when using these rules, we *choose* a new individual constant, i.e. one that does not occur before. Other individual constants may have been involved (though that was not the case in the two derivations above), but we can always choose one that is distinct from all of these.

Finally, we give rules for identity. Rule $(=)_1$ is an *axiom*, i.e. a rule without premises. An important note about the notation in rule $(=)_2$ is this: the premise $\varphi(s)$ may contain, as usual, occurrences of the term s. But in the conclusion, written $\varphi(t)$, we allow that only *some* (not necessarily *all*) occurrences of s are replaced by t. s and t are, of course, closed terms.

$$(=)_1 \qquad \frac{}{t = t}$$

$$(=)_2 \qquad \frac{s = t \qquad \varphi(s)}{\varphi(t)} \qquad\qquad \frac{t = s \qquad \varphi(s)}{\varphi(t)}$$

As an example, let us show how one can derive the *symmetry* of identity using these rules:

(17) $\vdash_{ND} \forall x \forall y (x = y \rightarrow y = x)$

The obvious plan is to derive $c = d \rightarrow d = c$, and then use $\forall$I (twice).

$$\dfrac{\dfrac{\dfrac{\dfrac{[c = d]^1 \qquad \dfrac{}{c = c}(=)_1}{d = c}(=)_2}{c = d \rightarrow d = c}\rightarrow\mathrm{I}_1}{\forall y (c = y \rightarrow y = c)}\forall\mathrm{I}}{\forall x \forall y (x = y \rightarrow y = x)}\forall\mathrm{I}$$

Observe how rule $(=)_2$ is used on the second line: let $\varphi(z)$ be the formula $z = c$. Then $\varphi(c)$ is the sentence $c = c$ (which is an axiom). And so with the assumption $c = d$, we use $(=)_2$ to conclude $\varphi(d)$, which is $d = c$.

The rest is as before, but note that the conditions for the first application of $\forall$I are indeed satisfied: d does not occur in $c = y \rightarrow y = c$, nor in any *undischarged* assumption of the derivation (it occurs in $c = d$, but that assumption is discharged before $\forall$I is used). Similarly for the second use of $\forall$I: c does not occur in $\forall y (x = y \rightarrow y = x)$, nor in any undischarged assumptions. c does indeed occur in $c = c$, but that sentence is *not an assumption*, so the constraints on the occurrence of constants do not apply.

3.1.3. Exercises to Chapter 3.1

Exercise 3.1.1
Construct suitable proof trees to show the following:

1. $\varphi \wedge \psi \vdash_{ND} \psi \wedge \varphi$
2. $\varphi \vee \psi \vdash_{ND} \psi \vee \varphi$
3. $\neg(\varphi \vee \psi) \vdash_{ND} \neg\varphi \wedge \neg\psi$
4. $\neg\varphi \wedge \neg\psi \vdash_{ND} \neg(\varphi \vee \psi)$

   [For 3, show $\neg(\varphi \vee \psi) \vdash_{ND} \neg\varphi$ and $\neg(\varphi \vee \psi) \vdash_{ND} \neg\psi$. 3 as well as 4 only use $\neg$I to deal with negation.]

5. $\varphi \to \psi \vdash_{ND} \neg\psi \to \neg\varphi$
6. $\neg\psi \to \neg\varphi \vdash_{ND} \varphi \to \psi$

   [5 uses $\neg$I, but 6 requires RAA.]

7. $\varphi \vdash_{ND} \neg\neg\varphi$ [RAA is not needed.]
8. $\vdash_{ND} (\varphi \to (\psi \to \chi)) \to ((\varphi \to \psi) \to (\varphi \to \chi))$
9. $\vdash_{ND} (\neg\psi \to \neg\varphi) \to ((\neg\psi \to \varphi) \to \psi)$

Exercise 3.1.2
Take the Law of Excluded Middle as an axiom (a rule without premises):

LEM: $\dfrac{}{\varphi \vee \neg\varphi}$

1. Show that RAA is derivable from LEM and the other rules (including EFQ).
2. *Give a direct derivation showing that the double negation rule DNE implies LEM (i.e without using the fact that DNE implies RAA which implies LEM), even without EFQ.
3. *Conclude that our natural deduction system for classical PL can be obtained from the system for intuitionistic PL by adding any one of RAA, DNE, or LEM.
4. Show that

   $$\vdash_{ND} (\varphi \to \psi) \vee (\psi \to \varphi)$$

   (This is not provable in intuitionistic PL.)

Exercise 3.1.3
The following tautology is called *Peirce's Law*:

$$((\varphi \to \psi) \to \varphi) \to \varphi$$

1. Check that it is indeed a tautology.

2. *Derive Peirce's Law in classical *ND*, (It is not derivable in intuitionistic propositional logic; see Exercise 3.1.6.) [Hint: Use RAA to derive φ, assuming $(\varphi \to \psi) \to \varphi$.]

Exercise 3.1.4 (intuitionistic propositional logic 1)

1. Using the BHK-interpretation (footnote 10), try to give an intuitive explanation of why

$$(\neg\varphi \vee \neg\psi) \to \neg(\varphi \wedge \psi)$$

   is intuitionistically valid.

2. Similarly, explain why

$$\neg(\varphi \wedge \psi) \to (\neg\varphi \vee \neg\psi)$$

   is *not* intuitionistically valid.

Exercise 3.1.5 (intuitionistic propositional logic 2)
Let *NDI* be the natural deduction system for the PL language containing (besides the assumption rule) the usual introduction and elimination rules for $\wedge$, $\vee$, and $\to$, the definition of negation (6), and the rule EFQ. Show

1. $\neg\varphi \vee \neg\psi \vdash_{NDI} \neg(\varphi \wedge \psi)$ (cf. Exercise 3.1.4:1.)

2. $\neg(\varphi \vee \psi) \vdash_{NDI} \neg\varphi \wedge \neg\psi$

3. $\neg\varphi \wedge \neg\psi \vdash_{NDI} \neg(\varphi \vee \psi)$

These are three parts of de Morgan's Laws. As indicated in Exercise 3.1.4:2, the fourth part, $\neg(\varphi \wedge \psi) \to (\neg\varphi \vee \neg\psi)$, is not provable in *NDI*.

Exercise 3.1.6 (intuitionistic propositional logic 3)
*Show that if Peirce's Law is added as an axiom to *NDI*, then LEM can be proved (so the system becomes equivalent to classical *ND*: Exercise 3.1.2). [Hint: Show $\vdash_{NDI} ((\varphi \vee \neg\varphi) \to \bot) \to (\varphi \vee \neg\varphi)$, using Exercise 3.1.5:2.]

Exercise 3.1.7 (intuitionistic propositional logic 4)
*Show the following:

1. $\varphi \vee \psi, \neg\varphi \vdash_{NDI} \psi$ (disjunctive syllogism)
2. $\vdash_{NDI} \varphi \to \neg\neg\varphi$
3. $\vdash_{NDI} \neg\neg\neg\varphi \leftrightarrow \neg\varphi$

   [Hint: Use 2 and Exercise 3.1.1:5, noting that it holds in *NDI*. To show $\vdash_{NDI} \psi \leftrightarrow \theta$, it is enough to show $\vdash_{NDI} \psi \to \theta$ and $\vdash_{NDI} \theta \to \psi$.]
4. $\neg\neg(\varphi \to \psi) \vdash_{NDI} \neg\neg\varphi \to \neg\neg\psi$

   [Hint: Use Exercise 3.1.1:5.]
5. $\neg\neg\varphi \to \neg\neg\psi \vdash_{NDI} \neg\neg(\varphi \to \psi)$

   [Hint: Assume $\neg(\varphi \to \psi)$ and derive a contradiction, then apply $\neg$I. Use the fact that $\neg\varphi \to (\varphi \to \psi)$ is valid (easily derived from EFQ), Exercise 3.1.1:5, and also derive $\neg\psi$ from $\neg(\varphi \to \psi)$.]

Exercise 3.1.8
Show

1. $\exists x(Px \vee Qx) \vdash_{ND} \exists xPx \vee \exists xQx$ [cf. (16)]
2. $\neg\exists xPx \vdash_{ND} \forall x\neg Px$ [cf. (15)]
3. $\exists x\exists yRxy \vdash_{ND} \exists y\exists xRxy$
4. $\exists x\forall yRxy \vdash_{ND} \forall y\exists xRxy$

Exercise 3.1.9
Show

1. $\forall x(\psi \to \varphi(x)) \vdash_{ND} \psi \to \forall x\varphi(x)$
2. $\forall x(\varphi(x) \to \psi) \vdash_{ND} \exists x\varphi(x) \to \psi$

Exercise 3.1.10
Show

1. $\vdash_{ND} \forall x\forall y\forall z((x = y \wedge y = z) \to x = z)$
2. $Pc \wedge \neg Pd \vdash_{ND} \exists x\exists y\, x \neq y$

Exercise 3.1.11
Let us say that the *meaning* of a propositional connective is its truth table. We ask: Are the meanings of the usual connectives *fixed* by their corresponding *ND* rules? Or could a non-standard truth table for, say, $\vee$, be *consistent with* those rules, in the sense that if we interpret $\vee$ according to this non-standard table, the rules would still *preserve truth*?

1. Show that the introduction and elimination rules for $\wedge$ fix the standard truth table for conjunction.

2. *Show that the same holds for $\vee$. [Hint: Use the following special case of $\vee$-elimination: $\varphi \vee \varphi/\varphi$.]

3. *Do the same for $\to$ and $\neg$. [Hint: $\psi/\varphi \to \psi$ and $/\varphi \to \varphi$ are special cases of $\to$I. In particular, consistency with $\to$I means that $\varphi \to \varphi$ always has value 1. And $\bot$ has value 0 by EFQ/RAA.]

3.2. Interlude: constants as parameters

The quantifier rules for *ND* can only be used efficiently if the vocabulary contains enough individual constants, and the same holds for the inference systems to be introduced in the two remaining sections of this chapter. But these individual constants are not used in the 'normal' way—to name a particular object in some intended interpretation—as, for example, the symbol 0 is used in arithmetical languages to name the smallest natural number. Rather, they are *parameters*: temporary names, during an argument, of objects assumed to exist, as when an assumption $\exists x\varphi(x)$ allows us to give a name c to an object satisfying $\varphi(x)$ that we know exists, though we may have no further information about it. Or when we let c name an 'arbitrary' object and derive $\varphi(c)$, from which we then conclude $\forall x\varphi(x)$.

These parameters do not occur in the premises or conclusions we are ultimately interested in, but are necessary tools during derivations. We shall therefore assume, unless otherwise noted, that *an unlimited supply of individual constants is available* (more precisely a countably infinite set of them), distinct from individual constants in the vocabularies we specify.

There is an alternative to this approach: use *free variables* as parameters. This has the advantage that no syntactic changes are necessary. For example, the rule $\forall$I would then be as follows:

$$(\forall\text{I}) \qquad \frac{\begin{array}{c}\vdots \\ \varphi(t)\end{array}}{\forall x\varphi(x)}$$

where t is an individual constant or variable not occurring in φ or in any undischarged assumptions in the derivation of $\forall x\varphi(x)$.

Another advantage is that this use of variables corresponds rather closely to actual mathematical reasoning. We may say "Suppose x is a prime number. Then ...", and continue reasoning about x until it is no longer needed, say, when we conclude "For all prime numbers x ...". (We will see examples of this kind of reasoning in Chapter 9.)

Some introductory logic textbooks adopt this approach, and thus allow formulas with free variables to be true in interpretations (which then means that they are satisfied by all assignments), and to appear in premises and conclusions of inference rules. This may be mostly a cosmetic change: in *ND* we would simply impose the same restrictions on the free variable in the rules ∀I and ∃E as we did on the constant c.

Nevertheless, we shall continue to uphold the intuition that only *sentences* are true or false in interpretations, and can appear in derivations. Thus we avail ourselves whenever necessary of 'special' individual constants used as parameters.[15]

3.3. A Hilbert system

We now present a type of inference system which historically predates natural deduction. It goes back to Frege's *Begriffsschrift* (1879), was used by Russell and Whitehead in their *Principia Mathematica* (1910-13), and in fully formalized form by David Hilbert in the early 20th century; these systems are usually called *Hilbert systems*. Conceptually, they encode a very natural and simple notion of inference, based on the idea of an *axiomatic system*. There are a couple of (logical) axioms and very few inference rules (just two in our system for first-order logic). Derivations are simply finite sequences of sentences, no annotations or decorations are needed. Indeed, a main advantage of Hilbert systems is that it is easy to give a fully precise definition of the notion of a derivation.[16]

The system of axioms and rules used here will be called H, but the next definition works for any Hilbert system:

---

[15]For example, Mendelson 2015, following Kleene 1952, adopts the free variable approach for a Hilbert style inference system (see the next section). Due to the way he formulates the rule for ∀-introduction, this leads to certain complications for the crucial Deduction Theorem (see Section 3.3.2 below and Mendelson 2015, pp. 70–71). But many early texts, including Frege's axiomatic system and Gentzen's version of natural deduction, use *different symbols* for free and bound variables; the free variables in deductions are often called 'eigenparameters'. This is essentially the same as our use of individual constants as parameters here.

[16]In the case of the system *ND*, we gave an informal explanation of what a proof tree is, sufficient to convey the idea and to enable one to do some derivations, but we didn't give a precise (inductive) definition.

Definition 3.3.1 (derivations)
A *derivation in H of φ from* Γ is a finite sequence of sentences whose last sentence is φ, and is such that each sentence in the sequence is either (i) an assumption in Γ, or (ii) an axiom of H, or (iii) follows from *earlier* sentences in the sequence by means of a rule in H.

Thus:

(18) $\Gamma \vdash_H \varphi$ iff there is a derivation in H of φ from Γ.

Hilbert systems turn out to be well adapted to a study of certain *properties* of inference, as we will see later. They are less suited for finding and displaying actual derivations, at least initially.

3.3.1. Axioms and rules

Again we start with propositional logic. Moreover, we use a language which has only two logical connectives: $\neg$ and $\rightarrow$. The inference system H then has just three axioms (or rather axiom schemes) and one rule (for the propositional part). As we know, sentences with other connectives have equivalents in this language, so we lose no expressive power. But we gain a certain conceptual simplicity. In the exercises we show how familiar laws involving the other connectives can be derived in H, and we also present a variant Hilbert system for the full language (which thus has more axioms, but still only one rule).

(Ax1) $\varphi \rightarrow (\psi \rightarrow \varphi)$

(Ax2) $(\varphi \rightarrow (\psi \rightarrow \chi)) \rightarrow ((\varphi \rightarrow \psi) \rightarrow (\varphi \rightarrow \chi))$

(Ax3) $(\neg\psi \rightarrow \neg\varphi) \rightarrow ((\neg\psi \rightarrow \varphi) \rightarrow \psi)$

(MP) From φ and $\varphi \rightarrow \psi$, ψ follows.

That's all. Ax1 is a familiar tautology, and Ax2 expresses an intuitively obvious property of implication. Ax3 is a version of RAA, expressed not as a rule but as an axiom: if $\neg\psi$ implies both $\neg\varphi$ and φ (i.e. implies a contradiction), then ψ holds. And MP is the familiar rule of Modus Ponens.

Note that the axioms are *schemes*: φ, ψ, χ can be replaced by arbitrary sentences. We already used schemes when formulating the *ND* rules, and most of our derivations were schematic too, using metavariables rather than actual object language sentences. (Alternatively, one can let Ax1–Ax3 be actual sentences, with sentence letters in place of metavariables, and add an extra rule of Uniform Substitution; see Exercise 3.3.10.)

Now for some examples. It trivially holds that

$$\varphi \vdash_H \varphi$$

since the sequence whose only element is φ is a derivation in H of φ from φ, according to Definition 3.3.1. But in contrast with *ND* we have no rule that automatically allows us to conclude

(19) $\vdash_H \varphi \to \varphi$

But we can *derive* $\varphi \to \varphi$, without assumptions, as follows:

(20)			
	1	$\varphi \to ((\varphi \to \varphi) \to \varphi)$	Ax1
	2	$(\varphi \to ((\varphi \to \varphi) \to \varphi)) \to ((\varphi \to (\varphi \to \varphi)) \to (\varphi \to \varphi))$	Ax2
	3	$(\varphi \to (\varphi \to \varphi)) \to (\varphi \to \varphi)$	MP from 1,2
	4	$\varphi \to (\varphi \to \varphi)$	Ax1
	5	$\varphi \to \varphi$	MP from 3,4

Here the middle column, read from top to bottom, is the actual derivation; the other two columns are just for explanation. Row 1 is an instance of Ax1, where ψ has been replaced by $\varphi \to \varphi$. And row 2 is Ax2, also with ψ replaced by $\varphi \to \varphi$, and χ by φ. Once you have figured out what replacements to make, the rest is easy.

Is this fairly complicated derivation of such a simple tautology really necessary? Couldn't we just add $\varphi \to \varphi$ as an extra axiom? We could, but then the axiom system would not be *independent*: one axiom would be derivable from the others. For studying the properties of a Hilbert system, it is best to have as few axioms as possible.

But it is not always easy to guess what replacements in the axioms lead to the desired result. Fortunately, this problem will gradually disappear. For one thing, we can use already derived sentences in derivations of other sentences. More precisely: if

$$\varphi_1, \ldots, \psi, \ldots, \chi$$

is a derivation χ from $\Gamma \cup \{\psi\}$ (in H; from now on we will usually omit this qualification), and

$$\psi_1, \ldots, \psi_k, \psi$$

is a derivation of ψ from Γ (or some subset of Γ), then clearly

(21) $\varphi_1, \ldots, \psi_1, \ldots, \psi_k, \psi, \ldots, \chi$

is a derivation of χ from Γ: every sentence in (21) is either an axiom or an element of Γ or follows from earlier sentences by MP.

Here is an example of this:

(22) $\vdash_H (\neg\varphi \to \varphi) \to \varphi$

1	$(\neg\varphi \to \neg\varphi) \to ((\neg\varphi \to \varphi) \to \varphi)$	Ax3 (with $\psi = \varphi$)
2	$\neg\varphi \to \neg\varphi$	an instance of (19)
3	$(\neg\varphi \to \varphi) \to \varphi$	MP from 1,2

So here the middle column is not the actual derivation; before the second sentence one should insert its derivation according to (20) (with $\neg\varphi$ in place of φ). But, since our goal is to show that *there is* a derivation (without assumptions) of the third sentence, there is no point in writing the entire derivation—it is enough to know that the second sentence is in fact derivable (without assumptions). Here is a slightly more involved example:

(23) $\neg\neg\varphi \vdash_H \varphi$

1	$\neg\neg\varphi$	assumption
2	$\neg\neg\varphi \to (\neg\varphi \to \neg\neg\varphi)$	Ax1
3	$\neg\varphi \to \neg\neg\varphi$	MP from 1,2
4	$(\neg\varphi \to \neg\neg\varphi) \to ((\neg\varphi \to \neg\varphi) \to \varphi)$	Ax3 (with $\psi = \neg\varphi$)
5	$(\neg\varphi \to \neg\varphi) \to \varphi$	MP from 3,4
6	$\neg\varphi \to \neg\varphi$	from (19)
7	φ	MP from 5,6

One thing that makes derivations in H complicated is that there is no rule allowing conditionalization of assumptions; no rule of $\to$-introduction. But in fact such a rule can be *derived*:

Theorem 3.3.2 (Deduction Theorem)
If $\Gamma, \varphi \vdash_H \psi$, *then* $\Gamma \vdash_H \varphi \to \psi$.

This is an important fact about Hilbert type systems. We postpone its proof until Section 3.3.2, but use it in examples below.

(24) $\varphi \to \psi, \psi \to \chi \vdash_H \varphi \to \chi$

This says that implication is (provably) transitive. We show (24) as follows.

1	$\varphi \to \psi$	assumption
2	$\psi \to \chi$	assumption
3	φ	assumption
4	ψ	MP from 1,3
5	χ	MP from 2,4

This shows that $\varphi \to \psi, \psi \to \chi, \varphi \vdash_H \chi$. So (24) follows directly from the Deduction Theorem. The argument is much shorter than a direct derivation of (24). Next:

(25) $\neg\psi \to \neg\varphi \vdash_H \varphi \to \psi$

By the Deduction Theorem, it is enough to show $\neg\psi \to \neg\varphi, \varphi \vdash_H \psi$:

1	$\neg\psi \to \neg\varphi$	assumption
2	φ	assumption
3	$\varphi \to (\neg\psi \to \varphi)$	Ax1
4	$\neg\psi \to \varphi$	MP from 2,3
5	$(\neg\psi \to \neg\varphi) \to ((\neg\psi \to \varphi) \to \psi)$	Ax3
6	$(\neg\psi \to \varphi) \to \psi$	MP from 1,5
7	ψ	MP from 4,6

(26) $\vdash_H \neg\neg\varphi \to \varphi$

This is an immediate consequence of (23) and the Deduction Theorem.

(27) $\vdash_H \varphi \to \neg\neg\varphi$

It is enough to show $\varphi \vdash_H \neg\neg\varphi$. The derivation is analogous to the one for (23), but uses (26) (rather than (19)):

1	φ	assumption
2	$\varphi \to (\neg\neg\neg\varphi \to \varphi)$	Ax1
3	$\neg\neg\neg\varphi \to \varphi$	MP from 1,2
4	$(\neg\neg\neg\varphi \to \neg\varphi) \to ((\neg\neg\neg\varphi \to \varphi) \to \neg\neg\varphi)$	Ax3
5	$\neg\neg\neg\varphi \to \neg\varphi$	instance of (26)
6	$(\neg\neg\neg\varphi \to \varphi) \to \neg\neg\varphi$	MP from 4,5
7	$\neg\neg\varphi$	MP from 3,6

(28) $\varphi \to \psi \vdash_H \neg\psi \to \neg\varphi$

Here we can use our earlier results:

1	$\varphi \to \psi$	assumption
2	$\psi \to \neg\neg\psi$	(27)
3	$\neg\neg\varphi \to \varphi$	(26)
4	$\neg\neg\varphi \to \neg\neg\psi$	with (24) (transitivity, twice) from 1,2,3
5	$\neg\psi \to \neg\varphi$	with (25) from 4

Similarly we obtain using (28) and (27):

(29) a. $\varphi \to \neg\psi \vdash_H \psi \to \neg\varphi$

b. $\neg\varphi \to \psi \vdash_H \neg\psi \to \varphi$

Let us also derive *Ex Falso Quodlibet* in the system H:

(30) $\varphi, \neg\varphi \vdash_H \psi$ (EFQ)

1	φ	assumption
2	$\neg\varphi$	assumption
3	$\varphi \to (\neg\psi \to \varphi)$	Ax1
4	$\neg\psi \to \varphi$	MP from 1,3
5	$\neg\varphi \to \psi$	from 4 with (29b)
6	ψ	MP from 2,5

As to $\wedge$ and $\vee$ we may, instead of seeing disjunctions and conjunctions as abbreviations, allow them in the language and add axioms guaranteeing that $\varphi \vee \psi \equiv_H \neg\varphi \to \psi$ and $\varphi \wedge \psi \equiv_H \neg(\varphi \to \neg\psi)$; see Exercise 3.3.2. But it is more natural to use axioms that correspond to the meaning of $\wedge$ and $\vee$ (Exercise 3.3.4).

To deal with the quantifiers in H we add four axiom schemes and one new rule. Below, ψ is a sentence, φ is a formula with at most x free, and t is a closed term.

(Ax4) $\forall x\varphi(x) \to \varphi(t)$

(Ax5) $\forall x(\psi \to \varphi(x)) \to (\psi \to \forall x\varphi(x))$

(Ax6) $\varphi(t) \to \exists x\varphi(x)$

(Ax7) $\forall x(\varphi(x) \to \psi) \to (\exists x\varphi(x) \to \psi)$

($R\forall$) $\forall x\varphi(x)$ follows from $\varphi(c)$, provided condition ($R\forall$*) holds.

Recall that Definition 3.3.1 specifies what it is for a finite sequence of sentences, ending with ψ, to be a *derivation of ψ from Γ*, where condition (iii) was "follows from earlier sentences in the sequence by means of a rule in H". What this means is clear for MP: there must be two sentences of the form χ and $\chi \to \psi$ earlier in the sequence. For $R\forall$, we stipulate that it means the following:

($R\forall$*) ψ has the form $\forall x\varphi(x)$ and a sentence of the form $\varphi(c)$ occurs earlier in the sequence, where c occurs neither in $\varphi(x)$ nor in sentences belonging to Γ that appear earlier in the sequence.

This corresponds to the conditions on c in the ND-rules $\forall$I and $\exists$E.

A first important fact is that the Deduction Theorem also holds for H with the new axioms and the rule $R\forall$. (It also holds when axioms for identity are added; see below.) This is shown in the next subsection. It means that all the propositional laws for H that we just derived are still valid. Here is a slightly involved example of a derivation involving quantifiers (see the exercises for more examples). We show:

(31) $\forall x\neg\varphi(x) \vdash_H \neg\exists x\varphi(x)$

(Compare the derivation of (15) in the preceding section.) Let c be an individual constant that does not occur in $\varphi(x)$.

1	$\forall x \neg\varphi(x)$	assumption
2	$\forall x \neg\varphi(x)) \to \neg\varphi(c)$	Ax4
3	$(\forall x \neg\varphi(x)) \to \neg\varphi(c)) \to (\varphi(c) \to \neg\forall x \neg\varphi(x))$	instance of (29)
4	$\varphi(c) \to \neg\forall x \neg\varphi(x)$	MP from 2,3
5	$\forall x(\varphi(x) \to \neg\forall x \neg\varphi(x))$	$R\forall$ from 4
6	$\forall x(\varphi(x) \to \neg\forall x \neg\varphi(x)) \to (\exists x\varphi(x) \to \neg\forall x \neg\varphi(x))$	Ax7
7	$\exists x\varphi(x) \to \neg\forall x \neg\varphi(x)$	MP from 5,6
8	$(\exists x\varphi(x) \to \neg\forall x \neg\varphi(x)) \to (\forall x \neg\varphi(x) \to \neg\exists x\varphi(x))$	instance of (29)
9	$\forall x \neg\varphi(x) \to \neg\exists x\varphi(x)$	MP from 7,8
10	$\neg\exists x\varphi(x)$	MP from 1,9

Note that the application of $R\forall$ at line 5 is correct: c does not occur in the formula $\varphi(x) \to \neg\forall x\neg\varphi(x)$, nor in any assumption. On the other hand, c does occur in axioms and other derived sentences before line 5, but this is permitted according to $R\forall^*$. Note further that only the free occurrences of x in the antecedent $\varphi(x)$ are bound by the leftmost occurrence of $\forall x$ on line 5; the occurrences of x in the consequent $\neg\forall x\neg\varphi(x)$ are already bound. Normally, one would choose another variable y here, but in this particular case we wanted to conclude $\neg\exists x\varphi(x)$ directly. Alternatively, we could first derive $\neg\exists y\varphi(y)$, and then from there $\neg\exists x\varphi(x)$.

The following is an immediate consequence of the formulation of the $R\forall$ rule:

(32) If $\Gamma \vdash_H \varphi(c)$, where c does not occur in Γ or in $\varphi(x)$, then $\Gamma \vdash_H \forall x\varphi(x)$.

We have a corrsponding fact for the existential quantifier:

(33) If $\Gamma, \varphi(c) \vdash_H \psi$, where c does not occur in Γ, $\varphi(x)$ or ψ, then we have $\Gamma, \exists x\varphi(x) \vdash_H \psi$.

Proof. Suppose $\Gamma, \varphi(c) \vdash_H \psi$, with c as above. By the Deduction Theorem, $\Gamma \vdash_H \varphi(c) \to \psi$. Since condition $R\forall^*$ is satisfied, it follows by the rule $R\forall$ that $\Gamma \vdash_H \forall x(\varphi(x) \to \psi)$. Using Ax7 and MP, we obtain $\Gamma \vdash_H \exists x\varphi(x) \to \psi$. So, using MP once more, we have $\Gamma, \exists x\varphi(x) \vdash_H \psi$. □

Finally, here are the axioms for identity:

(Ax8) $\forall x\, x = x$

(Ax9) $\forall x \forall y(x = y \to (\varphi(x) \to \varphi(y)))$

NB Here we are using $\varphi(x)$ and $\varphi(y)$ as we did $\varphi(s)$ and $\varphi(t)$ in the *ND*-rules for identity. We could also formulate the present axioms using closed terms as in *ND*; see Exercise 3.3.7. It is fairly easy to show:

(34) a. $\vdash_H \forall x \forall y(x = y \rightarrow y = x)$

b. $\vdash_H \forall x \forall y \forall z(x = y \wedge y = z \rightarrow x = z)$

c. If f is an n-ary function symbol,

$\vdash_H \forall x_1 \ldots x_n \forall y_1 \ldots \forall y_n (\bigwedge_{i=1}^{n} x_i = y_i \rightarrow fx_1 \ldots x_n = fy_1 \ldots y_n)$

3.3.2. The Deduction Theorem

In Chapter 2 we saw several examples of proof by *induction over formulas*: To show that *every* formula has a certain property P, you first show that atomic formlas have P, and then that *if* φ and ψ have P (the induction hypothesis) *then* also $\neg\varphi$, $\varphi \rightarrow \psi$, $\varphi \wedge \psi$, $\varphi \vee \psi$, $\forall x\varphi$, and $\exists x\varphi$ have property P.

A common way of proving things (in our metatheory) about inference systems is *induction over (the length of) derivations.* This method is particularly suited to Hilbert style systems, since derivations have such a simple structure. They also have the following useful property:

(35) If $\psi_0, \ldots, \psi_n$ is a derivation in H of ψ_n from Γ, then, for all $k \leqslant n$, $\psi_0, \ldots, \psi_k$ is a derivation in H of ψ_k from Γ.

That is, every *initial segment* of a derivation is also a derivation (from the same assumptions). This follows from Definition 3.3.1: rule applications only look at *earlier* sentences in the derivation sequence, and the requirement $R\forall^*$ is preserved for initial segments.

Now suppose you want to show that if $\Gamma \vdash_H \varphi$, then φ has property P. For this it is enough to show that the following holds, *for every* n, and all sentences $\psi_0, \ldots, \psi_n$:

(A_n) If $\psi_0, \ldots, \psi_n$ is a derivation in H of ψ_n from Γ, then ψ_n has property P.

The claim that (A_n) holds for every n can sometimes be proved by induction over the natural numbers. The base case is $n = 0$; then the derivation consists of a single sentence, so ψ_0 must be either a logical axiom or an element of Γ, and one needs to check that such sentences have property P. For the induction step it will in general be hard to show that (A_{n-1}) implies (A_n) for every n. This is because rule applications can use sentences arbitrarily far back in the sequence, so we will need to apply the induction hypothesis for derivations of length i, for any $i < n$, not just $i = n - 1$.

We get around this by slightly reformulating the induction hypothesis: instead of assuming (A_{n-1}), we assume that (A_i) holds for *all* $i < n$. This is so-called *strong induction*. That is, instead of showing that (A_{n-1}) implies (A_n) for every $n > 0$, we show, for every n, that if (A_i) holds for *all* $i < n$, then (A_n) holds. A nice thing about this formulation is that it covers the case $n = 0$ too: since there are no numbers smaller than 0, the antecedent "for all $i < 0$, (A_i) holds" is trivially true, so the implication is true iff (A_0) is true. Summarizing, *if* we can show, for all n,

(36) If (A_i) holds for $i < n$ (the induction hypothesis), then (A_n)

then we can be sure that for all n, (A_n) holds, which is what we wanted to prove. This holds for any property of numbers. For properties like (A_n) above, where n is the length of a certain derivation, the fact that initial segments of derivations are also derivations simplifies matters considerably.

An instructive application of this method is the proof of the Deduction Theorem (Theorem 3.3.2), repeated here:

(37) If $\Gamma, \varphi \vdash_H \psi$, then $\Gamma \vdash_H \varphi \to \psi$.

Proof. In this case, the property (A_n) is the following:

(A_n) If $\psi_0, \ldots, \psi_n$ is a derivation in H of ψ_n from $\Gamma \cup \{\varphi\}$, then $\Gamma \vdash_H \varphi \to \psi_n$.

If we can show that (A_n) holds for every n, then (37) follows. We use strong induction. Thus, take any n, and assume that (A_i) holds for all $i < n$ (induction hypothesis). We must show that then (A_n) holds too.

Now ψ_n is either an element of Γ, or it is φ, or it is a logical axiom (Ax1–Ax9), or it follows from earlier sentences in $\psi_0, \ldots, \psi_n$ by MP or $R\forall$. We look at each case in turn.

(a) $\psi_n \in \Gamma$: Then $\Gamma \vdash_H \psi_n$. But $\psi_n \to (\varphi \to \psi_n)$ is an axiom (Ax1). Thus, using MP, we see that $\Gamma \vdash \varphi \to \psi_n$.

(b) $\psi_n = \varphi$: In this case, what needs to be shown is $\Gamma \vdash \varphi \to \varphi$. But we already know that $\vdash_H \varphi \to \varphi$ without any assumptions (see (19) in Section 3.3.1), and thus $\Gamma \vdash_H \varphi \to \varphi$.

(c) ψ_n is an axiom: Then $\vdash_H \psi_n$, and just as in case (a) we get $\vdash_H \varphi \to \psi_n$, and hence $\Gamma \vdash_H \varphi \to \psi_n$.

(d) ψ_n was obtained with MP, which means that there are $i, j < n$ such that $\psi_j = \psi_i \to \psi_n$. The induction hypothesis entails that $\Gamma \vdash_H \varphi \to \psi_i$ and $\Gamma \vdash_H \varphi \to (\psi_i \to \psi_n)$. But

$$(\varphi \to (\psi_i \to \psi_n)) \to ((\varphi \to \psi_i) \to (\varphi \to \psi_n))$$

is Ax2. So using MP we first obtain $\Gamma \vdash_H (\varphi \to \psi_i) \to (\varphi \to \psi_n)$, and then $\Gamma \vdash_H \varphi \to \psi_n$.

(e) ψ_n was obtained with $R\forall$, so ψ_n has the form $\forall x\theta(x)$ and there is $i < n$ such that $\psi_i = \theta(c)$, where c satisfies condition $R\forall$*: c does not occur in $\theta(x)$ or in φ or in the sentences in Γ. By the induction hypothesis, $\Gamma \vdash_H \varphi \to \theta(c)$. But then, with $R\forall$, we have $\Gamma \vdash_H \forall x(\varphi \to \theta(x))$. And then, using Axiom Ax5 and MP, we get $\Gamma \vdash_H \varphi \to \forall x\theta(x)$, that is, $\Gamma \vdash_H \varphi \to \psi_n$.

This conclude the proof. □

Note that the only axioms used in this proof are Ax1, Ax2, and Ax5. It follows that the Deduction Theorem holds for any Hilbert style system where these are derivable, and whose only rules are MP and $R\forall$.

3.3.3. *H versus ND

In this section we show that *H* and *ND*, although based on different ideas about derivation, are extensionally equivalent: if φ can be derived from Γ in one of the systems, φ can be derived from Γ in the other system. The proof, in both directions, uses induction over derivations.

Lemma 3.3.3
If $\Gamma \vdash_H \varphi$, *then* $\Gamma \vdash_{ND} \varphi$.

Proof. Again, it is enough to show that for each n:

(B_n) If $\psi_0, \ldots, \psi_n$ is a derivation in *H* of ψ_n from Γ, then $\Gamma \vdash_{ND} \psi_n$.

So fix n, and suppose (B_i) holds for $i < n$. We must show (B_n). There are a few cases to consider. If $\psi_n \in \Gamma$, then $\Gamma \vdash_{ND} \psi_n$ by the assumption rule (A). Next, we must check that each of the axioms Ax1–Ax9 is derivable in *ND* (indeed without assumptions). But these are facts that we have already shown, of left as exercises to show. Ax1 is (3) in Section 3.1. Ax2 and Ax3 are 8 and 9, respectively, in Exercise 3.1.1. Ax4 follows directly from the rules ∀E and →I, and Ax6 from ∃I and →I. Ax5 and Ax7 are 1 and 2, respectively, in Exercise 3.1.9. And Ax8 and Ax9 follow easily from the identity rules in *ND*, together with (→I and) ∀I.

The next case is that ψ_n was obtained by MP from earlier sentences, which according to the induction hypothesis are derivable from Γ in *ND*. Since Modus Ponens is a rule in *ND* too (i.e. →E), it easily follows that ψ_n is derivable from Γ in *ND*.

The final case is when $R\forall$ was used to get $\psi_n = \forall x\theta(x)$, so there is $i < n$ such that $\psi_i = \theta(c)$, where c does not occur in $\theta(x)$ or in the sentences in Γ. By the induction hypothesis, $\Gamma \vdash_{ND} \theta(c)$. But this means that the conditions for applying $\forall$I are satisfied, which gives $\Gamma \vdash_{ND} \forall x\theta(x)$. □

Lemma 3.3.4
If $\Gamma \vdash_{ND} \varphi$, *then* $\Gamma \vdash_H \varphi$.

Proof. (Outline) We didn't give a really precise definition of derivation in *ND*, but essentially, what one must do is to show that for each *ND* rule, if the premises of the rule are derivable in H from Γ, then so is the conclusion. For example, suppose we are looking at a rule R with two premises, like $\wedge$I, or $\exists$E (in the latter case the rule allows discharging an assumption). Then we need to show:

(38) If the last step in a derivation of φ from Γ in *ND* is an application of R with φ as conclusion and φ_1, φ_2 as premises, and if $\Gamma, \psi_i \vdash_H \varphi_i$ for $i = 1, 2$, where ψ_i are assumptions in the *ND*-derivation of φ_i that may be discharged at the application of R, then $\Gamma \vdash_H \varphi$.

Similarly for other rule forms. Now we formulated H for a language with just $\neg$ and $\rightarrow$ as propositional connectives (but see Exercise 3.3.4), so we think of $\wedge$ and $\vee$ as defined. How this works in H is described in Exercise 3.3.2; using this one takes care of the introduction and elimination rules for $\wedge$ and $\vee$. For $\rightarrow$E and $\rightarrow$I we use MP and the Deduction Theorem, respectively. Let us look at $\vee E$ as an example: here φ is derived from three premises: $\varphi_1 = \theta_1 \vee \theta_2$, $\varphi_2 = \varphi$ (normally) derived with θ_1 as an assumption, and $\varphi_3 = \varphi$ (normally) derived with θ_2 as an assumption. This means that the assumption in (the corresponding version of) (38), that is, the induction hypothesis, is that we have $\Gamma \vdash_H \theta_1 \vee \theta_2$, $\Gamma, \theta_1 \vdash_H \varphi$, and $\Gamma, \theta_2 \vdash_H \varphi$. From this we easily see that $\Gamma \vdash_H \varphi$.

As to the rules for negation, we defined $\neg\psi$ as $\psi \rightarrow \bot$ in Section 3.1; if instead $\neg$ were taken as a primitive symbol one can choose $\neg$I and RAA as rules for negation, where the symbol $\bot$ in these rules is replaced by some fixed contradictory sentence θ_0, for example, $\theta_0 = \exists x\, x \neq x$ (so that $\vdash_H \neg\theta_0$). In the case when φ in (38) is obtained with R = $\neg$I, φ has the form $\neg\psi$, where the induction hypothesis now is that $\Gamma, \psi \vdash_H \theta_0$. Thus, $\Gamma \vdash_H \psi \rightarrow \theta_0$, which together with $\vdash_H \neg\theta_0$ gives $\vdash_H \neg\psi$. The case R = RAA is similar.

That (38) holds when R is one of the quantifier rules is seen with the help of (32), (33) and Exercise 3.3.5. Finally, the identity rules in *ND* are dealt with using the identity axioms in H. □

Thus, we have shown:

Theorem 3.3.5
ND and H are equivalent, i.e. for every sentence φ and set of sentences Γ (in some vocabulary L), we have $\Gamma \vdash_H \varphi$ if and only if $\Gamma \vdash_{ND} \varphi$.

3.3.4. Exercises to Chapter 3.3

Exercise 3.3.1
Construct derivations in H that verify the following claims. (You may use the Deduction Theorem and earlier established results.)

1. $\neg(\varphi \to \psi) \vdash_H \varphi$
   [Start with $\vdash \neg\varphi \to (\varphi \to \psi)$ (from EFQ and the Deduction Theorem).]
2. $\neg(\varphi \to \psi) \vdash_H \neg\psi$ [Use Ax1.]
3. $\varphi \to (\psi \to \chi) \vdash_H \psi \to (\varphi \to \chi)$

Exercise 3.3.2
1. Given that $\varphi \wedge \psi$ is an abbreviation of $\neg(\varphi \to \neg\psi)$, and $\varphi \vee \psi$ an abbreviation of $\neg\varphi \to \psi$, show $\varphi \wedge \psi \vdash_H \varphi$ and $\varphi \wedge \psi \vdash_H \psi$. In other words, what is to be shown [use Exercise 3.3.1] is
   (a) $\neg(\varphi \to \neg\psi) \vdash_H \varphi$
   (b) $\neg(\varphi \to \neg\psi) \vdash_H \psi$
2. Show
   (a) $\vdash_H \varphi \to (\psi \to (\varphi \wedge \psi))$
   [Start from $\varphi, \varphi \to \neg\psi \vdash_H \neg\psi$, use Deduction Theorem and (29).]
3. Similarly, show
   (a) $\varphi \vdash_H \varphi \vee \psi$
   (b) $\psi \vdash_H \varphi \vee \psi$
   (c) $\vdash_H \varphi \vee \neg\varphi$ (LEM)
   (d) $\vdash_H \varphi \vee \psi, \neg\varphi \vdash_H \psi$ (disjunctive syllogism)
   (e) $\varphi \to \chi, \psi \to \chi \vdash_H (\varphi \vee \psi) \to \chi$
   (f) If $\Gamma, \varphi \vdash_H \psi$, and $\Gamma, \neg\varphi \vdash_H \psi$, then $\Gamma \vdash_H \psi$.

Exercise 3.3.3
*Show

$$\vdash_H ((\varphi \to \psi) \to \varphi) \to \varphi \quad \text{(Peirce's Law)}$$

Exercise 3.3.4 (alternative axioms for propositional logic)
Let H' be the inference system for propositional logic with the connectives $\neg, \wedge, \vee, \rightarrow$ obtained from H (or propositional logic) by replacing Ax3 with the following axioms:

(PL3) $(\varphi \wedge \psi) \rightarrow \varphi$

(PL4) $(\varphi \wedge \psi) \rightarrow \psi$

(PL5) $\varphi \rightarrow (\psi \rightarrow (\varphi \wedge \psi))$

(PL6) $\varphi \rightarrow \varphi \vee \psi$

(PL7) $\psi \rightarrow \varphi \vee \psi$

(PL8) $((\varphi \rightarrow \chi) \wedge (\psi \rightarrow \chi)) \rightarrow ((\varphi \vee \psi) \rightarrow \chi)$

(PL9) $(\varphi \wedge \neg\varphi) \rightarrow \psi$

(PL10) $\neg\neg\varphi \rightarrow \varphi$

*Show that H and H' are equivalent. [A strict proof uses induction over the length of derivations; Section 3.3.3. Note that the Deduction Theorem holds for H'.]

Exercise 3.3.5
Show (where t is a closed term):

1. If $\Gamma \vdash_H \forall x\varphi(x)$, then $\Gamma \vdash_H \varphi(t)$.
2. If $\Gamma \vdash_H \varphi(t)$, then $\Gamma \vdash_H \exists x\varphi(x)$.
3. If $\Gamma, \varphi(t) \vdash_H \psi$, then $\Gamma, \forall x\varphi(x) \vdash_H \psi$.

Exercise 3.3.6
Show (using, among other things, Exercise 3.3.5):

1. $\vdash_H \forall x(\varphi(x) \rightarrow \psi(x)) \rightarrow (\forall x\varphi(x) \rightarrow \forall x\psi(x))$
2. $\forall x\forall yRxy \vdash_H \forall y\forall xRxy$
3. $\exists x\exists yRxy \vdash_H \exists y\exists xRxy$
   [First, show $Rcd \vdash_H \exists y\exists xRxy$ and then use (33).]
4. $\exists y\forall xRxy \vdash_H \forall x\exists yRxy$
   [Show $\forall xRxd \vdash_H \forall x\exists yRxy$ and use (33).]

Exercise 3.3.7 (alternative identity axioms)
Show that H is equivalent to the system obtained by replacing Ax8 and Ax9 with the following axioms, where s and t are closed terms.

(Ax8′) $t = t$
(Ax9′) $s = t \rightarrow (\varphi(s) \rightarrow \varphi(t))$

Exercise 3.3.8
Show that (34) holds.

Exercise 3.3.9
When t is a closed term and $\varphi(x)$ has at most x free, show

1. $\vdash_H \varphi(t) \leftrightarrow \exists x(x = t \wedge \varphi(x))$
2. $\vdash_H \varphi(t) \leftrightarrow \forall x(x = t \rightarrow \varphi(x))$

Exercise 3.3.10
*We axiomatized propositional logic in the Hilbert system H with three *axiom schemes*, Ax1–Ax3, and one rule, MP. Thus the number of axioms (object language sentences of these forms) is infinite. An alternative is to have three *axioms*, namely (where p, q, r are fixed sentence letters),

(A1) $p \rightarrow (q \rightarrow p)$

(A2) $(p \rightarrow (q \rightarrow r)) \rightarrow ((p \rightarrow q) \rightarrow (p \rightarrow r))$

(A3) $(\neg q \rightarrow \neg p) \rightarrow ((\neg q \rightarrow p) \rightarrow q)$

and two rules: MP and a *Uniform Substitution rule* S. Let $\varphi = \varphi(q_1, \ldots, q_n)$ mean that the sentence letters in φ are among $q_1, \ldots, q_n$. Also, let $\varphi(\psi_1/q_1, \ldots, \psi_n/q_n)$ be the result of (simultaneously) replacing all occurrences of $q_1, \ldots, q_n$ in φ with the sentences $\psi_1, \ldots, \psi_n$, respectively. Restrict attention to derivations *without assumptions*. Then rule S says that $\varphi(\psi_1/q_1, \ldots, \psi_n/q_n)$ follows from $\varphi(q_1, \ldots, q_n)$, for any sentences $\psi_1, \ldots, \psi_n$. Let H^s be this variant of H. Show:

1. If $\vdash_H \varphi(q_1, \ldots, q_n)$, then $\vdash_H \varphi(\psi_1/q_1, \ldots, \psi_n/q_n)$. [Use induction over the length of derivations.]

2. For every sentence φ in propositional logic, we have $\vdash_H \varphi$ iff $\vdash_{H^s} \varphi$. [Induction over the length of derivations.]

3. Why doesn't rule S work if we allow assumptions? How could we amend it to work for derivations with assumptions?

Exercise 3.3.11

1. Explain how it follows from the definitions of the relations $\vdash_{ND}$ and $\vdash_H$ that these relations are *monotone*, in the sense that if $\Gamma \vdash_{ND} \varphi$ and $\Gamma \subseteq \Delta$, then $\Delta \vdash_{ND} \varphi$, and similarly for $\vdash_H$.

2. Suppose $\psi_0, \ldots, \psi_n$ is a derivation in H (of ψ_n) from Γ, and let θ be any sentence. Does it follow that $\theta, \psi_0, \ldots, \psi_n$ is a derivation in H (of ψ_n) from Γ? If not always, under what circumstances does it follow?

Exercise 3.3.12 (intuitionistic propositional logic 5)
*There are interesting so-called *negative translations* from intuitionistic to classical logic. Here we look at the simplest one, *Glivenko's Theorem*: the double negation of any theorem in classical propositional logic is a theorem in intuitionistic propositional logic.

We take H' from Exercise 3.3.4 to be our classical system. The intuitionistic version, call it $H'I$, is obtained by replacing the double negation axiom, PL10, by $(\varphi \to \psi) \to ((\varphi \to \neg\psi) \to \neg\varphi)$ (corresponding to $\neg$I). In Exercises 3.1.4 – 3.1.7 we looked at the natural deduction version *NDI*. One can show that *NDI* and $H'I$ are equivalent, so the results established for *NDI* hold for $H'I$ too; we use this below. Thus, the task is to show that for any PL-formula φ,

(GT) $\quad \vdash_{H'} \varphi \text{ iff } \vdash_{H'I} \neg\neg\varphi$

The right-to-left direction of (GT) is easy. The other direction is by induction over theorems in H'. This means that we need to check two things: (a) if φ is an axiom in H', then $\vdash_{H'I} \neg\neg\varphi$; and (b) if $\vdash_{H'I} \neg\neg\varphi$ and $\vdash_{H'I} \neg\neg(\varphi \to \psi)$, then $\vdash_{H'I} \neg\neg\psi$.

1. Check that (a) holds when φ is one of Ax1, Ax2, PL1 – PL9.
2. Prove that (a) holds also for PL10: show $\vdash_{H'I} \neg\neg(\neg\neg\varphi \to \varphi)$. [Hint: Use (the $H'I$ versions of) Exercise 3.1.7: 5 and 3.]
3. Verify that (b) holds. [Hint: use Exercise 3.1.7: 4.]

Exercise 3.3.13
Since $p, p \to q \vdash_H q$, the Deduction Theorem immediately tells us that

$$p \vdash_H (p \to q) \to q$$

To appreciate the use of the Deduction Theorem, write a full derivation (sequence of sentences) in H establishing this fact. [Hint: For a strategy, look at the proof of the Deduction Theorem.]

Part II

Completeness

4 Completeness: PL

The goal of this chapter and the next is to show that for all sets of sentences Γ and all sentences φ (in some vocabulary L), the following holds:

(1) $\Gamma \vdash_H \varphi$ iff $\Gamma \models \varphi$

That is, the inference system H is *sound* (left-to-right) and *complete* (right-to-left). By Theorem 3.3.5, the same holds for the system *ND*.

As we said in the introductory chapter, (1) is by no means trivial. The right-hand side says that *all interpretations* making (all sentences in) Γ true also make φ true. The left-hand side says that *there exists a derivation* in H of φ from Γ. The two sides seem to be about different things, interpretations and derivations, respectively, and in addition there is universal quantification in one case and existential quantification in the other.

Actually, soundness is easy to verify, since the axioms in H are logically true, and the rules preserve truth; for the record we give a precise statement in Section 4.1 below. Soundness is a minimal requirement on any inference system; if you cannot be sure that the system takes you from true premises to true conclusions, it is not worth much. Completeness, on the other hand, says that the system (in this case H) doesn't miss any facts about logical consequence: the axioms and the rules—which are *syntactic* in the sense that they only refer to the form of the sentences involved, not to their meaning—manage to *exactly* capture the *semantic* concept of logical consequence.

It is quite remarkable that these two very different ideas about how to explain 'what follows from what' turn out to be (extensionally) equivalent (see also Exercise 5.6.8).[1] How can the information that no interpretations make the sentences in Γ true and φ false be used to construct a derivation of φ from Γ?

[1]There are logical systems for which completeness fails, for example, *second-order logic*, where you also can quantify over sets of individuals. That is, one can still formulate natural inference rules and axioms for second-order logic, but no system of rules can capture exactly validity or consequence in second-order logic.

In this chapter we show how this can be done in the case of propositional logic, where interpretations are assignments of truth values to sentences letters. At least when the number of premises is finite, there are only finitely many sentence letters involved, and hence only finitely many possible interpretations of these, so the problem seems more tractable for propositional logic. We may also note that in propositional logic, (1) entails that the system H is *decidable*: there is an algorithm for deciding, for any finite set of sentences Γ and any sentence φ, whether there is a derivation of φ from Γ or not. One such algorithm is the usual truth table method.

The completeness of (a system for) propositional logic was first shown by Paul Bernays in 1918 and (independently) by Emil Post in 1920. Here we shall use a method introduced by Leon Henkin in 1945, which works also for first-order logic; indeed it introduces ideas that are widely applicable. (For a different proof, see Exercise 4.8.12.)

Since we are talking about completeness with respect to the system H, we use the same logical connectives as in Chapter 3.3: $\neg$ and $\rightarrow$ are primitive; the others defined in terms of these.

4.1. Soundness

The following result applies to both PL and FOL. Let Γ be a set of sentences and φ a sentence in some vocabulary L.

Theorem 4.1.1 (Soundness of first-order logic)
If $\Gamma \vdash_H \varphi$, then $\Gamma \models \varphi$.

Proof. The proof is by induction on the length of derivations in H. Thus, we must show that (a) if φ is an axiom or an element of Γ, then $\Gamma \models \varphi$; (b) if φ follows with MP from sentences ψ and $\psi \rightarrow \varphi$, where we already know that $\Gamma \models \psi$ and $\Gamma \models \psi \rightarrow \varphi$, then $\Gamma \models \varphi$; and (c) if $\varphi = \forall x \theta(x)$ is derived from $\theta(c)$ with the rule $R\forall$, where condition $R\forall^*$ is satisfied and we already know that $\Gamma \models \theta(c)$, then $\Gamma \models \varphi$.

As to (a), it is trivial that the elements of a set of sentences are consequences of that set, and we already noted in Chapter 2 (explicitly in some cases, in others implicitly or in exercises) that Ax1–Ax9 are logical truths (and hence logical consequences of Γ). (b) is obviously true, and we formulated (c) as (42b) in Chapter 2.3.3 (and Exercise 2.4.20). □

It may seem that this proof is circular, because we 'showed' that certain logical principles are valid by appealing to those very principles (plus mathematical induction). But that is not so. What we did show was not that the logical principles are valid, which is essentially obvious, but that our formal implementation of these principles is correct.

Even if the soundness of an inference system is often rather obvious, and easy to prove (as in the case of H), it provides a very useful method of establishing that a certain sentence *cannot* be derived from certain premises. It suffices to find a *counter-example*: an interpretation where the premises are true and the conclusion false. Finding a counter-example can be much simpler than showing by syntactic means that no suitable derivation in the system exists.

4.2. Derivability and consistency

Back to completeness for propositional logic. Our problem seems to be that given that no interpretation makes the sentences in Γ true and φ false, we must find a derivation in H of φ from Γ. The first step will be to reformulate this problem.

We say that a set Γ of sentences is consistent (with respect to an inference system, in this case H) if no contradiction is derivable from it. Let $\bot$ be a fixed contradiction, say,

(2) $\quad \bot =_{\mathrm{def}} \neg(p_0 \rightarrow p_0)$

(or any other sentence φ_0 such that $\vdash_H \neg\varphi_0$).[2] Thus:

Definition 4.2.1 (consistency)
Γ is *consistent* if $\Gamma \nvdash_H \bot$. Otherwise, i.e. if $\Gamma \vdash_H \bot$, Γ is *inconsistent*.

There is a simple connection between consistency and derivability:

Lemma 4.2.2
$\Gamma \vdash_H \varphi$ iff $\Gamma \cup \{\neg\varphi\}$ is inconsistent.

Proof. Suppose first that $\Gamma \cup \{\neg\varphi\}$ is inconsistent, so $\Gamma, \neg\varphi \vdash_H \bot$. By the Deduction Theorem, $\Gamma \vdash_H \neg\varphi \rightarrow \bot$. By (29) in Chapter 3.3, $\Gamma \vdash_H \neg\bot \rightarrow \varphi$. Since $\vdash_H \neg\bot$, we have $\Gamma \vdash_H \varphi$.

In the other direction, suppose $\Gamma \vdash_H \varphi$. Then $\Gamma, \neg\varphi \vdash_H \varphi$ (adding a premise changes nothing). And trivially, $\Gamma, \neg\varphi \vdash_H \neg\varphi$, so by EFQ (see (30), Chapter 3.3), we obtain $\Gamma, \neg\varphi \vdash_H \bot$. □

This means that in order to show completeness, i.e. that $\Gamma \models \varphi$ implies $\Gamma \vdash_H \varphi$, it suffices to show that $\Gamma \models \varphi$ implies that $\Gamma \cup \{\neg\varphi\}$ is inconsistent. But now we recall, from (12) in Chapter 2.2.3, that

[2]So in contrast with Chapter 3.1, $\bot$ is not a primitive symbol here but a name of a particular sentence.

$$\Gamma \models \varphi \text{ iff } \Gamma \cup \{\neg\varphi\} \text{ is not satisfiable.}$$

Together with Lemma 4.2.2 this yields that in order to prove completeness, it is enough to show that if $\Gamma \cup \{\neg\varphi\}$ is not satisfiable, then $\Gamma \cup \{\neg\varphi\}$ is inconsistent. After contraposition, what we want to show is:

$$\text{If } \Gamma \cup \{\neg\varphi\} \text{ is consistent, then } \Gamma \cup \{\neg\varphi\} \text{ is satisfiable.}$$

And this means that the Completeness Theorem follows from the following fundamental result:

Lemma 4.2.3 (Consistency Lemma)
Every consistent set of sentences is satisfiable.

So in what follows we focus on this lemma.

4.3. Maximal consistent sets

We have reformulated our problem. Instead of, given that $\Gamma \models \varphi$, trying to find a derivation in H of φ from Γ, which doesn't seem very easy, our task is now the following: given any set Δ of sentences, about which we only know that no contradiction can be derived from it, to construct an interpretation (assignment of truth values) V which makes all sentences in Δ true.

How to construct V? The idea is to let Δ decide which sentence letters should be true. So, if $p \in \Delta$, we set $V(p) = 1$, and if $\neg p \in \Delta$, we set $V(p) = 0$. Do this for all sentence letters occurring in sentences in Δ. Note that the consistency of Δ guarantees that no letter will be assigned both 0 and 1. Will this construction make all sentences in Δ true in V?

Usually not. The problem is that Δ may contain too few sentences. For example, suppose $\neg\neg p \in \Delta$ but $p \notin \Delta$. Clearly we must have $V(p) = 1$ in this case too. Or suppose $p \in \Delta$ and $p \to q \in \Delta$, but $q \notin \Delta$. We have $\neg q \notin \Delta$, since Δ is consistent, but Δ lacks *explicit* information that q is true.

An obvious solution, in the latter case, is to *add* q, i.e. to consider $\Delta' = \Delta \cup \{q\}$. Δ' must also be consistent: if $\Delta' \vdash_H \bot$, i.e. $\Delta, q \vdash_H \bot$, we would have $\Delta \vdash_H \bot$, since $\Delta \vdash_H q$, which contradicts the consistency of Δ. And if Δ' is satisfiable, so is Δ.

In this case we actually had $\Delta \vdash_H q$ even though $q \notin \Delta$, so clearly we are forced to make q true in V, and thus to add q. In other cases, there may be no conclusive information one way or the other. For example, suppose $p \vee q \in \Delta$, but no other sentence containing p or q is in Δ. Then we could add p, or q, or both: we must make at least one of them true. So there is a choice, and nothing tells us (in this case) how to make it.

Summing up, the ambition is to add, for each sentence letter p occurring in sentences in Δ, either p or $\neg p$, while maintaining consistency. This will be accomplished in a rather unsophisticated way. We shall add *all sentences*—not just atomic sentences and their negations—which can be added without breaking consistency. As we saw, there is usually no unique way to do this. But we can choose a *fixed enumeration* of all sentences in the language, go through them one by one, and add them if it is consistent to do so, otherwise not.

This is an infinite construction, since there are infinitely many sentences in the language. (And Δ may be infinite too.) But we proceed by induction, which, as we know, is a finite way of dealing with the infinite (metaphorically speaking).

By the Locality Lemma for propositional logic (Lemma 2.2.6), we can relativize the construction to any vocabulary L, i.e. to any set L of sentence letters. So in what follows, we fix L and let Δ be a set of L-sentences. We begin by introducing a new concept.

Definition 4.3.1 (maximal consistent sets)
Δ is *maximal consistent* if Δ is consistent, and for every L-sentence $\psi \notin \Delta$ it holds that $\Delta \cup \{\psi\}$ is inconsistent.

Thus, a maximal consistent set is as large as can be: adding just one more sentence will break the consistency (the set will 'explode'). A first question might be: are there really any maximal consistent sets? But here is a simple, and important, example:

Example 4.3.2
Let V be an L-interpretation and let

$$\Delta = \{\psi \colon \psi \text{ is true in } V\}$$

Δ is obviously consistent. It is also maximal consistent: if ψ is an L-sentence not in Δ, then $V \not\models \psi$, which means that $V \models \neg\psi$, which means that $\neg\psi \in \Delta$, from which it follows that $\Delta \cup \{\psi\}$ is inconsistent.

So there are plenty of maximal consistent sets, but this kind of example doesn't help with our current task: we must *first* construe a maximal consistent set, and *then* define our interpretation from it. But *suppose* our construction has succeeded. Are we done then? We shall see that this is indeed the case. First we note some characteristic properties of maximal consistent sets (in our fixed vocabulary L):

Lemma 4.3.3 (properties of maximal consistent sets)
Let Δ be a maximal consistent set. Then, for all sentences φ, ψ:

(a) *$\varphi \notin \Delta$ iff $\neg\varphi \in \Delta$.*

(b) *If $\Delta \vdash_H \varphi$, then $\varphi \in \Delta$.*

(c) $\varphi \to \psi \in \Delta$ *iff* $\varphi \notin \Delta$ or $\psi \in \Delta$.

Proof. (a) says that *exactly one* of φ and $\neg\varphi$ is in Δ. Of course both cannot be there, since Δ is consistent. But if none of them were in Δ, both $\Delta \cup \{\varphi\}$ and $\Delta \cup \{\neg\varphi\}$ would be inconsistent, i.e. $\Delta, \varphi \vdash_H \bot$ and $\Delta, \neg\varphi \vdash_H \bot$. But this means that $\Delta \vdash_H \bot$ (see Exercise 3.3.2:3(f)), contrary to what we assumed.

(b) is a direct consequence of (a): if $\Delta \vdash_H \varphi$ and $\varphi \notin \Delta$, then $\neg\varphi \in \Delta$, which would make Δ inconsistent.

As to (c), suppose first that $\varphi \to \psi \notin \Delta$. By (a), $\neg(\varphi \to \psi) \in \Delta$. But we know (Exercise 3.3.1) that $\neg(\varphi \to \psi) \vdash_H \varphi$ and $\neg(\varphi \to \psi) \vdash_H \neg\psi$, so it follows with (b) that $\varphi \in \Delta$ and $\neg\psi \in \Delta$, i.e. $\psi \notin \Delta$, which gives the negation of the right-hand side of (c). Conversely, if $\varphi \to \psi \in \Delta$ and $\varphi \in \Delta$, then $\psi \in \Delta$ by MP and (b). In other words, if $\varphi \to \psi \in \Delta$, then either $\varphi \notin \Delta$ or $\psi \in \Delta$. □

4.4. Building the interpretation

Now assume that we have a maximal consistent set Δ. We build a corresponding interpretation V_Δ of the sentence letters in L as indicated at the beginning of the previous section:

$$(3) \qquad V_\Delta(p) = \begin{cases} 1 & \text{if } p \in \Delta \\ 0 & \text{if } p \notin \Delta \quad \text{(i.e. if } \neg p \in \Delta) \end{cases}$$

Our next result, the Truth Lemma, shows that the construction succeeds: all sentences in Δ are true in V_Δ, so Δ is satisfiable.

Lemma 4.4.1 (Truth Lemma)
For every L-sentence φ we have: $V_\Delta \models \varphi$ iff $\varphi \in \Delta$.

Proof. This is shown by induction over L-sentences.

Base case: φ is a sentence letter p. The claim follows directly from the construction of V_Δ.

Induction step: φ is $\neg\psi$, where we assume (induction hypothesis) that $V_\Delta \models \psi$ iff $\psi \in \Delta$. Thus: $V_\Delta \models \varphi$ iff $V_\Delta \models \neg\psi$ iff $V_\Delta \not\models \psi$ iff $\psi \notin \Delta$ (ind. hyp.) iff $\neg\psi \in \Delta$ (Lemma 4.3.3(a)) iff $\varphi \in \Delta$.

Induction step: φ is $\psi \to \chi$, where we assume (induction hypothesis) that the claim holds for ψ and for χ. Using Lemma 4.3.3(c), the induction hypothesis, and the truth definition, we obtain: $\varphi \in \Delta$ iff $\psi \notin \Delta$ or $\chi \in \Delta$ iff $V_\Delta \not\models \psi$ or $V_\Delta \models \chi$ iff $V_\Delta \models \varphi$. □

So every sentence in Δ is true in V_Δ, which was our goal. This claim is actually weaker that the claim in the Truth Lemma, but it is the stronger claim that is provable by induction. This is a common situation: one needs to find a claim that can be proved by induction, and that claim will often be stronger than the claim one was after in the first place.[3]

4.5. Lindenbaum's Lemma

The only thing remaining for our completeness proof is:[4]

Lemma 4.5.1 (Lindenbaum's Lemma)
Every consistent set of sentences can be extended to a maximal consistent set.

Proof. Let Δ be a consistent set of L-sentences. The idea is to add as many L-sentences as we can without breaking consistency. Let

$$\varphi_0, \varphi_1, \varphi_2, \ldots$$

be a fixed enumeration of *all* L-sentences. It doesn't matter in which order we enumerate them; the important thing is that every L-sentence occurs at least once in the sequence.[5] Now we define by induction a sequence of sets of sentences $\Delta_0, \Delta_1, \Delta_2, \ldots$ in the following way:

$$\Delta_0 = \Delta$$
$$\Delta_{n+1} = \begin{cases} \Delta_n \cup \{\varphi_n\} & \text{if } \Delta_n \cup \{\varphi_n\} \text{ is consistent} \\ \Delta_n & \text{otherwise} \end{cases}$$

Let

$$\Delta^* = \bigcup_{n \geqslant 0} \Delta_n$$

So we start with φ_0, check if it is consistent to add it to $\Delta = \Delta_0$, if so we do that (otherwise not), continue with φ_1, etc. So every L-sentence will eventually be dealt with, and added if it was consistent to do so at the step it was considered. Let us look at the properties of Δ^*.

(4) $\quad \Delta \subseteq \ldots \subseteq \Delta_n \subseteq \Delta_{n+1} \subseteq \ldots \subseteq \Delta^*$

This is immediate from the construction. Likewise, it is immediate that each Δ_n is consistent. Furthermore:

(5) $\quad \Delta^*$ is consistent.

[3] Exercise 2.4.10 gave another example of this.

[4] The name of this kind of result derives from the Polish logician Adolf Lindenbaum.

[5] How do we know there is such an enumeration? The key observation is that sentences are finite sequences of symbols, taken from a countable supply of symbols. Chapter 16.4.2 explains how one can enumerate all pairs, all triples, etc. of these symbols, and similarly all finite sequences of them.

Otherwise, $\Delta^* \vdash_H \bot$. But derivations are finite, and can only use finitely many premises from Δ^*. These premises are either in Δ or have been added during the construction. But this means that there is some n such that all the premises from Δ^* used in the derivation of $\bot$ belong to Δ_n. Therefore, $\Delta_n \vdash_H \bot$, which is impossible, since Δ_n is consistent. Finally:

(6) Δ^* is maximal consistent.

Suppose $\psi \notin \Delta^*$. We must show that $\Delta^* \cup \{\psi\}$ is inconsistent. This is where we use that ψ is φ_n for some n. So φ_n was *not* added at step $n+1$, which must have been because $\Delta_n \cup \{\varphi_n\}$ was *in*consistent. But if $\Delta_n, \varphi_n \vdash_H \bot$, then clearly $\Delta^*, \varphi_n \vdash_H \bot$, since $\Delta_n \subseteq \Delta^*$. That is, $\Delta^* \cup \{\psi\}$ is inconsistent. This completes the proof. □

4.6. Overview

Let us summarize. Our goal was to show that if $\Gamma \models \varphi$, then $\Gamma \vdash_H \varphi$. The reformulation in Section 4.2 entailed that it is enough to show :

If $\Gamma \cup \{\neg\varphi\}$ is consistent, then $\Gamma \cup \{\neg\varphi\}$ is satisfiable.

This follows from the Consistency Lemma, which says that *every* consistent set of sentences is satisfiable. So we needed to find, for any consistent set Δ, an interpretation making all the sentences in Δ true.

We saw that this task can be accomplished if we assume that Δ is not only consistent but maximal consistent. Then, if the atomic sentences in Δ get the value 1 and other atomic sentences (in L) the value 0, the Truth Lemma shows that all sentences in Δ are true in this interpretation, which we called V_Δ.

Lindenbaum's Lemma now says that we can *extend* Δ to a maximal consistent set Δ^*. So all the sentences in Δ^* will be true in V_{Δ^*}, and in particular all the sentences in Δ are true in V_{Δ^*}. In other words, Δ is satisfiable, we have proved Lemma 4.2.2, and hence:

Theorem 4.6.1 (Completeness of propositional logic)
The system H for PL is complete: if $\Gamma \models \varphi$, then $\Gamma \vdash_H \varphi$.

4.7. *Digression: maximal consistent sets as possible worlds

In this chapter we have gone from regarding *sentences* (in this case, PL-sentences) as syntactic expressions which can be true or false, and occur as premises and conclusions in arguments, to considering *sets of sentences* as objects that play the semantic role of determining truth and falsity. A maximal consistent set Δ can be seen as a complete description of a *possible world*: everything there is to know about that world, if expressible as a sentence φ in our formal language, is settled by Δ: φ is true in the world if $\varphi \in \Delta$, and if not, then $\neg\varphi \in \Delta$.

This is the basic idea behind *possible worlds semantics*. The idea has roots in Wittgenstein's *Tractatus*, and was made explicit by Rudolf Carnap in the 1940s.[6] Carnap called a set S of atomic or negated atomic sentences, such that for each p (in the vocabulary L), exactly one of p and $\neg p$ is in S, a *state description*. Clearly, such a set S is consistent (by soundness, since it is satisfiable), and it is easy to see that there is a *unique* maximal consistent set extending it; see Exercise 4.8.9. So state descriptions determine possible worlds, and we can talk of sentences being true or false *at* possible worlds.

In modern possible worlds semantics, semantic values of sentences are not 0 and 1 but sets of worlds, more precisely, subsets of some given set W. A valuation V now assigns subsets of W to sentence letters, and is extended to all sentences by a truth definition. Let $[\![\varphi]\!]^{W,V}$ be the value of φ relative to W and V. For $w \in W$, φ is *true at* w, written $W, V, w \models \varphi$, iff $w \in [\![\varphi]\!]^{W,V}$. Here it is not assumed that worlds are maximal consistent sets of sentences; W can be *any non-empty set* of objects (called worlds, states, points, etc.). But maximal consistent sets still play an important role in modern intensional logic.

To get a glimpse of how this happens, consider a basic modal propositional language with sentences of the form

$$\varphi := p \mid \neg\varphi \mid \varphi \to \varphi \mid \Box\varphi$$

with a new unary connective $\Box$. This is an all-purpose language for various kinds of applications. $\Box\varphi$ can be thought as saying that φ is *necessary* (classical modal logic), φ is *provable* (in some theory; provability logic), φ is *known* by an agent (epistemic logic), φ is *obligatory* (deontic logic), φ holds at all *future times* (temporal logic), etc. The truth definition is standard on $\neg$ and $\to$, but, depending on the application, needs some extra machinery to deal with $\Box$, which we don't go into here. φ is *valid* (on W) if φ is true at all worlds under all valuations.

A *modal logic* in this language is a set L of sentences containing all tautologies and closed under Modus Ponens. L may contain further axioms (such as $\Box\varphi \to \varphi$, saying that if something is known it is true under the epistemic interpretation) and obey further rules (such as inferring $\Box\varphi$ from φ, saying that if something is provable it is necessary under the modal interpretation). One usually writes $\vdash_{\mathsf{L}} \varphi$ for $\varphi \in \mathsf{L}$.

---

[6]See Supplement F of Leitgeb and Carus 2021 for historical and technical details.

Now a completeness question arises: is it the case that whenever φ is valid (relative to some class of interpretations suitable for L), we have $\vdash_{\mathsf{L}} \varphi$? And exactly as for PL, a positive answer follows if one can establish a Consistency Lemma, finding for each consistent set of sentences an interpretation, which is now a set of worlds with whatever extra machinery is needed, for which a Truth Lemma holds.

In this interpretation, called the *canonical* interpretation (or model) we take the maximal consistent sets to *be* the worlds. That is, the domain W_c (c for 'canonical') consists of all maximal consistent sets of sentences, according to L, in the basic modal language.[7] The corresponding canonical valuation V_c assigns to p the set of maximal consistent sets Δ such that $p \in \Delta$. Given that the 'extra machinery' is in place, we may be able to prove a Truth Lemma, successively establishing by induction:

$W_c, V_c, \Delta \models p$ iff $p \in \Delta$ (by definition)

$W_c, V_c, \Delta \models \neg\varphi$ iff $\neg\varphi \in \Delta$ (as in Lemma 4.3.3)

$W_c, V_c, \Delta \models \varphi \to \psi$ iff $\varphi \to \psi \in \Delta$ (as in Lemma 4.3.3)

$W_c, V_c, \Delta \models \Box\varphi$ iff $\Box\varphi \in \Delta$ (the hard part, using the 'extra macinery')

Furthermore, Lindenbaum's Lemma still holds, and so completeness of L follows in the same way as for PL.

Almost all completeness proofs in intensional logic today use a canonical model construction. And so, Henkin's strategy for proving completeness of a logic finds a particularly natural application in this area, where maximal consistent sets of sentences can themselves be seen as possible worlds.[8]

4.8. Exercises to Chapter 4

Exercise 4.8.1
Show:

1. $\nvdash_H (p \to q) \to p$
2. $p \wedge (q \vee r)\,,\, q \vee (p \wedge r) \nvdash_H q$
3. $\forall x Px \to Rcd \nvdash_H \forall x(Px \to Rcd)$
4. $Qc\,,\, Qd \nvdash_H \exists x \exists y(x \neq y)$

[7] More precisely, Δ is consistent if $\Delta \nvdash_{\mathsf{L}} \bot$, in the sense that there are no $\psi_1, \ldots, \psi_n \in \Delta$ such that $\vdash_{\mathsf{L}} \psi_1 \wedge \ldots \wedge \psi_n \to \bot$.

[8] Of course, we have only given a *very* rough idea of the role of maximal consistent sets in possible worlds semantics. Full details can be found in introductory texts to modal logic, such as Blackburn, de Rijke, and Venema 2001 or van Benthem 2010.

Exercise 4.8.2
Show that the following three claims are equivalent, where Γ is a set of sentences:

a. Γ is consistent.

b. There is no sentence φ s.t. both $\Gamma \vdash_H \varphi$ and $\Gamma \vdash_H \neg\varphi$.

c. There is a sentence ψ such that $\Gamma \nvdash_H \psi$.

[Hint: Consider the negations of these claims.]

Exercise 4.8.3
We saw that the Consistency Lemma implies the Completeness Theorem. Does the converse hold too?

Exercise 4.8.4
Verify the following properties of a maximal consistent set Δ:

1. $\varphi \wedge \psi \in \Delta$ iff $\varphi \in \Delta$ and $\psi \in \Delta$
2. $\varphi \vee \psi \in \Delta$ iff $\varphi \in \Delta$ or $\psi \in \Delta$

[Express $\varphi \wedge \psi$ and $\varphi \vee \psi$ in terms of $\neg$ and $\rightarrow$, and use Lemma 4.3.3.] Now define: $C_\varphi = \{\Delta : \Delta \text{ is max. consistent and } \varphi \in \Delta\}$. Conclude that

3. $C_{\varphi\wedge\psi} = C_\varphi \cap C_\psi$
4. $C_{\varphi\vee\psi} = C_\varphi \cup C_\psi$
5. $C_{\neg\varphi} = \overline{C_\varphi}$

Exercise 4.8.5
Given the situation described in Section 4.4, explain why an inductive proof of (*) would not work.

(*) For every L-sentence φ, if $\varphi \in \Delta$, then $V_\Delta \models \varphi$.

Exercise 4.8.6
Prove the following corollary to the Completeness Theorem:

(7) If $\Gamma \models \varphi$, there is a finite subset Γ_0 of Γ such that $\Gamma_0 \models \varphi$.

When we defined logical consequence for propositional logic (Definition 2.2.7) we did not assume that the set of premises was finite. (7) shows that we actually could have made that assumption.

Exercise 4.8.7
Consider the situation sketched at the beginning of Section 4.3, with a consistent set Δ containing $p \vee q$ but neither p nor q, nor any other sentences involving p or q. Discuss which properties of our fixed

enumeration would add p but not q to Δ, or q but not p, or both p and q, when Δ is extended to a maximal consistent set as in the proof of Lindenbaum's Lemma.

Exercise 4.8.8

1. Explain why no maximal consistent set of sentences can be finite.
2. Lindenbaum's Lemma shows the *existence* of a maximal consistent extension of a consistent set of sentences. Can this extension ever be *unique*? Give an example where it is not unique.

Exercise 4.8.9

Let Δ be a consistent set of L-sentences such that for each sentence letter p in L, either $\Delta \vdash p$ or $\Delta \vdash \neg p$. Suppose Δ' and Δ'' are maximal consistent sets of L-sentences such that $\Delta \subseteq \Delta'$ and $\Delta \subseteq \Delta''$. Show that $\Delta' = \Delta''$. [Hint: Induction over L-sentences.]

Exercise 4.8.10

Let $\mathcal{L}_n$ be the set of all formulas in propositional logic containing at most $p_1, \ldots, p_n$, and let $\Delta = \{\varphi \in \mathcal{L}_n : \varphi \text{ is a tautology}\}$. Is Δ

1. consistent?
2. maximal consistent?

Exercise 4.8.11 (a more general version of Lindenbaum's Lemma)

Let $\mathcal{L} = \{\varphi_0, \varphi_1, \varphi_2, \ldots\}$ be a (countably infinite) set of sentences in some language, and suppose $\vdash$ is a relation between subsets of $\mathcal{L}$ and elements of $\mathcal{L}$, about which the only thing we know is the following:

(fin) $\Gamma \vdash \varphi$ iff there is a finite subset Γ_0 of Γ such that $\Gamma_0 \vdash \varphi$

(a) Show that $\vdash$ is *monotone*, i.e. that if $\Gamma \vdash \varphi$ and $\Gamma \subseteq \Delta$ then $\Delta \vdash \varphi$.

(b) *Suppose $\Delta \subseteq \mathcal{L}$ and $\theta \in \mathcal{L}$ are such that $\Delta \nvdash \theta$. Show that there is a maximal extension of Δ with the same property, i.e. a set $\Delta^* \subseteq \mathcal{L}$ such that (i) $\Delta \subseteq \Delta^*$, (ii) $\Delta^* \nvdash \theta$, and (iii) if $\psi \notin \Delta^*$, then $\Delta^* \cup \{\psi\} \vdash \theta$. [Hint: Use the method of proof of Lindenbaum's Lemma.]

Exercise 4.8.12 (another completeness proof)

*Recall the notation from Exercise 2.4.5(c). We revise and extend it as follows: if V is a valuation of $p_1, \ldots, p_n$ and ψ is a formula containing at most the sentence letters $p_1, \ldots, p_n$, let $\psi^V = \psi$ if ψ is true in V, and $\psi^V = \neg\psi$ if ψ is false in V. So the result of that exercise was that if φ contains exactly $p_1, \ldots, p_n$, then φ is logically equivalent to the disjunction all conjunctions $p_1^V \wedge \ldots \wedge p_n^V$ such that V is a valuation making φ true. (This is a disjunctive normal form of φ.)

(a) Show that if ψ is as above and V is any valuation of $p_1, \ldots, p_n$, then $p_1^V, \ldots, p_n^V \vdash_H \psi^V$.

[Hint: Use induction on the complexity of ψ. When ψ is $\neg\psi_1$ or $\psi_1 \to \psi_2$, where we are assuming that $p_1^V, \ldots, p_n^V \vdash_H \psi_1^V$ and that $p_1^V, \ldots, p_n^V \vdash_H \psi_2^V$ (induction hypothesis), treat each possible combination of truth values of ψ_1 and ψ_2 separately.]

(b) Use (a) to show that if $\models \varphi$, then $\vdash_H \varphi$.

[Hint: Suppose φ contains exactly $p_1, \ldots, p_n$. Since $\models \varphi$, we have that for all V, $\varphi^V = \varphi$. Each row in the truth table for φ is a valuation V, and all (of the 2^n) valuations give φ the value 1. Take two rows (valuations) V and V' that differ only on p_1. By (a), $p_1, p_2^V, \ldots, p_n^V \vdash_H \varphi$ and $\neg p_1, p_2^V, \ldots, p_n^V \vdash_H \varphi$. Conclude that $p_2^V, \ldots, p_n^V \vdash_H \varphi$. Continue to eliminate the dependence on $p_2, p_3, \ldots$ in this way, eventually obtaining $\vdash \varphi$.]

(c) Conclude from (b) that if $\psi_1, \ldots, \psi_k \models \varphi$, then $\psi_1, \ldots, \psi_k \vdash_H \varphi$.

Exercise 4.8.13 (Post completeness)
*Consider the inference system H^s, with three axioms (not schemes) and two rules (MP and Uniform Substitution), defined in Exercise 3.3.10. Show that H^s has the following property:

(*) If $\nvdash_{H^s} \varphi$, then the system $H^s + \varphi$ obtained by adding φ as a new axiom, is inconsistent (a contradiction is derivable).

This property of inference systems is called *Post completeness.*

[Hint: If $\nvdash_{H^s} \varphi$ then (by Completeness and Exercise 3.3.10) there is an interpretation V in which φ is false. Let φ' be the result of replacing each sentence letter p in φ such that $V(p) = 1$ by $p \to p$, and each sentence letter q in φ such that $V(q) = 0$ by $\neg(q \to q)$. Show that φ' is a contradiction.]

Explain why the system H is not Post complete in this sense.

Exercise 4.8.14
*Let $\mathcal{S}$ be the set of all *consistent* sets of sentences (not only the maximal consistent ones), in some given vocabulary L of sentence letters. Show that the following holds, for all $\Gamma \in \mathcal{S}$ and all L-sentences φ, ψ:

(a) $\Gamma \vdash_H \varphi \to \psi$ iff for every $\Gamma' \in \mathcal{S}$ such that $\Gamma \subseteq \Gamma'$ we have that if $\Gamma' \vdash_H \varphi$, then $\Gamma' \vdash_H \psi$.

(b) $\Gamma \vdash_H \neg\varphi$ iff for every $\Gamma' \in \mathcal{S}$ such that $\Gamma \subseteq \Gamma'$ we have $\Gamma' \nvdash_H \varphi$.

Exercise 4.8.15 (Interpolation Theorem for PL)
*Suppose $\varphi \models \psi$. The *Interpolation Theorem* says that there is a formula θ, an *interpolant*, containing only non-logical symbols (in this case sentence letters) common to both φ and ψ, such that $\varphi \models \theta$ and $\theta \models \psi$.[9] Writing $at(\varphi)$ for the set of sentence letters (atoms) occurring in φ:

Theorem 4.8.16
If $\varphi \models \psi$ there is θ such that $at(\theta) \subseteq at(\varphi) \cap at(\psi)$ and $\varphi \models \theta$ and $\theta \models \varphi$.

We indicate a proof of this theorem by induction on $n = |at(\varphi) - at(\psi)|$, the number of sentence letters in φ but not in ψ. For this proof it is convenient to assume that the *falsum* connective $\bot$ (and hence $\top = \neg\bot$) is a primitive connective in the language.

1. Show that if $n = 0$ we can take $\theta = \varphi$.

2. Suppose the result holds for n, and that $|at(\varphi) - at(\psi)| = n + 1$. Take any $q \in at(\varphi) - at(\psi)$, and let φ' be the formula

   $$\varphi(\top/q) \vee \varphi(\bot/q)$$ [10]

   Show that $|at(\varphi') - at(\psi)| = n$ and $\varphi' \models \psi$.
   [Hint: if V' is a valuation of $at(\varphi') \cup at(\psi)$ such that $V'(\varphi') = 1$, then, depending on whether $V'(\varphi(\top/q)) = 1$ or $V'(\varphi(\bot/q)) = 1$, extend V' to a valuation V on $at(\varphi) \cup at(\psi)$ such that $V(\varphi) = 1$, and use the assumption and Locality.]

3. Show that $\varphi \models \varphi'$. [Similarly.]

4. Use $\varphi' \models \psi$ and the induction hypothesis to find an interpolant which, by the above, is also an interpolant for $\varphi \models \psi$.

5. This proves the theorem. Show as a corollary that if $\varphi \models \psi$ and $at(\varphi) \cap at(\psi) = \varnothing$, then either φ is a contradiction or ψ is a tautology.

---

[9] This is a significant fact about PL, or any logic that has an interpolation theorem. Via the completeness theorem, it says that if ψ is provable from φ, there is a 'direct' proof of ψ. It has numerous applications in mathematical logic, database theory, complexity theory (How hard is it to *compute* an interpolant?), automated reasoning, and other areas, but these lie beyond the scope of this book.

[10] Here $\varphi(\chi/q)$ is the result of replacing all occurrences of q in φ by χ.

5 Completeness: FOL

We have arrived at the main event of Part II, the completeness of first-order logic. As noted, this was first proved by Gödel in 1930, but we shall use a method originating with Henkin in 1945. Indeed, this is the method we already used for the case of propositional logic.

The facts about consistency and maximal consistency are exactly as in the previous chapter. Thus, all we need to prove is the first-order version of the Consistency Lemma. One difference is that first-order interpretations are more complex objects than mere assignments of truth values: we need to find a universe, and to interpret individual constants and predicate and function symbols in that universe. Another difference is that when proving Lindenbaum's Lemma, we must take quantified sentences into account.

5.1. Models

Before we begin, a terminological change. In what follows we will usually say *model* instead of *interpretation*. This is a standard and, as we will see in the next chapter, very natural terminology. We say

$\mathcal{M}$ is a model of φ

if the sentence φ is true in $\mathcal{M}$, i.e. if $\mathcal{M} \models \varphi$. And we say

$\mathcal{M}$ is a model of Γ

also written $\mathcal{M} \models \Gamma$, when *all* sentences in Γ are true in $\mathcal{M}$. Then, instead of saying that Γ is satisfiable we can say that Γ *has a model*.

And since the Consistency Lemma is about satisfiability of sets of sentences, we shall rename it the *Model Existence Theorem*:

Theorem 5.1.1 (Model Existence Theorem)
Every consistent set of sentences has a model.

To prove this, the idea is still to let a maximal consistent set Δ of L-sentences determine the model. Suppose the individual constants in L are c_1, c_2, c_3, and that P, R are the predicate symbols, where

P is unary and R is binary. Take any domain with three elements, $M = \{a_1, a_2, a_3\}$, and let $c_i^{\mathcal{M}} = a_i$, $i = 1, 2, 3$. Also, let $P^{\mathcal{M}}(a_i)$ hold iff $P(c_i) \in \Delta$, and similarly, let $R^{\mathcal{M}}(a_i, a_j)$ hold iff $R(c_i, c_j) \in \Delta$. The plan is that this should give a model where all sentences in Δ are true.

We can make things even simpler. It doesn't matter which three elements constitute the universe, all that matters is that they are denoted by the individual constants. So we shall simply let the individual constants *themselves* be the elements of the domain M. This may seem a bit strange, but it is not an arbitrary choice, and we are really building the model from the syntactic 'material' in Δ. So c_1, c_2, c_3 will now play two roles: as symbols in the language, and as objects that these symbols are naming. Of course, every individual constant will name itself. Thus, if $M = \{c_1, c_2, c_3\}$, we let $c_i^{\mathcal{M}} = c_i$, and, as before, $P^{\mathcal{M}}(c_i)$ iff $P(c_i) \in \Delta$ and $R^{\mathcal{M}}(c_i, c_j)$ iff $R(c_i, c_j) \in \Delta$.

Does this work? It works for atomic sentences formed with P and R in our example (and their negations). But not necessarily for complex sentences, even if we would assume that Δ is maximal consistent. For example, it could be that Δ contains the sentence $\exists x Px$, as well as the sentences $\neg Pc_1, \neg Pc_2, \neg Pc_3$. Then Pc_1, Pc_2, Pc_3 will be false in $\mathcal{M}$, but $\exists x Px$ could still be true in a model containing *other* individuals than the ones denoted by c_1, c_2, c_3.[1] So our model with $M = \{c_1, c_2, c_3\}$ will not do.

The solution to this problem is to enlarge the vocabulary L by adding new individual constants. In fact, we must add infinitely many new individual constants, one for each formula in Δ of the form $\exists x \psi(x)$. (Recall that maximal consistent sets are infinite; Exercise 4.8.8.) Such a constant c, for which $\psi(c)$ is true, is called a *witness* to $\exists x \psi(x)$.

There is another problem. Suppose the sentence $c_1 = c_2$ belongs to Δ. This sentence is false in our model $\mathcal{M}$, since $c_1^{\mathcal{M}}$ and $c_2^{\mathcal{M}}$, i.e. c_1 and c_2, are *different* objects (symbols). The solution to this problem requires yet another construction. But in order to focus on the essentials of Henkin's proof of completeness, we start by considering first-order logic *without identity*, i.e. FOL$^-$, where this problem doesn't arise.

5.2. Structure of the proof

Let us give a name to the property that all existentially quantified sentences have witnesses.

[1] $\Gamma = \{\neg Pc_1, \neg Pc_2, \neg Pc_3, \exists x Px\}$ is a *consistent* set of sentences, hence a subset of a maximal consistent set. The domain of a model making all sentences in Γ true must, if c_1, c_2, c_3 denote different individuals, have at least four elements.

Definition 5.2.1
A set of L-sentences Δ is *$\exists$-complete* if for every sentence $\exists x\psi(x) \in \Delta$ there is an individual constant c in L such that $\psi(c) \in \Delta$.

So we need a set of sentences that is not only maximal consistent but also $\exists$-complete. Therefore, Lindenbaum's Lemma is as follows.

Lemma 5.2.2 (Lindenbaum's Lemma)
Every consistent set Δ of L-sentences can be extended to a maximal consistent and $\exists$-complete set of L'-sentences, where L' is obtained by adding countably many individual constants to L.

If Δ is both maximal consistent and $\exists$-complete, we can use the construction of a model $\mathcal{M}_\Delta$ sketched above, and prove:

Lemma 5.2.3 (Truth Lemma)
If Δ is a maximal consistent and $\exists$-complete set of L'-sentences, then, for every L'-sentence φ, $\varphi \in \Delta$ iff $\mathcal{M}_\Delta \models \varphi$.

Now the Model Existence Theorem (and thereby the Completeness Theorem) follows exactly as before: extend the consistent set Δ of L-sentences to a maximal consistent and $\exists$-complete set Δ^* of L'-sentences, then build the model $\mathcal{M}_{\Delta^*}$; it will follow that all L'-sentences in Δ^* are true in $\mathcal{M}_{\Delta^*}$. But $\Delta \subseteq \Delta^*$, and $L \subseteq L'$, so every L-sentence in Δ is an element of Δ^*, and thus true in $\mathcal{M}_{\Delta^*}$. In other words, $\mathcal{M}_{\Delta^*}$ is a model of Δ.[2]

5.3. Model construction and Truth Lemma

Let Δ be a set of L-sentences (in FOL$^-$), where L contains at least one individual constant but no function symbols. Here is our model $\mathcal{M}_\Delta$:

Definition 5.3.1 (construction of $\mathcal{M}_\Delta$)
Let $M_\Delta = \{c\colon c \in L\}$. Also:

1. if c is an individual constant in L, $c^{\mathcal{M}_\Delta} = c$.
2. if P is an n-ary predicate symbol in L,
   $P^{\mathcal{M}_\Delta}(c_1, \ldots, c_n)$ iff $Pc_1 \ldots c_n \in \Delta$.

The Truth Lemma says that for any vocabulary L, if Δ is maximal consistent and $\exists$-complete set of L-sentences, then $\varphi \in \Delta$ iff $\mathcal{M}_\Delta \models \varphi$.

Proof of the Truth Lemma: As before, this is shown by induction. But in FOL one cannot use induction on sentences. Instead, we show the following more general claim by induction on *formulas*; the Truth Lemma becomes a special case.

[2]If we want a model of Δ in the original vocabulary L, simply restrict the interpretation function of $\mathcal{M}_{\Delta^*}$ from L' to the subset L. The result is called a *reduct* of $\mathcal{M}_{\Delta^*}$. By Locality (Lemma 2.3.17), the reduct is also a model of Δ.

(1) For all L-formulas $\varphi = \varphi(x_1, \ldots, x_n)$ and all $c_1, \ldots, c_n \in M_\Delta$ we have: $\varphi(c_1, \ldots, c_n) \in \Delta$ iff $\mathcal{M}_\Delta \models \varphi[c_1, \ldots, c_n]$.

On the left-hand side we have the *sentence* obtained by replacing all free occurrences of $x_1, \ldots, x_n$ by $c_1, \ldots, c_n$, respectively, whereas on the right-hand side, $c_1, \ldots, c_n$ appear in their role as elements of the model's domain, satisfying the *formula* $\varphi(x_1, \ldots, x_n)$ in $\mathcal{M}_\Delta$. We shall write $\overline{c} = c_1, \ldots, c_n$.

Base step: If φ is atomic, say $Pt_1 \ldots t_k$, (1) holds by the construction of $\mathcal{M}_\Delta$ (Definition 5.3.1). This should be clear but it is instructive to check an example. Since there are no function symbols, each t_i is either an individual constant or a variable. So say that $k = 3$ and $n = 4$ and our atomic formula $\varphi(x_1, x_2, x_3, x_4)$ is $Pc_3x_1x_3$.[3] Then $\varphi(c_1, c_2, c_3, c_4)$ is $Pc_3c_1c_3$. And $Pc_3x_1x_3$ is satisfied in $\mathcal{M}_\Delta$ by c_1, c_2, c_3, c_4 (which are assigned to x_1, x_2, x_3, x_4, respectively) iff $P^{\mathcal{M}_\Delta}(c_3^{\mathcal{M}_\Delta}, c_1, c_3)$ holds, that is, iff $P^{\mathcal{M}_\Delta}(c_3, c_1, c_3)$ holds, which, by Definition 5.3.1, means that $Pc_3c_1c_3 \in \Delta$.[4]

Induction step: φ is $\neg\psi$ or $\psi \to \chi$. Then the claim follows in exactly the same way as in the proof of Lemma 4.4.1, using the maximal consistency of Δ.[5] We only have to note that, for example, the formula $(\psi \to \chi)(x_1, \ldots, x_n)$ can be written $\psi(x_1, \ldots, x_n) \to \chi(x_1, \ldots, x_n)$, and thus $(\psi \to \chi)(\overline{c})$ is $\psi(\overline{c}) \to \chi(\overline{c})$.

Induction step: φ is $\exists x\psi(x, \overline{x})$. Then:

$$\begin{array}{lll} \exists x\psi(x, \overline{c}) \in \Delta & \text{iff} & \text{for some } d \in M_\Delta,\ \psi(d, \overline{c}) \in \Delta \\ & \text{iff} & \text{for some } d \in M_\Delta,\ \mathcal{M}_\Delta \models \psi[d, \overline{c}] \quad \text{(ind. hyp.)} \\ & \text{iff} & \mathcal{M}_\Delta \models \exists x\psi[x, \overline{c}] \qquad \text{(truth def.)} \end{array}$$

The first equivalence, from left to right, uses the $\exists$-completeness of Δ. In the other direction, if $\psi(d, \overline{c}) \in \Delta$, then $\exists x\psi(x, \overline{c}) \in \Delta$ follows from the fact that $\psi(d, \overline{c}) \vdash_H \exists x\psi(x, \overline{c})$, and the maximal consistency of Δ together with Lemma 4.3.3(b).

The case when φ is $\forall x\psi(x, \overline{x})$ is similar and left as an exercise. This proves (1), and the Truth Lemma is the special case when φ has no free variables. □

---

[3]So only x_1 and x_3 occur (free) in φ, but that's completely in accord with writing φ as $\varphi(x_1, x_2, x_3, x_4)$.

[4]Following the truth definition 2.3.13, we would write $P^{\mathcal{M}_\Delta}(c_3^{\mathcal{M}_\Delta,[\sigma]}, x_1^{\mathcal{M}_\Delta,[\sigma]}, x_3^{\mathcal{M}_\Delta,[\sigma]})$, where $\sigma(x_i) = c_i$, for $i = 1, 2, 3, 4$. This is the same as $P^{\mathcal{M}_\Delta}(c_3, c_1, c_3)$.

[5]The crucial properties of maximal consistent sets spelled out in Lemma 4.3.3 were proved for PL, but the lemma clearly holds for FOL-sentences as well, since the propositional reasoning used is available in FOL too.

5.4. Proof of Lindenbaum's Lemma

The proof idea is the same as in the propositional case (Lemma 4.5.1), but we must modify the construction in order to obtain $\exists$-completeness as well as maximal consistency. So we start with a consistent set Δ of L-sentences and add countably many new individual constants: $L' = L \cup \{d_0, d_1, d_2, \ldots\}$, where the d_i are not elements of L. Let

$$\varphi_0, \varphi_1, \varphi_2, \ldots$$

be a fixed enumeration of all L'-sentences. We define the sets of L'-sentences $\Delta_0, \Delta_1, \Delta_2, \ldots$ in the following way:

(2) *step* 0: $\Delta_0 = \Delta$.

step $n+1$: Suppose Δ_n is defined:

If $\Delta_n \cup \{\varphi_n\}$ is inconsistent, let $\Delta_{n+1} = \Delta_n$.

If $\Delta_n \cup \{\varphi_n\}$ is consistent and φ_n is not an existentially quantified sentence, let $\Delta_{n+1} = \Delta_n \cup \{\varphi_n\}$.

If $\Delta_n \cup \{\varphi_n\}$ is consistent and φ_n is of the form $\exists x\psi(x)$, let $\Delta_{n+1} = \Delta_n \cup \{\varphi_n\} \cup \{\psi(d_i)\}$, where d_i is a *new* individual constant, i.e. one that does not occur in Δ_n or in φ_n.

Note that we can always find a new individual constant in the last case. This is because the individual constants in Δ belong to L, and L' has infinitely many new individual constants, but only finitely many of them can occur in sentences that have been added at steps $0, \ldots, n$.

As be fore, we let

$$\Delta^* = \bigcup_{n \geqslant 0} \Delta_n$$

It follows directly from the construction that

(3) $\Delta \subseteq \ldots \subseteq \Delta_n \subseteq \Delta_{n+1} \subseteq \ldots \subseteq \Delta^*$

Furthermore:

(4) Each Δ_n is consistent.

Proof. That Δ_0 is consistent is an assumption. The construction (2) shows directly that Δ_{n+1} is consistent if Δ_n is, except in the case when $\varphi_n = \exists x\psi(x)$. So suppose $\Delta_{n+1} = \Delta_n \cup \{\exists x\psi(x), \psi(d_i)\}$, where the set $\Delta_n \cup \{\exists x\psi(x)\}$ is consistent and d_i is new. Suppose that Δ_{n+1} is *not* consistent, i.e. that $\Delta_n, \exists x\psi(x), \psi(d_i) \vdash_H \bot$. But then, by (33) in Chapter 3.3.1 and the fact that d_i does not occur in Δ_n or $\psi(x)$ or $\bot$, we would have $\Delta_n, \exists x\psi(x), \exists x\psi(x) \vdash_H \bot$, i.e. $\Delta_n, \exists x\psi(x) \vdash_H \bot$, contradicting our assumption. This proves (4).

Exactly as in the propositional case, it now follows that

(5) Δ^* is consistent.

It also follows, in just the same way as before, that

(6) Δ^* is maximal consistent.

For if $\psi \notin \Delta^*$, and ψ is the sentence φ_n, then ψ was *not* added at step $n + 1$, which can only be because $\Delta_n \cup \{\psi\}$ is inconsistent, and thus $\Delta^* \cup \{\psi\}$ is also inconsistent.

So it only remains to verify:

(7) Δ^* is $\exists$-complete.

But this follows directly from the construction. If $\exists x\psi(x)$ is an L'-sentence in Δ^*, then $\exists x\psi(x)$ is φ_n for some n, so at step $n + 1$, $\exists x\psi(x)$ must have been added, and therefore also $\psi(d)$, for some (new) individual constant d. This concludes the proof of Lindenbaum's Lemma. □

Thus, if the sentences in Γ and φ are first-order sentences without identity, we have shown that $\Gamma \models \varphi$ implies $\Gamma \vdash_H \varphi$. That is, we have shown that FOL$^-$ is complete.

5.5. Bringing in identity

As noted, this proof doesn't quite work for first-order logic with identity. If it should be the case that $c = d \in \Delta$, where c and d are *different* individual constants, then $c = d$ will be false in $\mathcal{M}_\Delta$, if $\mathcal{M}_\Delta$ is built as in Definition 5.3.1. So we must alter the construction so that, in this case, $c^{\mathcal{M}_\Delta} = d^{\mathcal{M}_\Delta}$. This is accomplished with a device which is familiar in mathematics, but which we will describe in detail here.

Now we also allow the vocabulary L to contain function symbols. Define the following relation between *closed* L-terms s, t (no variables):

$$s \sim t \text{ iff } s = t \in \Delta$$

We need the following lemma.

Lemma 5.5.1
If Δ is maximal consistent, then:

(a) *$\sim$ is an equivalence relation: reflexive, symmetric, transitive.*

(b) *If P is an n-ary predicate symbol in L, and $s_i \sim t_i$ for $i = 1, \ldots, n$, then $Ps_1 \ldots s_n \in \Delta$ iff $Pt_1 \ldots t_n \in \Delta$.*

(c) *If f is an n-ary function symbol in L, and $s_i \sim t_i$ for $i = 1, \ldots, n$, then $f(s_1, \ldots, s_n) \sim f(t_1, \ldots, t_n)$.*

Proof. (a): Since a maximal consistent set contains all sentences derivable form it, Ax8 (Chapter 3.3.1) implies that $t = t \in \Delta$, that is, $t \sim t$, so $\sim$ is reflexive. As to symmetry, suppose $s = t \in \Delta$; we must show $t = s \in \Delta$. But this follows by maximal consistency, since $s = t \vdash_H t = s$ (cf. (17) in Chapter 3.1). Similarly, transitivity follows from the fact that $s = t, t = u \vdash_H s = u$.

(b) follows by repeated application of Ax9: we let $\varphi(x_1)$ be the formula $Px_1 s_2 \ldots s_n$. Then $\varphi(s_1) \in \Delta$ and $s_1 = t_1 \in \Delta$, from which it follows as before that $\varphi(t_1)$, i.e. $Pt_1 s_2 \ldots s_n$, is an element of Δ. In this way we successively replace one term at a time.

Note that this argument works just as well for an arbitrary formula $\psi(x_1, \ldots, x_n)$ instead of the atomic $Px_1 \ldots x_n$. We can use this to prove (c): let $\psi(x_1, \ldots, x_n)$ be the formula $f(s_1, \ldots, s_n) = f(x_1, \ldots, x_n)$, so $\psi(s_1, \ldots, s_n)$ is a logical truth. Now reason as in the proof of (b), starting with $\psi_1(x_1, s_2, \ldots, s_n)$. □

If T_L is the set of closed terms in L, the relation $\sim$ (given that Δ is maximal consistent) yields a *partition* of T_L into (non-empty and pairwise disjoint) *equivalence classes* (see Chapter 16.3); the equivalence class of t will be written $|t|$:

$$|t| = \{s : s \sim t\}$$

Now we modify the construction of the model $\mathcal{M}_\Delta$ (Definition 5.3.1) by taking equivalence classes of closed terms, not the terms themselves, as the individuals in our domain:[6]

Definition 5.5.2 (modified construction of $\mathcal{M}_\Delta$)
Let $M_\Delta = \{|t| : t \in T_L\}$. Also:

1. If c is an individual constant in L, and thus in T_L, let $c^{\mathcal{M}_\Delta} = |c|$.
2. If P is an n-ary predicate symbol in L, we let $P^{\mathcal{M}_\Delta}(|t_1|, \ldots, |t_n|)$ iff $Pt_1 \ldots t_n \in \Delta$.
3. If f is an n-ary function symbol in L, let $f^{\mathcal{M}_\Delta}(|t_1|, \ldots, |t_n|) = |f(t_1, \ldots, t_n)|$.

Here we must check that 2 and 3 in this definition are correct. In 2 we are supposed to explain which n-tuples of equivalence classes belong to the relation $P^{\mathcal{M}_\Delta}$, but we expressed this by means of the terms themselves, not their equivalence classes. Similarly for 3. So we must verify that our definition is *independent* of the choice of terms, in other words, that

[6] In mathematical terms, $\sim$ is a is congruence relation on the algebra of closed L-terms (Lemma 5.5.1 (a) and (c)), and M_Δ is the domain of the corresponding quotient algebra.

(8) if $|s_i| = |t_i]$ for $i = 1, \ldots, n$, then
a. $Ps_1 \ldots s_n \in \Delta$ iff $Pt_1 \ldots t_n \in \Delta$
b. $|f(s_1, \ldots, s_n)| = |f(t_1, \ldots, t_n)|$

But (when Δ is maximal consistent) that is exactly what Lemma 5.5.1(b) and (c) tell us!

Now suppose as before that Δ is both maximal consistent and $\exists$-complete. The Truth Lemma is again proved by induction: the claim that must be proved this time is:

(9) For all L-formulas $\varphi(x_1, \ldots, x_n)$ and all $|t_1|, \ldots, |t_n| \in \mathcal{M}_\Delta$:
$\varphi(t_1, \ldots, t_n) \in \Delta$ iff $\mathcal{M}_\Delta \models \varphi[|t_1|, \ldots, |t_n|]$.

In particular, if φ is a sentence without free variables,

$$\varphi \in \Delta \text{ iff } \mathcal{M}_\Delta \models \varphi$$

so the Truth Lemma follows from (9).

In order to prove (9) we must first establish a fact about the interpretation of closed terms. Let s be a term with variables among $x_1, \ldots, x_n$, so we can write $s = s(x_1, \ldots, x_n)$. If $t_1, \ldots, t_n$ are closed terms, then $s(t_1, \ldots, t_n)$ is a closed term, which is interpreted in the model M_Δ. Recall from Definition 2.3.12 that $s^{\mathcal{M}_\Delta,[a_1,\ldots,a_n]}$ stands for the interpretation of s in $\mathcal{M}_\Delta$ relative to the assignment of $a_1, \ldots, a_n$ to $x_1, \ldots, x_n$, respectively. In the present case, $a_1, \ldots, a_n$ are equivalence classes $|t_1|, \ldots, |t_n|$.

We abbreviate: $\overline{x} = x_1, \ldots, x_n$, $\overline{t} = t_1, \ldots, t_n$, and $\overline{|t|} = |t_1|, \ldots, |t_n|$. What we need is the following.

(10) $|s(\overline{t})| = s^{\mathcal{M}_\Delta,[\overline{|t|}]}$

In other words, the equivalence class of the closed term $s(\overline{t})$ is exactly the interpretation in $\mathcal{M}_\Delta$ of the open term $s = s(\overline{x})$, relative to the assignment of $\overline{|t|}$ to $\overline{x}$. This should be fairly clear, but for the record we give a proof by induction over L-terms.

Proof of (10): We apply induction over s (cf. Definition 2.3.12). If s is an individual constant c, we have

$$|s(\overline{t})| = |c(\overline{t})| = |c| = c^{\mathcal{M}_\Delta} = c^{\mathcal{M}_\Delta,[\overline{|t|}]}$$

If s is one of the variables, say $s = x_i$, then

$$|s(\overline{t})| = |x_i(\overline{t})| = |t_i| = x_i^{\mathcal{M}_\Delta,[\overline{|t|}]}$$

Note that $x_i(\overline{t})$ is the result of replacing all occurrences of $x_1, \ldots, x_n$ in x_i by $t_1, \ldots, t_n$, respectively. The only occurrence is x_i itself, so the result is just t_i.

These are the base steps. For the induction step, assume that $s = f(s_1, \ldots, s_k)$, which means that $s(\overline{t}) = f(s_1(\overline{t}), \ldots, s_k(\overline{t}))$. We have:

$$\begin{array}{rcll}
|s(\overline{t})| & = & |f(s_1(\overline{t}), \ldots, s_k(\overline{t}))| & \\
& = & f^{\mathcal{M}_\Delta}(|s_1(\overline{t})|, \ldots, |s_k(\overline{t})|) & \text{(Def. 5.5.2, 3)} \\
& = & f^{\mathcal{M}_\Delta}(s_1^{\mathcal{M}_\Delta,[\overline{|t|}]}, \ldots, s_k^{\mathcal{M}_\Delta,[\overline{|t|}]}) & \text{(ind. hyp.)} \\
& = & f(s_1, \ldots, s_k)^{\mathcal{M}_\Delta,[\overline{|t|}]} & \text{(Def. 2.3.12, (iii))} \\
& = & s^{\mathcal{M}_\Delta,[\overline{|t|}]} & \square
\end{array}$$

This proves (10). Now we can return to the proof of (9). If φ is atomic, of the form $Ps_1 \ldots s_k$, where $s_1, \ldots, s_k$ may contain the variables $x_1, \ldots, x_n = \overline{x}$, we have:

$$\begin{array}{rll}
Ps_1 \ldots s_k(\overline{t}) \in \Delta & \text{iff} \;\; Ps_1(\overline{t}) \ldots s_k(\overline{t}) \in \Delta & \\
& \text{iff} \;\; P^{\mathcal{M}_\Delta}(|s_1(\overline{t})|, \ldots, |s_k(\overline{t})|) & \text{(Def. 5.5.2, 2)} \\
& \text{iff} \;\; P^{\mathcal{M}_\Delta}(s_1^{\mathcal{M}_\Delta,[\overline{|t|}]}, \ldots, s_k^{\mathcal{M}_\Delta,[\overline{|t|}]}) & \text{(by (10))} \\
& \text{iff} \;\; \mathcal{M}_\Delta \models Ps_1 \ldots s_k\,[\overline{|t|}] & \text{(Def. 2.3.13 (ii))}
\end{array}$$

The second base case, when φ has the form $s_1 = s_2$, is left as an exercise. The cases when φ is $\neg\psi$ or $\psi \to \chi$ are dealt with in exactly the same way as in the earlier proof of the Truth Lemma. Now consider the case when φ is $\exists x\psi(x, \overline{x})$, and so $\varphi(t_1, \ldots, t_n) = \varphi(\overline{t}) = \exists x\psi(x, \overline{t})$. Let us look at the two implications in (9) separately.

$$\begin{array}{rcll}
\exists x\psi(x, \overline{t}) \in \Delta & \Rightarrow & \text{for some ind. const. } c,\ \psi(c, \overline{t}) \in \Delta & (\exists\text{-compl.}) \\
& \Rightarrow & \text{for some ind. const. } c,\ \mathcal{M}_\Delta \models \psi\,[|c|, \overline{|t|}] & \text{(ind. hyp.)} \\
& \Rightarrow & \mathcal{M}_\Delta \models \exists x\psi\,[x, \overline{|t|}] & \text{(truth def.)}
\end{array}$$

Conversely:

$$\begin{array}{rcll}
\mathcal{M}_\Delta \models \exists x\psi\,[x, \overline{|t|}] & \Rightarrow & \text{for some } |s|,\ \mathcal{M}_\Delta \models \psi\,[|s|, \overline{|t|}] & \text{(truth def.)} \\
& \Rightarrow & \text{for some } |s|,\ \psi(s, \overline{t}) \in \Delta & \text{(ind. hyp.)} \\
& \Rightarrow & \exists x\psi(x, \overline{t}) \in \Delta &
\end{array}$$

The last step follows from the fact that Δ is maximal consistent: since $\psi(s, \overline{t}) \vdash_H \exists x\psi(x, \overline{t})$ and $\psi(s, \overline{t}) \in \Delta$, we obtain $\Delta \vdash_H \exists x\psi(x, \overline{t})$, and thus $\exists x\psi(x, \overline{t}) \in \Delta$.

The case when φ is $\forall x\psi(x, \overline{x})$ is left as an exercise. □

We have proved

Lemma 5.5.3 (Truth Lemma for FOL)
If Δ is maximal consistent and $\exists$-complete, then $\varphi \in \Delta$ iff $\mathcal{M}_\Delta \models \varphi$.

So there are a few details to check in order to show that the (modified) model construction and the Truth Lemma work also for first-order logic with identity. But that is all we need! The proof of Lindenbaum's Lemma is word by word as in Section 5.4; that the formulas may contain identity plays no role there. Thus, the completeness proof for FOL is finished:

Theorem 5.5.4 (Completeness of first-order logic)
The system H for first-order logic (with or without identity) is complete: if $\Gamma \models \varphi$, then $\Gamma \vdash_H \varphi$.

5.6. Exercises to Chapter 5

Exercise 5.6.1
Let the vocabulary L contain the binary predicate symbols R and S, and suppose that Γ is a maximal consistent set of L-sentences *not* containing the sentence $\exists z Szz \rightarrow \forall x \forall y (Rxy \vee Ryx)$. Can we conclude anything about whether the sentence $\exists x \exists y \neg (Rxy \vee Ryx)$ belongs to Γ or not?

Exercise 5.6.2
Let $\Gamma = \{\exists x Px, Qc, \forall y(Qy \rightarrow \neg Py)\}$, in the vocabulary $L = \{P, Q, c\}$.

1. Can Γ be extended to a $\exists$-complete and consistent set of sentences in the vocabulary L?
2. What if the vocabulary instead is $L' = \{P, Q, c, d\}$?

Exercise 5.6.3
Define a notion of $\forall$-completeness similarly to $\exists$-completeness, and show that maximal consistent sets are always $\forall$-complete in this sense.

Exercise 5.6.4
(a) Carry through the argument in the induction step of the proof of the Truth Lemma when φ has the form $\forall x \psi(x)$. (b) Same task for first-order logic with identity.

Exercise 5.6.5

(a) Suppose Γ is a consistent set of L-sentences, that $\exists x \varphi(x)$ is an L-sentence in Γ, and that d is an individual constant not in L. Show that $\Gamma \cup \{\varphi(d)\}$ is consistent.

(b) Let Δ be a consistent set of L-sentences in first-order logic with identity, let Δ^* be a maximal consistent and $\exists$-complete set of L'-sentences construed as indicated at the end of Section 5.5 (i.e. as in (2) in Section 5.4), where $L' = L \cup C$, and $C = \{d_0, d_1, d_2, \ldots\}$ is a set of new individual constants. Show that if t is any closed L-term, there is $d_i \in C$ such that $d_i = t \in \Delta^*$. [Hint: use the construction of Δ^*.]

Exercise 5.6.6
The *weak completeness theorem* is:

(11) If a sentence φ is valid, then it is provable (in some standard inference system, such as H), i.e. $\models \varphi$ implies $\vdash_H \varphi$.

(The *strong* version, which we have proved, involves logical consequence instead of validity, and sets of sentences rather than a single sentence.) Consider

(12) Every sentence φ is either refutable in H or true in some model

(where φ is *refutable in H* if $\vdash_H \neg\varphi$). Show that (11) and (12) are equivalent.

Gödel in 1930 proved (12), by considering sentences in prenex normal form (Exercise 2.4.28), and then reducing the problem further to sentences of the form $\forall x_1 \ldots \forall x_n \exists y_1 \ldots \exists y_m \psi$, where ψ is quantifier-free.

Exercise 5.6.7 (completeness for uncountable languages)
*(This exercise presupposes familiarity with ordinal and cardinal numbers.) So far we assumed that each vocabulary L is *countable* (see Chapter 16.4), and so the set of L-formulas is countably infinite. This is reasonable as long as logical consequence is related to actual reasoning. For model-theoretic purposes, however (see the next chapter), it is useful to note that essentially the same proof of the Model Existence Theorem (and hence of completeness) can be given for vocabularies of any cardinality.

So let L be a vocabulary such that the set of L-formulas has cardinality κ.[7] Suppose Δ is a consistent set of L-sentences, and let $L' = L \cup C$, where C is a set of new (not occurring in Δ) individual constants of cardinality κ. Let $\{\varphi_\alpha : \alpha < \kappa\}$ be the set of all L'-sentences. Define a sequence of sets Δ_α for each ordinal $\alpha < \kappa$ as follows:

(13) $\Delta_0 = \Delta$

Suppose Δ_β is defined for $\beta < \alpha$. If $\alpha = \beta + 1$, then:

if $\Delta_\beta \cup \{\varphi_\beta\}$ is inconsistent, let $\Delta_\alpha = \Delta_\beta$;

if $\Delta_\beta \cup \{\varphi_\beta\}$ is consistent and φ_β is not an existentially quantified sentence, let $\Delta_\alpha = \Delta_\beta \cup \{\varphi_\beta\}$;

if $\Delta_\beta \cup \{\varphi_\beta\}$ is consistent and φ_β is of the form $\exists x \psi(x)$, let $\Delta_\alpha = \Delta_\beta \cup \{\varphi_\beta\} \cup \{\psi(d)\}$, where d is a *new* individual constant, i.e. one that does not occur in Δ_β or in φ_β.

If α is a limit number, let $\Delta_\alpha = \bigcup_{\beta<\alpha} \Delta_\beta$.

[7] In general, if $|L|$ is the cardinality of L, the cardinality of the set of L-formulas is $|L| + \aleph_0$, which is equal to $|L|$, if L is infinite (and equal to $\aleph_0$ if L is finite).

1. Letting $\Delta^* = \bigcup_{\alpha<\kappa} \Delta_\alpha$, show (using transfinite induction) that the conclusion of Lindenbaum's Lemma holds: Δ^* is maximal consistent and $\exists$-complete.
2. Conclude that the proof of completeness of FOL carries over to this setting.

Exercise 5.6.8 (squeezing)
*The definition of logical consequence quantifies over interpretations or, as we now say, models. Since our metatheory is set theory, models are sets. But there are collections which are not sets (see Chapter 16.1) and the intuitive notion of consequence seems to quantify over all kinds of interpretations, regardless of whether they are sets or not: *every* interpretation making the premises true also makes the conclusion true. The class V of all sets, for example, might very well be the domain of an (intuitive) interpretation. Let $\models^I$ denote this consequence relation. Assume further that a strong form of soundness holds: if $\Gamma \vdash_H \varphi$, then $\Gamma \models^I \varphi$. Show that the Completeness Theorem implies that the intuitive and the model-theoretic notions of logical consequence coincide for FOL. (This observation, due to Georg Kreisel, is often called *Kreisel's squeezing argument*.)

6 Model theory

In this chapter our perspective changes. So far, the relation $\models$ between models and sentences has served to explain the meaning of the logical constants (as given in the truth definition, Definition 2.3.13), and to define logical truth and consequence. Now we will study it for its own sake. A model is a domain (universe) with various individuals, relations and functions. Put differently, a model is a mathematical *structure*.

Many properties of models—but not all, as we will see—can be described in a first-order language. There are two natural questions to ask in this context:

- Given a model (or a class of models), which sentences are true in it (in all models in the class)?
- Given a sentence, or a *theory*, i.e. a set of sentences, which models does it have? Which different kinds of models?

Such questions concern the *expressive power* of our logic. For example, is it possible to express that a set has exactly three elements? The answer is Yes (provided we have identity in the logic): there is a sentence whose models are precisely those $\mathcal{M} = (M, A)$ (where $A \subseteq M$) such that A has exactly three elements. Can you express that an order relation is *dense* (that between two elements there is always a third)? Yes: in a vocabulary with a binary predicate symbol. Can we express that a set is *finite*? Answer: No, and we will see that this follows from the results in the preceding chapter. That an ordered set is *well-founded* (see Exercise 16.3.7)? No: that too follows from results we have proved, as we will see. What if we restrict our attention to finite models, and ask if the property of a set having an *even* number of elements is expressible? The answer is again No; this will be shown in Section 6.10.2.

We begin with some examples of what *can* be expressed in first-order logic.

6.1. Expressing numerical claims

It is a simple but important fact about first-order logic with identity that, for every natural number n, we can express the statement that a set A has at least/exactly/at most n elements. We let

$$|A|$$

denote the number of elements in A, also called the *cardinality* of A (Chapter 16.5.1). Thus, the sentence

$$\exists x \exists y (x \neq y \wedge Px \wedge Py)$$

expresses, in every model $\mathcal{M} = (M, P^{\mathcal{M}})$, that $P^{\mathcal{M}}$ has at least two elements, i.e. that $|P^{\mathcal{M}}| \geqslant 2$. This can be generalized to any number $n \geqslant 1$. Let

(1) $\exists_{\geqslant n} x \, \psi(x)$

where $\psi(x)$ is a formula with at most x free, abbreviate

(2) $\exists x_1 \ldots \exists x_n (\bigwedge_{1 \leqslant i < j \leqslant n} x_i \neq x_j \;\wedge\; \bigwedge_{1 \leqslant i \leqslant n} \psi(x_i))$

Here we have written a long conjunction in a more compact way; for example, $\bigwedge_{1 \leqslant i < j \leqslant 4} x_i \neq x_j$ is short for

$$x_1 \neq x_2 \wedge x_1 \neq x_3 \wedge x_1 \neq x_4 \wedge x_2 \neq x_3 \wedge x_2 \neq x_4 \wedge x_3 \neq x_4$$

(We disregard here the order between the conjuncts, and similarly for long disjunctions.) So the sentence $\exists_{\geqslant n} x Px$ *says* that (the interpretation of) P has *at least* n elements, in the precise sense that

$$(M, A) \models \exists_{\geqslant n} x Px \text{ iff } |A| \geqslant n.$$ [1]

It is then also clear that if we let

$$\exists_{\leqslant n} x \, \psi(x)$$

abbreviate $\neg \exists_{\geqslant n+1} x \, \psi(x)$, and

$$\exists_{=n} x \, \psi(x)$$

abbreviate $\exists_{\geqslant n} x \, \psi(x) \wedge \exists_{\leqslant n} x \, \psi(x)$, the sentence $\exists_{\leqslant n} x Px$ says that P has *at most* n elements, and $\exists_{=n} x Px$ says that it has *exactly* n elements.

We can also use (1) when $\psi = \psi(x, y_1, \ldots, y_n)$ is a formula with free variables besides x. Then in a model $\mathcal{M}$, for each $a_1, \ldots, a_n \in M$, (1) says that at least n elements satisfy $\psi[x, a_1, \ldots, a_n]$ in $\mathcal{M}$.

The *cardinality of a model* $\mathcal{M}$ is the cardinality of its domain M. So we can express that $\mathcal{M}$ has at least n elements with the sentence

[1] Again, $\mathcal{M} = (M, A)$ is a model for the vocabulary $L = \{P\}$, where P is a unary predicate symbol, and where $P^{\mathcal{M}} = A$.

(3) $\exists_{\geqslant n} x\, x = x$

and similarly for exactly/at most n elements. In this case we may leave out all the conjuncts $x_i = x_i$ in (2), i.e. those corresponding to $\psi(x_i)$, since they are always satisfied. In other words, we can let $\exists_{\geqslant n} x\, x = x$ abbreviate

(4) $\exists x_1 \ldots \exists x_n \bigwedge_{1 \leqslant i < j \leqslant n} x_i \neq x_j$

An obvious next question is if we can also express in first-order logic that a model (or a set) is *finite*, or that it is *infinite*. Clearly, if the former can be expressed by a sentence, so can the latter (by the negation of that sentence). In Section 6.7 below we will see that one *cannot* express these statements, but that in a weaker sense, infinity, but not finitude, is expressible.

6.1.1. Numerical quantifiers

The expression $\exists_{\geqslant n} x P x$ abbreviates a sentence containing n quantifiers and a long conjunction (see also Exercise 6.13.1). Alternatively, we could add a quantifier

$$\exists_{\geqslant n}$$

as a *new logical symbol*, for every n, and treat it in the same way as we did $\forall$ and $\exists$. That is, if ψ is any formula and x is a variable, then

$$\exists_{\geqslant n} x\, \psi$$

is a formula, with the truth condition

(5) $\mathcal{M} \models \exists_{\geqslant n} x\, \psi[x, \overline{a}]$ iff
there are at least n elements a in M such that $\mathcal{M} \models \psi\,[a, \overline{a}]$

With these new *numerical quantifiers*, $\exists_{\geqslant n} x P x$ is a well-formed sentence (not an abbreviation), with a single bound variable, saying that $P^{\mathcal{M}}$ has at least n elements. Sometimes it is practical to add such quantifiers.[2] The expressive power does not increase: everything you can express with these new quantifiers can also be expressed with a sentence containing the usual $\forall$ and $\exists$, plus identity. But 'efficiency' increases: statements about numbers become *much shorter* if one allows numerical quantifiers. This can be important for computer implementations of logic.

Other types of new quantifiers can also be added to FOL, for example, a quantifier Q_0 such that $Q_0 x$ says 'for infinitely many x'. But this quantifier is *not* expressible in FOL. More examples are given in Section 6.9 below.

[2] An example dating back to the early days of predicate logic is that one often uses $\exists! x P x$ to express that there is *exactly one* x such that Px.

6.2. Order relations

The concept of an order, and many properties of orders, are easily expressed in FOL (Appendix 16.3.2 has information about orders). A (non-strict) *partial order* is a binary relation which is reflexive, anti-symmetric, and transitive. If R is a binary predicate symbol, these properties are expressed by the following first-order sentences:

(6) a. $\forall x Rxx$
b. $\forall x \forall y(Rxy \wedge Ryx \rightarrow x = y)$
c. $\forall x \forall y \forall z(Rxy \wedge Ryz \rightarrow Rxz)$

In other words, sentence (6b) is true in a model $\mathcal{M} = (M, R)$ iff R is anti-symmetric, etc., so the conjunction of (6a) – (6c) is true in (M, R) iff R is a (non-strict) partial order in M.

Here we are being a bit sloppy: we first used 'R' as a formal predicate symbol, and then the same 'R' for the relation interpreting this predicate symbol. We really should have written $R^{\mathcal{M}}$ for the latter. But this particular sloppiness is often useful, and should not cause confusion.

We often write

$$xRy$$

instead of Rxy, (as we already do for $=$). And with (partial or total) order relations we mostly use $\leqslant$ instead of R (and $<$ in the strict case). So, for example, (6b) can be formulated

$$\forall x \forall y(x \leqslant y \wedge y \leqslant x \rightarrow x = y)$$

All this is to increase readability and intuitive understanding. It works well, as long as one is clear about the fact that we on the one hand are talking about sentences, i.e. syntactic expressions in a formal language, and on the other hand about models in which these sentences are true or false.

Here are more examples of properties of (non-strict) partial orders expressible in FOL:

(7) a. $\forall x \forall y(x \leqslant y \vee y \leqslant x)$ expresses that the order is *total*.
b. $\exists x \forall y(x \leqslant y)$ expresses that it has a *least element*.
c. $\forall x \forall y((x \leqslant y \wedge x \neq y) \rightarrow \exists z(x \leqslant z \wedge x \neq z \wedge z \leqslant y \wedge z \neq y))$ expresses that it is *dense*.

With a strict relation $<$, density becomes simpler:

$$\forall x \forall y(x < y \rightarrow \exists z(x < z \wedge z < y))$$

We obtain this directly from (7c) by the usual way of going from a non-strict (partial) order $\leqslant$ to the corresponding strict relation $<$: $x < y$ is equivalent to $x \leqslant y \wedge x \neq y$. In the other direction, $x \leqslant y$ is equivalent to $x < y \vee x = y$.

6.3. Equivalence relations

Let Eq be the conjunction of the following sentences, where E is a binary predicate symbol:

$$\forall x\, xEx$$
$$\forall x \forall y (xEy \rightarrow yEx)$$
$$\forall x \forall y \forall z (xEy \wedge yEz \ \rightarrow \ xEz)$$

Then *Eq* is true in a model $\mathcal{M} = (M, E)$ iff E is an *equivalence relation* (reflexive, symmetric, transitive) in M. Appendix 16.3.3 describes how such a relation splits M into *equivalence classes*, where, for $a \in M$,

$$[a]_E = \{b \in M : aEb\}$$

is the equivalence class of a. Put differently, the equivalence classes form a *partition* of M (into non-empty and pairwise disjoint subsets), and conversely, every partition of M corresponds to an equivalence relation in M (where two elements are equivalent iff they belong to the same partition set).

One can classify an equivalence relation in terms of how many equivalence classes it has, and how many elements there are in each class. Up to a point, this can be expressed in FOL.

Let us look at some examples. The sentence

(8) $\quad \forall x \forall y\, xEy$

describes the *universal relation*, which obviously is an equivalence relation. In every model of (8) all elements of M are equivalent (related by E), that is, $E = M^2$. (Again we are using E both for the formal predicate symbol and its interpretation in a model.) We actually don't need *Eq* as an axiom, since the universal relation is reflexive, symmetric, och transitive. There is just one equivalence class: the whole M. Regardless of the cardinality of M, (8) characterizes the universal equivalence relation: for every model (M, E),

$$(M, E) \models \forall x \forall y\, xEy \ \text{ iff } \ E = M^2$$

Similarly, the next sentence uniquely characterizes the *smallest* equivalence relation on a domain M, namely, the identity relation:

(9) $\quad \forall x \forall y (xEy \leftrightarrow x = y)$

This sentence says that each individual is equivalent to itself and to no other individual in the domain:

$(M, E) \models \forall x \forall y (xEy \leftrightarrow x = y)$ iff
E is the identity relation on M, i.e. $E = \{(a, a) : a \in M\}$.

Here there are as many equivalence classes as there are elements of M, and every equivalence class has exactly one element: $[a]_E = \{a\}$.

Now suppose we want to say that *there are at least three equivalence classes*. This is the same as saying that there are at least three elements in the domain *not* related by E:

(10) $\exists x \exists y \exists z (\neg xEy \wedge \neg xEz \wedge \neg yEz)$

For if E is an equivalence relation and there are three non-equivalent individuals, these belong to different equivalence classes, so there are at least three such. Conversely, if there are at least three equivalence classes, there are at least three non-equivalent individuals: choose any member of each of the three equivalence classes. In other words:

(11) $(M, E) \models Eq \wedge \exists x \exists y \exists z (\neg xEy \wedge \neg xEz \wedge \neg yEz)$ iff
E is an equivalence relation in M with at least three equivalence classes.

Let $E_{\geqslant 3}$ be the sentence (10). More generally (see also Exercise 6.13.3):

(12) Let $E_{\geqslant n}$ be the sentence $\exists x_1 \ldots \exists x_n \bigwedge_{1 \leqslant i < j \leqslant n} \neg x_i E x_j$.

Then we have:

(13) If $(M, E) \models Eq$, i.e. E is an equivalence relation in M, then:
$(M, E) \models E_{\geqslant n}$ iff E has at least n equivalence classes.

Can we express that there are infinitely many equivalence classes? Not by one sentence, but let

$$\Delta = \{E_{\geqslant 1}, E_{\geqslant 2}, E_{\geqslant 3}, \ldots\}$$

Then

$(M, E) \models \{Eq\} \cup \Delta$ iff E is an equivalence relation in M with infinitely many equivalence classes.

Remember that $\mathcal{M} \models \Gamma$ means that *all* sentences in Γ are true in $\mathcal{M}$. So $(M, E) \models \{Eq\} \cup \Delta$ means, first, that Eq is true in (M, E), i.e. that E is an equivalence relation in M, and, second, that for each n there are at least n equivalence classes, which is true iff there are infinitely many equivalence classes.

Now let us see what we can say in FOL about the number of elements in an equivalence class. That there are at least three elements in the equivalence class of a, for example, means that there are at least three distinct elements equivalent with a. We can express this by a formula with a free variable corresponding to a, using the formulas (1) in Section 6.1, where $\psi = \psi(x, y)$ is the formula yEx:

$$\exists_{\geqslant 3} y\, yEx$$

If $\mathcal{M} = (M, E) \vDash Eq$, we have that a satisfies $\exists_{\geqslant 3} y\, yEx$ in $\mathcal{M}$ iff at least three elements of M stand in the relation E to a, i.e. iff $|[a]_E| \geqslant 3$. In general, if $\mathcal{M}$ is a model of *Eq*, then for all $a \in M$,

(14) $\quad \mathcal{M} \vDash \exists_{\geqslant n} y\, yEx\, [a] \text{ iff } |[a]_E| \geqslant n.$ [3]

In a similar way we can express that the equivalence class of a has at most n, or exactly n, elements.

This allows us in certain cases to describe an equivalence relation completely in terms of the number of equivalence classes, and the number of their elements. Here is an example; see also Exercise 6.13.4. The following sentence says that, given that E is an equivalence relation, there are exactly three equivalence classes, one of which has one element and the other two have two elements.

(15) $$\begin{aligned}&\exists x \exists y \exists z(\neg xEy \wedge \neg xEz \wedge \neg yEz \wedge \\ &\exists_{=1} v\, vEx \wedge \exists_{=2} v\, vEy \wedge \exists_{=2} v\, vEz \wedge \forall u(uEx \vee uEy \vee uEz))\end{aligned}$$

The first three conjuncts say that x, y, z belong to different equivalence classes, the following three conjuncts give the number of elements of the equivalence classes of x, y, z, respectively, and the final conjunct says that every element of the domain is equivalent to one of x, y, z, which entails that there are no other equivalence classes.

Note that the fact that sentence (15) is true in a model $\mathcal{M}$ says nothing about *which* elements M consists of, nor about which of them have equivalence classes with one or two elements. *Every* model where there are exactly three equivalence classes, one with one element and two with two elements, is a model of (15).

This is indeed what one should expect. All models of *Eq* in which (15) is true have the *same structure*, independently of which objects constitute the domain. Put differently, they are *isomorphic*. Sentences in FOL cannot distinguish isomorphic models. We will now make precise the idea about 'same structure', i.e. isomorphic models, and prove the claim just made.

---

[3] Here we have to live with a small collision of notation: on the left-hand side, $[a]$ stands for the sequence whose only element is a, which is assigned to the variable x (see the truth definition in Chapter 2.3.2). On the right-hand side, $[a]_E$ is the equivalence class of a: $[a]_E = \{b \in M : aEb\}$.

6.4. Isomorphic models

Let $\mathcal{M}$ and $\mathcal{M}'$ be two models for the same vocabulary L. That they have the same structure means, *first*, that there is a way to map each element of M to a unique element of M' in such a way that no elements of M' 'remain', and, *second*, that the interpretation of the symbols in L is the same in $\mathcal{M}$ and $\mathcal{M}'$, *relative to* this map.

More precisely, the first requirement is that there is a *one-one correspondence*, or a *bijection*, h, from M to M'; see Chapter 16.2 for explanations and examples. If P is, say, a binary predicate symbol in L, the second requirement is that for all $a, b \in M$,

$$P^{\mathcal{M}}(a,b) \text{ iff } P^{\mathcal{M}'}(h(a),h(b))$$

Here is the full definition.

Definition 6.4.1 (isomorphisms)
h is an *isomorphism* from $\mathcal{M}$ to $\mathcal{M}'$ if the following holds:

1. h is a bijection from M to M'.
2. If $c \in L$, then $c^{\mathcal{M}'} = h(c^{\mathcal{M}})$.
3. If P is an n-ary predicate symbol in L, and $a_1, \dots, a_n \in M$, then $P^{\mathcal{M}}(a_1,\dots,a_n) \Leftrightarrow P^{\mathcal{M}'}(h(a_1),\dots,h(a_n))$.
4. If f is an n-ary function symbol in L, and $a_1, \dots, a_n \in M$, then $h(f^{\mathcal{M}}(a_1,\dots,a_n)) = f^{\mathcal{M}'}(h(a_1),\dots,h(a_n))$.

We say that $\mathcal{M}$ and $\mathcal{M}'$ are *isomorphic*, in symbols,

$$\mathcal{M} \cong \mathcal{M}'$$

if there is an isomorphism from $\mathcal{M}$ to $\mathcal{M}'$, and we write $h\colon \mathcal{M} \cong \mathcal{M}'$ for "h is an isomorphism from $\mathcal{M}$ to $\mathcal{M}'$." It is left as an exercise to show that the relation $\cong$ is an equivalence relation among L-models. So we can just as well say that h is an isomorphism *between* $\mathcal{M}$ *and* $\mathcal{M}'$.

6.4.1. The Isomorphism Lemma

Now our goal is to show that FOL sentences *cannot distinguish isomorphic models*, in other words, that if $\mathcal{M} \cong \mathcal{M}'$, then:

$$\mathcal{M} \models \varphi \text{ iff } \mathcal{M}' \models \varphi$$

for every L-sentence φ. As usual, general claims about *sentences* cannot be proved directly by induction. The solution, as the reader is hopefully beginning to recognize, is to show a more general claim about *formulas*, which has the desired claim as a special case. In fact, this time the more general claim turns out to have independent interest (for example, Lemma 6.5.1 below). Let $\mathcal{M}$ and $\mathcal{M}'$ be L-models.

Lemma 6.4.2 (Isomorphism Lemma)
If $h\colon \mathcal{M} \cong \mathcal{M}'$, then for all L-formulas $\varphi(x_1,\ldots,x_n)$ and all $a_1,\ldots,a_n \in M$,

$$\mathcal{M} \models \varphi\,[a_1,\ldots,a_n] \text{ iff } \mathcal{M}' \models \varphi\,[h(a_1),\ldots,h(a_n)]$$

In particular, for every L-sentence φ,

$$\mathcal{M} \models \varphi \text{ iff } \mathcal{M}' \models \varphi$$

Proof. We abbreviate $x_1,\ldots,x_n$ as $\overline{x}$, $a_1,\ldots,a_n$ as $\overline{a}$, and similarly $h(a_1),\ldots,h(a_n)$ as $h(\overline{a})$. For simplicity, let us deal only with the case that L has no function symbols. First, observe that for every L-term t with variables among $x_1,\ldots,x_n$ we have (recall the notation from Chapter 2.3.2)

(16) $\quad h(t^{\mathcal{M},[\overline{a}]}) = t^{\mathcal{M}',[h(\overline{a})]}$

For if t is a variable x_i, then $h(x_i^{\mathcal{M},[\overline{a}]}) = h(a_i) = x_i^{\mathcal{M}',[h(\overline{a})]}$, and if t is an individual constant c, then $h(c^{\mathcal{M},[\overline{a}]}) = h(c^{\mathcal{M}}) = c^{\mathcal{M}'} = c^{\mathcal{M}',[h(\overline{a})]}$.

Now we can begin the inductive proof. The base step is that φ is atomic. If φ is $Pt_1\ldots t_k$, we have:

$$\begin{aligned}
\mathcal{M} \models Pt_1\ldots t_k\,[\overline{a}] &\Leftrightarrow P^{\mathcal{M}}(t_1^{\mathcal{M},[\overline{a}]},\ldots,t_k^{\mathcal{M},[\overline{a}]}) && \text{(truth def.)}\\
&\Leftrightarrow P^{\mathcal{M}'}(h(t_1^{\mathcal{M},[\overline{a}]}),\ldots,h(t_k^{\mathcal{M},[\overline{a}]})) && \text{(Def. 6.4.1)}\\
&\Leftrightarrow P^{\mathcal{M}'}(t_1^{\mathcal{M}',[h(\overline{a})]},\ldots,t_k^{\mathcal{M}',[h(\overline{a})]}) && \text{(by (16))}\\
&\Leftrightarrow \mathcal{M}' \models Pt_1\ldots t_k\,[h(\overline{a})] && \text{(truth def.)}
\end{aligned}$$

And if φ is $t_1 = t_2$:

$$\begin{aligned}
\mathcal{M} \models t_1 = t_2\,[\overline{a}] &\Leftrightarrow t_1^{\mathcal{M},[\overline{a}]} = t_2^{\mathcal{M},[\overline{a}]} && \text{(truth def.)}\\
&\Leftrightarrow h(t_1^{\mathcal{M},[\overline{a}]}) = h(t_2^{\mathcal{M},[\overline{a}]}) && \text{(since } h \text{ is injective!)}\\
&\Leftrightarrow t_1^{\mathcal{M}',[h(\overline{a})]} = t_2^{\mathcal{M}',[h(\overline{a})]} && \text{(by (16))}\\
&\Leftrightarrow \mathcal{M}' \models t_1 = t_2\,[h(\overline{a})] && \text{(truth def.)}
\end{aligned}$$

Now suppose φ is $(\psi \wedge \theta)$, and that the claim holds for ψ and θ (induction hypothesis). We have:

$$\begin{aligned}
\mathcal{M} \models (\psi \wedge \theta)\,[\overline{a}] &\Leftrightarrow \mathcal{M} \models \psi\,[\overline{a}] \text{ and } \mathcal{M} \models \theta\,[\overline{a}] &&\\
&\Leftrightarrow \mathcal{M}' \models \psi\,[h(\overline{a})] \text{ and } \mathcal{M}' \models \theta\,[h(\overline{a})] && \text{(ind. hyp.)}\\
&\Leftrightarrow \mathcal{M}' \models (\psi \wedge \theta)\,[h(\overline{a})] &&
\end{aligned}$$

The other propositional connectives are dealt with similarly. It remains to account for quantified formulas. Suppose φ is $\exists y\psi(y,\overline{x})$, and that the claim holds for ψ (induction hypothesis). Reason as follows::

$$\begin{aligned}
\mathcal{M} \models \exists y\psi[y,\overline{a}] &\Rightarrow \text{for some } b \in M,\ \mathcal{M} \models \psi\,[b,\overline{a}] && \text{(truth def.)}\\
&\Rightarrow \text{for some } b \in M,\ \mathcal{M}' \models \psi\,[h(b),h(\overline{a})] && \text{(ind. hyp.)}\\
&\Rightarrow \text{for some } b' \in M',\ \mathcal{M}' \models \psi\,[b',h(\overline{a})] && \text{(let } b' = h(b))\\
&\Rightarrow \mathcal{M}' \models \exists y\psi[y,h(\overline{a})] && \text{(truth def.)}
\end{aligned}$$

In the other direction we have:

$$\begin{aligned}
\mathcal{M}' \models \exists y\psi[y, h(\overline{a})] \quad &\Rightarrow \quad \text{for some } b' \in M',\ \mathcal{M}' \models \psi\,[b', h(\overline{a})] \ \text{(truth def.)}\\
&\Rightarrow \quad \text{for some } b \in M,\ \mathcal{M}' \models \psi\,[h(b), h(\overline{a})]\\
&\qquad\qquad\qquad \text{(since } h \text{ is surjective!)}\\
&\Rightarrow \quad \text{for some } b \in M,\ \mathcal{M} \models \psi\,[b, \overline{a}] \quad \text{(ind. hyp.)}\\
&\Rightarrow \quad \mathcal{M} \models \exists y\psi[y, \overline{a}] \qquad \text{(truth def.)}
\end{aligned}$$

The remaining case, $\varphi = \forall y\psi$, is similar. □

One consequence of this result is that since it doesn't matter which elements the domain contains, one can always choose some objects that are easy to deal with. In model theory one often uses the natural numbers. For a countably infinite domain, we can always choose $\{0, 1, 2, \ldots\}$. And if we need a finite domain with n elements, we can take, for example, $\{0, 1, \ldots, n-1\}$; see Exercises 6.13.7 and 6.13.8.

6.4.2. Examples

Example 6.4.3 (ordered sets)
An *ordered set* is a set with a total order relation. In other words, it is (in the non-strict case) a model of the form $(M, \leqslant)$ in which sentences (6) and (7a) in Section 6.2 are true. If one represents the order in a diagram where 'to the left of' means 'smaller than' (this is described in Chapter 16.3.2), it is often easy to see if two ordered sets are isomorphic or not. To show that they are isomorphic, one needs to find a suitable bijection, one that preserves the order. This can often be seen directly in the diagram. The following ordered sets are all isomorphic.

a. 0 1 2 3 4 ...

b. 0 2 4 6 8 ...

c. 2 3 5 7 11 ... (prime numbers in order of magnitude)

In the first case, the bijection is $h(n) = 2n$. That h is an isomorphism follows from the fact that, for all n, m, $n < m$ iff $2n < 2m$. And that a. and c. are isomorphic is seen by the function $h(n) = p_n$, where p_n is the n:th prime number (and you start with the 0:th, i.e. with 2).[4]

To show that two ordered sets are *not* isomorphic it is enough, according to the Isomorphism Lemma, to find a sentence (in the vocabulary $L = \{\leqslant\}$) which is true in the one set but false in the other. This is a very useful method. The following ordered sets, which all have $\mathbb{N} = \{0, 1, 2, \ldots\}$ as their domain, are not isomorphic:

[4]That h in the latter case is a bijection uses the fact (proved by Euclid) that there are infinitely many prime numbers; see Chapter 8.6 and Exercise 8.9.15.

a. 0 1 2 3 ...

b. ... 3 2 1 0

c. ... 4 2 0 1 3 5 ...

The first order has a least but not a greatest element, the second has a greatest but not a least element, and the third has neither a least nor a greatest element. This means that the sentences $\exists x \forall y\, x \leqslant y$ and $\exists x \forall y\, y \leqslant x$ have different truth values in these models, which therefore cannot be isomorphic. For more examples, see Exercise 6.13.9.

Example 6.4.4 (equivalence relations)
If two finite models $\mathcal{M} = (M, E)$ and $\mathcal{M}' = (M', E')$ of *Eq* are such that (a) the have the same finite number of equivalence classes, and (b) for every n they have the same number of equivalence classes with n element, then they are isomorphic. For we can match, for every n, the equivalence classes with n elements in $\mathcal{M}$ with the corresponding equivalence classes with n elements in $\mathcal{M}'$. Since corresponding equivalence classes have the same number of elements, there is a bijection between each such pair of equivalence classes. And since the equivalence classes are pairwise disjoint and together exhaust M and M', respectively, we can join all these bijections to one big bijection h between M and M'.[5] Then h will be such that aEb holds in $\mathcal{M}$ iff $h(a)E'h(b)$ holds in $\mathcal{M}'$, which means precisely that $h\colon \mathcal{M} \cong \mathcal{M}'$.

Conversely, if, $\mathcal{M}$ and $\mathcal{M}'$ (finite models of *Eq*) are isomorphic there is a bijection h from M to M' such that for all $a, b \in M$, we have $aEb \Leftrightarrow h(a)E'h(b)$. This means that $|[a]_E| = |[h(a)]_E|$ for each $a \in M$, since the fact that h is an isomorphism entails that the restriction of h to the equivalence class $[a]_E$ is a bijection from $[a]_E$ to $[h(a)]_{E'}$. But then it follows that $\mathcal{M}$ and $\mathcal{M}'$ have the same number of equivalence classes, and that for each n, they have the same number of equivalence classes with n elements.

What about infinite models? We restrict attention here to *countably infinite* or *denumerable* models: $M = \{a_0, a_1, a_2, \ldots\}$. In such a model there are countably many equivalence classes: $[a_0]_E, [a_1]_E, [a_2]_E, \ldots$.[6] Of these, some may be identical (perhaps all, if $E = M^2$; perhaps none, if E is the identity relation): if a_iEa_j, then $[a_i]_E = [a_j]_E$. But the situation is the same as in the finite case: two models $\mathcal{M}$ and $\mathcal{M}'$ of this kind are isomorphic if they have the same number (finite or denumerable) of equivalence classes of the same (finite or denumerable) cardinality. For in both the finite and the infinite case,

[5] Set-theoretically, this means that h is the *union* of the bijections between the corresponding equivalence classes; see Chapter 16.2.

[6] Remember that *countable* in this book means 'finite or with as many elements as $\mathbb{N}$'.

that two sets have the same number of elements means that they are *equinumerous* (see Chapter 16.4), i.e. that there is a bijection between them.

We can systematize this information about countable models of *Eq* in the following way. Let ω denote the number of elements in a countably infinite set (all such sets are equinumerous).

Definition 6.4.5 (signature of an equivalence relation)
The *signature* of a countable model $\mathcal{M}$ of *Eq* is a countably infinite sequence of numbers $\sigma^{\mathcal{M}} = (\sigma_0^{\mathcal{M}}, \sigma_1^{\mathcal{M}}, \sigma_2^{\mathcal{M}}, \ldots)$, where

$\sigma_0^{\mathcal{M}}$ is the number of equivalence classes in $\mathcal{M}$ with ω elements;

$\sigma_1^{\mathcal{M}}$ is the number of equivalence classes in $\mathcal{M}$ with 1 element;

...

$\sigma_n^{\mathcal{M}}$ is the number of equivalence classes in $\mathcal{M}$ with n elements;

...

Each $\sigma_k^{\mathcal{M}}$ is thus either a natural number $\geqslant 0$ or ω. For example, if M is countably infinite and $\mathcal{M} = (M, M^2)$, then

$$\sigma^{\mathcal{M}} = (1, 0, 0, 0, \ldots)$$

Signatures work for finite models too. If M is finite, say, $|M| = 5$, we obtain, for $\mathcal{M} = (M, M^2)$, $\sigma^{\mathcal{M}} = (0, 0, 0, 0, 0, 1, 0, 0, \ldots)$.

If M is countably infinite and $\mathcal{M} = (M, =)$, then

$$\sigma^{\mathcal{M}} = (0, \omega, 0, 0, 0, \ldots)$$

(whereas if $|M| = 5$, we obtain in this case $\sigma^{\mathcal{M}} = (0, 5, 0, 0, 0, \ldots)$.)

We have the following general result:

Fact 6.4.6
If $\mathcal{M}$ and $\mathcal{M}'$ are countable models of Eq, $\mathcal{M} \cong \mathcal{M}'$ iff $\sigma^{\mathcal{M}} = \sigma^{\mathcal{M}'}$.

The proof is essentially the same as in the finite case that we sketched above; see Exercise 6.13.11.

6.5. *Definability

Given a model $\mathcal{M}$ for a vocabulary L, a model-theorist asks which L-sentences are true in $\mathcal{M}$. A related and equally interesting question is which sets are definable in $\mathcal{M}$. Here a subset B of M is *definable* if there is a formula $\varphi(x)$ with one free variable which defines it, i.e. such that

$$B = \{b \in M : \mathcal{M} \models \varphi[b]\}$$

Similarly for definable relations over M. Note that if M is infinite there are uncountably many subsets of M, but only countably many of these can be definable, since there are only countably many L-formulas.

Trivially, M and $\varnothing$ are always definable (by $x = x$ and $x \neq x$, respectively). And if A, B are definable, so are $A \cap B$, $A \cup B$, and $\overline{A}$ (i.e. $M - A$). If $\mathbb{N}$ is the set of natural numbers and $<$ the usual ordering, the number 0, or more exactly the set $\{0\}$, is definable:

$$n = 0 \Leftrightarrow (\mathbb{N}, <) \models \neg\exists y\, y < x\, [n]$$

Similarly, every natural number m is definable: since for $m > 0$, m is the only number satisfying the formula $\exists_{=m} y\, y < x$ in $(\mathbb{N}, <)$. On the other hand, if the domain is $\mathbb{Z} = \{\ldots, -2, -1, 0, 1, 2, \ldots\}$, the set of integers, then no integer is definable in $(\mathbb{Z}, <)$; in fact, one can show that no subset of $\mathbb{Z}$ is definable in $(\mathbb{Z}, <)$ except $\mathbb{Z}$ and $\varnothing$. The set of even numbers is not definable in $(\mathbb{N}, <)$, but it is definable in the model $(\mathbb{N}, +)$: n is even iff $(\mathbb{N}, +) \models \exists y\, y + y = x\, [n]$. In Parts III and IV of this book we will be particularly interested in sets and relations definable in the standard model of arithmetic, $\mathcal{N} = (\mathbb{N}, 0, +, \cdot, s)$ (see Example 6.6.5 below); the so-called *arithmetical sets.*

A more general notion of definability is relative to parameters. If $a_1, \ldots, a_n \in M$, we say a set B *is definable with parameters* $a_1, \ldots, a_n$ *in* $\mathcal{M}$ if there is a formula $\varphi(x, x_1, \ldots, x_n)$ such that

$$B = \{b \in M : \mathcal{M} \models \varphi\, [b, a_1, \ldots, a_n]\}$$

To show that a set is definable in a model (perhaps with parameters), you need to come up with a defining formula. To show that it is *not* definable is usually harder. The following lemma is sometimes helpful. An *automorphism* on $\mathcal{M}$ is an isomorphism from $\mathcal{M}$ to $\mathcal{M}$.

Lemma 6.5.1
Suppose the set B is definable with parameters $a_1, \ldots, a_n$ in M. Then, for every automorphism h on $\mathcal{M}$ such that $h(a_i) = a_i$ for $i = 1, \ldots, n$, we have $b \in B \Leftrightarrow h(b) \in B$.

Proof. This is a direct consequence of the Isomorphism Lemma. Suppose $\varphi(x, x_1, \ldots, x_n)$ defines B in $\mathcal{M}$ with parameters $a_1, \ldots, a_n$. Then $b \in B \Leftrightarrow \mathcal{M} \models \varphi\, [b, a_1, \ldots, a_n] \Leftrightarrow \mathcal{M} \models \varphi\, [h(b), h(a_1), \ldots, h(a_n)]$ (by the Isomorphism Lemma) $\Leftrightarrow \mathcal{M} \models \varphi\, [h(b), a_1, \ldots, a_n]$ (by the assumption about h) $\Leftrightarrow h(b) \in B$. □

Thus, if you can find an automorphism h on $\mathcal{M}$ such that $b \in B$ but $h(b) \notin B$, then B is not definable in $\mathcal{M}$. We can use this to show that, for example, the number 3 (the set $\{3\}$) is not definable (without parameters) in $(\mathbb{Z}, <)$: let $h(k) = k + 1$ for all $k \in \mathbb{Z}$. h is a bijection from $\mathbb{Z}$ to $\mathbb{Z}$, and $k < m \Leftrightarrow k + 1 < m + 1$, so h is an automorphism on

$(\mathbb{Z}, <)$, but $3 \in \{3\}$ whereas $h(3) \notin \{3\}$, so $\{3\}$ is not definable. Clearly this argument works for every integer, so no element of the domain is definable in $(\mathbb{Z}, <)$ (without parameters).[7]

Let $\mathcal{M} = (M, A)$ be a model for the vocabulary $L = \{P\}$ where P is unary. We can use Lemma 6.5.1 to see exactly which sets are definable (with parameters) in $\mathcal{M}$. Let the *parts* of $\mathcal{M}$ be the sets $\emptyset$, A, $M - A$, and M. Obviously the parts are definable in $\mathcal{M}$. Given parameters $a_1, \ldots, a_n \in M$, we say that an $\{a_1, \ldots, a_n\}$*-variant* of a subset B of M is a set B' obtained from B by adding or deleting some of the $a_1, \ldots, a_n$. Then, if B is definable in $\mathcal{M}$ with parameters $a_1, \ldots, a_n$, so is B'. For example, if $\varphi(x, x_1, \ldots, x_n)$ defines B in $\mathcal{M}$ from $a_1, \ldots, a_n$, and $B' = (B \cup \{a_2\}) - \{a_3\}$, then B' is defined by the formula

$$(\varphi(x, x_1, \ldots, x_n) \vee x = x_2) \wedge x \neq x_3$$

Proposition 6.5.2
The sets definable in $\mathcal{M} = (M, A)$ *with parameters* $a_1, \ldots, a_n$ *are exactly the* $\{a_1, \ldots, a_n\}$*-variants of the parts of* $\mathcal{M}$.

Proof. We saw that these sets are all definable in $\mathcal{M}$ from $a_1, \ldots, a_n$. In the other direction, suppose B is definable in $\mathcal{M}$ with parameters $a_1, \ldots, a_n$, and let $B' = B - \{a_1, \ldots, a_n\}$. We show that B' is an $\{a_1, \ldots, a_n\}$-variant of some part of $\mathcal{M}$; it then follows that so is B. We may assume $B' \neq \emptyset$. Then there is a smallest of the remaining three parts such that B' is a subset of it; suppose $B' \subseteq A$ (the other two cases are similar). By assumption, there is $b \in B'$ such that $b \neq a_1, \ldots, a_n$. Now suppose for contradiction that B' is *not* an $\{a_1, \ldots, a_n\}$-variant of A. So there is $b' \in A - B'$ such that $b' \neq a_1, \ldots, a_n$. Let h be the function from M to M which switches b and b' but leaves all other elements of M as they are. Then h is an automorphism on $\mathcal{M}$ such that $h(a_i) = a_i$ for $i = 1, \ldots, n$. So it follows from Lemma 6.5.1 that $b \in B \Leftrightarrow h(b) \in B$. But $b \in B$ and $h(b) = b' \notin B$; this is our contradiction. □

This proposition can be generalized (with a suitable revision of the notion of part) to models of the form $(M, A_1, \ldots, A_k)$ where all the A_i are subsets of M, so-called *monadic* models. So it is clear which sets are definable (with parameters) in monadic models. But for non-monadic models, finding out which sets are definable can be a very difficult task.

---

[7] See also Exercise 6.13.14. This method works only when the model has non-trivial automorphisms. The model $(\mathbb{N}, <)$ doesn't have any, i.e. the only automorphism on $(\mathbb{N}, <)$ is the identity function (Exercise 6.13.12), so to show, for example, that the set of even numbers is not definable in $(\mathbb{N}, <)$, one must rely on other methods.

6.6. Theories

A (first-order) *theory* is simply a set T of sentences in some vocabulary L_T. We often call the sentences in T *axioms*, and the sentences derivable from T *theorems*.[8] Here we of course mean 'derivable in one of the usual inference systems for FOL', e.g. H (Chapter 3.3). Let $\vdash$ stand for derivability in some such system. By the Completeness Theorem, the theorems of T are exactly the logical consequences of T:

$$T \models \varphi \text{ iff } T \vdash \varphi$$

Our earlier notions of *consistency* (no contradiction is derivable from T) and *satisfiability* (T has a model) apply directly to theories, and by the results in Chapter 5 we know that T is consistent iff T is satisfiable. *In*consistent theories are of course rather uninteresting: in such a theory T, *all* L_T-sentences are theorems.

In order to specify a theory T, you have to specify its vocabulary L_T, and its axioms. Here are a few examples.

Example 6.6.1
If $L_0 = \emptyset$, i.e. L_0 is the *empty vocabulary*, the L_0-sentences are exactly the sentences that can be formed from atomic formulas of the form $x = y$ by means of connectives and quantifiers. For example, $\exists_{\geqslant 10} x\, x = x$ is such a sentence, and

$$\{\exists_{\geqslant 10} x\, x = x\},$$

let us call it $T_{\geqslant 10}$, is a theory in this vocabulary. Models for L_0 consist of a domain and nothing else; $\mathcal{M} = M$. So two such models are isomorphic if and only if they are equinumerous, i.e. if there is a bijection between them. $T_{\geqslant 10}$ is 'the theory of models with at least 10 elements', and there are of course many non-isomorphic such models. However, consider the following theory in the same vocabulary:

$$T_{=10} = \{\exists_{=10} x\, x = x\}$$

Models of $T_{=10}$ are simply sets with 10 elements—all such models are isomorphic!

Example 6.6.2
Let *EQ* be the theory whose cocabulary is $L_{EQ} = \{E\}$, where E is a binary predicate symbol, and whose axiom is the sentence *Eq* (Section 6.3), i.e. *EQ* = {*Eq*}. *EQ* is *the theory of one equivalence relation;*

[8]We use $T, T', \ldots$ for theories, although we previously used $\Gamma, \Delta, \ldots$ for sets of sentences. This is just notation; when we think of a set of sentences as a theory it is natural to use T.

its models are exactly structures of the form (M, E), where E is an equivalence relation on M. By adding more axioms, we can specify further properties of the equivalence relation. For example,

$$T_\omega = EQ \cup \{E_{\geqslant n} : n = 1, 2, \ldots\}$$

(see (13) in Section 6.3) is the theory of equivalence relations with infinitely many equivalence classes. The domain of a model of T_ω must be infinite. It cannot, for example, have (exactly) 100 elements. This means that the sentence

$$\neg\exists_{=100} x\, x = x$$

is a logical consequence of T_ω, and hence a theorem in T_ω.

Let us go through this reasoning in some detail. Every model $\mathcal{M} = (M, E)$ of T_ω is an equivalence relation with infinitely many equivalence classes. In particular, since the sentence $E_{\geqslant 101}$ is true in $\mathcal{M}$, there has to be at least 101 non-equivalent elements in M. So these elements are all distinct, and therefore the sentence $\exists_{\geqslant 101} x\, x = x$ is true in $\mathcal{M}$, which means that $\neg\exists_{=100} x\, x = x$ is also true in $\mathcal{M}$. This model-theoretic argument shows that $T_\omega \vDash \neg\exists_{=100} x\, x = x$: in every model of the axioms, the conclusion $\neg\exists_{=100} x\, x = x$ is true. Thus, by the Completeness Theorem, $T_\omega \vdash_H \neg\exists_{=100} x\, x = x$. So there is a derivation in H of $\neg\exists_{=100} x\, x = x$ from T_ω (more precisely, from $\{Eq, E_{\geqslant 101}\}$), but in this case it would be more cumbersome to construct such a derivation than to give the simple model-theoretic argument above.

Example 6.6.3 (*PO*, *LO*, and *DeLO*)
Let *PO* be the theory of (non-strict) *partial orders*, i.e. $L_{PO} = \{R\}$, where R is a binary predicate symbol, and *PO* consists of the three sentences in (6), saying that R is reflexive, anti-symmetric, and transitive. As usual we use $\leqslant$ for R and $<$ for its strict version.

Another example is the theory *LO* of (strict) *linear* or *total* orders, with axioms saying that $<$ is irreflexive, transitive, and total. We already saw examples of non-isomorphic models of *LO*, even non-isomorphic models whose domain is $\mathbb{N}$ (see Example 6.4.3 and exercises to this chapter and to Chapter 16.3).

The theory *DeLO* of *dense linear orders without first or last element* is obtained by adding to *LO* the axioms:

$$\forall x \exists y\, x < y$$

$$\forall x \exists y\, y < x$$

$$\forall x \forall y (x < y \rightarrow \exists z (x < z \wedge z < y))$$

The positive rational numbers with their usual order, $\mathcal{Q}^+ = (\mathbb{Q}^+, <)$, is a model of *DeLO*. The positive real numbers with their usual order, $\mathcal{R}^+ = (\mathbb{R}^+, <)$, is also a model of *DeLO*. These models are not even candidates for being isomorphic, since $\mathbb{Q}^+$ is countable while $\mathbb{R}^+$ is uncountable (see Chapter 16.5), so there can be no bijection between them. But we will see that all *countable* models of the theory *DeLO* are isomorphic (this is an old result by Cantor).

Example 6.6.4 (algebras)
Models for vocabularies without predicate symbols, apart from =, are called *algebras*. In this context one often thinks of individual constants as 0-ary function symbols, so the vocbulary is a set of function symbols, and the atomic formulas are all identities of the form $s = t$, called *equations*. Usually one is not interested in particular algebraic structures but in classes of algebras defined by universally quantified equations (these classes are called *varieties*) or other axioms. For example, a *monoid* is an algebra of the form $(M, 1, \cdot)$, where $1 \in M$ and $\cdot$ is binary operation on M, satisfying the axioms:[9]

(17) a. $x \cdot (y \cdot z) = (x \cdot y) \cdot z$ (associativity)
b. $x \cdot 1 = 1 \cdot x = x$ (1 is a unit element)

The natural numbers (or integers, or rational or real numbers) is a monoid with $\cdot$ as multiplication, but many other kinds of monoids arise in various context. For another example, let A be any set of symbols in A, and let A^* be the set of *finite strings* of symbols, including the empty string, written ϵ. If $\cdot$ is the *concatenation* operation,[10] then $(A^*, \epsilon, \cdot)$ is a monoid. We will have more to say about strings of symbols in Chapter 11.

A final example: a monoid in which every element has an *inverse* is a *group*. That is, a group satisfies axioms (17a) and (17b), and in addition

(17) c. $\forall x \exists y\, x \cdot y = y \cdot x = 1$ (existence of inverse)

Here we used the monoid vocabulary. If we want to describe groups using only equations, we add instead a unary function symbol, written $^{-1}$, and the axiom:

(17) c.′ $x \cdot x^{-1} = x^{-1} \cdot x = 1$

The reason this gives essentially the same result is that it follows from axiom (17)c. and the monoid axioms that the inverse must be *unique*.[11]

---

[9] Here we have, for readability, not written the universal quantifiers implicit in these axioms. The first axiom, for example, is really $\forall x \forall y \forall z\, x \cdot (y \cdot z) = (x \cdot y) \cdot z$.

[10] The concatenation of a string $a_1 \dots a_n$ with a string $b_1 \dots b_m$ is the string $a_1 \dots a_n b_1 \dots b_m$.

[11] Suppose y and y' are inverses of x. Then: $y = y \cdot 1 = y \cdot (x \cdot y') = (y \cdot x) \cdot y' = 1 \cdot y' = y'$.

Example 6.6.5 (Peano Arithmetic)
Let $L_{PA} = \{0, +, \cdot, '\}$, where $+$ and $\cdot$ are binary function symbols, $'$ is a unary function symbol, and 0 is an individual constant, and let *PA* be the following set of axioms:[12]

$$(18) \qquad \begin{aligned} & x' \neq 0 \\ & x' = y' \rightarrow x = y \\ & x + 0 = x \\ & x + y' = (x + y)' \\ & x \cdot 0 = 0 \\ & x \cdot y' = (x \cdot y) + x \\ & (\varphi(0) \wedge \forall x(\varphi(x) \rightarrow \varphi(x')) \rightarrow \forall x \varphi(x) \end{aligned}$$

The intended model of *PA* is the *standard model of arithmetic*,

$$\mathcal{N} = (\mathbb{N}, 0, +, \cdot, s)$$

i.e. the natural numbers with zero, addition, multiplication, the successor function s interpreting $'$ (so $s(n) = n + 1$ for every n).[13] The first six axioms of *PA* express familiar properties of 0, addition, multiplication and successor. Indeed, the third and fourth axioms give an (inductive) *definition* of addition, and similarly the fifth and sixth axioms define multiplication. The last axiom, the *Induction Axiom*, is a *scheme*: for every formula $\varphi(x)$ in L_{PA} we have an axiom of this form. Thus, the theory *PA* has infinitely many axioms. Amazingly, this simple theory suffices to prove most of what is known about number theory in mathematics. We will learn more about *PA* in Part III of this book.

Example 6.6.6 (set theory)
Set theory can be formulated as a first-order theory in the vocabulary $L = \{\in\}$, where $\in$ is a binary predicate symbol intended to denote the element-hood relation. A common axiomatization is *ZFC* (where C indicates that the Axiom of Choice in included); some of the axioms are discussed in Chapter 16.1. We shall not give all the axioms here, only a few examples:

$$\forall x \forall y(\forall z(z \in x \leftrightarrow z \in y) \rightarrow x = y) \qquad \text{(Extensionality axiom)}$$
$$\exists x \forall y\, y \notin x \qquad \text{(existence of the empty set; (4) in Ch. 16.1)}$$

---

[12]In the final induction axiom scheme, φ may contain other free variables, which are then universally quantified, besides x. See Chapter 9.

[13]Here we again used the 'sloppy' notation: in the description of $\mathcal{N}$, the symbols, in order, stand for the number 0, the addition function, the multiplication function, the successor function, while in the specification of the vocabulary L_{PA} these are *symbols* which (in the model $\mathcal{N}$) are interpreted as these numbers and functions. $\mathbb{N}$ is a standard notation for the set of natural numbers. Note that the model $(\mathbb{N}, 0, +)$ is monoid.

$$\forall x \forall y \exists z \forall u (u \in z \leftrightarrow (u = x \vee u = y)) \text{ (Pair Axiom; Ch. 16.1 (3))}$$

$$\forall x \exists y \forall z (z \in y \leftrightarrow (z \in x \wedge \varphi(z))) \text{ (Separation axiom; Ch. 16.1 (2))}$$

Note that in the 'intended model' of *ZFC*, the universe consists only of sets. It would be easy (and is sometimes practical) to recognize objects in the universe that are not sets, so-called *urelements*. Then we can have sets of urelements, but the $\in$ relation never holds between urelements, nor between sets and urelements. An extra unary predicate symbol U, and a few additional axioms, describe this situation.

It is not important for our purposes here to list all the axioms of *ZFC*. The main fact to remember is that even though it is first-order theory with a minimal vocabulary, it suffices to derive (at least in principle) almost all known facts of modern mathematics. In this sense, first-order logic is all the logic you need for classical mathematics.

Example 6.6.7 (theory of a model)
Let $\mathcal{M}$ be any model, for some vocabulary L. The *theory of* $\mathcal{M}$, in symbols $Th(\mathcal{M})$, is the set of all L-sentences true in $\mathcal{M}$:

$$Th(\mathcal{M}) = \{\varphi \colon \mathcal{M} \models \varphi\}$$

We encountered this kind of theory earlier, when we were introducing *maximal consistent sets* in Chapter 4.3. $Th(\mathcal{M})$ is maximal consistent: if φ is an L-sentence not in $Th(\mathcal{M})$, then φ is not true in $\mathcal{M}$, that is, $\mathcal{M} \models \neg\varphi$, so it would be inconsistent to add φ to $Th(\mathcal{M})$.

Theories of this form are quite different from the earlier examples, where we simply listed the axioms, or, in the case of the Induction Axiom for *PA* and the axiom of Separation for *ZFC*, specified their syntactic form as an axiom scheme. But regarding $Th(\mathcal{M})$ we have no control of the *form* of the axioms; the only thing we know about them is that they are true in $\mathcal{M}$.

For example, $Th(\mathcal{N})$ is the set of *true arithmetical sentences* (in the vocabulary L_{PA}). There are many unsolved questions in number theory. A simple example is *Goldbach's Conjecture*: every even number > 2 can be written as the sum of two prime numbers. This simple statement is easy to formulate in L_{PA}. But no one knows (so far) if it is true.[14] If it is true, it belongs to $Th(\mathcal{N})$, if not, its negation belongs to $Th(\mathcal{N})$. So although we can easily define $Th(\mathcal{N})$, there is a sense in which we do not *know* which axioms it contains.

6.6.1. Axiomatizable theories

In light of the last example, we see that a natural question to ask of a theory is whether there is a mechanical method for recognizing its

[14] As far as one has been able to check (using computers), no counter-example has been found. But this doesn't mean that none exists, and there is no proof that it doesn't, although weaker versions of the conjecture have been proved.

axioms. Let us say that a set Γ of L-sentences is *decidable* if there is an effective mechanical method for deciding if an arbitrary L-sentence φ belongs to Γ or not.

This is not (yet) a precise definition, since we have not specified 'mechanical method'. We will do this in Part IV. But for now, an intuitive understanding suffices. Every *finite* set of sentences is decidable: if $\Gamma = \{\psi_1, \ldots, \psi_n\}$ we can check (in principle), by successively comparing φ with each of these sentences, if φ belongs to Γ or not. But a countable set of sentences $\Delta = \{\psi_1, \psi_2, \ldots\}$ need not be decidable, not even if there is a mechanical method for *generating* $\psi_1, \psi_2, \ldots$. For suppose we have an L-sentence φ and start the generation to see if φ belongs to Δ. If φ does belong to Δ, this method gives a positive result: sooner or later we run into φ. But if $\varphi \notin \Delta$ we will look forever without finding an answer. So this procedure does not *after a finite number of steps* give an answer Yes or No to the question if φ belongs to Δ, and that is precisely what decidability requires.

But of course there are infinite and still decidable sets of sentences. Two examples are the theories T_ω and *PA* described earlier: here we know exactly what *form* an axiom has, and it is rather easy to design a method (e.g. a computer program) for deciding whether an arbitrary sentence (in the respective vocabularies) has this form or not.

So shall we say that T is axiomatizable if its set of axioms, i.e. T, is decidable? It could be the case that being an axiom in T is not decidable, but there is *another* set T' of axioms, which *is* decidable, and has the same theorems as T. The following definition allows for this.

Definition 6.6.8 (axiomatizability)

1. Two theories T and T' in the same vocabulary L are *equivalent* if they have the same theorems, i.e. if $T \vdash \varphi \Leftrightarrow T' \vdash \varphi$, for every L-sentence φ.
2. T is *axiomatizable* if there is a decidable set of axioms T' equivalent to T. If there is a finite such set T', we say that T is *finitely axiomatizable.*

The theories $T_{\geqslant 10}$, *EQ*, *PO*, *LO*, *DeLO* above have finitely many axioms, so they are finitely axiomatizable. The theories T_ω, *PA*, and *ZFC* have infinite but decidable sets of axioms so they are axiomatizable. We may still ask if they are finitely axiomatizable, i.e. if we can replace the axioms we gave by some equivalent finite sets of axioms. One can show that this is not possible—T_ω, *PA*, and *ZFC* are *not* finitely axiomatizable—but we will not enter into this question here. Concerning theories of the form $Th(\mathcal{M})$, finally, some are axiomatizable but many are not. For example, we will show in Part III that $Th(\mathcal{N})$ is not axiomatizable.

6.6.2. Categorical theories

We began this chapter by saying that it is natural to ask of a theory T how many models it has. Now we know that the first question must be: how many *non-isomorphic* models does T have? For if T has a model at all—if it is consistent—it has infinitely many models, because there are infinitely many isomorphic copies of any model.

One extreme case is when *all* models of T are isomorphic. This means that T completely determines which kinds of structures make its axioms true. In this case we say that T is *categorical*.

The theory

$$T_{=10} = \{\exists_{=10} x\, x = x\}$$

in the empty vocabulary is an example. Here a model is just a non-empty set M, and two such models are isomorphic iff they are equinumerous (have the same number of elements). But the axiom in $T_{=10}$ says that M has exactly ten elements, so all sets with ten elements are models of $T_{=10}$, and no other sets are: $T_{=10}$ is categorical.

We will see that this situation can only arise with finite models. More precisely, theories that have infinite models have models in every infinite cardinality. Therefore, the more interesting concept is categoricity for models of a fixed cardinality. In particular, we will look at the countably infinite models of these theories. Thus:

Definition 6.6.9 (categoricity)

1. T is *categorical* if all models of T are isomorphic.
2. T is *countably categorical* (or *$\aleph_0$-categorical*) if all countably infinite models of T are isomorphic.[15]

Since our language doesn't distinguish isomorphic models, we can say that a countably categorical theory has *just one* countably infinite model. We will soon see some examples of such theories.

A theory like *EQ* is obviously *not* countably categorical: there are so many different kinds of (non-isomorphic) equivalence relations on, for example, $\mathbb{N}$. And it is not meant to be; *EQ* just serves to axiomatize the property of being an equivalence relation. Similarly for the theories *PO* and *LO*. But the situation changes, as we will see, when more axioms are added to these theories.

[15] In this case we do not demand that all models of a given finite cardinality—if there are any—are isomorphic. The general notion, for any infinite cardinal κ, is that T is *κ-categorical* if all models of T of cardinal κ are isomorphic.

The situation is quite different with *PA*, which is meant to capture the essentials of elementary arithmetic: addition, multiplication, proof by induction. And as we said, *PA* in fact proves almost all known arithmetical truths. So it would be nice if it were countably categorical, i.e. if the standard model $\mathcal{N}$ were its only countably infinite model. But the opposite is the case: besides the standard model, *PA* has an extremely varied collection of countable *non-standard models*. And this is not because one has forgotten to add some axioms. It turns out that even if we take the whole $Th(\mathcal{N})$ as axioms, it does not help: even this theory has very many (in a precise sense: as many as possible) non-standard models. This may seem like a strange result, and one might wonder how such a fact could ever be proved. But in Section 6.7 we will see that this fact follows (with a very quick argument!) from something we already proved, namely, the Model Existence Theorem.

The study of non-standard models of arithmetic is an active branch of model theory. Set theory as well turns out to have many different kinds of models (though here it is not so easy to say which is *the* standard model), and the study of these is a central part of modern mathematical logic.[16]

6.6.3. Complete theories

A weaker but still quite reasonable demand on a theory like *PA* could be that every sentence φ in L_{PA} is decided by *PA*, in the sense that either φ or $\neg\varphi$ is a theorem in *PA*. Such a theory is said to be *complete*:

Definition 6.6.10 (complete theories)
T is *complete* if for every sentence φ in T:s vocabulary we have that either $T \vdash \varphi$ or $T \vdash \neg\varphi$.[17]

Just as for categoricity it is often obvious that a theory is *not* complete, because it is not intended to decide for every sentence in the language if it holds or not. Consider again the theory *EQ*. Most particular claims about equivalence relations are not decided by *EQ*. As an example, take the sentence $E_{\geqslant 3}$, expressing the there are at least three equivalence classes. We have $EQ \nvdash E_{\geqslant 3}$ *and* $EQ \nvdash \neg E_{\geqslant 3}$. To see this, recall that to prove that something is not a theorem it is enough to

[16] As the last sentence indicates, the study of axiomatic set theory takes place in set theory itself, giving a particular flavor to this branch of logic.

[17] As noted already in Chapter 1, this is a different use of "complete" than when we say that a *logic*, or rather an *inference system* for a logic, is complete. The latter means that all logical consequences of a set of assumptions can be derived in the system from those assumptions. When we say that that $T \models \varphi$ is equivalent to $T \vdash \varphi$, we are talking about (soundness and) completeness in the latter sense. But this has nothing to do with whether a *theory* expressed in such a logical language is complete in the sense of Definition 6.6.3. One has to learn to live with this ambiguity of "complete" (though sometimes the term *negation complete* is used for theories).

find a counter-example. So any equivalence relation with, say, just two equivalence classes is a counter-example to $EQ \vdash E_{\geqslant 3}$: the axiom Eq is true but the sentence $E_{\geqslant 3}$ is false. And any equivalence relation with, say, four equivalence classes is a counter-example to $EQ \vdash \neg E_{\geqslant 3}$.

Not even the theory T_ω of an equivalence relation with infinitely many equivalence classes is complete, since it says nothing about how many elements there are in these equivalence classes. So a sentence saying that there is an equivalence class with three members, for example, is not decided by T_ω.

How can one show that a theory *is* complete? To begin to answer that question we shall need the following important concept:

Definition 6.6.11 (elementary equivalence)
Two models $\mathcal{M}$ and $\mathcal{M}'$ for the same vocabulary L are *elementarily equivalent*, in symbols,

$$\mathcal{M} \equiv \mathcal{M}'$$

if the same L-sentences are true in them, i.e. for every L-sentence φ it holds that $\mathcal{M} \models \varphi$ iff $\mathcal{M}' \models \varphi$.

The following alternative characterization of elementary equivalence is almost immediate (see Example 6.6.7):

(19) $\quad \mathcal{M} \equiv \mathcal{M}'$ iff $\mathcal{M}' \models Th(\mathcal{M})$

Proof. $\mathcal{M} \equiv \mathcal{M}'$, then every sentence in $Th(\mathcal{M})$ is true in $\mathcal{M}'$, so we have $\mathcal{M}' \models Th(\mathcal{M})$. In the other direction, suppose $\mathcal{M}' \models Th(\mathcal{M})$. If $\mathcal{M} \models \varphi$, then $\varphi \in Th(\mathcal{M})$, so $\mathcal{M}' \models \varphi$. If $\mathcal{M} \not\models \varphi$, then $\mathcal{M} \models \neg\varphi$, so $\neg\varphi \in Th(\mathcal{M})$, and thus $\mathcal{M}' \models \neg\varphi$, i.e. $\mathcal{M}' \not\models \varphi$. Hence, $\mathcal{M} \equiv \mathcal{M}'$. □

Being elementarily equivalent is weaker than being isomorphic:

Lemma 6.6.12
If $\mathcal{M} \cong \mathcal{M}'$, then $\mathcal{M} \equiv \mathcal{M}'$.

Proof. This is a direct consequence of the Isomorphism Lemma. □

We will see that in many cases we have elementary equivalence without isomorphism (provided the models are infinite; see Exercise 6.13.21). But first we give a useful characterization of completeness in terms of elementary equivalence:

Lemma 6.6.13
T is complete iff all models of T are elementarily equivalent.

Proof. Suppose T is complete and that $\mathcal{M}$ and $\mathcal{M}'$ are two models of T. Let φ be any L_T-sentence. Either we have $T \models \varphi$ or $T \models \neg\varphi$. In the former case, φ is true in both $\mathcal{M}$ and $\mathcal{M}'$, since both are models of T. In the latter case, φ is false in both $\mathcal{M}$ and $\mathcal{M}'$. In other words, $\mathcal{M} \models \varphi$ iff $\mathcal{M}' \models \varphi$. So $\mathcal{M}$ and $\mathcal{M}'$ are elementarily equivalent.

Conversely, suppose that T is *not* complete. Then there is an L_T-sentence φ such that $T \not\models \varphi$ and $T \not\models \neg\varphi$. By the definition of logical consequence, this means that there is a model $\mathcal{M}$ of T in which φ is false, and a model $\mathcal{M}'$ of T in which $\neg\varphi$ is false, i.e. φ is true. So $\mathcal{M}$ and $\mathcal{M}'$ are models of T that are not elementarily equivalent. □

So one way to prove completeness is the following.

Lemma 6.6.14
If T is categorical (all models of T are isomorphic), then T is complete.

Proof. This follows directly from Lemma 6.6.12 and Lemma 6.6.13. □

As an example, the theory $T_{=10} = \{\exists_{=10}x\, x = x\}$ (Section 6.6.2) is complete: for *every* FOL-sentence φ without non-logical symbols we have either $T_{=10} \vdash \varphi$ or $T_{=10} \vdash \neg\varphi$.

Unfortunately, Lemma 6.6.14 is not useful for theories with infinite models—and so far all our examples, except $T_{=10}$, have been theories that allow (and sometimes require) infinite models! But we will see that there is a variant of Lemma 6.6.14, called *Vaught's Test* (Lemma 6.8.5), that can sometimes be used in these cases.

What about *PA*? In Part III we will show that *PA* is about as *incomplete* as can be. The proof of this uses other methods than the purely model-theoretic ones. But we shall see in the next section that some interesting, and quite surprising, facts about *PA* can be shown with simple model-theoretic methods.

6.7. The Compactness Theorem

Derivations in formal inference systems are finite, whereas the concept of logical consequence was defined for possibly infinite sets of premises. But the Completeness Theorem says that all logical consequences of any set of premises can be derived (in H, say) from them, and such a derivation only uses finitely many of the premises. This has the following remarkable consequence.[18]

[18] It is called the Compactness Theorem because it expresses compactness in the topological sense relative to a certain topology. (Fix a vocabulary L and let $\mathcal{S}_L$ be the set of maximal consistent sets of L-sentences. Then let $U(\varphi) = \{\Gamma \in \mathcal{S}_L : \varphi \in \Gamma\}$. The collection of the $U(\varphi)$ forms a basis for a topology on $\mathcal{S}_L$, and the compactness of this topology (every cover has a finite subcover) turns out to be equivalent to the Compactness Theorem in logic.) This is not something we discuss here, but the name of the theorem is standard.

Theorem 6.7.1 (Compactness Theorem)
If every finite subset of a set Γ of sentences has a model, then Γ has a model.

Proof. We prove the contraposition of the claim. So suppose Γ does *not* have a model. Then Γ is inconsistent, by the Model Existence Theorem (Theorem 5.1.1). That is, a contradiction can be derived from Γ. But derivations are finite, so a contradiction can be derived from some finite subset Γ_0 of Γ. Thus, Γ_0 has no model (is unsatisfiable). So there is a finite subset of Γ which has no model. □

Observe that the Compactness Theorem is only about truth in models, and says nothing about derivations. Our *proof* relies on facts about derivations, but not the result itself.[19] In model theory, the Compactness Theorem is a powerful method of showing the *existence* of models (of a sentence, or a theory). Here is a first example.

Corollary 6.7.2
If a set Γ of sentences has arbitrarily large finite models, then Γ also has an infinite model.

Proof. The assumption is that for every n, Γ has a model with at least n elements. Now consider the following set of sentences:

$$\Delta = \Gamma \cup \{\exists_{\geqslant k} x\, x = x \colon k = 1, 2, \ldots\}$$

Every *finite* subset Δ_0 of Δ has a model. This is because Δ_0 contains, besides sentences from Γ, only finitely many sentences of the form $\exists_{\geqslant k} x\, x = x$; say that n is the largest number such that $\exists_{\geqslant n} x\, x = x$ is in Δ_0. By assumption, Δ_0 has a model. By the Compactness Theorem, Δ has a model $\mathcal{M}$. $\mathcal{M}$ is a model of Γ (since $\Gamma \subseteq \Delta$), and $\mathcal{M}$ is infinite (since *all* the sentences $\exists_{\geqslant k} x\, x = x$ are true in $\mathcal{M}$). □

This is a typical use of the Compactness Theorem: to show that a set Γ of sentences has a model with a certain property, we add sentences to Γ which somehow express that property, and then try to show that every finite subset of the enlarged set has a model. Note that this type of argument is non-constructive: the Compactness Theorem says that a model *exists*, but nothing about how it can be constructed.

Corollary 6.7.2 confirms something we claimed but did not prove earlier: the notion of being finite cannot be expressed in first-order logic, not even by an infinite set of sentences:

[19]There are other proofs of the theorem that don't make the detour via the Completeness Theorem (for example, the proof hinted at in the preceding footnote).

Corollary 6.7.3
There is no set of sentences Γ, in any vocabulary L, such that for all L-models, $\mathcal{M} \models \Gamma$ iff $\mathcal{M}$ is finite.

Proof. Assume that there were such a set. Then it would have arbitrarily large finite models. Therefore it must have an infinite model, contradicting the assumption. □

Note that when we say that 'A is infinite' is not expressible in FOL, we mean that no FOL-sentence in a vocabulary $\{P\}$ of one unary predicate symbol expresses this. Similarly for saying that infinity *is* expressible by a set of FOL-sentences. It is another matter that with the help of *extra non-logical symbols*, we can write single sentences which only have infinite models. For example, if we add a binary predicate symbol R, and a sentence saying that R is a dense linear order on P, or a linear order on P in which every element has an immediate successor, then all models $\mathcal{M}$ of this sentence are such that $P^{\mathcal{M}}$ is infinite.

In this context, the following terminology is useful.

Definition 6.7.4 (reducts and expansions)
If $\mathcal{M}$ is a model for the vocabulary L, $L' \subseteq L$, and $\mathcal{M}'$ is obtained from $\mathcal{M}$ by deleting the interpretations of the symbols in $L - L'$, then $\mathcal{M}'$ is called a *reduct* of $\mathcal{M}$.[20] Similarly, $\mathcal{M}$ is called an *expansion* of $\mathcal{M}'$.

So we can say that although infinity is not definable by a single sentence in FOL, it is *definable with extra predicates* by a single sentence, in the following sense:

(20) Let $\mathcal{M} = (M, A)$ be a model where $A \subseteq M$, and let R be a binary predicate symbol. Then there is a sentence θ in the vocabulary $\{P, R\}$ such that A is infinite iff there is $S \subseteq M^2$ such that θ is true in the expansion $\mathcal{M}' = (M, A, S)$.

We just saw that the right-to-left direction in (20) holds, and in the other direction we can always add, say, a dense order on an infinite set A. On the other hand, Corollary 6.7.3 shows that 'A is finite' is not definable, *not even with extra predicates*, by any set of FOL-sentences.

We have assumed so far that our vocabularies are *countable* (finite or equinumerous with N), and hence that the number of L-formulas is countably infinite. But in principle we may allow uncountable vocabularies, indeed vocabularies of any infinite cardinality.[21] That may not make much sense when we talk about derivations and completeness,

[20] Recall that officially $\mathcal{M} = (M, I)$, where I is an interpretation function with domain L. So $\mathcal{M}' = (M, I')$, where I' is the restriction of I to L'.

[21] If L is a vocabulary of cardinality κ, where κ is infinite, then the set of L-formulas also has cardinality κ.

but it is very useful in model theory. In fact, the Completeness Theorem can be proved, with essentially the same argument as before, for vocabularies of arbitrary cardinality (this was done is Exercise 5.6.7). It follows that the Compactness Theorem also holds for arbitrary vocabularies. The next result (sometimes called the Upward Löwenheim-Skolem-Tarski theorem) uses this fact.

Theorem 6.7.5
*If a set of sentences has an infinite model, then it has an uncountable model. *In fact, it has a model of arbitrarily large infinite cardinality.*

Proof. Suppose a set Γ of L-sentences has an infinite model $\mathcal{M}$. Now add uncountably many new individual constants to L. We could, for example, let $L' = L \cup \{c_i : i \in \mathbb{R}\}$, so that the new constants are indexed by the real numbers, which we know are uncountably many (see (51) in Chapter 16.5). More generally, for any infinite cardinal κ, let I be a set of that cardinality, add κ new constants $\{c_i : i \in I\}$, and let

$$\Delta = \Gamma \cup \{c_i \neq c_j : i, j \in I, i \neq j\}$$

Then every finite subset Δ_0 of Δ has a model: just take the model $\mathcal{M}$ and interpret the finitely many new individual constants occurring in Δ_0 as different elements of M; this is possible since M is infinite. Thus, by the (general version of the) Compactness Theorem, Δ has a model $\mathcal{M}'$. $\mathcal{M}'$ is a model of Γ, and M' is uncountable; since *all* the sentences $c_i \neq c_j$ are true in $\mathcal{M}'$, it must have at least the size of I.[22] □

For another important illustration of this way of using the Compactness Theorem, see Exercise 6.13.25.

We shall give another rather remarkable application of the Compactness Theorem: the existence of non-standard models of arithmetic. By again adding new sentences we show that there are non-standard models not only of *PA* but of *Th*($\mathcal{N}$). *All* true arithmetical sentences (i.e. true in the standard model $\mathcal{N}$) are true in such a model, which means that the model is elementarily equivalent to $\mathcal{N}$, but it is still not isomorphic to $\mathcal{N}$. What makes this interesting is that we can find a *countably infinite* non-standard model (an uncountable model is trivially not isomorphic to $\mathcal{N}$). And to be able to draw this conclusion, we first need one more application of the Completeness Theorem, or rather, the proof of the Completeness Theorem.

[22]More precisely: the function $f : I \rightarrow M'$ defined by $f(i) = c_i^{\mathcal{M}'}$ for $i \in I$ is injective (one-one). Then M' must have at least as many elements as I (see Chapter 16.5.1).

6.8. The Löwenheim-Skolem Theorem

In what follows we only consider countable vocabularies. By Fact 16.4.6 in Chapter 16.4, there are then countably many L-terms, and a countably infinite number of L-formulas.

Theorem 6.8.1 (Löwenheim-Skolem Theorem)
If a set of sentences Γ has a model, it has a countable model. Specifically, if Γ has an infinite model, then Γ has a countably infinite model.

Proof. If Γ has a model, then Γ is consistent. Construct a model of Γ according to the proof of the Model Existence Theorem (Chapter 5.3 and 5.5). In the case of logic without identity, the domain consists of a countably infinite set of individual constants, and for logic with identity it consists of equivalence classes of closed terms. In the former case, the model is countably infinite. In the latter case it may also be finite, depending on how many terms have been identified (belong to the same equivalence class), but in any case it is countable. This proves the first claim.

If Γ has an infinite model, then $\Delta = \Gamma \cup \{\exists_{\geqslant k} x\, x = x : k = 1, 2, \ldots\}$ has a model (indeed the same model), and is therefore consistent. This time the model of Δ constructed in the proof of the Model Existence Theorem must be infinite, but it is still countable. This proves the second claim. □

In combination with the Upward Löwenheim-Skolem-Tarski theorem (Theorem 6.7.5), the Löwenheim-Skolem Theorem entails that first-order logic cannot distinguish countable and uncountable sets. (More generally, it cannot distinguish infinite cardinalities.) Also note the following corollary.

Corollary 6.8.2
Every infinite model has an elementarily equivalent countably infinite model.

Proof. Let $\mathcal{M}$ be infinite. We have $\mathcal{M} \models Th(\mathcal{M})$, so by the Löwenheim-Skolem Theorem, there is a countably infinite model $\mathcal{M}_0$ such that $\mathcal{M}_0 \models Th(\mathcal{M})$. But this means, as we saw in (19), that $\mathcal{M} \equiv \mathcal{M}_0$. □

Now we can prove the result about non-standard models of arithmetic. First some notation: recall that L_{PA} contains the individual constant 0 and the successor function $'$. We introduce the *numerals* $\mathbf{0}, \mathbf{1}, \mathbf{2}, \ldots$ by

$$\begin{aligned}\mathbf{0} &= 0\\ \mathbf{1} &= 0'\\ \mathbf{2} &= 0''\\ &\ldots\end{aligned}$$

Theorem 6.8.3 (Skolem)
There is a countably infinite model of $Th(\mathcal{N})$ not isomorphic to $\mathcal{N}$.

Proof. Let c be a new individual constant, and let

$$\Delta = Th(\mathcal{N}) \cup \{c \neq \mathbf{n} : n = 0, 1, 2, \ldots\}$$

Δ is a set of sentences such that every finite subset Δ_0 of Δ has a model: simply take $\mathcal{N}$ and interpret c as a number greater than all n such that the sentence $c \neq \mathbf{n}$ belongs to Δ_0. By compactness, Δ has a model $\mathcal{M}$. By the Löwenheim-Skolem Theorem, we can assume that $\mathcal{M}$ is countably infinite. $\mathcal{M}$ is a model for the vocabulary $L_{PA} \cup \{c\}$; let $\mathcal{M}'$ be the reduct of $\mathcal{M}$ to L_{PA} (Definition 6.7.4). Then $\mathcal{M}'$ is a model of $Th(\mathcal{N})$, which clearly cannot be isomorphic to $\mathcal{N}$, since it contains a 'number' ($c^{\mathcal{M}}$) which is distinct from all the standard numbers ($\mathbf{0}^{\mathcal{M}}, \mathbf{1}^{\mathcal{M}}, \mathbf{2}^{\mathcal{M}}, \ldots$) in $\mathcal{M}$.[23] □

The model $\mathcal{M}$ contains the *standard numbers* $\mathbf{0}^{\mathcal{M}}, \mathbf{1}^{\mathcal{M}}, \mathbf{2}^{\mathcal{M}}, \ldots$, which are isomorphic to $0, 1, 2, \ldots$ in $\mathcal{N}$. But it also contains $c^{\mathcal{M}}$, which is a *non-standard number*, greater than all the standard numbers. And since all the usual arithmetical truths hold in $\mathcal{M}$, it also contains $(c + \mathbf{1})^{\mathcal{M}}, (c + \mathbf{2})^{\mathcal{M}}, \ldots$, and $(c + c)^{\mathcal{M}}, (c \cdot c)^{\mathcal{M}}$, etc.; thus infinitely many non-standard numbers.

Example 6.8.4 (Skolem's Paradox)
Thoralf Skolem (Norwegian logican, 1887–1963) also noted that Theorem 6.8.1 entails that set theory, e.g. the theory *ZFC*, has a countable model, say $\mathcal{M}$. But in *ZFC* one can *prove* that there are uncountable sets, for example, that the power set of N, $\mathcal{P}(N)$, is uncountable (see Chapter 16.5.) How is this possible? It seems paradoxical, and this state of affairs is often called Skolem's Paradox. But it is merely an apparent paradox. The sentence in *ZFC* expressing that $\mathcal{P}(N)$ is uncountable, that is, that there is no surjective function from N to $\mathcal{P}(N)$ (Chapter 16.4) can be proved in *ZFC* and is therefore true in $\mathcal{M}$:

$$\mathcal{M} \models \neg\exists x(\text{“}x \text{ is a surjective function from } N \text{ to } \mathcal{P}(N)\text{”})$$

[23] In more detail, if h were an isomorphism from $\mathcal{N}$ to $\mathcal{M}'$, then we would have $h(n) = \mathbf{n}^{\mathcal{M}'} = \mathbf{n}^{\mathcal{M}}$ for every n. But $c^{\mathcal{M}} \in M$, and $c^{\mathcal{M}}$ is distinct from $\mathbf{n}^{\mathcal{M}}$ for every n. So h cannot be surjective, contradicting the assumption that it was an isomorphism.

But this only means that *in the domain of* $\mathcal{M}$ there exists no such function. In reality there is such a function, because in reality M *is* in fact countable. From *inside* $\mathcal{M}$ one cannot 'see' that the domain is countable, even though in fact it is.

So there is no paradox, but the study of models of set theory is a main area of mathematical logic, and the contrast between what holds *in* such a model and what one can know *about* it is ever present.

Finally, we can now give a result announced earlier, which can sometimes be used to show completeness of a theory.

Lemma 6.8.5 (Vaught's Test)
If a theory T has no finite models and is countably categorical, then T is complete.

Proof. Assume T is *not* complete. By Lemma 6.6.13 there are models $\mathcal{M}, \mathcal{M}'$ of T such that $\mathcal{M} \not\equiv \mathcal{M}'$. By assumption, $\mathcal{M}$ and $\mathcal{M}'$ are infinite. And by the Löwenheim-Skolem Theorem, we may in fact assume that $\mathcal{M}$ and $\mathcal{M}'$ are countably infinite.[24] Since T is countably categorical, $\mathcal{M}$ and $\mathcal{M}'$ must be isomorphic, but this contradicts Lemma 6.6.12. So our assumption was wrong, and T must be complete. □

As examples we may take some theories about equivalence relations: Fact 6.4.6 showed that countable models of *Eq* with the same signature are isomorphic. So if the theory can fix the signature of its countable models, it will be countably categorical. For example:

(21) $T = \{Eq, \forall x \exists_{=5} y\, yEx, E_{\geqslant 1}, E_{\geqslant 2}, E_{\geqslant 3}, \ldots\}$ is complete.

Proof. The axioms of T say, besides that E is an equivalence relation, that every element's equivalence class has exactly 5 elements, and that there are infinitely many equivalence classes. This determines the signature as

$$(0, 0, 0, 0, 0, \omega, 0, 0, 0, \ldots)$$

and no models of T can be finite. So completeness follows by Vaught's Test. □

Another example is the theory *DeLO* of dense linear orders without first or last elements. Georg Cantor showed that all countably infinite orders of this kind are isomorphic, i.e. that *DeLO* is countably categorical; we will state a generalization of this result in Section 6.10.2. So all countable such orders are isomorphic to $(\mathbb{Q}^+, <)$, the usual order of the positive rational numbers. Since the order is dense, *DeLO* has no finite models, so by Vaught's Test we get:

[24] Since $\mathcal{M} \not\equiv \mathcal{M}'$ there is a sentence φ such that $\mathcal{M} \models T \cup \{\varphi\}$ and $\mathcal{M}' \models T \cup \{\neg\varphi\}$. By the Löwenheim-Skolem Theorem, we may assume that $\mathcal{M}$ and $\mathcal{M}'$ are countable.

(22) *DeLO* is a complete theory.

There are, however, many complete theories with only infinite models that are not countably categorical (see Exercises 6.13.17 and 6.13.38). So to show that they are complete, different methods must be used. One way is to use Lemma 6.6.13 and explore feasible ways of proving that two models are elementarily equivalent. We outline this method in Section 6.10.

6.9. Other quantifiers

In Section 6.1.1 we mentioned the possibily of adding quantifiers $\exists_{\geqslant n}$ to the FOL language, and also as quantifier Q_0 expressing 'infinitely many'. In each case, we add a new quantifier *symbol* to the logical constants, i.e. a new variable-binding operator, and a corresponding clause in the truth definition. This is in fact what we already did for the existential quantifier: a *formation rule,*

If φ is formula and x is a variable, $\exists x\varphi$ is a formula.

and a corresponding clause (Chapter 2.3.2; we are simplifying a bit here, ignoring possible free variables in $\exists x\psi(x)$):

$\mathcal{M} \models \exists x\psi(x)$ iff there is $a \in M$ such that $\mathcal{M} \models \psi[a]$

Similarly for $\forall$. We can do the same for Q_0:

(23) a. If φ is formula and x is a variable, $Q_0x\varphi$ is an formula.

b. $\mathcal{M} \models Q_0x\psi(x)$ iff there are infinitely many $a \in M$ s.t. $\mathcal{M} \models \psi[a]$

The quantifiers $\exists_{\geqslant n}$ can be officially added in the same way. But the difference is that whereas each $\exists_{\geqslant n}$ is *definable* in FOL, in the sense that there is a FOL-sentence ψ with a unary P as its only non-logical symbol, such that $\exists_{\geqslant n}xPx$ is logically equivalent to ψ, there is no such FOL-sentence for Q_0xPx. This follows from our earlier results in this chapter. Consider the sentence

$\neg Q_0xPx$

which, according to (23), is true in $\mathcal{M} = (M, A)$ iff A is *finite*. By Corollary 6.7.3, no FOL-sentence—indeed, no set of FOL-sentences—has this property!

6.9.1. Generalized quantifiers

Q_0 and the $\exists_{\geqslant n}$ are examples of *generalized quantifiers*. To add such a quantifier to FOL, you add a new quantifier symbol Q, and a new clause in the truth definition specifying what Q means. But what do quantifiers mean? Note that the right-hand side in the defining clause for Q_0, and for $\exists_{\geqslant n}$, and for $\exists$, and for $\forall$, are *conditions on a set*: the set $A = \{a \in M : \mathcal{M} \models \psi[a]\}$. In other words, it is a *second-order property*: that A is infinite, that A has at least n elements, that A is non-empty, and that A contains all of M. Two more examples, with A as above:

(24) $\mathcal{M} \models Q^R x\psi(x)$ iff $|A| > |M-A|$ (the *Rescher quantifier*)

(25) $\mathcal{M} \models Q_{\text{even}} x\psi(x)$ iff $|A|$ is an even number

In general, corresponding to the symbol Q we have a (generalized) quantifier $\mathcal{Q}$, which with each domain M associates a set $\mathcal{Q}_M$ of subsets of M, as in the examples above, with the correspondig clause in the truth definition:

(26) $\mathcal{M} \models Qx\psi(x)$ iff $\{a \in M : \mathcal{M} \models \psi[a]\} \in \mathcal{Q}_M$

Thus, $\exists_M = \{A \subseteq M : A \neq \varnothing\}$, $(\mathcal{Q}_0)_M = \{A \subseteq M : A \text{ is infinite}\}$, $(\exists_{\geqslant n})_M = \{A \subseteq M : |A| \geqslant n\}$, $(\mathcal{Q}_{\text{even}})_M = \{A \subseteq M : |A| \text{ is even}\}$, etc.

Generalized quantifiers in this sense were introduced in Mostowski 1957. Lindström 1966 realized that they are a special case of a more general concept.[25] First, a generalized quantifier can relate *two* (or more) sets, rather than being a property of one. Then Qx applies to two (or more) fomulas, binding free occurrences of x in each. So in the binary case the formation rule is: if φ, ψ are formulas and x is a variable, $Qx(\varphi, \psi)$ is a formula. Now $\mathcal{Q}_M$ is a binary relation between subsets of M. Here are two examples: letting $A = \{a \in M : \mathcal{M} \models \varphi[a]\}$ and $B = \{a \in M : \mathcal{M} \models \psi[a]\}$, define

(27) $\mathcal{M} \models Ix(\varphi, \psi)(x)$ iff $|A| = |B|$ (the *Härtig* quantifier)

(28) $\mathcal{M} \models \textit{most}\, x(\varphi, \psi)(x)$ iff $|A \cap B| > |A-B|$

The name of the last quantifier comes from its corresponding expression in English: a sentence of the form "Most As are B" is naturally taken to mean that the number of As that are B is greater than the number of As that are not B (see the next subsection). Interestingly, it can be shown that neither *most* nor the Härtig quantifier can be defined by any number of quantifiers that express properties of sets.

Even more generally, Q can stand for a *property of relations*, or a *relation between relations*. We give two examples. The *well-order quantifier* expresses a property of binary relations:

[25] Actually, the idea of treating quantifiers semantically as second-order relations, and syntactically as variable-binding operators, goes back to Frege 1879.

(29) $\mathcal{M} \models Wxy\psi(x,y)$ iff $\{(a,b) \in M^2 : \mathcal{M} \models \psi[a,b]\}$ is a well-order

(see Exercise 6.13.25 for explanation). Wxy binds all free occurrences of x and y in ψ. Our final example is, on each M, the following relation $\mathcal{B}_M$ between two subsets C, D of M and a binary relation R over M:

(30) $\mathcal{B}_M(C,D,R) \Leftrightarrow \exists X,Y \subseteq M[most_M(C,X)\ \&\ most_M(D,Y)$
$\&\ X \times Y \subseteq R]$

Corresponding formulas have the form $Bx, y, zu(\varphi(x), \psi(y), \theta(z,u))$. The significance of this quantifier is explained in the next subsection.

These examples should convey the basic idea of what a generalized quantifier $\mathcal{Q}$ is, and how one can add it to the FOL language, resulting in the logical language FOL($\mathcal{Q}$). Note that since we have a well-defined language and a notion of truth in a model, logical consequence in FOL($\mathcal{Q}$) is defined as usual: $\Gamma \models_{\text{FOL}(\mathcal{Q})} \varphi$ iff every model making all sentences in Γ true also makes φ true.[26]

At this point the reader may ask: Why not just add some of these quantifiers to FOL, so that we get a more expressive language to begin with? The reason is that, although we gain in expressive power, the resulting logics are less well-behaved. For example, *compactness fails for* FOL($\mathcal{Q}_0$). To see this, consider

$$\Delta = \{\exists_{\geqslant n} xPx : n = 1, 2, \ldots\} \cup \{\neg Q_0 xPx\}$$

Clearly, every finite subset of Δ has a model, but Δ itself has no model. In Chapter 15 we will see that the Completeness Theorem also fails for FOL($\mathcal{Q}_0$): there is no inference system in the sense of Chapter 3 which captures the relation $\models_{\text{FOL}(\mathcal{Q}_0)}$ using axioms and rules. On the other hand, one can show that the Löwenheim-Skolem Theorem still holds.

In fact, a famous result in model theory, Lindström's Theorem, shows that this state of affairs is *unavoidable*: if a logic properly extends FOL, at least one of the Compactness Theorem (or the Completeness Theorem) and the Löwenheim-Skolem Theorem must fail. So the balance between expressive power and useful properties, when designing a logical language, is a delicate one. We outline a proof of Lindström's Theorem in Section 6.11 below.

6.9.2. Quantifiers and natural language

Consider these sentences.

[26]There are several introductions to generalized quantifiers in the literature. For example, Westerståhl 2019 gives an overview, and Peters and Westerståhl 2006 is book-length treatment.

(31) a. All logicians run.
b. No mathematicians dance.
c. Most students jog.

Sentences (31a) and (31b) can be 'formalized' in FOL as $\forall x(Lx \rightarrow Rx)$ and $\neg\exists x(Mx \wedge Dx)$, respectively. The truth conditions seem right, but how accurate are these translations? One could argue that there is no *implication* in (31a), and no *conjunction* in (31b). In fact, these English sentences don't seem to contain any propositional connectives. Furthermore, there is no corresponding translation of (31c).[27]

The following translations not only get (31c) right, but are more faithful to the originals.

(32) a. $all\, x(Lx, Rx)$
b. $no\, x(Mx, Dx)$
c. $most\, x(Sx, Jx)$

Here we have used the generalized quantifier *most* from (28), and the Aristotelian quantifiers *all* and *no*, defined by $all_M(A, B) \Leftrightarrow A \subseteq B$, and $no_M(A, B) \Leftrightarrow A \cap B = \varnothing$.[28] The latter two are obviously definable in FOL; nevertheless they correspond to the English *determiners* "all" and "no". (The FOL quantifiers $\forall$ and $\exists$ can be seen as translations of "everything" and "something".) English has a rich class of determiners; including complex determiners we have, for example:

> all, some, no, at least five, no more that ten, exactly seven, the twentyfive, all but five, a dozen, most, many, few, several, more than two-thirds of the, less than ten percent of the, John's, some of Mary's, an even number of, infinitely many, ...

All of these phrases have the following two properties: syntactically, they combine with a *noun* (N) to form a *noun phrase* (NP, sometimes called a *determiner phrase*, DP); semantically, they are interpreted as generalized quantifiers taking two sets as arguments, so-called *type* $\langle 1, 1\rangle$ *quantifiers*. Furthermore, corresponding NPs like

> some boys, no more than ten applicants, all but five professors, several poodles, the twentyfive dogs, some of Mary's cats, more than two-thirds of the citizens, ...

are then interpreted as type $\langle 1\rangle$ quantifiers, which take one set argument, and are obtained by 'freezing' the first argument of the type

[27] This is a fact of logic; see Exercise 6.13.41.

[28] Aristotelian *syllogistics* is about (some of) the logical behavior of the four (generalized) quantifiers *all*, *no*, *some*, and *not all*.

$\langle 1, 1 \rangle$ quantifier to the set denoted by the N.[29] For example, the NP "three cats" will denote the set of subsets of the domain containing exactly three cats. This means in turn that the sentence

(33) Three cats meowed.

which has the linguistic structure

(34) $[_{\text{S}}\,[_{\text{NP}}\,[_{\text{Det}}\text{ three}]\,[_{\text{N}}\text{ cats}]]\,[_{\text{VP}}\text{ meowed}]]$,

gets a *compositional* interpretation: the set denoted by the VP (verb phrase) is claimed to belong to the set of sets denoted by the NP.[30]

Formal semantics aims at compositionally interpreting natural language expressions, following their linguistic structure. We see how this works for (33): the interpretations of "three" (a relation between sets) and "cats" (a set A) are composed to the interpretation of "three cats" (a set of sets), which in turn is composed with the interpretation of "meowed" (a set B) to yield a truth value (True, if B belongs to the NP interpretation, otherwise False). The interpretation follows the subject-predicate [NP VP] structure of the sentence, and the [Det N] structure of the noun phrase.[31]

In fact, one of the starting points of modern formal semantics was Richard Montague's realization in the late 1960's that NPs can uniformly be taken to denote type $\langle 1 \rangle$ quantifiers. Somewhat later it became clear that the model-theoretic approach to generalized quantifiers had in fact numerous applications to natural language semantics.

---

[29]This typing system of generalized quantifiers should be almost self-explanatory. Thus, a quantifier of type $\langle 1, 1, 1 \rangle$ is on every domain M a ternary relation between subsets of M. The same idea is used for quantifiers which are relations between relations. For example, the quantifiers in (29) and (30) have types $\langle 2 \rangle$ and $\langle 1, 1, 2 \rangle$, respectively.

[30]The example is very simple, but compare with the translation into FOL:

$$\exists x \exists y \exists z (Cx \wedge Cy \wedge Cz \wedge Mx \wedge My \wedge Mz \wedge x \neq y \wedge y \neq z \wedge x \neq z \\ \wedge \forall u (Cu \wedge Mu \rightarrow u = x \vee u = y \vee u = z))$$

[31]The principle of compositionality says:

(PoC) The meaning of a complex expression is determined by the meanings of its (immediate) parts and the mode of composition.

Of course, the notions of 'expression', 'part', 'mode (rule) of composition', and 'meaning' have to be specified in order for (PoC) to be true, or false, of a language. But the syntactic structure (34) is rather clear, and in the present case we can take the meaning of determiners to be type $\langle 1, 1 \rangle$ quantifiers, the meaning of nouns and (intransitive) verbs to be subsets of the domain of discourse, and the meaning of sentences to be truth values. This works nicely for simple sentences like (33). How to best derive compositionally the meanings of sentences with transitive verbs and quantified objects, like

(i) Every critic reviewed three films.

is a much debated issue in formal semantics. (Note that (i) is ambiguous.)

Here is one illustration. As we saw, the structure of sentences with quantified subject NPs can be written

(35) $[_S [_{NP} [_{Det}\ \mathcal{Q}] [_N\ A]] [_{VP}\ B]]$

with the truth condition (on a given domain M) that $\mathcal{Q}_M(A, B)$ holds. Here $\mathcal{Q}$ is any type $\langle 1, 1\rangle$ quantifier, and $A, B \subseteq M$. But are all type $\langle 1, 1\rangle$ quantifiers eligible as possible denotations of determiners? The answer is No: as the structure (35) indicates, the sets A and B play different roles. A belongs to the subject, restricting the determiner as it were; B comes from the VP. It turns out that there is a clear semantic counterpart of this: $\mathcal{Q}$ is *conservative* in the following sense:

Definition 6.9.1 (conservativity)
A type $\langle 1, 1\rangle$ quantifier $\mathcal{Q}$ is *conservative* if for all M and all $A, B \subseteq M$,

(CONSERV) $\mathcal{Q}_M(A, B)$ iff $\mathcal{Q}_M(A, A \cap B)$

That is, only those Bs which are in A matter for the truth value of (35). This corresponds to an obvious enough fact, namely, that sentences of the form (36a) and (36b) are trivially equivalent:

(36) a. *Q* As are *B*.
b. *Q* As are As that are *B*

The reader can easily check this with examples from the list of determiners above. But many mathematically natural type $\langle 1, 1\rangle$ quantifiers, such as the Härtig quantifier $\mathcal{I}$, are not conservative, and hence not possible interpretations of natural language determiners.

There is a lot more to say about this intriguing application of logic to the study of natural languages, but we shall leave the topic here, with a final example. It has been argued that not only *monadic* quantifiers, i.e. those standing for relations between *sets*, are needed for an adequate analysis of some natural language sentences, but also 'polyadic' quantifiers. One example is the following.

(37) Most boys in my class and most girls in your class know each other.

Barwise 1978 argued that (37) means that there is a large set X of boys in my class (containing more than half of them), and a large set Y of girls in your class, such that for every pair (a, b) with $a \in X$ and $b \in Y$, a knows b and b knows a. These are exactly the truth conditions given by the quantifier $\mathcal{B}$ in (30). Moreover, it can be shown that $\mathcal{B}$ is not definable from any finite number of monadic quantifiers.[32]

[32]The volume Montague 1974 collects Montague's pioneering papers in formal semantics. One of the first, and still very readable, papers connecting generalized quantifier theory to natural language semantics was Barwise and Cooper 1981; the articles in

The next two sections of this chapter are more technical than the others. They can safely be skipped, but I would still recommend a cursory reading, since most proofs are omitted anyway, and the results are quite fascinating.

6.10. *Back-and-forth characterization of elementary equivalence

In model theory one often wants to show that two models are elementarily equivalent, $\mathcal{M} \equiv \mathcal{M}'$, but this can be non-trivial, partly because proofs by induction over formulas don't work, since $\equiv$ is about *sentences*. But there is a useful alternative characterization of this relation. We give a brief account in this section, skipping many details. This characterization can be described in terms of a simple *game*, played by two players, called *Duplicator* (D) and *Spoiler* (S), respectively. These games are called EF-games, in honor of Andrzej Ehrenfeucht and Roland Fraïssé, who invented the method.

6.10.1. EF-games

We are given two models $\mathcal{M}$ and $\mathcal{M}'$ for the same vocabulary L. In this section we assume that the vocabulary is *finite*, and, for simplicity, *relational*: it contains only predicate symbols. If $a_1, \ldots, a_n \in M$ and $a'_1, \ldots, a'_n \in M'$, we write

$$(a_1, \ldots, a_n) \cong (a'_1, \ldots, a'_n)$$

if, for all $i_1, \ldots, i_k$ among $1, \ldots, n$, (i) $a_{i_1} = a_{i_2} \Leftrightarrow a'_{i_1} = a'_{i_2}$, and (ii) if $P \in L$ is k-ary, then $P^{\mathcal{M}}(a_{i_1}, \ldots, a_{i_k}) \Leftrightarrow P^{\mathcal{M}'}(a'_{i_1}, \ldots, a'_{i_k})$. The map $a_i \mapsto a'_i$ is then called a *partial isomorphism* from $\mathcal{M}$ to $\mathcal{M}'$.[33]

Definition 6.10.1 (the $EF^n(\mathcal{M}, \mathcal{M}')$ game)
The game $EF^n(\mathcal{M}, \mathcal{M}')$ is played in n *rounds*. In each round, S makes a move by choosing one of $\mathcal{M}, \mathcal{M}'$ and picking an element in it, and D then responds by picking an element in the *other* model. (Any elements in the domains can be picked, also ones that have been picked before.) After m rounds ($m \leqslant n$), elements $a_1, a'_1, a_2, a'_2, \ldots, a_m, a'_m$ have been picked, where the a_i are in M and the a'_i in M'. If we

van Benthem 1986 give several further developments. An overview of the area is Peters and Westerståhl 2006. The undefinability of $\mathcal{B}$ from monadic quantifiers was proved in Hella, Väänänen, and Westerståhl 1997.

[33]It is an isomorphism between the *submodel* of $\mathcal{M}$ with domain $\{a_1, \ldots, a_n\}$ and the corresponding submodel of $\mathcal{M}'$.

have $(a_1, \ldots, a_m) \not\cong (a'_1, \ldots, a'_m)$, then S wins the game instantly. If S doesn't win after n rounds, i.e. if $(a_1, \ldots, a_n) \cong (a'_1, \ldots, a'_n)$, D wins. A player loses iff the other player wins.

The purpose of the game is that D tries to show that $\mathcal{M}$ and $\mathcal{M}'$ are similar, and S tries to show they are different. Who can win depends on the models, and also of the length n of the game. What interests us is not so much particular plays of the game, but which player has a *winning strategy*: a method of picking elements so that (s)he wins no matter how the opponent plays. It is a well-known fact of game theory that in this kind of game, exactly one of the players has a winning strategy.

For example, let $\mathcal{M} = (M, A)$ and $\mathcal{M}' = (M', A')$, where $A \subseteq M$ has k elements, and $M - A$, A', and $M' - A'$ each has more than k elements. Then D has a winning strategy in $EF^k(\mathcal{M}, \mathcal{M}')$, but not in $EF^{k+1}(\mathcal{M}, \mathcal{M}')$ (Exercise 6.13.35). For another example, let $\mathcal{M} = (\mathbb{N}, <)$ and $\mathcal{M}' = (\mathbb{Q}, <)$. These models are very different so it should be easy for S to win. Indeed, he can always win in 3 rounds: let him pick, say, 5 and 6 in $\mathbb{N}$ in the first two rounds; D must respond with rational numbers b_5 and b_6. Then S picks a rational number *between* b_5 and b_6 in the third round, and now D cannot respond without losing. (More examples in Exercise 6.13.37.)

Write

$$\mathcal{M} \sim_n \mathcal{M}'$$

if D has a winning strategy in $EF^n(\mathcal{M}, \mathcal{M}')$. We will now see that, *up to a point*, this means that the same sentences are true in $\mathcal{M}$ and $\mathcal{M}'$. Let the *quantifier depth*, $qd(\varphi)$, of a FOL-formula φ be the number of 'nestings' of quantifiers in φ. A precise definition is as follows:

(38) a. If φ is atomic, $qd(\varphi) = 0$.
b. $qd(\neg\varphi) = qd(\varphi)$
c. $qd(\varphi \to \psi) = max(qd(\varphi), qd(\psi))$
d. $qd(\exists x\varphi) = qd(\forall x\varphi) = qd(\varphi) + 1$

For example, the quantifier depth of $\exists xPxy \to \neg\forall yRyzu$ is 1, and the quantifier depth of $\forall z(Pz \to \exists yR_1zy) \to \exists uR_2uvz$ is 2. We state without proof the following intuitively plausible fact (recall that the vocabulary L is finite).

Fact 6.10.2
For any k and n, there are only finitely many non-equivalent formulas with free variables among $x_1, \ldots, x_k$ and quantifier depth at most n.

Now let

$$\mathcal{M} \equiv_n \mathcal{M}'$$

mean that the same sentences of quantifier depth at most n are true in $\mathcal{M}$ and $\mathcal{M}'$. Thus, $\mathcal{M} \equiv \mathcal{M}'$ holds iff for all $n \geqslant 1$, $\mathcal{M} \equiv_n \mathcal{M}'$. $\equiv_n$ is clearly an equivalence relation among models for the vocabulary L, and it follows from Fact 6.10.2 that there are only finitely many equivalence classes.

The main results about these notions are the next two theorems. The proofs rely on Fact 6.10.2, but will not be given here.[34]

Theorem 6.10.3
$\mathcal{M} \sim_n \mathcal{M}'$ iff $\mathcal{M} \equiv_n \mathcal{M}'$.

The *infinite* game $EF^\omega(\mathcal{M}, \mathcal{M}')$ is as the finite game, except that there is no upper bound for the number of rounds. This means that the game can go on forever, which is precisely what it takes for D to win.[35] Write $\mathcal{M} \sim_\omega \mathcal{M}'$ if D has a winning strategy in this game. Clearly, $\mathcal{M} \sim_\omega \mathcal{M}'$ implies $\mathcal{M} \sim_n \mathcal{M}'$ for each n, but the converse is not true (see Exercise 6.13.40). We also have:

Theorem 6.10.4
If $\mathcal{M}$ and $\mathcal{M}'$ are countably infinite and $\mathcal{M} \sim_\omega \mathcal{M}'$, then $\mathcal{M} \cong \mathcal{M}'$.

6.10.2. Three applications

We give three typical applications of this machinery. First, it can be used to show that a theory is *complete*. This is not surprising, since one way to show completeness of T is to show that all models of T are elementarily equivalent (Lemma 6.6.13). Here is an example. Let χ_n be a sentence in the vocabulary $\{E\}$ saying that E is an equivalence relation such that there is is exactly one equivalence class with exactly n members. Let

$$T = \{\chi_n : n = 1, 2, \ldots\}$$

T is complete. To prove this, let $\mathcal{M} = (M, E)$ and $\mathcal{M}' = (M', E')$ be models of T. So E and E' are equivalence relations such that for every $n \geqslant 1$ there is exactly one equivalence class with n members. But we know nothing about the number of equivalence classes with infinitely many members. This shows that T is not countably categorical, so we cannot use Vaught's Test to prove completeness. But we can, for each n, design a winning strategy for D in the game $EF^n(\mathcal{M}, \mathcal{M}')$. The interesting case is when S picks an element in an infinite equivalence

[34] Most textbooks covering a first-year course in model theory treat EF-games and their application in detail. Although the basic facts are quite elementary, they are usually presented in a mathematical context; Hodges 1997, Ch. 3, is a good example. A slightly less technical account, which centers around the use of games in logic, is Väänänen 2011.

[35] It is still the case that these infinite games are *determined*: exactly one of Duplicator and Spoiler has a winning strategy.

class in one of the models (assuming there is one). But even if the other model doesn't have any infinite equivalence classes, it still has arbitrarily large finite equivalence classes, so D can always respond with a suitable element in one of these. We leave the details to Exercise 6.13.38(a). By Theorem 6.10.3, for each n, $\mathcal{M} \equiv_n \mathcal{M}'$, so $\mathcal{M} \equiv \mathcal{M}'$, as was to be shown. See also Exercises 6.13.38(b) and 6.13.40.

Next, Theorem 6.10.3 also provides a useful way of showing certain negative facts about the expressive power of FOL. Let us prove a claim made in the introduction to this chapter: that the property of a set containing an *even* number fo elements is not expressible in FOL. Put differently, the quantifier $\mathcal{Q}_{\text{even}}$ is not definable in FOL. We reason as follows. Suppose there was a FOL-sentence φ in the vocabulary $\{P\}$ (P unary) such that for all models $\mathcal{M} = (M, A)$,

(a) $(M, A) \models \varphi$ iff $|A|$ is even

Let φ have quantifier depth n. We produce two models (M, A) and (M', A') such that (i) exactly one of $|A|, |A'|$ is even, and (ii) we have $(M, A) \equiv_n (M', A')$. This contradicts (a), since φ is either true in both models or false in both. So there can be no such sentence. To find two such models is almost trivial. For example, let $|M| = |M'| = 2n + 1$, and let $A \subseteq M$ have n elements and $A' \subseteq M$ have $n+1$ elements. Then exactly one of $|A|, |A'|$ is even, but it is easy to see that Duplicator has a winning strategy in $EF^n((M, A), (M, A'))$ (cf. Exercise 6.13.35).

Finally, an easy application of Theorem 6.10.4 is that the theory *DeLO* of dense linear orderings without endpoints is countably categorical (hence complete by Vaught's Test). Let $(M, <)$ and $(M', <')$ be countable models of *DeLO*. We need to design a strategy for D so that, at each step, whatever element S picks in one of the models, D can always respond with an element in the other model which stands in the same order relations (so to speak) to the already picked elements. This is possible precisely because in both models, for every element there is a smaller one, and a greater one, and between two elements there is always a third. It follows that $\mathcal{M} \sim_\omega \mathcal{M}'$, and thus $\mathcal{M} \cong \mathcal{M}'$.

6.10.3. A formulation without games

Characterizing elementary equivalence with EF-games is quite intuitive. But the use of games is not necessary. We formulate an equivalent characterization without games here, mainly because it is used for the proof of Lindström's Theorem in the next section. Let $\mathcal{M}$ and $\mathcal{M}'$ for the same (finite and relational) vocabulary be given.

Definition 6.10.5
A *back-and-forth sequence of length n for* $\mathcal{M}, \mathcal{M}'$ is a sequence of relations $I_k \subseteq M^k \times (M')^k$, $k < n$, such that

(i) $()I_0()$

(ii) If $(a_0, \ldots, a_{k-1})I_k(a'_0, \ldots, a'_{k-1})$, then for every $a_k \in M$ ($a'_k \in M'$) there is $a'_k \in M'$ ($a_k \in M$) such that $(a_0, \ldots, a_k)I_{k+1}(a'_0, \ldots, a'_k)$.

(iii) $(a_0, \ldots, a_{k-1})I_k(a'_0, \ldots, a'_{k-1})$ implies that for all atomic formulas $\varphi(x_0, \ldots, x_{k-1})$, $\mathcal{M} \models \varphi[a_0, \ldots, a_{k-1}]$ iff $\mathcal{M}' \models \varphi[a'_0, \ldots, a'_{k-1}]$.

We write

$$\mathcal{M} \cong_n \mathcal{M}'$$

if there exists a back-and-forth sequence of length n for $\mathcal{M}, \mathcal{M}'$. Likewise, $\mathcal{M} \cong_\omega \mathcal{M}'$ means that there is an infinite sequence of relations I_n, for $n = 0, 1, 2, \ldots$, as in Definition 6.10.5. Note that condition (iii) above implies that $a_i = a_j \Leftrightarrow a'_i = a'_j$ for $i, j < k$ (use identity formulas), and that the function $a_i \mapsto a'_i$ is a partial isomorphism from $\mathcal{M}$ to $\mathcal{M}'$. So the next fact shouldn't be too surprising (we omit the proof).

Lemma 6.10.6

(a) $\mathcal{M} \cong_n \mathcal{M}'$ *iff* $\mathcal{M} \sim_n \mathcal{M}'$.

(b) $\mathcal{M} \cong_\omega \mathcal{M}'$ *iff* $\mathcal{M} \sim_\omega \mathcal{M}'$.

6.11. *Lindström's Theorem

A *logic with generalized quantifiers* is one of the form FOL($\mathcal{Q}, \mathcal{Q}', \ldots$), where we have added any number of quantifiers $\mathcal{Q}, \mathcal{Q}', \ldots$ to FOL, each with its own variable-binding operator in the language and the corresponding syntactic formation rule and semantic clause in the truth definition, as described in Section 6.9. In this section, a *logic* is a logic with generalized quantifiers.[36] We use $\mathcal{L}, \mathcal{L}', \ldots$ for logics.

We can compare the expressive power of logic as follows. Let

(39) $\quad \mathcal{L} \leqslant \mathcal{L}'$

mean that $\mathcal{L}'$ is *at least as strong as* $\mathcal{L}$, or an *extension* of $\mathcal{L}$, in the sense that for every $\mathcal{L}$-sentence φ there is a logically equivalent $\mathcal{L}'$-sentence ψ:[37] for all models $\mathcal{M}$, we have $\mathcal{M} \models \varphi$ iff $\mathcal{M} \models \psi$. Thus, for all $\mathcal{L}$,

---

[36]The results in Lindström 1969 are formulated for a more abstract notion of a logic, but this level of generality is sufficient for our purposes here. Basically, a *logic*—in the model-theoretic sense—can be identified with a set of objects called *sentences*, a class of objects called *models*, and a 'truth' relation $\models$ between models and sentences, subject to certain conditions. In the case of logics with generalized quantifiers we only need to specify the various quantifiers: the sentences are given by the familiar formation rules, the models are the usual first-order models, and $\models$ comes from the inductive definition of satisfaction. Note that all logics, also in the abstract sense, determine a semantic *consequence relation*: preservation of truth for all models.

[37]Here, of course, an $\mathcal{L}$-sentence is a sentence in the language of $\mathcal{L}$, in *some* vocabulary (which we don't make explicit here).

FOL $\leqslant \mathcal{L}$

We write $\mathcal{L} < \mathcal{L}'$ when $\mathcal{L} \leqslant \mathcal{L}'$ and $\mathcal{L}' \nleqslant \mathcal{L}$, and $\mathcal{L} \equiv \mathcal{L}'$ when $\mathcal{L} \leqslant \mathcal{L}'$ and $\mathcal{L}' \leqslant \mathcal{L}$. So, in a clear sense, $\mathcal{L} \equiv \mathcal{L}'$ means that $\mathcal{L}$ and $\mathcal{L}'$ have the *same expressive power*: everything you can say in one of them can also be said in the other (though perhaps with a very different sentence).

For the logics considered here, there is another way to express (39). In Section 6.9 we indicated what it means for a quantifier $\mathcal{Q}$ to be *definable* in FOL. This immediately extends to definability in any logic $\mathcal{L}$. Here is an example. Exercise 6.13.34 asks the reader to find a FOL($\mathcal{I}$)-sentence in the vocabulary $\{P\}$ which is logically equivalent to the FOL($\mathcal{Q}_0$)-sentence $Q_0 x Px$. That such a sentences exists is precisely what it means for $\mathcal{Q}_0$ to be *definable* in FOL($\mathcal{I}$) (more examples in Exercise 6.13.42). Now it is fairly easy to check that the following holds.

(40) FOL($\mathcal{Q}, \mathcal{Q}', \ldots$) $\leqslant \mathcal{L}$ iff each of $\mathcal{Q}, \mathcal{Q}', \ldots$ is definable in $\mathcal{L}$.

For example, FOL($\mathcal{Q}_0$) $\leqslant$ FOL($\mathcal{I}$).[38]

Next, consider the following properties of logics:[39]

(41) a. $\mathcal{L}$ has the *Löwenheim property* if every $\mathcal{L}$-sentence which has an infinite model also has a countably infinite model.

b. $\mathcal{L}$ has the *compactness property* if whenever every finite subset of a countable set Δ of $\mathcal{L}$-sentences has a model, Δ also has a model.

We can now state one of the results in Lindström 1969.

Theorem 6.11.1 (Lindström)
If a logic $\mathcal{L}$ (extending FOL as above) has both the Löwenheim and compactness properties, then $\mathcal{L} \equiv$ FOL.

The plan of the proof is as follows. Suppose $\mathcal{L}$ has the Löwenheim property, but is *not* equivalent to FOL. We show that then $\mathcal{L}$ is not compact. First, the assumption that $\mathcal{L} \nleqslant$ FOL will be seen to imply (except in a case we deal with separately) that there is an $\mathcal{L}$-sentence φ such that for each n there are models $\mathcal{M}_n, \mathcal{M}'_n$ such that $\mathcal{M}_n \models \varphi$, $\mathcal{M}_n \models \neg\varphi$, and $\mathcal{M}_n \cong_n \mathcal{M}'_n$. For simplicity, let the only non-logical symbol of φ be a binary predicate symbol R, so we write φ as $\varphi(R)$.[40] Next, using some extra non-logical symbols and some coding machinery, we can write an $\mathcal{L}$-sentence ψ which 'describes'

[38]One can show that FOL($\mathcal{I}$) $\nleqslant$ FOL($\mathcal{Q}_0$), so FOL($\mathcal{Q}_0$) $<$ FOL($\mathcal{I}$). That is, FOL($\mathcal{I}$) is *more expressive* than FOL($\mathcal{Q}_0$).

[39](41a) is weaker than the Löwenheim-Skolem theorem we proved for FOL, which was about *sets* of sentences.

[40]In the general case, only finitely many predicate symbols occur in φ, which is why the results of Section 6.10.3 for finite vocabularies apply in the argument to follow.

the facts stated above: a unary predicate symbol P will simulate an initial segment of the natural numbers, and ψ says "for all x in P there is a back-and-forth sequence of length x for a model for $\{R\}$ and a model for $\{R'\}$", where R' is a new binary predicate symbol. Let θ be $\psi \wedge \varphi(R) \wedge \neg\varphi(R')$. The result is that models $\mathcal{C}$ of θ (which must be infinite) will have two reducts $\mathcal{A}$ and $\mathcal{A}'$ (to the vocabularies $\{R\}$ and $\{R'\}$, respectively; see Definition 6.7.4) such that $\mathcal{A} \models \varphi(R)$, $\mathcal{A}' \models \neg\varphi(R')$, and a back-and-forth sequence of length $|P^{\mathcal{C}}|$ for $\mathcal{A}, \mathcal{A}'$. By the Löwenheim property, we can assume that these models are countably infinite. It will be easy to see that for each k, θ has models $\mathcal{C}$ such that $|P^{\mathcal{C}}| \geqslant k$. But θ can have no model where $P^{\mathcal{C}}$ is infinite, for that would mean that there is a back-and-forth sequence of length ω for $\mathcal{A}, \mathcal{A}'$, which by Theorem 6.10.4 entails that $\mathcal{A} \cong \mathcal{A}'$, which is impossible since $\mathcal{A} \models \varphi(R)$ and $\mathcal{A}' \models \neg\varphi(R')$. Well, but then the set $\{\theta\} \cup \{\exists_{\geqslant n} x Px : n = 1, 2, \ldots\}$ is a counter-example to compactness.

We now provide a bit more detail. Let $\mathcal{L}_1 \leqslant_{\text{inf}} \mathcal{L}_2$ mean that every $\mathcal{L}_1$-sentence has the same *infinite* models as some $\mathcal{L}_2$-sentence. We are assuming $\mathcal{L} \nleqslant$ FOL. Let us first deal with the case owhen $\mathcal{L} \leqslant_{\text{inf}}$ FOL. So there is an $\mathcal{L}$-sentence φ_1 which has the same infinite models as some FOL-sentence ψ_1, but not the same finite models as any FOL-sentence. Let θ_1 be the $\mathcal{L}$-sentence $\neg(\varphi_1 \leftrightarrow \psi_1)$. So θ_1 has no infinite models, but it is not hard to show that it has arbitrarily large finite models (Exercise 6.13.44). This means that compactness fails for $\mathcal{L}$, and we are done.

So from now on, assume that $\mathcal{L} \nleqslant_{\text{inf}}$ FOL, and that $\varphi = \varphi(R)$ is an $\mathcal{L}$-sentence which does not have the same infinite models as any FOL-sentence. Then, as promised:

(42) For each n there are countably infinite models $\mathcal{M}_n, \mathcal{M}'_n$ such that $\mathcal{M}_n \models \varphi$, $\mathcal{M}'_n \models \neg\varphi$, and $\mathcal{M}_n \cong_n \mathcal{M}'_n$.

Proof. By Theorem 6.10.3 and Lemma 6.10.6, it is enough to show that there are countably infinite models $\mathcal{M}_n, \mathcal{M}'_n$ s.t. $\mathcal{M}_n \models \varphi$, $\mathcal{M}'_n \models \neg\varphi$, and $\mathcal{M}_n \equiv_n \mathcal{M}'_n$. Suppose not, i.e:

(a) If $\mathcal{A}$ and $\mathcal{B}$ are countably infinite models such that $\mathcal{A} \models \varphi$ and $\mathcal{A} \equiv_n \mathcal{B}$, then $\mathcal{B} \models \varphi$.

Recall from Section 6.10 that the class of models (for our vocabulary) is partitioned into finitely many equivalence classes under $\equiv_n$. In particular, this holds for the countably infinite models. Each such equivalence class E_i is characterized by a FOL-sentence, say ψ_i. By (a), φ is true in all countably infinite models in some of the equivalence classes, say $E_{k_1}, \ldots, E_{k_m}$, and false in all the others. It then follows that φ is true in the same countably infinite models as the FOL-sentence $\psi_{k_1} \vee \ldots \vee \psi_{k_m}$, and hence, by the Löwenheim property, in the same infinite models (Exercise 6.13.45). But this contradicts our assumption about φ. □

Next, we add a unary predicate symbol P, a binary $\leqslant$, and sentences saying that $\leqslant$ is a linear order of P with a smallest element, and such that every element that has a successor has an immediate successor. We also add a sentence enforcing that the universe C (say) is infinite (for example, a function symbol g and a sentence saying that g is a one-one map from C to $C - \{a\}$ for some a).

Finally, we need to describe a back-and-forth sequence of length x for each x such that Px. So we add a ternary predicate symbol S with the idea that $Sxab$ should mean that the relation I_x from Definition 6.10.5 holds between a and b. Here a, b should be sequences of length x, so we introduce a binary function symbol f and a sentence saying that for each a, $f(a, \cdot)$, written f_a, is a function from P to C. The idea is that, for $y < x$, $f_a(y)$ is (codes) the y:th element of the sequence a. Now we can write sentences corresponding to the conditions in Definition 6.10.5. For example, condition (iii) becomes a sentence saying:

> For all x, y, z, a, b, if $y, z < x$ and $Sxab$, then $R(f_a(y), f_a(z))$ iff $R'(f_b(y), f_b(z))$ and $f_a(y) = f_a(z)$ iff $f_b(y) = f_b(z)$.

Let ψ be the conjunction of all these (finitely many!) sentences,[41] and let θ be $\psi \wedge \varphi(R) \wedge \neg\varphi(R')$. If things have been done properly, we get:

(43) a. If $\mathcal{C} \models \theta$, then C is infinite and $P^{\mathcal{C}}$ is finite.
b. For every n there is a model $\mathcal{C}$ of θ such that $|P^{\mathcal{C}}| \geqslant n$.

Proof. For (b), we use (42), which tells us that the required back-and-forth sequence exists (for each n). (Let $C = \mathbb{N}$, and $P^{\mathcal{C}} = \{0, \ldots, n-1\}$.) For (a), assume there was a model $\mathcal{C}$ of θ such that $P^{\mathcal{C}}$ is infinite. We can add a new function symbol h and a sentence ρ saying that h is an injection from $P^{\mathcal{C}}$ to $P^{\mathcal{C}} - \{a\}$, for some $a \in P^{\mathcal{C}}$. So $\mathcal{C}$ can be expanded to a model $\mathcal{D}$ of $\theta' = \theta \wedge \rho$. By the Löwenheim property, we can assume that $\mathcal{D}$ is countably infinite. Our axioms about P and $\leqslant$ now guarantee that for every n there is $c_n \in P^{\mathcal{D}}$ with exactly n predecessors. Using this, and the other axioms from θ, we can define a back-and-forth sequence of length ω for $\mathcal{A}, \mathcal{A}'$, where $\mathcal{A} = (C, R^{\mathcal{D}})$ and $\mathcal{A}' = (C, (R')^{\mathcal{D}})$. By Theorem 6.10.4, this shows that $\mathcal{A} \cong \mathcal{A}'$, which contradicts the fact that $\mathcal{A} \models \varphi(R)$ and $\mathcal{A}' \models \neg\varphi(R')$. This completes the sketch of the proof of (43), and thereby of the theorem. □

[41] We used function symbols above, but clearly these can be replaced by predicate symbols with a corresponding rewording of the sentences.

Lindström proved several other characterizations of FOL, among them the following two. Say that $\mathcal{L}$ has the *Tarski property* if every sentence with an infinite model has an uncountable model. Also, $\mathcal{L}$ is *complete* if the set of valid $\mathcal{L}$-sentences is recursively enumerable, and we say that $\mathcal{L} \leqslant_{\text{eff}} \mathcal{L}'$ holds if there is a computable function f which for every $\mathcal{L}$-sentence φ finds a logically equivalent $\mathcal{L}'$-sentence $f(\varphi)$. These notions are explained in Part IV, but completeness of a logic essentially means that there is an inference system which generates exactly its valid sentences, so it certainly holds for FOL.

Theorem 6.11.2 (Lindström)

(a) *If $\mathcal{L}$ has the Löwenheim and Tarski properties, then $\mathcal{L} \equiv_{\mathit{inf}}$ FOL.*[42]

(b) *If FOL $\leqslant_{\text{eff}} \mathcal{L}$ and $\mathcal{L}$ has the Löwenheim property and is complete, then $\mathcal{L} \equiv_{\text{eff}}$ FOL.*

6.12. Concluding remarks

The last two sections have covered a bit more, if only in outline, than one may deem fitting for a short chapter on model theory. But it seemed appropriate to end this part of the book with Lindström's Theorems. These results show that our axiomatic presentation of FOL, followed by Henkin's proof of the Completeness Theorem, which in turn yields the Compactness Theorem and the Löwenheim-Skolem Theorem, really captures the essence of first-order logic.

At the same time, we have gotten a glimpse of stronger logical languages, obtained by adding generalized quantifiers to FOL, which then necessarily lose some of its nice properties. That doesn't make them uninteresting though, and these stronger languages have found many applications. In particular, we saw how logics like FOL(*most*) are useful tools in the study of natural language semantics.[43]

6.13. Exercises to Chapter 6

Exercise 6.13.1

1. How many conjuncts does (the sentence that we abbreviated by) $\exists_{\geqslant n} x\, x = x$ have, in the simplified version (4)?
2. How many conjuncts in the following sentence?

   (a) $\forall x_1 \ldots \forall x_{n-1} \exists x_n \bigwedge_{1 \leqslant i \leqslant n-1} x_i \neq x_n$
3. Show that $\exists_{\geqslant n} x\, x = x$ and (a) are logically equivalent.

[42] Simple extra conditions on $\mathcal{L}$ will guarantee the stronger conclusion $\mathcal{L} \equiv$ FOL.

[43] FOL(*most*) is not complete or compact, nor does it have the Löwenheim property!

Exercise 6.13.2
*Every finite subset of the set $\Gamma = \{\exists_{\geqslant n}\, x = x : n = 1, 2, \ldots\}$ has a finite model, but Γ has no finite model (though it has infinite models). Find a consistent set of FOL-sentences Δ in the empty vocabulary such that every *proper* subset of Δ (even if infinite) has a finite model, but Δ has no finite model.

Exercise 6.13.3
1. Definition (12) doesn't really work for $n = 1$. (Why?) Let $E_{\geqslant 1}$ be the sentence $\exists x_1\, x_1 = x_1$. Verify that (13) then holds for $n = 1$.
2. Show that the sentence $Eq \wedge E_{=1}$ is equivalent to the sentence in (8) (and thus characterizes the universal equivalence relation).

Exercise 6.13.4
1. Suppose $(M, E) \models Eq$ and that the sentence (15) is true in (M, E). How many elements are there in M?
2. Let $k_1, \ldots, k_n$ be natural numbers > 0, and consider the sentence

$$\exists x_1 \ldots \exists x_n (\bigwedge_{1 \leqslant i < j \leqslant n} \neg x_i E x_j \wedge \bigwedge_{1 \leqslant i \leqslant n} \exists_{=k_i} y\, y E x_i \wedge \forall z \bigvee_{1 \leqslant i \leqslant n} z E x_i)$$

   What does this sentence say in a model of *Eq*?
3. Specify a sentence θ_{mn} which is true in a model of *Eq* iff there are at least m equivalence classes with exactly n elements ($m, n > 0$).

Exercise 6.13.5
Show that the relation $\cong$ is an equivalence relation (in the class of models for a given vocabulary L).

Exercise 6.13.6
Show that (16) in the proof of the Isomorphism Lemma holds also if the vocabulary contains function symbols.

Exercise 6.13.7
Let $L = \{P, Q\}$, with P, Q unary, and define $\mathcal{M}$ by $M = \{$England, Germany, Sweden, France, Italy, Holland$\}$, $P^{\mathcal{M}}$ is the property of being a monarchy, and $Q^{\mathcal{M}}$ the property of having the Euro as currency.[44] Construe a model isomorphic to $\mathcal{M}$ with domain $\{0, 1, 2, 3, 4, 5\}$. How many such models (with that domain) are there?

Exercise 6.13.8
Show that every countable model $\mathcal{M}$ is isomorphic to a model whose domain is a subset of $\mathbb{N}$.

[44] Background info: England, Sweden, and Holland are monarchies; Germany, France, Italy, and Holland use the Euro.

Exercise 6.13.9
Which pairs of the following ordered sets are isomorphic?

1. 0 1 2 3 4 ...
2. 1 6 11 16 21 ...
3. 0 2 4 ... 1 3 5 ...
4. 0 3 6 ...... 7 4 1 2 5 8 ...

Exercise 6.13.10
Show that if $\mathcal{M} = (M, E)$ is a model of *Eq*, then:

$$M \text{ is finite iff } \sigma_0^{\mathcal{M}} = 0 \text{ and } \sum_{n \geqslant 1} \sigma_n^{\mathcal{M}} \text{ is a natural number.}$$

Exercise 6.13.11
Prove Fact 6.4.6.

Exercise 6.13.12
Show that the only automorphism h on $(\mathbb{N}, <)$ is the identity function, $h(n) = n$. [Hint: Assume h is an automorphism on $(\mathbb{N}, <)$, and start by showing that $h(0) = 0$.]

Exercise 6.13.13
Show: if A is definable in $\mathcal{M}$ with parameter a, and a is definable in $\mathcal{M}$ without parameters, then A is definable in $\mathcal{M}$ without parameters.

Exercise 6.13.14

1. Is any integer definable in $(\mathbb{Z}, <)$ *with* parameters?
2. Show that 0 is definable (without parameters) in the model $(\mathbb{Z}, +)$.
3. Show that no integer other than 0 is definable (without parameters) in $(\mathbb{Z}, +)$. [Hint: Consider $h(a) = -a$.]
4. *Show that every element of the domain is definable (without parameters) in the model $(\mathbb{Z}, +, \cdot)$. [Hint: Start by defining 1.] Models with this property are called *pointwise definable*.

Exercise 6.13.15
*Consider definability without parameters in $\mathcal{M} = (\mathbb{R}, 0, 1, +, \cdot)$ (where $\mathbb{R}$ is the set of real numbers).

1. Show that the order relation is definable.
2. Show that every integer is definable.
3. Show that every rational number is definable.
4. Show that $\sqrt{2}$ is definable.

(One can show that exactly the algebraic numbers are definable in $\mathcal{M}$.)

Exercise 6.13.16

1. Let $L = \{c_1, c_2\}$ (where c_1, c_2 are individual constants), and $T = \{\neg c_1 = c_2\}$. Show that T is not categorical. Can we add another L-sentence φ such that $T \cup \{\varphi\}$ is categorical?
2. Is the theory $T_{\leqslant n} = \{\exists_{\leqslant n} x\, x = x\}$ categorical for some n?
3. Give an example of a categorical theory in the vocabulary $L = \{E\}$, where E is a binary predicate symbol (intended for an equivalence relation).

Exercise 6.13.17

Which (if any) of the following theories (in the vocabulary $L = \{E\}$) are countably categorical? [Hint: Fact 6.4.6 may be used.]

1. $T = \{\forall x \forall y (xEy \leftrightarrow x = y)\}$
2. $T' = \{Eq\} \cup \{E_{\geqslant 2n} : n = 1, 2, \ldots\}$
3. $T'' = \{Eq, \forall x \exists_{=2} y\, yEx, E_{\geqslant 1}, E_{\geqslant 2}, E_{\geqslant 3}, \ldots\}$
4. $T''' = \{Eq, \forall x \exists_{=10} y\, yEx\}$
5. $T'''' = \{Eq\} \cup \{\theta_{mn} : m \geqslant 1, n \geqslant 1\}$, where θ_{mn} is the sentence in Exercise 6.13.4:3.

(See also Exercises 6.13.24 and 6.13.38.)

Exercise 6.13.18

Explain why the theories *PO* and *LO* (Section 6.6) are not complete.

Exercise 6.13.19

If T is a theory in the vocabulary L, let

$$Thm_T = \{\varphi\colon \varphi \text{ is an } L\text{-sentence and } T \vdash \varphi\}$$

Show that a consistent theory T is complete iff there is a model $\mathcal{M}$ for L such that $Thm_T = Th(\mathcal{M})$. [Hint: Use Lemma 6.6.13.]

Exercise 6.13.20

Define the relation $\Rrightarrow$ between models for a vocabulary L as follows:

$$\mathcal{M} \Rrightarrow \mathcal{M}' \text{ iff for every } L\text{-sentence } \varphi,\ \mathcal{M} \models \varphi \text{ implies } \mathcal{M}' \models \varphi.$$

Show that $\mathcal{M} \Rrightarrow \mathcal{M}'$ iff $\mathcal{M} \equiv \mathcal{M}'$.

Exercise 6.13.21

*Show that if $\mathcal{M}$ is a finite model for a finite vocabulary L (that we assume to be relational, for simplicity), then there is an L-sentence $\theta_{\mathcal{M}}$ such that for all models $\mathcal{M}'$ for L, $\mathcal{M}' \models \theta_{\mathcal{M}} \Leftrightarrow \mathcal{M}' \cong \mathcal{M}$. Conclude that if two models, one of which is finite, are elementarily equivalent, then they are isomorphic.

Exercise 6.13.22
If T is a set of L-sentences and $\mathcal{C}$ a class of models for L, define

$$Th(\mathcal{C}) = \{\varphi\colon \text{ for all } \mathcal{M} \in \mathcal{C},\ \mathcal{M} \models \varphi\}$$
$$Mod(T) = \{\mathcal{M}\colon \text{ for all } \varphi \in T,\ \mathcal{M} \models \varphi\}$$

(So $Th(\{\mathcal{M}\})$ is what we have written $Th(\mathcal{M})$.) Note that (19) says that $\mathcal{M} \equiv \mathcal{M}'$ iff $\mathcal{M}' \in Mod(Th(\mathcal{M}))$.

1. Show that the following connection (called a *Galois connection*) holds between these notions:

   (G) $\mathcal{C} \subseteq Mod(T)$ iff $T \subseteq Th(\mathcal{C})$

2. Conclude from (G) that:[45]
   - $T \subseteq Th(Mod(T))$
   - $\mathcal{C} \subseteq Mod(Th(\mathcal{C}))$
   - $T \subseteq T'$ implies $Mod(T') \subseteq Mod(T)$
   - $\mathcal{C} \subseteq \mathcal{C}'$ implies $Th(\mathcal{C}') \subseteq Th(\mathcal{C})$

3. Show that $Thm_T = Th(Mod(T))$ holds (see Exercise 6.13.19 for notation), and check that this fact is essentially a formulation of the completeness of FOL.

Exercise 6.13.23

(a) Show that every countable set of sentences in FOL$^-$ (FOL without identity) which has a model, has a countably infinite model.

(b) Using (a), show that identity is not definable in FOL$^-$, in the strong sense that there can be *no* set of sentences Γ in a language without identity whose vocabulary contains at least one binary predicate symbol R such that, for every model $\mathcal{M}$,

$$\mathcal{M} \models \Gamma \text{ iff } R^{\mathcal{M}} = \{(a,a)\colon a \in M\} \text{ (the identity relation in } M)$$

Exercise 6.13.24
Which of the theories in Exercise 6.13.17, 1–4, are complete? [Hint: Vaught's Test may be used in some cases.]

Exercise 6.13.25 (undefinability of well-order)
A totally ordered set $(M,<)$ is *well-ordered* if there is no infinite descending chain in M, i.e. if there are no $a_0, a_1, a_2, \ldots \in M$ such that $a_0 > a_1 > a_2 > \ldots$. A paradigm example is the standard order of the natural numbers. Show that the notion of well-order cannot be expressed in first-order logic: there is no set of sentences Γ in the vocabulary $L = \{<\}$ such that for all $\mathcal{M} = (M,<)$,

$$(M,<) \models \Gamma \text{ iff } (M,<) \text{ is well-ordered}$$

[45] These facts can be easily inferred directly from the truth definition, but the point is that they follow from (G).

[Hint: Assume the contrary, add new constants $c_0, c_1, c_2, \ldots$ to L, add suitable sentences to Γ, and use compactness.]

Exercise 6.13.26
Suppose T_1 and T_2 are theories such that $T_1 \cup T_2$ has no model. Show that there is a sentence φ such that $T_1 \models \varphi$ and $T_2 \models \neg\varphi$. [Hint: By compactness there is a finite $T_0 \subseteq T_1 \cup T_2$ which has no model.]

Exercise 6.13.27
Suppose T_1 and T_2 are theories in some vocabulary L such that for all L-models we have: $\mathcal{M} \models T_1$ iff $\mathcal{M} \not\models T_2$. Show that T_1 and T_2 are finitely axiomatizable. [Hint: Use Exercise 6.13.26.]

Exercise 6.13.28
*That T is finitely axiomatizable means that there is a finite theory T_0 such that T and T_0 are equivalent. Show that T_0 in that case be can chosen as a subset of T. [Hint: Use compactness. Note that T_0 is equivalent to $\{\varphi\}$ for some φ, so $T \cup \{\neg\varphi\}$ has no model.]

Exercise 6.13.29 (EC and EC$_\Delta$ classes)
*Fix a vocabulary L and recall the notation from Exercise 6.13.22. A class K of models is EC (an *elementary class*) if $K = Mod(\varphi)$ for some φ. K is EC$_\Delta$ (a *δ-elementary class*) if $K = Mod(\Gamma)$ for some set Γ of sentences. Write $\overline{K}$ for the class of models for L which are not in K.

(a) Suppose K is EC$_\Delta$ and has arbitrarily large finite members. Show:

  (a1) K contains an infinite member.

  (a2) The class of infinite members of K is EC$_\Delta$ but not EC. (Use Exercise 6.13.28.)

  (a3) Conclude that, for example, the class of finite linear orders is not EC$_\Delta$, and the class of infinite linear orders, although EC$_\Delta$, is not EC.

(b) Show that $K \in$ EC iff $K \in$ EC$_\Delta$ and $\overline{K} \in$ EC$_\Delta$.
[Hint: If $K = Mod(\Gamma_1)$ and $\overline{K} = Mod(\Gamma_2)$, $\Gamma_1 \cup \Gamma_2$ has no model.]

Exercise 6.13.30
Suppose φ and ψ are sentences such that for all countable (i.e. finite or countably infinite) models $\mathcal{M}$, $\mathcal{M} \models \varphi$ iff $\mathcal{M} \models \psi$. Show that φ and ψ are logically equivalent. [Hint: Use the Löwenheim-Skolem Theorem.]

Exercise 6.13.31
Consider the property *extension* of type $\langle 1, 1\rangle$ quantifiers:

(EXT) If $A, B \subseteq M \subseteq M'$, then $Q_M(A, B) \Leftrightarrow Q_{M'}(A, B)$.

Define *extension* for quantifiers of any type. Most quantifiers that turn up in a natural language context are EXT. Check this with the examples we have given. Show that although *every* is EXT, $\forall$ is not. Is $\exists$ EXT?

Exercise 6.13.32
The *relativization* of a type $\langle 1 \rangle$ quantifier $\mathcal{Q}$ is the type $\langle 1, 1 \rangle$ quantifier $\mathcal{Q}^{rel}$ defined by

$$\mathcal{Q}^{rel}_M(A, B) \text{ iff } \mathcal{Q}_A(A \cap B)$$

Show that a type $\langle 1, 1 \rangle$ quantifier is CONSERV and EXT if and only if it is the relativization of some type $\langle 1 \rangle$ quantifier.

Exercise 6.13.33
*Find a FOL($\mathcal{I}$)-sentence which is logically equivalent to $Q_0 x P x$. [Hint: Use fact (44) in the Appendix.] Conclude that the compactness theorem fails for FOL($\mathcal{I}$). What about the Löwenheim-Skolem Theorem?

Exercise 6.13.34
Use Exercise 6.13.25 to show that compactness fails for FOL($\mathcal{W}$).

Exercise 6.13.35
Show that $\mathcal{M} \sim_k \mathcal{M}'$ holds, but not $\mathcal{M} \sim_{k+1} \mathcal{M}'$, for the two models described directly after Definition 6.10.1.

Exercise 6.13.36
(a) Show that $\mathcal{M} \sim_\omega \mathcal{M}'$ implies that for all n, $\mathcal{M} \sim_n \mathcal{M}'$.
(b) Show that $\mathcal{M} \cong \mathcal{M}'$ implies $\mathcal{M} \sim_\omega \mathcal{M}'$.

Exercise 6.13.37
* $\mathbb{N}$, $\mathbb{Z}$, $\mathbb{Q}$, $\mathbb{R}$ are the natural numbers, the integers, the rational numbers, and the real numbers, respectively. Let $\mathbf{N} = (\mathbb{N}, <)$, and similarly for $\mathbf{Z}$, $\mathbf{Q}$, and $\mathbf{R}$. Write $\mathbf{N} + \mathbf{N}$ for the linear order obtained by placing a copy of $\mathbf{N}$ directly after $\mathbf{N}$, and similarly for the other ordered structures above. Thus, for example, $\mathbf{N} + \mathbf{N}$ is (isomorphic to) the order

$$0 \;\; 2 \;\; 4 \;\; \ldots \;\; 1 \;\; 3 \;\; 5 \;\; \ldots$$

Which of Duplicator and Spoiler has a winning strategy in the following games?
(a) $EF^2(\mathbf{N}, \mathbf{Q})$
(b) $EF^2(\mathbf{N}, \mathbf{Z})$
(c) $EF^3(\mathbf{Z}, \mathbf{Q})$
(d) $EF^n(\mathbf{Q}, \mathbf{R})$
(e) $EF^2(\mathbf{N}, \mathbf{N} + \mathbf{N})$ and $EF^3(\mathbf{N}, \mathbf{N} + \mathbf{N})$

Exercise 6.13.38

(a) Describe in more detail the winning strategy for Duplicator in the completeness proof of the theory T in Section 6.10.2.

(b) Show by similar reasoning that the theory T'''' in Exercise 6.13.17 is also complete.

Exercise 6.13.39

Give a more detailed description of the winning strategy for Duplicator in the game $EF^{\omega}((M,<),(M',<'))$ indicated in Section 6.10.2.

Exercise 6.13.40

*Let *DiLO* be the theory of *discrete linear orders*, i.e. linear orders such that every element has an immediate successor and an immediate predecessor. The typical model of *DiLO* is **Z** (see Exercise 6.13.37). If $(M,<)$ is a model of *DiLO*, $a, b \in M$, and $a \leqslant b$, let the *distance* between a and b, written $|(a,b)|$, be the number of $c \in M$ such that $a \leqslant c \leqslant b$. In **Z** all distances are finite, but other models of *DiLO* may also have infinite distances between elements.

1. Show that *DiLO* has only infinite models, but is not countably categorical. [Hint: consider **Z** and **Z** + **Z**.]
2. Let $(M,<)$, $(M',<')$ be models of *DiLO*. Prove that we have $(M,<) \sim_n (M',<')$ for every n (and hence, by Theorem 6.10.3, that *DiLO* is complete). Also show that it does *not* follow that $(M,<) \sim_{\omega} (M',<')$.

   [Hint: The idea for Duplicator's winning strategy is to maintain suitable distances between chosen elements. In detail: to see to it that for $1 \leqslant i \leqslant n$, when $(a_1,a'_1),\ldots,(a_i,a'_i)$ have been picked (not necessarily in that order), where $a_1 \leqslant \ldots \leqslant a_i$ and $a'_1 \leqslant \ldots \leqslant a'_i$, we have, for $1 \leqslant j < i$, that if $|(a_j,a_{j+1})| < 2^{n-i+1}$ or $|(a'_j,a'_{j+1})| < 2^{n-i+1}$, then $|(a_j,a_{j+1})| = |(a'_j,a'_{j+1})|$. Describe informally a strategy which has this result.]

Exercise 6.13.41

In Section 6.9.1 we showed that $\mathcal{Q}_0$ ('infinitely many') is not definable in FOL, using the fact that the compactness theorem holds for FOL.

(a) Give another proof of this fact along the lines of the proof in Section 6.10.2 that $\mathcal{Q}_{\text{even}}$ is not definable in FOL.

(b) Do the same for the Rescher quantifier $\mathcal{Q}^R$ (Section 6.9.1).

(c) Similarly for the quantifiers $\mathcal{I}$ (the Härtig quantifier) and *most*. [Comment: for *most*, you may show that $\mathcal{Q}^R$ is definable from *most* and use (a). Or you may do a direct construction.]

Exercise 6.13.42
Let *more* be the quantifier defined by $more_M(A, B) \Leftrightarrow |A| > |B|$. Show:

1. $\mathcal{I}$ and *more* are not conservative (Section 6.9.2).
2. *most* and $\mathcal{I}$ are both definable in FOL(*more*).
3. *Over *finite* domains, *more* is definable in FOL(*most*).
4. * FOL(*more*) $\equiv$ FOL($most$, $\mathcal{Q}_0$). [Hint: Use $\mathcal{Q}_0$ to distinguish the cases when A is finite and A is infinite. In the finite case, use 3 above, and in the infinite case, use a similar definition of *more*.]

Exercise 6.13.43
Let φ be an $\mathcal{L}$-sentence in some logic $\mathcal{L}$. Show that for each n there is a FOL-sentence $\chi_{\varphi,n}$ such that for all models $\mathcal{M}$ (for the finite relational vocabulary L_φ of φ) with $|M| \leqslant n$, we have $\mathcal{M} \models \varphi \leftrightarrow \chi_{\varphi,n}$. Thus, over models whose size is below a fixed finite number, every $\mathcal{L}$-sentence is expressible in FOL. [Hint: Use the sentences $\theta_{\mathcal{M}'}$ (for finite $\mathcal{M}'$) from Exercise 6.13.21, noting that up to isomorphism, there are only finitely many models for L_φ of size $\leqslant n$.]

Exercise 6.13.44
Suppose that φ_1 is an $\mathcal{L}$-sentence which is not equivalent to any FOL-sentence over finite models. Show that for every FOL-sentence ψ_1, the sentence $\theta_1 = \neg(\varphi_1 \leftrightarrow \psi_1)$ has arbitrarily large finite models. [Hint: Assume the opposite and use the preceding exercise.]

Exercise 6.13.45
Suppose $\mathcal{L}$ has the Löwenheim property, and that φ is an $\mathcal{L}$-sentence which has the same countably infinite models as some FOL-sentence ψ. Show that φ has the same infinite models as ψ.

Part III

Incompleteness

7 Overview of incompleteness and undecidability

7.1. Background to Parts III and IV

The first half of the 1930s was a decisive epoch in modern logic. In what may be seen as the first textbook on first-order predicate logic (Hilbert and Ackermann 1928),[1] Hilbert and Ackermann had asked if their axiomatization was *complete*: if all logical truths could be derived in their system. As we have seen, Gödel showed in 1930 that the answer was Yes, a result that was to highlight the particular properties of first-order logic, and eventually, via the Compactness theorem and (with Henkin's completeness proof) the Löwenheim-Skolem Theorem, lay the foundations of the model-theoretic approach to logic that started picking up speed in the 1950s. And one year later, 1931, Gödel showed that there can be no *complete axiomatization* of mathematics: every formal system axiomatizing a mathematical theory which contains a certain amount of elementary arithmetic is such that, if the system is *consistent*—free from contradiction—there are true arithmetical statements that cannot be proved in the system. Furthermore, the consistency of such a system cannot be proved in the system itself.

7.1.1. Incompleteness

The incompleteness theorems came as a severe blow to a program in the foundations of mathematics pursued by Hilbert, Bernays, and others in the first decades of the 20th century: *Hilbert's Program*. In view of the discovery of paradoxes in early formulations of set theory, and of discussions about the role of the infinite in mathematics, the aim of the program was to vindicate mathematical theories, including

[1] Although Hilbert and Ackermann still saw FOL as merely a *fragment* of logic, located at the bottom of the type hierarchy.

Cantor's transfinite set theory, by *proving by finitary means that they are consistent*. The first step, to *formalize* such theories, had already been undertaken by Frege, Russell and Whitehead, Hilbert himself, and others. Proofs could then be seen as finite configurations of symbols, construed according to precise rules, and these configurations could presumably be studied with finitary methods. The second step, to show that no such proof could end, say, with the sentence $0 \neq 0$, seemed quite realistic. However, even though it was a matter of debate exactly what methods were 'finitary', most people came to agree that the system *PA* of *Peano Arithmetic* contains these methods, and (according to some) much more. Then Gödel's second theorem shows that with these methods one cannot even prove that *PA* is consistent, let alone set theory.[2]

More generally, the incompleteness theorems seem to show that mathematical knowledge—even arithmetical knowledge—is in a sense *inexhaustible*: we cannot lay down axioms that once and for all fix our knowledge of arithmetical truths. For every attempt to do so in a theory T, based on axioms or principles we trust, we can always add the statement "and of course T is consistent", or rather its formal counterpart Con_T, but then Con_T (if true) will not be provable in T.[3]

Do these results show that we have some reason to *doubt* the consistency of, say, *PA*, or that proving consistency of a theory requires some special new kind of reasoning? Very much has been written about the consequences of Gödel's theorems, some of it speculative and fanciful. Few mathematical theorems, if any, have caught the attention of both scholars outside mathematics and the general public like Gödel's theorems. I will come back to their significance in Chapter 12.9; for now let me just affirm that the answer to the question just posed is No: the incompleteness theorems show no such thing.

Indeed, their main impact is *not* negative. They provide insights into what one can and cannot prove *in* (sufficiently strong) axiomatic theories, they introduce powerful methods for proving facts *about* such theories, and they have been cornerstones of logic ever since.

Moreover, the incompleteness theorems inspired Alan Turing and others to investigate the concept of computability (see below), leading to the emergence of a new discipline in logic and, eventually, to computer science. Finally, Hilbert's and his collaborators' efforts

[2]Hilberts' program, in its later stages, made a distinction between *real* and *ideal* mathematics, and the goal shifted to proving (by finitary means) *conservativity*: that real statements provable in an ideal theory T were already provable in another theory, say F, dealing only with real objects. But, already the *first* incompleteness theorem shows that this route to achieving conservativity will not work: the sentence Gödel constructed is about real objects and can be seen to be true. So if T is comprehensive enough the sentence should be provable in T, but it is unprovable already in F. For an overview of Hilbert's program and the effect of the incompleteness theorems, see Zach 2019.

[3]Franzén 2004 is a very readable exposition of the incompleteness theorems, focusing on the aspect of inexhaustibility.

to analyze proofs was the starting point, especially in the hands of Gerhard Gentzen, of another major area in modern logic: *proof theory*.

Gödel's main technical innovation was, first, to *code*, using what is now called a *Gödel numbering*, metalogical statements about formulas, theories, derivability, etc. as arithmetical statements: the *arithmetization* of (meta)logic. Second, using a technique for *self reference*, which enables one to find sentences which in a precise sense refer to themselves, Gödel managed to construe an arithmetical sentence such that neither it nor its negation is derivable in the theory T under consideration (assuming T contains an appropriate amount of arithmetic): an *undecidable* sentence. In particular, Con_T is such a sentence.

This was a radically new way of proving incompleteness. And the method is general: it doesn't help to add that sentence (or its negation) to the axioms: Gödel's proof then immediately provides *another* sentence which is undecidable in the extended system.

It is instructive to compare the situation in euclidean geometry: here there was an axiom, the axiom of parallels, which mathematicians for centuries had tried to derive from Euclid's other axioms, without success. In 1868 Beltrami showed that it *cannot* be derived, by constructing a *model* in which the other axioms are true but the parallel axiom false. And since there are also models in which the other axioms are true and the parallel axiom is true as well, the negation of the parallel axiom isn't derivable either: it is *independent* of the other axioms. This method of proving that something is *not* derivable is the familiar method of counter-examples; we saw several simple applications of it in Part II. But for *PA* the situation was very different. There were no known ways of constructing models of *PA* that falsify some sentence that is true (or that one believes is true) in the standard model. Gödel's method is syntactic, and shows directly that in 'sufficiently strong' theories there must be undecidable sentences.[4]

7.1.2. Computability

The incompleteness theorems necessitated a revision of an old assumption that, explicitly or implicitly, had been made by many mathematicians throughout the ages: that all mathematical problems can in principle be solved. Hilbert famously expressed this attitude as follows in 1900, when presenting his list of 23 unsolved mathematical problems at the Second International Congress of Mathematicians in Paris:

[4]Gödel's proof is remarkable in that it explicitly construes an undecidable sentence, and shows that Con_T is an example. So does incompleteness essentially depend on a theory's ability to construct self-referential sentences? Not really. There are other incompleteness proofs that don't rely on self-referential sentences; in fact, the incompleteness phenomenon can be seen a general fact in computability theory (recursion theory) as we will see in Part IV. It is more adequate to say that the main tool for proving incompleteness is *diagonalization*. Self-reference is a particular application of diagonalization. All of this will become clear as we go along.

> This conviction of the solvability of every mathematical problem is a powerful incentive to the worker. We hear within us the perpetual call: There is the problem. Seek its solution. You can find it by pure reason, for in mathematics there is no *ignorabimus*.

But what exactly does it mean that a mathematical problem is solvable, or, more to the point, that it is *unsolvable*?

Gödel had assumed that the theories his proof applied to were such that the property of being (the Gödel number of) an axiom or a derivation was *primitive recursive* (see Chapter 8). But it was known that there are effectively computable sets and functions that are not primitive recursive, so the question was exactly which class of functions deserves the label 'computable'. Gödel, Jacques Herbrand, Alonzo Church, Emil Post, Rózsa Péter, and Stephen Kleene, among others, worked on this issue, and came up with partly different mathematical characterizations, which however all turned out to be (extensionally) equivalent; these functions are nowadays simply called *recursive*.

Meanwhile, Turing presented his famous analysis of the very concept of effective computability, in terms of what was soon to be called *Turing machines*. His analysis lays the foundation of modern computer science. It turned out that the Turing computable functions and relations are exactly the recursive ones. This fact, together with failed attempts to come up with computable functions that are not Turing computable, as well as the fact that the various other attempts to capture this class of functions mathematically were all equivalent, led to *Church-Turing's Thesis*, that is, that the effectively computable functions are exactly the Turing computable, or recursive, ones. And it became clear that Gödel's incompleteness results hold for all (sufficently strong) theories that are axiomatizable in the sense that their sets of axioms are recursive.

The Church-Turing Thesis also gives a precise definition of the concept of an *unsolvable problem*. The problem of deciding if a sentence in propositional logic is a tautology or not is solvable (by the method of truth tables): you can program a computer, or a Turing machine, that gives the correct answer in a finite number of steps. But the analogous problem for first-order logic is unsolvable. This was shown by Church and (independently) by Turing in 1936. So it is not just that we haven't so far been able to devise an effective method which, when applied to any first-order sentence, tells us whether that sentence is a logical truth or not. There is no point in even looking for such a method, because *there isn't one*—provided the Church-Turing Thesis is correct, which almost everyone believes.

Likewise, we get a definition of the concept of an *undecidable theory*: one for which the problem of deciding if an arbitrary sentence in the theory's language is a *theorem* or not is unsolvable. In other words, a theory whose set of (Gödel numbers of) theorems is not recursive. And this holds in spite of the fact that it is part of the very notion of a formal theory that its theorems are *effectively enumerable*: one can write a program which successively outputs each one of its theorems. But decidability doesn't follow. If a statement *is* in fact a theorem, it will eventually appear in the enumeration, but if it is *not* a theorem, we will never find out (at least not by this method).

The discovery that some easily formulated problems are unsolvable provided logic with rich new areas of research. Many theories are undecidable—for example, all theories for which the incompleteness theorems hold—but there are also interesting (non-trivially) decidable theories. And an undecidable problem can have a decidable subproblem; for example, first-order logic with only unary predicate symbols ($\mathrm{FOL}^{\mathrm{mon}}$) is decidable, and predicate logic where quantification is restricted to certain formats can be decidable.

But from the perspective of philosophy of logic and mathematics, it is the very concept of (un)decidability that is revolutionizing. Before this concept was introduced (discovered?) by Turing and others in the mid-1930s, it was simply impossible to even imagine what an in principle unsolvable problem could be. Now, however, it is a commonplace, and the study and classification of various kinds of unsolvable problems is part of the well developed area of logic called *recursion theory*, or *computability theory*.

7.1.3. Outline

Parts III and IV present the basic results about incompleteness and undecidability, along with the mathematical concepts, such as primitive recursive and recursive functions, used in their proofs. It is striking that the *ideas* behind these proofs are quite easy to understand, whereas it takes some detailed work to see how these ideas can actually be implemented. For this reason, Section 7.2 of this chapter gives a rather comprehensive overview of the results and the ideas behind them. The remaining chapters provide details, but also take the results quite a bit further.

Thus, Chapter 8 presents primitive recursive functions and relations. In the process, we cover some elementary number-theoretic facts, notably about division and prime numbers, and use these to *code finite sequences* of numbers. Such coding is essential to what follows; the reader needs to know *how* it works, but not necessarily all the details of *why* it works: starred sections can be skipped or skimmed.

Chapter 9 treats Peano arithmetic, the theory *PA* we already met. The goal here is to convey a sense, by means of simple examples, of how proofs in *PA* can be done, and specifically how the induction axiom is used. We also prove some specific facts to be used later. Then there is a chapter about representability in *PA* of primitive recursive functions (Chapter 10), and one about arithmetization, i.e. about how metalogical properties and relations via Gödel numbering are recast as (usually) primitive recursive properties and relations among numbers, and hence representable in *PA* (Chapter 11).

This lays the foundation for a first version of the incompleteness theorems, presented in Chapter 12, together with several related results, such as Tarski's theorem about the undefinability of truth, Löb's theorem, as well as formalized versions of some of these theorems. We also extend the incompleteness theorems to theories that do not explicitly contain arithmetic, such as set theory. The chapter ends with a discussion of the philosophical significance of incompleteness.

For the fully general version of these results one needs, as we said, a precise concept of a *decidable* or *solvable* problem. This is dealt with in Part IV, where Chapter 13 introduces both (partial) recursive functions and Turing computable functions, and gives a fairly detailed proof that these two classes of functions coincide. It is then straightforward to show that all recursive functions and relations are representable in *PA*, and thus to extend the results of Chapter 12 to this more general setting.

Chapter 14 focuses on *undecidability*. We show that the theories proved to be incomplete in earlier chapters are also undecidable, and we discuss a (seemingly) different class of undecidable problems, such as the halting problem. Furthermore, we observe that it is sufficient to use a *finitely axiomatizable* subtheory of *PA*—in particular, the theory *Q*, or *Robinson Arithmetic*—in order to define all recursive functions; this leads to the undecidability of first-order logic. We also introduce a classification of formulas in terms of quantifier complexity, and show that all recursive functions are representable in *Q* by formulas of very low complexity (Σ_1-formulas). In this context we take a brief look at some other weak arithmetical theories, between *Q* and *PA*.

Chapter 15, finally, introduces *recursively enumerable* sets and relations, and further generalizations of the earlier results that this concept makes possible. The chapter gives a first glimpse of computability theory. We introduce the classification in the *arithmetical hierarchy* of unsolvable problems, together with basic results such as the Enumeration Theorem, the s-m-n theorem, and the Recursion Theorem (Fixed Point Theorem). We show how to compare unsolvable problems by means of the notion of m-reducibility, and discuss Post's Problem (for m-reducibility), as well as so-called productive and creative sets, and we end by showing how facts about these sets provide a still more abstract and general view of the incompleteness and undecidability phenomena in logic.

7.2. Road to incompleteness

A preliminary version of the incompleteness theorems is as follows.

Theorem 7.2.1 (incompleteness theorems: preliminary version) *Every consistent formal system F containing a certain amount of arithmetic is incomplete: there are arithmetical statements in F which can neither be proved or disproved in F. Also, the arithmetical sentence expressing that F is consistent is unprovable in F.*

To arrive at precise formulations, several things need to be made clear. Our strategy will be to start with special cases, and then see how they generalize. *First*, by a 'formal system' we will simply mean a first-order theory T (as defined in Chapter 6.6) such that the property of being an element (axiom) of T is effectively computable. *Second*, by 'effectively computable' we understand in Part III *primitive recursive* (explained in Chapter 8); in Part IV we replace this with *recursive*.[5]

Third, as regards 'contains a certain amount of arithmetic', we first assume that the theories concerned have the *same* vocabulary as *PA*: $L_{PA} = \{0, +, \cdot, '\}$, and that 'containing' arithmetic simply means being an *extension* of *PA*, or even some weaker theory in L_{PA}. Having established the theorem for such theories, we will then see how it generalizes to other theories, such as set theory, into which a certain amount of elementary arithmetic can be *translated*. The undecidable sentences that we find are then translations of arithmetical sentences.

All the main ideas of the proof of the incompleteness theorems are present in the special case we start with. Once these have been understood, applying them to more general cases is mostly straightforward.

7.2.1. First-order theories

A first-order theory as defined in Chapter 6.6 is simply a set T of sentences that we call *axioms*, in some vocabulary. We let L_T be the set of non-logical symbols that occur in sentences in T. The *theorems* of T are the L_T-sentences derivable or provable in T, and we define:

$$Thm_T = \{\varphi\colon \varphi \text{ is an } L_T\text{-sentence and } T \vdash \varphi\}$$

A theory T' in the same vocabulary as T is an extension of T if everything provable in T is also provable in T':

[5]The effective computability requirement is essential, but not the use of first-order theories. For example, the results apply equally to theories expressed in *second-order logic*, where we can quantify not only over individuals but also over sets and relations between individuals.

Definition 7.2.2 (extension of a theory)
T' is an *extension* of T if $L_{T'} = L_T$ and $Thm_T \subseteq Thm_{T'}$.[6]

For example, if FO_L is the set of logical truths in the vocabulary L, then FO_L is the smallest L-theory: every theory T with $L_T = L$ is an extension of FO_L.

In Definition 6.6.8, we said that a theory is (finitely) *axiomatizable* if it is equivalent to a theory with an effectively computable (finite) set of axioms. Our focus will be on such sets of axioms, so an *axiomatized* theory is an effectively computable set of axioms. In particular, *finite* theories are axiomatized.

Even with merely an intuitive understanding of 'effectively computable', we note the following important connection between the notions of axiomatizability, decidability, and completeness:

Lemma 7.2.3
If T is axiomatizable and complete, then T is decidable.

Proof. A strict proof will come later (Chapter 15.2), but it is really only important to understand the intuitive argument, which comes here: Let T' be an axiomatized theory equivalent to T. So T' is also complete. Since T' is effectively computable, it is not hard to see that one can *effectively enumerate* all derivations from its axioms, say, $D_1, D_2, D_3, \ldots$. Now proceed as follows. Given any L_T-sentence φ, start the enumeration, and check at step i if the derivation D_i is a derivation of φ (ends with φ, if we use a Hilbert system) or of $\neg\varphi$. Since T' is complete, either φ or $\neg\varphi$ is derivable, so this process will halt after a finite number of steps, and we have described a decision method for theoremhood in T', and hence in T. □

This is a good time to emphasize that the words *decidable* and *undecidable* are used in two completely different senses in logic. In one sense, they apply to *theories*, and concern the existence, or not, of an effective method to verify if an arbitrary sentence is a theorem in the theory or not. In the other sense, they apply to *sentences* relative to a theory: φ is decidable in T if either $T \vdash \varphi$ or $T \vdash \neg\varphi$, and so φ is undecidable in T if neither holds. Thus, T is complete if every L_T-sentence is decidable in T, and incomplete otherwise.

This can be confusing, but the terminology is standard. There is a connection between the two meanings of '(un)decidable' though, precisely Lemma 7.2.3: if an axiomatizable theory T is undecidable, then there must be a sentence which is undecidable in T.

[6]Recall that Definition 6.6.8 called T and T' of the same vocabulary *equivalent* if $Thm_T = Thm_{T'}$. For the notion of extension, one sometimes merely requires that L_T is a subset of $L_{T'}$, so that every L_T-sentence is an $L_{T'}$-sentence, but not necessarily vice versa. Most of what we say later about extensions of theories holds for this more general notion of extension, or is easily adapted to that notion.

7.2.2. Arithmetical theories and truth

For much of the remainder of this book we restrict attention to theories in the arithmetical vocabulary $L_{PA} = \{0,', +, \cdot\}$. As before, $\mathcal{N}$ is the *standard model* of *PA*, and $Th(\mathcal{N})$ is the set of L_{PA}-sentences true in $\mathcal{N}$.

An *arithmetical formula* is an L_{PA}-formula, an *arithmetical term* is an L_{PA}-term, and an *arithmetical theory* is a theory in the vocabulary L_{PA}. An L_{PA}-sentence is *true* if it is true in $\mathcal{N}$, and an arithmetical theory is *true* if all its axioms are true. $Th(\mathcal{N})$ is a true theory. But, as we have emphasized, it is one thing to know what it *means* for a sentence to be true, and quite another to *know* that it is in fact true. For the latter (unless the truth of the sentence is self-evident), we have to *derive* it from sentences (and so ultimately from axioms) that we know are true, by means of rules that preserve truth. For this to be feasible, a minimum requirement is that the theory used for deriving truths is axiomatizable, and we will soon see that $Th(\mathcal{N})$ is *not* axiomatizable. So we turn to axiomatized theories such as *PA*, whose axioms were specified in Chapter 6.6. *PA* turns out to be a very powerful theory—most of what is known in elementary number theory is provable in it. It might seem quite plausible that *PA*, or some axiomatized extension of *PA*, suffices to prove *all* arithmetical truths. That is why the question of its completeness is so significant.

7.2.3. The incompleteness theorems

The first incompleteness theorem, in the special case we are now considering, is as follows.[7]

Theorem 7.2.4 (First Incompleteness Theorem)
Every consistent axiomatizable extension of PA is incomplete.

This theorem has several significant consequences:

- $Th(\mathcal{N})$ is a consistent and complete extension of *PA*. So it follows that $Th(\mathcal{N})$ is *not* axiomatizable. And since axioms and theorems coincide in $Th(\mathcal{N})$, it also follows that $Th(\mathcal{N})$ is *undecidable*.

- Since every arithmetical sentence is either true or false (in $\mathcal{N}$), it follows that in every consistent axiomatizable extension T of *PA*, there is a *true* sentence which cannot be derived in T.

- *PA* is an axiomatizable theory. So, given that it is consistent, it is incomplete. But this isn't because we forgot some axiom. If new (true) axioms are added, then, as long as the set of axioms remains decidable, we obtain a consistent and axiomatizable extension of *PA*, which is again incomplete.

[7] As we will see, Gödel's version of the theorem was slightly weaker.

In a slogan, the first incompleteness theorem says that there is an unbridgeable gap between *truth* and *proof*.

A further important observation is the following. *PA* has infinitely many axioms, but an analysis of the proof of Theorem 7.2.4 reveals that the full strength of *PA* is not needed, indeed only finitely many of the axioms are used. In other words, there is a finitely axiomatizable subtheory of *PA* such that Theorem 7.2.4 holds when *PA* is replaced by that theory. A particularly simple example of a theory that suffices is *Robinson's Arithmetic*, usually called Q. This theory and its properties will be presented in Chapter 14.[8]

There are various ways to prove Theorem 7.2.4. One is to first show the following result (see Exercise 7.3.12).

Theorem 7.2.5
Every consistent extension of PA (indeed, of Q) is undecidable.

Here we do not require the theory to be axiomatizable, so, for example, $Th(\mathcal{N})$ is undecidable by this result. But *if* the theory is also axiomatizable, then it cannot be complete, by Theorem 7.2.5 together with Lemma 7.2.3. So Theorem 7.2.4 follows from Theorem 7.2.5.

This proof tells us that a sentence that can neither be proved nor disproved *exists*, but it doesn't provide us with an example. Gödel's method was instead to construct an undecidable sentence directly. The construction is interesting in itself, and easy to understand.

The basic idea comes from an analogy with the Liar Paradox: a sentence that says about itself that it is false. For example, in English:

(1) This sentence is false.

or

(2) Sentence (2) is false.

If (2) is true, then what it claims is correct, and thus it is false. But if (2) is false, then that is exactly what (2) says, so it is true. Paradox!

Gödel's idea is to construct a sentence saying not 'I am false', but 'I am not provable in T', where T is a consistent axiomatizable extension of *PA*. Let G be such a sentence. More precisely, suppose (a) that we can find an arithmetical formula $Pr_T(y)$ ('*Pr*' for 'provable') which

---

[8]As we noted, the incompleteness of *PA* is remarkable because *PA* is such a *strong* theory. The incompleteness of Q itself, on the other hand, is not at all remarkable, since Q is a very *weak* theory. It is easy to show that familiar laws of arithmetic, such as $\forall x \forall y(x + y = y + x)$, are not provable in Q (and neither are their negations). What is remarkable about Q is that Theorem 7.2.4 holds with Q instead of *PA*, which yields the incompleteness of all (consistent axiomatizable) extensions of Q, including *PA*.

in some reasonable sense expresses that y is (a name of) a sentence provable in T, and (b) that we are able to construct an arithmetical sentence G saying about itself that it is not provable in T, in the sense that

(3) $\quad PA \vdash G \leftrightarrow \neg Pr_T(\ulcorner G \urcorner)$

where $\ulcorner G \urcorner$ is a name of G.

That $Pr_T(y)$ 'expresses provability in T' should, as a minimum, entail the following, for any sentence φ:

(I) $\quad$ If $T \vdash \varphi$, then $T \vdash Pr_T(\ulcorner \varphi \urcorner)$.

Gödel noted that (under a certain assumption; see below), the converse holds too:

(II) $\quad$ If $T \vdash Pr_T(\ulcorner \varphi \urcorner)$, then $T \vdash \varphi$.

Now, *if* G were provable in T, that is, if $T \vdash G$, then $T \vdash Pr_T(\ulcorner G \urcorner)$ by (I). But (3) then implies that $T \vdash \neg G$, contradicting the assumption that T is consistent.

Hence, $T \nvdash G$. And since that is exactly what G says, G is a true sentence, and we have found a *true but unprovable* sentence.

Moreover, $\neg G$ is *false*, so if we if simply assume that T is true (proves only true sentences), it follows directly that $T \nvdash \neg G$, and so T is incomplete.

Instead of making this assumption, Gödel used the weaker (II). If $T \vdash \neg G$, then, again by (3), $T \vdash Pr_T(\ulcorner G \urcorner)$. Thus, by (II), $T \vdash G$, once again contradicting consistency. □

The *second* incompleteness theorem is about what it takes to show that *PA* and stronger theories are consistent. But isn't it clear that *PA* *is* consistent, since its axioms are true, hence its theorems are true, and no contradiction can be true? It is indeed clear, and the argument just made can be formalized, and the consistency of *PA* can be proved in set theory. More precisely, we can prove in set theory that *every theorem of PA is true in* $\mathcal{N}$, from which consistency follows immediately. But the crux is that this argument cannot be carried out in *PA*, since the concept of truth in $\mathcal{N}$ is not arithmetically definable. This fact, the *undefinability of truth*, is an easy consequence of the arithmetization and diagonalization techniques, known as Tarski's Theorem: Theorem 7.2.8 below. The proof is a direct translation of the Liar argument into the arithmetical language.

Gödel's second theorem doesn't make the detour via truth but concerns the syntactic notion of consistency. If T is an axiomatizable extension of *PA*, we can express the consistency of T using the formula $Pr_T(y)$ above: let Con_T be the sentence $\neg Pr_T(\ulcorner 0 \neq 0 \urcorner)$.

Theorem 7.2.6 (Second Incompleteness Theorem)
If T is a consistent axiomatizable extension of PA, then $T \nvdash Con_T$.

The proof idea of the second incompleteness theorem is also very simple; conceptually, it is an easy consequence of the proof of the first half of the first theorem, which established that if G is provable in T, then T is inconsistent. Now formalize this whole argument in *PA*. This should be possible, since the argument relies only on elementary reasoning that, via Gödel numbering, can be carried out with the tools available in *PA*. The result should then be:

$$PA \vdash Pr_T(\ulcorner G \urcorner) \rightarrow \neg Con_T$$

Then, using (3), we obtain

$$(4) \quad PA \vdash Con_T \rightarrow G$$

Since T is an extension of *PA*, we get $T \vdash Con_T \rightarrow G$. But this means that if Con_T is provable in T, so is G, which contradicts the first incompleteness theorem. Thus, $T \nvdash Con_T$. □

7.2.4. To do

We now have a fairly long to do-list, if we want to implement the previous informal arguments. First on the list is the coding of metalogical reasoning that the argument relies on.

Gödel numbering

We must effectively assign numbers to arithmetical terms, formulas, sentences, and proofs. Suppose this is done, and let

$$\#(u) = \text{the Gödel number of } u$$

Now properties and relations among syntactic objects become properties and relations among numbers. For example:

$var(n)$ iff n is the Gödel number of a variable

$fml(n)$ iff n is the Gödel number of an L_{PA}-formula

$ax_T(n)$ iff n is the Gödel number of an axiom in the theory T

$prf_T(m, n)$ iff m is the Gödel number of a proof in T of the sentence with Gödel number n

Representability

The next step is to show that all these properties and relations can be represented by arithmetical formulas, in the following precise sense. Recall that the *numeral* of the number n, written

$$\mathbf{n}$$

is the term

$$0^{\prime\prime\cdots\prime}$$

(with n occurrences of $'$). We say that a relation $R(n_1, \ldots, n_k)$ among numbers is *representable in T*, if there is an L_{PA}-formula $\psi(x_1, \ldots, x_k)$ such that

a. If $R(n_1, \ldots, n_k)$, then $T \vdash \psi(\mathbf{n}_1, \ldots, \mathbf{n}_k)$.

b. If not $R(n_1, \ldots, n_k)$, then $T \vdash \neg\psi(\mathbf{n}_1, \ldots, \mathbf{n}_k)$.

When this holds, we say that $\psi(x_1, \ldots, x_k)$ *represents* R in T.

We must show that all the metalogical properties and relations that we need are indeed representable in this sense in *PA*. This will be done by showing that they all are computable, in the precise sense of being *recursive*, in fact in most cases *primitive recursive*.

Recursive functions and relations

We start by defining the primitive recursive functions and relations, and then show that all of these are representable in *PA*. (This is what Gödel did in his 1931 proof.) In fact, we first define the primitive recursive *functions*, and then extend this to *relations* by saying that a relation R is primitive recursive if its *characteristic function* c_R is primitive recursive, where c_R is defined as follows:

$$(5) \qquad c_R(n_1, \ldots, n_k) = \begin{cases} 1 & \text{if } R(n_1, \ldots, n_k) \\ 0 & \text{if not } R(n_1, \ldots, n_k) \end{cases}$$

We will see that if ax_T is primitive recursive, so is the relation prf_T, and hence this relation is representable in *PA*, which is precisely what we need for the incompleteness theorems.

Since there are effectively computable functions that are not primitive recursive (we will give examples), this does not yet give us Theorem 7.2.4, which talks about *axiomatizable* extensions of *PA*, and thus extensions T such that ax_T is effectively computable. To get there we have to do more work: define the *recursive* functions and relations and show that these are the same as the *Turing computable* functions. Then Church-Turing's Thesis makes sense, and we can identify the effectively computable functions and relations with the recursive functions and relations, and show that all of these are representable in *PA*.

Self reference

A final step remains in order to prove incompleteness. With the methods just described we can easily find an arithmetical sentence saying that a certain sentence is provable, or not provable, in T. But how can we find a sentence saying something about *itself*? It turns out that that this can always be done, in the following precise sense:

Lemma 7.2.7 (Self Reference or Diagonal Lemma)
For every L_{PA}-formula $\psi(y)$ with the single free variable y, there is a sentence φ such that

$$PA \vdash \varphi \leftrightarrow \psi(\ulcorner\varphi\urcorner)$$

This may look like magic, but the simple proof is given in Chapter 12.1. Now, if $Prf_T(x, y)$ is a formula representing the relation prf_T in *PA*, let $\psi(y)$ be the formula

$$\neg\exists x Prf_T(x, y)$$

which says that the sentence (with Gödel number) y is not provable in T.[9] Then, by the Diagonal Lemma, there is a sentence, G say, such that

(6) $\quad PA \vdash G \leftrightarrow \neg\exists x Prf_T(x, \ulcorner G\urcorner)$

Now the reasoning in the first half of the informal proof above of Theorem 7.2.4 goes through. Suppose $T \vdash G$. Then there is a proof of G in T, say with Gödel number m, so if $\#(G)$ is the Gödel number of G, we have that $prf_T(m, \#(G))$ holds. Since the relation prf_T is representable in *PA*, it follows that $PA \vdash Prf_T(\mathrm{m}, \ulcorner G\urcorner)$, where $\ulcorner G\urcorner$ is the numeral of $\#(G)$. By ordinary logic, this means that $PA \vdash \exists x Prf_T(x, \ulcorner G\urcorner)$, and hence, by (6),

$$PA \vdash \neg G$$

But T is an extension of *PA*, so $T \vdash \neg G$, which means that T is inconsistent, contrary to assumption. Thus, $T \nvdash G$.

What about the claim that $T \nvdash \neg G$? Here Gödel had to use a slightly stronger notion than consistency, so-called ω-consistency. This implies principle (II) from Section 7.2.3 above:

(II) $\quad$ If $T \vdash \exists x Prf_T(x, \ulcorner\varphi\urcorner)$, then $T \vdash \varphi$.

As we saw there, this immediately yields that $T \nvdash \neg G$. In 1936, J. Barkley Rosser showed that if one uses a more complex self-referential sentence (now called a *Rosser sentence*), consistency is sufficient for the whole argument to go through, as we will see in Chapter 12.3.

Tarski's theorem on the undefinability of truth

An almost immediate application of the Diagonal Lemma is Tarski's observation that there can be no truth definition in the arithmetical

[9] So $\exists x Prf_T(x, y)$ is the formula we called $Pr_T(y)$ in the informal argument earlier.

language. Here, a *truth definition in T* is a formula $Tr(y)$ with one free variable such that for every arithmetical sentence φ,

(7) $\quad T \vdash \varphi \leftrightarrow Tr(\ulcorner\varphi\urcorner)$

Theorem 7.2.8 (Tarski's Theorem)
If T is a consistent extension of PA (indeed of Q), there is no truth definition in T.

Proof. Suppose $Tr(y)$ is a truth definition in T. The Diagonal Lemma applied to the formula $\neg Tr(x)$ yields a sentence ψ such that

$$PA \vdash \psi \leftrightarrow \neg Tr(\ulcorner\psi\urcorner)$$

(Compare the Liar Paradox!) But together with (7) for $\varphi = \psi$, this leads to a contradiction in T. □

Note that this result holds for all consistent extensions of T, in particular of $Th(\mathcal{N})$. So even with all true arithmetical sentences at our disposal, no arithmetical formula can define arithmetical truth.

The Truth Teller and Löb's Theorem

Once you see the proof of Gödel's first theorem it is natural to ask: What about a sentence C that says of itself that it *is* provable in T?

$$T \vdash C \leftrightarrow \exists x Prf_T(x, \ulcorner C\urcorner)$$

C exists by the Diagonal Lemma. Compare the *Truth Teller*:

(8) $\quad$ This sentence is true.

(8) is not paradoxical, but we have no obvious way of assigning it a truth value. C is the analogous sentence about provability, and here too we seem to have no intuitions about whether it is true or false. But C is an arithmetical sentence, so it must be either true or false in $\mathcal{N}$. Here is a surprising fact, which was proved by Martin Löb using an analogy to another paradox (Curry's paradox; see Exercise 7.3.5 for the paradox and Chapter 12.5 for the proof).

Theorem 7.2.9 (Löb's Theorem)
If T is a consistent and axiomatizable extension of PA, and ψ is a sentence such that $T \vdash \exists x Prf_T(x, \ulcorner\psi\urcorner) \rightarrow \psi$, then $T \vdash \psi$.

It follows that C is a theorem in T! But the theorem also says something more interesting. Intuitively, $\exists x Prf_T(x, \ulcorner\psi\urcorner) \rightarrow \psi$ expresses that T is *correct*: if a sentence ψ is provable then ψ is true. It may seem reasonable that T could prove its own correctness, in the sense that

(9) $T \vdash \exists x Prf_T(x, \ulcorner\psi\urcorner) \to \psi$

would hold for all sentences ψ. But Löb's Theorem says that this only holds for sentences ψ which are already provable in T. It follows that no consistent theory of this kind can prove its own correctness.

Undecidability of first-order logic

Using Theorem 7.2.5, one can give a proof that first-order logic is undecidable. Consider first-order logic in the arithmetical vocabulary, FOL_{PA}. So in FOL_{PA}, considered as a theory, only the logical truths in the vocabulary L_{PA} are theorems.

Theorem 7.2.10
FOL_{PA} is undecidable.

Proof. By Theorem 7.2.5, the theory Q is undecidable. Let θ_Q be the conjunction of the (finitely many) axioms of Q. Then we have, for every arithmetical sentence φ,

$$Q \vdash \varphi \text{ iff } \theta_Q \vdash \varphi \text{ iff } FOL_{PA} \vdash \theta_Q \to \varphi$$

Now if there were an effective method for deciding FOL_{PA}, we could use it to decide Q: for any arithmetical sentence φ, just check if $\theta_Q \to \varphi$ is logically true. But since Q is undecidable, there is no such method. □

This is for first-order logic in the arithmetical vocabulary. But the result extends to first-order logic in almost any vocabulary; see Chapter 14.3.

This concludes our tour of the main ideas and results related to Gödel's incompleteness theorems and their proofs.

7.3. Exercises to Chapter 7

Exercise 7.3.1

1. Explain why a set of sentences Γ is satisfiable iff, for some sentence φ, we have $\Gamma \not\models \varphi$.
2. Explain why $Th(\mathcal{N})$ (a) is complete; (b) has no finite models.

Exercise 7.3.2
The Liar paradox was stated explicitly by Eubulides (4th century BC). It is sometimes confused with the so-called Epimenedes' paradox, which goes as follows: Epimenedes, who is Cretan (i.e. from the isle of Crete) said: "All Cretans are liars". Explain why Epimenedes' statement is *not* paradoxical.

Exercise 7.3.3
Formulate a paradoxical *pair* of sentences, such that each sentence says something about the truth or falsity of the *other* sentence.

Exercise 7.3.4 (Extended Liar)
About the Liar Paradox: couldn't it be the case that (2) in Section 7.2.3 is *neither true nor false*? Suppose we allow this third possibility: a sentence can be *true*, *false*, or *undefined*. Then consider sentence (10).

(10) Sentence (10) is not true.

Show that (10) also leads to paradox (the so-called *Extended Liar*), even though a third 'truth value' is allowed.

Exercise 7.3.5 (Curry's paradox)
Let φ be the sentence "The Moon is made of cheese" (or "2+2=5", or any other sentence). Suppose we have a sentence saying "If I am true, then φ". That is:

(11) $(11) \rightarrow \varphi$

Give an informal argument, starting from (11), that φ must be true, i.e. that the Moon is made of cheese.

Exercise 7.3.6 (a Russell variant of Curry's paradox)
This variant of Curry's paradox (due to George Boolos) shows its affinity with Russell's paradox. Define the set A as follows: $A = \{x :$ if $x \in x$ then $\varphi\}$ (where φ is any sentence, for example, "The Moon is made of cheese"). Argue informally that φ must be true.

Exercise 7.3.7 (Yablo's paradox)
Consider a list of sentences $\varphi_0, \varphi_1, \varphi_2, \ldots$ saying the following:

(φ_0) φ_i is false for $i > 0$.

(φ_1) φ_i is false for $i > 1$.

$\vdots$

(φ_n) φ_i is false for $i > n$.

$\vdots$

Note that none of these sentences refers to itself, only to sentences further down the list. Show that this situation nevertheless leads to paradox.

Exercise 7.3.8
Give an example of a consistent and axiomatizable extension of *PA* in which some false sentence is a theorem. [Hint: Use the proof of the first Incompleteness Theorem.]

Exercise 7.3.9

The *graph* of a k-ary function f is the $(k{+}1)$-ary relation G_f defined by

$$G_f(n_1, \dots, n_k, m) \Leftrightarrow f(n_1, \dots, n_k) = m$$

Let T be a consistent extension of *PA*. Show that a relation R is representable in T if and only if the graph of its characteristic function c_R is representable in T. [Thus, if some formula represents R in T, find a formula that represents G_{c_R} in T, and vice versa.]

Exercise 7.3.10

1. Show that Löb's Theorem implies the second incompleteness theorem (Theorem 7.2.6).

2. Show that if

   $$T \vdash \exists x Prf_T(x, \ulcorner\psi\urcorner) \rightarrow \psi$$

   holds for all sentences ψ, then $T \vdash Con_T$.

Exercise 7.3.11

Write (as we will do later) $T + \varphi$ for the theory $T \cup \{\varphi\}$. Suppose we have established that if T is a consistent and axiomatizable extension of *PA*, then for all sentences φ,

(a) $\quad PA \vdash \neg\exists x Prf_T(x, \ulcorner\varphi\urcorner) \rightarrow Con_{T+\neg\varphi}$

Note that this is a formalization of one direction of the familiar fact that $T \vdash \varphi$ iff $T \cup \{\neg\varphi\}$ is inconsistent, and we will in fact prove this formalization later; see Chapter 12.6. Show that Theorem 7.2.6 in combination with (a) yields Löb's Theorem.

Exercise 7.3.12

1. Show that if T is a consistent extension of *PA*, then the set thm_T is not representable in T. [Hint: Use the Diagonal Lemma, similarly to the proof of Theorem 7.2.8.]

2. Use this, and the fact (to be shown later) that all decidable relations are representable in *PA*, to prove Theorem 7.2.5.

8 Primitive recursive functions and relations

The first step on the way to showing that metalogical properties and relations are representable, via coding, in *PA*, is to identify the class of primitive recursive functions and relations. That is the topic of the present chapter.

The main feature of this class of functions is that it is closed under defining functions by induction, here called *primitive recursion*. Specifying the class is a part of elementary number theory. It necessarily involves some detailed work, not all of which is necessary in order to grasp the main picture. With some experience from typical examples, one can learn to 'see' that a certain function is primitive recursive, without relying on a detailed proof of this fact. Accordingly, much detail may be skipped or skimmed on a first reading.

A note about notation: in this chapter I use $x, y, z, \ldots$ as variables over natural numbers, when they occur as arguments of primitive recursive functions. We are not concerned here with formal theories expressed in a first-order language, but with an informal presentation using standard mathematical notation. The relation between our work here and first-order theories such as *PA* will be spelled out in the following chapters.

8.1. Basic functions

All functions discussed here take arguments and values in the set $\mathbb{N} = \{0, 1, 2, \ldots\}$ of natural numbers. The primitive recursive functions are specified by first declaring some basic functions to be primitive recursive, and then obtaining the rest by composition and primitive recursion. One possibility would be to take addition and multiplication as basic, but it is of some interest that certain even simpler functions suffice. Once the class of primitive recursive functions is defined, a relation R is said to be primitive recursive if its characteristic function c_R (see (5) in the previous chapter) is primitive recursive.

Definition 8.1.1 (basic functions)

1. The *zero* function Z, defined by

   $$Z(x) = 0$$

   for all natural numbers x. (Phrases like "for all natural numbers x" will be implicit in what follows.)

2. The *successor* function s, defined by

   $$s(x) = x + 1$$

3. The *identity* functions id_i^n, for $n \geqslant 1$ and $1 \leqslant i \leqslant n$, defined by

   $$id_i^n(x_1, \ldots, x_i, \ldots, x_n) = x_i$$

Z and s are unary functions, whereas id_i^n is n-ary. The identity functions (note that there is an infinite number of them) are also called *projection functions*. For example:

$$id_1^1(x) = x$$
$$id_1^2(x, y) = x, \quad id_2^2(x, y) = y$$
$$id_2^3(x, y, z) = y$$

8.2. Composition

Composition is a standard way of forming new functions from given ones. If, for example,

$$f(x, y, z) = x + y + z$$

then we may define the function h by

(1) $$h(x, y) = f(x, s(y), id_2^2(x, y)) = x + s(y) + id_2^2(x, y) = x + 2y + 1$$

Here we have replaced y by $s(y)$ and z by $id_2^2(x, y)$, and then calculated the result. The general format for composition is as follows:[1]

Definition 8.2.1 (function composition)
If f is an m-ary function and $g_1, \ldots, g_m$ are n-ary functions, define an n-ary function h by

(Cn) $h(x_1, \ldots, x_n) = f(g_1(x_1, \ldots, x_n), \ldots, g_m(x_1, \ldots, x_n))$

We also introduce an official *name* of h:

[1]Function composition is often seen as a binary operation on functions: if f and g are functions from $\mathbb{N}$ to $\mathbb{N}$, then $f \circ g$ is the function defined by $f \circ g(x) = f(g(x))$; see Chapter 16.2. This is a special case of the more general notion of function composition defined here.

$$h = \text{Cn}[f, g_1, \ldots, g_m]$$

In (Cn), all arguments of f are replaced by functions, whereas in (1), x was not replaced. And y was replaced by a unary function, while z was replaced by a binary function. But (1) is still an instance of (Cn), since we can let $g_1(x, y)$ be $id^2_1(x, y)$, while $g_2(x, y) = id^2_2(x, s(y))$, and $g_3(x, y) = id^2_2(x, y)$.

g_2 too is obtained by composition. In order to see that its definition follows the scheme (Cn), define $s_1(x, y) = s(id^2_2(x, y)) = s(y)$. Then:

$$g_2(x, y) = id^2_2(id^2_1(x, y), s_1(x, y)) = id^2_2(x, s(y)) = s(y)$$

So s_1 is defined by composition of s with id^2_2, and then g_2 is defined by composition of id^2_2 with id^2_1 and s_1. Using the official names of these functions:

$$\begin{aligned} s_1 &= \text{Cn}[s, id^2_2] \\ g_2 &= \text{Cn}[id^2_2, id^2_1, s_1] = \text{Cn}[id^2_2, id^2_1, \text{Cn}[s, id^2_2]] \end{aligned}$$

Then the whole description of how the function h in (1) is obtained from the function f and basic functions by repeated use of the composition scheme (Cn) is explicit in the expression

(2) $\quad h = \text{Cn}[f, id^2_1, \text{Cn}[id^2_2, id^2_1, \text{Cn}[s, id^2_2]], id^2_2]$

We call the right-hand side of (2) a *function description* of h. It specifies exactly how h was formed, given f and certain basic functions.

WARNING: Function descriptions are not for practical use! When the defined functions are complex, descriptions quickly become unreadable. For practical purposes we *always* use the standard notation, as in (1). The use of function descriptions are a bit like the use of formal derivations in the system H: to establish that a sentence is derivable from certain axioms we use lemmas, previously derived facts, knowledge about what one can do in H, etc.—we almost never write down the actual derivation, which might consist of hundreds of sentences. We establish that a derivation *exists*, without having to write it down. Similarly, when a function is defined from functions already defined from functions ... defined from basic functions, using composition and primitive recursion (below), we know that a function description *exists*, explicitly stating each step in the definition.

This knowledge can be useful, not for establishing that some particular function is primitive recursive, but when we want to make general statements about *all* primitive recursive functions. One example is given in Exercise 8.9.29.

In the general format for composition in Definition 8.2.1, all the 'replacing' functions must have the same arity, and every argument of f

must be replaced. But this can always be achieved using the identity functions. In particular, an n-ary function can also be considered as an m-ary function for $m > n$, just as we above considered the successor function s as the binary function s_1. But there is a point in having one general format that covers all cases.

Starting from the basic functions, not many interesting functions can be defined by composition. But we can at least get the *constant functions*. Z is the constant function 0, and

$$h(x) = s(Z(x)) = \mathrm{Cn}[s, Z](x) = 0 + 1 = 1$$

is the constant function 1. In general, if $const_n$ is the constant function n, we define:

(3) a. $const_0 = Z$
b. $const_{n+1} = \mathrm{Cn}[s, const_n]$

These are infinitely many functions: one for each n. Can't we make n an argument too, and thus have just one binary function:

(4) $const_x(y) = x$

for all x, y? Yes, but for that we need the scheme of primitive recursion.

8.3. Primitive recursion

The operation that allows one to define a great number of interesting functions is *definition by induction*, here called primitive recursion. A typical example is *addition*. In this definition and below we use $'$ instead of s for the successor function, i.e.

$$x' = s(x)$$

just to increase readabilty. And for binary functions we often use the usual infix notation: $x + y$ instead of $+(x, y)$. Thus:

$$(5)\quad \begin{cases} x + 0 &= x \\ x + y' &= (x + y)' \end{cases}$$

This is recursion (induction) over y. First we specify the value for $y = 0$ (x fixed). Then, *given* that $x + y$ is defined, we specify the value of $x+y'$. Now we can *compute* +. For any numbers x, y we can calculate the sum $x + y$ in a finite number of steps, by successively computing $x + 0, x + 1, x + 2, \ldots, x + (y - 1), x + y$, according to (5).

(5) defines addition from basic functions using primitive recursion and composition. Schematically, the definition has the form

$$(6) \quad \begin{cases} h(x,0) &= f(x) \\ h(x,y') &= g(x,y,h(x,y)) \end{cases}$$

Thus, in (5), $f(x) = id_1^1(x)$ and $g(x,y,z) = z'$. We write

$$h = \text{Pr}[f,g]$$

This gives us function descriptions —that is, names— of functions defined by primitive recursion. As an example, let us give the function description for addition as defined above. $f = id_1^1$ is a basic function. g can be obtained by composition from basic functions as follows:

$$g(x,y,z) = s(z) = s(id_3^3(x,y,z)) = \text{Cn}[s, id_3^3](x,y,z)$$

and thus,

$$x + y = \text{Pr}[id_1^1, \text{Cn}[s, id_3^3]](x,y)$$

or simply,

$$(7) \quad + = \text{Pr}[id_1^1, \text{Cn}[s, id_3^3]]$$

Now we can define *multiplication* and *exponentiation* by primitive recursion:

$$(8) \quad \begin{cases} x \cdot 0 &= 0 \\ x \cdot y' &= x \cdot y + x \end{cases}$$

$$(9) \quad \begin{cases} x^0 &= 1 \\ x^{y'} &= x^y \cdot x \end{cases}$$

To write (8) in the format (6), let

$$g(x,y,z) = z + x = id_3^3(x,y,z) + id_1^3(x,y,z) = \text{Cn}[+, id_3^3, id_1^3](x,y,z)$$

Then:

$$(10) \quad x \cdot y = \text{Pr}[Z, \text{Cn}[+, id_3^3, id_1^3]](x,y)$$

So if we replace + in (10) by the function description (7), we obtain a full description of how the multiplication function can be obtained:

$$\cdot \; = \text{Pr}[Z, \text{Cn}[\text{Pr}[id_1^1, \text{Cn}[s, id_3^3]], id_3^3, id_1^3]]$$

But from now on we heed the warning above, and will *not* write down official function descriptions anymore! Instead, we use standard notation as in (5), (8), and (9). Here is the official format for primitive recursion:

Definition 8.3.1 (primitive recursion)
Let f be an n-ary function (including the case $n = 0$; then f is a constant, i.e. a number), and g an $(n+2)$-ary function. The $(n+1)$-ary function h is defined by *primitive recursion* from f and g if

$$\begin{cases} h(x_1, \ldots, x_n, 0) & = & f(x_1, \ldots, x_n) \\ h(x_1, \ldots, x_n, y') & = & g(x_1, \ldots, x_n, y, h(x_1, \ldots, x_n, y)) \end{cases} \tag{11}$$

Officially:

$$h = \mathrm{Pr}[f, g]$$

Now we can define the class of primitive recursive functions and relations. Recall that the *characteristic function* of an n-ary relation R among natural numbers is the n-ary function c_R defined by

$$c_R(x_1, \ldots, x_n) = \begin{cases} 1 & \text{if } R(x_1, \ldots, x_n) \\ 0 & \text{if not } R(x_1, \ldots, x_n) \end{cases}$$

Definition 8.3.2 (primitive recursive functions and relations)

1. An n-ary number-theoretic function is *primitive recursive* if it can be obtained from the basic functions with a finite number of applications of composition and primitive recursion.

   Equivalently, it is primitive recursive if it has a *primitive recursive function description*, i.e. a function description containing only names of basic functions, Cn[...], and Pr[...].[2]

2. An n-ary relation R between numbers is *primitive recursive* if its characteristic function c_R is primitive recursive.

We shall use several specific primitive recursive functions and relations in what follows, and the rest of the chapter is concerned with defining them. First, however, a digression.

8.4. *(Incredibly) fast growing functions

(8) and (9) show a pattern that can be iterated. To see this it is convenient to write exponentiation in a linear notation: $x^y = x \uparrow y$. Then (9) becomes

[2]The definition in terms of function descriptions is still informal, since we haven't really specified exactly how these are formed. Also, we haven't separated in the notation a function *description* from the function it denotes. See Exercise 8.9.2 for a formally correct version.

$$(12)\qquad \begin{cases} x \uparrow 0 &= 1 \\ x \uparrow y' &= x \cdot (x \uparrow y) \end{cases}$$

Next, we define *superexponentiation*, $x \Uparrow y$, in the analogous way:

$$(13)\qquad \begin{cases} x \Uparrow 0 &= 1 \\ x \Uparrow y' &= x \uparrow (x \Uparrow y) \end{cases}$$

Thus,

$$(14)\qquad x \Uparrow y = x^{x^{\cdot^{\cdot^{\cdot^{x}}}}} \qquad \text{(with } y \text{ stacked } x\text{'s)}$$

which means that $\Uparrow$ is a function that grows quite fast. For example:

$$\begin{aligned} &3 \cdot 3 = 9 \\ &3 \uparrow 3 = 3^3 = 27 \\ &3 \Uparrow 3 = 3^{3^3} = 3^{27} = 7.625.597.484.987 \end{aligned}$$

We can go on in the same way! Instead of using up-arrows with more and more vertical lines, we introduce the following notation (originating with Donald Knuth):

$$(15)\qquad \begin{cases} x \uparrow_0 y &= x \cdot y \\ x \uparrow_1 y &= x^y \\ x \uparrow_{n+1} 0 &= 1 \\ x \uparrow_{n+1} y' &= x \uparrow_n (x \uparrow_{n+1} y) \end{cases}$$

By induction, we see that all of the functions $\uparrow_n$ are primitive recursive. $\uparrow_3$ grows *much faster* than $\uparrow_2$, i.e. than $\Uparrow$. Already $3 \uparrow_3 3$ is a very large number: as in (14), with a stack of 7625597484987 3:s!

The larger these numbers get, the harder it is to find some perspicuous notation for them. For $\uparrow_3$ one can use so-called *tetration*: write (14) as ${}^{y}x$, i.e.

$${}^{y}x = x \uparrow_2 y$$

with stacks to the left, so that, for example, ${}^{3}3 = 7625597484987$, and

$${}^{({}^{3}3)}3 = 3 \uparrow_3 3$$

In the same way:

$$\begin{aligned} &{}^{1}4 = 4 \\ &{}^{2}4 = 4^4 = 256 \\ &{}^{3}4 = 4^{(4^4)} = 4^{256} \\ &{}^{4}4 = 4^{(4^{(4^4)})} = 4^{(4^{256})} \end{aligned}$$

At this point, a natural next step is to let n be a third argument to the function. Define:

(16) $\alpha(x, y, z) = x \uparrow_z y$

α is *computable*: given x, y, z we can, by successively applying the primitive recursive functions $\uparrow_0, \uparrow_1, \ldots, \uparrow_{z-1}$, compute $\alpha(x, y, z)$. This computation that can hardly be carried out in practice, since $\alpha(x, y, z)$ even with small values of x, y, z is an inconceivably large number, but in principle we know how to do it. So is α also primitive recursive?

The answer is No: one can show that α (which is a variant of the so-called Ackermann function) is *not* primitive recursive. Here is an informal argument. A primitive recursive function has a primitive recursive function description, containing a *fixed* number of applications of primitive recursion, i.e. of occurrences of Pr[...]. But the number of applications of primitive recursion needed to calculate $\alpha(x, y, z)$ *depends on* z (indeed, z applications are needed). So no finite primitive recursive function description manages to describe this calculation.

Of course this is not a proof (we haven't shown that some other function description cannot do the job), and we shall not enter into a detailed argument. The idea is to show that the function $\alpha_0(x) = \alpha(x, x, x)$ *grows faster* than any unary primitive recursive function. Then α_0 cannot be primitive recursive, and hence neither can α. The result shows that the primitive recursive functions do not exhaust the computable functions. Interestingly, *that* is something one can rather easily give a strict proof of, with a method that involves so-called *diagonalization* rather than fast growing functions; see Exercise 8.9.29. As we have already hinted (Lemma 7.2.7), diagonalization is a major trick in logic and in computability theory.

8.5. Examples of primitive recursive functions and relations

We now give several examples of primitive recursive functions and relations that we will need, as well as useful methods for showing that a function or relation is primitive recursive.

(17) The function $x! = 1 \cdot 2 \cdot 3 \cdot \ldots \cdot x$ is primitive recursive.

$x!$ is read "x-factorial". (17) defines this function, but not in a way that allows us to immediately see that it is primitive recursive. This is due to the occurrence of ... in (17), which has no place in a primitive recursive function description. But we can give an alternative definition:

$$\begin{cases} 0! & = & 1 \\ (y')! & = & y! \cdot y' \end{cases}$$

This is a definition of the *same* function by primitive recursion (the case $n = 0$ in Definition 8.3.1) in terms of multiplication and the successor function, which we already know are primitive recursive. Next:

(18) If f is primitive recursive, then so is

$$h(x, y) = \sum_{i=0}^{y} f(x, i) = f(x, 0) + \ldots + f(x, y)$$

Again, this definition doesn't show directly that h is primitive recursive, but we can give an equivalent definition of h as follows:

$$(19) \quad \begin{cases} h(x, 0) & = & f(x, 0) \\ h(x, y') & = & h(x, y) + f(x, y') \end{cases}$$

Now it is clear, first, that (19) really is an alternative definition of h in (18), and, second, that it can be written in the general format for primitive recursion ((11) in Definition 8.3.1). The latter means that there is a 3-ary primitive recursive function g such that $h(x, y) + f(x, y') = g(x, y, h(x, y))$; in other words that the function $g(x, y, z) = z + f(x, y')$ is primitive recursive (given that f is), which in turn follows from the fact that it can be obtained by composition from identity functions, addition, s, and f.

In a similar way we see that (20) holds.

(20) If f is primitive recursive, then so is

$$p(x, y) = \prod_{i=0}^{y} f(x, i) = f(x, 0) \cdot \ldots \cdot f(x, y)$$

From now on we will use definitions of the type (19) without explaining in detail how they can be written in the standard format (11). However, we state as a lemma the fact that given a primitive recursive function, one can switch the order of variables, identify variables, and remove variables; the result is still primitive recursive:

Lemma 8.5.1
Let f be a k-ary primitive recursive function, and let $x_1, \ldots, x_n$ be distinct variables. Choose variables $y_1, \ldots, y_k$ among $x_1, \ldots, x_n$ (the same variable may be chosen several times). Then the function

$$g(x_1, \ldots, x_n) = f(y_1, \ldots, y_k)$$

is primitive recursive.

Proof. Suppose $y_i = x_{m_i}$ for $1 \leqslant i \leqslant k$, so $y_i = id^n_{m_i}(x_1, \ldots, x_n)$. Then:

$$g(x_1, \ldots, x_n) = f(id^n_{m_1}(x_1, \ldots, x_n), \ldots, id^n_{m_k}(x_1, \ldots, x_n))$$

that is, $g = \text{Cn}[f, id^n_{m_1}, \ldots, id^n_{m_k}]$. □

For example, if $f(x_1, x_2, x_3)$ is primitive recursive, the following functions are also primitive recursive:

$$g_1(x_1, x_2, x_3) = f(x_3, x_2, x_1) \quad \text{(permutation of variables)}$$
$$g_2(x_1, x_2) = f(x_1, x_2, x_1) \quad \text{(identification of variables)}$$
$$g_3(x_1, x_2, x_3, x_4) = f(x_1, x_2, x_3) \quad \text{('dummy'-variables)}$$

8.5.1. Predecessors, subtraction, sign functions, etc.

Here is a list of further primitive recursive functions and relations: first a direct definition, then a reformulated definition showing—as the reader can check—it is primitive recursive.

(21) $$\mathit{pred}(x) = \begin{cases} x - 1 & \text{if } x > 0 \\ 0 & \text{if } x = 0 \end{cases}$$

$$\begin{cases} \mathit{pred}(0) & = & 0 \\ \mathit{pred}(x') & = & x \end{cases}$$

(22) $$x \dot{-} y = \begin{cases} x - y & \text{if } x \geqslant y \\ 0 & \text{if } x < y \end{cases}$$

$$\begin{cases} x \dot{-} 0 & = & x \\ x \dot{-} y' & = & \mathit{pred}(x \dot{-} y) \end{cases}$$

(23) $$|x - y| = \begin{cases} x - y & \text{if } x \geqslant y \\ y - x & \text{if } x < y \end{cases}$$

$$|x - y| = (x \dot{-} y) + (y \dot{-} x)$$

(24) $$sg(x) = \begin{cases} 0 & \text{if } x = 0 \\ 1 & \text{if } x > 0 \end{cases}$$

$$\begin{cases} sg(0) & = & 0 \\ sg(x') & = & 1 \end{cases}$$

(25) $\overline{sg}(x) = \begin{cases} 1 & \text{if } x = 0 \\ 0 & \text{if } x > 0 \end{cases}$

$$\overline{sg}(x) = 1 \dot{-} sg(x)$$

(26) $x = y$

$$c_{=}(x, y) = \overline{sg}(|x - y|)$$

(The characteristic function of = is primitive recursive.)

(27) $x < y$

$$c_{<}(x, y) = sg(y \dot{-} x)$$

8.5.2. Booleans, bounded quantification and μ-operator, definition by cases

Negation, conjunction, etc. of (n-ary) relations are defined as usual. We also introduce *bounded* variants of universal and existential quantification:

(28) $\exists y_{y<z} R(x_1, \ldots, x_n, y)$ iff there is $y < z$ s.t. $R(x_1, \ldots, x_n, y)$

That is: if R is $(n+1)$-ary, we define a new $(n+1)$-ary relation S by

$$S(x_1, \ldots, x_n, z) \Leftrightarrow \exists y (y < z \wedge R(x_1, \ldots, x_n, y))$$

Similarly for bounded universal quantification:

(29) $\forall y_{y<z} R(x_1, \ldots, x_n, y) \Leftrightarrow \forall y (y < z \rightarrow R(x_1, \ldots, x_n, y))$

Another very useful operator is the *bounded μ-operator*: given an $(n+1)$-ary function f, define (writing $\overline{x}$ instead $x_1, \ldots, x_n$):

(30) $\mu\, y_{y<z}(f(\overline{x}, y) = 0) = \begin{cases} \text{the smallest } y < z \text{ s.t. } f(\overline{x}, y) = 0 \\ \qquad\qquad \text{if there is such a } y \\ z \qquad\quad \text{otherwise} \end{cases}$

So $\mu\, y_{y<z}(f(\overline{x}, y) = 0)$ is a function $g(\overline{x}, z)$ which finds the smallest $y < z$ for which $f(\overline{x}, y) = 0$, if there is such a number; otherwise it returns z. We can also use the bounded μ-operator with relations:

(31) $\mu\, y_{y<z}\, R(\overline{x}, y)$

is the smallest $y < z$ for which $R(\overline{x}, y)$ holds, if there is such a number; otherwise z. In fact, this is a special case of (30):

(32) $\mu\, y_{y<z}\, R(\overline{x}, y) = \mu\, y_{y<z}\, (\overline{sg}(c_R(\overline{x}, y)) = 0)$

Finally, a very common way to define functions is *definition by cases*:

$$(33)\qquad f(\overline{x}) = \begin{cases} g_1(\overline{x}) & \text{if} \quad S_1(\overline{x}) \\ \cdot & \\ \cdot & \\ g_k(\overline{x}) & \text{if} \quad S_k(\overline{x}) \end{cases}$$

Here $g_1, \ldots, g_k$ are given functions, and $S_1, \ldots, S_k$ are given relations with the property that for every sequence $\overline{x}$ of numbers, *exactly one* of the conditions $S_1(\overline{x}), \ldots, S_k(\overline{x})$ is satisfied.

Lemma 8.5.2
A relation or function defined from primitive recursive functions and relations using boolean operations, bounded μ-operator, bounded quantification, or definition by cases, is primitive recursive.

Proof. For boolean operations we have

$$c_{\neg R}(\overline{x}) = 1 \dot{-} c_R(\overline{x})$$
$$c_{R_1 \wedge R_2}(\overline{x}) = c_{R_1}(\overline{x}) \cdot c_{R_2}(\overline{x})$$

Other boolean operations can be treated as defined in terms of $\neg$ and $\wedge$. Next, if $g(\overline{x}, z) = \mu\, y_{y<z}(f(\overline{x}, y) = 0)$, a little thought verifies that

$$(34)\qquad \begin{cases} g(\overline{x}, 0) & = & 0 \\ g(\overline{x}, z') & = & g(\overline{x}, z) + sg(f(\overline{x}, g(\overline{x}, z))) \end{cases}$$

This shows that the bounded μ-operator applied to a primitive recursive function yields a new primitive recursive function. According to (32), the same holds for $\mu\, y_{y<z}\, R(\overline{x}, y)$. For bounded existential quantification we observe:

$$(35)\qquad \exists y_{y<z}\, R(\overline{x}, y) \ \text{iff} \ \mu\, y_{y<z}\, R(\overline{x}, y) < z$$

(35) shows that we can define the relation $\exists y_{y<z}\, R(\overline{x}, y)$ by *substitution* of a primitive recursive function (here, the function $\mu\, y_{y<z}\, R(\overline{x}, y)$) in a primitive recursive relation (here, the relation $u < z$). That such substitution always leads to a new primitive recursive relation is seen as follows: if S is a k-ary relation and $f_1, \ldots, f_k$ are n-ary functions, and the relation R is defined by

$$R(\overline{x}) \Leftrightarrow S(f_1(\overline{x}), \ldots, f_k(\overline{x}))$$

then we have

$$c_R = \mathrm{Cn}[c_S, f_1, \ldots, f_k] \quad (\text{i.e. } c_R(\overline{x}) = c_S(f_1(\overline{x}), \ldots, f_k(\overline{x})))$$

For bounded universal quantification, the claim follows by

$$\forall y_{y<z} R(\overline{x}, y) \Leftrightarrow \neg\exists y_{y<z} \neg R(\overline{x}, y)$$

Finally, suppose f is defined by cases as in (33). Then:

$$f(\overline{x}) = g_1(\overline{x}) \cdot c_{S_1}(\overline{x}) + \ldots + g_k(\overline{x}) \cdot c_{S_k}(\overline{x})$$

This proves the lemma. □

In (28) the bound is strict, but the non-strict case works as well:

(36) $\exists y_{y \leqslant z} R(\overline{x}, y)$ iff $\exists y_{y<z} R(\overline{x}, y) \vee R(\overline{x}, z)$

Similarly for bounded universal quantification.

In what follows we use Lemma 8.5.2 and other facts established in this section without explicit mention.

8.6. Division

This section contains some elementary facts about division and prime numbers, most of them going back to ancient times. We need them for coding finite sequences, which is crucial for what follows. But the fine details can be a distraction from our main purpose, and proofs in the starred subsections can safely be skipped without losing the thread.

8.6.1. Remainder and quotient

The relation 'y divides x', which we write $y|x$, is obviously primitive recursive (writing yz for $y \cdot z$):

$$y|x \text{ iff } \exists z_{z \leqslant x}(x = yz)$$

Note that for simplicity we allow $0|0$. Here are two easily verified properties of the relation $|$:

(37) Suppose $x > y$.

a. If $z|x$ and $z|y$, then $z|x-y$.

b. If $z|x-y$ and $z|y$, then $z|x$.

From school mathematics we know that if we divide any natural number x by $y > 0$ we get a unique *quotient* q and *remainder* r. More precisely, there is a unique pair of natural numbers q, r, such that

$$x = qy + r \ \& \ r < y$$

This fact lets us define two functions quo and rem, where $quo(x, y) = q$ and $rem(x, y) = r$. To make these functions total we must also stipulate a value when $y = 0$; we let $quo(x, 0) = 0$ and $rem(x, 0) = x$. So our official definition of these functions is as follows.

(38) $$rem(x,y) = \begin{cases} \mu z_{z<y} \exists w_{w \leqslant x} (x = w \cdot y + z) & \text{if } y \neq 0 \\ x & \text{if } y = 0 \end{cases}$$

(39) $$quo(x,y) = \begin{cases} \mu w_{w \leqslant x} \exists z_{z<y} (x = w \cdot y + z) & \text{if } y \neq 0 \\ 0 & \text{if } y = 0 \end{cases}$$

It follows that *quo* and *rem* are primitive recursive.

8.6.2. *Using the integers

Some facts about subtraction (obviously) but also division become easier to state if we work with the set $\mathbb{Z} = \{\ldots, -2, -1, 0, 1, 2, \ldots\}$ of *integers* rather than just the natural numbers $\mathbb{N} = \{0, 1, 2, \ldots\}$. If a, b are both negative, dividing a by b is the same as dividing the positive $-a$ by the positive $-b$, just as before. If a is negative and b positive (or vice versa), there are by the above unique natural numbers q, r such that $-a = qb + r$, with $0 \leqslant r < b$. Thus, $a = -qb - r$. So, when $r > 0$, one may take the quotient to be the negative $-q$ and the remainder to be the negative $-r$.[3]

Thus, we can extend the relation $y|x$ (including fact (37)) to integers. Under both definitions of the remainder, $b|a$ holds iff the remainder of division of a by b is 0.[4]

8.6.3. *Greatest common divisor

If x, y are positive numbers, $gcd(x, y)$ is the greatest number which divides both x and y. For example, $gcd(34, 51) = 17$, $gcd(34, 50) = 2$, and $gcd(34, 49) = 1$. gcd is primitive recursive (cf. Exercise 8.9.9):

(40) $$gcd(x,y) = \mu z_{z \leqslant max(x,y)} (z|x \wedge z|y \wedge \forall u_{u \leqslant max(x,y)} (u > z \rightarrow \neg(u|x \wedge u|y))$$

Since every positive number divides 0 (and we stipulated that $0|0$), this definition also gives $gcd(x, 0) = gcd(0, x) = x$, which seems right.

Around 300 B.C., Euclid devised an *algorithm* for calculating the greatest common divisor of (positive) x and y:

> Given the pair (x, y), if $x \neq y$, choose the largest of them, say x, and consider the pair $(x–y, y)$ (similarly if y is largest). Continue in this way until we obtain a pair (z, z). Then $z = gcd(x, y)$.

---

[3]If we want the remainder to always be a natural number, we may instead stipulate that the quotient be $-(q+1)$. Then, since $a = -(q+1)b + (b-r)$, the remainder $b-r$ is positive or 0.

[4]In this section we use a, b, c as variables for integers, whereas $x, y, \ldots$ vary as before over natural numbers.

It is a nice exercise to prove by induction that the algorithm eventually stops with a pair of equal numbers, and that this number is the *gcd*. Here we will give another characterization of the *gcd*. Thus, given positive x, y, let

$$I(x, y) = \{xa + yb\colon\ a, b \in \mathbb{Z}\}$$

We note some properties of $I(x, y)$.

(41) a. If $a, b \in I(x, y)$, then $a + b \in I(x, y)$.
b. If $a \in I(x, y)$, then $ab \in I(x, y)$ for all $b \in \mathbb{Z}$.

Let x_0 be the smallest positive number in $I(x, y)$ (there is such a number since clearly $x, y \in I(x, y)$). Then we have:

(42) If $a \in I(x, y)$, then $x_0 | a$.

The proof of (41) and (42) is Exercise 8.9.11. Next:

(43) $gcd(x, y) \in I(x, y)$

Proof. Using Euclid's algorithm for calculating $gcd(x, y)$, it follows from (41) (since $x, y \in I(x, y)$) that $gcd(x, y) \in I(x, y)$. □

(44) If $a \in I(x, y)$, then $gcd(x, y) | a$.

Proof. Immediate from the fact that $gcd(x, y) | x$ and $gcd(x, y) | y$. □

(42) – (44) yield the following fact.

Lemma 8.6.1 (Bézout's lemma)
Suppose $x, y > 0$.

(i) $gcd(x, y) = x_0 =$ *the smallest positive number in* $I(x, y)$.

(ii) $gcd(x, y) = 1$ *iff there are* $a, b \in \mathbb{Z}$ *such that* $xa + yb = 1$.

Proof. (i) Since $gcd(x, y)$ belongs to $I(x, y)$, is positive, and divides every number in $I(x, y)$, it must be the smallest positive number in $I(x, y)$. (ii) The left-to-right direction is by (43) and the definition of $I(x, y)$. The other direction follows from (i). □

Definition 8.6.2
x and y are *relative prime* (or *coprime*) if $gcd(x, y) = 1$.

A number $p > 1$ is a *prime number* if it has no positive divisors except 1 and p. Equivalently, p is prime iff for every x strictly between 1 and p, $gcd(x, p) = 1$. We can now prove the following classical result:

Lemma 8.6.3 (Euclid's lemma)
If p and x are relative prime and $p|xy$, then $p|y$. In particular, if p is prime and $p|xy$, then $p|x$ or $p|y$.

Proof. We may assume $x, y > 0$. Suppose $gcd(x, p) = 1$. By Bézout's lemma (ii), there are a, b such that $xa + pb = 1$, and thus $xya + pyb = y$. Since $p|pyb$ and $p|xya$ (by the assumption), we have $p|y$. For the second claim, if $gcd(x, p) > 1$, then, since p is prime, we must have $p|x$. □

Here is another consequence of Bézout's lemma:

(45) If $x|z$ and $y|z$ and x and y are relative prime, then $xy|z$.

Proof. As above, there are a, b such that $xa + yb = 1$, so $xaz + ybz = z$. By assumption, there are q_1, q_2 such that $z = xq_1 = yq_2$. Then, it follows that $xayq_2 + ybxq_1 = xy(aq_2 + bq_1) = z$, so $xy|z$. □

8.6.4. *Congruence classes

Two integers a, b are *congruent modulo n* (where n is positive), written

$$a \equiv b \ mod(n)$$

if n divides $a - b$. The following (left as exercises) is easily verified.

(46) a. Congruence mod. n is an equivalence relation (for all n).

b. If $a_1 \equiv b_1 \ mod(n)$ and $a_2 \equiv b_2 \ mod(n)$, then $a_1 + a_2 \equiv b_1 + b_2 \ mod(n)$ and $a_1 a_2 \equiv b_1 b_2 \ mod(n)$.

The equivalence classes $[a] = \{b : a \equiv b \ mod(n)\}$ are called *congruence classes $mod(n)$*, and (46) entails that addition and multiplication transfer directly to congruence classes, with $[a] + [b] = [a + b]$ and $[a] \cdot [b] = [ab]$. Working with congruence classes is fundamental in number theory. Here we shall only talk about congruence in the statement and proof of a classical result about division, the Chinese remainder theorem, which in turn was used by Gödel in order to to code finite sequences of numbers (see Section 8.7).

8.6.5. Enumerating the prime numbers

Clearly, the property of being a prime number is primitive recursive:

(47) $prime(x)$ iff $1 < x \wedge \forall y_{y<x}(1 < y \rightarrow \neg\, y|x)$

We can enumerate the prime numbers in order of magnitude by a primitive recursive function π, where $\pi(x)$ = the $(x+1)$:st prime:

(48) $$\begin{cases} \pi(0) & = & 2 \\ \pi(x') & = & \mu\, y_{y<\pi(x)!+2}\, (\pi(x) < y \wedge \mathit{prime}(y)) \end{cases}$$

This definition relies on another result proved by Euclid, namely, that if x is a prime number, there is a prime number strictly between x and $x!+2$. (For a proof, see Exercise 8.9.15.) Using what we now know about how to construct primitive recursive functions, we see that π as defined in (48) is primitive recursive. Strictly speaking, this follows without Euclid's result. What that result shows is that π really enumerates the primes in order of magnitude.

8.6.6. *The fundamental theorem of arithmetic

Theorem 8.6.4 (Fundamental Theorem of Arithmetic)
Every number $x > 1$ can be uniquely written as a product of primes:

(49) $$x = 2^{x_0} \cdot 3^{x_1} \cdot \ldots \cdot \pi(k-1)^{x_{k-1}}$$

where $x_{k-1} > 0$. The other x_i can be 0 or not; what is uniquely determined by x is the sequence $(x_0, \ldots, x_{k-1})$. (49) is called the prime factorization *of x.*

For example:

$$\begin{aligned} 26 &= 2^1 \cdot 3^0 \cdot 5^0 \cdot 7^0 \cdot 11^0 \cdot 13^1 \\ 27 &= 2^0 \cdot 3^3 \\ 1001 &= 2^0 \cdot 3^0 \cdot 5^0 \cdot 7^1 \cdot 11^1 \cdot 13^1 \\ 1200 &= 2^4 \cdot 3^1 \cdot 5^2 \end{aligned}$$

Statements of this theorem often leave out the prime numbers with exponent 0, so that e.g. $1001 = 7^1 \cdot 11^1 \cdot 13^1$. Then x is divisible by all the primes in its prime factorization. For our purposes it is convenient to include all the primes up to $\pi(k-1)$.

To prove the Fundamental Theorem one needs to show existence and uniqueness of the prime factorization. Both use induction. As to existence, assume $x > 2$ and x is not a prime; otherwise the result is immediate. Then there are y, z such that $1 < y, z < x$ and $x = yz$. By induction hypothesis, y and z are products of primes, so it follows that x is a product of primes, which clearly can be written in the form (49).

For uniqueness, suppose $x = 2^{x_0} \cdot \ldots \cdot \pi(k-1)^{x_{k-1}} = 2^{y_0} \cdot \ldots \cdot \pi(k-1)^{y_{k-1}}$; by allowing suitable exponents to be 0 we may assume both factorizations have the same length k. We must show $x_i = y_i$ for $i = 0, \ldots, k-1$. Suppose $x_0 \neq y_0$, say $x_0 < y_0$. It follows that $3^{x_1} \cdot \ldots \cdot \pi(k-1)^{x_{k-1}} = 2^{y_0 - x_0} \cdot 3^{y_1} \cdot \ldots \cdot \pi(k-1)^{y_{k-1}}$. Thus, $2^{y_0-x_0}$ divides $3^{x_1} \cdot \ldots \cdot \pi(k-1)^{x_{k-1}}$. Since $2^{y_0-x_0}$ and 3^{x_1} are relative prime, it follows by Euclid's lemma that $2^{y_0-x_0}$ divides $5^{x_2} \cdot \ldots \cdot \pi(k-1)^{x_{k-1}}$. Going on in the same way we see that $2^{y_0-x_0}$ divides $\pi(k-1)^{x_{k-1}}$, which is impossible. So $x_0 = y_0$. Similarly (by induction) for the other pairs x_i, y_i. □

8.6.7. *The Chinese remainder theorem

The first statement of this theorem appears in the book *Sunzi SuanJiang* in the 3rd century, written by an unknown author named Sunzi. It is stated as a puzzle:

> There are certain things whose number is unknown. If we count them by threes, we have two left over; by fives, we have three left over; and by sevens, two are left over. How many things are there?

The claim is that the question has a unique answer, i.e. that there is a unique number x satisfying $rem(x, 3) = 2$, $rem(x, 5) = 3$, and $rem(x, 7) = 2$; to get uniqueness we should add the condition that $0 \leqslant x < 3 \cdot 5 \cdot 7 = 105$. In fact, that number is $x = 23$.

The general claim is as follows:

Theorem 8.6.5 (Chinese remainder theorem)
Let $x_1, \ldots, x_k$ be positive and pairwise relative prime, and let p be the product $x_1 \cdot \ldots \cdot x_k$. For $a_1, \ldots, a_k \in \mathbb{Z}$, consider the system of equations

$$\text{(i)} \qquad \begin{array}{l} x \equiv a_1 \; mod(x_1) \\ \vdots \\ x \equiv a_k \; mod(x_k) \end{array}$$

Then (i) is solvable, and if x, y are solutions to (i), then $x \equiv y \; mod(p)$. In particular, there is a unique solution if it is required that $0 \leqslant x < p$.

Proof. Uniqueness: Suppose x and y are both solutions to (i). Then $rem(x, x_i) = rem(y, x_i) = a_i$ for each i, from which it follows that each x_i divides $x - y$. Since $x_1, \ldots, x_k$ are pairwise relative prime, by repeated use of (45) we see that the product p also divides $x - y$, i.e. $x \equiv y \; mod(p)$.

Existence: Consider first the case $k = 2$. By Bézout's lemma there are b, c such that $bx_1 + cx_2 = 1$. Let $x = a_1cx_2 + a_2bx_1$. Then:

$$x = a_1cx_2 + a_2bx_1 = a_1(1 - bx_1) + a_2bx_1 = a_1 + (a_2 - a_1)bx_1$$

This shows that x_1 divides $x - a_1$, i.e. $x \equiv a_1 \; mod(x_1)$. Similarly, $x \equiv a_2 \; mod(x_2)$. So we found a solution for $k = 2$. For $k = 3$, suppose s is a solution to the first two equations. By the uniqueness part, the equation $x \equiv s \; mod(x_1x_2)$ has a solution, say t. Note that

t also solves the first two equations.[5] Furthermore, if x_1, x_2, x_3 are pairwise relative prime, it follows by Euclid's lemma that x_1x_2 and x_3 are relative prime. So we only need to solve the pair of equations $x \equiv s\ mod(x_1x_2)$ and $x \equiv a_3\ mod(x_3)$, and we are back to case $k = 2$. Continuing in this way completes the proof. □

Getting back to Sunzi's question, his equations are

$$\begin{aligned} x &\equiv 2\ mod(3) \\ x &\equiv 3\ mod(5) \\ x &\equiv 2\ mod(7) \end{aligned}$$

For the first two equations, since $2{\cdot}3 - 1{\cdot}5 = 1$, a solution by the above proof is $x = -2{\cdot}1{\cdot}5 + 3{\cdot}2{\cdot}3 = 8$. Next, we need to solve $x \equiv 8\ mod(15)$ and $x \equiv 2\ mod(7)$. By the same method, since $1{\cdot}15 - 2{\cdot}7 = 1$, we obtain $x = -8\cdot2\cdot7 + 2\cdot1\cdot15 = -82$. We want the smallest positive solution, which is $-82 + 3{\cdot}5{\cdot}7 = 23$.

8.7. Coding finite sequences

Since terms and formulas are finite strings of symbols, and proofs are finite sequences of sentences, it is crucial for Gödel's proof of the incompleteness theorems to be able to code finite sequences of numbers. The code numbers are called *sequence numbers*. There are many ways to define sequence numbers; in this section we present two. Both involve basic arithmetical facts about prime numbers and division as specified in the preceding section. To understand Gödel's proof, it is not necessary to be familiar with all of these facts, or all the details of the codings. The main thing to take home is that, in both cases, the set of sequence numbers is primitive recursive, and there are primitive recursive functions giving the *length* of the coded sequence, the *i:th element* of the sequence, and the *concatenation* of two sequences.

8.7.1. Coding with exponentiation and prime numbers

This coding relies on the Fundamental Theorem of Arithmetic. To a sequence of numbers $x_0, \ldots, x_{k-1}$ we assign the number $2^{x_0+1} \cdot 3^{x_1+1} \cdot \ldots \cdot \pi(k-1)^{x_{k-1}+1}$. (The reason for adding 1 to the exponents is to be able to code sequences containing 0.) In more detail, for each $k \geqslant 0$ we define a k-ary function $\langle\cdot\rangle^k$ by

(50)
$$\begin{aligned} \langle x_0, \ldots, x_{k-1}\rangle^k &= 2^{x_0+1} \cdot 3^{x_1+1} \cdot \ldots \cdot \pi(k-1)^{x_{k-1}+1} \quad (k > 0) \\ \langle\rangle^0 &= 1 \end{aligned}$$

[5] We have $s - a_1 = q_1x_1$ and $t - s = qx_1x_2$. It follows that $t - a_1 = t - s + q_1x_1 = qx_1x_2 - q_1x_1 = x_1(qx_1 + q_1)$, so $x_1 | t - a_1$, and similarly $x_2 | t - a_2$.

Using the Fundamental Theorem, we see that the coding is one-one: different sequences get different code numbers. More precisely:

Fact 8.7.1
$\langle x_0, \ldots, x_{k-1} \rangle^k = \langle y_0, \ldots, y_{m-1} \rangle^m$ *iff* $k = m$ *and* $x_i = y_i$ *for* $i < k$.

Each of the coding functions $\langle \rangle^k$ is primitive recursive (Exercise 8.9.17). Often we just write $\langle x_0, \ldots, x_{k-1} \rangle$, since the arity is apparent anyway. We say that x is a *sequence number* if it codes some finite sequence of numbers:

(51) $sq(x)$ iff $x = \langle x_0, \ldots, x_{k-1} \rangle^k$ for some k and some $x_0, \ldots, x_{k-1}$

The following clearly holds:

(52) a. $k < \langle x_0, \ldots, x_{k-1} \rangle$
b. $x_i < \langle x_0, \ldots, x_{k-1} \rangle$ for $i < k$

Each $x > 1$ has a unique prime factorization, but for x to be a sequence number it must be the case that from a certain number k in the prime factorization of x, the exponent of $\pi(k)$ is 0, whereas for all $i < k$ the exponent is greater than 0. This yields the following characterization, which shows that sq is primitive recursive.

(53) $sq(x)$ iff $x = 1 \vee (x > 1 \wedge \forall y_{y<x}(\pi(y)|x \rightarrow \pi(y \dot{-} 1)|x))$

If $x = \langle x_0, \ldots, x_{k-1} \rangle$ is a sequence number, we say that k is the *length* of x, and x_i is the *i:th element* of x. We need primitive recursive functions that pick out the length, and for each i smaller than the length, the i:th element of a sequence x. These functions are written $lh(x)$ and $(x)_i$. Thus, they should have the following properties:

(54) a. $lh(\langle x_0, \ldots, x_{k-1} \rangle) = k$
b. $(\langle x_0, \ldots, x_{k-1} \rangle)_i = x_i$, for $i < k$

$lh(x)$ and $(x)_i$ can be defined, for arbitrary numbers as arguments (not only sequence numbers), as follows:

(55) a. $lh(x) = \mu y_{y<x} \neg \pi(y) \mid x$ if $x > 0$, and $lh(0) = 1$.
b. $(x)_i = \mu y_{y<x} \neg \pi(i)^{y+2} \mid x$

Note that $(x)_i$ is a 2-place function, with x and i as arguments—we can call it a *decoding* function.[6] If $x = \langle x_0, \ldots, x_{k-1} \rangle$ and $i < k$, then $\pi(i)^{x_i+1}$ divides x, but $\pi(i)^{x_i+2}$ doesn't. So (55b) ensures that (54b) holds. Similarly for (55a) and (54a); note that $lh(\langle \rangle) = 0$. Clearly the functions defined in (55) are primitive recursive.

[6]The notation $(x)_i$ is classical, although sometimes not very practical.

Concatenation, written $*$, is an important operation on sequences:

(56) $\langle x_0, \ldots, x_{n-1}\rangle * \langle y_0, \ldots, y_{m-1}\rangle = \langle x_0, \ldots, x_{n-1}, y_0, \ldots, y_{m-1}\rangle$

When x and y are sequence numbers, we can find a primitive recursive upper bound for their concatenation, i.e. a primitive recursive function P such that if $sq(x)$ and $sq(y)$, then $x*y \leqslant P(x,y)$ (Exercise 8.9.19). The following explicit definition shows that $*$ is primitive recursive:[7]

(57) $$x * y = \mu z_{z \leqslant P(x,y)}(lh(z) = lh(x) + lh(y) \wedge \forall i_{i<lh(x)}((z)_i = (x)_i) \wedge \forall i_{i<lh(y)}((z)_{lh(x)+i} = (y)_i))$$

Furthermore, one verifies that concatenation is *associative*, i.e.:

(58) $x * (y * z) = (x * y) * z$

Thus, we can drop parentheses and write $x * y * z$.

8.7.2. *Coding with the β function: 1

Sequence coding using prime factorization is easy and intuitive. For some purposes, however, we want a coding that only uses addition and multiplication, but not exponentiation. Such a coding was designed by Gödel. Let β be the 3-place function defined as follows:

(β) $\beta(x, y, i) = rem(x, y\cdot(i+1)+1)$

That is, $\beta(x, y, i)$ is the remainder when the number x is divided by $y\cdot(i+1)+1$. Section 8.6.1 showed that the functions *rem* and *quo* are primitive recursive, and thus so is the β function. Note that

(59) $\beta(x, y, i) \leqslant x$ for all x, y, i.

Gödel showed that by means of the β function, every finite sequence of numbers can be coded by *two* numbers:

Lemma 8.7.2 (β function lemma)
For every sequence $a_0, \ldots, a_{k-1}$ of numbers there are numbers x, y such that $\beta(x, y, i) = a_i$ for $i < k$.

The proof uses the Chinese remainder theorem. For this coding too we need functions picking out the length and the i:th element of a sequence. As to the length, we use the trick of putting it first in the sequence.[8] Thus, to code $a_0, \ldots, a_{k-1}$, we apply the β function lemma to the sequence $k, a_0, \ldots, a_{k-1}$. This gives us two numbers x, y such that $\beta(x, y, 0) = k$ and $\beta(x, y, i+1) = a_i$ for $i < k$.

[7] Alternatively, one can define $x * y$ by primitive recursion; this does not require P.

[8] We could have used the same trick for the coding in Section 8.7.1, instead of the direct calculation of the length function in (55a). With the β-style coding, however, there is no obvious way to retrieve k from a pair (x, y) coding $a_0, \ldots, a_{k-1}$.

Can't we code a sequence by *one* number rather than two? Of course we can, once we have a suitable *pairing function*. We explain how this is done in the next subsection. Before that, we prove the β function lemma (feel free to skip).

Proof of the β function lemma.
Given $a_0, \ldots, a_{k-1}$, let $a = max(k, a_0, \ldots, a_{k-1})$, and let $y = a!$.

Claim: If $0 \leqslant i < j \leqslant k - 1$, then the numbers $1 + (i + 1)y$ and $1 + (j + 1)y$ are relative prime.

For suppose p is a prime dividing both of these numbers. Then p divides their difference, which is $(j - i)y$, so by Euclid's lemma (Lemma 8.6.3), p divides $j - i$ or p divides y. But if p divides y, then it divides both $(j + 1)y$ and $1 + (j + 1)y$, so it divides 1, which is impossible. Moreover, $j - i$ divides y by construction, so p cannot divide $j - i$ either. This proves the Claim.

Thus, the numbers $b_i = 1 + (i + 1)y$ are pairwise relative prime. By the Chinese remainder theorem, there is a number x such that we have $x \equiv a_i \; mod(b_i)$ for $i = 0, \ldots, k - 1$. This means that $\beta(x, y, i) = rem(x, y \cdot (i+1)+1) = rem(x, b_i) = a_i$, since $0 \leqslant a_i < b_i$. □

We shall need an upper bound for x, y in the β function lemma. Let b be greater than $max(k, a_0, \ldots, a_{k-1})$. Inspecting the above proof, we see that $x, y < (1 + (b + 1)b!)^b$. Thus, for each k there is a primitive recursive function B_k such that for x, y as in the β function lemma:

(60) $\quad x, y < B_k(a_0, \ldots, a_{k-1})$

8.7.3. *Coding with the β function: 2

Cantor observed that the set $\mathbb{N}^2 = \{(x, y) : x, y \in \mathbb{N}\}$ of ordered pairs of natural numbers is equinumerous with $\mathbb{N}$. The simple bijection, here denoted OP, from $\mathbb{N}^2$ to $\mathbb{N}$ can be seen in a diagram were $\mathbb{N}^2$ is displayed as an infinite square whose pairs are enumerated along the diagonals; see Chapter 16.4.2. We have:

(61) $\quad OP(x, y) = (x+y)(x+y+1)/2 + x$

It is clear from the diagram that each pair (x, y) is assigned a unique number, and each natural number is the image of a unique pair. So there are two inverse functions π_1 and π_2 such that for all x, y,

(62) $\quad \pi_1(OP(x, y)) = x \quad \text{and} \quad \pi_2(OP(x, y)) = y$

We have that $x, y \leqslant OP(x, y)$, $\pi_1(z) \leqslant z$, $\pi_2(z) \leqslant z$, and the functions OP, π_1, and π_2 are primitive recursive (Exercise 8.9.20). Now we can combine the β function and OP to code finite sequences. To distinguish it from the earlier sequence coding we use the superscript $^{\beta}$. First, revise the β function as follows:

(63) $\beta'(z,i) = \beta(\pi_1(z), \pi_2(z), i)$

Then:

(64) $\langle\rangle^{\beta,0} = 1$, and for $k > 0$, the k-ary function $\langle\cdot\rangle^{\beta,k}$ is defined by
$\langle x_0, \ldots, x_{k-1}\rangle^{\beta,k} = \mu z_{z<B}(\beta'(z,0) = k \wedge \forall i_{i<k}\beta'(z,i+1) = x_i)$

Here $B = B_k(x_0, \ldots, x_{k-1})$ as in (60). Now we easily get length and decoding functions:

(65) a. $lh^{\beta}(z) = \beta'(z,0)$
b. $(z)^{\beta}_i = \beta'(z,i+1)$

We have $lh^{\beta}(z) \leqslant z$ and $(z)^{\beta}_i \leqslant z$ for all z, i.[9] Moreover, (65) shows that we can define the set of 'β-style' sequence numbers as follows:

(66) $sq^{\beta}(x)$ iff $\forall y_{y<x}(lh^{\beta}(y) \neq lh^{\beta}(x) \vee \exists i_{i<lh^{\beta}(x)}(y)^{\beta}_i \neq (x)^{\beta}_i)$

Finally, we deal with concatenation just as before in (57), but using the β-versions of the length and i:th element functions. This again requires us to find a primitive recursive function G (in place of the earlier P), giving an upper bound $G(x,y)$ for $x *^{\beta} y$, when $sq^{\beta}(x)$ and $sq^{\beta}(y)$. The argument leading up to (60) shows how this can be done.[10]

8.7.4. *Coding by iterating the pairing function

The reader might reasonably ask: if we can code pairs with the simple pairing function OP, why not code triples etc. by iterating this function—i.e. the code of (x, y) is $OP(x, y)$, the code of (x, y, z) is then $OP(OP(x, y), z)$, and so on for all finite sequences of numbers?

This has the disadvantage that each number x will be the code of a unique n-tuple for each $n \geqslant 2$, so the coding is not injective. But we can solve this by the same trick as with the β function: think of $(x_0, \ldots, x_{n-1})$ as the sequence $(n, x_0, \ldots, x_{n-1})$. In this way one can inductively define a bijection between $\mathbb{N}$ and the set of finite sequences of elements of $\mathbb{N}$, using OP. The problem, however, is *decoding*: it is not so obvious how to define decoding functions as in (55b) and (65b) for this style of coding. Since decoding is essential in what follows, we stick with the two kinds of sequence coding already described.[11]

---

[9]Since $\beta(\pi_1(z), \pi_2(z), i) \leqslant \pi_1(z) \leqslant z$.

[10]When $sq^{\beta}(x)$, use $F(x) = 1 + lh^{\beta}(x) + \Sigma_{i<lh^{\beta}(x)}(x)^{\beta}_i$ as the value of b in the argument just before (60). Then it is easy to define $G(x,y)$ in terms of $F(x)$ and $F(y)$.

[11]That decoding is not obvious doesn't mean it's not possible. In fact, it *is* possible, though with some difficulty. Smoryński 1991 has a detailed discussion of various

8.8. Course-of-values recursion

One often defines a function f by recursion in such a way that $f(\overline{x}, y)$ is specified not in terms of $f(\overline{x}, y-1)$, but of $f(\overline{x}, 0)$, ..., $f(\overline{x}, y-1)$. To formulate this properly we first define an operation that collects all the $f(\overline{x}, i)$ for $i < y$. Given f, let:[12]

$$\overline{f}(x_1, \ldots, x_n, y) = \langle f(x_1, \ldots, x_n, 0), \ldots, f(x_1, \ldots, x_n, y-1)\rangle \tag{67}$$

Now $\overline{f}$ can be defined with primitive recursion from f, as follows:

$$\begin{cases} \overline{f}(x_1, \ldots, x_n, 0) & = & 1 \\ \overline{f}(x_1, \ldots, x_n, y') & = & \overline{f}(x_1, \ldots, x_n, y) * \langle f(x_1, \ldots, x_n, y)\rangle \end{cases} \tag{68}$$

Thus, if f is primitive recursive, so is $\overline{f}$.

Definition 8.8.1 (course-of-values recursion)
f is defined by *course-of-values recursion from* g, h if

$$\text{(cov)} \quad \begin{cases} f(x_1, \ldots, x_n, 0) & = & g(x_1, \ldots, x_n) \\ f(x_1, \ldots, x_n, y) & = & h(x_1, \ldots, x_n, y, \overline{f}(x_1, \ldots, x_n, y)) \text{ for } y > 0 \end{cases}$$

The next fact shows that course-of-values recursion doesn't lead out of the class of primitive recursive functions.

Fact 8.8.2
If g and h are primitive recursive, so is the function f defined by (cov).

Proof. Since h is primitive recursive, the following is a primitive recursive definition of $\overline{f}$ (compare (68), writing $\overline{x}$ for $x_1, \ldots, x_n$):

$$\begin{cases} \overline{f}(\overline{x}, 0) & = & 1 \\ \overline{f}(\overline{x}, y') & = & \overline{f}(\overline{x}, y) * \langle h(\overline{x}, y, \overline{f}(\overline{x}, y))\rangle \end{cases} \tag{69}$$

In more detail: the function h_0 defined by

$$h_0(\overline{x}, y, z) = z * \langle h(\overline{x}, y, z)\rangle$$

is primitive recursive. So the second line in (69) becomes $\overline{f}(\overline{x}, y') = h_0(\overline{x}, y, \overline{f}(\overline{x}, y))$. From this we see that $\overline{f}$ is primitive recursive. And since f is obtained in (cov) by definition by cases from primitive recursive functions and relations (the cases are $y = 0$ and $y > 0$), it follows that f is also primitive recursive. □

---

methods of sequence coding. He argues that, in a clear if not completely precise sense, coding with the β function is the *simplest* possible coding scheme.

[12]We use prime factorization coding here, but exactly the same results would be obtained with β function coding.

One can also define primitive recursive relations by course-of-values recursion; see Exercise 8.9.26. Course-of-values recursion will be a useful tool in Chapter 11, e.g. for showing that the set of (Gödel numbers of) arithmetical terms and formulas are primitive recursive.

8.9. Exercises to Chapter 8

Exercise 8.9.1
Explain how an n-ary function f can be written as an m-ary function, for $m > n$, using the identity functions and composition.

Exercise 8.9.2
*Let FD_n be the set of function descriptions of n-ary primitive recursive functions. Give an inductive definition of the sets FD_n (induction over the complexity of descriptions), at the same time describing the unique primitive recursive function that each description denotes. Here are two examples:

1. (The symbol) $Z \in FD_1$, and Z denotes the function giving the value 0 for each argument.
2. If $G_1, \ldots, G_m \in FD_n$, $F \in FD_m$, G_i denotes g_i, and F denotes f, then $\mathrm{Cn}[F, G_1, \ldots, G_m] \in FD_n$, and $\mathrm{Cn}[F, G_1, \ldots, G_m]$ denotes the function h defined by

   (Cn) $h(x_1, \ldots, x_n) = f(g_1(x_1, \ldots, x_n), \ldots, g_m(x_1, \ldots, x_n))$

Thus, add the remaining clauses in the definition. [Note in particular what is needed to deal with the case $n = 0$ in Definition 8.3.1.] This simultaneously defines the set of function descriptions ($= \bigcup_{n \geqslant 0} FD_n$) and the set of primitive recursive functions.

Exercise 8.9.3
Show that every primitive recursive function has infinitely many function descriptions.

Exercise 8.9.4
Define the 2-place constant function in (4) with primitive recursion.

Exercise 8.9.5

1. Show that $x \uparrow_n 1 = x$ for all x and n.
2. Verify that $x \uparrow_2 y = x^{x^{\cdot^{\cdot^{\cdot^{x}}}}}$ with a stack of y occurrences of x.

Exercise 8.9.6
Give an explicit function description of the factorial function $x!$.

Exercise 8.9.7
Define the product function $\prod_{i=0}^{y} f(x, i)$ in (20) by primitive recursion.

Exercise 8.9.8
Check that (34) really defines the desired function.

Exercise 8.9.9

1. Prove that in order to show that f, defined by cases as in (33), is primitive recursive, we don't need to assume that the relation S_k is primitive recursive.
2. Show that the function $max(x, y)$ = the maximum of x and y is primitive recursive.
3. More generally, show by induction on k that $max_k(x_0, \ldots, x_{k-1})$ = the maximum of $x_0, \ldots, x_{k-1}$ is a primitive recursive function.

Exercise 8.9.10
Show that every finite set is primitive recursive. [If $A = \{a_1, \ldots, a_n\}$, define c_A by cases.]

Exercise 8.9.11
Show that (41) holds. Using this, prove (42). [Hint: Let $z = qx_0 + r$, where r, according to the stipulation in Section 8.6.2, is non-negative. Deduce from (41) that $r \in I(x, y)$, and then that $r = 0$.]

Exercise 8.9.12
Show that Euclid's lemma (Lemma 8.6.3) actually characterizes the primes, i.e., for $p > 1$,

(70) p is a prime iff for all $x, y > 0$, $p|xy$ implies $p|x$ or $p|y$.

[Hint: From right to left, prove the contraposition.]

Exercise 8.9.13
Verify that (46) holds.

Exercise 8.9.14
Prove the following alternative characterization of primality:

$$x \text{ is prime iff } x > 1 \text{ and for all } y, z \text{ we have } x \neq (y + 2)(z + 2)$$

Exercise 8.9.15 (infinity of prime numbers)

1. *Prove (the version given here of) Euclid's theorem about the infinity of primes: For every prime number x there is a prime number y such that $x < y \leqslant x!+1$. [Hint: The crucial observation is that $x! + 1$ is not divisible by any z such that $2 \leqslant z \leqslant x$.]

2. *Let $p_1, \ldots, p_n$ be an arbitrary list of prime numbers, and let $p = p_1 \cdot \ldots \cdot p_n$. Show that $p + 1$ is either a prime number or divisible by a prime number not in the list. Conclude that there are infinitely many primes. [This is essentially Euclid's original proof.]

Exercise 8.9.16
Prove Fact 8.7.1, using the Fundamental Theorem of Arithmetic.

Exercise 8.9.17
Check that the coding functions defined in (50) are primitive recursive, and that the inequalities in (52) hold.

Exercise 8.9.18

1. Explain why the functions in (55) are primitive recursive.
2. Verify that (54a) holds, and that $lh(\langle\rangle) = 0$.

Exercise 8.9.19

1. Define a primitive recursive function P such that $sq(x)$ & $sq(y)$ implies that $x * y \leqslant P(x, y)$. [Hint: Use the fact that if $sq(x)$, then

$$x = 2^{(x)_0+1} \cdot \ldots \cdot \pi(lh(x) - 1)^{(x)_{lh(x)-1}+1} \leqslant \pi(lh(x) - 1)^{lh(x)+\Sigma_{i<lh(x)}(x)_i} = F(x)$$

   F is primitive recursive. Similarly find a bound for $x * y$.]

2. Show that concatenation as defined here is associative (i.e. (58)).

Exercise 8.9.20
Show that the function OP and its inverses π_1 and π_2 are primitive recursive, and that $x, y \leqslant OP(x, y)$, $\pi_1(z) \leqslant z$, and $\pi_2(z) \leqslant z$.

Exercise 8.9.21 (a coding of finite sets)
*Let $\mathbb{N}^{<\omega}$ be the set of finite sets of natural numbers. The *canonical index* of a finite set A is defined by the function ci as follows:

$$\begin{cases} ci(\varnothing) & = \quad 0 \\ ci(\{x_0, \ldots, x_{n-1}\}) & = \quad 2^{x_0} + \ldots + 2^{x_{n-1}}, \text{where } x_0 < \ldots < x_{n-1} \end{cases}$$

Show that ci is a bijection from $\mathbb{N}^{<\omega}$ to $\mathbb{N}$. [Hint: use the binary representation of natural numbers.] Its inverse is usually written D, so D_x = the set with canonical index x.

Exercise 8.9.22
Show that the following functions are primitive recursive: *fst*(x) and *lst*(x) are the first and last elements, respectively, in the sequence coded by x (when x is a sequence number).

Exercise 8.9.23 (contraction of functions and relations)
Sequence coding can be used to transform k-place to 1-place functions: if f is k-place, define the function $\langle f \rangle$, called the *contraction* of f, by

$$\langle f \rangle(x) = f((x)_0, \ldots, (x)_{k-1})$$

Show:

$$f(x_0, \ldots, x_{k-1}) = \langle f \rangle(\langle x_0, \ldots, x_{k-1} \rangle)$$

Conclude that f is primitive recursive iff $\langle f \rangle$ is primitive recursive. Do the same thing for contraction of relations.

Exercise 8.9.24 (contraction of quantifiers)
Using the preceding exercise, show:

$$\exists x_0 \ldots \exists x_{k-1} R(x_0, \ldots, x_{k-1}) \Leftrightarrow \exists x \langle R \rangle(x)$$
$$\forall x_0 \ldots \forall x_{k-1} R(x_0, \ldots, x_{k-1}) \Leftrightarrow \forall x \langle R \rangle(x)$$

Exercise 8.9.25 (c-o-v recursion: example)
The *Fibonacci series* 1, 1, 2, 3, 5, 8, 13, 21, 34, ... is defined so that the next number is the sum of the two earlier ones:

$$\begin{cases} Fi(0) & = & 1 \\ Fi(1) & = & 1 \\ Fi(x) & = & Fi(x-2) + Fi(x-1) \text{ for } x \geqslant 2 \end{cases}$$

Show that *Fi* is primitive recursive. [Hint: Use definition by cases and course-of-values recursion.]

Exercise 8.9.26 (c-o-v recursion for relations)
Let R be defined by

$$R(x_1, \ldots, x_n, y) \Leftrightarrow S(x_1, \ldots, x_n, y, \overline{c_R}(x_1, \ldots, x_n, y))$$

where S is primitive recursive. Show that R is primitive recursive. [Hint: $c_R(x_1, \ldots, x_n, y) = c_S(x_1, \ldots, x_n, y, \overline{c_R}(x_1, \ldots, x_n, y))$]

Exercise 8.9.27 (c-o-v recursion for relations: example)
Suppose R is defined by

$$R(x, y) \Leftrightarrow \exists z_{z<y}(R(x, z) \wedge S(x, y, z))$$

where S is primitive recursive. Show that R is primitive recursive. [Hint: Use course-of-values recursion as in the preceding exercise, recalling that for $z < y$, $(\overline{c_R}(x, y))_z = c_R(x, z)$.]

Exercise 8.9.28 (simultaneous recursion)
*Let the functions f_1, f_2 be defined by *simultaneous recursion*:

$$\begin{cases} f_1(x,0) &= g_1(x) \\ f_2(x,0) &= g_2(x) \\ f_1(x,y') &= h_1(x,y,f_1(x,y),f_2(x,y)) \\ f_2(x,y') &= h_2(x,y,f_1(x,y),f_2(x,y)) \end{cases}$$

Show that if g_1, g_2, h_1, h_2 are primitive recursive, so are f_1 and f_2. [Hint: Use coding to give a primitive recursive definition of $f(x,y) = \langle f_1(x,y), f_2(x,y)\rangle$.]

Exercise 8.9.29 (a computable but not primitive recursive function)

(a) Sketch a way to effectively code all primitive recursive functions. [Code their function descriptions.]

(b) If not every number is the code of some primitive recursive function (the coding function is not surjective), show how one can make the coding surjective (onto $\mathbb{N}$) and still effective. [Choose some primitive recursive function and give it lots of codes.]

(c) Suppose we have an effective coding $[n]$ such that

$$[0], [1], [2], \ldots$$

is an effective enumeration of all 1-ary primitive recursive functions. (So for every 1-ary primitive recursive function f there is a number e such that $[e] = f$.) Define

$$Ev_1(e,x) = [e](x)$$

Show that Ev_1 is not primitive recursive. Conclude that there is a 1-ary function which is computable but not primitive recursive.

9 Peano Arithmetic

This chapter is devoted to first-order arithmetic as presented in the theory *PA*. To get a feeling for how the induction axiom is used, we go through proofs of some basic properties of addition, multiplication, and order, and some particular *PA* theorems that will be useful later.

The main goal is to give a sense of how one can *reason in PA*. This does not mean that we present detailed derivations in the Hilbert system H from the *PA* axioms. Rather, we reason informally, making sure at each step that the inference machinery of H can handle the corresponding formal steps. The best way to see how this works is to look at examples.

Reasoning in *PA*, we often omit the universal quantifiers at the front of sentences. For example, we write axiom (PA2) below as $x' = y' \to x = y$, although the actual axiom is $\forall x \forall y(x' = y' \to x = y)$. This improves readability, and also allows us to treat universally quantified variables as parameters during derivations, as we will see.

Observe that in this chapter—in contrast with the preceding one!—the letters $x, y, z, \ldots$ are formal variables in the language of the first-order theory *PA*,[1] whereas $k, m, n, \ldots$ stand for natural numbers.

9.1. The axioms of *PA*

Let us repeat, and name, the axioms of *PA*:

(PA1) $x' \neq 0$

(PA2) $x' = y' \to x = y$

(PA3) $x + 0 = x$

(PA4) $x + y' = (x + y)'$

(PA5) $x \cdot 0 = 0$

(PA6) $x \cdot y' = (x \cdot y) + x$

(IND) $(\varphi(0, \overline{y}) \wedge \forall x(\varphi(x, \overline{y}) \to \varphi(x', \overline{y}))) \to \forall x \varphi(x, \overline{y})$

[1]Or, to be more precise, $x, y, z, \ldots$ are metavariables for the actual formal variables, which come from the list $v_0, v_1, v_2, \ldots$.

The induction axiom (IND) is a *scheme*, so *PA* has infinitely many axioms. The formula $\varphi(x, \overline{y})$ in (IND) may contain other free variables $\overline{y} = y_1, \ldots, y_n$ besides x, which in that case are universally quantified. Here is a first (but not very typical) example of the use of (IND):

(1) $\quad PA \vdash x \neq 0 \rightarrow \exists y\, x = y'$

In other words: every number, except 0, is the successor of some number. This is of course *true*: we can reach every number by starting from 0 and apply the successor function. But it doesn't *follow* from (PA1) and (PA2) alone. With the help of (IND), however, it does follow.

Proof of (1). Let $\varphi(x)$ be the formula $x \neq 0 \rightarrow \exists y\, x = y'$. The base step is to show $\varphi(0)$, i.e. $0 \neq 0 \rightarrow \exists y\, 0 = y'$. But the antecedent $0 \neq 0$ is logically false: its negation is derivable in H without assumptions. Therefore, $\varphi(0)$ too is derivable in H, hence also in *PA*.

As to the induction step, $\forall x \varphi(x')$ also happens to be logically true, since $\forall x \exists y\, x' = y'$ is logically true.[2] But that means that

$$\forall x(\varphi(x) \rightarrow \varphi(x'))$$

is logically true, hence derivable in *PA*. So we have shown that both conjuncts in the antecedent of this instance of (IND) are derivable (even without *PA*:s axioms—that's why this example is atypical!), and it follows from (IND) that $\forall x \varphi(x)$ is derivable in *PA*, as desired. □

(1) is the claim that *there is* a derivation of $\forall x(x \neq 0 \rightarrow \exists y\, x = y')$ from the axioms of *PA*. We didn't prove that claim by actually exhibiting such a derivation. Instead, we gave a—hopefully convincing—argument that a derivation indeed exists, with indications of how one could construct it. For example, we helped ourselves to the fact that all logical truths are derivable in *PA*. And we showed that both conjuncts of the antecedent of (IND) applied to our formula $\varphi(x)$ are derivable. Since the consequent of this instance of (IND) is our desired sentence, this suffices.

9.2. Properties of addition and multiplication

Addition and multiplication are *commutative* and *associative* operations:

$$n + m = m + n$$
$$n + (m + k) = (n + m) + k$$

[2] $\forall x \exists y\, x = y$ is logically true, and therefore so is $\forall x \exists y\, x' = y'$. By completeness, we have $\vdash_H \forall x \exists y\, x' = y'$. Or, directly in H, derive $\forall x \exists y\, x = y$ from the first identity axiom, and then $\forall x \exists y\, x' = y'$ from the second (cf. (34c) in Chapter 3).

and similarly for multiplication. Let us see that the counterparts of these claims in the arithmetical language are provable in *PA*. This is done in several steps; we check how the induction axiom is used at each step. Again, the arguments are informal but can be seen as instructions for finding formal derivations. Besides Modus Ponens, the Deduction Theorem, and universal instantiation (from $\forall x\varphi(x)$ to $\varphi(t)$), in particular substitution of identicals is used a lot in such derivations (i.e. that if $s = t$ and $\varphi(s)$ have been derived, $\varphi(t)$ follows).

(2) $\quad PA \vdash 0 + x = x$

Proof. Let $\varphi(x)$ be the formula $0 + x = x$.

$$\begin{array}{rrcll} \varphi(0): & 0+0 & = & 0 & \text{(from (PA3))} \\ \text{suppose } \varphi(x): & 0+x & = & x & \text{(ind. hyp.)} \\ \text{then} & 0+x' & = & (0+x)' & \text{(by (PA4))} \\ \varphi(x'): & & = & x' & \text{(using ind. hyp.)} \end{array}$$

In other words, $\varphi(0)$ holds by (PA3), and we show $\varphi(x) \rightarrow \varphi(x')$ by assuming $\varphi(x)$ (the induction hypothesis) and deriving $\varphi(x')$, using axiom (PA4) and substitution of identicals (replacing $0+x$ by x). The Deduction Theorem then gives $\varphi(x) \rightarrow \varphi(x')$.[3] Thereby it is clear that $\forall x\varphi(x)$, that is, $\forall x(0 + x = x)$, follows with (IND). □

From now on I will not write $\varphi(0), \varphi(x)$, etc. to the left, and neither the conclusion that $\forall x\varphi(x)$ follows using (IND).

(3) $\quad PA \vdash y + x' = y' + x$

Proof. Induction on x. Here $\varphi(x, y)$ is the formula $y + x' = y' + x$, and we use (IND) with y as a universally quantified parameter. Base step:

$$\begin{array}{rcll} y+0' & = & (y+0)' & \text{(PA4)} \\ & = & y' & \text{(PA3)} \\ & = & y'+0 & \text{(PA3)} \end{array}$$

Induction step: show that if $y + x' = y' + x$, then $y + x'' = y' + x'$.

$$\begin{array}{rcll} y+x'' & = & (y+x')' & \text{(PA4)} \\ & = & (y'+x)' & \text{(ind. hyp.)} \\ & = & y'+x' & \text{(PA4)} \end{array}$$

□

[3]In a formal derivation we would introduce a new individual constant (parameter) c and show, with the reasoning in the induction step above, that $PA \vdash \varphi(c) \rightarrow \varphi(c')$. Then the rule $R\forall$ in H gives $PA \vdash \forall x(\varphi(x) \rightarrow \varphi(x'))$. As stated in Chapter 3.2, we presuppose that fresh individual constants are always available as parameters. In the informal reasoning above, on the other hand, we simply used x as a parameter.

(4) $\quad PA \vdash x + y = y + x$

Proof. Induction on y. Base step:

$$\begin{aligned} x + 0 &= x && \text{(PA3)} \\ &= 0 + x && \text{(by (2))} \end{aligned}$$

Induction step:

$$\begin{aligned} x + y' &= (x + y)' && \text{(PA4)} \\ &= (y + x)' && \text{(ind. hyp.)} \\ &= y + x' && \text{(PA4)} \\ &= y' + x && \text{(by (3))} \end{aligned}$$

□

Thus, three applications of the induction axiom were required to prove that addition is commutative. The proof that it is associative needs only one application of (IND):

(5) $\quad PA \vdash x + (y + z) = (x + y) + z$

Proof. Induction on z. Base step:

$$\begin{aligned} x + (y + 0) &= x + y && \text{(PA3)} \\ &= (x + y) + 0 && \text{(PA3)} \end{aligned}$$

Here we used (PA3) twice: first to replace $y + 0$ with y, and then to replace $x + y$ with $(x + y) + 0$. The induction step uses (PA4) three times:

$$\begin{aligned} x + (y + z') &= x + (y + z)' && \text{(PA4)} \\ &= (x + (y + z))' && \text{(PA4)} \\ &= ((x + y) + z)' && \text{(ind. hyp.)} \\ &= (x + y) + z' && \text{(PA4)} \end{aligned}$$

□

The proofs of the corresponding claims for multiplication are left as exercises (with some hints in Exercise 9.10.1):

(6) $\quad PA \vdash x \cdot y = y \cdot x$

(7) $\quad PA \vdash x \cdot (y \cdot z) = (x \cdot y) \cdot z$

(8) $\quad PA \vdash x \cdot (y + z) = x \cdot y + x \cdot z$

The following fact will be used in the next section.

(9) $\quad PA \vdash x + y' \neq x$

9.3. Digression: 2+2=4

To appreciate the difference between informal reasoning in *PA*, which shows that *there is* a proof, and actual proofs in *PA*, let's prove that 2+2=4, i.e. that

(10) $PA \vdash 0'' + 0'' = 0''''$

Informally, this follows with two applications of (PA4) and one application of (PA3):

$$\begin{aligned} 0'' + 0'' &= (0'' + 0')' && \text{from (PA4)} \\ &= (0'' + 0)'' && \text{from (PA4)} \\ &= 0'''' && \text{from (PA3)} \end{aligned}$$

The applications of $\forall$-elimination and substitution of identities involved here are tacit but the reasoning is totally convincing. As may be expected, a formal proof in the natural deduction system *ND* is rather simple:

(11)
$$\dfrac{\dfrac{\dfrac{\dfrac{\forall x \forall y\, x + y' = (x+y)'}{\forall y\, 0'' + y' = (0''+y)'}}{0'' + 0'' = (0'' + 0')'} \qquad \dfrac{\dfrac{\forall x \forall y\, x + y' = (x+y)'}{\forall y\, 0'' + y' = (0''+y)'}}{0'' + 0' = (0'' + 0)'}}{0'' + 0'' = (0'' + 0)''} \qquad \dfrac{\forall x\, x + 0 = x}{0'' + 0 = 0''}}{0'' + 0'' = 0''''}$$

Recall the second identity rule:

$$\dfrac{s = t \qquad \varphi(s)}{\varphi(t)}$$

At the first application of this rule in (11), s is $0''+0'$, t is $(0''+0)'$, and $\varphi(z)$ is $0''+0'' = z'$. At the second application, s is $0''+0$, t is $0''$, and $\varphi(u)$ is $0''+0'' = u''$.

Unfortunately, a precise formal description of *ND* proofs is somewhat complicated, which is why we are using the Hilbert system H instead. This will pay off later (Chapter 11.7), but the price is that actual proofs become long and unwieldy. That's why we *never* display actual proofs but rely on informal reasoning in *PA*, as above. But just to bring the point home, let us make *one* exception and write down a formal proof in H of 2+2=4. The reason it gets so long is that $\forall$-elimination is not a rule but an axiom in H, and likewise substitution of identities is the axiom

$$\forall x \forall y (x = y \to (\varphi(x) \to \varphi(y)))$$

Here is a proof, a sequence of 24 sentences, without explanations of where each sentence comes from, i.e. if it is a *PA* axiom, a logical axiom, or results from applying a rule to earlier sentences—these explanations are helpful but do not belong to the official derivation.

(12)
$$\begin{array}{l}
\forall x \forall y\, x+y' = (x+y)' \\
\forall x \forall y (x+y' = (x+y)' \to \forall y\, 0''+y' = (0''+y)') \\
\forall y\, 0''+y' = (0''+y)' \\
\forall y (0''+y' = (0''+y)' \to 0''+0'' = (0''+0')') \\
0''+0'' = (0''+0')' \\
\forall y (0''+y' = (0''+y)' \to 0''+0' = (0''+0)') \\
0''+0' = (0''+0)' \\
\forall z \forall u (z = u \to (0''+0'' = z' \to 0''+0'' = u')) \\
\forall z \forall u (z = u \to (0''+0'' = z' \to 0''+0'' = u')) \to \\
\qquad \forall u (0''+0' = u \to (0''+0'' = (0''+0')' \to 0''+0'' = u')) \\
\forall u (0''+0' = u \to (0''+0'' = (0''+0')' \to 0''+0'' = u')) \\
\forall u (0''+0' = u \to (0''+0'' = (0''+0')' \to 0''+0'' = u')) \to \\
\qquad 0''+0' = (0''+0)' \to (0''+0'' = (0''+0')' \to 0''+0'' = \\
\qquad (0''+0)'') \\
0''+0' = (0''+0)' \to (0''+0'' = (0''+0')' \to 0''+0'' = (0''+0)'') \\
0''+0'' = (0''+0')' \to 0''+0'' = (0''+0)'' \\
0''+0'' = (0''+0)'' \\
\forall x\, x+0 = x \\
\forall x (x+0 = x \to 0''+0 = 0'') \\
0''+0 = 0'' \\
\forall v \forall w (v = w \to (0''+0'' = v'' \to 0''+0'' = w'')) \\
\forall v \forall w (v = w \to (0''+0'' = v'' \to 0''+0'' = w'')) \to \\
\qquad \forall w (0''+0 = w \to (0''+0'' = (0''+0)'' \to 0''+0'' = w'')) \\
\forall w (0''+0 = w \to (0''+0'' = (0''+0)'' \to 0''+0'' = w'')) \\
\forall w (0''+0 = w \to (0''+0'' = (0''+0)'' \to 0''+0'' = w'')) \to \\
\qquad 0''+0 = 0'' \to (0''+0'' = (0''+0)'' \to 0''+0'' = 0'''') \\
0''+0 = 0'' \to (0''+0'' = (0''+0)'' \to 0''+0'' = 0'''') \\
0''+0'' = (0''+0)'' \to 0''+0'' = 0'''' \\
0''+0'' = 0''''
\end{array}$$

Hopefully, this example is both instructive and deterring.

9.4. The order relation in *PA*

L_{PA} doesn't have a symbol for the usual order between natural numbers, but this order can be defined:

(13) a. $x < y \leftrightarrow_{\text{def}} \exists z\, x + z' = y$

b. $x \leqslant y \leftrightarrow_{\text{def}} x < y'$

Strictly speaking, there are two ways to view these definitions. Either one considers all expressions $x < y$ (and more generally $s < t$, where s, t are L_{PA}-terms) as *abbreviations* of the corresponding L_{PA}-

formulas, and similarly for $\leqslant$. Or, one *adds* $<$ and $\leqslant$ as new binary predicate symbols, and likewise $x < y \leftrightarrow \exists z\, x + z' = y$ as well as $x \leqslant y \leftrightarrow x < y'$ to the axioms. One can verify in general that adding new predicate (or function) symbols with their defining axioms doesn't have any unexpected consequences. More precisely, it doesn't let you prove any new theorems in the old vocabulary; this is a general fact about adding defined symbols in first-order logic and has nothing *per se* to do with *PA*; see Exercises 9.10.11 and 9.10.12, and the discussion in Section 9.9.2 below. For most purposes it doesn't matter much which perspective we choose.

We note:

(14) a. $PA \vdash x = y \vee x < y \leftrightarrow x < y'$

b. $PA \vdash x \leqslant y \leftrightarrow \exists z\, x + z = y$

c. $PA \vdash x \leqslant y' \leftrightarrow (x \leqslant y \vee x = y')$

Proof. Reason informally in *PA*. (a) First observe that $x < x'$ is provable, since $x + 0' = (x + 0)' = x'$ (axioms (PA4) and (PA3)). So if $x = y$ we have $x < y'$, whereas if $x < y$ there is z such that $x + z' = y$, and hence $(x + z')' = y'$, which entails that $x + z'' = y'$, and so $x < y'$. This proves the left-to-right direction. In the other direction, suppose $x < y'$, so there is z such that $x + z' = y'$. This gives $(x + z)' = y'$ and hence, by axiom (PA2), $x + z = y$. If $z = 0$, we have $x = y$. If $z \neq 0$ there is, by (1), u such that $z = u'$, so $x + u' = y$, and thus $x < y$. This proves (a). The proofs of (b) and (c) are similar. □

We now show that the claim that $\leqslant$ is a total non-strict order (and hence that $<$ is a total strict order) can be proved in *PA*. That is the main message of this section, i.e. that (16)–(19) below hold; the proofs can be skipped if desired. First, two lemmas:

(15) a. $PA \vdash x + y = x \rightarrow y = 0$

b. $PA \vdash x \neq 0 \rightarrow x + y \neq 0$

Proof. (15a) is an easy consequence of (1) and (9). (15b) is an exercise. □

(16) $PA \vdash x \leqslant x$

Proof. We must show that $PA \vdash \exists z\, x + z = x$. But that follows from (PA3) (and $\exists$-introduction). □

(17) $PA \vdash (x \leqslant y \wedge y \leqslant x) \rightarrow x = y$

Proof. Assume $x \leqslant y$ and $y \leqslant x$. By (14b) there are z and u such that $x + z = y$ and $y + u = x$. Thus, using (5), $x + (z + u) = (x + z) + u =$

$y + u = x$. Then it follows from (15a) that $z + u = 0$, and therefore, by (15b), that $z = 0$. In other words, $x + 0 = y$, which according to (PA3) means that $x = y$. □

The reasoning in the above proof is entirely informal. It should be clear by now that each step in the argument can be carried out 'inside' *PA*. The proof that we gave above is a proof of (17), i.e. of the fact that *there is a derivation* in H of the sentence $\forall x \forall y((x \leqslant y \wedge y \leqslant x) \rightarrow x = y)$ from the axioms of *PA*. This is an informal proof in our metalanguage of the existence of a formal derivation in the system H.

(18) $PA \vdash (x \leqslant y \wedge y \leqslant z) \rightarrow x \leqslant z$

Proof. Assume that $x \leqslant y$ and $y \leqslant z$. So there are u and v such that $x + u = y$ and $y + v = z$. Thus, $x + (u + v) = (x + u) + v = y + v = z$. And from $x + (u + v) = z$ it follows that $\exists w(x + w = z)$, i.e. $x \leqslant z$. □

(19) $PA \vdash x \leqslant y \vee y \leqslant x$

Proof. Induction on y. For the base step we must show $x \leqslant 0 \vee 0 \leqslant x$. But this follows from the fact that $0 \leqslant x$ holds (which in turn follows from the definition of $\leqslant$ and (2)). For the induction step we assume that $x \leqslant y \vee y \leqslant x$ holds, and show that $x \leqslant y' \vee y' \leqslant x$ follows. We reason by cases.[4]

Case 1: $x \leqslant y$. Then there is z such that $x + z = y$. Thus, with (PA4), $x + z' = (x + z)' = y'$, which means that $\exists v\, x + v = y'$, i.e. that $x \leqslant y'$, and hence $x \leqslant y' \vee y' \leqslant x$.

Case 2: $y \leqslant x$. There is u such that $y + u = x$. Now there are two subcases.

Case 2A: $u = 0$. From $y + 0 = x$ and (PA3) it then follows that $y = x$, which entails (since $x + 0' = x'$ by (PA4) and (PA3)), that $x \leqslant y'$, and hence $x \leqslant y' \vee y' \leqslant x$.

Case 2B: $u \neq 0$. Then it follows from (1) that $u = v'$ for some v. Therefore, $y + v' = x$. Using (3) we obtain $y' + v = x$, which means that $y' \leqslant x$, and thus again that $x \leqslant y' \vee y' \leqslant x$.

So in both cases the desired conclusion follows, which takes care of the induction step. □

These results are formulated for the non-strict order. For the strict order, we can show in *PA*, using (13), and (14) and the results about $\leqslant$, that $<$ is irreflexive, transitive, and total:

(20) $PA \vdash x < y \vee x = y \vee y < x$

[4]This is allowed, since $\varphi \vdash_H \theta$ and $\psi \vdash_H \theta$ implies $\varphi \vee \psi \vdash_H \theta$.

9.5. More on addition, multiplication, order

(21) a. $PA \vdash x \leqslant x + y$

b. $PA \vdash y \neq 0 \to x \leqslant x \cdot y$

(22) a. $PA \vdash x + y = 0 \to (x = 0 \wedge y = 0)$

b. $PA \vdash x \cdot y = 0 \to (x = 0 \vee y = 0)$

(23) a. $PA \vdash x + z = y + z \to x = y$

b. $PA \vdash (z \neq 0 \wedge x \cdot z = y \cdot z) \to x = y$

Proof. We show (23b) since the proof exemplifies a slightly more involved use of the induction axiom; the rest are exercises. So far, free variables besides the variable on which we perform induction have been fixed parameters during the whole argument. In the present case we do induction on y. There are two more variables, x and z, but only z is a fixed parameter. Namely, we let the induction formula be

$$\varphi(y, z) := \forall x((z \neq 0 \wedge x \cdot z = y \cdot z) \to x = y)$$

Base step: $y = 0$. Take any x and suppose $z \neq 0$ and $x \cdot z = 0 \cdot z$. But $0 \cdot z = 0$ ((6) and (PA5)), so $x \cdot z = 0$, and thus $x = 0$, by (22b) and the assumption that $z \neq 0$. Hence, $x = y$.

Induction step: Fix y (recall that z is fixed throughout) and suppose we have $\forall x((z \neq 0 \wedge x \cdot z = y \cdot z) \to x = y)$; this is the induction hypothesis. Now take x such that $z \neq 0 \wedge x \cdot z = y' \cdot z$. We must show $x = y'$. Since $z \neq 0$ it follows from (22b) (since $y' \neq 0$ by (PA1)) that $y' \cdot z \neq 0$, and hence that $x \cdot z \neq 0$, from which we conclude that $x \neq 0$ (since $0 \cdot z = 0$). By (1), there is w such that $x = w'$. So we have $w' \cdot z = y' \cdot z$, which by axiom (PA6) (and (6)) means that $w \cdot z + z = y \cdot z + z$. By (23a) we obtain $w \cdot z = y \cdot z$. And now we can use our induction hypothesis to conclude that $w = y$. Note that this hypothesis is that *for all* x we have that if $z \neq 0$ and $x \cdot z = y \cdot z$, then $x = y$, which we now apply to w. Thus (where x is again our selected parameter), $x = w' = y'$. □

9.6. Bounded quantification in *PA*

We can introduce bounded quantifiers in the formal language of *PA*, just as we did informally in Chapter 8.5.2:

(24)
$$\exists y_{y \leqslant z} \varphi(\overline{x}, y) := \exists y(y \leqslant z \wedge \varphi(\overline{x}, y))$$
$$\forall y_{y \leqslant z} \varphi(\overline{x}, y) := \forall y(y \leqslant z \to \varphi(\overline{x}, y))$$

Note that $\exists y_{y \leqslant z}\varphi(\overline{x}, y)$ and $\forall y_{y \leqslant z}\varphi(\overline{x}, y)$ are formulas whose free variables are among $\overline{x}, z$. Now recall the *numerals* $\mathbf{0}, \mathbf{1}, \mathbf{2}, \ldots$ that we introduced earlier (e.g. Chapter 7.2.4) as 'canonical' terms referring to numbers: $\mathbf{0} = 0$ (i.e. the *symbol* '0'), $\mathbf{1} = 0'$, $\mathbf{2} = 0''$, ... For every number n we have:

(25) $\quad PA \vdash x \leqslant \mathbf{n} \leftrightarrow (x = \mathbf{0} \vee \ldots \vee x = \mathbf{n})$

Proof. We prove this by induction in the metalanguage, i.e. induction over n. Base step: $n = 0$. We must show $PA \vdash x \leqslant \mathbf{0} \leftrightarrow x = \mathbf{0}$, but this is an easy consequence of earlier results. Induction step: Assume

$$x \leqslant \mathbf{n} \leftrightarrow (x = \mathbf{0} \vee \ldots \vee x = \mathbf{n})$$

We must show

$$x \leqslant \mathbf{n}' \leftrightarrow (x = \mathbf{0} \vee \ldots \vee x = \mathbf{n} \vee x = \mathbf{n}')$$

which follows directly from the induction hypothesis and (14c) (with $y = \mathbf{n}$). □

Now we can show the following (where we leave out in the notation possible free variables in φ besides x):

(26) a. $PA \vdash \exists x_{x \leqslant \mathbf{n}}\varphi(x) \leftrightarrow (\varphi(\mathbf{0}) \vee \ldots \vee \varphi(\mathbf{n}))$

b. $PA \vdash \forall x_{x \leqslant \mathbf{n}}\varphi(x) \leftrightarrow (\varphi(\mathbf{0}) \wedge \ldots \wedge \varphi(\mathbf{n}))$

Proof. The left-hand side in (26a) is $\exists x(x \leqslant \mathbf{n} \wedge \varphi(x))$, which according to (25) is equivalent to

$$\exists x((x = \mathbf{0} \vee \ldots \vee x = \mathbf{n}) \wedge \varphi(x))$$

which by a distributive law in propositional logic is equivalent to

$$\exists x((x = \mathbf{0} \wedge \varphi(x)) \vee \ldots \vee (x = \mathbf{n} \wedge \varphi(x)))$$

which in turn, by a law in FOL about how the existential quantifier distributes over disjunction, is equivalent to

$$\exists x(x = \mathbf{0} \wedge \varphi(x)) \vee \ldots \vee \exists x(x = \mathbf{n} \wedge \varphi(x))$$

But $\exists x(x = \mathbf{k} \wedge \varphi(x))$ is logically equivalent to $\varphi(\mathbf{k})$, so (26a) follows. And (26b) follows from (26a) by de Morgan's laws and the fact that $\forall x\psi$ is equivalent to $\neg\exists x\neg\psi$. □

Similarly, for $n > 0$:[5]

(27) a. $PA \vdash \exists x_{x < \mathbf{n}}\varphi(x) \leftrightarrow (\varphi(\mathbf{0}) \vee \ldots \vee \varphi(\mathbf{n-1}))$

b. $PA \vdash \forall x_{x < \mathbf{n}}\varphi(x) \leftrightarrow (\varphi(\mathbf{0}) \wedge \ldots \wedge \varphi(\mathbf{n-1}))$

[5]Here $\mathbf{n-1}$ stands for the term 0 followed by $n-1$ $'$:s; see Exercise 9.10.4 for another notation for numerals.

9.7. Closed terms in *PA*

A closed term in *PA*, i.e. an L_{PA}-term without variables, is built from 0 with the function symbols $+, \cdot, '$. This means that each such term has a unique natural number as *value*. For example, the value of

$$0''' \cdot (0' + 0'''')$$

i.e.

$$\mathbf{3} \cdot (\mathbf{1} + \mathbf{4})$$

is 15. We define the *value* $v(t)$ of a closed term t by induction:

Definition 9.7.1

1. $v(0) = 0$
2. $v(t') = v(t) + 1$
3. $v(s + t) = v(s) + v(t)$, and $v(s \cdot t) = v(s) \cdot v(t)$.[6]

We see immediately that

(28) $v(\mathbf{n}) = n$

The following is somewhat tedious but not hard to prove, for closed L_{PA}-terms t, s:[7]

(29) a. If $v(t) = n$, then $PA \vdash t = \mathbf{n}$, and if $v(t) \neq n$, $PA \vdash t \neq \mathbf{n}$.

b. If $v(t) \leqslant v(s)$, $PA \vdash t \leqslant s$, and if $v(t) \nleqslant v(s)$, $PA \vdash \neg t \leqslant s$.

Since identical terms can be substituted in H (i.e. if $s = t$ and $\varphi(s)$ are derivable, so is $\varphi(t)$), we can now obtain, for example, from (26a):

$$\text{If } v(t) = n, \text{ then } PA \vdash \exists x_{x \leqslant t}\varphi(x) \leftrightarrow (\varphi(\mathbf{0}) \vee \ldots \vee \varphi(\mathbf{n})).$$

9.8. Arithmetical definability

In Chapter 8 we encountered a host of number-theoretic relations and functions. Can these be expressed in our first-order arithmetical language in the vocabulary $L_{PA} = \{0, ', +, \cdot\}$? In many cases the answer is obvious, since we described these relations and functions explicitly using addition, multiplication, successor, and logical operations such as bounded quantification, all of which are available in the formal arithmetical language. To make our question precise, we use the concept of *definability in a model* from Chapter 6.5. Thus, we can ask which

[6]Observe that the signs $+$ and $\cdot$ on the left-hand side are symbols in L_{PA}, whereas on the right-hand side they stand for ordinary addition and multiplication.

[7]A proof of this in a weaker theory than *PA* is outlined in Exercise 14.8.14.

number-theoretic relations are definable in $\mathcal{N}$ (without parameters), the standard model of arithmetic.

Recall that a k-ary relation $R \subseteq M^k$ is definable in a model $\mathcal{M}$ for a vocabulaly L if there is an L-formula $\psi(x_1, \ldots, x_k)$ such that for all $a_1, \ldots, a_k \in M$,

$$R(a_1, \ldots, a_k) \text{ iff } \mathcal{M} \models \psi\,[a_1, \ldots, a_k]$$

In the case of $\mathcal{N}$, each number n in the domain is denoted by a numeral $\mathbf{n}$, so instead of saying that $n_1, \ldots, n_k$ satisfies the formula $\psi(x_1, \ldots, x_k)$ in $\mathcal{N}$, we can say that the sentence $\psi(\mathbf{n}_1, \ldots, \mathbf{n}_k)$ is true in $\mathcal{N}$.

The notion of truth in a model was defined formally in Chapter 2.3.2. Since currently we are only interested in the standard model $\mathcal{N}$, we simply say (as we already did in Chapter 7) that an arithmetical sentence is *true* (*false*) when it is true (false) in $\mathcal{N}$.

What about functions? We extend the notion of definability to functions by considering their graphs:

(30) If f is a k-ary function, the *graph* of f is the $(k+1)$-ary relation G_f defined by

$$G_f(n_1, \ldots, n_k, m) \text{ iff } f(n_1, \ldots, n_k) = m$$

Let us make all of this official:

Definition 9.8.1 (arithmetical relations and functions)
A k-ary number-theoretic relation R is *arithmetically definable*, or simply *arithmetical*, if there is an L_{PA}-formula $\psi(x_1, \ldots, x_k)$ such that

$$R(n_1, \ldots, n_k) \text{ iff } \psi(\mathbf{n}_1, \ldots, \mathbf{n}_k) \text{ is true}$$

for all $n_1, \ldots, n_k$,. A number-theoretic function is *arithmetically definable* if its graph is arithmetically definable.

For example, the order relation among numbers is arithmetical since, even though $<$ is not a primitive symbol in L_{PA}, it holds that $m < n$ iff $m + k' = n$ for some k, and so the formula $\exists z\, x + z' = y$ defines the relation $<$ in $\mathcal{N}$. Similarly, the relation $n|m$ (n divides m) is defined by the formula $\exists z\, y = x \cdot z$. And since n is a prime if $n > 1$ and no number between 1 and n divides it, the set of primes is defined by the formula $Prime(x) := \mathbf{1}{<}x \wedge \neg\exists y_{\mathbf{1}<y}(y{<}x \wedge y|x)$. That is:

$$n \text{ is a prime number iff } Prime(\mathbf{n}) \text{ is true.}$$

In this way, by just rewriting the informal definitions in the arithmetical language, we see that many number-theoretic relations are arithmetically definable. And similarly for explicitly defined functions. For example, the remainder and quotient function from Chapter 8.6.1 are arithmetical. Recall:

$$rem(m,n) = \begin{cases} \mu r_{r<n} \exists q_{q \leqslant m}(m = n \cdot q + r) & \text{if } n \neq 0 \\ m & \text{if } n = 0 \end{cases}$$

So the graph G_{rem} is given by

$$G_{rem}(m,n,k) \Leftrightarrow (n = 0 \wedge k = m) \vee (n \neq 0 \wedge k < n \wedge \exists q_{q \leqslant m}(m = n \cdot q + k))$$

which is defined in $\mathcal{N}$ by the formula

$$Rem(x, y, u) := (y = 0 \wedge u = x) \vee (y \neq 0 \wedge u < y \wedge \exists w_{w \leqslant x}(x = y \cdot w + u))$$

Similarly, functions defined with the bounded μ-operator from arithmetical functions or relations are arithmetical. Suppose, for example, that $f(m, n) = \mu p_{p<n} R(p, m)$. Then we have

$$G_f(m,n,k) \Leftrightarrow (k < n \wedge R(k,m) \wedge \forall q_{q<k} \neg R(q,m)) \vee (\neg \exists p_{p<n} R(p,m) \wedge k = n)$$

So if R is arithmetical, it is clear how find an L_{PA}-formula defining G_f.

There are uncountably many sets of natural numbers (Chapter 16.5) but only countably many arithmetical formulas, so there are plenty of non-arithmetical sets and relations among numbers. As a concrete example, we indicated in Chapter 7.2.4 a proof that the set (of Gödel numbers of sentences in) $Th(\mathcal{N})$ is not arithmetical (Theorem 7.2.8).

9.9. Representability in arithmetical theories

So far we have discussed how number-theoretic relations and functions can be expressed in the arithmetical language, relying on the notion of truth (in $\mathcal{N}$). We also want to see how these relations and functions can be dealt with in axiomatic arithmetical *theories*, such as *PA*. So in this section, T is a *consistent extension* of *PA*. That is, (a) no contradictions are derivable in T, (b) $L_T = L_{PA}$, and (c) all theorems of *PA* are theorems of T. (We are not assuming that T is axiomatizable.) The notion of a relation being representable in T was defined in Chapter 7.2.4, and is repeated below.

Definition 9.9.1 (representable relations)
A k-ary relation R is *representable in* T if there is an arithmetical formula $\varphi(x_1, \ldots, x_k)$ such that

(a) if $R(n_1, \ldots, n_k)$, then $T \vdash \varphi(\mathbf{n}_1, \ldots, \mathbf{n}_k)$, and
(b) if not $R(n_1, \ldots, n_k)$, then $T \vdash \neg\varphi(\mathbf{n}_1, \ldots, \mathbf{n}_k)$.

$\varphi(x_1, \ldots, x_k)$ is said to *represent* R in T. If the weaker condition

(c) $R(n_1, \ldots, n_k)$ iff $T \vdash \varphi(\mathbf{n}_1, \ldots, \mathbf{n}_k)$

holds, we say that $\varphi(x_1, \ldots, x_k)$ *weakly represents* R in T, and thus that R is *weakly representable* in T.

A few immediate comments:

- Representability implies weak representability (since T is consistent!), but the converse can fail, as we will see.
- If R is representable in T and T' is an extension of T, then R is representable in T'. This does *not* hold in general for weak representability.
- If $T = Th(\mathcal{N})$, then representability and weak representability both coincide with arithmetical definability.
- It follows from (28) and (29) the relations $m = n$, $m \leqslant n$, and $m < n$ are representable in T.

9.9.1. Representable functions

It would be natural to say that a function is representable in T if its graph is representable in T. It turns out, however, that for functions we shall have more use for a (seemingly) stronger condition.[8]

Definition 9.9.2 (representable functions)
A k-ary function f is *representable* in T if there is a formula $\varphi(x_1, \ldots, x_k, y)$ such that for all $n_1, \ldots, n_k, m$,

(d) if $f(n_1, \ldots, n_k) = m$, then $T \vdash \forall y(\varphi(\mathbf{n}_1, \ldots, \mathbf{n}_k, y) \leftrightarrow y = \mathbf{m})$.

But now it seems we have *two* notions of representability for functions. Fortunately, we can show that they in fact coincide.

Lemma 9.9.3
A function f is representable in T iff its graph G_f is representable in T.

Proof. For simplicity, suppose f is unary. First, if $\varphi(x, y)$ represents f in T as in (d) above, then clearly

(31) a. $f(n) = m$ implies $T \vdash \varphi(\mathbf{n}, \mathbf{m})$.
b. $f(n) \neq m$ implies $T \vdash \neg\varphi(\mathbf{n}, \mathbf{m})$.

[8]WARNING: The terminology concerning representability and definability varies in the literature. Some authors call representability *binumerability*, while weak representability is called *numerability*. Others use 'definable' where I have used 'representable', and vice versa (!). Additional variants occur. I have chosen to use *definable* in the model-theoretic sense (so arithmetically definable means definable in $\mathcal{N}$), and *representable* when provability in a theory is involved.

Thus, the same formula $\varphi(x, y)$ represents G_f in T.

The other direction is more interesting. Suppose that $\varphi(x, y)$ represents G_f in T, so that (31) holds. It does *not* follow that $\varphi(x, y)$ also represents f in T in the sense of (d). But we can find *another* formula $\tilde{\varphi}(x, y)$ that does represent f:

$$\tilde{\varphi}(x, y) := \varphi(x, y) \wedge \forall z_{z<y} \neg\varphi(x, z)$$

We show that (d) holds for $\tilde{\varphi}(x, y)$. So suppose $f(n) = m$. By (31):

(32) $T \vdash \varphi(\mathbf{n}, \mathbf{m})$

and

$$T \vdash \neg\varphi(\mathbf{n}, \mathbf{0}) \wedge \ldots \wedge \neg\varphi(\mathbf{n}, \mathbf{m}{-}\mathbf{1})$$

According to (27), the latter entails (since T is an extension of *PA*) that

(33) $T \vdash \forall z_{z<\mathbf{m}} \neg\varphi(\mathbf{n}, z)$

so we have $T \vdash \varphi(\mathbf{n}, \mathbf{m}) \wedge \forall z_{z<\mathbf{m}} \neg\varphi(\mathbf{n}, z)$, i.e.

(34) $T \vdash \tilde{\varphi}(\mathbf{n}, \mathbf{m})$

This means that $T \vdash y = \mathbf{m} \to \tilde{\varphi}(\mathbf{n}, y)$, so in order to show that (d) holds for $\tilde{\varphi}(x, y)$ it remains to prove the implication in the other direction, that is,

(35) $T \vdash \tilde{\varphi}(\mathbf{n}, y) \to y = \mathbf{m}$

We reason by cases 'inside T'; cf. the proof of (19). Suppose $\tilde{\varphi}(\mathbf{n}, y)$. If $\mathbf{m} < y$, it follows from the assumption (i.e. from $\forall z_{z<y} \neg\varphi(\mathbf{n}, z)$) that $\neg\varphi(\mathbf{n}, \mathbf{m})$, which contradicts (32). If $y < \mathbf{m}$, it follows from (33) that $\neg\varphi(\mathbf{n}, y)$, which contradicts the assumption that $\tilde{\varphi}(\mathbf{n}, y)$. So neither $\mathbf{m} < y$ nor $y < \mathbf{m}$ holds. But, by (20),

$$\mathbf{m} < y \vee \mathbf{m} = y \vee y < \mathbf{m}$$

Thus, $y = \mathbf{m}$, and we have shown (35). □

9.9.2. Strongly representable functions

There is a still stronger version of the requirement (d) on a representable function: add that the formula $\varphi(x_1, \ldots, x_k, y)$ also satisfies:

(e) $T \vdash \forall x_1 \ldots \forall x_k \exists_{=1} y \varphi(x_1, \ldots, x_k, y)$

Say that a formula φ satisfying (e) is *provably total in* T.

Definition 9.9.4
f is *strongly representable in* T if it is representable by a provably total formula in T.

When $\varphi(x_1, \ldots, x_k, y)$ is provably total in T, it is safe to add a new function symbol, say $\mathtt{f}$, to the vocabulary, with a *defining axiom*

$$(\mathtt{f\text{-}ax}) \quad \mathtt{f}x_1 \ldots x_k = y \leftrightarrow \varphi(x_1, \ldots, x_k, y)$$

Let T' be the theory T + ($\mathtt{f\text{-}ax}$), in the vocabulary $L_T \cup \{\mathtt{f}\}$. Safety here means two things: (i) Every L_T-sentence provable in T' is already provable in T; (ii) The new symbol $\mathtt{f}$ is *eliminable* in the sense that each $L_{T'}$-sentence is equivalent in T' to an L_T-sentence. T' is called an *extension by definitions* of T, and the fact that (i) and (ii) hold is a general feature of first-order logic; it is not particular to arithmetical theories. Similarly for predicate symbols: for any L_T-formula $\psi(x_1, \ldots, x_m)$ (no special condition needed) we may safely add a new m-ary predicate symbol $\mathtt{P}$ with the defining axiom

$$(\mathtt{P\text{-}ax}) \quad \mathtt{P}x_1 \ldots x_m \leftrightarrow \psi(x_1, \ldots, x_m)$$

These facts are covered in Exercises 9.10.11 and 9.10.12. Adding defined function and predicate symbols is a convenient way to shorten formulas and increase readability.

The interest in condition (e) is also due to the following fact.

Fact 9.9.5
If f is representable in T, then f is strongly representable in T.

Proof. Again, if $\varphi(\overline{x}, y)$ represents f in T, one can construct another formula $\varphi^*(\overline{x}, y)$ which strongly represents f in T. This time the construction is less natural; we leave as Exercise 9.10.10 to show that

$$\varphi^*(\overline{x}, y) := (\varphi(\overline{x}, y) \wedge \exists_{=1} z\, \varphi(\overline{x}, z)) \vee (y = 0 \wedge \neg \exists_{=1} z\, \varphi(\overline{x}, z))$$

strongly represents f in T. □

It is often important to have strongly representing formulas, but the construction in the proof above is rarely used in practice. Instead, one can usually find simple and natural formulas strongly representing the relevant functions. An obvious example is addition and multiplication: it is almost immediate that the formulas $x + y = z$ and $x \cdot y = z$ strongly represent these functions in *PA* (and hence in T). A less immediate example is the remainder function *rem*; we saw at the end of Section 9.8 that the formula

$$Rem(x, y, u) := (y = 0 \wedge u = x) \vee (y \neq 0 \wedge u < y \wedge \exists w_{w \leqslant x}(x = y \cdot w + u))$$

arithmetically defines (the graph of) this function. In fact:

(36) $Rem(x, y, u)$ strongly represents *rem* in *PA*.

Proof. It is easy to see that if $rem(n, m) = k$, then $PA \vdash Rem(\mathbf{n}, \mathbf{m}, \mathbf{k})$. So it remains to show

$$PA \vdash \forall x \forall y \exists_{=1} u \, Rem(x, y, u)$$

This has two parts, *existence* and *uniqueness*. We leave the existence part as an exercise, and show uniqueness here.

As usual we reason informally in *PA*. So assume $Rem(x, y, u)$ and $Rem(x, y, v)$. We must derive $u = v$. The argument is by cases. If $y = 0$, it follows directly that $u = x$ and $v = x$, so $u = v$. So assume $y \neq 0$. Then it follows by $Rem(x, y, u)$ and $Rem(x, y, v)$ that there are $c, d \leqslant x$ such that $u < y$ and $x = y \cdot c + u$, and $v < y$ and $x = y \cdot d + v$. Now distinguish three cases.

Case 1: $c = d$. Then $x = y \cdot c + u = y \cdot c + v$, from which it follows (by (23a) in Section 9.5 (and the commutativity of addition) that $u = v$.

Case 2: $c < d$. Then there is z such that $c + z = d$, and $z \neq 0$. Thus:

$$x = y \cdot c + u = y \cdot (c + z) + v = y \cdot c + y \cdot z + v$$

(using a distributive law). Again by (23a), we have

$$u = y \cdot z + v$$

Using (21a) and (21b) in the same section, we conclude (since $z \neq 0$)

$$u = y \cdot z + v \geqslant y \cdot z \geqslant y$$

But this contradicts our assumption that $u < y$.

Case 3: $d < c$. In a completely symmetric way one shows that this contradicts $v < y$.

Therefore, since $<$ is total, we must have $c = d$, and hence $u = v$. □

9.10. Exercises to Chapter 9

Exercise 9.10.1

1. Show that $PA \vdash 0 \cdot x = 0$
2. Show that $PA \vdash x' \cdot y = x \cdot y + y$ [Hint: use that addition is associative and commutative]
3. Use these facts to show (6). [Hint: induction on x.]
4. Prove (8).
5. Prove (7).

Exercise 9.10.2

1. Prove (9). [Hint: induction on x.]
2. Prove (14c). [Hint: earlier results suffice.]
3. Prove (15b).
4. Show (21). [Hint: for (b), use (1).]

5. Show (22). [Hint: induction on y.]
6. Show (23a). [Hint: induction on z.]

Exercise 9.10.3 (strong induction and least number principle)
The *Strong* Induction axiom and the *Least Number Principle* are the following schemes (suppressing possible additional free variables):

(S-IND) $\forall x(\forall y(y < x \rightarrow \varphi(y)) \rightarrow \varphi(x)) \rightarrow \forall x\varphi(x)$

(LNP) $\exists x\varphi(x) \rightarrow \exists x(\varphi(x) \wedge \forall y(y < x \rightarrow \neg\varphi(y)))$

(a) Show that (S-IND) and (LNP) are *logically* equivalent.

(b) *Show that (S-IND) follows from (IND) in *PA*. [Hint: use (IND) with the formula $\psi(x) := \forall y(y < x \rightarrow \varphi(y))$.]

Exercise 9.10.4 (numeral notation)
Our boldface notation for numerals has its limitations. For example, does the term $\mathbf{m} + \mathbf{n}$ contain the symbol '+'? Yes, but it would be good to also have a notation for the numeral consisting of 0 followed by $m+n$ primes. One option is to use overlining: then $\overline{m}+\overline{n}$ contains '+', but $\overline{m+n}$ does not. Show that with this notation, we could simplify condition (d) in Definition 9.9.2 as follows: for all $n_1, \ldots, n_k$,

(d′) $T \vdash \forall y(\varphi(\overline{n_1}, \ldots, \overline{n_k}, y) \leftrightarrow y = \overline{f(n_1, \ldots, n_k)})$.

Exercise 9.10.5
1. Show that the predecessor function *pred* is strongly represented in *PA* by the formula $(x = 0 \wedge y = 0) \vee x = y'$.
2. Show that the subtraction function $n \dot{-} m$ is strongly represented in *PA* by the formula $(x < y \wedge z = 0) \vee x = y + z$.
3. Find a formula strongly representing the function $|n - m|$ in *PA*.

Exercise 9.10.6
*Prove the existence part of (36), i.e. that $PA \vdash \forall x \forall y \exists u Rem(x, y, u)$.

[Hint: Reason in *PA* with induction on x. In the ind. step, pick x, y: by ind. hyp. there are u and $w \leqslant x$ s.t. $y = 0 \wedge u = x$ or $u < y \wedge x = y \cdot w + u$. You need to find v such that either $y = 0 \wedge v = x'$ or there is $w_1 \leqslant x'$ such that $v < y \wedge x' = y \cdot w_1 + v$. Distinguish the cases $y = 0$ and $y \neq 0$, and, in the latter case, distinguish the subcases $u' < y$ and $u' = y$.]

Exercise 9.10.7
Show that if T is a *true* theory, and if a function or relation is representable in T, then it is arithmetically definable.

The remaining exercises do not require that T is an extension of PA. In 9.10.8 – 9.10.10, T is any theory in the arithmetical vocabulary L_{PA}. In 9.10.11 –

9.10.12, T is any first-order theory. Thus, the claims in these exercises only require logical reasoning, not arithmetical reasoning.

Exercise 9.10.8

Suppose that the formula $\varphi(x)$ represents the set A in T.

1. Suppose $T \vdash \theta$. Show that the formula $\varphi'(x) := \varphi(x) \wedge \theta$ also represents A in T. Are $\varphi(x)$ and $\varphi'(x)$ equivalent in T?
2. Suppose instead that T in addition is a true theory, and that θ is true but unprovable in T. (The existence of such a θ could follow from the first incompleteness theorem.) Show that $\varphi'(x)$ arithmetically defines A, and that, if $A \neq \varnothing$, $\varphi(x)$ and $\varphi'(x)$ are not equivalent in T.
3. Now suppose that $T \nvdash \theta$ and $T \nvdash \neg\theta$. Show that $\varphi''(x) := \varphi(x) \vee \theta$ weakly represents A in T, and that, if $A \neq N$, $\varphi(x)$ and $\varphi''(x)$ are not equivalent in T.

Exercise 9.10.9

Show that conditions 1 and 2 are equivalent:

1. f is representable in T.
2. There is a formula $\varphi(x_1, \ldots, x_k, y)$ such that for all $n_1, \ldots, n_k$,
   (a) if $f(n_1, \ldots, n_k) = m$, then $T \vdash \varphi(\mathbf{n}_1, \ldots, \mathbf{n}_k, \mathbf{m})$; and
   (b) $T \vdash (\varphi(\mathbf{n}_1, \ldots, \mathbf{n}_k, y_1) \wedge \varphi(\mathbf{n}_1, \ldots, \mathbf{n}_k, y_2)) \rightarrow y_1 = y_2$

Exercise 9.10.10

Prove Fact 9.9.5; i.e. show that if $\varphi(x, y)$ represents f in T (assume for simplicity that f is 1-place), then $\varphi^*(x, y)$ strongly represents f in T:

1. Show that $f(n) = m$ implies $T \vdash \varphi^*(\mathbf{n}, \mathbf{m})$.
2. Show that $T \vdash \forall x \exists_{=1} y\, \varphi^*(x, y)$.

   [Hint: Reason in T: pick x and show $\exists_{=1} y\, \varphi^*(x, y)$ by distinguishing two cases: $\exists_{=1} z\, \varphi(x, z)$ and $\neg\exists_{=1} z\, \varphi(x, z)$. In both cases, show $\exists y \varphi^*(x, y)$ and that $\varphi^*(x, u) \wedge \varphi^*(x, w)$ implies $u = w$.]

Exercise 9.10.11 (extensions by definitions: conservativity)

1. Let T be any first-order theory and φ an L_T-formula such that

   $$T \vdash \forall x_1 \ldots \forall x_k \exists_{=1} y \varphi(x_1, \ldots, x_k, y)$$

   Form T' and $L_{T'}$ as in (`f-ax`) in Section 9.9.2. Show that T' is a *conservative extension* of T, in the sense that no new L_T-sentences can be proved in T':

   If θ is an L_T-sentence and $T' \vdash \theta$, then $T \vdash \theta$.

   [Use the completeness theorem and reason model-theoretically.]
2. Similarly for adding a new predicate symbol as in (`P-ax`).

Exercise 9.10.12 (extensions by definitions: eliminability)
*Suppose both f and P have been added as in the preceding exercise, so $L_{T'} = L_T \cup \{\mathtt{f}, \mathtt{P}\}$, and T' has the two new defining axioms. A theory formed in this way is called an *extension by definitions* of T. It is clear that T' is a conservative extension of T.

1. Show that for any model $\mathcal{M}$ of T, there is a unique expansion $\mathcal{M}'$ of $\mathcal{M}$ to the vocabulary $L_{T'}$ (same domain M and same interpretation of the L_T-symbols) which is a model of T'.
2. Call a formula *unnested* if all its atomic subformulas have one of the following forms: $x = y$, $Px_1 \dots x_n$, or $g(x_1, \dots, x_n) = y$ (when $n = 0$, this is $c = y$). Show that every formula (in any vocabulary) is logically equivalent to an unnested formula.

   [Start by recursively replacing atomic formulas χ of the form $g(t_1, \dots, t_n) = z$, where z does not occur in the t_i, by

   $$\chi^* := \exists y_1 \dots \exists y_n [(t_1 = y_1)^* \wedge \dots \wedge (t_n = y_n)^* \wedge g(y_1, \dots, y_n) = z]$$

   where the y_i are new (and $(c = y)^*$ is $c = y$, and $(x = y)^*$ is $x = y$). Then, for any terms s, t let $(s = t)^* = \exists u((s = u)^* \wedge (t = u)^*)$, and similarly,

   $$(Qt_1 \dots t_n)^* = \exists y_1 \dots \exists y_n [(t_1 = y_1)^* \wedge \dots \wedge (t_n = y_n)^* \wedge Qy_1 \dots y_n]$$

   The recursive definitions of $(\neg\theta)^*$, $(\theta_1 \wedge \theta_2)^*$, and $(\exists x\theta)^*$ are obvious. Prove by induction that for all formulas θ, all models $\mathcal{M}$, and all assignments σ in M, $\mathcal{M} \models \theta\,[\sigma]$ iff $\mathcal{M} \models \theta^*\,[\sigma]$.]
3. Show that the new symbols in $L_{T'}$ are *eliminable*, in the sense that for every $L_{T'}$-formula θ there is an L_T-formula $\theta^\dagger$ equivalent in T' to θ. [Hint: By 2. we can assume that θ is unnested. Let $\theta^\dagger$ result by

   replacing $\mathtt{P}x_1 \dots x_m$ by $\psi'(x_1, \dots, x_m)$
   replacing $\mathtt{f}(x_1 \dots x_k) = y$ by $\varphi'(x_1, \dots, x_k, y)$

   where ψ', φ' result from ψ, φ by bound variable changes (if necessary) to avoid variable clashes. Prove by induction that θ and $\theta^\dagger$ are satisfied by the same assignments in every model of T'.]
4. Conclude that for any $L_{T'}$-sentence θ, $T' \vdash \theta$ iff $T \vdash \theta^\dagger$.

These facts specify the sense in which adding new but defined non-logical symbols does not change a theory T in any *essential* way. Indeed, if one wants, one can regard the formulas in the expanded vocabulary as *abbreviations* of their translations into the original vocabulary as in 4. In practice, extensions by definitions are used all the time; think, for example, of all the new individual constants, function and predicate symbols one usually adds to the language of set theory, where the original vocabulary is simply $L_{ZF} = \{\in\}$.

10 Representability of primitive recursive functions

We now show that all primitive recursive functions (hence all primitive recursive relations) are representable in *PA*: (a) the basic functions are representable; (b) if $f, g_1, \ldots, g_n$ are representable, the composed function $\text{Cn}[f, g_1, \ldots, g_n]$ is also representable, and (c) if f, g are representable, so is $\text{Pr}[f, g]$. (a) and (b) are easy. (c) requires a bit of work.

10.1. The basic functions are representable

(1) a. The zero function Z is (strongly) represented in *PA* by the formula $y = 0$.

b. The successor function s is (strongly) represented in *PA* by the formula $y = x'$.

c. The identity function id_i^k is (strongly) represented in *PA* by the formula $y = x_i$.

Proof. We show c.; the others are exercises. We have

$$G_{id_i^k}(n_1, \ldots, n_k, m) \Leftrightarrow id_i^k(n_1, \ldots, n_k) = m \Leftrightarrow n_i = m$$

so we take $\varphi_{k,i}(x_1, \ldots, x_k, y)$ to be $y = x_i$.[1] We must show:

$$\text{If } id_i^k(n_1, \ldots, n_k) = m, \text{ then } PA \vdash \varphi_{k,i}(\mathbf{n}_1, \ldots, \mathbf{n}_k, y) \leftrightarrow y = \mathbf{m}$$

in other words,

$$\text{If } n_i = m, \text{ then } PA \vdash y = \mathbf{n}_i \leftrightarrow y = \mathbf{m}$$

[1]This formula only has x_i and y as free variables, but remember that writing it as $\varphi_{k,i}(x_1, \ldots, x_k, y)$ only indicates that the free variables of $\varphi_{k,i}$ are *among* $x_1, \ldots, x_k, y$.

But the sentence on the right is a trivial logical truth! For strong representability, we note that $\forall x_1 \dots \forall x_k \exists_{=1} y\, y = x_i$ is also a logical truth. □

10.2. Composition and representability

Let h be defined by composition from f and $g_1, \dots, g_m$ (Chapter 8.2):

(Cn) $h(k_1, \dots, k_n) = f(g_1(k_1, \dots, k_n), \dots, g_m(k_1, \dots, k_n))$

That is, $h = \mathrm{Cn}[f, g_1, \dots, g_m]$. It follows that:

(2) $h(k_1, \dots, k_n) = k$ iff there are $l_1, \dots, l_m$ such that $g_i(k_1, \dots, k_n) = l_i$ for $i = 1, \dots, m$, and $f(l_1, \dots, l_m) = k$.

Lemma 10.2.1
If $h = \mathrm{Cn}[f, g_1, \dots, g_n]$ and $f, g_1, \dots, g_n$ are (strongly) representable in PA, then h is also (strongly) representable in PA.

Proof. We look at the case $m = 1$ and $n = 2$; the general case is entirely similar. So $h(k_1, k_2) = f(g(k_1, k_2))$, and (2) becomes

(i) $h(k_1, k_2) = k$ iff there is m s.t. $g(k_1, k_2) = m$ and $f(m) = k$.

Suppose f and g are represented in *PA* by the formulas $\varphi_f(x, y)$ and $\varphi_g(x_1, x_2, z)$, respectively. That is:

(ii) If $f(m) = k$, then $PA \vdash \varphi_f(\mathbf{m}, y) \leftrightarrow y = \mathbf{k}$

(iii) If $g(k_1, k_2) = m$, then $PA \vdash \varphi_g(\mathbf{k_1}, \mathbf{k_2}, z) \leftrightarrow z = \mathbf{m}$

Then h is represented in *PA* by the formula $\exists z(\varphi_g(x_1, x_2, z) \wedge \varphi_f(z, y))$:

(iv) If $h(k_1, k_2) = k$, then $PA \vdash \exists z(\varphi_g(\mathbf{k_1}, \mathbf{k_2}, z) \wedge \varphi_f(z, y)) \leftrightarrow y = \mathbf{k}$

This is seen as follows. Suppose $h(k_1, k_2) = k$ and let m be as in (i). By (iii), the sentence in (iv) that we need to prove is equivalent in *PA* to

$$\exists z(z = \mathbf{m} \wedge \varphi_f(z, y)) \leftrightarrow y = \mathbf{k}$$

which is logically equivalent to

$$\varphi_f(\mathbf{m}, y) \leftrightarrow y = \mathbf{k}$$

which is provable in *PA* by (ii). The claim about strong representability is similar and left as an exercise. □

10.3. Representability of primitive recursion

Suppose $h = \text{Pr}[f, g]$, where we for simplicity let h be 2-ary, so

$$\begin{cases} h(n,0) &= f(n) \\ h(n,m') &= g(n,m,h(n,m)) \end{cases}$$

We must show that if f and g are representable in *PA*, so is h. Nothing in first-order languages lets us handle definitions of functions by recursion directly. Instead, we rewrite the primitive recursive definition as an *explicit* definition. That $h(n,m) = k$ means that there is a sequence of numbers $h(n,0), h(n,1), \ldots, h(n,m)$, where the first is $f(n)$, the last is k, and every number except the first is obtained from the preceding one with g:

(pr1) $h(n,m) = k \Leftrightarrow$

$$\begin{aligned} &\text{there are } a_0, \ldots, a_m \text{ such that} \\ &[a_0 = f(n) \wedge \\ &\forall i_{\,i<m}(a_{i+1} = g(n,i,a_i)) \wedge \\ &a_m = k] \end{aligned}$$

We can express this by coding $a_0, \ldots, a_m$ as a sequence number. And here we want to use the β function coding, as in Chapter 8.7.3, precisely because this coding relies only on properties of addition and multiplication, which are already part of the arithmetical language. Thus, if $b = \langle a_0, \ldots, a_m\rangle^\beta$ in (pr1), we have (see (65b) in Chapter 8.7.3) $a_i = \beta'(b, i+1)$ for $i \leqslant m$. Then we can rewrite (pr1) as follows:

(pr2) $h(n,m) = k \Leftrightarrow$

$$\begin{aligned} &\exists b\,[\beta'(b,1) = f(n) \wedge \\ &\forall i_{\,i<m}(\beta'(b,i+2) = g(n,i,\beta'(b,i+1)) \wedge \\ &\beta'(b,m+1) = k] \end{aligned}$$

The next observation is this:

(3) The function β' is strongly representable in *PA*.

Proof. First, (36) in Chapter 9.9.2 showed that the remainder function *rem* is strongly representable in *PA*, and since $\beta(b,c,i) = rem(b,(c\cdot i')')$, it follows that β is strongly representable in *PA* (by Lemma 10.2.1, since multiplication and successor are strongly representable in *PA*).

Next (skip this part if you didn't get through Chapter 8.7.3!), recall that $\beta'(b,i) = \beta(\pi_1(b), \pi_2(b), i)$, so it suffices to show that the functions π_1 and π_2 are strongly representable in *PA*. To see this, note first that the function *OP* (see Chapter 8.7.3) can be shown to be strongly represented in *PA* by the formula

$$\varphi_{OP}(x,y,z) := \ \mathbf{2}\cdot z = (x+y)(x+y+1) + \mathbf{2}\cdot x$$

Then it is easy to see that π_1 is strongly represented in *PA* by

$$\varphi_{\pi_1}(z,u) := \exists y_{y\leqslant z}\, \varphi_{OP}(u,y,z)$$

Similarly for π_2. □

Thus, there is an L_{PA}-formula $B(x,y,z)$ with these properties:

(4) a. If $\beta'(b,i) = k$, then $PA \vdash B(\mathbf{b},\mathbf{i},\mathbf{k})$.

b. $PA \vdash \forall x \forall y \exists_{=1} z B(x,y,z)$

Using $B(x,y,z)$, we can rewrite the right-hand side of (pr2) as an arithmetical formula. Note that the claim, for example, that $\beta'(b,1) = f(n)$ cannot be expressed directly in *PA*, since we don't have function symbols corresponding to β' and f, only formulas expressing their *graphs*. But using a quantifier solves this:

$$\exists w(B(\mathbf{b},\mathbf{1},w) \wedge \varphi_f(\mathbf{n},w))$$

So we see that the following formula corresponds to the right-hand side of (pr2) in the arithmetical language:

(5) $PrimRec_h(x_1,x_2,y) :=$

$$\begin{aligned}&\exists u[\exists w(B(u,\mathbf{1},w) \wedge \varphi_f(x_1,w)) \wedge\\&\forall z_{\,z<x_2} \exists w_0 \exists w_1 (B(u,z'',w_1) \wedge B(u,z',w_0) \wedge\\&\varphi_g(x_1,z,w_0,w_1)) \wedge B(u,x_2{}',y)]\end{aligned}$$

Now, the next and final step is to prove:

Lemma 10.3.1
If h = Pr$[f,g]$, where f,g are representable in PA, then h is representable in PA.

Then, with the facts proved earlier in this chapter, we have:

Theorem 10.3.2
Every primitive recursive function and relation is representable in PA.

Proof. Given the lemma, it only remains to check the claim about relations. A relation R is primitive recursive iff the characteristic function c_R is primitive recursive, so there is a formula $\psi(\overline{x},y)$ such that

$$c_R(\overline{n}) = m \Rightarrow PA \vdash \psi(\overline{\mathbf{n}},y) \leftrightarrow y = \mathbf{m}$$

Then it is easy to see that the formula $\psi(\overline{x},\mathbf{1})$ represents R in *PA*. □

A proof of Lemma 10.3.1 at this point is quite feasible; it involves some detailed reasoning in *PA* but no principal difficulties (see Exercises 10.5.4 and 10.5.5). However, we shall postpone the proof of Theorem 10.3.2 until Chapter 14.5, where we obtain a stronger result. For now, we content ourselves with the following weaker result, which is a direct consequence of our work in this chapter.

Theorem 10.3.3
Every primitive recursive function (hence every primitive recursive relation) is arithmetical.

Proof. Every function representable in *PA* is arithmetically definable (by the same formula). Thus, the basic functions are arithmetical, and a glance at the proof of Lemma 10.2.1 shows that the composition of arithmetical functions is arithmetical. Finally, if h is obtained with primitive recursion from arithmetical functions f and g, we have just seen that the formula $PrimRec_h$ arithmetically defines h—this is clear as soon as one realizes that $PrimRec_h$ is just a paraphrase of the right-hand side of (pr2) in the arithmetical language. □

This result is weaker but still not at all trivial, precisely because FOL has no machinery for inductive definitions. Instead, we had to rewrite such definitions as explicit ones, which involved quantifying over finite sequences of numbers, by means of Gödel's β-function.

Moreover, we will see later that the formulas involved in representing primitive recursive functions, as specified in this chapter, are of a very simple kind (so-called Σ_1-formulas), and for these simple formulas, arithmetical definability actually implies representability in *PA*. In this way, Theorem 10.3.2 turns out to follow from (an improved version of) Theorem 10.3.3.

10.4. Summary and comment

We have shown that all primitive recursive functions and relations are definable in the arithmetical vocabulary L_{PA}, making heavy use of coding finite sequences of number with Gödel's β-function. With a little extra work (most of the details are indicated in the exercises), we could have shown that these functions and relations are even representable in *PA*. Indeed, it is the stronger result about representability that we need for the incompleteness theorems in the next two chapters. So the reader will either have to take Theorem 10.3.2 on faith for the time being (which shouldn't be too hard since we did prove Theorem 10.3.3), or take the time to do Exercises 10.5.4 and 10.5.5.

At this point, however, the reader may ask: Was it really necessary to present *two* coding schemes, in particular the β-function relying on facts about congruence classes and the Chinese remainder theorem? Couldn't we be content with the simpler coding using prime factorizations? True, this requires the exponentiation function, but couldn't we simply add to *PA* a function symbol *exp* to the vocabulary, with the two defining axioms $exp(x, 0) = \mathbf{1}$ and $exp(x, y') = exp(x, y) \cdot x$?

Indeed we could. Then the β-function would not be needed, and the argument in Section 10.3 could use the simpler prime factorization coding. That would save some work. But there is a cost: the result would be *weaker*. It is of legitimate logical interest to see just *how much* is required of a formal system in which (most of) the vast area of number theory can be developed. And it is quite remarkable that axioms for addition, multiplication, and successor, together with induction, suffice for this, and that exponentiation can then be represented in *PA*—along with all other primitive recursive functions! That this is possible was an important by-product of Gödel's proof of the incompleteness results.

In fact, the situation is more remarkable still. We will see in Chapter 14.5.2 that you don't even need induction to represent all primitive recursive (indeed all recursive) functions; just one extra axiom, in addition to the first six Peano axioms, suffices.

10.5. Exercises to Chapter 10

Exercise 10.5.1
Verify that the basic functions Z and s are strongly representable in *PA*.

Exercise 10.5.2
Prove the 'strong' variant of Lemma 10.2.1. [Hint: The same formula works.]

Exercise 10.5.3
*Fill in the details of the proof of (3), i.e. the claims about the formulas strongly representing the functions *OP* and π_1.

Exercise 10.5.4 (proof of Lemma 10.3.1, part 1)
*Let h be defined by primitive recursion from f and g as in Section 10.3. Show that if $h(n, m) = k$, then $PA \vdash PrimRec_h(\mathbf{n}, \mathbf{m}, \mathbf{k})$.

[Hint: Let b be as in (pr2). Show that

$$PA \vdash \exists w(B(\mathbf{b}, \mathbf{1}, w) \wedge \varphi_f(\mathbf{n}, w))$$

Let $a_i = \beta'(b, i + 1)$ for $i \leqslant m$. Show, using (27) in Chapter 9.6, that

$$PA \vdash \forall z_{z<\mathbf{m}} \exists w_0 \exists w_1 (B(\mathbf{b}, z'', w_1) \wedge B(\mathbf{b}, z', w_0) \wedge \varphi_g(\mathbf{n}, z, w_0, w_1))$$

Finally, show

$$PA \vdash B(\mathbf{b}, \mathbf{m}', \mathbf{k})$$

and conclude that $PA \vdash PrimRec_h(\mathbf{n}, \mathbf{m}, \mathbf{k})$.]

Exercise 10.5.5 (proof of Lemma 10.3.1, part 2)
*To prove the lemma, it is now sufficient, given part 1, to show that if $h(n, m) = k$, then $PA \vdash \exists_{=1} y\, PrimRec_h(\mathbf{n}, \mathbf{m}, y)$. Use induction on m in the metalanguage.

[Hint: First prove the base step: $PA \vdash \exists_{=1} y\, PrimRec_h(\mathbf{n}, 0, y)$. For the induction step: assume

(a) $\quad PA \vdash \exists_{=1} y\, PrimRec_h(\mathbf{n}, \mathbf{m}, y)$

and show $PA \vdash \exists_{=1} y\, PrimRec_h(\mathbf{n}, \mathbf{m}', y)$. Let $k = h(n, m)$ and $j = h(n, m') = g(n, m, k)$. By the previous exercise (part 1) we have that $PA \vdash PrimRec_h(\mathbf{n}, \mathbf{m}, \mathbf{k})$. Since also $PA \vdash \varphi_g(\mathbf{n}, \mathbf{m}, \mathbf{k}, \mathbf{j})$, check that we obtain:

(b) $\quad PA \vdash PrimRec_h(\mathbf{n}, \mathbf{m}', \mathbf{j})$

Now reason in *PA*, and suppose $PrimRec_h(\mathbf{n}, \mathbf{m}', y)$. It is enough to derive $y = \mathbf{j}$. So there is u such that

(i) $\exists w(B(u, \mathbf{1}, w) \wedge \varphi_f(\mathbf{n}, w))$

(ii) $\forall z_{z \leqslant \mathbf{m}} \exists w_0 \exists w_1 (B(u, z'', w_1) \wedge B(u, z', w_0) \wedge \varphi_g(\mathbf{n}, z, w_0, w_1))$

(iii) $B(u, \mathbf{m}'', y)$

Reformulate (ii) as follows: there are z_0, z_1 such that

(ii)′ $\forall z_{z < \mathbf{m}} \exists w_0 \exists w_1 (B(u, z'', w_1) \wedge B(u, z', w_0) \wedge \varphi_g(\mathbf{n}, z, w_0, w_1)) \wedge$
$B(u, \mathbf{m}'', z_1) \wedge B(u, \mathbf{m}', z_0) \wedge \varphi_g(\mathbf{n}, \mathbf{m}, z_0, z_1)$

Show that it follows that

(c) $\quad PA \vdash PrimRec_h(\mathbf{n}, \mathbf{m}, z_0)$

Now use the induction hypothesis to conclude that $z_0 = \mathbf{k}$, and then that $\varphi_g(\mathbf{n}, \mathbf{m}, \mathbf{k}, z_1)$, and finally that $z_1 = \mathbf{j}$. This means that $B(u, \mathbf{m}'', \mathbf{j})$ holds. Since the formula $B(u, v, y)$ strongly represents β' in *PA*, we see that $y = \mathbf{j}$.]

11 Arithmetization

We now have the tools needed to code symbols, terms, formulas, and derivations in the arithmetical language (or the language of any (countable) voicabulary; see Section 11.6), thus transforming metalogical properties and relations into properties and relations between numbers, and then show that these properties and relations are representable in *PA*. This procedure is often called the *arithmetization of syntax* (or of metamathematics).

There are many ways to effect such a coding or *Gödel numbering*; we present one using the sequence coding based on prime factorizations from Chapter 8.7.1. But we could also have used the β-function coding, and there are other alternatives as well. Moreover, the coding of *symbols* is to a large extent arbitrary. So the translation of a meta-statement like "$\exists x\, x \neq y + 0$ is a formula" will be an L_{PA}-sentence φ which *depends* on the particular choice of coding.

We must be sure that this dependence is harmless—otherwise our results would have little value. For example, if we had used *another* coding, then our meta-statement would translate as *another* arithmetical sentence, say φ', but then it should be the case that φ is provable in *PA* iff φ' is provable in *PA*.[1]

The main requirement of any reasonable coding is that there is an effective method (an algorithm) for going from a formal expression to its code number, and also an effective method for going in the other direction. We need to be sure that our proposed coding satisfies this. And we should convince ourselves that if we had chosen another reasonable coding, our results would not be affected.

Although none of the facts stated are very surprising, this chapter is somewhat long because we attend to most of the nitty-gritty coding details. Many of these can be skipped without losing the understanding of what is going on.

[1]Indeed, since this particular meta-statement happens to be true, both translations should be provable in *PA*.

11.1. Gödel numbering of *PA*

If u is any formal expression (symbol, formula, proof, ...), its Gödel number will be denoted $\#(u)$. We start by defining the function # for *symbols*: logical, non-logical, and others:

(1) **coding of symbols**

u	(	)	$\neg$	$\rightarrow$	$\exists$	$\forall$	$=$	0	$'$	$+$	$\cdot$
v_i	d_i										
$\#(u)$	1	3	5	7	9	11	13	15	17	19	21
$2\cdot 3^{i+1}$	$2\cdot 5^{i+1}$										

(Other logical symbols can be regarded as defined.) Here $d_0, d_1, \ldots$ is the list of special individual constants that are used as parameters in derivations; see Chapter 3.2.

(2) **coding of symbol strings**

If $u_0 u_1 \ldots u_{k-1}$ is a string of symbols, then

$\#(u_0 u_1 \ldots u_{k-1}) = \langle \#(u_0), \#(u_1), \ldots, \#(u_{k-1}) \rangle$

Here $\langle \ldots \rangle$ is the function we used for sequence coding in Chapter 8.7.1, that is, $\langle n_0, \ldots, n_{k-1} \rangle = 2^{n_0+1} \cdot 3^{n_1+1} \cdot \ldots \cdot \pi(k-1)^{n_{k-1}+1}$. For example, take the sentence $0 \neq 1$, that is, $\neg 0 = 0'$. This is still not quite the official notation; recall that atomic formulas should have the form $Pt_1 \ldots t_n$, and functional terms are written $ft_1 \ldots t_n$, so, officially, this sentence is the string

$$\neg = 0'0$$

(You can see why we prefer the other notation!) Accordingly:

$$\#(\neg = 0'0) = 2^6 \cdot 3^{14} \cdot 5^{16} \cdot 7^{18} \cdot 11^{16}$$

And

$$\#(\exists v_2\, v_2 = 0) = \#(\exists v_2 = v_2 0) = 2^{10} \cdot 3^{2\cdot 3^3+1} \cdot 5^{14} \cdot 7^{2\cdot 3^3+1} \cdot 11^{16}$$

All symbols have odd numbers, except the variables $v_0, v_1, \ldots$, whose numbers are of the form $2\cdot 3^{i+1}$, and similarly for the special parameters. No symbol strings have Gödel numbers of that form (the exponents of 2 are different), so no symbol has the same number as any string. In particular, a symbol u and the string whose only element is u—call it temporarily $[u]$—will get different code numbers:

$$\#([u]) = 2^{\#(u)+1}$$

The only meaningful strings with one element are 0 and the variables and parameters, and we may distinguish in these cases between the *symbol* and the *term* consisting of the symbol: terms are always strings of symbols.

We code sequences of symbol strings in the same way:

coding of sequences of symbol strings

If $s_0, s_1, \ldots, s_{k-1}$ is a sequence of symbol strings, then

$\#(s_0, s_1, \ldots, s_{k-1}) = \langle \#(s_0), \#(s_1), \ldots, \#(s_{k-1}) \rangle$

Again we distinguish a symbol string from the sequence whose only element is that string; for example, between a *sentence* φ and the *derivation* whose only element is φ (e.g. if φ is a logical axiom): Hilbert style derivations are sequences of sentences.

The exponent of 2 in the Gödel number of a string will be an even number (recall that we always add 1 to the exponent), whereas the exponent of 2 in the Gödel number of a sequence of strings will be of the form $2^m \cdot y + 1$ (where $m \geqslant 2$), and hence an odd number. It follows that the function # is *injective.*

Our coding is clearly reasonable in the required sense: given an arbitrary symbol, symbol string, or sequence of symbols strings, we have just described an effective method to find its Gödel number. Conversely, given an arbitrary number n, check if n is the code of a symbol. If not, check if it is a sequence number (as we have seen, this is a primitive recursive property). If it is, we can inspect the unique prime factorization of x to see if it is the Gödel number of a formal expression, and, if that is the case, recover that expression.

What if we had chosen another reasonable coding scheme? Exercise 11.9.1 spells out the sense in which our results would still hold.

Our Gödel numbering results in very large code numbers. However, the *form* of these numbers, written with ordinary exponentiation notation, is quite perspicuous. Expressions like $2^{\#(u_0)+1} \cdot \ldots \cdot \pi(k-1)^{\#(u_{k-1})+1}$ can be seen as *names* rather than numbers. That is, the name is the syntactic expression itself, "$2^{\#(u_0)+1} \cdot \ldots \cdot \pi(k-1)^{\#(u_{k-1})+1}$", not the number it denotes. Then our coding method is an effective method for assigning such names to syntactic expressions, names that can be manipulated with mathematical methods. In a sense, what we have done is to give an effective *notation system* for syntactic objects.

11.2. Syntax as number theory

Now we can translate metalogical relations between formal expressions into relations between their corresponding Gödel numbers. We first specify the relation (or function) in words, and then with an arithmetical definition, which in most cases shows directly that it is primitive recursive.

Let *var* be the set of Gödel numbers of variables, where we think of variables as terms. The following shows that *var* is primitive recursive:

$$\begin{aligned} var(n) &\Leftrightarrow n \text{ is the number of a variable term} \\ &\Leftrightarrow \exists i_{i<n}\, n = \langle 2\cdot 3^{i+1}\rangle \end{aligned}$$

Similarly, we define the set *par* of Gödel numbers of parameters.

Recall the functions to handle finite sequences introduced in Chapter 8.7.1; in particular, the function $*$ which concatenates two sequences.

$$\begin{aligned} neg(n) &= \text{the negation of } n \text{ (i.e. the number of the result of placing } \neg \\ &\quad \text{in front of the string with number } n) \\ &= \langle 5\rangle * n \end{aligned}$$

$$\begin{aligned} impl(n,m) &= \text{the implication from } n \text{ to } m \text{ (correspondingly)} \\ &= \langle 1\rangle * n * \langle 7\rangle * m * \langle 3\rangle \end{aligned}$$

$$\begin{aligned} exquant(j,n) &= \text{the result of placing } \exists v_j \text{ in front of the string} \\ &\quad \text{with number } n \\ &= \langle 9, 2\cdot 3^{j+1}\rangle * n \end{aligned}$$

The function $allquant(j,n)$ is defined similarly. Thus, if φ and ψ are formulas, $neg(\#(\varphi))$ is the Gödel number of the formula $\neg\varphi$, $impl(\#(\varphi), \#(\psi))$ is the Gödel number of $(\varphi \rightarrow \psi)$, $exquant(j, \#(\varphi))$ is the Gödel number of $\exists v_j \varphi$, and $allquant(j, \#(\varphi))$ is the Gödel number of $\forall v_j \varphi$.

11.3. Terms and formulas

A *term* is either 0, or a variable v_j, or a parameter d_j, or of the form s', $s+t$, or $s \cdot t$, where s and t are terms. This can be expressed as a definition by *course-of-values recursion*, as presented in Chapter 8.8, where the value of a function $f(n,m)$ is defined not only in terms of $f(n,m-1)$ (for $m > 0$), but in terms of $f(n,k)$ for (some) $k < m$. We showed that functions defined in this way from primitive recursive functions are primitive recursive, and similarly for relations (see Exercises 8.9.26 and 8.9.27). The next definition of *term* shows that it is primitive recursive. Again we write complex terms in the official way, thus $+st$ instead of $s + t$, and similarly for $'s$ and $\cdot st$.

$$\begin{aligned} term(n) \;\Leftrightarrow\;& n = \langle 15\rangle \lor var(n) \lor par(n) \\ & \lor \exists m_{m<n}\,(term(m) \land n = \langle 17\rangle * m \\ & \lor \exists m_{m<n}\,\exists k_{k<n}\,(term(m) \land term(k) \land n = \langle 19\rangle * m * k) \\ & \lor \exists m_{m<n}\,\exists k_{k<n}\,(term(m) \land term(k) \land n = \langle 21\rangle * m * k) \end{aligned}$$

An *atomic formula* has the shape $s = t$ (officially, $=st$), where s and t are terms. Thus:

$$atom(n) \Leftrightarrow \exists k_{k<n}\,\exists m_{m<n}\,(term(k) \land term(m) \land n = \langle 13\rangle * k * m)$$

So *atom* is primitive recursive. And a *formula* is either atomic, or a negation, or an implication, or an existential or universal quantification applied to a formula. So we can define the set *fml* by course-of-values recursion:

$$\begin{aligned} fml(n) \;\Leftrightarrow\;& n \text{ is the Gödel number of a formula} \\ \Leftrightarrow\;& atom(n) \lor \exists m_{m<n}\,\exists k_{k<n}\,\exists j_{j<n}\,[fml(m) \land fml(k) \land \\ & (n = neg(m) \lor n = impl(m,k) \lor n = exquant(j,m) \lor n = allquant(j,m))] \end{aligned}$$

Thus, *fml* is primitive recursive. So are the following relations:

$$\begin{aligned} subterm(m,n) \;\Leftrightarrow\;& term(n) \text{ and } m \text{ is a subterm of } n \\ \Leftrightarrow\;& term(n) \land term(m) \land \exists j_{j<n}\exists k_{k<n}\, n = j * m * k \end{aligned}$$

$$\begin{aligned} subfml(m,n) \;\Leftrightarrow\;& fml(n) \text{ and } m \text{ is a subformula of } n \\ \Leftrightarrow\;& fml(n) \land fml(m) \land \exists j_{j<n}\exists k_{k<n}\, n = j * m * k \end{aligned}$$

Here, of course, "m is a subterm of n" means "m is the Gödel number of a subterm of the term with Gödel number n", etc. Note that, since every term (formula) is a subterm (subformula) of itself, we have that $subterm(m,n)$ or $subfml(m,n)$ implies $m \leqslant n$. So we also have:

$$propersubterm(m,n) \Leftrightarrow subterm(m,n) \land m < n$$

$$propersubfml(m,n) \Leftrightarrow subfml(m,n) \land m < n$$

11.4. Sentences

Now let us single out *sentences*, i.e. formulas without free variables. We start by giving the arithmetical version of the relation 'x occurs free in u', defined at the end of Chapter 2.3.1, where u may be a term or a formula.

For the vocabulary L_{PA}, the definition becomes:

$$
\begin{array}{lcl}
\mathit{oc\text{-}free}(j,n) & \Leftrightarrow & v_j \text{ occurs free in (the term or formula) } n \\
& \Leftrightarrow & n = \langle 2 \cdot 3^{j+1} \rangle \\
& \vee & \exists m_{m<n}[\mathit{subterm}(m,n) \wedge \mathit{oc\text{-}free}(j,m)] \\
& \vee & \exists m_{m<n} \exists k_{k<n}[\mathit{term}(m) \wedge \mathit{term}(k) \wedge n = \langle 13 \rangle * m * k \ \wedge \\
& & \qquad (\mathit{oc\text{-}free}(j,m) \vee \mathit{oc\text{-}free}(j,k))] \\
& \vee & \exists m_{m<n}[\mathit{fml}(m) \wedge n = \mathit{neg}(m) \wedge \mathit{oc\text{-}free}(j,m)] \\
& \vee & \exists m_{m<n} \exists k_{k<n}[\mathit{fml}(m) \wedge \mathit{fml}(k) \wedge n = \mathit{impl}(m,k) \ \wedge \\
& & \qquad (\mathit{oc\text{-}free}(j,m) \vee \mathit{oc\text{-}free}(j,k))] \\
& \vee & \exists m_{m<n} \exists i_{i<n}[\mathit{fml}(m) \wedge (n = \mathit{allquant}(i,m) \vee n = \mathit{exquant}(i,m)) \\
& & \wedge\ i \neq j \wedge \mathit{oc\text{-}free}(j,m)]
\end{array}
$$

The first disjunct says that v_j occurs free in v_j, and the second that if v_j occurs free in a proper subterm of a term t, then it occurs free in t. (In these cases "free" has no import.) The remaining disjuncts take care of atomic formulas (of the form $s = t$), and of negations, implications, and quantified formulas, following definition (26) in Chapter 2.3.1.

So this is a definition by course-of-values recursion of the relation *oc-free* from primitive recursive relations and functions, showing that *oc-free* is primitive recursive. Therefore, so is the set of Gödel numbers of sentences:

$$
\begin{array}{lcl}
\mathit{sent}(n) & \Leftrightarrow & n \text{ is the Gödel number of a sentence} \\
& \Leftrightarrow & \mathit{fml}(n) \wedge \neg \exists j_{j<n}\, \mathit{oc\text{-}free}(j,n)
\end{array}
$$

We shall also need the relation *oc-par* for occurrences of parameters:

$$\mathit{oc\text{-}par}(j,n) \Leftrightarrow d_j \text{ occurs in (the term or formula) } n$$

The primitive recursive definition of *oc-par* is left as an exercise (this is simpler, since there is no distinction between free and bound occurrences).

11.5. Axioms

Let

$$\mathit{logax}(n) \Leftrightarrow n \text{ is the number of a logical axiom}$$
$$\mathit{ax}_T(n) \Leftrightarrow n \text{ is the number of an axiom in } T$$

It is intuitively clear that *logax* is a primitive recursive set; the axioms are usually given as a small number of *schemes*, so there are infinitely many axioms, but they have easily recognizable forms, each of which should be describable with the primitive recursive functions and relations at our disposal. About the set ax_T we have *a priori* no information. But, for example, for the theory *PA* it is again intuitively clear that ax_{PA} should be primitive recursive: there are six axioms, and an axiom scheme of an easily recognizable form.

However, to deal with the quantifier axioms, or the induction scheme, we first have to show how *substitution* of terms for free variables can be handled. For example, consider the axiom scheme (Ax6):

(Ax6) $\quad \varphi(t) \to \exists x \varphi(x)$

Here $\varphi(x)$ is a formula in which at most x occurs free, and $\varphi(t)$ is the result of replacing all free occurrences of x by the closed term t. Since t contains no variables, this replacement is always permitted, but we still need to describe how the Gödel number of $\varphi(t)$ is obtained from that of $\varphi(x)$. And presumably we will also want to account for the general case, when t can be any term, provided, that is, that t is *free for* x *in* $\varphi(x)$ (see (23) in Chapter 2.3.1).

We will now go through this in detail, but this is for enthusiasts! The reader who feels confident that substitution can be handled with primitive recursive functions, and hence that the sets *logax* and ax_{PA} are primitive recursive—as well as the function *sub* given in (3) below—can go on to Section 11.7.

11.6. *Substitution

Our task is to transform the inductive definitions (28) and (29) in Chapter 2.3.1 into a definition of the corresponding substitution function on Gödel numbers by course-of-values recursion (we will use the same substitution function for both terms and formulas). That is, we want to show that the function *sub* is primitive recursive:

(3) $$sub(m,n,j) = \begin{cases} \text{the result of replacing each free occurrence of } v_j \text{ in } m \text{ by } n & \text{if } m \text{ is a term or a formula, } n \text{ is a term, and } n \text{ is free for } v_j \text{ in } m \\ 0 & \text{otherwise} \end{cases}$$

This kind of substitution should work for every vocabulary L, so *in this section* we assume L is an arbitrary fixed (countable) vocabulary whose symbols have been suitably Gödel numbered. That is, the relations *i-const*$_L$, *p-symb*$_L$, and *f-symb*$_L$ are primitive recursive, where, for example,

(4) $\quad$ *p-symb*$_L(k,m,n)$ iff n is the m:th k-ary predicate symbol

(This refers to a given listing of the non-logical symbols in L; see Exercise 11.9.6 for details.) To see what is involved, we first consider a toy example.

Example 11.6.1 (toy example of substitution)
Let $L = \{P, c\}$, where P is unary, and suppose the language has only two variables x, y. So the terms are just x, y, c. Further, suppose atomic formulas have the form Pt (no identity), and the only complex formulas are implications, written $\rightarrow\varphi\psi$ to avoid parentheses. There is a Gödel numbering, so let k_P be the number of P, k_c the number of c, and similarly for k_x, k_y, and $k_{\rightarrow}$. Terms and formulas are numbered as strings in the usual way, and the sets *term* of terms and *fml* of formulas are primitive recursive.

Now suppose we want to show that the function * below is primitive recursive:

$$m^* = \begin{cases} \text{the result of replacing } x \text{ with c in } m & \text{if } \mathit{fml}(m) \vee \mathit{term}(m) \\ 0 & \text{otherwise} \end{cases}$$

It would be natural to give an inductive definition as follows:

$$(5) \qquad m^* = \begin{cases} c & \text{if } m \text{ is } c \text{ or } x \\ y & \text{if } m \text{ is } y \\ Pt^* & \text{if } m \text{ is } Pt \\ \rightarrow\varphi^*\psi^* & \text{if } m \text{ is } \rightarrow\varphi\psi \\ 0 & \text{otherwise} \end{cases}$$

This is of course quite informal; for example, m is a *number*, not a symbol, so when we write e.g. "m is c" we really mean "m is the Gödel number of the term c" (so in this case, $m = \langle k_c \rangle$). But this is easily understood. Moreover, (5) is, or can be turned into, a definition by course-of-values recursion: in the third clause, m is the number of a formula Pt, for some term t, and the number of t is *smaller* than m (by our sequence coding), so assuming that * is already defined for that number is legitimate. Similarly for the fourth clause.

In order to actually rewrite this as a definition by course-of-values recursion, it is convenient to start with the relation $R(m, k) \Leftrightarrow m^* = k$, i.e. the *graph* of *. R can be defined as follows.

$$(6)\qquad R(m,k) \Leftrightarrow \begin{cases} ((term(m) \vee fml(m)) \wedge \\ [((m = \langle k_c\rangle \vee m = \langle k_x\rangle) \wedge k = \langle k_c\rangle) \\ \vee\ (m = \langle k_y\rangle \wedge k = m) \\ \vee\ \exists p_{p<m} \exists p'_{p'<k} (m = \langle k_P\rangle * p \wedge R(p,p') \wedge k = \langle k_P\rangle * p') \\ \vee\ \exists p_{p<m} \exists p'_{p'<k} \exists q_{q<m} \exists q'_{q'<k} (m = \langle k_\to\rangle * p * q \wedge \\ \qquad R(p,p') \wedge R(q,q') \wedge k = \langle k_\to\rangle * p' * q')]) \\ \vee \\ (\neg(term(m) \vee fml(m)) \wedge k = 0) \end{cases}$$

A little thought reveals that this is indeed the graph of *, but it is not quite given by course-of-values recursion as we defined it in Chapter 8.8. This is because the right-hand side involves $R(p,p')$ for $p < m$ and $p' < k$, so it is not course-of-values recursion over m, but rather over both m and k at the same time.

However, a final trick reduces this to recursion over just one variable: replace in (6) m by $(r)_0$ and k by $(r)_1$ (where r is a new number variable). Let $S(r) \Leftrightarrow R((r)_0, (r)_1)$. Now, for example, the fourth row of the right-hand side of (6) has a disjunct of the form:

$$\exists p_{p<(r)_0} \exists p'_{p'<(r)_1} (\ldots R(p,p') \ldots)$$

that is,

$$\exists p_{p<(r)_0} \exists p'_{p'<(r)_1} (\ldots S(2^{p+1} \cdot 3^{p'+1}) \ldots)$$

But if $p < (r)_0$ and $p' < (r)_1$, then $2^{p+1} \cdot 3^{p'+1} < r$. Similarly for the other disjunct involving R. Therefore, (6) transforms into a definition by ordinary course-of-values recursion of the unary relation S. This shows that S is primitive recursive. But then, so is R, since $R(m,k) \Leftrightarrow S(2^{m+1} \cdot 3^{k+1})$.

So the graph of the function * is primitive recursive. We cannot in general conclude from the fact that the graph of a function is primitive recursive that the function itself is primitive recursive.[2] However, in the case of substitution functions we can easily give a primitive recursive *upper bound* of the (Gödel number of) the formula or term resulting from the substitution. In this toy example we simply replaced occurrences of x in a string with number m by c, so we find a primitive recursive function g such that $m^* \leqslant g(m)$ (Exercise 11.9.7). This means that we can use the bounded μ-operator:

$$(7)\qquad m^* = \mu\, k_{k \leqslant g(m)} R(m,k)$$

[2]One can show that the graph G_α of the function α in Chapter 8.4 is primitive recursive, even though α is not.

which—finally!—shows that m^* is primitive recursive. If we instead replace ocurrences of x by any term with Gödel number n, the upper bound will be primitive recursive function of m and n. *End of toy example.*

Now let us get back to our function *sub*. Below we give an informal definition along the lines of (5) in the toy example. It will be fairly easy to see that this definition is correct (it mirrors (28) and (29) in Chapter 2.3.1), and essentially the same arguments as in that example (defining the graph of *sub* by course-of-values recursion on two variables, etc.) then show that *sub* is primitive recursive. So we will not repeat these arguments here. For brevity, we write $m(n/j)$ instead of $sub(m, n, j)$. Also, in all clauses except the last, we assume that $term_L(n)$ holds.[3]

$$(8) \qquad m(n/j) = \begin{cases} m & \text{if } \textit{i-const}_L(m) \text{ or } (var(m) \wedge m \text{ is not } v_j) \\ n & \text{if } m \text{ is } v_j \\ ft_1(n/j)\ldots t_k(n/j) & \text{if } m \text{ is } ft_1\ldots t_k \\ Pt_1(n/j)\ldots t_k(n/j) & \text{if } m \text{ is } Pt_1\ldots t_k \\ \neg\varphi(n/j) & \text{if } m \text{ is } \neg\varphi \\ (\varphi(n/j) \to \psi(n/j)) & \text{if } m \text{ is } (\varphi \to \psi) \\ m & \text{if } m \text{ is } \exists v_j\varphi \\ \exists v_i\varphi(n/j) & \text{if } m \text{ is } \exists v_i\varphi,\ i \neq j, \text{ and} \\ & \text{either } \neg \textit{oc-free}_L(i,n) \text{ or } \neg\textit{oc-free}_L(j,\varphi) \\ \forall v_i\varphi(n/j) & \text{if } m \text{ is } \forall v_i\varphi,\ i \neq j, \text{ and} \\ & \text{either } \neg \textit{oc-free}_L(i,n) \text{ or } \neg\textit{oc-free}_L(j,\varphi) \\ 0 & \text{otherwise} \end{cases}$$

The quantifier clauses ensure that if v_i is free in the term numbered n and v_j is free in φ, so the term is not free for v_j in the formula, then replacing v_j by n in $\exists v_i\varphi$ or $\forall v_i\varphi$ is not allowed, and so the substitution function returns the value 0, which is not the Gödel number of any well-formed L-expression.

Now we can give a primitive recursive characterization of the axiom scheme (Ax6), i.e. of the Gödel numbers of sentences of the form

[3] So when n is not the number of an L-term, $sub(m, n, j) = 0$. In (8) it is understood that $t_1, \ldots, t_k$ are L-terms and that φ, ψ are L-formulas. For example, the fourth clause should be taken as follows (see (4) for $p\text{-}symb_L$):

$$\text{(iv)} \quad \forall p_{p<m}\forall q_{q<m}\forall m'_{m'<m}\forall k_{k<m}[(p\text{-}symb_L(k,m',p) \wedge sq(q) \wedge lh(q) = k \wedge \forall i_{i<k} term_L((q)_i) \wedge m = p * q) \Rightarrow m(n/j) = p * \langle (q)_0(n/j), \ldots, (q)_{k-1}(n/j)\rangle^k]$$

In the consequent we did not simply write $m(n/j) = p * q(n/j)$, since substitution is defined for terms, not for sequences of terms (although it is clear how such a definition would go). If we write the consequent as $m(n/j) = p * \Pi_{i<k}\pi(i)^{(q)_i(n/j)+1}$, it becomes clearer that this is a legitimate part of a definition of $m(n/j)$ by course-of-values induction on m. Sticking (iv) into the actual definition is easier if we first define the graph of *sub*, as we saw in the toy example.

(Ax6) $\varphi(t/v_j) \to \exists v_j \varphi$

where t is a closed term and φ a formula with at most v_j free:[4]

$$\begin{aligned} \mathit{ax6}(k) \quad \Leftrightarrow \quad & \exists m_{m<k} \exists n_{n<k} \exists j_{j<k} [\mathit{fml}(m) \wedge \mathit{term}(n) \\ & \wedge \; \neg \exists i_{i<n} \mathit{oc\text{-}free}(i, n) \\ & \wedge \; \forall i_{i<m} (\mathit{oc\text{-}free}(i, m) \to i = j) \\ & \wedge \; k = \mathit{impl}(\mathit{sub}(m, n, j), \mathit{exquant}(j, m))] \end{aligned}$$

Similarly for other the logical axiom schemes involving substitution. Combining the descriptions of each axiom (scheme) in a long disjunction, we can now finally see that the set *logax* of logical axioms is primitive recursive.

In the logical schemes only closed terms are substituted. The induction scheme involves replacing variables by terms which contain variables: from $\varphi(x)$ to $\varphi(x')$. In this case there is still no problem of 'accidental binding' (since the only variable in the term x' is x), but in general one may need to stipulate that no such binding must occur. This can always be done by adding the requirement that $\mathit{sub}(m, n, j) \neq 0$ for the relevant m, n, j.

11.7. Proofs

A derivation, or a *proof*, as we will mostly call it from now on, in a theory T (in our Hilbert system) is a sequence $\varphi_0, \varphi_1, \ldots, \varphi_{k-1}$ of sentences where, for each $i < k$, φ_i is either a logical axiom, or an axiom in T (i.e. an element of T), or follows from earlier sentences in the sequence by means of some rule. It remains to describe the action of the inference rules in primitive recursive form. Modus Ponens (MP) is easy:

$$\begin{aligned} \mathit{mp}(k, m, n) \quad & \Leftrightarrow \quad \text{sentence number } n \text{ is obtained with MP from} \\ & \qquad \text{sentences number } k \text{ and } m \\ & \Leftrightarrow \quad m = \mathit{impl}(k, n) \end{aligned}$$

(The requirement that k and n are numbers of sentences will be added later.)

The other rule, $R\forall$, derives $\forall v_j \varphi$ from $\varphi(c/v_j)$, where c is a parameter satisfying a condition that involves the whole preceding derivation. Let us first define the following relation describing the syntactic properties of the terms and sentences involved:

$$\mathit{allrule}(j, k, l, p, q) \quad \Leftrightarrow \quad \mathit{fml}(k) \wedge \mathit{par}(l) \wedge p = \mathit{sub}(k, l, j) \wedge q = \mathit{allquant}(j, k)$$

So if k numbers φ and l numbers c, then p numbers $\varphi(c/v_j)$, and q is the number of $\forall v_j \varphi$.

[4] Below $\mathit{fml}(m)$ means $\mathit{fml}_{L_{PA}}(m)$ and similarly for *term* and *oc-free*.

Now we are ready to define the crucial proof relation. Let T be an artithmetical theory and let ax_T be the set of (Gödel numbers of) axioms of T.

(9) $prf_T(m,n)$

$$\Leftrightarrow \quad m \text{ is the number of a derivation in } T \text{ of sentence number } n$$

$$\Leftrightarrow \quad sq(m) \wedge \forall i_{i<lh(m)}(sent((m)_i) \wedge [logax((m)_i) \vee ax_T((m)_i)$$
$$\vee\ \exists k_{k<i}\exists j_{j<i}\, mp((m)_k,(m)_j,(m)_i)$$
$$\vee\ \exists k_{k<i}\exists j_{j<i}\exists l_{l<i}\exists p_{p<i}(allrule((m)_j,(m)_k,(m)_l,(m)_p,(m)_i) \wedge$$
$$\neg oc\text{-}par((m)_l,(m)_k) \wedge \forall q_{q<i}(ax_T((m)_q) \rightarrow \neg oc\text{-}par((m)_l,(m)_q)))])$$
$$\wedge\ (m)_{lh(m)\dot{-}1} = n$$

Here $(m)_l$ is the parameter in the application of $R\forall$, and the requirement that this parameter doesn't occur in the formula numbered $(m)_k$ or in earlier elements of T is explicitly stated.

This is an explicit, not a recursive, definition, and it immediately yields the following fundamental fact:

Lemma 11.7.1
If ax_T is primitive recursive, then prf_T is a primitive recursive relation.

Now we define:

$$thm_T(n) \quad \Leftrightarrow \quad n \text{ is the number of a theorem of } T$$
$$\Leftrightarrow \quad \exists m\, prf_T(m,n)$$

Here we *cannot* bound the length of the derivation (with number) m, since one cannot know in advance how long the derivation of a theorem in T will be. So we cannot conclude that thm_T is primitive recursive, even if ax_T is. On the contrary, in the 'normal' case, as we will see, the set of theorems in the arithmetical theories that interest us is not primitive recursive.

11.8. The formula $Prf_T(x,y)$

Even if the relation prf_T is primitive recursive, there will be many formulas representing it in *PA* (see Exercise 9.10.8). But there is a 'canonical' representing formula that we use in what follows.

To simplify notation we assume that we have introduced new function symbols in the vocabulary, corresponding to the functions $(m)_i$, lh, and $m\dot{-}n$. We use the same symbols for these, but underlined. Thus we write

$$\underline{(x)}_y$$

$$\underline{lh}(x)$$

$$x\underline{\dot{-}}y$$

These functions are representable in *PA*, indeed *strongly* representable (Fact 9.9.5), and therefore new function symbols can be added for them (together with their defining axioms), and used as if we are still working in *PA*.[5]

Suppose also that we have chosen fixed formulas $Sq(x)$, $Sent(x)$, $Mp(x,y,z)$, $Allrule(x,y,z,u,v)$, and $Oc\text{-}par(x,y)$ to represent the corresponding relations in *PA*. Then only one thing is missing in order to simply copy definition (9) in the arithmetical language, namely, a formula representing the set ax_T of (Gödel numbers of) axioms in T. In general, we have no information about this formula, so let $\tau(x)$ be any formula with one free variable. Then the formula $Prf_\tau(x,y)$ is defined as follows:

$$
\begin{aligned}
(10)\quad & Prf_\tau(x,y) := \\
& Sq(x) \wedge \forall z_{z<\underline{lh}(x)}(Sent((x)_{\underline{z}}) \wedge [Logax((x)_{\underline{z}}) \vee \tau((x)_{\underline{z}}) \\
& \quad \vee \exists u_{u<z}\exists v_{v<z}\, Mp((x)_{\underline{u}}, (x)_{\underline{v}}, (x)_{\underline{z}}) \\
& \quad \vee \exists u_{u<z}\exists v_{v<z}\exists w_{w<z}\exists s_{s<z}(Allrule((x)_{\underline{v}}, (x)_{\underline{u}}, (x)_{\underline{w}}, (x)_{\underline{s}}, (x)_{\underline{z}}) \wedge \\
& \qquad \neg Oc\text{-}par((x)_{\underline{w}}, (x)_{\underline{u}}) \wedge \forall t_{t<z}(Ax_T((x)_{\underline{t}}) \rightarrow \neg Oc\text{-}par((x)_{\underline{w}}, (x)_{\underline{t}}))))]) \\
& \wedge (x)_{\underline{lh}(x)\underline{\dot{-}}1} = y
\end{aligned}
$$

It is now straightforward, even if tedious, to verify the following.

Fact 11.8.1
If $\tau(x)$ represents ax_T in PA, then $Prf_\tau(x,y)$ represents prf_T in PA.

The formula $Prf_\tau(x,y)$ depends only on the choice of $\tau(x)$. In what follows, when T is a primitive recursive theory—that is, when ax_T is primitive recursive—we shall assume that some suitable formula $\tau(x)$ has been chosen which represents ax_T in *PA*. Exactly which formula is chosen is often immaterial (as long as it represents ax_T), but sometimes it does matter, and we shall note when that is the case. When T is a non-empty finite set, $T = \{\varphi_1, \ldots, \varphi_n\}$, we take $\tau(x)$ to be $x = \ulcorner\varphi_1\urcorner \vee \ldots \vee x = \ulcorner\varphi_n\urcorner$. When $T = \varnothing$, so we are dealing with logical truth, we take $\tau(x)$ to be $x \neq x$.

We shall use $Ax_T(x)$ to (ambiguously) denote any formula $\tau(x)$ as above, and we write

$$(11)\quad Prf_T(x,y)$$

instead of $Prf_{Ax_T}(x,y)$.

Here is an example of the use of $Prf_T(x,y)$. If φ is a sentence, we let

[5] More precisely, Exercises 9.10.11 and 9.10.12 showed (a) that the extended theory is a *conservative* extension of *PA* (or T), so no new L_{PA}-sentences are provable in it, and (b) that every sentence θ in the extended vocabulary can be *translated* to an L_{PA}-sentence $\theta^\dagger$ which is provably equivalent to it (in the extended theory). We may therefore think of sentences involving the new function symbols above as abbreviations of L_{PA}-sentences.

$$T + \varphi$$

be the theory obtained by adding φ as a new axiom, i.e. $T + \varphi = T \cup \{\varphi\}$. Also, $ax_{T+\varphi} = ax_T \cup \{\#(\varphi)\}$, and

$$Ax_{T+\varphi}(x) := Ax_T(x) \vee x = \ulcorner\varphi\urcorner$$

It is essentially immediate (Exercise 11.9.8) that if $Ax_T(x)$ represents ax_T in *PA*, then $Ax_{T+\varphi}(x)$ represents $ax_{T+\varphi}$ in *PA*. Finally, let

$$Prf_{T+\varphi}(x, y)$$

be defined as in (10) except that Ax_T is replaced with $Ax_{T+\varphi}$. Then $Prf_{T+\varphi}(x, y)$ is a 'canonical' formula representing the relation $prf_{T+\varphi}$ in *PA*.

Every proof of a sentence ψ in T is also a proof of ψ in $T + \varphi$. Now we can easily verify this (trivial) fact *in PA* (see also Exercise 11.9.10):

(12) $\quad PA \vdash \forall x(Prf_T(x, \ulcorner\psi\urcorner) \rightarrow Prf_{T+\varphi}(x, \ulcorner\psi\urcorner))$

Proof. Reason informally in *PA*. Suppose $Prf_T(x, \ulcorner\psi\urcorner)$, i.e. that the formula in (10) holds for $y = \ulcorner\psi\urcorner$. But if we in this formula replace the formula $Ax_T((x)_{\underline{z}})$ by the formula $Ax_T((x)_{\underline{z}}) \vee (x)_{\underline{z}} = \ulcorner\varphi\urcorner$, we obtain a *weaker* claim, indeed a claim that follows logically from $Prf_T(x, \ulcorner\psi\urcorner)$. And this claim is precisely $Prf_{T+\varphi}(x, \ulcorner\psi\urcorner)$. □

11.9. Exercises to Chapter 11

Exercise 11.9.1 (acceptable codings)
Our official coding yields two algorithms: one mapping each formal expression u to its Gödel number $\#(u)$, and one, say $\dagger$, mapping any number n to the formal expression $\dagger(n)$, if n is in the range of $\#$, and, say, to 0 if it is not. Thus, $\dagger(\#(u)) = u$, and, when n is in the range of $\#$, $\#(\dagger(n)) = n$.

Let C be another coding, with corresponding effective mappings $\#^C$ and $\dagger^C$. Call C *acceptable* (relative to our official coding) if there are primitive recursive functions h_1 and h_2 such that, for all formal expressions u, $h_1(\#(u)) = \#^C(u)$ and $h_2(\#^C(u)) = \#(u)$.

Thus, for example, the set *fml* of Gödel numbers of formulas according to our scheme will be different from the set fml^C of code numbers of formulas according to scheme C. Show that *fml* is primitive recursive iff fml^C is primitive recursive. Extend this to all relations and functions shown to be primitive recursive in this chapter.

Exercise 11.9.2
Check if the following numbers are Gödel numbers, and if so, of which formal expressions: $6, 64, 100, 2500 \cdot 3^{14}$.

Exercise 11.9.3
Define a primitive recursive function *num* such that for all n, $num(n)$ = the Gödel number of $\mathbf{n}$ (the numeral of n).

Exercise 11.9.4
Write course-of-values recursive definitions of the relations *subterm* and *subfml* from Section 11.3.

Exercise 11.9.5
Write a primitive recursive definition of the relation *oc-par* (Section 11.4).

Exercise 11.9.6
In Gödel-numbering non-logical constants in an arbitrary vocabulary L (see Section 11.6), we assume that there are countably many individual constants $c_0, c_1, c_2, \ldots$, and for each $k \geqslant 1$, countably many k-ary predicate symbols $P_0^k, P_1^k, P_2^k, \ldots$, and countably many k-ary function symbols $f_0^k, f_1^k, f_2^k, \ldots$. The relation (4) refers to this list:

$$p\text{-}symb_L(k, m, n) \text{ iff } n \text{ is the Gödel number of } P_m^k$$

and similarly for *f-symb*$_L$ and *i-const*$_L$. Assuming these relations are primitive recursive, show how to adapt the definitions of terms and formulas in Section 11.3 to yield primitive recursive sets *term*$_L$, *atom*$_L$, and *fml*$_L$.

Exercise 11.9.7
Define a primitive recursive function g that gives an upper bound as in (7) in Example 11.6.1.

Exercise 11.9.8
Check that if $\varphi(x)$ represents the set A in an arithmetical theory T, then the formula $\varphi(x) \vee x = \mathbf{k}$ represents the set $A \cup \{k\}$ in T.

Exercise 11.9.9
Outline a proof of Fact 11.8.1.

Exercise 11.9.10
Show that the argument for (12) in fact shows that

$$\vdash \forall x \forall y (Prf_T(x, y) \to Prf_{T+\varphi}(x, y))$$

that is, that (i) we can universally quantify $\ulcorner\psi\urcorner$, and (ii) *PA* is not needed, the sentence is a *logical* truth.

12 Incompleteness

Finally, we can now fill in the details of the informal proofs of Gödel's two incompleteness theorems given in Chapter 7.[1] Through arithmetization we are able to express metalogical statements in the arithmetical language—'translate' them to that language, if you will—and in many cases prove them in *PA* if they are true. For example, we translate the true claim

(1) "$\exists v_2\, v_2 = 0 + v_1$" is a formula

by first finding the Gödel number, say, $k = \#(\exists v_2\, v_2 = 0{+}v_1)$, and then choose a formula $Fml(x)$ representing the property *fml*—the existence of such a formula is guaranteed by Theorem 10.3.2 and the fact that *fml* is primitive recursive— which gives us the translation:

$$Fml(\mathbf{k})$$

which we also write $Fml(\ulcorner\exists v_2\, v_2 = 0 + v_1\urcorner)$. And since $\exists v_2\, v_2 = 0 + v_1$ really is a well-formed arithmetical formula, we have $fml(k)$, and since $Fml(x)$ does represent *fml* in *PA*, we get

$$PA \vdash Fml(\ulcorner\exists v_2\, v_2 = 0 + v_1\urcorner)$$

Thus, the translation of the true statement (1) is provable in *PA*. Similarly, we can translate the statement

(2) "$\forall x \forall y\, x + y = y + x$" is a theorem of *PA*

as

$$\exists x\, Prf_{PA}(x, \ulcorner\forall x \forall y\, x + y = y + x\urcorner)$$

[1] *Except* that we still don't have a fully adequate notion of an axiomatizable theory T—that will have to wait until Part IV.

where $\mathit{Prf}_{PA}(x,y)$ is the formula from Chapter 11.8.[2] A sentence is a theorem if *there is* a proof in *PA* of it, and hence a Gödel number of such a derivation. Moreover, since there actually is a derivation of this sentence in *PA* (as we saw in Chapter 9.2), with Gödel number m, say, and since $\mathit{Prf}_{PA}(x,y)$ represents prf_{PA} in *PA*, we have

$$PA \vdash \mathit{Prf}_{PA}(\mathbf{m}, \ulcorner \forall x \forall y\, x + y = y + x \urcorner)$$

and thus

(3) $\quad PA \vdash \exists x\, \mathit{Prf}_{PA}(x, \ulcorner \forall x \forall y\, x + y = y + x \urcorner)$

Thus, we are really working at three different levels:

1. The first level is where we make (meta-)claims about formal systems, provability in *PA*, consistency, etc.
2. At the second level, these claims become, via Gödel numbering, claims about natural numbers, sets and relations between natural numbers, etc.
3. Finally, at the third level, we are 'inside' some formal theory like *PA*, and can often find arithmetical sentences which can be seen as translations of our initial claims.

We just saw two examples of true claims whose translations are provable in *PA*. But now consider the equally true claim

(4) $\quad$ "$\forall y\, y + 0 = 0$" is not a theorem of *PA*.

The translation is just as simple as before, $\neg\exists x\, \mathit{Prf}_{PA}(x, \ulcorner \forall y\, y + 0 = 0 \urcorner)$, or equivalently,

(5) $\quad \forall x\, \neg \mathit{Prf}_{PA}(x, \ulcorner \forall y\, y + 0 = 0 \urcorner)$

Now, what we know is that since $\mathit{Prf}_{PA}(x,y)$ represents prf_{PA} in *PA*, and since there is no (Gödel number of) a proof of $\forall y\, y + 0 = 0$ in *PA*,

(6) $\quad$ for *every* number k we have $PA \vdash \neg \mathit{Prf}_{PA}(\mathbf{k}, \ulcorner \forall y\, y + 0 = 0 \urcorner)$.

But (6) does *not* imply that (5) is provable in *PA*!

So what is the situation, is (5) provable in *PA* or not? That's what Gödel's incompleteness theorems are about. Indeed, we already stated the answer in Chapter 7.2.3: sentence (5) ought to be equivalent to Con_{PA} (since a theory is consistent iff not every sentence is provable

[2] Note that $\ulcorner \forall x \forall y\, x + y = y + x \urcorner$ is a *numeral*, i.e. a closed term of the form $0''\cdots'$. In particular, it does *not* contain x or y. Thus, the existential quantifier in $\exists x\, \mathit{Prf}_{PA}(x, \ulcorner \forall x \forall y\, x + y = y + x \urcorner)$ only binds the variable x occurring free in the formula $\mathit{Prf}_{PA}(x, \ldots)$. Even if x should occur free in a formula $\varphi(x)$, that occurrence is *not* bound in the sentence $\exists x\, \mathit{Prf}_{PA}(x, \ulcorner \varphi(x) \urcorner)$, precisely because there are no occurrences (free or bound) of x in the numeral $\ulcorner \varphi(x) \urcorner$.

in it), and the second incompleteness theorem says that Con_{PA} is *not* provable (if *PA is* consistent). So (5) is not provable—even though, by (6), *every instance of it provable.*

There is huge difference between being able to prove a universally quantified arithmetical formula and being able to prove all its numerical instances. That is one of the lessons of Gödel's proof.[3]

12.1. The Diagonal Lemma

We have seen how a a sentence φ can express in *PA* the statement "there is no proof in T of sentence θ". But for Gödel's argument we need φ to say this *about itself*. Suppose $\psi(y)$ is a formula with one free variable, so $\psi(y)$ says, roughly, "y is ψ". If we replace y by the name of a sentence φ, then $\psi(\ulcorner\varphi\urcorner)$ says, in this sense, that φ is ψ. But the Gödel number of *that* sentence, i.e. $\psi(\ulcorner\varphi\urcorner)$, can of course not be the Gödel number of φ (different syntactic expressions have different Gödel numbers). However, we are not trying to have the two sentences have the *same* Gödel number (which is impossible); it suffices for them to be *provably equivalent*. And this can in fact be achieved, with a simple but ingenious use of substitution and diagonalization.[4]

Let x be a fixed variable, say, v_0, and recall the function $sub(m, n, j)$ from Chapter 11.6. Also, let *num* be the primitive recursive function (Exercise 11.9.3)

$$num(n) = \text{the Gödel number of the numeral } \mathbf{n}$$

Now let $sub_0(m, n) = sub(m, num(n), 0)$. Thus, sub_0 is a primitive recursive function such that

$$(7) \qquad sub_0(m,n) = \begin{cases} \text{the Gödel number of the result of replacing all free occurrences of } x \text{ in } m \text{ with } \mathbf{n} & \text{if } m \text{ is a formula or a term} \\ 0 & \text{otherwise} \end{cases}$$

More perspicuously (but less appropriately), we could write:

$$sub_0(m, n) = m(\mathbf{n}/x)$$

[3]Couldn't we add a *rule* saying that if $\varphi(\mathbf{n})$ is provable for all n, then $\forall x\varphi(x)$ is provable? We could, this rule is called the *ω-rule*, and it gives a much stronger logic, which has been studied. But it is not an inference system in our sense, since derivations in it can be infinite.

[4]Gödel proved the existence of a sentence asserting its own unprovability. Apparently it was Rudolph Carnap who pointed out that the construction works for any arithmetical formula with one free variable.

Since sub_0 is primitive recursive, it is represented in *PA* by some formula, say, $Sub_0(x_1, x_2, y)$: for all m, n, k, if $sub_0(m, n) = k$, then $PA \vdash \forall y(Sub_0(\mathbf{m}, \mathbf{n}, y) \leftrightarrow y = \mathbf{k})$. In particular, when m is the Gödel number of a formula $\theta(x)$ with x as its only free variable, we have

(8) $\quad PA \vdash \forall y(Sub_0(\ulcorner\theta\urcorner, \mathbf{n}, y) \leftrightarrow y = \ulcorner\theta(\mathbf{n})\urcorner)$

Lemma 12.1.1 (Diagonal or Self-Reference Lemma)
For every L_{PA}-formula $\psi(y)$ with the single free variable y, there is a sentence φ such that

(D) $\quad PA \vdash \varphi \leftrightarrow \psi(\ulcorner\varphi\urcorner)$

Proof. Given $\psi(y)$, let

$$\theta(x) := \exists y(Sub_0(x, x, y) \wedge \psi(y))$$

By (8), we have

(9) $\quad PA \vdash \forall y(Sub_0(\ulcorner\theta\urcorner, \ulcorner\theta\urcorner, y) \leftrightarrow y = \ulcorner\theta(\ulcorner\theta\urcorner)\urcorner)$

But then $\varphi := \theta(\ulcorner\theta\urcorner)$ is our desired sentence, as a few simple logical steps carried out in *PA* show:

$$\begin{array}{rll} \varphi & = & \theta(\ulcorner\theta\urcorner) \\ & = & \exists y(Sub_0(\ulcorner\theta\urcorner, \ulcorner\theta\urcorner, y) \wedge \psi(y)) \\ & \leftrightarrow & \exists y(y = \ulcorner\varphi\urcorner \wedge \psi(y)) \qquad \text{(by (9))} \\ & \leftrightarrow & \psi(\ulcorner\varphi\urcorner) \qquad \text{(by logic)} \end{array}$$

□

The 'diagonalization' in the proof is the identification of the first two variables in the formula Sub_0. This seemingly simple move is behind the proof of Cantor's theorem in set theory (Chapter 16.5.1), as well as Russell's paradox (Chapter 16.5.2), and we will see several applications of it later in this book. There are more general versions of the Diagonal Lemma; some are stated in Exercises 12.10.1 – 12.10.4.

As we saw in Chapter 7.2.4, Tarski's theorem that truth is not arithmetically definable (Theorem 7.2.8) is an easy but important application of the Diagonal Lemma, using essentially the argument in the Liar Paradox. And practically the same argument shows that the set of (Gödel numbers of) theorems in a consistent extension T of *PA* is not representable in T; this was Exercise 7.3.12:1, to be repeated and put to good use in Chapter 14.1. For now, we use Lemma 12.1.1 to prove the incompleteness theorems.

12.2. The first incompleteness theorem

In Chapter 7.2.3 we showed that if T is a consistent extension of *PA* and $Prf_T(x,y)$ represents the relation prf_T in T (where $Prf_T(x,y)$ is now the formula presented in Chapter 11.8), and if G is a sentence obtained by the Diagonal Lemma such that

(10) $\quad PA \vdash G \leftrightarrow \neg\exists x Prf_T(x, \ulcorner G \urcorner)$

then it follows that $T \nvdash G$: if $T \vdash G$, we get directly from (10) and the representability of prf_T that T is inconsistent.

In fact, only the first of the representability conditions is needed for this; it yields the principle we labeled (I):

(I) $\quad$ If $T \vdash \varphi$, then $T \vdash \exists x Prf_T(x, \ulcorner\varphi\urcorner)$.

Moreover, since G asserts its own unprovability in T, it is *true*, and so $\neg G$ is false. If we were to require that T only proves true sentences, it follows that $T \nvdash \neg G$, and thus T is incomplete.

But this is a semantic condition on T. Gödel wanted to use only syntactic conditions. In order to obtain the converse of (I), i.e.

(II) $\quad$ If $T \vdash \exists x Prf_T(x, \ulcorner\varphi\urcorner)$, then $T \vdash \varphi$.

he imposed a condition he called ω-consistency, stronger than consistency, but weaker than assuming only true sentences are provable.

Definition 12.2.1
An arithmetical theory T is *ω-consistent* if for every formula $\psi(x)$ which is such that $T \vdash \neg\psi(\mathbf{k})$ for every number k, we have $T \nvdash \exists x\psi(x)$. Otherwise T is *ω-inconsistent*.

Note that if T is *true*, i.e. all its axioms (and hence all its theorems) are true, then T is ω-consistent, since if $\psi(\mathbf{k})$ is false for every k, the sentence $\exists x\psi(x)$ obviously cannot be true. But false theories too can be ω-consistent, just as false theories can be consistent. In fact, ω-consistency implies consistency:

Fact 12.2.2
If T is ω-consistent, then T is consistent.

Proof. Let $\psi(x)$ be the formula $x \neq x$. We have $T \vdash \neg(\mathbf{k} \neq \mathbf{k})$ for every number k. By ω-consistency, $T \nvdash \exists x(x \neq x)$. But the existence of an unprovable sentence in T is equivalent to T being consistent. □

We will soon see that there are consistent but ω-inconsistent theories.

Let us formulate the version of the first incompleteness theorem that we are able to prove at this point. In what follows, we say that T is *primitive recursive* if the set ax_T of Gödel numbers of the elements of T is primitive recursive.

Theorem 12.2.3 (First incompleteness theorem, version 1)
If T is a consistent and primitive recursive extension of PA, and G is as in (10), then $T \nvdash G$. If T is ω-consistent, we also have $T \nvdash \neg G$.

Proof. The fact that $Prf_T(x, y)$ represents prf_T in *PA*, and hence in T, gives principle (I) and thereby the first claim. For the second claim, it is enough to show that if T is ω-consistent, the converse principle (II) holds. We prove the contraposition. So suppose φ is a sentence such that $T \nvdash \varphi$. Then no number is the code of a proof of φ in T, and therefore, by representability in T, we have:

For every k, $T \vdash \neg Prf_T(\mathbf{k}, \ulcorner\varphi\urcorner)$.

But then it follows by ω-consistency that $T \nvdash \exists x Prf_T(x, \ulcorner\varphi\urcorner)$, and hence that $T \nvdash \neg G$. □

Recall the following purely logical fact, which holds for every first-order theory T:

(11) $T \vdash \varphi$ iff $T + \neg\varphi$ is inconsistent.[5]

It follows that if T and G are as in Theorem 12.2.3, both $T + G$ and $T + \neg G$ are consistent extensions of *PA*. However:

(12) $T + \neg G$ is consistent but not ω-consistent.

Proof. As we saw, $\neg Prf_T(\mathbf{k}, \ulcorner G\urcorner)$ is provable in T, hence in $T + \neg G$, for every k, while $\neg G$, which is equivalent to $\exists x Prf_T(x, \ulcorner G\urcorner)$, is of course also provable in $T + \neg G$. □

In Chapter 7 we mentioned various ways in which the first incompleteness theorem can be strengthened, and what needs to be done in order to achieve this. To replace "primitive recursive" by "recursive", and thereby get an adequate notion of axiomatizable theory, we must define the recursive functions, as well as the Turing computable functions, and be convinced by the Church-Turing Thesis that this is the right notion. To apply the result to non-arithmetical theories like set theory, we must formulate a precise sense in which a theory can be said to 'contain' arithmetic. And to get the undecidability of first-order logic, we need to see that *PA* can be replaced in the result by a finitely axiomatized theory. All of this will be dealt with in due course. In this

[5] Here, as in Chapter 11.8, we write $T + \psi$ instead of $T \cup \{\psi\}$.

chapter, we shall first see how the assumption of ω-consistency can be removed, then discuss the second incompleteness theorem and Löb's Theorem, then say a little more about how these metalogical results can themselves be formalized in *PA*, and about how incompleteness extends to other theories. We end with a discussion of the philosophical and logical significance of the incompleteness theorems.

12.3. Rosser sentences

Gödel showed that the sentence

"I am not provable" (in T)

can neither be proved nor disproved in T, if T is an ω-consistent primitive recursive extension of *PA*. In 1936 J. Barkley Rosser showed that the sentence

"For every proof of me there is a shorter proof of my negation"

is also neither provable nor disprovable, but for this it suffices to assume that T is consistent. To express Rosser's sentence we use the following relation ('ref' for 'refutable'):

$\mathit{ref}_T(m,n)$ iff m is the Gödel number of a proof in T of the negation of the sentence with number n

Just as for prf_T, it is easy to see that if ax_T is primitive recursive, ref_T is also primitive recursive, so there is a ('canonical') formula $\mathit{Ref}_T(x,y)$ representing this relation in *PA*.

Now apply the Diagonal Lemma to the following formula:

$$\forall x(\mathit{Prf}_T(x,y) \to \exists z_{z<x}\, \mathit{Ref}_T(z,y))$$

This gives us a sentence, call it R, such that

$$\text{(13)} \qquad \mathit{PA} \vdash R \leftrightarrow \forall x(\mathit{Prf}_T(x,\ulcorner R\urcorner) \to \exists z_{z<x}\, \mathit{Ref}_T(z,\ulcorner R\urcorner))$$

Sentences of this and related forms are called *Rosser sentences*. Intuitively, a Rosser sentence cannot be provable, because otherwise its negation would also be provable, violating consistency. (So intuitively R is true, since the antecedent of the implication is false.) On the other hand, if m were a code number of a proof of $\neg R$, we would have (a) that no $x \leqslant m$ is the number of a proof of R (since R is not provable), and (b) that for every $x > m$ there is a smaller number (namely, m), which is (the number of) a proof of $\neg R$. But this means that for *every* x, either x is not the number of a proof of R, or there is a smaller number which is of a proof of $\neg R$, which according to (13) is exactly what R

says! So R would be provable, and again we would have a violation of consistency. Thus $\neg R$ cannot be provable either.

Actually, it is not hard to turn this informal argument into a real proof that if T and R are as described, then $T \nvdash R$ and $T \nvdash \neg R$. Suppose first that $T \vdash R$. So there is a proof, with number m, say, of R in T. As before, we obtain

$$T \vdash \mathit{Prf}_T(\mathbf{m}, \ulcorner R \urcorner)$$

By (13) and the assumption that $\vdash_T R$ it follows that

$$(14) \qquad T \vdash \exists z_{z<\mathbf{m}}\, \mathit{Ref}_T(z, \ulcorner R \urcorner)$$

But since T is consistent, no number k can be the number of a proof of $\neg R$. In particular:

for every $k < m$ we have $T \vdash \neg \mathit{Ref}_T(\mathbf{k}, \ulcorner R \urcorner)$.

Now we use (27) in Chapter 9.6, obtaining

$$(15) \qquad T \vdash \forall z_{z<\mathbf{m}}\, \neg \mathit{Ref}_T(z, \ulcorner R \urcorner)$$

But (47) and (15) contradict the consistency of T. Thus, $T \nvdash R$.

Next, suppose that $T \vdash \neg R$. Then there is a proof of $\neg R$, let its Gödel number be m. No number, in particular no number $\leqslant m$, is the number of a proof of R in T (by consistency). As above we get

$$(16) \qquad T \vdash \mathit{Ref}_T(\mathbf{m}, \ulcorner R \urcorner)$$

and with (26) in Chapter 9.6,

$$(17) \qquad T \vdash \forall x_{x \leqslant \mathbf{m}}\, \neg \mathit{Prf}_T(x, \ulcorner R \urcorner)$$

From (16) it follows by pure logic that

$$(18) \qquad T \vdash \forall x(\mathbf{m} < x \rightarrow \exists z_{z<x}\, \mathit{Ref}_T(z, \ulcorner R \urcorner))$$

But since $PA \vdash \forall x(x < \mathbf{m} \vee x = \mathbf{m} \vee \mathbf{m} < x)$, it follows from (17) and (18), by pure logic, that

$$T \vdash \forall x(\mathit{Prf}_T(x, \ulcorner R \urcorner) \rightarrow \exists z_{z<x}\, \mathit{Ref}_T(z, \ulcorner R \urcorner))$$

In other words, we have $T \vdash R$, again contradicting our assumption. Hence, $T \nvdash \neg R$. □

So we obtain an improved version of Theorem 12.2.3 where the assumption of ω-consistency is dropped:

Theorem 12.3.1 (First incompleteness theorem, version 2)
If T is a consistent and primitive recursive extension of PA, and R is as in (13), then $T \nvdash R$ and $T \nvdash \neg R$.

This is a *much* stronger result than what we obtained (by a simpler argument) under the assumption that T is true theory (only proves true sentences), since being consistent is a *much* weaker assumption than being true.

12.4. The second incompleteness theorem

Recall that we defined

(19) $\quad Con_T := \neg\exists x Prf_T(x, \ulcorner 0 \neq 0 \urcorner)$

expressing that T is consistent. As explained in Chapter 7.2.3, if we can formalize the first part of the proof of the first incompleteness theorem in *PA*, this would show that

$$PA \vdash \exists x Prf_T(x, \ulcorner G \urcorner) \to \neg Con_T$$

which, using (10), gives $PA \vdash Con_T \to G$. From the first part of Theorem 12.2.3 we could then conclude:

Theorem 12.4.1 (Second incompleteness theorem, version 1)
If T is a consistent primitive recursive extension of PA, then $T \nvdash Con_T$.

So 'only' the formalization of the first part of the proof of the first incompleteness theorem is missing. Even though it is not surprising that this can be done, the details are rarely written out in full. Gödel had promised a sequel to his 1931 paper where the proof would be given, but it never appeared (apparently because everyone was satisfied that the second incompleteness theorem was correct). Later Paul Bernays undertook to go through the proof, which led not to a direct formalization of the argument, but to the formulation of three properties of the provability predicate $\exists x Prf_T(x, y)$ that are sufficient for the proof to go through. These *derivability conditions* were simplified by Martin Löb in 1955. They are presented as (D1) – (D3) below.

Let us say that an arithmetical formula $B(y)$ ('B' for 'Beweis') is a *provability predicate for T* if it satisfies the following conditions: for all sentences φ, ψ:[6]

(D1) If $T \vdash \varphi$, then $T \vdash B(\ulcorner\varphi\urcorner)$.

(D2) $T \vdash B(\ulcorner\varphi\urcorner) \to (B(\ulcorner\varphi \to \psi\urcorner) \to B(\ulcorner\psi\urcorner))$

(D3) $T \vdash B(\ulcorner\varphi\urcorner) \to B(\ulcorner B(\ulcorner\varphi\urcorner)\urcorner)$

[6] A slightly stronger formulation is sometimes used, which replaces the second, third, and fourth occurrence of '$T \vdash$' in (D1) – (D3) (but not the first) with '$PA \vdash$'.

(D1) is familiar from before, and (D3) can be seen as the formalization of (D1) in T. (D2) is just provable closure under Modus Ponens.

It now has to be verified that $\exists x Prf_T(x, y)$ is a provability predicate in this sense for T. (D1) is, as we have seen, a simple consequence of the fact that $Prf_T(x, y)$ represents the relation prf_T in *PA*. (D2) is straightforward; a proof is indicated in Exercise 12.10.19. It is (D3) that requires some serious formalizing in *PA*, which we shall not go into here.[7]

Using (D1) – (D3) we can state and prove a general version of the second incompleteness theorem:

Theorem 12.4.2 (The second incompleteness theorem, version 2)
If T is a consistent extension of PA, and $B(y)$ is a provability predicate for T, then $T \nvdash \neg B(\ulcorner 0 \neq 0 \urcorner)$.

First a simple lemma, whose proof is left as an exercise.

Lemma 12.4.3
Under the assumptions in Theorem 12.4.2, we have

$$T \vdash B(\ulcorner \varphi \urcorner) \rightarrow (B(\ulcorner \neg\varphi \urcorner) \rightarrow B(\ulcorner 0 \neq 0 \urcorner))$$

Proof of Theorem 12.4.2: With the Diagonal Lemma we obtain a sentence, let us keep calling it G, such that $PA \vdash G \leftrightarrow \neg B(\ulcorner G \urcorner)$. So

$$T \vdash B(\ulcorner G \urcorner) \rightarrow \neg G$$

By (D1),

$$T \vdash B(\ulcorner B(\ulcorner G \urcorner) \rightarrow \neg G \urcorner)$$

Then, using (D2) and ordinary logic,

$$(20) \qquad T \vdash B(\ulcorner B(\ulcorner G \urcorner) \urcorner) \rightarrow B(\ulcorner \neg G \urcorner)$$

But by (D3) we have

$$T \vdash B(\ulcorner G \urcorner) \rightarrow B(\ulcorner B(\ulcorner G \urcorner) \urcorner)$$

So from (20) and logic,

$$T \vdash B(\ulcorner G \urcorner) \rightarrow B(\ulcorner \neg G \urcorner)$$

---

[7] The idea is to prove that

$$\text{(i)} \qquad PA \vdash \psi \rightarrow \exists x Prf_{PA}(x, \ulcorner \psi \urcorner)$$

for all Σ_1 sentences ψ (see Chapter 14.5). Since $\psi := \exists x Prf_T(x, \ulcorner \varphi \urcorner)$ is itself Σ_1, (D3) follows. (i) is a formalization of an important fact we shall prove in Chapter 14.5, namely, that all true Σ_1 sentences are provable in *PA* (in fact, in *Q*). A detailed but still accessible proof of (i) can be found in G. Boolos 1993.

By Lemma 12.4.3, this means that

$$T \vdash B(\ulcorner G \urcorner) \to B(\ulcorner 0 \neq 0 \urcorner)$$

Thus, by the definition of G,

$$(21) \qquad T \vdash \neg B(\ulcorner 0 \neq 0 \urcorner) \to G$$

But the argument in the first part of the proof of Gödel's first incompleteness theorem is still valid: if $T \vdash G$, then $T \vdash B(\ulcorner G \urcorner)$ (by (D1)), and thus, by the definition of G, $T \vdash \neg G$, i.e. T is inconsistent. Therefore, $T \nvdash G$. By (21), it follows that $T \nvdash \neg B(\ulcorner 0 \neq 0 \urcorner)$. □

12.4.1. *Reflexive theories

PA doesn't prove its own consistency, but 'almost': it does prove the consistency of each of its *finite* subtheories. To state this we introduce the following terminology. Let $\tau(y)$ be a formula with y as the only free variable, and let T be the theory arithmetically defined by $\tau(y)$. Then let $\tau|x(y)$ be the formula $\tau(y) \wedge y \leqslant x$, and let $T|\mathbf{k}$ be the theory defined by $\tau|\mathbf{k}(y)$. Thus, $T|\mathbf{k}$ is the finite subtheory $\{\varphi \in T : \#(\varphi) \leqslant k\}$.

An arithmetical theory T is called *reflexive* if for every k, $T \vdash Con_{T|\mathbf{k}}$. The following theorem is due to Andrzej Mostowski in 1952.

Theorem 12.4.4
Every consistent extension of PA is reflexive.

It is easy to see that $PA \vdash Con_T \leftrightarrow \forall x\, Con_{T|x}$, so $\forall x\, Con_{T|x}$ is not provable in T (when T is a consistent primitive recursive extension of *PA*), even though each instance is provable. The proof of Theorem 12.4.4 will not be discussed in this book, but we note:

Corollary 12.4.5
No consistent extension of PA—in particular not PA itself—is finitely axiomatizable.

Proof. Let T be a consistent extension of *PA*. If T were equivalent to a finite theory T_0, then T_0 would be a consistent primitive recursive extension of *PA*. By Mostowski's theorem, T_0 proves the consistency of each of its finite subtheories. But one of these finite subtheories is T_0 itself, so T_0 proves its own consistency, which contradicts the second incompleteness theorem. □

This is a characteristic property of *PA*: the fact that the induction axiom holds for arbitrarily complex formulas precludes a finite axiomatization. There are weaker theories in which the induction axiom is restricted to formulas of a certain shape, and although the natural axiomatization of these theories are infinite (since there are infinitely many formulas of that shape), they turn out to be finitely axiomatizable after all. We will say a bit more about this in Chapter 14.6.

12.4.2. *The sentence Con_T

Recall that Prf_T really should be written Prf_τ, where $\tau(x)$ is a formula representing ax_T in *PA* (see Chapter 11.8). Similarly, we should write Con_τ. Now, there are many formulas representing a given set in *PA*; some rather 'unnatural' examples were given in Exercise 9.10.8. For the first incompleteness theorem, it doesn't matter which formula we choose; the Gödel sentence G will depend on that formula, but it will always be an undecidable sentence in T, and the main point is that *there is* an undecidable sentence, not what exactly that sentence 'says'.

The second incompleteness theorem, on the other hand, is different: it mentions a specific sentence supposed to express the consistency of T. Because of incompleteness, there will be different formulas $\tau(x)$ and $\tau'(x)$ arithmetically defining ax_T which are not provably equivalent in T (see Exercise 9.10.8), and thereby such that Con_τ and $Con_{\tau'}$ are not equivalent in T. So which one should we choose?

This question was answered in Feferman 1960. First, Feferman showed that if we require $\tau(x)$ to be a rather simple formula: a so-called Σ_1-formula, then the second incompleteness theorem holds (in fact, (D3) holds of the formula $\exists x Prf_\tau(x, y)$; see footnote 7).[8] We will have more to say about these formulas in Section 12.9.1 below, and in Chapter 14.5, where we will also see that every primitive recursive set is representable in *PA* by a Σ_1-formula.

So the extra requirement on Con_T is no threat to the second incompleteness theorem, but it does raise the issue of what a 'correct' translation into the arithmetical language of a meta-logical claim is. Sometimes, mere extensional correctness—such as representability—is not enough. This was vividly demonstrated by another result in Feferman 1960. If $\tau(x)$ is a formula, define:

(22) $\quad \tau^*(x) := \tau(x) \wedge Con_{\tau|x}$

Theorem 12.4.6
Let T be a consistent axiomatizable extension of PA. If $\tau(x)$ represents ax_T in T, then $\tau^*(x)$ also represents ax_T in T, and $PA \vdash Con_{\tau^*}$.

The first claim follows from the fact that T is reflexive (Theorem 12.4.4). For the second claim, we can reason informally in *PA* as follows: Let p be any proof in T, and let φ be the axiom (according to $\tau^*(x)$) with the largest Gödel number that occurs in p. But we have $Con_{\tau|\ulcorner\varphi\urcorner}$, so the set of axioms occurring in the proof must be

[8] Actually, the theorem holds when τ is a Σ_1-formula *weakly* representing T in *PA*.

consistent. Thus, p cannot be a proof of a contradiction. (Well, that was *very* informal; you will have to take it on trust that the argument can in fact be formalized in *PA*.)

The construction (22) might look like a mere artifice. In fact, it has proved to be a valuable tool in the study of interpretability of arithmetical theories (see Section 12.8.1 below). For more about 'unnatural' consistency statements, see Exercises 12.10.21 – 12.10.23.

12.5. Löb's theorem

In Chapter 7.2.4 we mentioned Löb's Theorem, reformulated below, and the surprising answer it gives to the question of the status of a sentence saying "I am provable in *PA*": such a sentence must be provable in *PA*! Using the derivability conditions (D1) – (D3) from the preceding section, we can express Löb's Theorem as follows.

Theorem 12.5.1 (Löb's theorem)
If T is a consistent extension of PA, $B(y)$ is a provability predicate for T, and φ is a sentence such that $T \vdash B(\ulcorner\varphi\urcorner) \to \varphi$, then $T \vdash \varphi$.

It may be hard to see how remarkable this theorem is. If you are unaccustomed to the huge difference between truth and proof, $B(\ulcorner\varphi\urcorner) \to \varphi$ might seem a trivially true claim that should be provable for *any* sentence φ in a true theory T. And even if you are aware of this difference, it may look very plausible that for *at least one* unprovable sentence, T proves that *if* it were provable *then* it would be true. It seems bizarre that this should *never* happen, and that T only proves that implication in the trivial case when φ is already provable.[9]

There are (at least) two proofs of Löb's theorem; below we first give Löb's original proof, which is interesting (in fact, rather amazing) because it is based on an analogy with another semantic paradox: Curry's (or Löb's) Paradox. This paradox begins with a sentence saying "If I am true then φ", where φ is an *arbitrary* sentence (such as "The Moon is made of cheese", or "$0 \neq 0$"), and then proceeds to 'show' that φ must be true. We asked for the intuitive argument for this in Exercise 7.3.5. Now we will see that if "true" is replaced by "provable in T", the intuitive reasoning can be turned into a proof of Löb's Theorem.

Proof of Theorem 12.5.1. Suppose

(23) $\quad T \vdash B(\ulcorner\varphi\urcorner) \to \varphi$

[9]G. Boolos 1993, p. 54–55 lists five reasons we should think that Löb's theorem is "utterly astonishing".

By the Diagonal Lemma, applied to the formula $B(y) \rightarrow \varphi$, there is a sentence ψ such that

(24) $\quad PA \vdash \psi \leftrightarrow (B(\ulcorner\psi\urcorner) \rightarrow \varphi)$

("If I am provable then φ.") In particular, $T \vdash \psi \rightarrow (B(\ulcorner\psi\urcorner) \rightarrow \varphi)$, so by (D1),

$$T \vdash B(\ulcorner\psi \rightarrow (B(\ulcorner\psi\urcorner) \rightarrow \varphi)\urcorner)$$

Using (D2) and Modus Ponens twice, we obtain

$$T \vdash B(\ulcorner\psi\urcorner) \rightarrow (B(\ulcorner B(\ulcorner\psi\urcorner)\urcorner) \rightarrow B(\ulcorner\varphi\urcorner))$$

But according to (D3) we have $T \vdash B(\ulcorner\psi\urcorner) \rightarrow B(\ulcorner B(\ulcorner\psi\urcorner)\urcorner)$, and thus

(25) $\quad T \vdash B(\ulcorner\psi\urcorner) \rightarrow B(\ulcorner\varphi\urcorner)$

Our assumption (23) then gives

$$T \vdash B(\ulcorner\psi\urcorner) \rightarrow \varphi$$

But, by (24), this means that $T \vdash \psi$. Therefore, by (D1), $T \vdash B(\ulcorner\psi\urcorner)$. Using (24) again, we get $T \vdash \varphi$. $\square$

It is easy to see that Löb's theorem entails the second incompleteness theorem (let φ be $0 \neq 0$; this was Exercise 7.3.10).

A schema like

(26) $\quad \exists x Prf_T(x, \ulcorner\varphi\urcorner) \rightarrow \varphi$

(reverting now to the 'canonical' provability predicate $\exists x Prf_T(x, y)$) is called a *reflection principle*, and Löb's theorem shows that no reflection principle for T can be provable in T for all φ, if T is consistent. But each instance of (26) for *PA* is clearly *true*, and thus, like Con_{PA}, its addition to *PA* results in a stronger and still true theory. This step can be iterated, resulting in so-called *progressions* of arithmetical theories. The study of such progressions is quite interesting, and relates to the idea that arithmetical truth is *inexhaustible* that we alluded to in Chapter 7.1.1, but will not be pursued here (but see Franzén 2004, Chs. 13–15, for a fascinating account).

The second proof of Löb's Theorem is shorter, and derives it from the second incompleteness theorem. To state it, we assume that (27) below holds for any sentence ψ. It is a formalization of the fact that if ψ is not provable in T, then $T + \neg\psi$ is consistent; we defer the proof to the next section (Fact 12.6.3).

(27) $\quad PA \vdash \neg\exists x Prf_T(x, \ulcorner\psi\urcorner) \rightarrow Con_{T+\neg\psi}$

Second proof of Löb's Theorem. Suppose $T \vdash \exists x Prf_T(x, \ulcorner\varphi\urcorner) \to \varphi$. That is, $T \vdash \neg\varphi \to \neg\exists x Prf_T(x, \ulcorner\varphi\urcorner)$. By (27), and since T extends *PA*:

$$T + \neg\varphi \vdash Con_{T+\neg\varphi}$$

But $T + \neg\varphi$ is a primitive recursive extension of *PA*, so the second incompleteness theorem implies that $T + \neg\varphi$ is inconsistent. Thus, $T \vdash \varphi$. □

The original proof of Löb's theorem, however, has the advantage that it leads to a formalized version of the theorem, as we will see in the following section (Theorem 12.6.4).

12.6. *More about the provability predicate

In this section $T, T', \ldots$ are consistent primitive recursive extensions of *PA*. To save space, let

$$Pr_T(y) := \exists x Prf_T(x, y)$$

Also, let $\bot$ be the sentence $0 \neq 0$. So Con_T is $\neg Pr_T(\ulcorner\bot\urcorner)$. We use as before that $Pr_T(y)$ satisfies the derivability conditions (D1)–(D3).

In (12) in Chapter 11.8, we saw that $PA \vdash \forall x(Prf_T(x, \ulcorner\psi\urcorner) \to Prf_{T+\varphi}(x, \ulcorner\psi\urcorner))$, and strengthened this in Exercise 11.9.10 to:

(28) $\quad \vdash \forall x \forall y(Prf_T(x, y) \to Prf_{T+\varphi}(x, y))$

(So this sentence is a *logical* truth.) It follows immediately that

(29) $\quad \vdash \forall y(Pr_T(y) \to Pr_{T+\varphi}(y))$

The next fact is a slightly more general statement:

Fact 12.6.1

(a) $\vdash \forall x(Ax_T(x) \to Ax_{T'}(x)) \to \forall y(Pr_T(y) \to Pr_{T'}(y))$

(b) $\vdash \forall x(Ax_T(x) \to Ax_{T'}(x)) \to (Con_{T'} \to Con_T)$

Proof. Part (a) is immediate by looking at the definition of Prf_T and $Prf_{T'}$. Part (b) follows directly from (a). □

The following fact is useful.

Fact 12.6.2

$PA \vdash Pr_{T+\varphi}(\ulcorner\psi\urcorner) \leftrightarrow Pr_T(\ulcorner\varphi \to \psi\urcorner)$

Proof outline. The left-to-right direction is a formalization of the Deduction Theorem, and to prove it you have to check that the proof of that result can be carried out in *PA*. We shall not do that here, but a look at that proof by induction on the length of derivations in Chapter 3.3.2 should at least make it plausible that this proof can indeed be formalized in *PA*.

But we can prove the right-to-left direction. We reason in *PA*: suppose that $Pr_T(\ulcorner\varphi \rightarrow \psi\urcorner)$ holds. By (29), we have that $Pr_{T+\varphi}(\ulcorner\varphi \rightarrow \psi\urcorner)$. But we also have $Pr_{T+\varphi}(\ulcorner\varphi\urcorner)$; this follows with (D1), since, trivially, $T+\varphi \vdash \varphi$. But then we get from (D2) that $Pr_{T+\varphi}(\ulcorner\psi\urcorner)$. □

Here is a simple exercise in formalization, this time of the fact that $T \vdash \varphi$ iff $T + \neg\varphi$ is inconsistent:

Fact 12.6.3
$PA \vdash Pr_T(\ulcorner\varphi\urcorner) \leftrightarrow \neg Con_{T+\neg\varphi}$

Proof. Reason in *PA*. Suppose first $\neg Con_{T+\neg\varphi}$, i.e. $Pr_{T+\neg\varphi}(\ulcorner\bot\urcorner)$. By Fact 12.6.2, $Pr_T(\ulcorner\neg\varphi \rightarrow \bot\urcorner)$. Thus (Exercise 12.10.20), $Pr_T(\ulcorner\neg\bot \rightarrow \varphi\urcorner)$. But $Pr_T(\ulcorner\neg\bot\urcorner)$, by (D1), so $Pr_T(\ulcorner\varphi\urcorner)$, by (D2).

In the other direction, suppose $Pr_T(\ulcorner\varphi\urcorner)$. Then, by (29), $Pr_{T+\neg\varphi}(\ulcorner\varphi\urcorner)$. And clearly, $Pr_{T+\neg\varphi}(\ulcorner\neg\varphi\urcorner)$, so it follows that $Pr_{T+\neg\varphi}(\ulcorner\bot\urcorner)$, that is, $\neg Con_{T+\neg\varphi}$. □

Formalization in *PA* can be taken much further. For example, Facts 12.6.2 and 12.6.3 can be strengthened as follows:

(30) $PA \vdash \forall y \forall z(Pr_{T+y}(z) \leftrightarrow Pr_T(y \rightarrow z))$

(31) $PA \vdash \forall y(Pr_T(y) \leftrightarrow \neg Con_{T+\neg y})$

But we have not yet made any sense of formulas like these, even if their intended meaning should be clear. For example, "$y \rightarrow z$" is neither a formula nor a term in the language of *PA*. To remedy this, let $\dot{\rightarrow}$ be a new function symbol representing the primitive recursive function *impl* (Chapter 11.2). We saw in Chapter 11.8 how such function symbols can be introduced when the corresponding function is strongly representable in *PA* (although there we used underlining instead of a dot). We then have (writing $y \dot{\rightarrow} z$ rather than $\dot{\rightarrow} yz$), for any formulas φ, ψ that $PA \vdash \ulcorner\varphi \rightarrow \psi\urcorner = \ulcorner\varphi\urcorner \dot{\rightarrow} \ulcorner\psi\urcorner$. Similarly for $\dot{\neg}$.

Also, looking at the proof of (28), we can take $Prf_{T+y}(x,z)$ to be the formula obtained from $Prf_{T+\varphi}(x,z)$ by replacing $\ulcorner\varphi\urcorner$ with y. With these changes, (30) and (31) make perfect sense. This is still only the very beginning of the 'art of arithmetization', but we shall leave the subject with one more example of formalization, this time of Löb's theorem.[10] The idea (due to Georg Kreisel) is to make further use Löb's original proof the theorem.

Theorem 12.6.4 (formalized Löb's theorem)
$PA \vdash Pr_T(\ulcorner Pr_T(\ulcorner\varphi\urcorner) \to \varphi\urcorner) \to Pr_T(\ulcorner\varphi\urcorner)$

Proof. Let φ be any sentence. We use the sentence ψ constructed in the proof of Theorem 12.5.1. By (25), it follows that

$$PA \vdash (Pr_T(\ulcorner\varphi\urcorner) \to \varphi) \to (Pr_T(\ulcorner\psi\urcorner) \to \varphi)$$

Since $PA \vdash \psi \leftrightarrow (Pr_T(\ulcorner\psi\urcorner) \to \varphi)$, we have $PA \vdash (Pr_T(\ulcorner\varphi\urcorner) \to \varphi) \to \psi$. Using (D1) and (D2), we obtain

$$PA \vdash Pr_T(\ulcorner Pr_T(\ulcorner\varphi\urcorner) \to \varphi\urcorner) \to Pr_T(\ulcorner\psi\urcorner)$$

Now $PA \vdash Pr_T(\ulcorner Pr_T(\ulcorner\varphi\urcorner) \to \varphi\urcorner) \to Pr_T(\ulcorner\varphi\urcorner)$ follows from this and (25). □

12.7. *Provability and modal logic

This section is a brief digression (mostly without proofs) on the connections between the results in this chapter and modal logic. It will not be used later in the book. We fix $T = PA$, and may write $PA \vdash \varphi$ simply as $\vdash \varphi$. Likewise, we write $Pr(y)$ instead of $Pr_{PA}(y)$.[11]

12.7.1. A modal notation

Borrowing a symbol from modal logic, let us write $Pr(\ulcorner\varphi\urcorner)$ as $\Box\varphi$. For example, the formalized version of Löb's Theorem for PA becomes:

(32) $\quad \vdash \Box(\Box\varphi \to \varphi) \to \Box\varphi$

Similarly, the derivability conditions are:

(D1) If $\vdash \varphi$, then $\vdash \Box\varphi$

(D2) $\vdash \Box\varphi \to (\Box(\varphi \to \psi) \to \Box\psi)$

(D3) $\vdash \Box\varphi \to \Box\Box\varphi$

Also, Con_{PA} is $\neg\Box\bot$, so we can express a formalized version of the second incompleteness theorem as follows:

[10] See the exercises to this chapter for some further facts. A good (but advanced) presentation of this area of logic is Lindström 2003.

[11] For more details on the topic of this section, see G. S. Boolos, Burgess, and Jeffrey 2007, Ch. 27. For full details, see the classic introduction to provability logic, G. Boolos 1993.

(33) $\vdash \neg\Box\bot \to \neg\Box\neg\Box\bot$

We didn't state this in Section 12.5, but (33) actually follows from the formalized Löb's theorem. Let's see how the reasoning goes. First, note that $\Box\bot \to \bot$ is equivalent in propositional logic to $\neg\Box\bot$. So if we make this replacement in (32) (with $\bot$ as φ), we obtain

$$\vdash \Box\neg\Box\bot \to \Box\bot$$

But this is just the contraposition of (33). □

The point of all this is to make clear that much of our reasoning about provability in theories like *PA* is just propositional reasoning in a simple language with an additional 'connective' □. Here is one more example. By the Diagonal lemma, we obtained a sentence G such that

$$\vdash G \leftrightarrow \neg\Box G$$

Given this, it is immediate, by (D1), that $\nvdash G$: if $\vdash G$, then $\vdash \Box G$, and so $\vdash \neg G$, contradicting consistency (of *PA*). But we can say more. Lemma 12.4.3, if we take $\neg\varphi$ to be the same as $\varphi \to \bot$, becomes a special case of (D2):

(34) $\Box\varphi \to (\Box\neg\varphi \to \Box\bot)$

And now we can do the entire proof of the second incompleteness theorem (Theorem 12.4.2, for *PA*) in the simplified propositional format, with the result that

(35) $\vdash \neg\Box\bot \to G$

12.7.2. Basic modal logic

The connection between modal logic and incompleteness is more than a convenient notation. To state this, we start from the basic (propositional) modal language, whose set $\mathcal{L}$ of sentences is generated by:

$\mathcal{L}$: $\varphi := p \mid \bot \mid (\varphi \to \varphi) \mid \Box\varphi$

A *modal logic* is a set L of sentences in this language which contains all propositional tautologies and is closed under the rules of Modus Ponens (if $\varphi \in \mathsf{L}$ and $\varphi \to \psi \in \mathsf{L}$, then $\psi \in \mathsf{L}$) and Uniform Substitution (if $\varphi(p_1, \ldots, p_n) \in \mathsf{L}$, then $\varphi(\psi_1, \ldots, \psi_n) \in \mathsf{L}$ for all sentences $\psi_1, \ldots, \psi_n$). Instead of $\varphi \in \mathsf{L}$, we may write $\mathsf{L} \vdash \varphi$ and say that φ is a *theorem* of L.

The *basic modal logic* K is the smallest modal logic L which contains the axiom

K $\quad \Box(p \to q) \to (\Box p \to \Box q)$

and is closed under the rule of *Necessitation*:

Nec $\quad$ If $\varphi \in \mathsf{L}$ then $\Box\varphi \in \mathsf{L}$.

We see that these are essentially just our conditions (D2) and (D1) under new names! (D3) too has a traditional name in modal logic:[12]

4 $\quad \Box p \to \Box\Box p$

K4 is the logic where the 4 axiom has been added to K. It is now clear that much of the informal reasoning with $\Box$ above translates to formal reasoning in K4. To make this correspondence more precise, we proceed as follows.

A *realization* is any function ρ from the set $\{p_0, p_1, \ldots\}$ of sentence letters to the set of L_{PA}-sentences. Every realization ρ associates with every $\mathcal{L}$-sentence φ an arithmetical *translation* φ^ρ as follows:

(36)
a. $p^\rho = \rho(p)$
b. $\bot^\rho = \bot$
c. $(\varphi \to \psi)^\rho = (\varphi^\rho \to \psi^\rho)$
d. $(\Box\varphi)^\rho = Pr(\ulcorner\varphi^\rho\urcorner)$

We take $\neg\varphi$ to abbreviate $\varphi \to \bot$, and if we do the same in the arithmetical language, we see that $(\neg\varphi)^\rho = \neg\varphi^\rho$. The translation φ^ρ is uniquely determined by the realization ρ. Note that there are *letterless* sentences in $\mathcal{L}$, such as $\neg\Box\bot$; their translations are fixed and independent of realizations. For example, $(\neg\Box\bot)^\rho = \neg Pr(\ulcorner\bot\urcorner) = Con_{PA}$.

From our discussion so far, the following fact should come as no surprise. The proof is a straightforward induction on theorems in K4, using (D1) – (D3) for *PA*.

Lemma 12.7.1
If K4 $\vdash \varphi$, *then for all realizations* ρ, *we have* $PA \vdash \varphi^\rho$.

12.7.3. Provability logic

The connection between modal logic and arithmetical provability goes much deeper. The key turns out to be the formalized Löb's theorem. Adding the *Löb axiom*

L $\quad \Box(\Box p \to p) \to \Box p$

to K4 gives the so-called Gödel-Löb modal logic GL. Actually the 4 axiom is not needed; it turns out to be derivable from L (G. Boolos

[12]Here K and 4 are taken as single sentences, but the schematic versions in (D2) and (D3) follow by Uniform Substitution.

1993, Theorem 18). So (D1) – (D3) correspond to K4; GL is stronger.[13] Indeed, the logic GL has some remarkable properties. First, Lemma 12.7.1 generalizes:

Theorem 12.7.2 (arithmetical soundness theorem)
If $\mathsf{GL} \vdash \varphi$*, then for all realizations* ρ*, we have* $PA \vdash \varphi^\rho$*.*

A much deeper result is that the converse also holds: if $PA \vdash \varphi^\rho$ for all ρ, then $\mathsf{GL} \vdash \varphi$. This is Solovay's *arithmetical completeness theorem.*

Finally, a beautiful result about GL is the de Jongh - Sambin *fixed point theorem.* Below we do not give the full formulation, but a corollary which already is striking.

Theorem 12.7.3 (GL **fixed point theorem)**
Let $\varphi(p)$ *be an* $\mathcal{L}$*-sentence in which every occurrence of* p *is within the scope of an occurrence of* $\Box$*. Then there is an* $\mathcal{L}$*-sentence* ψ *— a* fixed point of $\varphi(p)$ *— in which* p *does not occur (and the only sentence letters in* ψ *are letters occurring in* $\varphi(p)$*) such that* $\mathsf{GL} \vdash \psi \leftrightarrow \varphi(\psi)$*.*

The full theorem shows that all fixed points of $\varphi(p)$ are equivalent in GL. Some proofs of the theorem (there are several) give algorithms for calculating fixed points. For example, the simplest fixed point of $\neg\Box p$ turns out to be the consistency sentence $\neg\Box\bot$. Now recall the Gödel sentence G, for which we have $PA \vdash G \leftrightarrow \neg Pr(\ulcorner G \urcorner)$. Let ρ be a realization such that $\rho(p) = G$. Thus, $PA \vdash (p \leftrightarrow \neg\Box p)^\rho$. Using the full formulation of the fixed point theorem (not given here), it then follows that

(37) $\quad PA \vdash G \leftrightarrow Con_{PA}$

We knew that the right-to-left direction is provable in PA (using (D1) – (D3)), but now we also get the left-to-right direction. This is just one instance of how the modal analysis can give insights into arithmetical provability (although this particular insight is easily proved directly: Exercise 12.10.8). There is much more to this story, but we shall leave it here.

12.8. Incompleteness for other theories

The incompleteness theorems also hold for many theories in other vocabularies: it suffices that they 'contain enough arithmetic' in some

[13] But didn't we earlier prove Löb's theorem from the assumptions (D1) – (D3)? Yes, but, *first*, that proof presupposed the self-referential sentence in (24). *Assuming* that for a given sentence φ there is a sentence ψ such that $\psi \leftrightarrow (\Box\psi \to \varphi)$, the rest of the proof can indeed be carried out in K4. But, *second*, this yields the *Löb rule*: from $\vdash \Box\varphi \to \varphi$, conclude $\vdash \varphi$. The *formalized* version L is not provable in K4. (Nevertheless, K4 plus the Löb rule turns out to be equivalent to GL; G. Boolos 1993, p. 59.)

suitable sense. An important example is set theory *ZF*, whose vocabulary is $\{\in\}$. As we have said, practically all results in classical mathematics can (in principle) be proved in *ZFC*: *ZF* extended by the Axiom of Choice. But *ZF* is primitive recursive, and the incompleteness theorems apply. So if *ZF* is consistent, there are sentences neither provable nor refutable in *ZF*; in particular, Con_{ZF} is such a sentence.

To see this, it sufficies to note that *PA* can be translated into *ZF*. First, translate the L_{PA}-terms. The idea is that 0 translates to $\varnothing$, $\mathbf{1} = 0'$ to $\{\varnothing\}$, $\mathbf{2} = 0''$ to $\{\varnothing, \{\varnothing\}\}$, $\mathbf{3} = 0'''$ to $\{\varnothing, \{\varnothing\}, \{\varnothing, \{\varnothing\}\}\}$, etc. So define a translation function $*$ such that $0^* = \varnothing$ and $(t')^* = t^* \cup \{t^*\}$. The symbols $+$ and $\cdot$ can also be translated as set-theoretic (defined) terms, and we obtain an inductive definition of t^* for every L_{PA}-term t. Let $N(x)$ be a set-theoretic formula expressing that x belongs to every set z such that $\varnothing \in z$ and for all y, if $y \in z$ then $y \cup \{y\} \in z$.[14] Then $N(x)$ says that x is a natural number, in the sense of *ZF*.

Next, we translate L_{PA}-formulas as follows:

$$\begin{aligned}
&(s = t)^* = (s^* = t^*)\\
&(\neg\varphi)^* = \neg\varphi^*\\
&(\varphi \to \psi)^* = (\varphi^* \to \psi^*)\\
&(\exists x\varphi)^* = \exists x(N(x) \wedge \varphi^*)\\
&(\forall x\varphi)^* = \exists x(N(x) \to \varphi^*)
\end{aligned}$$

It is not hard to show that the translations of all axioms in *PA* are theorems of *ZF*, and hence that

$$PA \vdash \varphi \quad \Rightarrow \quad ZF \vdash \varphi^*$$

Say that a set-theoretic formula is *arithmetical* if all its quantifiers are restricted to $N(x)$. In particular, formulas of the form φ^* are arithmetical. Now, by simply translating the proof we gave for *PA*, one shows that all primitive recursive functions are definable in *ZF* by arithmetical formulas.[15] This is enough to prove the Diagonal Lemma, and so one can construct a Rosser sentence which is neither provable nor disprovable in *ZF* (if *ZF* is consistent). Likewise, $ZF \nvdash Con_{ZF}$.

12.8.1. Interpretability

We can formulate this type of result more generally, via a notion of *interpretation* of one theory U into another theory T. The first part of the interpretation is a *translation* τ of L_U into L_T.[16] τ comes with a *domain*

[14]Put differently, $N = \bigcap\{z \colon \varnothing \in z \wedge \forall y(y \in z \to y \cup \{y\} \in z)\}$.

[15]In the sense that if f is primitive recursive and, say, 1-ary, there is an arithmetical formula $\psi(x, y)$ such that if $f(n) = m$, then $ZF \vdash \forall y(N(y) \to (\psi(\mathbf{n}^*, y) \leftrightarrow y = \mathbf{m}^*))$.

[16]Not to be confused with the translations from the modal to the arithmetical language we mentioned in Section 12.7.2. Also, in Chapters 2 – 4, we used the term "interpretation" for what we are now calling *models*: a domain and an assignment of

formula $\delta_\tau(x)$ in the vocabulary L_T (cf. $N(x)$ above), and maps every k-ary predicate symbol $P \in L_U$ to an L_T-formula $\psi_{P,\tau}(x_1, \ldots, x_k)$. Similarly, we assume that for every k-ary function symbol $f \in L_U$ there is a corresponding L_T-formula $\psi_{f,\tau}(x_1, \ldots, x_k, y)$, and for each individual constant $c \in L_U$ an L_T-formula $\psi_{c,\tau}(y)$. Now define the map τ on (certain) L_U-formulas as follows:

(38) a. $(x = y)^\tau := x = y$
b. $(x = c)^\tau := \psi_{c,\tau}(x)$
c. $(fx_1 \ldots x_k = y)^\tau := \psi_{f,\tau}(x_1, \ldots, x_k, y)$
d. $(Px_1 \ldots x_k)^\tau := \psi_{P,\tau}(x_1, \ldots, x_k)$
e. $(\neg\varphi)^\tau := \neg\varphi^\tau$
f. $(\varphi \to \psi)^\tau := \varphi^\tau \to \psi^\tau$
g. $(\exists x\varphi)^\tau := \exists x(\delta_\tau(x) \wedge \varphi^\tau)$
h. $(\forall x\varphi)^\tau := \forall x(\delta_\tau(x) \to \varphi^\tau)$

This translation applies only to formulas whose atomic subformulas are of a certain simple form: we called such formulas *unnested* in Exercise 9.10.12, and indicated a proof there that every formula is logically equivalent to an unnested formula (in the same vocabulary). Indeed there is a mechanical procedure for transforming any formula into an unnested equivalent. Using this, we can take τ to be a primitive recursive function mapping every L_U-formula φ to an L_T-formula φ^τ (of course, the map is really between the corresponding Gödel numbers).

Now, we say that such a translation τ is an *interpretation of* U *in* T if the following holds, for $f, c \in L_U$:[17]

(39) a. $T \vdash \exists x\delta_\tau(x)$
b. $T \vdash \exists x(\delta_\tau(x) \wedge \forall y(\psi_{c,\tau}(y) \leftrightarrow y = x))$
c. $T \vdash \forall\overline{x}(\delta_\tau(\overline{x}) \to \exists y(\delta_\tau(y) \wedge \forall z(\delta_\tau(z) \to (\psi_{f,\tau}(\overline{x}, z) \leftrightarrow z = y)))$
d. If $U \vdash \varphi$, then $T \vdash \varphi^\tau$.

So c. says that the L_T-formula $\psi_{f,\tau}(\overline{x}, y)$ corresponding to a function symbol f in L_U really defines a function (restricted to the domain $\delta_\tau(x)$) in T, and similarly $\psi_{c,\tau}(y)$ defines a unique object in $\delta_\tau(x)$.

We say that U *is interpretable in* T if there is an interpretation τ of U in T.[18] Clearly, the map $*$ indicated earlier shows that *PA* is

appropriate values to the non-logical symbols in a vocabulary. Obviously, the term is used here in a different (though related) sense.

[17]In c., $\forall\overline{x}$ is short for $\forall x_1 \ldots \forall x_k$, and $\delta_\tau(\overline{x})$ abbreviates $\delta_\tau(x_1) \wedge \ldots \wedge \delta_\tau(x_k)$.

[18]We have presented the notion of interpretability between theories essentially due to Tarski. Model theorists have since found use for more general notions. For example, the translation of = need not be identity but an arbitrary equivalence relation. Also, our interpretations are 1-dimensional, whereas an n-dimensional translation maps variables in L_U-formulas to n-tuples of variables in L_T-formulas. Requirement (39d) is sometimes too strong, and the map τ need not be (primitive) recursive. For a

interpretable in *ZF*. For example, $\delta_*(x)$ is the formula $N(x)$, and we have $\psi_{0,*}(y) := \forall x\, x \notin y$, and $\psi_{',\tau}(x,y) := \forall z(z \in y \leftrightarrow z \in x \vee z = x)$ (that is, $\psi_{',\tau}(x,y) := y = x \cup \{x\}$).

If T is an extension of U in the same vocabulary, or, a bit more generally, if $L_U \subseteq L_T$ and $Thm_U \subseteq Thm_T$, then trivially U is interpretable in T (by the identity interpretation). Next, let

$$U^\tau = \{\psi\colon \psi \text{ is an } L_U\text{-sentence and } T \vdash \psi^\tau\}$$

Then it is easy to show (Exercise 12.10.27):

(40) $U^\tau \vdash \varphi$ iff $T \vdash \varphi^\tau$

Furthermore:

(41) If U and T are primitive recursive and T is consistent, then U^τ is a consistent and primitive recursive extension of U.

Proof. That U^τ is an extension of U follows from (39d). If U^τ is inconsistent, there is an L_U-sentence φ such that $U^\tau \vdash \varphi$ and $U^\tau \vdash \neg\varphi$, which according to (38e) and (40) means that $T \vdash \varphi^\tau$ and $T \vdash \neg\varphi^\tau$, i.e. that T is inconsistent, contrary to assumption.

It remains to show that U^τ is primitive recursive. This doesn't follow directly from the definition of U^τ, since we in effect defined

(42) $ax_{U^\tau}(n)$ iff $\exists m\, prf_T(m, \tau(n))$

The relation prf_T is primitive recursive, but this doesn't make the set ax_{U^τ} primitive recursive. However, we will see later (Chapter 15.1.2) that there is an effective method to transform an axiom set defined as in (42) into an equivalent primitive recursive set of axioms. □

Now we can generalize the first incompleteness theorem again:

Theorem 12.8.1 (First incompleteness theorem, version 3)
If T a primitive recursive and consistent theory in which PA is interpretable, then T is incomplete.

Proof. If τ interprets *PA* in T, we can according to (41) apply Rosser's version of the first incompleteness theorem to the consistent primitive recursive extension PA^τ of *PA*. So there is an L_{PA}-sentence φ such that $PA^\tau \nvdash \varphi$ and $PA^\tau \nvdash \neg\varphi$. But then it follows by (40) that $T \nvdash \varphi^\tau$ and $T \nvdash \neg\varphi^\tau$, i.e. T is incomplete. □

---

mathematical account of various kinds of interpretations used in model theory, see Hodges 1993, Ch. 5.

The second incompleteness theorem can also be extended to theories in which *PA* is interpretable. There are further strengthenings of this theorem in terms of interpretability; we mention a few in the next subsection.

A theory T that 'contains enough arithmetic' in one of the senses discussed here has an *arithmetical component*. T could be a theory of physics, for example, which literally contains *PA*, but also has other non-logical symbols and other axioms concerning them. Or it could be a mathematical theory like *ZFC*, with none of the arithmetical non-logical symbols, but with the means to define them. The incompleteness theorems hold for all such theories. But note that the incompleteness concerns only the arithmetical part of the theories. That is, the Rosser sentence which is undecidable in T is an *arithmetical* sentence, in the sense of belonging to the arithmetical component of T:s language. Likewise, the sentence Con_T is arithmetical.

Thus, we cannot expect Gödel's incompleteness theorems, applied to such theories, to yield undecidable statements that are of interest for physics, or concern important properties of sets. There are indeed many interesting statements about sets that are undecidable in set theory; most well-known are the Axiom of Choice (AC) and the Continuum Hypothesis (CH). These were proved to be independent of *ZF* by the combined efforts of Gödel in 1938 and Paul Cohen in 1963. But the incompleteness theorems play no role in these proofs, which instead use elaborate constructions of models of *ZF*.

12.8.2. *Interpretability of consistency

Interpretability was originally introduced in logic in order to generalize facts about undecidability; we get to these facts in Chapter 14. But since then interpretations have been studied for their own sake, and proved to be powerful tools in arithmetized metalogic. There is an immediate connection to consistency: if U is interpretable in T and T is consistent, then U is consistent, as we have seen. But this connection goes much deeper, and in fact leads to significant strengthenings of the second incompleteness theorem. Without giving proofs, we will mention a few important results. Let

$$U \leqslant T$$

mean that U is interpretable in T. One checks that $\leqslant$ is a preorder (reflexive and transitive), and so the relation $\simeq$ defined by $U \simeq T \Leftrightarrow U \leqslant T \;\&\; T \leqslant U$ is an equivalence relation, whose equivalence classes are called *degrees of interpretability*. Write $deg(T)$ for the degree of T.

The degrees are partially ordered by $\leqslant$, where $deg(U) \leqslant deg(T)$ iff $U \leqslant T$,[19] a partial order with an intricate and complex structure.[20]

Some examples of (non)interpretability:

- As we have seen, $PA \leqslant ZF$.
- On the other hand, $ZF \nleqslant PA$. For if $ZF \leqslant PA$, then not only would the consistency of PA imply that of ZF, but this fact would be provable in ZF: $ZF \vdash Con_{PA} \rightarrow Con_{ZF}$. But the consistency of PA can be proved in ZF: $ZF \vdash Con_{PA}$. But then $ZF \vdash Con_{ZF}$, which contradicts the second incompleteness theorem.
- The model construction in Gödel's proof that AC and CH are consistent with ZF actually shows that $ZF + \text{AC} + \text{CH} \leqslant ZF$.
- And one of the proofs that AC and CH are independent of ZF can be used to show that $ZF + \neg\text{AC} + \neg\text{CH} \leqslant ZF$.

Now, here is a first generalization of the second incompleteness theorem. In what follows, T and U are consistent primitive recursive extensions of PA.[21]

(43) $\quad T + Con_T \nleqslant T$

Since, trivially, $T \vdash \varphi$ implies $T + \varphi \leqslant T$, it follows immediately from (43) that $T \nvdash Con_T$.

Many positive results about the existence of interpretations build on the next fact, which is a formal version of the *completeness theorem* for first-order logic. The proof amounts to a (by no means trivial) formalization in *PA* of Henkin's proof of the Model Existence Theorem (Theorem 5.1.1).

(44) $\quad U \leqslant T + Con_U$

An interpretation of U in T can be seen as a construction of a model of U inside T (see Exercise 12.10.29 for a precise formulation of this). So (44) 'says' that if U is assumed to be consistent, it has a model.

A striking application of (44) is the following.

(45) $\quad T + \neg Con_T \leqslant T$

A simple proof of (45) is indicated in Exercise 12.10.32. Interestingly, completeness and incompleteness come together in this result. Note that if we had $T \vdash Con_T$, then $T + \neg Con_T$ would be inconsistent,

[19] See Exercise 16.3.11 in the Appendix for the general facts about pre-orders, equivalence relations, and partial orders used here.

[20] See e.g. Lindström 2003, Ch. 7.

[21] The results below come from Feferman 1960. A modern overview can be found, for example, in Lindström 2003, Ch. 6.

and hence not interpretable in T (which we assumed to be consistent), so (45) indeed generalizes the second incompleteness theorem, but it says more. We end with a quote from Visser 2014, a paper which deals precisely with this and related results: "[(45)] says, in metaphorical paraphrase, that it is not just the case that a theory fails to prove its own consistency, but that a theory actively holds its own inconsistency for possible".

12.9. What do Gödel's theorems mean?

Hopefully, this chapter has given an idea not only of the proofs of the incompleteness theorems but also the fruitfulness of the techniques employed, and the possibility of applying these tools and techniques for various purposes. The next part of the book pursues some of these applications. We end this part with a discussion of some philosophical issues raised by the inompleteness phenomena. We will not deal with the more fanciful claims that have been made,[22], nor will we say more about the consequences of Gödel's theorems for Hilbert's Program than we did in Chapter 7.1.1. But we shall address a few natural questions that arise when one stops to think about the import of the incompleteness theorems.

12.9.1. Goldbach-like statements

Recall Goldbach's Conjecture: every even number greater than 2 is the sum of two prime numbers. Checking, of any individual number, whether it is even and if so the sum of two primes is a mechanical procedure that gives a result in a finite number of steps. In other words, there is a *algorithm* for doing this check. Borrowing a term from Torkel Franzén (see note 22), let us say that a statement is *Goldbach-like* if it is of the form "Every natural number has property P", where P is an algorithmic property. In the arithmetical first-order language, the conjecture is

$$\forall x(x > \mathbf{2} \wedge Even(x) \rightarrow \exists y_{y<x} \exists z_{z<x}(Prime(y) \wedge Prime(z) \wedge y + z = x))$$

where $Even(x)$ and $Prime(x)$ are the obvious arithmetical formulas. Here is another famous Goldbach-like claim, *Fermat's Theorem*:[23]

[22]Such as the claim that they show that the human mind is not a 'machine', which has engendered a huge debate. This debate and other imagined or real consequences of the incompleteness theorems are discussed at length in Franzén 2005, which is the best book I know of that explains, in an informal yet precise way, the import of Gödel's theorems. The discussion in this section is inspired by that book.

[23]There is no primitive function symbol for exponentiation in L_{PA}, but since exponentiation is primitive recursive, it is (strongly) definable in *PA*, so when we write x^u we are in effect using the defining formula for exponentiation, or a new function symbol whose introduction is warranted by that formula.

$$\forall x \forall y \forall z \forall u (x > 0 \wedge y > 0 \wedge z > 0 \wedge u > \mathbf{2} \rightarrow x^u + y^u \neq z^u)$$

(We may allow several universal quantifiers in Goldbach-like claims.) And here is an example of a statement which is *not* Goldbach-like, the *Twin Prime Conjecture*:

$$\forall x \exists y (y > x \wedge \mathit{Prime}(y) \wedge \mathit{Prime}(y + \mathbf{2}))$$

This fails to be Goldbach-like because of the existential quantifier: there is no (known) algorithmic procedure for deciding if *there exist* twin primes greater than x. Fermat's Theorem was proved in 1995 by Andrew Wiles.[24] Goldbach's Conjecture and the Twin Prime Conjecture are still open.

These arithmetical statements are of interest here, since the undecidable Gödel and Rosser sentences, as well as the sentence Con_T, turn out to express Goldbach-like statements. For example, Con_T is

$$\forall x \neg \mathit{Prf}_T(x, \ulcorner \bot \urcorner)$$

Since $\mathit{Prf}_T(x, y)$ represents the primitive recursive (hence algorithmic) relation prf_T in *PA*, Con_T is Goldbach-like.

We can apply these notions of quantifier complexity directly to arithmetical formulas as follows. Say that such a formula is *bounded* if all its quantifiers are bounded: either of the form $\forall x (x < t \rightarrow \ldots)$ or of the form $\exists y (y < t \wedge \ldots)$. Next, a formula is Π_1 if it has the form

$$\forall x_1 \ldots \forall x_n \psi$$

where ψ is bounded, and it is Σ_1 if it has the form

$$\exists x_1 \ldots \exists x_n \theta$$

where θ is bounded.[25] It is easy to see that all bounded sentences are decidable in *PA*. So it makes sense to identify *Goldbach-like* arithmetical sentences with Π_1 sentences. The two theorems below we will be proved in Chapter 14.5.

Theorem 12.9.1
All primitive recursive relations and functions are representable in PA (in fact, in the much weaker theory Q; Chapter 14.4) by Σ_1 formulas.

If the primitive recursive relations prf_T and ref_T are represented in *PA* by Σ_1 formulas $\mathit{Prf}_T(x, y)$ and $\mathit{Ref}_T(x, y)$, we see that $\neg \exists x \mathit{Prf}_T(x, \ulcorner G \urcorner)$, Con_T, and $\forall x (\mathit{Prf}_T(x, \ulcorner R \urcorner) \rightarrow \exists y_{y<x} \mathit{Ref}_T(y, \ulcorner R \urcorner))$ are all (logically equivalent to) Π_1 sentences, when T is a primitive recursive extension of *PA*.

[24] Wiles' 125 pages long proof relies on advanced mathematical theories far beyond arithmetic. It is not known if the proof can be done in *PA*, though some mathematicians suspect that it can.

[25] These definitions are preliminary and will be made precise in Chapter 14.5.

Goldbach-like (Π_1) sentences have the interesting property that if they are *false*, that fact is provable in *PA* (indeed, in Q). This follows from the following fundamental result which, together with Theorem 12.9.1, highlights the importance of Σ_1 formulas in arithmetization.

Theorem 12.9.2
All true Σ_1 sentences are provable in PA (in Q).

Thus, if there is some very large even number which is *not* the sum of two primes, i.e. if Goldbach's Conjecture is false, then this can be proved in *PA*. (We have no reason at present to suppose this to be the case.) Similarly for any true claim that a theory T (a primitive recursive extension of *PA*) is *not* consistent. On the other hand, if there is some number such that for every prime number p larger than it, $p+2$ is not a prime number, i.e. if the Twin Prime Conjecture is false, that would give no information about whether or not this is provable in *PA*, since this conjecture has a more complex form than Goldbach-like statements.

12.9.2. Truth and consistency

The incompleteness theorems do *not* prove that the Gödel sentence G for a theory T (say, a primitive recursive extension of *PA*), or the sentence Con_T, is true. What they prove, or rather, what they entail, is: "*if* T is consistent, *then* G and Con_T are true". The truth of G and Con_T follows only if we can also prove that T is consistent.

Gödel's theorems apply to *consistent* theories (of a certain kind), not only to true theories. Just knowing that a theory is consistent is not a good reason to trust it. Many consistent theories prove false theorems. Suppose $T \nvdash Con_T$. Then $T' = T + \neg Con_T$ is consistent. Trivially, $T' \vdash \neg Con_T$. And since T' obtained by adding an axiom to T, Fact 12.6.1(b) shows that $\vdash Con_{T'} \rightarrow Con_T$, from which it follows that $T' \vdash \neg Con_{T'}$. So T' proves that it is *in*consistent, which is patently false.

But can we really know that, say, Con_{PA} is true, given that *PA* is consistent? Isn't truth a notion based on intuition, or models, rather than proof? Well, *first*, recall that 'true' here means 'true in the model $\mathcal{N}$', and truth in models or interpretations is a straightforward mathematical notion that we defined back in Chapter 2. If you think that notion is suspicious, then you must think the semantics of first-order logic in general is suspicious.

Second, recall that Con_{PA} is a Goldbach-like sentence. To prove that it is true we have to show that every natural number has a certain computable property (the property of not being a Gödel number of a proof in *PA* of $0 \neq 0$). This is an arithmetical claim, no different in kind from Goldbach's Conjecture or Fermat's Theorem. Such claims can (sometimes) be proved by mathematical methods. To say that Goldbach's conjecture is *true* is no more than saying that every even number greater than 2 is the sum of two primes. We don't know if this is actually so, but we certainly know what a proof of it would have to establish. In the case of Con_{PA} and Fermat's Theorem we do know that they are both true, even though one of them, and perhaps both, are not provable in *PA*. We know this because it can be *proved*, by reasoning that mathematicians trust.

We can be more specific. The argument "All *PA* axioms are true (in $\mathcal{N}$), hence all theorems of *PA* are true, no contradiction is true, hence no contradiction is a theorem of *PA*" can be formalized and proved in a mathematical theory. It can be carried out in a set theory such as *ZFC*, but in fact a much weaker theory suffices. In any case, that theory contains only axioms that most mathematicians accept.

There is also a syntactic proof of the consistency of *PA*, given by Gentzen in 1936. This goes by way of a careful analysis of derivations in *PA*, relative to an inference system suitable for that purpose (not our Hilbert system). The analysis uses *ordinal numbers*, which are numbers generalizing the *finite* ordinal (natural) numbers 0,1,2,... to *transfinite* ordinal numbers. The smallest transfinite ordinal number is ω, which represents the standard order of the natural numbers, and so ordinary induction as we have used it in this book is *induction up to* ω. Gentzen's proof requires induction up to a larger ordinal number, called ϵ_0 (which is still very low in the transfinite ordinal hierarchy). Again, this induction principle is not something mathematicians usually doubt.

Gentzen's proof also refutes the claim that a proof of the consistency of T must be carried out in a theory *stronger* than T. In fact, his proof can be formalized in a theory which has a stronger induction axiom that *PA*, but does not prove certain *PA*-theorems, so it is not an extension of *PA*. In general, it makes no sense to require that a consistency proof of a theory is always carried out in a stronger theory. For example, $PA + \neg Con_{PA}$ is consistent, but there would be no point in proving this in a theory containing $PA + \neg Con_{PA}$, since such a theory proves false statements. Instead, we prove that *if* *PA* is consistent, then $PA + \neg Con_{PA}$ is consistent; this reasoning can actually be carried out inside *PA* (see Exercise 12.10.25).

These observations should make it clear that proving consistency does not require some special new techniques, or some new kind of mathematical insight or intuition. It can be done with ordinary mathematical methods.

A final important point is that the second incompleteness theorem by itself doesn't give us any reason to *doubt* the consistency of *PA* (or any primitive recursive extension of *PA*). If someone actually doubted this, it would presumably be because he or she thinks the induction axiom is problematic. The second theorem just says that *if* *PA* is consistent *then* this cannot be proved in *PA*. That fact alone should do nothing to reinforce such doubts. Of course, it doesn't alleviate them either, so to such a person we could only say that the consistency of *PA* can be proved by methods most mathematicians accept, but these methods might then not be accepted by our doubter.

The situation is different in set theory. Most mathematicians believe that *ZFC* is consistent, but the reason for this is not that they agree on a mathematical proof of this fact. Some think the *ZFC* axioms are self-evidently true, but many would not agree to that. If we make the assumption that all generally accepted mathematical arguments can be carried out in *ZFC*, then the second incompleteness theorem entails that *the consistency of ZFC cannot be proved by a generally accepted mathematical argument*. This is of course a philosophically significant consequence of the theorem.

The consistency of *ZFC* can be proved if certain axioms about the existence of very large cardinals are added to *ZFC*. (It suffices to add the smallest so-called *inaccessible* cardinal.) But these axioms do not have the status of being generally accepted, and in any case they raise the issue of the consistency of *ZFC* + such axioms. The reason most mathematicians believe in the consistency of *ZFC* is that no inconsistency has been found, despite an immense amount of work in the theory, that the axioms are designed to avoid known ways to generate contradiction, etc. These are probably good reasons, but they do not amount to a mathematical proof.

12.10. Exercises to Chapter 12

Exercise 12.10.1
In the proof of the Diagonal Lemma, let instead $\theta(x)$ be the formula

$$\forall y(Sub_0(x,x,y) \rightarrow \psi(y))$$

Show that in this case too we have, with $\varphi = \theta(\ulcorner\theta\urcorner)$, $PA \vdash \varphi \leftrightarrow \psi(\ulcorner\varphi\urcorner)$.

Exercise 12.10.2
Show that the following stronger version of the Diagonal Lemma holds:

(D1) If $\psi(y, x_1, \ldots, x_n)$ is a formula with exactly $y, x_1, \ldots, x_n$ as free variables, then there is a formula $\varphi(x_1, \ldots, x_n)$ with exactly $x_1, \ldots, x_n$ as free variables, such that:

$$PA \vdash \varphi(x_1, \ldots, x_n) \leftrightarrow \psi(\ulcorner\varphi(x_1, \ldots, x_n)\urcorner, x_1, \ldots, x_n)$$

[Hint: essentially the same proof works.]

Exercise 12.10.3
Let $\psi(x, y)$ be any formula. Show that there is a sentence φ such that

$$PA \vdash \varphi \leftrightarrow \psi(\ulcorner\varphi\urcorner, \ulcorner\neg\varphi\urcorner)$$

[Hint: The function *neg* (Chapter 11.2) is representable in *PA*. Use the Diagonal Lemma on a suitable formula.]

Exercise 12.10.4 (another diagonal lemma)
If x is v_0 and y is v_1, recall that $sub_0(m,n) = sub(m, num(n), 0) = m(\mathbf{n}/x)$. Similarly, let

$$sub_1(m, n_0, n_1) = sub(sub(m, num(n_1), 1), num(n_0), 0) = m(\mathbf{n_1}/y)(\mathbf{n_0}/x)$$

So sub_1 is primitive recursive. Let the formula $Sub_1(y, x_0, x_1, z)$ represent it in *PA*. Show that if $\theta(x,y)$ has the free variables shown, we have, for all n,

(a) $\quad PA \vdash \forall z(Sub_1(\ulcorner\theta\urcorner, \mathbf{n}, \ulcorner\theta\urcorner, z) \leftrightarrow z = \ulcorner\theta(\mathbf{n}, \ulcorner\theta\urcorner)\urcorner)$

[Hint: First show $PA \vdash \forall z(Sub_1(\ulcorner\theta\urcorner, \mathbf{n}, \mathbf{k}, z) \leftrightarrow z = \ulcorner\theta(\mathbf{n}, \mathbf{k})\urcorner)$.] Then use (a) to prove the following Diagonal Lemma:

(46) If $\psi(x,y)$ is any formula with the free variables shown, there is a formula $\varphi(x)$ such that, for all n,

$$PA \vdash \varphi(\mathbf{n}) \leftrightarrow \psi(\mathbf{n}, \ulcorner\varphi(\mathbf{n})\urcorner)$$

[Hint: Start with the formula $\theta(x,y) := \exists z(Sub_1(y,x,y,z) \wedge \psi(x,z))$, and let $\varphi(x) := \theta(x, \ulcorner\theta\urcorner)$.]

Exercise 12.10.5
Say that an arithmetical sentence φ is *humanly provable* if there is a primitive recursive extension T of *PA* with true axioms, which is such that $T \vdash \varphi$. Do the incompleteness theorems show that there are true arithmetical sentences which are not humanly provable?

Exercise 12.10.6
Consider the theory $T = PA + \{\mathbf{n} < c \colon n = 0, 1, 2, \ldots\}$ in the vocabulary $L = L_{PA} \cup \{c\}$. Show that T is consistent but ω-inconsistent.

Exercise 12.10.7 (length of proofs 1)
If f is a 1-ary function we say that a theory T is *f-bounded* if

$$thm_T(n) \Leftrightarrow \text{there is } m' \leqslant f(n) \text{ such that } prf_T(m', n)$$

That is, if $T \vdash \varphi$, then there is a derivation of φ whose length—which we here identify with its Gödel number—is at most $f(\#(\varphi))$.

1. Show that if T is a primitive recursive extension of *PA*, there is no primitive recursive function f such that T is f-bounded. [Hint: Either use the fact that thm_T is not representable in T (Exercise 7.3.12), or construct directly a sentence ψ saying "There is no proof of ψ in T of length $\leqslant f(\#(\psi))$".]

2. Let f be, for example, one of the incredibly fast growing primitive recursive functions discussed in Chapter 8.4 (e.g. $f(n) = n \uparrow_{100} n$, remember that already $4 \uparrow_4 4$ is a ridiculously large number). Conclude that there are theorems φ in T such that—roughly speaking—the length of the shortest proof of φ is incredibly much longer than (the Gödel number of) φ itself.

Exercise 12.10.8 (explicitly definable fixed points)
Let T be a primitive recursive extension of *PA*.

1. Show that for any sentence φ, $PA \vdash \neg Pr_T(\ulcorner\varphi\urcorner) \rightarrow Con_T$.

2. Conclude that if G is as in (10), then $PA \vdash Con_T \leftrightarrow G$.

(Informal arguments suffice.) If $\psi(y)$ is a formula and φ a sentence such that $PA \vdash \varphi \leftrightarrow \psi(\ulcorner\varphi\urcorner)$, we say that φ is a *fixed point* of $\psi(y)$. Thus, the Gödel sentence G is a fixed point of $\neg Pr_T(y)$, and we have just concluded that G is also *explicitly definable*, i.e. equivalent in *PA* to a sentence that does not involve self-reference.

3. Show that the Henkin sentence H, where $PA \vdash H \leftrightarrow Pr_T(\ulcorner H\urcorner)$, is also explicitly definable in this sense. [Use Löb's Theorem.]

4. Given a sentence φ such that $PA \vdash Pr_T(\ulcorner\varphi\urcorner) \rightarrow \varphi$, show that the fixed point ψ of the formula $Pr_T(y) \rightarrow \varphi$ used in the proof of Löb's Theorem is also explicitly definable.

Exercise 12.10.9
*The Gödel sentence G is equivalent in *PA* to a sentence of the form $\forall y \psi(y)$, where for all n, $PA \vdash \psi(\mathbf{n})$, even though $PA \nvdash \forall y \psi(y)$. Use G to find a formula $\theta(y)$ such that $PA \vdash \exists y \theta(y)$ even though for every n, $PA \nvdash \theta(\mathbf{n})$.

Exercise 12.10.10
Suppose the formula $\psi(y)$ is such that for every sentence φ, we have:

a. if $T \vdash \varphi$, then $T \vdash \psi(\ulcorner\varphi\urcorner)$

b. $T \vdash \psi(\ulcorner\varphi\urcorner) \rightarrow \varphi$

Show that if this holds and T is an extension of *PA*, then T is inconsistent. [Hint: use the Diagonal Lemma on a suitable formula.]

Exercise 12.10.11
Let $T = PA + \neg Con_{PA}$, and let T' be obtained by adding all instances of the reflection principle

(Rfn) $\quad \exists x Prf_T(x, \ulcorner\varphi\urcorner) \rightarrow \varphi$

as axioms. Show that T' is inconsistent.

Exercise 12.10.12
Let an *explicit reflection scheme* for T have the form

$$\text{(ERfn)}\ \mathit{Prf}_T(\mathbf{m}, \ulcorner\varphi\urcorner) \to \varphi$$

Show that if T is a primitive recursive extension of *PA*, then for all m and all φ, the explicit reflection scheme is provable in T. [Hint: distinguish the cases $\mathit{prf}_T(m, \#(\varphi))$ and not $\mathit{prf}_T(m, \#(\varphi))$.]

Exercise 12.10.13

1. Let $\mathit{Prf}'_T(x, y)$ be the formula

   $$\mathit{Prf}_T(x, y) \wedge \forall z_{z<x} \neg \mathit{Ref}_T(z, y)$$

   where T is a primitive recursive extension of *PA*. Show that this formula also represents the relation prf_T in *PA*.

2. Express sentence R from Section 12.3 in terms of $\mathit{Prf}'_T(x, y)$.

Exercise 12.10.14 (another Rosser sentence)
Let R' be a sentence (which exists by the Diagonal Lemma) such that

(47) $\quad \mathit{PA} \vdash R' \leftrightarrow \exists x(\mathit{Ref}_T(x, \ulcorner R'\urcorner) \wedge \forall z_{z<x} \neg \mathit{Prf}_T(z, \ulcorner R'\urcorner))$

1. Explain why R' is false (with T as before).

2. Show that Theorem 12.3.1 holds with R' in place of R. [Hint: A similar argument works.]

Sentences satisfying (47) are also called Rosser sentences.

Exercise 12.10.15 (monoconsistency 1)
*Say that a set X of sentences is *monoconsistent with* T if for all $\psi \in X$, $T + \psi$ is consistent. (This notion and the results in this and the next exercise are due to Per Lindström.) For example, if ψ is undecidable in T, then $\{\psi, \neg\psi\}$ is monoconsistent with T. Prove the following, assuming that T is a consistent primitive recursive extension of *PA*:

(48) If there is a primitive recursive relation R such that $k \in X \Leftrightarrow \exists m R(m, k)$ [this says that X is *recursively enumerable*; see Chapter 15.1], and X is monoconsistent with T, then there is a sentence φ such that $\varphi, \neg\varphi \notin X$.

[Hint: Similar to the proof of Rosser's theorem. Suppose $\rho(x, y)$ represents R in *PA*, and let φ be a sentence such that (cf. Exercise 12.10.3):

(a) $\quad \mathit{PA} \vdash \varphi \leftrightarrow \forall x(\rho(x, \ulcorner\varphi\urcorner) \to \exists z_{z\leqslant x} \rho(z, \ulcorner\neg\varphi\urcorner))$

Suppose for *reductio* that $\varphi \in X$ or $\neg\varphi \in X$, and let m be the smallest number such that either $R(m, \#(\varphi))$ or $R(m, \#(\neg\varphi))$.
Case 1: $R(m, \#(\neg\varphi))$, and so $\neg\varphi \in X$ and for all $k < m$, not $R(k, \#(\varphi))$, i.e. $PA \vdash \neg\rho(\mathbf{k}, \ulcorner\varphi\urcorner)$. Use this and (a) to derive $PA \vdash \varphi$, which contradicts the assumptions that $\neg\varphi \in X$ and X is monoconsistent with T.
Case 2: $R(m, \#(\varphi))$. Use a similar argument to contradict monoconsistency with T.]

Exercise 12.10.16 (monoconsistency 2)

1. Let T be a consistent primitive recursive extension of *PA*. Show that Rosser's Theorem for T is a special case of (48).
2. Prove the following strengthening of Rosser's Theorem:

(49) Let $T_0, T_1, T_2, \ldots$ be primitive recursive extensions of *PA* s.t. there is a primitive recursive relation R s.t. $n \in ax_{T_k} \Leftrightarrow R(k, n)$. Using the fact (to be proved in Chapter 15) that then there is a primitive recursive relation S s.t. $n \in thm_{T_k} \Leftrightarrow \exists m S(k, m, n)$, show that there is a sentence φ which is undecidable in all the theories T_k. [Hint: Use (48), noting that $n \in thm_{T_k} \Leftrightarrow \exists p S'(p, n)$, where $S'(p, n) \Leftrightarrow S((p)_0, (p)_1, n)$.]

Exercise 12.10.17 (length of proofs 2)

*Let T be a primitive recursive extension of *PA*, and f any primitive recursive function such that $m \leqslant f(m)$ for all m. Suppose $T \nvdash \varphi$. Show that there is a sentence θ such that $T \vdash \theta$ and there is a proof with Gödel number q of θ in $T + \varphi$ such that no proof of θ in T is shorter than $f(q)$.

[Outline: Suppose $\chi_f(x, y)$ represents f in *PA*, and let ψ be such that

$$PA \vdash \psi \leftrightarrow \exists x \exists y (Prf_{T+\varphi}(x, \ulcorner\varphi \vee \psi\urcorner) \wedge \chi_f(x, y) \wedge \forall z_{z \leqslant x+y} \neg Prf_T(z, \ulcorner\varphi \vee \psi\urcorner))$$

(ψ exists by a suitable adaption of the Diagonal Lemma; cf. Exercise 12.10.3.) Let $\theta := \varphi \vee \psi$. Suppose $T \nvdash \theta$. But $T + \varphi \vdash \theta$. Use this to show that $T \vdash \psi$, which contradicts the assumption that $T \nvdash \theta$.

Thus, $T \vdash \theta$. Let q be the number of the shortest proof in $T + \varphi$ of θ. Suppose that there is a proof $\leqslant f(q)$ of θ in T. In a similar fashion, show that then $T \vdash \neg\psi$, which, since $T \vdash \theta$, entails that $T \vdash \varphi$, again a contradiction.]

In other words, if $T + \varphi$ properly extends T, then there are theorems of T which have 'much shorter' proofs in $T + \varphi$.

Exercise 12.10.18

In Chapter 6.8 we used the Compactness Theorem to show the existence of non-standard models of *PA* (indeed, of $Th(\mathcal{N})$).

(a) Show that (assuming *PA* is consistent) Rosser's Theorem implies the existence of non-standard models of *PA*.

(b) Let R be the Rosser sentence for *PA*. Show that there is a model of *PA* in which there is a *non-standard proof* of R, i.e. a proof whose Gödel number is non-standard. (NB A *non-standard number* in a model $\mathcal{M}$ of *PA* is an element a of M such that $a \neq \mathbf{n}^{\mathcal{M}}$ for all n.)

Exercise 12.10.19
Show that derivability condition (D2) holds for $\exists x Prf_T(x, y)$.

Exercise 12.10.20

1. Show that Lemma 12.4.3 follows with (D1) and (D2) from the fact that $\varphi \to (\neg\varphi \to 0 \neq 0)$ is a logical truth.
2. Show that it also follows that:

$$\text{If } T \vdash B(\ulcorner \neg\varphi \to \psi \urcorner), \text{ then } T \vdash B(\ulcorner \neg\psi \to \varphi \urcorner)$$

Exercise 12.10.21

(a) Show that the formula $B(y) := \; y = y$ is a provability predicate (satisfies (D1) – (D3)) for every theory T. (So the fact that $B(y)$ is a provability predicate doesn't always mean that the formula has something to do with proofs!)

(b) Explain why the conclusion in Theorem 12.4.1 is trivially true in this case.

(c) One property that the formula $B(y)$ in (a) lacks is:

(*) If $T \vdash B(\ulcorner \varphi \urcorner)$, then $T \vdash \varphi$.

Suppose the set ax_T is representable in T. Let $B(y)$ be the formula $\exists x Prf_T(x, y)$, and assume that $B(y)$ is a provability predicate for T. Show that if T is ω-consistent , then (*) holds.

Exercise 12.10.22
Consider the formula

$$B^*(y) =_{\text{def}} \exists x Prf_T(x, y) \wedge Con_T$$

(T is as usual a consistent primitive recursive extension of *PA*.)

(a) Show that $B^*(y)$ arithmetically defines the set of theorems of T, i.e. that for all sentences φ we have

$$T \vdash \varphi \text{ iff } B^*(\ulcorner \varphi \urcorner) \text{ is true}$$

(b) Let Con_T^* be like Con_T, except that $B^*(y)$ is used instead of the usual provability predicate: $Con_T^* := \neg B^*(\ulcorner 0 \neq 0 \urcorner)$. Show that

$$T \vdash Con_T^*$$

(c) Explain how one of (D1) – (D3) fails for $B^*(y)$.

Exercise 12.10.23
Here is a variant of the preceding exercise. Suppose $Ax_T(x)$ represents ax_T in T and define

$$Ax^*_T(x) := Ax_T(x) \wedge Con_T$$

1. Show that $Ax^*_T(x)$ arithmetically defines ax_T (cf. Exercise 9.10.8), but does not even weakly represent ax_T in T.

2. *Argue informally in T that no contradiction is derivable from the $Ax^*_T(x)$ axioms, and conclude that $T \vdash Con_{Ax^*_T}$.

   [Hint: you may use the fact that *PA* proves that predicate logic (in the vocabulary L_{PA}) is consistent, i.e., with the notation of Chapter 11.8, that $PA \vdash Con_{\varnothing}$.]

The last three exercises, as well as the more striking result in Section 12.4.2 (more striking, since there we used $Con_{\tau *}$ with a formula $\tau^*(y)$ that *represents* ax_T in *PA*), illustrate the 'intensionality' of arithmetization: the unprovability of consistency (and similar statements) only holds if you choose the 'right' way to formalize the consistency statement. Several other parameters might also play a role, such as the chosen coding, and the proof of the Diagonal Lemma (which of the infinitely many fixed point is chosen). For a nice discussion of these issues, and especially the role of self-reference, see Halbach and Visser 2014a,b.

Exercise 12.10.24
(a) Show that $\top$ (i.e. $\neg\bot$) is a fixed point of the formula $\varphi(p) := \Box p$ in GL (in fact, in K).

(b) *Show that $\Box q \to q$ is a fixed point in GL of $\varphi(p) := \Box p \to q$. In other words, show that

$$(\dagger)\ \mathsf{GL} \vdash (\Box q \to q) \leftrightarrow (\Box(\Box q \to q) \to q)$$

[Hint: Reason informally in GL, using the L axiom, propositional reasoning, and the fact that in any modal logic extending K we have that $\vdash \psi \to \theta$ implies $\vdash \Box\psi \to \Box\theta$.].

(c) Conclude from (b) that for every L_{PA}-sentence φ there is a sentence ψ such that $PA \vdash \psi \leftrightarrow (Pr(\ulcorner\psi\urcorner) \to \varphi)$ (cf. (24) in the proof of Löb's theorem), and indeed that an example of such a sentence ψ is $Pr(\ulcorner\varphi\urcorner) \to \varphi$.

[Hint: Use the arithmetical soundness theorem (Theorem 12.7.2).]

Exercise 12.10.8 asked you to prove these facts directly (without modal reasoning).

Exercise 12.10.25 (formalized second incompleteness theorem)
*Prove that the following holds, when T is a primitive recursive extension of *PA*:

$$PA \vdash Con_T \rightarrow Con_{T+\neg Con_T}$$

[Hint: Let G be the Gödel sentence as in (10). Use the fact (proof of Theorem 12.4.1) that $PA \vdash Con_T \rightarrow G$ to show $PA \vdash Pr_T(\ulcorner Con_T \urcorner) \rightarrow \neg Con_T$ (use (D1) and (D2)); then apply Fact 12.6.3.] Explain why this is a formalized version of Gödel's second incompleteness theorem.

Exercise 12.10.26
Consider the following argument:

(**) Suppose there was a proof of $0 \neq 0$ in *PA*. Since proofs are finite, there would then be a proof of $0 \neq 0$ in a finite subtheory PA_0 of *PA*. But, by reflexivity (which we assume), *PA* proves that PA_0 is consistent. This is a contradiction. Hence, there is no proof in *PA* of $0 \neq 0$.

This seems correct, and the argument uses only notions that can be expressed L_{PA}. But by the second incompleteness theorem, no formalization of (**) is provable in *PA* (assuming *PA* is consistent). Try to explain at which point(s) a formalization of (**) would fail.

The next six exercises concern the notion of interpretability introduced in Sections 12.8.1 and 12.8.2.

Exercise 12.10.27
Show that (40) holds when τ is an interpretation of *PA* in T. (Use the Deduction Theorem.)

Exercise 12.10.28
Convince yourself that the relation $U \leqslant T$ is transitive.

Exercise 12.10.29
Let τ be a translation of L_U into L_T, where the theories U, T are as in Section 12.8.2. For every model $\mathcal{M}$ for L_T, τ induces a model $\tau\mathcal{M}$ for L_U with domain $\tau M = \{a \in M : \mathcal{M} \models \delta_\tau(x)\,[a]\}$, in the obvious way: if $P \in L_U$ is a k-ary predicate symbol, then, for $a_1, \ldots, a_k \in \tau M$,

$$P^{\tau\mathcal{M}}(a_1, \ldots, a_k) \text{ iff } \mathcal{M} \models \psi_P\,[a_1, \ldots, a_k]$$

1. Describe how, provided that the L_T-sentences mentioned in (39)a.–c. are true in $\mathcal{M}$, individual constants and function symbols of L_U can be interpreted in $\tau\mathcal{M}$.

2. Show that, under the same provision as above, for every L_U-formula $\varphi(x_1, \ldots, x_n)$ and all $a_1, \ldots, a_n \in \tau M$, we have

$$\tau\mathcal{M} \models \varphi\,[a_1, \ldots, a_n] \text{ iff } \mathcal{M} \models \varphi^\tau\,[a_1, \ldots, a_n]$$

   [Induction over L_U-formulas.]

3. Suppose T satísfies the requirements (39)a.–c. Show that the following are equivalent:

   (a) For every L_U-sentence φ, if $U \vdash \varphi$, then $T \vdash \varphi^\tau$. (In other words, τ is an interpretation of U in T.)

   (b) For every model $\mathcal{M}$ of T, $\tau\mathcal{M}$ is a model of U.

Exercise 12.10.30 (disjunctive interpretations 1)
*Show that if φ is an L_T-sentence, and $U \leqslant T + \varphi$ and $U \leqslant T + \neg\varphi$, then $U \leqslant T$.

[Hint: suppose $\tau : U \leqslant T + \varphi$ and $\sigma : U \leqslant T + \neg\varphi$. Define a translation $\tau\langle\varphi\rangle\sigma$ from L_U into L_T as follows: $\delta_{\tau\langle\varphi\rangle\sigma}(x)$ is $(\delta_\tau(x) \wedge \varphi) \vee (\delta_\sigma(x) \wedge \neg\varphi)$, and, for $P \in L_U$, $\psi_{P,\tau\langle\varphi\rangle\sigma}(\overline{x})$ is $(\psi_{P,\tau}(\overline{x}) \wedge \varphi) \vee (\psi_{P,\sigma}(\overline{x}) \wedge \neg\varphi)$ (and similarly for function symbols and individual constants). Show that $\tau\langle\varphi\rangle\sigma$ is an interpretation of U in T, i.e. that (39) holds for the map $\tau\langle\varphi\rangle\sigma$, given that it holds for τ and for σ. For a.–c. this is straightforward even if a bit messy. For d., prove that for any L_U-sentence θ, we have $T + \varphi \vdash \theta^{\tau\langle\varphi\rangle\sigma} \leftrightarrow \theta^\tau$, and $T + \neg\varphi \vdash \theta^{\tau\langle\varphi\rangle\sigma} \leftrightarrow \theta^\sigma$.]

Exercise 12.10.31 (disjunctive interpretations 2)
*More generally, show that if $U \leqslant T + \varphi_1$ and $U \leqslant T + \varphi_2$, then $U \leqslant T + \varphi_1 \vee \varphi_2$. [Hint: Similar to the previous exercise.]

Exercise 12.10.32 (proof of (45))
Using Exercises 12.10.30 and 12.10.25, apply (44) (the arithmetized completeness theorem) to prove (45), i.e. that $T + \neg Con_T \not\leqslant T$ (when T is a consistent primitive recursive extension of PA). [Hint: Let $U = T + \neg Con_T$ and show that $U \leqslant T + Con_T$ and $U \leqslant T + \neg Con_T$. This simple proof of (45) was found (independently) by Albert Visser and Per Lindström.]

Exercise 12.10.33 (second-order logic)
Second-order logic adds variables $X, Y, \ldots$ over sets of individuals (more generally, variables for relations between individuals), and quantification $\forall X\psi$ and $\exists X\psi$ over sets. This greatly increases expressive power.

(a) *Write a second-order sentence in the vocabulary $\{P\}$ (P unary) which expresses that P is infinite. [Hint: Use the fact that a set A is infinite if there is $a \in A$ such that $|A| = |A - \{a\}|$.]

In second-order logic, the induction axiom scheme (IND) can be replaced by a *single* axiom:

$$\forall X(X(0) \wedge \forall y(X(y) \to X(y')) \to \forall x X(x))$$

Together with a few other axioms (including the first six Peano axioms), we get a primitive recursive *second-order Peano Arithmetic, PA^2*.

(b) Show that the first incompleteness theorem in Rosser's version holds for PA^2.

(c) A well-known result by Dedekind states that PA^2 is *categorical*: all its models are isomorphic (to $\mathcal{N}$). Conclude from (b) that the *completeness theorem* fails for second-order logic.

Part IV

Computability

13 Decidability

So far we have seen primitive recursive functions as typical examples of effectively computable functions. Via Gödel numbering, many metalogical properties and relations become primitive recursive properties and relations, which can be represented in an arithmetical theory like *PA*. But we also saw that there are effectively computable functions that are *not* primitive recursive (Chapter 8.4 and Exercise 8.9.29). In other words, we have not yet fully captured the concept of effective computability, and thereby neither the concept of *decidability*.

Intuitively, a set A of natural numbers—for example, the set of Gödel numbers of theorems in some theory—is *decidable* if its characteristic function c_A is effectively computable, that is, if there is an effective method to decide, for any given n, if $c_A(n)$ is 1 or 0.

In 1936 Alan Turing proposed a precise definition of the notion of effective computability, in terms of what have since been called *Turing machines*. A Turing machine M works with a (potentially) infinite *tape* divided into discrete *cells*. M *scans* one cell at a time, and can *write* a symbol in it (deleting the symbol already there, if there was one). Alternatively, it can *move* one step to the left or right. At each moment, M is in one of a finite number of *states*, and its action at that moment is determined solely by the state and the symbol in the scanned cell. These two parameters also determine M:s *next state*. So M can be identified with a finite list of *instructions*, each beginning with a state and a symbol, and specifying (a) if M is to write a new symbol or move left or right, and (b) the next state. Finally, one of the states is a terminal state: when M reaches this state it *stops*.

Natural numbers can be represented on a machine tape, for example, letting the number n be represented by $n + 1$ successive 1:s (surrounded by empty cells). Then M can be said to *compute* a function f_M: start M with the representation of n and nothing else on the tape (say, scanning the rightmost 1, and in a designated *start state*); if M stops after a finite numbers of steps with nothing but the representation of a number m on the tape, then $f_M(n) = m$ (precise details will follow in a moment). We cannot always be sure, however, that M stops after a finite number of steps; if it never stops, $f_M(n)$ is *undefined*. In other words, if we want each Turing machine M to compute a unique function f_M, then we must allow that f_M may be a *partial* function (see Appendix 16.2.1).[1]

The *Church-Turing Thesis*, proposed in 1936 as a 'working hypothesis' by Alan Turing and Alonzo Church, is that the intuitive notion of effective computability coincides with the mathematically precise notion 'computable by a Turing machine'. This can hardly be *proved*, since the intuitive notion is, precisely, intuitive. But the thesis is generally accepted, even though its methodological status is still discussed.[2]

As mentioned in Chapter 7.1, there are various kinds of *evidence* for Church-Turing's Thesis. One is that every function so far encountered in practice which has seemed intuitively computable has been shown to be Turing computable. Another is that all known methods for defining new computable functions from given computable functions in fact correspond to methods for defining new Turing machines from given ones. A third kind of rather strong evidence is that other mathematical definitions of the notion of effective computability—and there are several such definitions, based on quite different ideas—have turned out to be equivalent to Turing's definition, in the sense that they define the *same* class of functions. As Gödel remarked, this means that "one has for the first time succeeded in giving an absolute definition of an interesting epistemological notion, i.e. one not depending on the formalism chosen." (Gödel 1946, p. 150)

As Gödel indicates, Turing's characterization stands apart from the others. It does not refer to any particular formalism, or to mathematical systems of equations (as some other characterizations do). In particular, it doesn't refer to *recursion* in any form. It only uses elementary and extremely basic steps of computation.

One alternative definition is in terms of *recursive functions*. These are obtained from the basic functions Z, s, and id_i^n with composition and primitive recursion as before, but with one new operation: the *unbounded μ-operator*:[3] if f is already shown to be recursive, then h defined below is also recursive:

$$h(x) = \mu y(f(x,y) = 0) = \text{the smallest } y \text{ such that } f(x,y) = 0$$

[1] Can't we just restrict attention to Turing machines that do stop, on every input, after a finite number of steps? No: one of the basic observations of Turing is that the problem of deciding whether an arbitrary Turing machine stops or not—the so-called *halting problem*—is *itself* unsolvable. As we will see in Chapter 14.7, this is in fact easy to prove, once the relevant notions are in place. But the upshot is that the use of partial functions is essential in the context of computability.

[2] In fact, there exist recent proposals for proving Church-Turing's Thesis. Kripke 2013 argues that it follows from Gödel's completeness theorem.(!) Dershowitz and Gurevich 2008 lays down axioms concerning the notion of *computation* which are taken to be self-evident, and to entail the Thesis. For an exposition of the discussion around Church-Turing's Thesis, see Copeland 2017.

[3] Recall from Chapter 8 that the *bounded* μ-operator $g(x,z) = \mu y_{y<z}(f(x,y) = 0)$ yields a primitive recursive function g, if f is primitive recursive.

Here $h(x)$ is undefined if $f(x, y) \neq 0$ for all y, or if $f(x, z)$ is undefined for some z smaller than the smallest u such that $f(x, u) = 0$, so h may again be a *partial* function.

It is a remarkable and useful fact that a (partial) function is computable by a Turing machine if and only if it is recursive. In this chapter we shall first see how this fact lets us formulate more general—and more interesting—versions of the incompleteness theorems. We present the relevant definitions and results, and explain how they can be used, without going into detailed proofs. In the remainder of the chapter, which can be skipped at first reading, we will see how these results can be proved.

13.1. Decidability 1: definitions and facts

13.1.1. Turing machines

As just said, a Turing machine can be visualized as a device writing symbols on a tape divided into cells. We restrict attention to the case when there are just two symbols, 0 and 1, where 0 can be thought of as 'blank'.[4] In other words, empty cells are represented by 0 and the machine can change 0 to 1, or vice versa. The tape is infinite in both directions,[5] but at each step of the computation all but a finite number of the cells will be empty. For example, the tape could look like this:

$$\ldots\ 0\ 0\ 0\ 1\ 1\ 0\ 0\ 1\ 1\ 1\ 1\ 0\ 0\ 0\ \ldots$$

At each step the machine scans exactly one cell. A finite number of *states* $q_0, q_1, \ldots, q_{k-1}$ $(k \geqslant 1)$ belong to the machine, and its action at each step is determined by the state it is in and the scanned symbol. We will take q_0 to be the *start state*:[6] all computations are started with the machine in state q_0. We could also have designated terminal states; for now we just stipulate that the computation *halts* whenever it is in a state-symbol combination for which it has no instruction to act. In fact, the machine can be identified with a finite list of instructions.

Each *instruction* has one of the following three forms, where q_i, q_j are states and s_m, s_p are symbols (in our case, 0 or 1). When the symbol s_m is scanned in state q_i, the instructions are as follows:

(1)
a. $q_i s_m s_p q_j$ "write symbol s_p and assume state q_j"
b. $q_i s_m L q_j$ "go one step left and assume state q_j"
c. $q_i s_m R q_j$ "go one step right and assume state q_j"

[4]This turns out to be no limitation: machines with two symbols compute the *same* functions (on the natural numbers) as machines with any finite number of symbols.

[5]Or at least potentially infinite: extra cells can always be 'glued on' whenever needed.

[6]Except when we *compose* Turing machines; see below.

Finally, we require the machine, i.e. the list of instructions, to be *deterministic*: for each pair (q_i, s_m) there is *at most one* instruction starting with $q_i s_m$.[7] That's all! Here is an example:

Example 13.1.1
The machine

(2) $M = \{q_0 0 1 q_1, q_0 1 1 q_1, q_1 1 R q_0\}$

fills the tape to the right of (and including) the start cell with 1:s; when started it never stops. In more detail: in the start state q_0, M writes a 1 regardless of what symbol in the scanned cell, and shifts to state q_1. In q_1, since it is now looking at a 1, it goes one step right and shifts back to state q_0, so the whole process begins again. Etc.

As we said, a number n is represented on the tape by $n + 1$ consequtive 1:s, surrounded by at least one 0 at both ends. Similarly, a sequence of numbers $(n_0, \ldots, n_{k-1})$ is represented by corresponding sequences of 1:s with a 0 in between. For example, the tape

(3) ... 0 0 0 1 1 1 0 1 0 1 1 1 1 1 0 0 0 ...

represents the sequence $(2, 0, 4)$.

Now we say that a Turing machine M *computes* a 1-place number-theoretic function f if, whenever M is started in *standard position* on a tape representing the number n, which means that M is in state q_0 and scans the *rightmost* 1 in the representation of n, then M halts after a finite number of steps, at which point the tape represents the number $f(n)$. Similarly if f is a k-place function and the initial tape represents $(n_0, \ldots, n_{k-1})$: then M starts scanning the rightmost 1 in the representation of n_{k-1}. A few examples will explain how this works.

Example 13.1.2
Let us build a Turing machine that computes the successor function s. This is easy: the machine just needs to add a 1 to the right and stop. Note that the cell to the right of the start cell contains a 0. So the following machine does the job:

$$M = \{q_0 1 R q_0, q_0 0 1 q_1\}$$

No instruction starts with q_1: when the machine reaches q_1, it stops.

---

[7] One can also allow *indeterminstic* Turing machines, which can 'choose' between several instruction beginning with the same state-symbol pair. It can be shown that this does not change the class of computable functions. However, indeterministic machines can be faster (use fewer steps) than deterministic ones.

Example 13.1.3
Here is a machine that *adds* numbers, that is, computes the 2-place function $n + m$. The simple idea is as follows: start on the representation of (n, m), look for the first 0 to the left of the representation of m, and write a 1 there. Then proceed to the 0 to the left of the representation of n. Now we have $n + 1 + 1 + m + 1$ consequtive 1:s on the tape, which are *two* too many: we want to represent the number $n + m$. So the machine needs to delete two 1:s, and then stop:

$$M = \{q_0 1 L q_1, q_1 1 L q_1, q_1 0 1 q_2, q_2 1 L q_2, q_2 0 R q_3, q_3 1 0 q_3, q_3 0 R q_4, q_4 1 0 q_4\}$$

Here we have used as few states as possible: when M has taken two steps to the right and written 0 it is still in state q_4. But no instruction starts with $q_4 0$, so M stops. We would of course have achieved the same effect if the last instruction had been, say, $q_4 1 0 q_5$.

As this example illustrates, if a function is computed by some Turing machine, there are always many *other* Turing machines that compute the same function; see Exercises 13.3.1 and 13.3.2.

Example 13.1.4
Now let's build a subtraction machine, computing the function $n \dot{-} m$, which outputs $n - m$ if $n \geqslant m$ and 0 otherwise. This is a bit more complicated. Given (n, m), the idea is to delete one 1 at a time at both ends of the representations of n and m, until one of them is exhausted. There are two cases. If the 1:s in the representation of m are used up first, or the 1:s in both disappear at the same time, then $n \geqslant m$, so if we add one 1 to what's left of the representation of n we will have $n - m + 1$ consequtive 1:s, as desired. If the 1:s in the representation of n are used up first, then $n < m$, so we must end with just one 1 on the tape. This procedure requires quite a number of instructions, but if we split them into *subroutines* it becomes easy to see how things work. Note that the main subroutine of deleting one 1 at both ends is *repeated* until something on the tape (the presence of 0 in a certain cell) tells the machine to exit and go to one of the two final routines.[8]

	$q_0 1 0 q_0$	
	$q_0 0 L q_1$	
M_1	$q_1 1 L q_1$	
	$q_1 0 L q_2$	"Delete one 1, go left to the first cell left of the 0 between (what remains of) n and m."

[8]Such procedures are built into most modern programming languages. The point here is that they can be written in the extremely basic 'language' of Turing machines.

	$q_2 1 L q_3$	
	$q_3 1 L q_3$	
M_2	$q_3 0 R q_4$	
	$q_4 1 0 q_5$	"If there is a 1 there, continue left across the 1:s and delete the leftmost one."
	$q_2 0 R q_2$	
	$q_2 1 0 q_{10}$	
	$q_{10} 0 R q_{11}$	
M_3	$q_{11} 1 0 q_{10}$	
	$q_{11} 0 L q_{12}$	
	$q_{12} 0 1 q_{25}$	"If there is a 0 (so nothing remains of n), go right, delete all 1:s except the last one, and stop."
	$q_5 0 R q_6$	
M_4	$q_6 1 R q_6$	
	$q_6 0 R q_7$	"In case M_2, go back to the 0 between the two sequences and take one step to the right."
	$q_7 1 R q_8$	
M_5	$q_8 1 R q_8$	
	$q_8 0 L q_0$	"If there is a 1 there, find the rightmost 1; apply M_1."
	$q_7 0 L q_9$	
M_6	$q_9 0 1 q_{25}$	"If there is a 0 there (so nothing remains of m), go one step left, write 1, and stop."

Here q_{25} is used as a terminal state. The following diagram illustrates the computation:

(4)

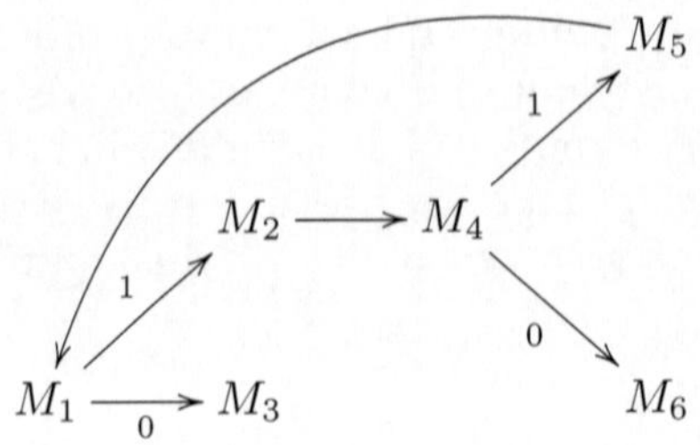

We are now starting to see how Turing machines can be used to compute functions, not very efficiently perhaps, but it works. We also see how a complex machine can be split into subroutines, each of which could be thought of as a separate machine. In other words, we see how Turing machines in principle can be composed: one can choose the states in such a way that the terminal state of one machine is the start state of the next machine.

The functions computed so far are all primitive recursive, in particular they are *total*, and for all appropriate inputs, the corresponding machines halt in an appropriate position in a finite number of steps. But it is easy to build Turing machines that, once started, never stop; see Example 13.1.1. Likewise, a Turing machine might stop with an output number on the tape when started on an *even* number, but never stop, or stop with no number represented, when the input is (the representation of) an *odd* number. Such a machine would compute a *partial* function, whose domain is the set of even numbers.

A *partial function f from* $\mathbb{N}$ *to* $\mathbb{N}$ takes values in $\mathbb{N}$, and has a subset of $\mathbb{N}$ as domain: $dom(f) = \{n\colon \exists m\, f(n) = m\} = \{n\colon f(n) \text{ is defined}\} \subseteq \mathbb{N}$. f is *total* if $dom(f) = \mathbb{N}$. Similarly for n-ary functions.

Allowing partial functions has the pleasant effect that, for every $k \geqslant 1$, *every* Turing machine computes a unique k-ary partial function:

Definition 13.1.5 (computable functions)
Let M be a Turing machine and $k \geqslant 1$. M computes a k-ary partial function f defined as follows. Start M in standard position on (the representation of) a k-tuple $(n_0, \ldots, n_{k-1})$. If M halts in a finite number of steps with (the representation of) a number m and nothing else on the tape, then $f(n_0, \ldots, n_{k-1}) = m$. Otherwise—i.e. if M never halts, or halts on a tape which does not represent a number—$f(n_0, \ldots, n_{k-1})$ is undefined. We say that a k-ary partial function is *Turing computable*, or simply *computable*, if it is computed by some Turing machine.

Consider the incredibly fast growing function $\alpha(m, n, k) = m \uparrow_k n$ from Chapter 8.4 (a variant of the Ackermann function). We argued that α is not primitive recursive but intuitively computable. By the Church-Turing Thesis, it should be computable by some Turing machine. And indeed one can build a Turing machine computing α, though we will not attempt that here. It is not necessary to rely on the Thesis in this case, and, as we said before, all intuitively computable functions that one has come across turn out out be Turing computable. The Church-Turing Thesis serves rather as a heuristic in these cases. On the other hand, if we want to show that some given function is *not* effectively computable, the Thesis is essential, as we will see.

The concept of a Turing machine computation is robust in the sense that one can change various details in the definition without changing the class of computable functions. Here is a useful variant:

Definition 13.1.6 (strongly computable functions)
A Turing machine M *strongly computes* a k-ary partial function f if it computes f and in addition the following holds, when M is started in standard position on $(n_0, \ldots, n_{k-1})$:

1. No cell to the left of the representation of $(n_0, \ldots, n_{k-1})$ is scanned during the computation (whether it halts or not).
2. The state in M with the largest index, say q_m, is a *terminal state* in the sense that (a) none of M:s instructions begins with q_m, and (b) M halts only when it is in state q_m.
3. M halts only when it is in standard position on some number (i.e. the number $f(n_0, \ldots, n_{k-1})$).

A machine satisfying 1 – 3 is called a *strong* Turing machine.

Condition 1 means that we may assume the tape to be infinite in only one direction (to the right). We will see later that computability implies strong computability, so this is no limitation.

To illustrate the use of the notion of strong computability, let us consider how to show that if $f, g_1, \ldots, g_m$ are strongly computable, say by Turing machines $M_f, M_{g_1}, \ldots, M_{g_m}$, then the composed function $h = \mathrm{Cn}[f, g_1, \ldots, g_m]$, i.e.

$$h(n_0, \ldots, n_{k-1}) = f(g_1(n_0, \ldots, n_{k-1}), \ldots, g_m(n_0, \ldots, n_{k-1}))$$

is also strongly computable. To this end we need routines that can *copy* (the representation of) a k-tuple, or chosen parts of it, immediately to the right (with a 0 in between). Strong Turing machines doing this kind of copying are not hard to build, but the details are left for Section 13.2. We can then compose the relevant routines so that the following happens. Let the initial situation be

$$, n_0, \ldots, \underline{n_{k-1}},$$

Here the tape is depicted in a more compact way. n_i stands for a sequence of $n_i + 1$ consequtive 1:s, and each comma stands for 0. Underlining n_i means that the rightmost 1 in the representation of n_i is scanned in the situation. Now a few situations in the computation of h can be described as follows:

$, n_0, \ldots, \underline{n_{k-1}},$	start
$, n_0, \ldots, n_{k-1}, \underline{n_0, \ldots, n_{k-1}},$	copy
$, n_0, \ldots, n_{k-1}, \underline{g_1(n_0, \ldots, n_{k-1})},$	M_{g_1}
$, n_0, \ldots, n_{k-1}, g_1(n_0, \ldots, n_{k-1}), n_0, \ldots, \underline{n_{k-1}},$	copy
$, n_0, \ldots, n_{k-1}, g_1(n_0, \ldots, n_{k-1}), \underline{g_2(n_0, \ldots, n_{k-1})},$	M_{g_2}
$\vdots$	$\vdots$
$, n_0, \ldots, n_{k-1}, g_1(n_0, \ldots, n_{k-1}), \ldots, \underline{g_m(n_0, \ldots, n_{k-1})},$	M_{g_m}
$, n_0, \ldots, n_{k-1}, \underline{f(g_1(n_0, \ldots, n_{k-1}), \ldots, g_m(n_0, \ldots, n_{k-1}))},$	M_f
$, \underline{f(g_1(n_0, \ldots, n_{k-1}), \ldots, g_m(n_0, \ldots, n_{k-1}))},$	delete

The final deletion can be done by a strong machine computing the basic function id^{k+1}_{k+1}. The first copying is of the whole k-tuple, the second copies the k first elements of a $(k+1)$-tuple, etc. Note that it is essential that strong machines are used in the computation, in particular that no cells to the left of the arguments of a function are involved during the computation of the value for that argument. Note also that after computing $g_i(n_0, \ldots, n_{k-1})$, some empty cells may have been created between n_{k-1} and $g_i(n_0, \ldots, n_{k-1})$; in the illustration we have tacitly assumed that some routine 'moves' the function value to the left so that such 'holes' are filled.

If $f, g_1, \ldots, g_m$ are partial, the composition $h = \mathrm{Cn}[f, g_1, \ldots, g_m]$ is also partial. More precisely, $h(n_0, \ldots, n_{k-1})$ is defined if and only if each $g_i(n_0, \ldots, n_{k-1})$ is defined, say with the values $p_1, \ldots, p_m$ respectively, and $f(p_1, \ldots, p_m)$ is defined. The Turing machine indicated above strongly computes this partial function: if some $g_i(n_0, \ldots, n_{k-1})$ should be undefined then M_{g_i} will not stop for this input (since M_{g_i} is strong), and therefore the whole computation will go on forever. The same holds if f is undefined for the given arguments.

We will see later that using similar composition of subroutines one can show that a function defined with primitive recursion from strongly computable functions is also strongly computable. It follows that all primitive recursive functions are strongly computable.

13.1.2. Recursive functions

As mentioned in the introduction to this chapter, the recursive functions are obtained by adding a new way to construct functions, the *unbounded μ-operator*, or simply the *μ-operator*. That is, if f is a $(k+1)$-ary function we define a new k-ary function,

$$g(\overline{x}) = \mu y(f(\overline{x}, y) = 0)$$

as follows:[9]

$$(5) \qquad \mu y(f(\overline{x}, y) = 0) = \begin{cases} u & \text{if } f(\overline{x}, u) = 0 \text{ and for all } z < u \\ & f(\overline{x}, z) \text{ is defined and } > 0 \\ \text{undefined} & \text{otherwise} \end{cases}$$

As we noted, even if f is total, $\mu y(f(\overline{x}, y) = 0)$ may be partial: if for some $\overline{x}$ there is no u such that $f(\overline{x}, u) = 0$, *or* if there is a smallest such number u but $f(\overline{x}, z)$ is undefined for some $z < u$, then $\mu y(f(\overline{x}, y) = 0)$ is undefined. The reason for this stipulation is that we want $\mu y(f(\overline{x}, y) = 0)$ to be computable when f is computable.

[9] In this subsection and the next we revert to the practice from Chapter 8 to use $x, y, z, \ldots$ as variables for numbers. The sequence $x_0, \ldots, x_{k-1}$ is abbreviated $\overline{x}$.

But the only way, intuitively at least, to compute $\mu y(f(\overline{x}, y) = 0)$ is to successively compute $f(\overline{x}, 0), f(\overline{x}, 1), \ldots$, and stop when we get to a u such that $f(\overline{x}, u) = 0$. This will only work if $f(\overline{x}, z)$ is defined for $z < u$.

If $g(\overline{x}) = \mu y(f(\overline{x}, y) = 0)$, we let

Mu$[f]$

be the *function description* of g.

As in the bounded case, the unbounded μ-operator can also be applied to relations. Since relations are total (i.e. their characteristic functions are total), we obtain:

$$(6) \qquad \mu y R(\overline{x}, y) = \begin{cases} u & \text{if } R(\overline{x}, u) \text{ and for all } z < u, \neg R(\overline{x}, z) \\ \text{undefined} & \text{if there is no } z \text{ such that } R(\overline{x}, z) \end{cases}$$

As before, this operator is definable from the one given in (5):

$$(7) \qquad \mu y R(\overline{x}, y) = \mu y(\overline{\text{sg}}(c_R(\overline{x}, y)) = 0)$$

We now extend Definition 8.3.2 of primitive recursive functions to partial recursive functions:

Definition 13.1.7 (partial recursive functions)

1. A partial function is *recursive* if it can be obtained from the basic functions with a finite number of applications of composition, primitive recursion, and the μ-operator.[10]
2. Equivalently, a partial function is *recursive* if if it has a *recursive function description*, i.e. a function description in terms of basic functions, Cn[-], Pr[-], and Mu[-].
3. A relation R is *recursive* if c_R is recursive.

Note on terminology: Functions can be total or partial, and each kind can be recursive. In the literature one often uses *partial recursive* for the property of partial functions defined above, and reserves *recursive* for total functions. Thus the definition would begin "A function is *partial recursive* if it can be obtained ...". (There is no change in item 3, since relations are always total.) I am not following that usage here, but

[10]We explained above how composition of partial functions is defined. Similarly, if h is defined by primitive recursion,

$$h(\overline{x}, 0) = f(\overline{x})$$
$$h(\overline{x}, y') = g(\overline{x}, y, h(\overline{x}, y))$$

where f and g are partial, it is understood that if $g(\overline{x}, y, h(\overline{x}, y))$ (or $f(\overline{x})$) is undefined, then $h(\overline{x}, y')$ (or $h(\overline{x}, 0)$) is undefined. In this case $h(\overline{x}, z)$ will be undefined for all $z > y$ (or all z).

prefer to specify explicitly (when it is not obvious from the context) if a recursive function is partial or total.

Primitive recursive functions are thus (total and) recursive. Lemma 8.5.2 described ways to form new primitive recursive functions and relations from given primitive recursive functions and relations. These results hold for *total* recursive functions as well:

Lemma 13.1.8
A relation or function defined from total recursive functions and relations by means of boolean operations, bounded quantification, the bounded μ-operator, or definition by cases, is (total and) recursive.

Proof. In each case the earlier proof works. For example, with the same argument as before one sees that substitution of a total recursive function in a recursive relation yields a new recursive relation. Likewise, if f is defined by cases from total recursive functions $g_1, \ldots, g_k$ and recursive conditions $S_1, \ldots, S_k$, we have as before

$$(8) \qquad f(\overline{x}) = g_1(\overline{x}) \cdot c_{S_1}(\overline{x}) + \ldots + g_k(\overline{x}) \cdot c_{S_k}(\overline{x})$$

which shows that f is total, and that it is recursive since it is obtained by composition with multiplication and addition of the given recursive functions. □

The argument above for definition by cases doesn't work if the g_i are *partial* functions. For example, suppose $S_1(\overline{x})$ holds, and so $c_{S_1}(\overline{x}) = 1$, whereas $c_{S_i}(\overline{x}) = 0$ for $i \neq 1$. If $g_2(\overline{x})$ is undefined but $g_1(\overline{x})$ is defined, then the right-hand side of (8) is undefined (recall how composition of partial functions was defined). But a reasonable way to interpret definition by cases, i.e.

$$(9) \qquad f(\overline{x}) = \begin{cases} g_1(\overline{x}) & \text{if} \quad S_1(\overline{x}) \\ \cdot & \\ \cdot & \\ g_k(\overline{x}) & \text{if} \quad S_k(\overline{x}) \end{cases}$$

in this situation, is that $f(\overline{x}) = g_1(\overline{x})$, and in general that (9) defines a recursive *partial* function. In fact, it is true that the class of partial recursive functions is closed under definition by cases, but a different argument is required to show this, which we come back to in Chapter 15 (see Fact 15.6.2).

13.1.3. Turing computability versus recursivity

In this section we state important facts concerning the relations between Turing computability and recursivity. Detailed proofs are given in Section 13.2. First:

Theorem 13.1.9
Every recursive (partial) function is strongly Turing computable.

The proof is by induction over recursive function descriptions. We already saw that the initial (basic) functions are strongly computable, and we explained how to show that function composition preserves strong computability. In the case of primitive recursion it is again possible—though it takes a bit of work—to build a Turing machine which, given machines that strongly compute the functions f and g in terms of which h is defined by primitive recursion, successively computes $h(\overline{x}, 0), h(\overline{x}, 1), \ldots, h(\overline{x}, y-1), h(\overline{x}, y)$ when these are defined (Section 13.2.1). Finally, the case of the μ-operator is handled similarly, but the construction is simpler.

The converse of Theorem 13.1.9 follows from the following fundamental result, due to Stephen C. Kleene.

Theorem 13.1.10 (Kleene's Normal Form theorem)
There is an $(n+2)$-ary primitive recursive relation T_n and a unary primitive recursive function U such that the following holds: for each n-ary partial Turing computable function f there is a number e, called an index for f, such that

(a) $f(\overline{x})$ *is defined iff* $\exists y T_n(e, \overline{x}, y)$

(b) $f(\overline{x}) = U(\mu y T_n(e, \overline{x}, y))$

We see directly from (b) that f is recursive.[11] And since strong computability implies computability we have:

Corollary 13.1.11
The following are equivalent, for a partial function f:

1. *f is recursive.*
2. *f is strongly Turing computable.*
3. *f is Turing computable.*

The proof of the Normal Form theorem is actually straightforward: e is simply the Gödel number (code) of a Turing maching M that computes f, and $T_n(e, \overline{x}, y)$ says that y codes a computation with M: a sequence of situations starting with $\overline{x}$ being scanned in standard

[11] We also see, via Theorem 13.1.9, that every partial recursive function can be obtained from primitive recursive functions with just *one* application of the μ-operator.

position and ending with a situation where a number (and nothing else) is represented on the tape. U extracts this number, i.e. $f(\overline{x})$, from y.

Theorem 13.1.10 has many interesting consequences; we return to some of them later. For now we shall use it to draw a conclusion needed in the next subsection.

A *total* recursive function is, according to our definition, a function with a recursive function description that happens to be defined for all arguments. But one cannot simply look at the function description in order to see if it describes a total function or not. This entails in particular that so far we cannot show by induction that all total recursive functions have some property (see Exercise 13.3.9). There is, however, another way to characterize the total recursive functions which allows inductive arguments of this kind.

Let us say that a $(k+1)$-ary total function is *regular* if for every $\overline{x}$ there is a number y such that $f(\overline{x}, y) = 0$. If f is regular, $g(\overline{x}) = \mu y(f(\overline{x}, y) = 0)$ will be a *total* function.

Definition 13.1.12 (μ-recursive functions)
A function is *μ-recursive* if it can be obtained from the basic functions with a finite number of applications of composition, primitive recursion, and the μ-operator applied to regular functions.[12]

Note that since the basic functions are total, and the μ-operator is only applied to regular functions, all μ-recursive functions are total. Also, clearly all primitive recursive functions are μ-recursive.

For total functions, we now have two definitions of recursivity, both involving the μ-operator, but in the second case only applied to regular functions. Fortunately, we can use the Normal Form Theorem to show that these definitions yield the same class of functions:

Fact 13.1.13
A total function is recursive if and only if it is μ-recursive.

Proof. That μ-recursive functions are recursive follows directly from the definitions. Conversely, suppose g is recursive and total. By Theorem 13.1.10, there is a number e such that $g(\overline{x}) = U(\mu y T_n(e, \overline{x}, y))$, and since g is total it follows that for every $\overline{x}$ there is a y such that $T_n(e, \overline{x}, y)$, i.e. such that $\overline{sg}(c_{T_n}(e, \overline{x}, y)) = 0$. In other words, the function f defined by $f(\overline{x}, y) = \overline{sg}(c_{T_n}(e, \overline{x}, y))$ is a regular primitive recursive function, hence a regular μ-recursive function. Since $g(\overline{x}) = U(\mu y(f(\overline{x}, y) = 0))$, it follows that g is μ-recursive. □

[12] As already noted, the terminology concerning recursive functions is not uniform in the literature. Instead of 'μ-recursive', sometimes 'general recursive' or simply 'recursive' is used. We keep using 'recursive' for partial functions (hence also for total ones), as in Definition 13.1.7.

13.1.4. Representability of recursive functions

In the context of definability, or representability in an arithmetical theory, we are usually interested in total functions, and we saw in Chapter 10 that all primitive recursive functions are representable in *PA*. More precisely, we showed that the basic functions are representable in *PA*, and that the class of functions representable in *PA* is closed under composition and definition by primitive recursion.

Theorem 13.1.14
All total recursive functions are representable in PA, and all recursive relations are representable in PA.

Proof. The second claim follows from that first as in the proof of Theorem 10.3.2. To prove the first claim we use Fact 13.1.13. Thus, it only remains to verify that the class of functions representable in *PA* is closed under the allowed form of definition with the μ-operator. That is, we must show that if $g(\overline{n}) = \mu k(f(\overline{n}, k) = 0)$, where f is regular and representable in *PA*, say by a formula $\varphi_f(\overline{x}, y, z)$, then g is also representable in *PA*. We claim that g is represented in *PA* by the formula

$$\psi(\overline{x}, y) := \varphi_f(\overline{x}, y, 0) \wedge \forall z_{z<y} \neg \varphi_f(\overline{x}, z, 0)$$

Suppose $g(\overline{n}) = k$. Then $f(\overline{n}, k) = 0$ and for each $i < k$ we have $f(\overline{n}, i) \neq 0$. Since φ_f defines f we obtain that $PA \vdash \varphi_f(\overline{\mathbf{n}}, \mathbf{k}, 0)$, and for each $i < k$ that $PA \vdash \neg\varphi_f(\overline{\mathbf{n}}, \mathbf{i}, 0)$.

This shows (see Chapter 9.6) that $PA \vdash \psi(\overline{\mathbf{n}}, \mathbf{k})$. It remains only to prove uniqueness, i.e. that

$$PA \vdash \psi(\overline{\mathbf{n}}, y) \rightarrow y = \mathbf{k}$$

But this follows with reasoning by cases in *PA*, based on the fact that

$$PA \vdash y < \mathbf{k} \vee y = \mathbf{k} \vee \mathbf{k} < y$$

It is rather easy to see that the cases $y < \mathbf{k}$ and $\mathbf{k} < y$ are incompatible with the definition of ψ and the fact that $PA \vdash \psi(\overline{\mathbf{n}}, \mathbf{k})$. □

Earlier we showed that if ax_T, the set of Gödel numbers of axioms of the theory T, is primitive recursive, then the relation prf_T, where $prf_T(m, n) \Leftrightarrow m$ is the number of a proof in T of the sentence with number n, is also primitive recursive (Lemma 11.7.1). With exactly the same argument, and Lemma 13.1.8, we now see that the corresponding fact holds for recursive sets of axioms:

Lemma 13.1.15
If ax_T is recursive, then prf_T is a recursive relation.

13.1.5. The incompleteness theorems revisited

Now that we have the concepts of Turing computability and recursivity we can—finally—provide an exact definition of what we mean by an axiomatizable theory, i.e. we can make Definition 6.6.8 precise.

Definition 13.1.16 (axiomatizable theories)
A theory T is *recursive* if the set ax_T is recursive. T is *axiomatizable* if it is equivalent to a recursive theory.

This definition is not specific for theories in the vocabulary L_{PA}; it applies to theories in any vocabulary L, as long as L itself is recursive, so that Gödel numbering along the usual lines works. Neither does it depend on exactly which version of Gödel numbering is used, as long as it is 'effective' (see Exercise 11.9.1).

If the Church-Turing Thesis is correct, Definition 13.1.16 captures exactly the idea that a theory is axiomatizable if it can be axiomatized in such a way that there is an effective method for deciding if a sentence is an axiom or not. And now we can generalize the incompleteness theorems to axiomatizable theories. That is, we can eliminate the earlier, unmotivated, restriction to *primitive* recursive theories.

It follows from Theorem 13.1.14 and Lemma 13.1.15 that if T is recursive there is a formula $Prf_T(x,y)$ (construed as in Chapter 11.8) representing the relation prf_T in PA. And that's all we need to carry through the earlier arguments. Let G as before be a sentence such that

$$PA \vdash G \leftrightarrow \neg\exists x Prf_T(x, \ulcorner G \urcorner)$$

Theorem 13.1.17 (Gödel's first incompleteness theorem, version 1.1)
If T is a consistent recursive extension of PA, then $T \nvdash G$. If, in addition, T is ω-consistent, we also have $T \nvdash \neg G$.

Rosser's Theorem, Theorem 12.3.1, is generalized in exactly the same way. In fact, *all* the results proved in Chapter 12, including those in the exercises, stay true if "primitive recursive" is replaced by "recursive"! This holds in particular for the second incompleteness theorem, Theorem 12.4.1, and more generally for the following fact:

Theorem 13.1.18
If T is a consistent recursive extension of PA, the formula $\exists x Prf_T(x,y)$ is a provability predicate for T.[13]

These generalizations can be obtained by suitable adaptions of the proofs in the primitive recursive case. But there is also a general

[13]Here it is assumed as before that the formula $\tau(x)$ representing T in PA is 'natural'; more precisely, that it is a Σ_1-formula; see Chapter 12.4.2.

result, known as Craig's Theorem, which entails that, surprisingly, any recursive theory is equivalent to a primitive recursive theory. The proof of this fact relies on Kleene's Normal Form theorem, but is quite simple, as we will see in Chapter 15.1.2.

Let us end by mentioning that the converse of Theorem 13.1.14 also holds: if a relation is representable in *PA*, it is recursive. In fact:

Theorem 13.1.19
For every consistent recursive extension T of PA it holds that a relation is representable in T if and only if it is recursive.

The proof is given in Chapter 15.2.

13.2. *Decidability 2: details

We now provide more details for the proof that the Turing computable functions are exactly the recursive ones, starting with Theorem 13.1.9.

13.2.1. Recursive functions are strongly computable

As we saw in Section 13.1.3 we need Turing machines performing certain routines, such as copying a number to the right of a sequence of numbers. And we must describe how to 'compose' Turing machines.

Suppose two operations are to be performed in sequence, and that M_1 performs the first and M_2 the second, where both M_1 and M_2 are strong. Let the terminal state in M_1 be q_k. Then let

$$M_1 \to M_2$$

('M_1 followed by M_2') be the strong Turing machine consisting of (a) the quadruples in M_1, (b) the quadruples in M_2 modified so that q_i is replaced by q_{i+k}. It follows directly from the definition that

$$(M_1 \to M_2) \to M_3 \;=\; M_1 \to (M_2 \to M_3)$$

so parentheses can be left out. Also, let $M^k \;:=\; M \to M \to \ldots \to M$ (k copies of M).

Example 13.2.1 (identity functions)
Suppose $(n_0, \ldots, n_{k-1})$ is represented on the tape. Consider the following machines (starting at the rightmost cell as usual):

	$q_0 1 0 q_1$	
M_1	$q_0 0 L q_2$	
	$q_1 0 L q_0$	delete a block of 1:s, go left to first 1 of next block
M_2	$q_0 1 L q_0$	
	$q_0 0 L q_1$	pass by a block of 1:s, go left to first 1 of next block

M_3	$q_0 0 R q_0$ $q_0 1 R q_1$ $q_1 1 L q_1$ $q_1 0 L q_2$ go right to remaining block of 1:s, halt on rightmost 1

Now consider the following Turing machine:

$$\mathcal{ID}_{k,i} \; = \; M_1^{k-i-1} \rightarrow M_2 \rightarrow M_1^i \rightarrow M_3$$

(10) $\mathcal{ID}_{k,i}$ strongly computes the identity function id_i^k.

We sometimes want to let the output of a machine M be the input of *either* M' *or* M'', depending on some circumstance during the computation with M. Then let M have *two* terminal states q_k and $q_{k'}$, say, the largest and the next largest state of M, which then satisfy a condition corresponding to 2 in Definition 13.1.6. If q_k is the start state of M' and $q_{k'}$ the start state of M'', we write the composed machine

$$\begin{array}{ccc} & & M' \\ & \nearrow & \\ M & & \\ & \searrow & \\ & & M'' \end{array}$$

We leave to the interested reader a more precise description of this composed Turing machine. Next, we sketch the definitions of a number of machines performing certain useful routines. A *hole* one the tape is a sequence of *at least two* 0:s occurring between 1:s.

Example 13.2.2 (move a number left)
We need a machine $\mathcal{B}$ which, when started on a number in standard position, moves the number to the left so that the hole (if there is one) between the number and the closest 1 to the left is filled. $\mathcal{B}$ is obtained by composing some simpler subroutines:

$\mathcal{B}_1$ Delete 1, find the first 0 to the left, write 1, go one step left. If a 0 (1) is scanned, go one step right and halt in the first (second) terminal state.

$\mathcal{B}_2$ Go to the right in standard position.

$\mathcal{B}_3$ Delete 1 and go one step right.

$\mathcal{A}$ Find the first 1 to the right, write 1 and stop.

Machine $\mathcal{B}_1$ has the following instructions:

$q_0 1 0 q_0$
$q_0 0 L q_1$
$q_1 1 L q_1$
$q_1 0 1 q_2$

$$q_2 1 L q_3$$
$$q_3 0 R q_5$$
$$q_3 1 R q_4$$

where q_5 is the first and q_4 the second terminal state. The instructions for the other machines are left as exercises. Now define:

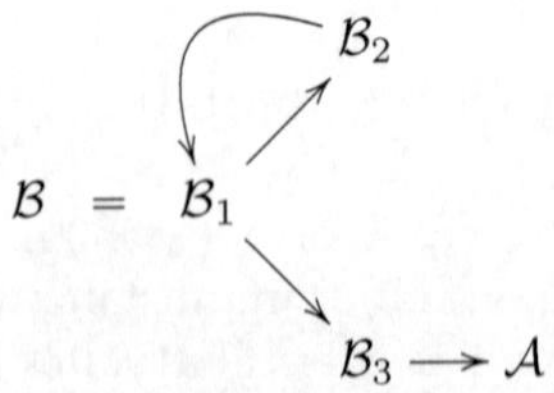

Example 13.2.3 (copy)
The machine $\mathcal{I}_k$ shall, when started on $(n_0, \ldots, n_{k-1})$ in standard position, copy n_0 immediately to the right of the k-tuple and halt in standard position on the copy, i.e. in standard position on $(n_0, \ldots, n_{k-1}, n_0)$. The constructions of the following subroutines are left as exercises:

$\mathcal{C}$ Go two steps right and write 1.

$\mathcal{D}$ Go to standard position on the next number to the left.

$\mathcal{E}$ Check if the scanned number is 0; if Yes, halt in terminal position 1; if No, halt in terminal position 2.

$\mathcal{F}$ Delete 1 and go one step left.

$\mathcal{G}$ Go to standard position on the next number to the right.

$\mathcal{H}$ Fill the hole to the next number to the right with 1:s.

Then we define:

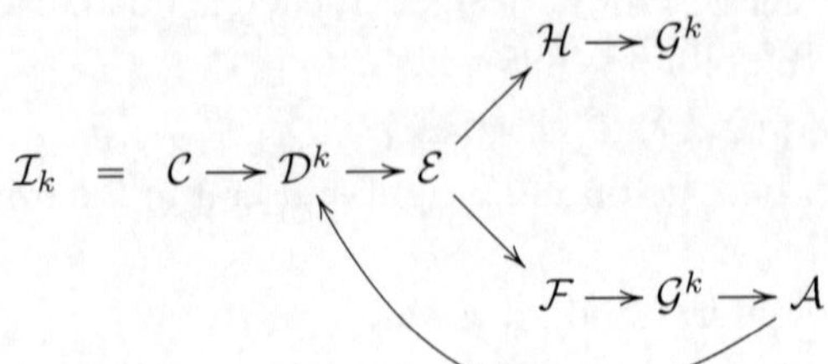

Example 13.2.4 (more copying)
By repeated use of $\mathcal{I}_k$ we can copy chosen parts of a sequence of numbers. For example:

(11) $(\mathcal{I}_4)^4$ copies a whole quaduple once.

(12) $\mathcal{I}_4 \rightarrow \mathcal{I}_2$ copies the first and fourth element of the quadruple.

With the machines now at our disposal it is easy to build the Turing machine for computing composition of functions that was sketched at the end of Section 13.1.3 (Exercise 13.3.15).

Example 13.2.5 (copy with hole)
The machine $\mathfrak{K}_m$ shall, when started on an m-tuple in standard position, copy the whole m-tuple to the right with a hole consisting of two 0:s in between. We have:

$$\mathfrak{K}_m \;=\; \mathcal{A} \rightarrow \mathcal{I}^m_m \rightarrow \mathcal{F} \rightarrow \mathcal{D}^m \rightarrow \mathcal{F} \rightarrow \mathcal{G}^m$$

Example 13.2.6
Machine $\mathcal{L}$ will, when started on a number n in standard position, delete all 1:s to the left of n until the first encountered hole (if there is one); then it returns to standard position on n. (Exercise)

Now we have all that is needed for describing a Turing machine that (strongly) computes a function defined with primitive recursion. Thus, assume that

$$\begin{aligned} h(n,0) &= f(n) \\ h(n,m') &= g(n,m,h(n,m)) \end{aligned}$$

where f and g are computed by the strong machines M_f and M_g (the case when h has higher arity is analogous). The plan is as follows. To get $h(n,m)$ we must first have $h(n,m-1)$, for which we must first have $h(n,m-2)$, etc. Therefore we generate $0,1,2,\ldots$ on the tape and use first M_f and then M_g to successively compute $h(n,0), h(n,1), \ldots$. To know when to stop, we simultaneously generate $m, m-1, m-2, \ldots$, and halt the procedure when this number is 0. Here is an illustration of the computation (where we have assumed that $m > 0$):

Tape	Step
$, n, \underline{m},$	(input)
$, n, m, , n, \underline{m},$	$\mathfrak{K}_2$: copy n,m with a hole
$, n, m, , n, m, \underline{n},$	$\mathcal{I}_2$
$, n, m, , n, m, \underline{h(n,0)},$	$M_f \to \mathcal{B}$: compute $h(n,0) = f(n)$
$, n, m, , n, m, h(n,0), n, \underline{m},$	$\mathcal{I}_3^2 \to \mathcal{E}$: generate n,m; check if $m = 0$
$, n, m, , n, m, h(n,0), n, m, \underline{0},$	$\mathcal{C}$: generate 0
$, n, m, , n, m, h(n,0), n, m, 0, n, 0, \underline{h(n,0)},$	$\mathcal{I}_3 \to \mathcal{I}_2 \to \mathcal{I}_6$
$, n, m, , n, m, h(n,0), n, m, 0, \underline{h(n,1)},$	$M_g \to \mathcal{B}$: compute $h(n,1)$
$, n, m, , n, m, h(n,0), n, m, 0, h(n,1), n, \underline{m-1},$	$\mathcal{I}_4^2 \to \mathcal{F} \to \mathcal{E}$: generate $n, m-1$; check if $m-1 = 0$
$, n, m, , n, m, h(n,0), n, m, 0, h(n,1), n, m-1, \underline{1},$	$\mathcal{I}^4 \to \mathcal{A}$: generate 1
$, n, m, , n, m, h(n,0), n, m, 0, h(n,1), n, m-1, 1, n, 1, \underline{h(n,1)},$	$\mathcal{I}_3 \to \mathcal{I}_2 \to \mathcal{I}_6$
$, n, m, , n, m, h(n,0), n, m, 0, h(n,1), n, m-1, 1, \underline{h(n,2)},$	$M_g \to \mathcal{B}$: compute $h(n,2)$
$\vdots$	$\vdots$
$, n, m, , \ldots\ldots\ldots, h(n,m), n, \underline{m-m},$	$\mathcal{I}_4^2 \to \mathcal{F} \to \mathcal{E}$: generate $n, m-m$; check if $m-m = 0$
$, n, m, , \ldots\ldots\ldots, h(n,m), n, m-m, \underline{h(n,m)},$	$\mathcal{I}_3$
$, n, m, \underline{h(n,m)},$	$\mathcal{L} \to \mathcal{B}$
$, \underline{h(n,m)},$	$\mathcal{ID}_{3,3}$ (output)

We see that the machine computing h looks as follows:

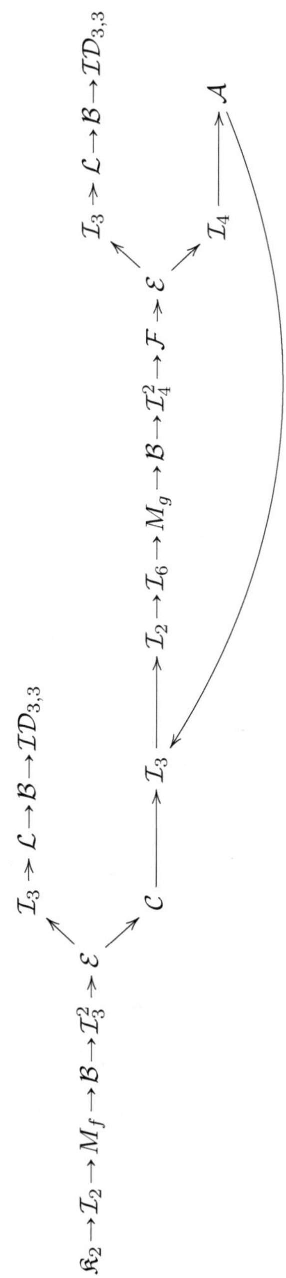

If $f(n)$ or one of $g(n, i, h(n, i))$ for $i < m$ is undefined, the computation will go on forever, and it is clear that the other conditions for being a strong Turing machine are also satisfied.

To prove Theorem 13.1.9, it only remains to construe a strong Turing machine that computes $\mu k(f(\overline{n}, k) = 0)$, given that f is regular and computed by a strong machine M_f. This is easier than the case of primitive recursion, and is left as an exercise.

13.2.2. Computable functions are recursive

Our final task is to describe the primitive recursive relation T_n and the primitive recursive function U in Kleene's Normal Form theorem (Theorem 13.1.10). We start with a Gödel numbering: quadruples are numbered with sequence numbers (as in Chapter 8.7.1), say (where i, j are arbitrary natural numbers and p, r are 0 or 1):

$$\begin{aligned} \#(q_i p r q_j) &= \langle i, p, r, j \rangle \\ \#(q_i p L q_j) &= \langle i, p, 2, j \rangle \\ \#(q_i p R q_j) &= \langle i, p, 3, j \rangle \end{aligned}$$

Then Turing machines are coded as finite sequence of quadruples.[14]

The next step is to code *situations*, where a situation contains the configuration of the tape at a certain moment, the scanned cell, and the machine state. Remember that at each moment all but a finite number of the cells are empty (have a 0). So a situation looks as follows:

$$\begin{array}{c} \ldots\ 0\ 0\ u_{r-1}\ \ldots\ u_0\ p\ v_0\ \ldots\ v_{s-1}\ 0\ 0\ \ldots \\ q_i \end{array} \tag{13}$$

where $u_0, \ldots, u_{r-1}, v_0, \ldots, v_{s-1}$, and p are 0 or 1. Also, either $u_{r-1} = 1$ or each of $u_0, \ldots, u_{r-1}$ is 0, and similarly for $v_0, \ldots, v_{s-1}$ (this is needed to make situations unique). We let the tape to the left of the scanned cell get the number

$$u = \langle 0, u_{r-1}, \ldots, u_0 \rangle$$

whereas the tape to the right gets the number

$$v = \langle v_0, \ldots, v_{s-1}, 0 \rangle$$

Finally, the whole situation in (13) has code number

$$\langle u, i, p, v \rangle$$

[14] A Turing machine is a *set* of quadruples, so with the present coding, the same machine will get several different code numbers. This is not a problem; what matters is that different machines get different code numbers. The coding scheme we choose for Turing machines and their behavior (below) is just one of many possible. As long as these codings are reasonable (Exercise 11.9.1), our results don't depend on this choice.

If the machine-tape is in this situation, and the machine has the instruction $q_i p r q_j$ (where r is 0 or 1), the next situation will be

$$\begin{array}{c} \ldots\ 0\ 0\ u_{r-1}\ \ldots\ u_0\ r\ v_0\ \ldots\ v_{s-1}\ 0\ 0\ \ldots \\ q_j \end{array}$$

whose code number is $\langle u, j, r, v\rangle$. If instead the instruction is $q_i p L q_j$, the next situation is

$$\begin{array}{c} \ldots\ 0\ 0\ u_{r-1}\ \ldots\ u_1\ u_0\ p\ v_0\ \ldots\ v_{s-1}\ 0\ 0\ \ldots \\ q_j \end{array}$$

with code $\langle in(u,1), j, u_0, \langle p\rangle * v\rangle$, where *in* is a primitive recursive function such that $in(\langle a_0, \ldots, a_{k-1}\rangle, 1) = \langle a_0, \ldots, a_{k-2}\rangle$. Similarly if the instruction is $q_i p R q_j$.

It should now be clear that there are primitive recursive functions *write, left, right* such that if w is the number of a situation, then

$$\begin{aligned} &write(\langle i, p, r, j\rangle, w) \\ &left(\langle i, p, 2, j\rangle, w) \\ &right(\langle i, p, 3, j\rangle, w) \end{aligned}$$

is the number of the *next* situation as above. Now define:

$fit(q, w)$ iff q is (the number of) a quadruple that fits situation w

That is, if w is as in (13), the quadruple must begin with $q_i p$; in other words, $(q)_0 = (w)_1$ och $(q)_1 = (w)_2$. So *fit* is a primitive recursive relation. Furthermore, there is a primitive recursive relation *suit* such that if e is (the number of) a Turing machine, then

$suit(e, w)$ iff machine e contains a quadruple q such that $fit(q, w)$

Indeed, we can let $suit(e, w) \Leftrightarrow \exists i_{i<lh(e)} fit((e)_i, w)$. In a similar way we find a primitive recursive function *apply* such that $apply(e, w)$ = the number of the (unique) quadruple in machine number e that fits w, whenever $suit(e, w)$.

With these functions and relations at hand it is not hard to define a primitive recursive function *next* such that if e is the number of a Turing machine and w the number of a situation:

$$next(e, w) = \begin{cases} \text{the number of the next situation (by } e) & \text{if } suit(e, w) \\ 0 & \text{otherwise} \end{cases}$$

Note that when $next(e, w) = 0$, w is a terminal situation: no instruction fits. Finally, let

$start_k(n_0, \ldots, n_{k-1})$ = the number of the situation in which $(n_0, \ldots, n_{k-1})$ is in standard position in state q_0

and

$$standpos(w) \text{ iff in situation } w, \text{ some number is in standard pos.}$$

start och *standpos* are primitive recursive. And we can define a primitive recursive function *st* such that if $standpos(w)$, then

$$st(w)$$

is the number which is in standard position.

At last, we are able to define the relations T_k. Consider for simplicity the case $k = 1$:

$$\begin{aligned} T_1(e, n, m) \quad \Leftrightarrow \quad & sq(m) \wedge (m)_0 = start_1(n) \wedge \\ & \forall i_{i<lh(m)\dot{-}1}((m)_{i+1} > 0 \wedge (m)_{i+1} = next(e, (m)_i)) \wedge \\ & next(e, (m)_{lh(m)\dot{-}1}) = 0 \wedge standpos((m)_{lh(m)\dot{-}1}) \end{aligned}$$

In other words, when e is the number of a machine M, $T_1(e, n, m)$ holds if and only if, when M is started on n in the start situation $w_0 = start_1(n)$, the tape goes through a sequence of situations coded by m, $m = \langle w_0, \ldots, w_{k-1} \rangle$, and halts in a terminal situation $w_{k-1} = (m)_{k-1}$ where some number is in standard position.

So if we let U be the primitive recursive function defined by

$$U(m) = st((m)_{lh(m)\dot{-}1})$$

then $U(m)$ is the value $f(n)$, where f is the 1-place function computed by M. If on the other hand $f(n)$ is undefined, i.e. the computation goes on forever or halts in a situation where no number is in standard position, then there is no m such that $T_1(e, n, m)$. It follows that:

$$f(n) = U(\mu m\, T_1(e, n, m))$$

and Theorem 13.1.10 is proved. □

13.3. Exercises to Chapter 13

Exercise 13.3.1

1. Construct a Turing machine that computes addition but, in contrast with Example 13.1.3, starts by deleting the rightmost 1.
2. Why can't you start by deleting two 1:s to the right instead?

Exercise 13.3.2
Explain why every computable is computed by infinitely many Turing machines.

Exercise 13.3.3
Show that the following functions are strongly computable:

1. $f(n) = n + 3$
2. the basic function Z, i.e. $Z(n) = 0$ for all n.
3. the basic function id_i^k, where $id_i^k(n_0, \ldots, n_{k-1}) = n_i$, and $i < k$.

Exercise 13.3.4
Redefine the machine in Example 13.1.4 so that it instead computes the partial function $n - m$, i.e.

$$n - m = \begin{cases} n - m & \text{if } n \geqslant m \\ \text{undefined} & \text{if } n < m \end{cases}$$

Exercise 13.3.5
Construct a Turing machine that computes multiplication.

Exercise 13.3.6
Explain why all primitive recursive functions are total.

Exercise 13.3.7
Recall Goldbach's Conjecture (Chapter 12.9.1). Let the function h be defined as follows.

$$h(n) = \begin{cases} 1 & \text{if Goldbach's Conjecture is true} \\ 0 & \text{if Goldbach's Conjecture is false} \end{cases}$$

Is h Turing computable?

Exercise 13.3.8
Give explicit descriptions of the following functions (for which arguments they are defined and what the values are in that case):

1. $\mu y(x \cdot y = 0)$
2. $\mu y(x + y = 0)$
3. $\mu y(x^y = 0)$

Exercise 13.3.9
Suppose h is defined by composition from partial functions $f, g_1, \ldots, g_m$, $h = \text{Cn}[f, g_1, \ldots, g_m]$, and that h is a total function. Does it follow that $g_1, \ldots, g_m$ are total? Does it follow that f is total?

Exercise 13.3.10
Is it the case that a total function f is regular iff the function $\mu y(f(\overline{x}, y) = 0)$ is total?

Exercise 13.3.11
Complete the proof of Theorem 13.1.14.

Exercise 13.3.12
Verify that (10) is true.

Exercise 13.3.13
Check that machine $\mathcal{B}$ in Example 13.2.2 does what it is supposed to.

Exercise 13.3.14
Similarly for Examples 13.2.3 – 13.2.6.

Exercise 13.3.15
Check that the Turing machine for strongly computing $\mathrm{Cn}[f, g_1, \ldots, g_m]$ indicated at the end of Section 13.1.3 can be defined as follows (where $g_1, \ldots, g_m$ are k-ary):

$$\mathcal{I}_k^k \to M_{g_1} \to \mathcal{B} \to \mathcal{I}_{k+1}^k \to M_{g_2} \to \mathcal{B} \to \ldots \to \mathcal{I}_{k+m-1}^k \to M_{g_m} \to \mathcal{B} \to M_f \to \mathcal{B} \to \mathcal{ID}_{k+1,k+1}$$

Exercise 13.3.16
Sketch a computation routine which shows that the class of strongly computable functions is closed under definition with the μ-operator from regular functions.

Exercise 13.3.17
Show that the functions *start* and *st*, and the relation *standpos* (Section 13.2.2), are primitive recursive.

14 Undecidability

Via the Church-Turing Thesis we have a precise concept of decidability. Thus, our concept of *undecidability* is just as precise. If we can show that a certain problem—or via coding, a certain set of numbers—is *not* recursive, we may conclude, this time with essential use of the Church-Turing Thesis, that there *doesn't exist* any effective method to solve the problem, not just that we so far haven't been able to find one.

It turns out that logic contains many unsolvable problems, and in this chapter we will encounter a few of them. Some of these are tied to questions about how Turing machines work. But we start with the problem of deciding whether a sentence is provable in a certain theory T or not. Recall the set thm_T:

$$thm_T(n) \text{ iff } n \text{ is the Gödel number of a theorem of } T$$

or, equivalently,

$$thm_T(n) \Leftrightarrow \exists m\, prf_T(m, n)$$

Definition 14.0.1 (undecidable theories)
A theory T is *decidable* if thm_T is recursive; otherwise T is *undecidable*.

We begin by looking at theories in the vocabulary L_{PA}, but thm_T and prf_T can of course be defined for any axiomatizable theory whose sentences and derivations can be Gödel numbered.

14.1. Undecidable extensions of *PA*

The following simple application of the Diagonal Lemma is reminiscent of the proof of Tarski's Theorem (Theorem 7.2.8); in fact, that was Exercise 7.3.12.

Lemma 14.1.1
If T is a consistent extension of PA, thm_T is not representable in T.

Proof. Suppose there was a formula $\psi(y)$ representing thm_T in T, i.e. if $thm_T(n)$ then $T \vdash \psi(\mathbf{n})$, and if not $thm_T(n)$ then $T \vdash \neg\psi(\mathbf{n})$. By the Diagonal Lemma there is a sentence φ such that $PA \vdash \varphi \leftrightarrow \neg\psi(\ulcorner\varphi\urcorner)$, and so, since T is an extension of *PA*,

(1) $\quad T \vdash \varphi \leftrightarrow \neg\psi(\ulcorner\varphi\urcorner)$

This means that if $T \vdash \varphi$, then $T \vdash \psi(\ulcorner\varphi\urcorner)$ and so, by (1), $T \vdash \neg\varphi$, which contradicts the consistency of T. Thus, $T \nvdash \varphi$. But then we have $T \vdash \neg\psi(\ulcorner\varphi\urcorner)$ and thus, again by (1), $T \vdash \varphi$, contradicting what we just showed. So there can be no formula representing thm_T in T. □

Corollary 14.1.2
Every consistent extension of PA is undecidable.

Proof. Immediate from Theorem 13.1.14 and Lemma 14.1.1. □

Definition 14.1.3 (essential undecidability)
A theory T is *essentially undecidable* if every consistent extension of T is undecidable.

Corollary 14.1.2 says that *PA* is essentially undecidable. We noted already in Chapter 7.2 that this fact, together with Lemma 7.2.3, gives another proof of incompleteness (but without exhibiting any undecidable sentences), since axiomatizable complete theories are decidable.

What exactly is the role of *PA* in Corollary 14.1.2? It is clear from the proof that two properties of a theory T_0 suffice in order to replace *PA* by T_0 in the corollary: (a) the Diagonal Lemma holds for T_0, and (b) all (total) recursive functions (hence all recursive relations) are representable in T_0. In fact, (b) implies (a). Given (b), not only does Corollary 14.1.2 hold, but also the first incompleteness theorem for T_0:

Proposition 14.1.4
If T_0 is a consistent L_{PA}-theory in which all recursive functions are representable, then the first incompleteness theorem, in the strongest version we have seen so far, holds with PA replaced by T_0. Also, T_0 is essentially undecidable.

Proof. Let T_0 be as assumed. Thus, prf_T is representable in T_0, when T is a consistent recursive extension of T_0. Second, the primitive recursive function sub_0 in the proof of the Diagonal Lemma (Chapter 12.1) is representable in T_0, and a quick look at that proof shows that this is all we need for the Diagonal Lemma to hold for T_0.

Now consider the (updated) version of the first incompleteness theorem, i.e. Theorem 13.1.17. Just as before there is a sentence G such that $T_0 \vdash G \leftrightarrow \neg\exists x Prf_T(x, \ulcorner G\urcorner)$, and the proof that $T \nvdash G$, and, if T_0 is ω-consistent, that $T \nvdash \neg G$, are exactly as before. The second (Rosser's) version of the incompleteness theorem goes through too, as does the most general third version; i.e. Theorem 12.8.1 (where "primitive recursive" is replaced by "recursive").

That T_0 is essentially undecidable follows exactly as for *PA*.[1] □

Note that this result concerns the *first* incompleteness theorem. The *second* incompleteness theorem requires more of T_0 than all recursive functions being representable: we also need to be able to show that $\exists x Prf_T(x, y)$ is a provability predicate. This requires in particular use of the induction axiom of *PA*.

However, focusing on the first incompleteness theorem and on undecidability, we are led to the following very natural question: What does it take for an arithmetical theory to be able to represent all recursive functions? As we will see (Section 14.4 below), somewhat surprisingly this doesn't require any use of induction at all.

14.2. Finitely axiomatizable arithmetical theories

A theory is *finitely axiomatizable* if it is equivalent to a finite theory (a theory consisting of finitely many axioms). *PA* is *not* finitely axiomatizable: the induction axiom (scheme) cannot be replaced by finitely many axioms; see Chapter 12.4.1. However, in order to prove that all recursive functions are representable in *PA*, only finitely many of *PA*:s axioms are actually used.

If one goes through the proofs that the basic functions are representable in *PA*, and that the class of representable functions in *PA* is closed under composition, definition with primitive recursion, and with the μ-operator applied to regular functions, it becomes clear that it suffices to have the following:

- the six axioms (PA1) – (PA6) of *PA* (Chapter 9.1);
- some (but not all) basic properties of addition and multiplication according to Chapter 9.2 and 9.5;
- basic properties of the order relation ($<$ and $\leqslant$) as in Chapter 9.4, in particular that the order is total;

[1] Don't we need to assume that T_0 is recursive? Actually, the proof doesn't rely on that, since it is about consistent recursive extensions of T_0. For example, $Th(\mathcal{N})$ is a consistent and complete L_{PA}-theory in which all recursive functions are representable. But that doesn't contradict the Proposition, since there are no consistent recursive extensions of $Th(\mathcal{N})$. On the other hand, in principle T_0 could be a weaker non-recursive theory in which all recursive functions are representable; it would still be true that all consistent recursive extensions of T_0 are incomplete. In practice, of course, we are only interested in the case when T_0 is recursive (axiomatizable).

- properties of closed terms as in Chapter 9.7;
- the following properties of bounded quantification (Chapter 9.6):

$$\exists x_{x \leqslant \mathbf{n}} \varphi(x) \leftrightarrow (\varphi(\mathbf{0}) \vee \ldots \vee \varphi(\mathbf{n}))$$
$$\forall x_{x \leqslant \mathbf{n}} \varphi(x) \leftrightarrow (\varphi(\mathbf{0}) \wedge \ldots \wedge \varphi(\mathbf{n}))$$

The most complex part of the proof was closure under definition by primitive recursion; here we used that Gödel's β-function (actually the function β') is strongly representable, which essentially follows from the fact that the remainder function *rem* is strongly representable, which is proved using the resources listed above (see Chapter 10.3).[2]

Some of these results were proved by induction. But the proofs only use particular, and finitely many, instances of the induction scheme (IND). This leads to the following conclusion:

Theorem 14.2.1
There is a finite subtheory, say PA_0, of PA such that all recursive functions are representable in PA_0.

PA_0 consists of the axioms (PA1) – (PA6) together with the instances of the induction scheme needed to prove the above results.

So it follows from Proposition 14.1.4 that the first incompleteness theorem (in its various versions) holds for a finite subtheory of *PA*, which is also essentially undecidable. One might think that this is not a very sensational result. But as we saw already in Chapter 7.2.4, precisely the fact that the number of axioms is finite allows us to draw an interesting conclusion.

14.3. The undecidability of first-order logic

We start by repeating the argument essentially made already in Chapter 7.2.4. FOL_{PA} is predicate logic in the vocabulary $L_{PA} = \{0, +, \cdot, '\}$, so it is a theory with the empty set of non-logical axioms. We write $FOL_{PA} \vdash \varphi$, or simply $\vdash \varphi$, to say that φ is a theorem of this theory, which is to say that φ is a *logical truth*: $\models \varphi$. Thus:

$$thm_{FOL_{PA}}(\#(\varphi)) \text{ iff } \vdash \varphi$$

Now let θ be the conjunction of the axioms of the theory PA_0 (or some other finite theory in which all recursive functions are definable, such as the theory Q presented later). Then we have, for every arithmetical sentence φ, and using the Deduction Theorem,

[2] We deferred this proof to Exercises 10.5.4 and 10.5.5, since we will obtain a stronger result later in the present chapter.

$$PA_0 \vdash \varphi \text{ iff } \theta \vdash \varphi \text{ iff } \vdash \theta \to \varphi$$

If there were an effective method for deciding FOL_{PA}, we could use it to decide PA_0: for any arithmetical sentence φ, just check if $\theta \to \varphi$ is logically true. But since PA_0 is undecidable, there is no such method. We have shown that

(2) First-order logic in the vocabulary L_{PA} is undecidable.

The argument just given was informal. To be more formal (which is not really necessary, once you are used to this kind of argument), we could reason as follows. Let k_0 be the Gödel number of θ, and recall the primitive recursive relation *impl* that we defined in Chapter 11.2. Then we have, for all n,

$$thm_{PA_0}(n) \Leftrightarrow thm_{FOL_{PA}}(impl(k_0, n))$$

This shows that if $thm_{FOL_{PA}}$ were recursive, then the set thm_{PA_0} would also be recursive. But by Proposition 14.1.4 and Theorem 14.2.1, the latter set is *not* recursive. □

Now consider an arbitrary vocabulary L containing at least one individual constant and one unary and two binary function symbols. We may assume (without loss of generality) that these are precisely the symbols $0, ', +, \cdot$, although now we say nothing about how they are to be interpreted. L may contain any other non-logical symbols, but every L_{PA}-sentence is also an L-sentence. Let FOL_L be predicate logic in the vocabulary L.

Theorem 14.3.1 (Church, Turing)
FOL_L is undecidable.

Proof. This follows from (2) and the fact that FOL_L is a *conservative extension* of FOL_{PA}, in the sense that if an L_{PA}-sentence is derivable in FOL_L, it is already derivable in FOL_{PA}.[3] For this in turn means that:

$$thm_{FOL_{PA}}(n) \Leftrightarrow thm_{FOL_L}(n) \wedge sent_{L_{PA}}(n)$$

where $sent_{L_{PA}}$ is the set of Gödel numbers of L_{PA}-sentences. And since this set is (primitive) recursive it follows that thm_{FOL_L} is *not* recursive, because $thm_{FOL_{PA}}$ is not recursive. □

This result can be improved: one can show, for example, that it suffices for L to contain at least one binary predicate symbol to make

[3]Since being provable in FOL_{PA} or FOL_L is the same as being a logical truth (by the completeness theorem), and since the truth of a sentence in a model only depends on the interpretation of the non-logical symbols occurring in that sentence (locality), it readily follows that FOL_L is a conservative extension of FOL_{PA}.

FOL_L undecidable. On the other hand, predicate logic with only unary predicate symbols (and no function symbols; so-called *monadic* predicate logic) is decidable.

14.3.1. *Digression: some decidable theories

The fact that predicate logic is undecidable, and that all consistent extensions of PA_0 are undecidable, might suggest that all interesting first-order theories are undecidable. But this is far from the case: we give a few examples of decidable theories (without proofs, but see Exercises 14.8.6 – 14.8.8).

Example 14.3.2 (*DeLO*)
We claimed in Chapter 6.8 that the theory *DeLO* of dense linear orders without endpoints is complete, indeed that it is countably categorical; an argument for this was indicated in Chapter 6.10.2. As we have seen (Lemma 7.2.3), it follows that *DeLO* is decidable. A proof of the completeness of *DeLO* by means of *quantifier elimination* is outlined in Exercise 14.8.7.

Example 14.3.3 (theory of the successor function)
Let S be the theory in the vocabulary $L_S = \{0,'\}$ consisting of the following (infinitely many) axioms:

$$\begin{array}{l} 0 \neq x' \\ x' = y' \to x = y \\ x \neq 0 \to \exists y\, x = y' \\ x' \neq x, x'' \neq x, x''' \neq x, \ldots \end{array}$$

Then S is complete: for every L_S-sentence φ, we have either $S \vdash \varphi$ or $S \vdash \neg\varphi$. This can also be shown by quantifier elimination (Exercise 14.8.8). Hence, S is decidable. One can show that S is not finitely axiomatizable (Exercise 14.8.9).

Example 14.3.4 (Presburger arithmetic)
Presburger arithmetic (let us call the theory *PB*) is Peano arithmetic without multiplication. So $L_{PB} = \{0, +,'\}$, and the axioms are as in *PA* except for (PA5) and (PA6); the induction scheme (IND) remains, but of course only for L_{PB}-formulas. *PB* is much stronger than S, but much weaker than *PA*. Nothing about, for example, division or prime numbers can be proved in it, since this requires multiplication. But the theory has interesting logical properties.

- *PB* is complete, and thus decidable (Mojźesz Presburger 1929).
- *PB* is not finitely axiomatizable.
- FOL_{PB}, i.e. predicate logic in the vocabulary L_{PB}, is undecidable. (Boris Trakhtenbrot 1953)

While *PB* is a weak decidable theory, our final example is very strong, in the sense that it contains addition and multiplication and gives a complete (first-order) description of the real numbers.

Example 14.3.5 (Real closed fields)
The vocabulary of this theory, let us call it *RCF*, is $L_{RCF} = \{0, 1, +, \cdot, <\}$. The axioms are:

- The operations $+$ and $\cdot$ are associative, commutative, and the distributive law $x(y + z) = xy + xz$ holds.[4]
- $x + 0 = x$ and $\exists y(x + y = 0)$ (existence of $-x$)
- $x \cdot 1 = x$, and $xy = 0 \rightarrow x = 0 \vee y = 0$, and $x \neq 0 \rightarrow \exists y(xy = 1)$ (existence of x^{-1})
- $1 \neq 0, 1 + 1 \neq 0, 1 + 1 + 1 \neq 0$, etc.
- $<$ is a total order
- $x < y \rightarrow x + z < y + z$, and $x < y \wedge 0 < z \rightarrow xz < yz$
- $0 < x \rightarrow \exists y(x = y^2)$ (every positive number has a square root)
- $x_n \neq 0 \rightarrow \exists y(x_n y^n + x_{n-1} y^{n-1} + \ldots + x_1 y + x_0 = 0)$, for each odd number n. (Every polynomial whose largest exponent is odd has a root.)

The real numbers with the corresponding operations, i.e. the model $\mathcal{R} = (\mathbb{R}, 0, 1, +, \cdot, <)$, is indeed a model of *RCF*. Tarski showed in 1948 that *R* is complete, which means that $Th(\mathcal{R}) = \{\varphi : RCF \vdash \varphi\}$, and as above that *RCF* is a decidable theory.

Since $\mathbb{N} \subseteq \mathbb{R}$ it may seem strange that *RCF* is decidable and PA_0 is not. Put differently, that $Th(\mathcal{R})$ is a rather 'simple' set while $Th(\mathcal{N})$ is a very 'complex' set; we just saw that $Th(\mathcal{N})$ is not recursive (Corollary 14.1.2), but actually we know from Tarski's Theorem that it is not even arithmetically definable. Part of the explanation is that, even though the terms $0, 1, 1+1, 1+1+1, \ldots$ belong to the theory, there is no way to *define* the natural numbers in *RCF*. In other words, there is no L_{RCF}-formula $\psi(x)$ which is satisfied in the model $\mathcal{R}$ by exactly the natural numbers. (If there were such a formula, *RCF* would contain arithmetic in the sense of Chapter 12.8 and thus be incomplete.)

So first-order logic is undecidable (in most vocabularies), but if you add certain axioms you get a decidable theory, whereas with other axioms the theory becomes undecidable. The borderline between decidable and undecidable extensions of FOL is more elusive than one might think.

[4] xy means $x \cdot y$, and x^n means $xx \ldots x$ with n occurrences of x.

14.4. Robinson arithmetic

There is a finite arithmetical theory which is much weaker, and simpler, than PA_0, but which has the property that all recursive functions are representable in it. In particular, it contains no induction axioms. This theory is known as *Robinson arithmetic*, and usually called Q.

Q has seven axioms:

- (PA1) – (PA6) (the first six axioms in *PA*)
- (Q7) $x \neq 0 \rightarrow \exists y(x = y')$

Recall that (Q7) was our first example of a sentence provable by induction in *PA*; (1) in Chapter 9.

Q is a *very weak* teori: very few general statements can be proved. For example, we have

$$Q \nvdash 0 + x = x$$
$$Q \nvdash x \neq x'$$

(see Exercises 14.8.15 and 14.8.16). It follows that Q is incomplete, but for the trivial reason that there are simple arithmetical truths that it cannot prove.

However, very few general statements are needed to show that all recursive functions are definable. What is needed are *instantiations with closed terms* of these statements. For example, $x + y = y + x$ is not a theorem of Q, but for all numerals m, n we have

$$Q \vdash \mathrm{m} + \mathrm{n} = \mathrm{n} + \mathrm{m}$$

More generally, if s, t are closed terms then, where $v(t)$ is the *value* of t, defined in Chapter 9.7, we have (see Exercise 14.8.14):

(3) a. if $v(s) = v(t)$, then $Q \vdash s = t$
b. if $v(s) \neq v(t)$, then $Q \vdash s \neq t$
c. if $v(s) < v(t)$, then $Q \vdash s < t$
d. if $v(s) \nless v(t)$, then $Q \vdash \neg s < t$

As before, the formulas $x < y$ and $x \leqslant y$ are treated as defined, either as abbreviations or as added symbols with the axioms

(4) a. $x < y \leftrightarrow \exists z(x + z' = y)$
b. $x \leqslant y \leftrightarrow x < y'$

We also have:

(5) a. $Q \vdash x < y' \leftrightarrow x = y \vee x < y$
b. $Q \vdash x \leqslant y \leftrightarrow \exists z(x + z = y)$

c. $Q \vdash x \leqslant y' \leftrightarrow x \leqslant y \vee x = y'$

d. $Q \vdash \neg x < 0$

e. $Q \vdash x < x'$

f. $Q \vdash x \neq 0 \rightarrow \exists y(y < x \wedge x = y')$

Proof. For (a)–(c), note that all the steps in the proof of (14) in Chapter 9.4 can be carried out in Q. For (d), if $x < 0$ there is z such that $x + z' = 0$, so $(x + z)' = 0$, which contradicts (PA1). For (e), by (PA4) and (PA3), $x + 0' = (x + 0)' = x'$, so $x < x'$. Finally, (f) follows from (Q7) and (e). □

Furthermore, for every number m:

(6) $Q \vdash x \leqslant \mathbf{m} \leftrightarrow x = 0 \vee \ldots \vee x = \mathbf{m}$

(Exercise 14.8.13). We may conclude, *exactly* as in Chapter 9.6 (i.e. the argument there works when you reason in Q instead of *PA*), that

(7) a. $Q \vdash \exists x_{x<\mathbf{m}}\varphi(x) \leftrightarrow \varphi(\mathbf{0}) \vee \ldots \vee \varphi(\mathbf{m{-}1})$

b. $Q \vdash \forall x_{x<\mathbf{m}}\varphi(x) \leftrightarrow \varphi(\mathbf{0}) \wedge \ldots \wedge \varphi(\mathbf{m{-}1})$

In Q it is not possible to prove that the order relation is total, i.e. that $x < y \vee x = y \vee y < x$, but we do have, for every m:

(8) $Q \vdash x < \mathbf{m} \vee x = \mathbf{m} \vee \mathbf{m} < x$

Proof. First, by an argument very similar to the one that proves (6), one obtains

(9) $Q \vdash \mathbf{m} < x \leftrightarrow x \neq 0 \wedge \ldots \wedge x \neq \mathbf{m}$

Then by (6) and de Morgan's laws, $Q \vdash \neg x \leqslant \mathbf{m} \rightarrow x \neq 0 \wedge \ldots \wedge x \neq \mathbf{m}$, so by (9) we get $Q \vdash \neg x \leqslant \mathbf{m} \rightarrow \mathbf{m} < x$, i.e. $Q \vdash x \leqslant \mathbf{m} \vee \mathbf{m} < x$. By (5a) and (4b), we have $Q \vdash x \leqslant y \leftrightarrow x < y \vee x = y$, and the result follows. □

We shall eventually prove that all recursive functions are representable in Q. In fact, this is *almost* clear from the proof we gave that all recursive functions are representable in *PA*. What *is* clear is that if we make a simple addition to Q, the proof goes through. One such addition would be the axiom stating that $<$ is a strict total order. Or it could be a weaker axiom saying that the formula $Rem(x, y, u)$ *strongly* represents the remainder function *rem* (see Chapter 9.9.2). Let Q^* be any of these theories.

Lemma 14.4.1
All recursive functions are representable in Q^*.

Proof. This is seen by simply looking carefully at our proof that all recursive functions are representable in *PA*. Clearly, the formulas we gave representing the basic functions (Chapter 10.1) work in Q (and hence in Q^*) as well. And if a function is defined by composition from functions representable in Q (or Q^*), then it is easily seen that the formula shown in Chapter 10.2 to represent it in *PA* actually represents it in Q (Q^*). The same holds when a function h is defined by the μ-operator from a regular function representable in Q (Q^*): the formula used in the proof of Theorem 13.1.14 in fact represents h in Q (Q^*); this uses precisely (7) and (8) but nothing else. Finally, suppose h is defined by primitive recursion from functions representable in Q^*, as in Chapter 10.3. A look at the proof (which we relegated to Exercises 10.5.4 and 10.5.5) reveals that we essentially used the fact that Gödel's β function is *strongly* representable in *PA*, which is a direct consequence of the strong representability of the remainder function *rem* in *PA*. Apart from that, only reasoning available in Q is used. But the proof, in Chapter 9.9.2, that *rem* is strongly representable only relies on the totality axiom and reasoning that can be done in Q. □

To get this result for Q involves a little more work. From one point of view, the choice between Q and Q^* (or PA_0) is immaterial: what matters is only that these theories are finitely axiomatized. But from another point of view it really is a remarkable fact that it suffices to add the seemingly trivial axiom (Q7) to the first six Peano axioms in order to represent all recursive functions. Besides, proving this will give us the opportunity to introduce a classification of arithmetical formulas which (as we saw in Chapter 12.9.1) is interesting in itself.

14.5. Representability by Σ_1 formulas

Our objective in this section is to prove not only that all recursive functions are representable in Q, but that they are representable by particularly simple formulas: Σ_1 formulas. These were introduced informally in Chapter 12.9.1, and we start by making precise and extending the classification given there.[5]

[5]The terminology and exact definitions of various classes of Δ_0, Σ_1, and Π_1 formulas vary slightly in the literature in ways which are sometimes confusing. (In fact, it's hard to find two textbooks which give exactly the same definition of these classes of formulas!) Some authors allow more formulas in Δ_0, some fewer, and some use 'Σ_1' for what we will call 'generalized Σ_1'. Other notational variants occur. Fortunately, these differences do not matter for the main results we shall prove, such as Theorems 14.5.6 and 14.5.11 below. But it's best to read the definitions carefully.

14.5.1. Δ_0, Σ_1, and Π_1 formulas

Definition 14.5.1 ($\Delta_0, \Sigma_1, \Pi_1$)

1. The class of Δ_0 *formulas* is the smallest class of L_{PA}-formulas containing all atomic formulas—where we now count both $s = t$ and $s < t$ as atomic—and closed under boolean connectives, as well as under bounded quantification: if $\varphi \in \Delta_0$, then $\forall x_{x<t}\varphi \in \Delta_0$ and $\exists x_{x<t}\varphi \in \Delta_0$, where t is any term not containing x.[6] More concisely: Δ_0 formulas are those arithmetical formulas all of whose quantifiers are bounded.

2. φ is a Σ_1 *formula* (a Π_1 *formula*) if φ is Δ_0 or has the form $\exists x\psi$ ($\forall x\psi$), where ψ is Δ_0.

3. φ is a *generalized* Σ_1 (Π_1) *formula* if φ is obtained from Δ_0 formulas by means of conjunction, disjunction, bounded quantification, and existential (universal) quantification.

Note that 1. and 3. are inductive definitions (although written somewhat informally); this will be important below. It is easy to see that each of the sets of (Gödel numbers of) formulas defined above is primitive recursive.

Examples:

1. The formulas in (3)–(9) are Δ_0 formulas. But note that this holds for the *formulas*, not the *sentences* (which in this case are theorems of Q) obtained by universally quantifying the free variables; these are Π_1 sentences.

2. The formulas we called Σ_1 (Π_1) in Chapter 12.9.1 are generalized Σ_1 (Π_1) according to the present definition, since we allowed a prefix of finitely many existential (universal) quantifiers. We will soon see that the difference between Σ_1 (Π_1) and generalized Σ_1 (Π_1) is negligible in many contexts.

3. Let:

$$Even(x) := \exists y_{y<x'}\, x = y + y$$

$$Prime(x) := \mathbf{1} < x \wedge \forall y_{y<x}(\mathbf{1} < y \rightarrow \neg\exists z_{z<x}(\mathbf{1} < z \wedge x = yz))$$

These are Δ_0 formulas, and thus Goldbach's Conjecture, i.e.

$$\forall x(Even(x) \wedge \mathbf{2} < x \rightarrow \exists y_{y<x}\exists z_{z<x}(Prime(y) \wedge Prime(z) \wedge x = y+z))$$

is a Π_1 sentence.

[6] Since $x < t := \exists z\, x + z = t$, we are in fact allowing unbounded existential quantifiers in Δ_0 formulas, but only in this particular position. Alternatively, we could have extended the vocabulary with the $<$ symbol and added the defining axiom to the relevant theories. To see that the restriction on x is necessary, consider the formula $\exists x(x \leqslant x \wedge \varphi)$ (i.e. $\exists x(x < x' \wedge \varphi)$). This is equivalent in Q to $\exists x\varphi$, which has an unbounded existential quantifier, and which we definitely do not want in Δ_0.

4. Suppose $\varphi_f(z, y)$ and $\varphi_g(x_1, x_2, z)$ are generalized Σ_1 formulas representing the functions f and g in T. As noted in the proof of Theorem 14.4.1 above, when T is an extension of Q, the formula

$$\theta(x_1, x_2, y) := \exists z(\varphi_g(x_1 m, x_2, z) \wedge \varphi_f(z, y))$$

then represents the composed function $h = \mathrm{Cn}[f, g]$ in T, and we see that $\theta(x_1, x_2, y)$ is also a generalized Σ_1 formula. If we instead assume that $\varphi_f(z, y)$ and $\varphi_g(x_1, x_2, z)$ are Δ_0 formulas, we conclude that $\theta(x_1, x_2, y)$ is a Σ_1 formula.

5. If $\varphi(x)$ is a formula in any of the classes defined in Definition 14.5.1 and t is any term, then $\varphi(t)$ is a formula in the same class.

6. The negation of a (generalized) Σ_1 (Π_1) formula is logically equivalent to a (generalized) Π_1 (Σ_1) formula.

The last two claims can be proved by easy inductions but are intuitively clear. For example, consider $\neg\varphi$, where φ is a generalized Σ_1 formula. We 'move' the negation inwards by the following laws: $\neg\exists x\psi \equiv \forall x\neg\psi$, $\neg\exists x_{x<t}\psi \equiv \forall x_{x<t}\neg\psi$, $\neg(\psi \wedge \theta) \equiv \neg\psi \vee \neg\theta$, and similarly for bounded universal quantification and disjunction. Eventually all negation signs will be in front of Δ_0 formulas. But negations of Δ_0 formulas are Δ_0, and it is clear that the result is a generalized Π_1 formula.

By Theorem 14.3.1, logical equivalence in general is undecidable,[7] but in this case there is a mechanical—indeed primitive recursive—procedure that transforms any negated (generalized) Σ_1 (Π_1) formula into a logically equivalent (generalized) Π_1 (Σ_1) formula.

Now, before we get to representability in Q, it will be convenient to look at the weaker notion of *arithmetical definability*, as defined in Chapter 9.8: a k-ary function f is *arithmetically definable* if there is an arithmetical formula $\varphi(x_1, \ldots, x_k, y)$ such that for all $n_1, \ldots, n_k, m$,

$$f(n_1, \ldots, n_k) = m \text{ iff the sentence } \varphi(\mathbf{n}_1, \ldots, \mathbf{n}_k, \mathbf{m}) \text{ is true}$$

Put differently, $\varphi(x_1, \ldots, x_k, y)$ represents the graph of f (the relation $G_f(n_1, \ldots, n_k, m) \Leftrightarrow f(n_1, \ldots, n_k) = m$) in $Th(\mathcal{N})$. Also, let us say that two formulas $\psi(x_1, \ldots, x_k)$ and $\theta(x_1, \ldots, x_k)$ are *arithmetically equivalent* if, for all numbers $n_1, \ldots, n_k$,

$$\varphi(\mathbf{n}_1, \ldots, \mathbf{n}_k) \text{ is true iff } \psi(\mathbf{n}_1, \ldots, \mathbf{n}_k) \text{ is true.}$$

Clearly, if $\varphi(x_1, \ldots, x_k, y)$ arithmetically defines a function f, every formula arithmetically equivalent to $\varphi(x_1, \ldots, x_k, y)$ also defines f.

[7] If logical equivalence were decidable then logical validity would be decidable too, since φ is logically valid iff φ is logically equivalent to $\top$.

One reason for introducing the class of generalized Σ_1 formulas was that one can directly see that the following holds.

Lemma 14.5.2
Every recursive function is arithmetically definable by a generalized Σ_1 formula.

Proof. The (total) recursive functions were defined inductively from the basic functions, and, just following the proof of Theorem 14.4.1 that all recursive functions are representable in the theory we there called Q^*, we observe that the basic functions are represented by Δ_0 formulas, and that at each inductive step we used formulas obtained by conjunction, disjunction, bounded quantification, and existential quantification. This shows that all recursive functions are representable in Q^* by generalized Σ_1 formulas. But then (since all Q^*-theorems are true) the same formulas arithmetically define these functions. □

Now, 'generalized Σ_1' can be replaced by 'Σ_1' in this result.

Lemma 14.5.3
Every generalized Σ_1 formula is arithmetically equivalent to a Σ_1 formula.

Proof. We prove this by induction over generalized Σ_1 formulas. Δ_0 formulas are Σ_1 formulas by definition, so the base step is clear. For the induction steps, suppose first $\varphi(\overline{x})$ has the form $\exists y \psi(y, \overline{x})$, where $\psi(y, \overline{x})$ by induction hypothesis is arithmetically equivalent to a Σ_1 formula, say, $\exists z \theta(z, y, \overline{x})$, where θ is Δ_0. So $\varphi(\overline{x})$ is arithmetically equivalent to $\exists y \exists z \theta(z, y, \overline{x})$. But now observe:

$$\exists y \exists z \theta(z, y, \overline{x}) \text{ is arithmetically equivalent to } \exists u \exists y_{y<u} \exists z_{z<u} \theta(z, y, \overline{x})$$

and the formula to the right is Σ_1.

Next, suppose $\varphi(\overline{x})$ is a conjunction $\psi_1(\overline{x}) \wedge \psi_2(\overline{x})$, where $\psi_1(\overline{x})$ is arithmetically equivalent to $\exists y \theta_1(y, \overline{x})$ and $\psi_2(\overline{x})$ is arithmetically equivalent to $\exists z \theta_2(z, \overline{x})$, where θ_1, θ_2 are Δ_0 and we are assuming, as we clearly may, that y and z are distinct variables. Then we have:

$$\exists y \theta_1(y, \overline{x}) \wedge \exists z \theta_2(z, \overline{x}) \text{ is logically equivalent to } \exists y \exists z (\theta_1(y, \overline{x}) \wedge \theta_2(z, \overline{x}))$$

We just saw how to 'contract' two existential quantifiers to one, so it follows that $\varphi(\overline{x})$ is arithmetically equivalent to a Σ_1 formula. The case when $\varphi(\overline{x})$ is a disjunction is similar.

Next, suppose $\varphi(\overline{x})$ is a bounded universally quantified formula $\forall y_{y<t} \psi(y, \overline{x})$, where $\psi(y, \overline{x})$ is arithmetically equivalent to $\exists z \theta(z, y, \overline{x})$ and $\theta(z, y, \overline{x})$ is Δ_0. Since in a finite set of numbers there is a largest one, we have

(10) $\forall y_{y<t}\exists z\theta(z, y, \overline{x})$ is arithm. equivalent to $\exists u\forall y_{y<t}\exists z_{z<u}\theta(z, y, \overline{x})$

which is a Σ_1 formula. The case when $\varphi(\overline{x})$ is $\exists y_{y<t}\psi(x)$ is trivial, since we can just permute the existential quantifiers. This takes care of the last induction step, and the lemma is proved. □

Corollary 14.5.4
Every recursive function (hence every recursive relation) is arithmetically definable by a Σ_1 formula.

14.5.2. Σ_1-completeness and its consequences

We must now improve Corollary 14.5.4 by replacing 'arithmetically definable' by 'representable in Q'. A crucial step is the next important fact about Q, mentioned already in Chapter 12.9.1. First, a definition.

Definition 14.5.5 (Σ_1-soundness and Σ_1-completeness)
An arithmetical theory T is Σ_1-*sound* if every generalized Σ_1 sentence that T proves is true. T is Σ_1-*complete* if the converse holds, i.e. T proves all true generalized Σ_1 sentences.

Trivially, Q—like all true theories—is Σ_1-sound. Σ_1-soundness is related to ω-*consistency*; see Exercises 14.8.17 and 14.8.22.

Theorem 14.5.6 (Σ_1-completeness of Q)
Q is Σ_1-complete.

Proof. We prove this by induction along the definition of generalized Σ_1 formulas. The base case is Δ_0 formulas, so we start by showing that the following claim holds, by induction over Δ_0 sentences:[8]

(11) If φ is Δ_0 and true, $Q \vdash \varphi$, and if φ is Δ_0 and false, $Q \vdash \neg\varphi$.

Atomic sentences are of the form $s = t$ or $s < t$, and since $s = t$ is true iff $v(s) = v(t)$, and $s < t$ is true iff $v(s) < v(t)$, the result follows from (3). If φ is $\neg\psi$, then φ is true entails that ψ is false, so $Q \vdash \neg\psi$ by induction hypothesis, and φ is false entails that ψ is true, so $Q \vdash \psi$ by induction hypothesis, and hence $Q \vdash \neg\neg\psi$. The case when φ is a conjunction is similar.

Now consider bounded quantification. Suppose φ is $\forall x_{x<t}\psi(x)$, where $\psi(x)$ is Δ_0. Since φ is a sentence and x does not occur in t, t must be a closed term, say that $v(t) = n$. Then φ is equivalent in Q to $\forall x_{x<\mathbf{n}}\psi(x)$, which in turn is equivalen in Q to $\psi(\mathbf{0}) \wedge \ldots \wedge \psi(\mathbf{n}-\mathbf{1})$,

[8] As we have seen, in general one cannot prove claims about FOL *sentences* directly by induction, but has to prove a more general claim about *formulas*. In this case, however, we are talking about truth in the model $\mathcal{N}$, in which every object has a name. To prove a claim about a sentence of the form $\exists x\varphi(x)$, for example, it is enough to use the induction hypothesis about *sentences* of the form $\varphi(\mathbf{n})$.

by (7). So if φ is true, all of these conjuncts are true, and hence provable in Q by induction hypotheses, i.e. $Q \vdash \varphi$. If φ is false, then $\exists x_{x<\mathbf{n}} \neg\psi(x)$ is true, so $\neg\psi(\mathbf{k})$ is true for some $k < n$, which by induction hypothesis entails that $Q \vdash \neg\psi(\mathbf{0}) \vee \ldots \vee \neg\psi(\mathbf{n-1})$, so again by (7), $Q \vdash \exists x_{x<\mathbf{n}} \neg\psi(x)$, and this sentence is equivalent in Q to $\neg\varphi$. The case when φ is $\exists x_{x<t}\psi(x)$ is similar. This proves (11).

For the induction steps in the proof of the theorem, if φ is a true generalized Σ_1 conjunction, the conjuncts are true generalized Σ_1 sentences, hence provable in Q by induction hypothesis, so φ is also provable in Q. Similarly for disjunctions.

Next, suppose φ is $\exists x\psi(x)$. If φ is true, then $\psi(\mathbf{n})$ is true for some n, hence provable in Q by induction hypothesis, so $Q \vdash \exists x\psi(x)$. A variation of this argument shows that if φ is $\exists x_{x<t}\psi(x)$, the truth of φ entails its provability in Q. Finally, suppose φ is $\forall x_{x<t}\psi(x)$, where $\psi(x)$ is a generalized Σ_1 formula. If φ is true and $v(t) = n$, then, by induction hypothesis, $Q \vdash \psi(\mathbf{k})$ for all $k < n$. As above, it follows that $Q \vdash \forall x_{x<\mathbf{n}}\psi(x)$, which is equivalent in Q to φ. □

We pause to observe that the proof consists of two straightforward inductive arguments. So one expects it to be formalizable in *PA*. This is indeed the case, although the details require some thought. We shall not go into those details here but merely state the result.[9]

Theorem 14.5.7 (formalized Σ_1-completeness)
If φ is a generalized Σ_1 sentence, then $PA \vdash \varphi \rightarrow Pr_Q(\ulcorner\varphi\urcorner)$.

Here is a corollary to the above proof (which dealt with Δ_0 *sentences*, but the argument for Δ_0 *formulas* is analogous):

Corollary 14.5.8
Q decides all Δ_0 formulas. That is, if $\varphi(x_1, \ldots, x_n)$ is Δ_0, then for all $k_1, \ldots, k_n$, either $Q \vdash \varphi(\mathbf{k_1}, \ldots, \mathbf{k_n})$ or $Q \vdash \neg\varphi(\mathbf{k_1}, \ldots, \mathbf{k_n})$.

Now we shall focus on the functions arithmetically definable by Δ_0 formulas. Using the Σ_1-completeness of Q we can establish:

Lemma 14.5.9
If a function is arithmetically definable by a Δ_0 formula, then it is representable in Q by a Δ_0 formula.

Proof. Suppose that f is arithmetically defined by the Δ_0 formula $\varphi(x, y)$ (consider the unary case for simplicity). The claim is not that $\varphi(x, y)$ represents f in Q, but that *another* Δ_0 formula $\psi(x, y)$ does just that. In fact, we have already seen how to construe $\psi(x, y)$:

[9] A detailed proof can be found in G. Boolos 1993, pp. 46–49, although the definition of Σ_1 formulas there is slightly different.

$$\psi(x, y) := \varphi(x, y) \wedge \forall z_{z<y} \neg \varphi(x, z)$$

$\psi(x, y)$ is also a Δ_0 formula. The proof of Lemma 9.9.3 showed that if $\varphi(x, y)$ represents the graph of f in *PA*, then $\psi(x, y)$ represents f in *PA*. Moreover, a quick look at that proof makes it clear that it goes through already in Q (indeed, only (7) and (8) are needed). Now, since $\varphi(x, y)$ is a Δ_0 formula arithmetically defining f, it follows from Theorem 14.5.6 that $\varphi(x, y)$ represents the graph of f in Q. In detail: If $f(n) = m$ then $\varphi(\mathbf{n}, \mathbf{m})$ is true, and since it is a Δ_0 formula (thus a Σ_1 formula), it is provable in Q. And if $f(n) \neq m$, then $\neg\varphi(\mathbf{n}, \mathbf{m})$ is true, and also a Δ_0 formula, therefore provable in Q. Thus, by the argument in the proof of Lemma 9.9.3, $\psi(x, y)$ represents f in Q. □

It may seem that we are still far from the goal, since recursive functions are *not* in general arithmetically defined by Δ_0 formulas. But a final lemma shows that they 'almost' are![10]

Lemma 14.5.10
Every recursive function can be obtained as a composition of functions arithmetically defined by Δ_0 formulas.

Proof. Let f be a recursive function (1-place, for simplicity). By Corollary 14.5.4, f is arithmetically defined by a Σ_1 formula, say,

$$f(n) = m \text{ iff } \exists z \psi(\mathbf{n}, \mathbf{m}, z) \text{ is true,}$$

where $\psi(x, y, z)$ is Δ_0. Define the 1-place function g by

$$g(n) = \mu p \exists m_{m \leqslant p} \exists k_{k \leqslant p} \psi(\mathbf{n}, \mathbf{m}, \mathbf{k}) \text{ is true}$$

Note that $g(n)$ is total, since f is total. Also, g is arithmetically defined by the following Δ_0 formula:

$$\varphi_g(x, u) := \exists y_{y \leqslant u} \exists z_{z \leqslant u} \psi(x, y, z) \wedge \forall v_{v<u} \neg \exists y_{y \leqslant v} \exists z_{z \leqslant v} \psi(x, y, z)$$

Next, define the 2-place function h as follows:

$$h(n, p) = \mu m_{m \leqslant p} \exists k_{k \leqslant p} \psi(\mathbf{n}, \mathbf{m}, \mathbf{k}) \text{ is true}$$

h is arithmetically defined by the Δ_0 formula

$$\varphi_h(x, u, y) := \exists z_{z \leqslant u} \psi(x, y, z) \wedge \forall v_{v<y} \neg \exists z_{z \leqslant u} \psi(x, v, z)$$

The point of all this is that the following holds:

$$f(n) = h(n, g(n))$$

[10] I have taken this nice technical lemma, and its use to prove Theorem 14.5.11 below, from G. S. Boolos, Burgess, and Jeffrey 2007.

To see this, suppose $f(n) = m$, let k be the smallest number such that $\psi(\mathbf{n}, \mathbf{m}, \mathbf{k})$ is true, and let $p = max(m, k)$. Then $g(n) = p$. Also, $h(n, p) = m$.

Thus, f is obtained by composition from h and g. □

Let us take stock. Suppose f is a recursive function. We just saw that (in the unary case) $f(n) = h(n, g(n))$, where g, h are arithmetically definable by Δ_0 formulas. By Lemma 14.5.9, g, h are representable in Q by Δ_0 formulas. Moreover, as we observed in Example 4. after Definition 14.5.1, the composed function f is then represented in Q by a Σ_1 formula. We have proved:

Theorem 14.5.11
Every recursive function (and hence every recursive relation) is representable in Q by a Σ_1 formula.

There is more to be said about representability in arithmetical theories and complexity of the representing formulas. For example, one can show that all *primitive* recursive functions are *strongly* representable in *PA* by Σ_1 formulas. Functions which have this property are called *provably recursive in PA*. It is not the case that all recursive functions are provably recursive in *PA*.[11]

We end this subsection by noting that as an immediate consequence of Theorem 14.5.11 and our earlier results on incompleteness and undecidability, we obtain:

Theorem 14.5.12
(a) *If T is a consistent axiomatizable extension of Q, then T is incomplete. Similarly if Q is interpretable in T.*
(b) *Q is essentially undecidable.*

14.5.3. Complexity of some familiar formulas

Recall the 'canonical' formula $Prf_\tau(x, y)$ from (10) in Chapter 11.8, which faithfully corresponds to the natural definition of the proof relation prf_T, where $\tau(x)$ corresponds to ax_T. It is straightforward to see that the proof of Fact 11.8.1 (which we left to Exercise 11.9.9) works already for Q. That is, if $\tau(x)$ represents ax_T in Q, then $Prf_\tau(x, y)$ represents prf_T in Q. What can we say about the complexity of $Prf_\tau(x, y)$?

A careful look at the definition reveals that only Δ_0 formulas, conjunction, disjunction, bounded quantification, and existential quantification are used. Since we had some extra function symbols in (10), this

[11] Recall that we showed in Chapter 9.9.2 that every function representable in *PA* is strongly representable in *PA*. But the strongly representing formula used in that proof is not Σ_1.

might not be completely obvious, so let us check one case. One conjunct in the definition was $Sent((x)_{\underline{z}})$, where $(x)_{\underline{z}}$ uses a new function symbol to interpret the decoding function $(n)_i$ (the i:th member of the sequence coded by n). Let us write $(n)_i$ more readably as $dec(n, i)$. By Theorem 14.5.11, there is a Σ_1 formula $Dec(x_1, x_2, y)$ such that if $dec(n, i) = m$. then

$$Q \vdash Dec(\mathbf{n}, \mathbf{i}, y) \leftrightarrow y = \mathbf{m}$$

It follows that we can see $Sent((x)_{\underline{z}})$ as an abbreviation for

$$\exists w(Dec(x, z, w) \wedge Sent(w))$$

The upshot of this, in view of Theorem 14.5.11, is this:

Fact 14.5.13
If $\tau(x)$ is a generalized Σ_1 formula, then so is $Prf_\tau(x, y)$.

Thus, for example, $Con_T := \neg\exists x Prf_T(x, \ulcorner\bot\urcorner)$ is (logically equivalent to) a generalized Π_1 formula.

Next, consider the Gödel sentence G and related sentences. First, we rephrase and strengthen the Diagonal Lemma (Lemma 12.1.1).

Lemma 14.5.14 (strengthened Diagonal Lemma)

(a) *For every formula $\psi(y)$ there is a sentence φ such that*

$$Q \vdash \varphi \leftrightarrow \psi(\ulcorner\varphi\urcorner)$$

(b) *If $\psi(y)$ is generalized Σ_1 (Π_1), then φ can be chosen to be generalized Σ_1 (Π_1).*

(c) *Suppose T is a recursive extension of Q s.t. $T \vdash x \leqslant y \vee y \leqslant x$. Then, if $\psi(y)$ is Σ_1 (Π_1), a sentence φ such that $T \vdash \varphi \leftrightarrow \psi(\ulcorner\varphi\urcorner)$ can be chosen to be Σ_1 (Π_1).*

Proof. (a): By Theorem 14.5.11, the function sub_0 is representable in Q by a Σ_1 formula $Sub_0(x_1, x_2, y)$, and we have already noted (e.g. in the proof of Proposition 14.1.4) that this is all it takes for the proof of the Diagonal Lemma to go through.

(b): Recall that in that proof, we let $\theta(x) := \exists y(Sub_0(x, x, y) \wedge \psi(y))$ and then took $\varphi := \theta(\ulcorner\theta\urcorner)$. So if $\psi(y)$ is generalized Σ_1, then $\theta(x)$ is also generalized Σ_1, and thus, so is φ. In Exercise 12.10.1 we asked the reader for a variant of the proof which instead starts from $\theta'(x) := \forall y(Sub_0(x, x, y) \rightarrow \psi(y))$, and again lets $\varphi' := \theta'(\ulcorner\theta'\urcorner)$. In this case, it follows that if $\psi(y)$ is generalized Π_1, so is φ'.

(c): Now suppose that $\psi(y)$ is Σ_1, say, $\psi(y) := \exists z\psi'(z, y)$, where ψ' is Δ_0. We already assumed that $Sub_0(x_1, x_2, y)$ is Σ_1: $Sub_0(x_1, x_2, y) := \exists w\, \chi(w, x_1, x_2, y)$, where χ is Δ_0. This time, let

$$\theta_0(x) := \exists y \exists z \exists w(\chi(w, x, x, y) \wedge \psi'(z, y))$$

Note that $\theta_0(x)$ is logically equivalent to $\theta(x)$. Now the claim in (c) follows from the next little lemma. □

Lemma 14.5.15
If T is a recursive extension of Q such that $T \vdash x \leqslant y \vee y \leqslant x$, then every formula of the form $\exists x_1 \ldots \exists x_n \psi$, where ψ is Δ_0, is equivalent in T to a Σ_1 formula. Similarly for the Π_1 case.

Proof. It is clearly enough to show the following:

(12) $\quad T \vdash \exists x \exists y \psi(x, y) \leftrightarrow \exists z \exists x_{x \leqslant z} \exists y_{y \leqslant z} \psi(x, y)$

The right-to-left direction is a simple logical truth. For the left-to-right direction, reason in T: assume $\psi(x, y)$ and distinguish two cases. If $x \leqslant y$, then, taking $z = y$, we obtain $x \leqslant z$ and $y \leqslant z$ and $\psi(x, y)$, as desired. If $y \leqslant x$, the argument is similar. Since $x \leqslant y \vee y \leqslant x$ holds, we are done. The proof for $\forall x \forall y \psi(x, y)$ is similar: now the left-to-right direction is trivial, and the other direction needs an argument distinguishing the cases $x \leqslant y$ and $y \leqslant x$. □

In the next section we will see what one must add to Q in order to prove that every generalized Σ_1 formula is equivalent to a Σ_1 formula.

Now recall the Gödel sentence G and the Rosser sentence R (relative to a consistent recursive extension T of Q):

$$Q \vdash G \leftrightarrow \neg \exists x Prf_T(x, \ulcorner G \urcorner)$$
$$Q \vdash R \leftrightarrow \forall x(Prf_T(x, \ulcorner R \urcorner) \rightarrow \forall z_{z<x} Ref_T(x, \ulcorner R \urcorner))$$

It follows that G and R can be taken to be generalized Π_1 sentences. In a theory as in Lemma 14.5.14(c), they can be chosen as Π_1 sentences.

14.6. *Weak systems of arithmetic

Q is a very weak theory, but adding the induction axiom scheme yields the very strong theory *PA*. We get intermediate theories by adding induction restricted to classes of 'simple' formulas. This, and other kinds of addition to Q, leads to the study of *weak systems of arithmetic*, which is an active research area in logic. We just give a few examples here.[12]

The theory *I(open)* is obtained by adding to Q the induction scheme for open (quantifier-free) L_{PA}-formulas:

[12] An encyclopedic source of information about weak arithmetical theories is Hájek and Pudlák 1993. For the facts mentioned here, see in particular Ch. I.1 (a), (c), (d), and Ch. IV.3.

For all open formulas $\varphi(x, \overline{y})$,

$$(\varphi(0, \overline{y}) \wedge \forall x(\varphi(x, \overline{y}) \to \varphi(x', \overline{y})) \to \forall x \varphi(x, \overline{y})$$

To see what can be proved in *I(open)*, consider the theorems of *PA* proved by induction in Chapter 9. Whenever the relevant formula was quantifier-free (as it was in most cases), the same proof works in *I(open)*. For example, take the proof of

$$x + y = y + x$$

In Chapter 9.2, this was obtained using three instances of (IND), on the formulas $0 + x = x$, $y + x' = y' + x$ (induction on x), and $x + y = y + x$ (induction on y), respectively. All of these are quantifier-free, so $\forall x \forall y(x + y = y + x)$ is a theorem of *I(open)*.

In the context of weak systems of arithmetic, we take $<$ (or $\leqslant$) to be a primitive symbol. In particular, the formula $x \leqslant y \vee y \leqslant x$ is quantifier-free, which means that the totality of the order of the natural numbers, that is, $\forall x \forall y(x \leqslant y \vee y \leqslant x)$, is provable in *I(open)*, with the proof from Chapter 9.4. Similarly for many of the results in that chapter. One apparent exception was the proof in Chapter 9.5 of $\forall x \forall y \forall z((z \neq 0 \wedge x \cdot z = y \cdot z) \to x = y)$. The induction formula was

$$\forall x((z \neq 0 \wedge x \cdot z = y \cdot z) \to x = y)$$

which is Π_1, so that proof doesn't work in *I(open)*. However, there is in fact another proof of that sentence in *I(open)*, which instead uses the induction formula $x < y \wedge z \neq 0 \to x \cdot z < y \cdot z$.[13]

Since *I(open)* proves that $\leqslant$ is total, Lemma 14.5.15 applies to this theory, so a sequence of existential (universal) quantifiers can be *contracted* to one.

The theory $I\Delta_0$ (also called $I\Sigma_0$) allows all Δ_0 formulas in the induction scheme. Here is an example of what can be proved in $I\Delta_0$:

(13) *Least Number Principle* for Δ_0-formulas: if $\varphi(x)$ is Δ_0, then:

$$I\Delta_0 \vdash \exists x \varphi(x) \to \exists x(\varphi(x) \wedge \forall y_{y<x} \neg\varphi(y))$$

The proof assumes $\exists x(\varphi(x) \wedge \forall x(\varphi(x) \to \exists y_{y<x}\varphi(y)))$, and derives a contradiction by applying induction to the Δ_0 formula $\forall y_{y<x} \neg\varphi(y)$. Conversely, it also holds that the Least Number Principle for Δ_0 formulas implies the induction scheme for Δ_0 formulas. Many facts about division are also provable in $I\Delta_0$, such as Euclid's Lemma (Lemma 8.6.3).

---

[13]So here is a situation where it matters whether $<$ is a primitive symbol or not. Only in the former case can we claim that $\forall x \forall y \forall z((z \neq 0 \wedge x \cdot z = y \cdot z) \to x = y)$ is provable in *I(open)*.

The next theory, $I\Sigma_1$, allows induction on Σ_1 formulas. As a first example, we show that the equivalence (10), the truth of which was used in the previous section, can be proved in $I\Sigma_1$.[14]

($B\Sigma_1$) If $\theta(x, y)$ is Σ_1, $I\Sigma_1 \vdash \forall x_{x \leqslant u} \exists y \theta(x, y) \to \exists z \forall x_{x \leqslant u} \exists y_{y \leqslant z} \theta(x, y)$

Proof. It is enough to prove the (seemingly weaker) principle

($B\Sigma_0$) If $\theta(x, y)$ is Δ_0, $I\Sigma_1 \vdash \forall x_{x \leqslant u} \exists y \theta(x, y) \to \exists z \forall x_{x \leqslant u} \exists y_{y \leqslant z} \theta(x, y)$

for then ($B\Sigma_1$) follows by contraction of quantifiers. Reason in $I\Sigma_1$: assume $\forall x_{x \leqslant u} \exists y \theta(x, y)$, and prove

(*) $w \leqslant u \to \exists z \forall x_{x \leqslant w} \exists y_{y \leqslant z} \theta(x, y)$

by induction on w; then the result follows with $w = u$. Note that (*) is (logically equivalent to) a Σ_1 formula. If $w = 0$, the consequent $\exists z \exists y_{y \leqslant z} \theta(0, y)$ follows directly from our assumption (let $z = y$). For the induction step, suppose (*) holds, and take w such that $w' \leqslant u$. Since $w \leqslant u$, there is z_0 such that $\forall x_{x \leqslant w} \exists y_{y \leqslant z_0} \theta(x, y)$, by induction hypothesis. And by the assumption, there is y_0 such that $\theta(w', y_0)$. So if we let $z = max(z_0, y_0)$, it follows (since $z_0 \leqslant y_0 \vee y_0 \leqslant z_0$ holds in $I\Sigma_1$) that for every $x \leqslant w'$ there is $y \leqslant z$ such that $\theta(x, y)$. □

As a consequence, the set of formulas provably equivalent to Σ_1 formulas in the theory $I\Sigma_1$ is closed under bounded quantification: we just proved the case of bounded universal quantification, and the case of bounded existential quantification is trivial, since $\exists x_{x \leqslant u} \exists y \theta(x, y)$ is logically equivalent to $\exists y \exists x_{x \leqslant u} \theta(x, y)$. In fact, it is not hard to see that the whole argument in the proof of Lemma 14.5.3 can be carried out in $I\Sigma_1$, so that:

(14) Every generalized Σ_1 formula is provably equivalent in $I\Sigma_1$ to a Σ_1 formula.

Exercise 14.8.22 describes how this leads to a strengthening of Gödel's first incompleteness theorem for theories containing $I\Sigma_1$.

$I\Sigma_1$ is a rather strong theory. The exponentiation function, say, $exp(n, m) = n^m$, is expressible in it, in a slightly weaker sense than that of Chapter 9.9, but it can still be used to code finite sequences. Therefore, much of the arithmetization used in the proofs of the incompleteness theorems can be carried out *inside* $I\Sigma_1$. This can be applied to prove results along the lines of the second incompleteness theorem, which required precisely a formalization of the argument

[14]Below, θ may contain other free variables besides x, y. Note that the converse implication holds in all theories, since it is a logical truth.

that the consistency of T implies the Gödel sentence G.[15] Another application is the construction of a *partial truth definition* in $I\Sigma_1$. In particular, there is a formula $Tr_1(y)$ such that for all Σ_1 sentences φ we have:

(15) $\quad I\Sigma_1 \vdash \varphi \leftrightarrow Tr_1(\ulcorner\varphi\urcorner)$

This is a consequence of the fact that the Tarskian definition of satisfaction can be formalized for Σ_1 formulas; there is a formula $Sat_1(u, v)$ (which itself is Σ_1) such that (a formalized version of) the following can be proved in $I\Sigma_1$:

(16) 'If $Sat_1(u, v)$, then u is a Σ_1-formula, v is an assignment, and
if u is $x = y$, $Sat_1(u, v)$ iff $v(x) = v(y)$, and similarly for $x < y$;[16]
if u is $\neg x$, $Sat_1(u, v)$ iff not $Sat_1(x, v)$; similarly for conjunctions;
if u is $\forall z_{z<t}\, x$, $Sat_1(u, v)$ iff for each assignment v_0 that differs from v at most at the variable z and is such that if $v_0(z) < v_0(t)$ then $Sat_1(x, v_0)$;
if u is $\exists z\, x$, $Sat_1(u, v)$ iff there is y such that if v_1 is like v except that $v_1(z) = y$, then $Sat_1(x, v_1)$.'

So $Tr_1(y)$ is a truth definition for Σ_1 sentences. We know from Tarski's Theorem (Theorem 7.2.8) that there can be no truth definition for *all* sentences, but partial truth definitions are indeed possible, also in relatively weak arithmetical theories. Here is one striking application of partial truth definitions.

Call a *set* of natural numbers Σ_1 if it is arithmetically definable by a Σ_1 formula.[17] As we just saw, in $I\Sigma_1$ proves a formalized version of the claim "$Sat_1(u, v)$ satisfies Tarski's satisfaction conditions for Σ_1 formulas". This is a single provable sentence, say ψ, so there is a finite subtheory I_1 of $I\Sigma_1$ such that $I_1 \vdash \psi$. Using this, one can, via suitable coding, prove in I_1 a formalization of the following claim, call it θ:

'For all Σ_1 sets X, if $X(0)$ and $\forall y(X(y) \rightarrow X(y'))$, then $\forall y X(y)$.'

Now it is not very hard to see (when all the details are in place) that θ in fact implies in I_1 each instance of the Σ_1-induction scheme. Thus, we conclude:

[15] One can prove in $I\Sigma_1$ that there are infinitely many primes, but it is not known if this is provable in $I\Delta_0$. Concerning exponentiation, it turns out that the *graph* of the exponentiation function, i.e. the relation $n^m = k$, can in fact be expressed in $I\Delta_0$ (though this is far from trivial), and this can be used to code syntax already in $I\Delta_0$; see Hájek and Pudlák 1993, Ch. V.

[16] That is, if u is (the Gödel number of) an identity formula then u is satisfied by the assignment v iff the value of the left-hand side under v is equal to the value of the right-hand side under v, etc.

[17] We will have more to say about Σ_1 sets in the next chapter.

(17) $I\Sigma_1$ is finitely axiomatizable.

This is surprising, at least in view of the fact that the Σ_1-induction scheme is an infinite set of axioms (one for each Σ_1 formula). There are many other applications of partial truth definitions, but we leave the topic here. As a final consideration about $I\Sigma_1$, recall our remark (that we didn't substantiate) at the end of Section 14.5.2 that all primitive recursive are *provably recursive* (= strongly representable by Σ_1 formulas) in *PA*. In fact, this holds already for $I\Sigma_1$. Moreover, the converse is also true (we shall not try to even sketch the proof), and so an important fact about $I\Sigma_1$ is:

(18) A function is prim. recursive iff it is provably recursive in $I\Sigma_1$.

14.7. Undecidability of the halting problem

We end this chapter by looking at another kind of undecidable problems, related to Turing machines. A Turing machine is just a finite set of quadruples with symbols from a countable alphabet.[18] It follows (cf. Appendix 16.4) that one can *effective enumerate* all Turing machines,

$$M_0, M_1, M_2, \ldots$$

i.e. that there is a systematic way to generate all finite sets of quadruples that define Turing machines.[19]

Since each Turing machine computes a 1-place partial function, we thus obtain an effective enumeration

$$f_0, f_1, f_2, \ldots$$

of all computable 1-place partial functions, and similarly an effective enumeration of all computable k-place partial functions for each $k \geqslant 1$.

A diagonal argument now shows that it is really necessary to include all *partial* computable functions in any such enumeration: let the function g be defined by

$$g(n) = f_n(n) + 1$$

g is intuitively computable: given n, find machine M_n in the list, start M_n on input n, and add 1 to the result. By the Church-Turing Thesis, g must be in the list, say, $g = f_i$. Thus,

[18] In the version of Turing machines described in Chapter 13.1.3 only the number of states, $q_0, q_1, q_2, \ldots$, is countable. In other versions one may for practical reasons have access to a supply $s_0, s_1, s_2, \ldots$ of symbols that can be written on the tape, whereas we only had 0 and 1. Such design differences do not affect which functions are computable.

[19] Recall that Turing machines are *deterministic* sets of quadruples, i.e. that for each state q_i and each symbol s_j there is at most one quadruple in the set starting with $q_i s_j$.

(19) $f_i(n) = f_n(n) + 1$

But this is impossible for $n = i$! We conclude that $g(i) = f_i(i)$ must be *undefined*.

Implicit in the above argument is the fact that the problem of deciding whether a given Turing machine computes a total function or not, and the problem of deciding whether it halts or not for a given input, cannot themselves be decided by an algorithm. Let us express this in a more precise way. Define

$$Tot = \{n\colon M_n \text{ computes a total 1-place function}\}$$

Then we have

(20) The set *Tot* is undecidable (not recursive).

Proof. If *Tot* were decidable we could generate a sublist $N_0, N_1, N_2, \ldots$ from $M_0, M_1, M_2, \ldots$, by successively deleting all M_i that do not compute a total function. Then the diagonalization argument above would yield a total function g not generated by any N_i. This is a contradiction—provided g is actually computable. So from Church-Turing's Thesis it follows that *Tot* is an example of an undecidable set (problem). □

Here is our second example: the *halting problem* is to decide whether an arbitrary Turing machine M_m with an arbitrary input n eventually stops or not. Thus:

$$H(m,n) \Leftrightarrow M_m \text{ with input } n \text{ stops after a finite number of steps}$$

Now we can show:

(21) The halting problem is unsolvable (i.e. H is not recursive).

Proof. Define the function h as follows:

$$h(n) = \begin{cases} f_n(n) + 1 & \text{if } H(n,n) \text{ and } M_n\text{'s output} \\ & \text{is a number in standard position} \\ 0 & \text{otherwise} \end{cases}$$

First observe that h is total: it returns a value for every number n. But now we can again see that h cannot be one of $f_0, f_1, \ldots$. For *suppose* $h = f_i$. In particular, $h(i)$ is defined (since h is total). That is, M_i with input i halts with the number $f_i(i)$ as output, which means that the first condition in the definition of h is satisfied. But that means that $f_i(i) = h(i) = f_i(i) + 1$, a contradiction.

This yields our conclusion about the halting problem. *If* H were a decidable relation, we would be able to decide if the first condition in the definition of h was satisfied or not, i.e. (a) if $H(n,n)$ holds, and, in case $H(n,n)$ holds, (b) if machine M_n's output, on input n, is a number. (We just have to check if the tape represents a number or not.) But then the function h would be computable, and thus appear in the list $f_0, f_1, \ldots$, which we just saw is impossible. Thus, H is not decidable. □

An immediate corollary (of the proof) is that the set

$$K = \{n \colon H(n, n)\}$$

is not recursive either. The set K represents what we may call the *diagonalized halting problem*. It plays a basic role in the theory of recursively enumerable sets, as we will see in the next chapter.

We see that diagonalization is a crucial tool for finding actual examples of undecidable problems.[20] This seems to be a general phenomenon. Note that all our examples of undecidable theories build on diagonalization, namely, Lemma 14.1.1, which in turn uses the Diagonal Lemma.

In this section we have relied heavily on the Church-Turing Thesis. But many of these uses were *inessential*: for example, in the proof of (20) we claimed that if *Tot* were decidable one could effectively enumerate a certain sublist of $M_0, M_1, M_2, \ldots$. Instead, we could have actually given the detailed specification of that list, given that *Tot* were a recursive set. This sort of use of the Thesis is just a convenience—actually, it is *very* convenient, and used all the time! An *essential* use of the Thesis, on the other hand, is when we, from the fact that a set which codes a certain problem is shown to be non-recursive, conclude that the problem is unsolvable, in other words that *there exists no algorithm* for solving it.

14.8. Exercises to Chapter 14

Exercise 14.8.1
Give an example of an arithmetical theory which is undecidable but not essentially undecidable.

Exercise 14.8.2
Show that if T is essentially undecidable and T' is a consistent extension of T, then T' is essentially undecidable.

Exercise 14.8.3
Say that T' is a *finite extension* of T if T' is obtained by adding finitely many axioms (in the same vocabulary) to T. Show that if T' is a finite extension of T, and T' is undecidable, then T is undecidable.

[20] That *there exist* undecidable problems, i.e. non-recursive sets of numbers, on the other hand, is trivial. There are countably many Turing machines, but uncountably many sets of natural numbers (see Appendix 16.5), so in fact uncountably many non-recursive sets of natural numbers.

Exercise 14.8.4
Let T_1 and T_2 be theories in the same vocabulary. We say that T_1 and T_2 are *compatible* if the theory $T_1 \cup T_2$ is consistent. Show:

1. If T is compatible with Q, then T is undecidable.
2. If T is a *true* theory in the vocabulary L_{PA} (i.e. all axioms in T are true), then T is undecidable.

Exercise 14.8.5
*We have seen (and will prove in a precise way in the next chapter) that if T is axiomatizable and complete, then T is decidable. On the other hand, there are decidable (hence axiomatizable) incomplete theories. Show that the following nevertheless holds: Every consistent decidable theory has a complete, decidable consistent extension. [Hint: Use a construction as in the proof of Lindenbaum's Lemma.]

The next five exercises concern theories mentioned in Section 14.3.1.

Exercise 14.8.6 (quantifier elimination 1)
A theory T *has quantifier elimination* if every L_T-formula is equivalent in T to a quantifier-free L_T-formula with at most the same free variables.

1. Show that if every L_T-formula of the form $\exists x \psi$ is equivalent in T to a quantifier-free L_T-formula with at most the same free variables, then T has quantifier elimination. [Hint: write ψ in disjunctive normal form (see Exercise 2.4.6)]
2. Show that if T has quantifier elimination and all quantifier-free sentences are decidable in T (i.e. for all quantifier-free sentences ψ, either $T \vdash \psi$ or $T \vdash \neg\psi$), then T is complete.
3. Verify that the complete—and hence decidable—theory $T_{=10} = \{\exists_{=10} x\, x = x\}$ in the empty vocabulary (Chapter 6.6) does *not* have quantifier elimination.
4. Show that the theory $T^* = \{\exists_{\geqslant n} x\, x = x : n = 1, 2, \ldots\}$ in the empty vocabulary has quantifier elimination, as follows:
   (a) Show that it suffices to show that each formula $\exists x \psi$, where ψ is a conjunction of literals (atomic or negated atomic formulas) is equivalent in T^* to a quantifier-free formula.
   (b) Then show that we can assume these literals all have the form $x = y$ or $x \neq z$, where y, z are variables distinct from x, and use this to draw the desired conclusion.

   Conclude that T^* is complete and decidable (it is the 'theory of infinite domains').

Exercise 14.8.7 (quantifier elimination 2)
*Show that the theory *DeLO* has quantifier elimination. Conclude that *DeLO* is complete and decidable.

[Hint: First eliminate negated literals from conjunctions of literals, by replacing $\neg y < z$ with $y = z \vee z < y$, and $y \neq z$ with $y < z \vee z < y$ (using the totality axiom). Then, the disjuncts of the disjunctive normal form (when $\exists x$ has been distributed inside) have the form $\exists x\theta$, where θ is a conjunction of formulas of the form $z < y$, $z = y$ (these can be moved outside as before), $x < x$, $x = x$, $x < y$, $x = y$, and $y < x$. Proceed from there.]

Exercise 14.8.8 (quantifier elimination 3)
*Show that the theory S in Example 14.3.3 has quantifier elimination.

[Proof outline: Write s^0x for x, and, for $n > 0$, write s^nx for $x'\cdots'$ with n primes. All terms have the form s^nt, where t is either 0 or a variable. For a formula $\exists x\psi$ where ψ is a conjunction of literals we may assume as before that each conjunct contains x. Thus, all literals in ψ may be assumed to have the form $s^nx = s^mt$ or the negation of this. We can furthermore assume t is distinct from x, since $s^nx = s^nx$ is equivalent to $0 = 0$ in S, and for $n \neq m$, $s^nx = s^mx$ is equivalent to $0 \neq 0$ in S. Now distinguish two cases: either all conjuncts are negations, or some conjunct is not a negation. In the first case, show that $\exists x\psi$ is equivalent in S to 0=0. In the second case there is a conjunct δ of the form $s^mx = t$, where t does not contain x. Replace δ by $t \neq 0 \wedge \ldots \wedge t \neq s^{m-1}0$, and replace the equation in each other conjunct, say $(\neg)s^kx = u$, with $(\neg)s^{k+m}x = s^mu$, which becomes $(\neg)s^kt = s^mu$. Explain why this yields a formula not containing x which is equivalent in S to $\exists x\psi$.]

Exercise 14.8.9
Show that the theory S is not finitely axiomatizable, by using the fact, proved in Exercise 6.13.28 by means of the Compactness theorem, that if S were finitely axiomatizable, it would be axiomatized by a finite subset of S.

Exercise 14.8.10
Show how to express in the vocabulary L_{PB} (i.e. without multiplication) the statement "every number is odd or even".

Exercise 14.8.11
Let L_0 be the vocabulary $\{+, \cdot\}$. Show that the individual constant 0 and the unary function symbol $'$ are arithmetically definable in L_0. That is, for $'$ you need to find an L_0-formula $\varphi(x, y)$ such that

- $m = n + 1$ iff $\varphi(\mathbf{n}, \mathbf{m})$ is true
- $\forall x \exists_{=1} y \varphi(x, y)$ is true

and similarly for 0.

Exercise 14.8.12
Prove:

1. $Q \vdash x + y = 0 \rightarrow x = 0 \wedge y = 0$
2. $Q \vdash x \cdot y = 0 \rightarrow x = 0 \vee y = 0$

[Hint: prove the contrapositions, using axiom (Q7).]

Exercise 14.8.13 (proofs of (6) and (9))
The proofs are by induction (in the metalanguage) on m. Reason informally in Q, using (5). For (6), the base step is $Q \vdash x \leqslant 0 \leftrightarrow x = 0$. The induction step is that, assuming $Q \vdash x \leqslant \mathbf{m} \leftrightarrow x = 0 \vee \ldots \vee x = \mathbf{m}$, we have $Q \vdash x \leqslant \mathbf{m}' \leftrightarrow x = 0 \vee \ldots \vee x = \mathbf{m} \vee x = \mathbf{m}'$. The proof of (9) is similar.

Exercise 14.8.14 (proof of (3))
In this exercise we write $\overline{n}$ for the numeral n of n. For example, $\overline{3+5}$ is the term consisting of 0 followed by eight primes; it does not contain the symbol +. Prove:

1. $Q \vdash \overline{n} + \overline{m} = \overline{n+m}$
2. $Q \vdash \overline{n} \cdot \overline{m} = \overline{n \cdot m}$
3. If $n < m$, then $Q \vdash \overline{n} \neq \overline{m}$ and $Q \vdash \overline{n} < \overline{m}$
4. If $n \nless m$, then $Q \vdash \neg \overline{n} < \overline{m}$

[For 1–3, use metalanguage induction on m. For 4, use (6), (8), (9).]
Then prove that when $t(x_1, \ldots, x_n)$ is any term:

5. $Q \vdash t(\overline{k_1}, \ldots, \overline{k_n}) = \overline{v(t(\overline{k_1}, \ldots, \overline{k_n}))}$

and use this to conclude that (3) holds.

Exercise 14.8.15
Consider a model whose domain is $\mathbb{N} \cup \{a, b\}$, where $a, b \notin \mathbb{N}$, and where the individual constant 0 is interpreted as the number 0, and the successor function symbol $'$ is interpreted as the function s^*, where $s^*(n) = n + 1$ for all numbers n, while $s * (a) = a$ and $s^*(b) = b$. Moreover, the addition symbol + is interpreted as the function $+^*$, where $m +^* n = m + n$ for all numbers m, n, and $a +^* n = a, b +^* n = b$, whereas $u +^* a = b$ and $u +^* b = a$ for all u in the domain.

1. Show that axioms (P1) – (P4) and (Q7) are true in this model.
2. Show that the sentence $\forall x(0 + x = x)$ is false in the model.
3. Define a function $\cdot^*$ in the domain such that (P5) and (P6) are true in the expanded model.
4. Conclude that $\forall x(0 + x = x)$ is not a theorem of Q.
5. Show that neither is $\neg\forall x(0 + x = x)$ a theorem of Q.
6. Show that the order relation is not total in this model, i.e. that the sentence $\exists x \exists y(\neg x \leqslant y \wedge \neg y \leqslant x)$ is true in it.

Exercise 14.8.16
*This exercise presupposes some knowledge of cardinal arithmetic. Consider the model whose domain is the cardinal numbers (or the set of cardinal numbers $< \aleph_\omega$), where 0 is interpreted as 0, + and $\cdot$ as cardinal addition and multiplication, and $'$ as the operation +1.

1. Show that all axioms of Q are true in this model.
2. Conclude that $\forall x(x \neq x')$ is not provable in Q. (Even though Q proves $\forall x(x < x')$!)

Exercise 14.8.17 (on Σ_1-soundness)

1. Show that if T is Σ_1-sound, then T is consistent, and check that Σ_1-soundness implies that T does not *dis*prove (prove the negation of) any true Π_1 sentence.
2. Show that if T is an ω-consistent extension of Q, then all Σ_1 sentences provable in T are true. (So the second part of the first incompleteness theorem (Theorem 12.2.3 or Theorem 13.1.17) goes through under this assumption.)

Exercise 14.8.18 (Σ_1-definable functions are Π_1-definable)
Suppose the function f (unary, for simplicity) is arithmetically definable by a Σ_1 formula. Show that f is also arithmetically definable by a Π_1 formula.

[Hint: We have $f(n) = m$ iff $\varphi(\mathbf{n}, \mathbf{m})$ is true. Hence also: $f(n) \neq m$ iff $\exists z(z \neq \mathbf{m} \wedge \varphi(\mathbf{n}, z))$ is true.]

The next three exercises use the Σ_1-completeness of Q.

Exercise 14.8.19
Show the following:

1. A Π_1 sentence φ is true if and only if φ is consistent with Q (i.e. $Q + \varphi$ is consistent).
2. If T extends Q, then T is consistent iff T is Π_1-sound (proves only true generalized Π_1 sentences).
3. Conclude that if Goldbach's Conjecture is undecidable in *PA*, then it is true!

Exercise 14.8.20
If $\varphi(x)$ and $\psi(y)$ are formulas with the free variables shown, let

$$\chi := \forall x(\varphi(x) \rightarrow \exists y_{y \leqslant x}\psi(y))$$
$$\theta := \forall y(\psi(y) \rightarrow \exists x_{x<y}\varphi(x))$$

Show the following.

(a) $PA \vdash \chi \vee \theta$

[Reason in *PA*: assume $\neg\chi$ and $\neg\theta$, and derive a contradiction.]

(b) $PA \vdash \chi \wedge \theta \rightarrow \forall x \neg\varphi(x)$

[Hint: Use the the least number principle in *PA* (Exercise 9.10.3).]

(c) If $\varphi(x)$ and $\psi(y)$ are Δ_0, and $\exists x\varphi(x)$ and $\forall y \neg\psi(y)$ are true, then $PA \vdash \theta$.

[Hint: Show that $\neg\chi$ is a true Σ_1 sentence.]

Exercise 14.8.21
Use Σ_1-completeness and Exercise 14.8.20 (c) to give another proof of Rosser's version of the incompleteness theorem, when T is a consistent recursive extension of *PA* (Theorem 12.3.1).

[Hint: $\psi(y) := Prf_T(y, \ulcorner R \urcorner)$ and $\varphi(x) := Ref_T(x, \ulcorner R \urcorner)$ are Δ_0, where R is as in (13), Chapter 12.3, except that *PA* is replaced by Q . By consistency, $T \vdash R$ implies $T \nvdash \neg R$; now use (13) and Σ_1-completeness to derive a contradiction. And $T \vdash \neg R$ implies $T \nvdash R$; use (13) and Exercise 14.8.20 (c).]

Exercise 14.8.22 (1-consistency)
*A theory T is called *1-consistent* if for every Δ_0 formula $\varphi(x)$ s.t. $T \vdash \neg\varphi(\mathrm{m})$ for all m, we have $T \nvdash \exists x\varphi(x)$. In other words, 1-consistency is ω-consistency for Δ_0 formulas.

1. Show that 1-consistency entails consistency.
2. Prove the following improved version of the first incompleteness theorem:

   If T is a 1-consistent recursive extension of $I\Sigma_1$, and

   $$T \vdash G \leftrightarrow \neg\exists x Prf_T(x, \ulcorner G \urcorner)$$

   then $T \nvdash G$ and $T \nvdash \neg G$.

   [Hint: $T \nvdash G$ is as usual. For the second claim, assume the contrary, use the first claim, (14), and Lemma 14.5.15.]

Exercise 14.8.23 (1-consistency and Σ_1-soundness)
*Let T be a consistent recursive extension of Q. Show the following:

(22) T is 1-consistent iff T proves only true Σ_1 sentences.

[Hint: In both directions, use Σ_1-completeness.]

Exercise 14.8.24
*Show that the formula $Tr_1(y)$ in (15) cannot be equivalent in Q to a Δ_0 formula. [Hint: Compare the proof of Tarski's Theorem (Theorem 7.2.8), and use Lemma 14.5.14.]

Exercise 14.8.25 (partially conservative sentences)
*Let T be a consistent recursive extension of *PA*. We say that a sentence φ is *Π_1-conservative over T* (*Σ_1-conservative over T*) if adding φ as an

axiom doesn't make any new Π_1 sentences (Σ_1 sentences) provable, i.e. if ψ is Π_1 (Σ_1), then $T + \varphi \vdash \psi$ entails $T \vdash \psi$. This holds trivially if $T \vdash \varphi$, so the interesting cases are when $T \nvdash \varphi$.

1. Explain why Con_T is not Π_1-conservative over T.
2. Show that if φ is Π_1-conservative over T and ψ is Σ_1, then φ is Π_1-conservative over $T + \psi$. Similarly with Π_1 and Σ_1 interchanged.
3. Suppose that T is Σ_1-sound and that ψ is Π_1. Show that the following are equivalent:
   (a) ψ is Σ_1-conservative over T
   (b) ψ is true
   (c) $T + \psi$ is consistent

So if T is Σ_1-sound, then Con_T is Σ_1-conservative over T. By the incompleteness theorems, we know that neither Con_T nor $\neg Con_T$ is provable in T. Show:

4. (Kreisel) $\neg Con_T$ is Π_1-conservative over T.

[Proof outline: We use Theorem 14.5.7 (provable Σ_1-completeness). Suppose ψ is Π_1 and $T + \neg Con_T \vdash \psi$; show $T \vdash \psi$. We have

(a) $\quad T \vdash \neg\psi \rightarrow Con_T$

Conclude

(b) $\quad PA \vdash Pr_T(\ulcorner\neg\psi\urcorner) \rightarrow Pr_T(\ulcorner Con_T\urcorner)$

(use (D1), (D2) in Chapter 12.4). Show that it follows (Fact 12.6.3) that

(c) $\quad PA \vdash Pr_T(\ulcorner\neg\psi\urcorner) \rightarrow \neg Con_{T+\neg Con_T}$

By provable Σ_1-completeness, $PA \vdash \neg\psi \rightarrow Pr_T(\ulcorner\neg\psi\urcorner)$, and by the formalized second incompleteness theorem (Exercise 12.10.25), we have $PA + Con_T \vdash Con_{T+\neg Con_T}$. Conclude that

(d) $\quad PA \vdash \neg\psi \rightarrow \neg Con_T$

and hence that $T \vdash \psi$.]

Exercise 14.8.26

1. We saw in Exercise 8.9.29 that there is an effective enumeration of all primitive recursive functions. What is the conclusion if the diagonalization argument in Section 14.7 is applied to this enumeration?
2. Show that there is no effective enumeration of all μ-recursive functions.

15 Computability theory

The incompleteness and undecidability results proved by Gödel, Turing, Church, and others in the 1930s sparked a new discipline in logic that became known as *recursion theory*; today usually called *computability theory*. It abstracts from syntactic objects like sentences or theories, and focuses on properties of the corresponding (Gödel) numbers and sets of numbers. For example, Gödel's proof of the first incompleteness theorem starts from a set of code numbers of theorems of a certain theory T and effectively produces the code number of a sentence (the undecidable sentence G) *not* in that set. Can we give a general description of this property, and of which sets have it? For another example, we have two main examples of non-recursive sets: the set of theorems of T as above, and the (diagonalized) halting problem. How are these related? Is one more 'difficult' that the other? Can we even make sense of such a notion of difficulty?

This final chapter gives a taste of computability theory. In particular, we provide answers to the questions above. For example, we show that the halting problem and the undercidable set of theorems of, say, *PA* are—in a precise sense—*equally* difficult (indeed they can be seen as the same problem), but that there are undecidable problems which are *less* difficult, and others which are *more* difficult.

The main new concept involved in these developments—that of a *recursively enumerable* set—is in fact already implicit in much of what we have said. We have spoken about effectively decidable sets, or problems, coded as sets of numbers, and given two formal definitions of this notion (Definitions 13.1.5 and 13.1.7), which turned out to be extensionally equivalent (Corollary 13.1.11), and which according to the Church-Turing Thesis are exact counterparts of the intuitive notion of effective decidability. Now consider one main example of an *un*decidable set/problem: the set thm_T of (code numbers of) theorems of some axiomatizable extension T of Q. This set, however, although not decidable, is closely tied to a decidable relation; we may call it *semi-decidable*.

There are two ways to think about this notion. The first is that there is a decidable binary relation such that our set is obtained by existential quantification, in this case also called *projection*, from that relation. This is precisely the case for thm_T:

$$thm_T(n) \Leftrightarrow \exists m\, prf_T(m, n)$$

Since $prf_T(m, n)$ is recursive, we can try to find out if $thm_T(n)$ holds by successively deciding $prf_T(0, n)?$, $prf_T(1, n)?$, $prf_T(2, n)?$, ... As soon as we get the answer Yes, we know that $thm_T(n)$ holds. But if $thm_T(n)$ does *not* hold, we never get an answer. A slightly different way of describing the procedure is that we can effectively generate all proofs in T, and check if one of them ends with the sentence φ whose code number is n. Again, if φ is in fact provable in T, we will eventually (after a finite number of steps) find this out, but if not, the procedure goes on forever: it is 'semi-effective'.

The second way to think of semi-decidability is in terms of *enumerations*. If a set can be effectively enumerated there is, as we just saw, a way of testing membership in it, which gives a result whenever the answer is Yes. Enumerability of a (non-empty) set A in the set-theoretic sense (see Appendix 16.4) is the property that there is a surjective function f from N to A, i.e. such that $A = range(f) = \{f(0), f(1), f(2), \ldots\}$. Now we simply add the requirement that f should be *recursive*.

This second idea of semi-decidability entails the first, since if $A = range(f)$, we have:

(1) $\quad n \in A \Leftrightarrow \exists m\, n = f(m)$

and if f is recursive, the relation $n = f(m)$ is recursive. The next section will show that these two ideas in fact give the same result. In that section and in the following ones we provide several additional characterizations of this important notion. In Section 15.2 we apply it to two left-overs from earlier chapters. One is a proof that every axiomatizable and complete theory is decidable—Lemma 7.2.3. To be sure, the informal argument we gave is already convincing. But we shall see that the more abstract proof is even simpler. The second left-over is Theorem 13.1.19, which implies that a relation is recursive iff it is representable in some (hence in every) consistent axiomatizable extension of *PA* (indeed Q). We also obtain a corresponding characterization of recursive enumerability in terms of *weak* representability.

The remaining sections of the chapter give glimpses of the fascinating landscape of computability theory, and more can be found in the exercises. In particular, we study a natural way of comparing the 'difficulty' of unsolvable problems, so-called many-one reducibility.

And we close the circle with a section that reconnects the abstract theory once again with logic, adding a new perspective of the work in earlier chapters.[1]

15.1. Recursively enumerable sets

We use the following terminology, when A is a set of natural numbers.

Definition 15.1.1 (recursively enumerable and semi-recursive sets)

1. A is *recursively enumerable* (often abbreviated *r.e.*, or RE), if $A = \emptyset$ or there is a total recursive function f such that $A = range(f) = \{f(0), f(1), f(2), \ldots\}$.
2. A is *semi-recursive* if there is a recursive relation R such that $n \in A \Leftrightarrow \exists m\, R(n, m)$.

First, we note:

(2) If A is recursive, then A is semi-recursive.

Proof. If A is recursive, the relation R defined by $R(n, m) \Leftrightarrow n \in A \wedge m = m$ is also recursive, and trivially, $n \in A \Leftrightarrow \exists m\, R(n, m)$. □

On the other hand, the set thm_T of any consistent extension of Q is a semi-recursive set which is not recursive (Theorem 14.5.12).

15.1.1. Basic properties

The next theorem gives three important characterizations of recursive enumerability.

Theorem 15.1.2 (basic theorem on recursively enumerable sets) *The following claims about a set A are equivalent:*

(a) *A is recursively enumerable.*

(b) *A is semi-recursive.*

(c) *A is the domain of a partial recursive function (in other words, $A = dom(f) = \{n\colon \exists m\, f(n) = m\}$ for some partial recursive f).*

Proof. (a) ⇒ (b): If $A = \emptyset$, then A is obviously recursive, hence semi-recursive. If $A = range(f)$ for some total recursive f, we saw in (1) that it directly follows that A is semi-recursive.

(b) ⇒ (c): If $n \in A \Leftrightarrow \exists m\, R(n, m)$ for some recursive relation R, it follows that the (partial) recursive function

[1] The main omissions in this overview chapter are relative recursiveness, the notion of Turing reducibility, and the jump operator.

$$f(n) = \mu m\, R(n, m)$$

has A as domain: $n \in dom(f) \Leftrightarrow \exists m\, R(n, m) \Leftrightarrow n \in A$.

(c) $\Rightarrow$ (a): Suppose $A = dom(g)$ for a partial recursive function g. So there is a Turing machine M_e which strongly computes g, but for some arguments the computation may never stop. We give an informal description of a procedure which successively generates a list of numbers which constitute A, when $A \neq \emptyset$:

Step 1: Carry out 1 step in the computation of $g(0)$. If the computation halts within 1 step, add 0 to the list.

Step $n+1$: Carry out $n+1$ steps in each one of the computations of $g(0), \ldots, g(n)$. For any of these that halts within $n+1$ steps, add its *input* to the list.[2]

Now define f as follows:

$$f(0) = \text{the first element of the list}$$

$$f(n+1) = \begin{cases} \mu m\,[m \text{ was added during step} \\ n+1 \text{ and } m \neq f(0), \ldots, f(n)] & \text{if such an } m \text{ exists} \\ f(0) & \text{otherwise} \end{cases}$$

By the Church-Turing Thesis we may conclude that f is recursive, and it follows from the construction that f is total if $A \neq \emptyset$. It is also clear from the construction that $range(f) = dom(g)$. □

So being the range of a *total* recursive function is (for non-empty sets) the same as being the domain of a *partial* recursive function. The proof above used Church-Turing's Thesis, but again it is an *inessential* use: it is often (very) much simpler to describe informally an algorithm for computing a certain function than to explicitly design a Turing machine that computes it, or to show that the function is recursive according to Definition 13.1.7. With a certain amount of experience, one may trust that a direct construction is possible, the details of which, however, would be long and tedious to write down. This way of using the Thesis is very common.

In what follows we shall not distinguish semi-recursivity, recursive enumerability, and being the domain of a partial recursive function; we use the definition best suited for the occasion, and we usually use 'recursively enumerable' as the common label. Here is an application of Theorem 15.1.2 and an earlier result:

---

[2]This sort of procedure is called *dove-tailing*: we want to carry out an infinite number of computations, some of which may never stop, so we cannot do them one at a time, but instead we perform n steps in the first n computations, for $n = 0, 1, 2, \ldots$. Eventually, each step in each computation will be performed.

Fact 15.1.3
In the definition of semi-recursivity, R can be taken as a primitive recursive relation.

Proof. If A is semi-recursive then A is the domain of a partial recursive function f. By Kleene's Normal Form Theorem (Theorem 13.1.10), f has an index e, i.e. we have $f(n) = U(\mu k\, T_1(e, n, k))$. This means that

$$\begin{aligned} n \in A &\Leftrightarrow \exists m(f(n) = m) \\ &\Leftrightarrow \exists m \exists k(T_1(e,n,k) \wedge U(k) = m) \\ &\Leftrightarrow \exists p(T_1(e,n,(p)_1) \wedge U((p)_1) = (p)_0) \quad (\text{let } p = \langle m, k \rangle) \end{aligned}$$

Since T_1 and U are primitive recursive, the relation given by $R(p, n) \Leftrightarrow T_1(e, n, (p)_1) \wedge U((p)_1) = (p)_0$ is also primitive recursive. □

Corollary 15.1.4
A is recursively enumerable if and only if $A = \varnothing$ or $A = range(f)$ for some primitive recursive function f.

Proof. We need to show that if A is recursively enumerable and non-empty, there is a primitive recursive function f such that $A = range(f)$. By Fact 15.1.3 there is a primitive recursive relation R s.t. $n \in A \Leftrightarrow \exists m\, R(n, m)$. Take any number m_0 in A and define g as follows:

$$g(n,m) = \begin{cases} n & \text{if } R(n,m) \\ m_0 & \text{otherwise} \end{cases}$$

Then g is primitive recursive and $range(g) = \{g(n, m) \colon n, m \in \mathbf{N}\} = A$. In order to transform g into a 1-place function we define:

$$f(k) = \begin{cases} g((k)_0, (k)_1) & \text{if } \exists n_{n \leqslant k} \exists m_{m \leqslant k}\, k = \langle n, m \rangle \\ m_0 & \text{otherwise} \end{cases}$$

Then f is primitive recursive. Also, a moment's thought should make it clear that $range(f) = range(g) = A$. □

Exercises 15.14.1 and 15.14.4 – 15.14.6 present further useful properties of recursively enumerable sets. Next comes a nice application of Corollary 15.1.4.

15.1.2. Craig's Theorem

In Chapter 12 we proved the incompleteness theorems and related results for *primitive* recursive extensions of *PA*, i.e. such that ax_T is primitive recursive. In Chapter 13 we defined recursivity and pointed out that the same proofs of incompleteness etc. worked for recursive theories. Since there are recursive sets (and theories) that are not primitive recursive, one might justifiably think that these second versions of the theorems are *stronger*. Curiously, they are not! This is a consequence of a simple but ingenious observation, usually called Craig's Theorem.

The key to this result is the fact, which we ask the reader to prove in Exercise 15.14.5, that a set which is enumerated by a *strictly increasing* primitive recursive function f (such that $m < n$ implies $f(m) < f(n)$) must be primitive recursive.

Theorem 15.1.5 (Craig's Theorem)
For every recursively enumerable theory T (i.e. such that ax_T is recursively enumerable) we can effectively find a primitive recursive theory which is equivalent to T.

Proof. Suppose T is recursively enumerable. By Corollary 15.1.4 there is a primitive recursive function f s.t. $ax_T = \{f(0), f(1), f(2), \ldots\} = \{\#(\varphi_0), \#(\varphi_1), \#(\varphi_2), \ldots\}$, where $\#(\varphi_i) = f(i)$. If ax_T is finite there is nothing to prove, so assume ax_T is infinite. Let

$$T_0 = \{\varphi_0,\ \varphi_0 \wedge \varphi_1,\ \varphi_0 \wedge \varphi_1 \wedge \varphi_2,\ \ldots\}$$

Clearly T_0 and T are equivalent (they prove the same theorems). But ax_{T_0} is enumerated by a strictly increasing function, say g, since we have $\#(\varphi_0) < \#(\varphi_0 \wedge \varphi_1) < \#(\varphi_0 \wedge \varphi_1 \wedge \varphi_2) < \ldots$. It should be obvious that g is primitive recursive.[3] We conclude that ax_{T_0} is primitive recursive. □

Recursive theories are recursively enumerable. Thus:

Corollary 15.1.6
All axiomatizable theories can be axiomatized by primitive recursive sets of axioms.

So it was not necessary, after all, to redo the proofs of the incompleteness theorems for the case of axiomatizable theories: the results follow from the primitive recursive case by Craig's Theorem. This is a nice illustration of the usefulness of recursive function-theoretic notions in logic.

[3] In more detail, g can be defined by primitive recursion from f and primitive recursive functions, as follows, where $\#(\wedge) = n_0$ (recall that $*$ is the concatenation function, and that 1 and 3 are the Gödel numbers of the left and right parenthesis):

$$\begin{cases} g(0) & = & f(0) \\ g(n+1) & = & \langle 1 \rangle * g(n) * \langle n_0 \rangle * f(n+1) * \langle 3 \rangle \end{cases}$$

15.1.3. Sets versus relations

So far we have only talked about sets, but the concept of recursive enumerability, under its various guises, transfers to relations. There are two (equivalent) ways to think about this generalization. The first is to say that a k-ary relation R is semi-recursive if there is a $(k+1)$-ary recursive relation S such that $R(n_1, \ldots, n_k) \Leftrightarrow \exists m\, S(n_1, \ldots, n_k, m)$, and similarly to replace condition (c) in Theorem 15.1.2 by saying that R is the domain of a k-ary partial recursive function. It's a little less clear what to do with the 'listing' definition of recursive enumerability, but that problem disappears on the second approach, which is also more easy to state in a systematic way.

This approach simply uses coding (and decoding), by some of the coding schemes we have seen. For example, OP is a bijection from $\mathbb{N}^2$ to $\mathbb{N}$ (Chapter 8.7.3); if we call it OP_2 we can use it to define a bijection OP_k from $\mathbb{N}^k$ to $\mathbb{N}$, for each $k \geqslant 2$. Thus, the inverse function OP_k^{-1} is a bijection from $\mathbb{N}$ to $\mathbb{N}^k$. All these functions are primitive recursive. Therefore, if we start from a unary (partial) recursive function f, then $f \circ OP_k$ is a k-ary (partial) recursive function, and if g is a k-ary (partial) recursive function, then $OP_k^{-1} \circ g$ is a unary (partial) recursive function.

Now we can revise Definition 15.1.1(a) in the following way: a k-ary relation R (that is, a set of k-tuples of numbers) is recursively enumerable if $R = \varnothing$ or there is a unary total recursive function f such that $R = range(OP_k^{-1} \circ f) = \{OP_k^{-1}(f(0)), OP_k^{-1}(f(1)), \ldots\}$.

We will not go through further details of this, but usually state our results for sets, keeping in mind that a generalization to relations is often straightforward. One way to phrase these facts is that the notion of *dimension* plays no role in computability theory: 1-ary and k-ary relations behave in the same way.[4]

15.2. Post's Lemma

The next result shows that we can define recursivity in terms of recursive enumerability (instead of the other way around, as above).[5]

Theorem 15.2.1 (Post's Lemma)
A set is recursive iff both it and its complement are recursively enumerable.[6]

[4]For a slightly more detailed account, see Rogers 1967, Ch. 5.

[5]Emil Post (1887–1954) was a pioneer in logic, abstract algebra, and theory of recursive functions. Lemma 15.2.1 is occasionally called *Post's Theorem*, but that name is usually given to another, much deeper, result by Post, about the arithmetical hierarchy (Section 15.4).

[6]So the notion of recursive enumerability could be taken as conceptually prior to recursivity, *provided* we have an independent way to define the recursively enumerable

Proof. One direction is trivial: if A is recursive then so is $\overline{A}$, and we have already noted that recursive sets are recursively enumerable. In the other direction, there is an obvious informal argument: if A is enumerated by a recursive function f, and $\overline{A}$ is enumerated by a recursive function g, then we can decide if n belongs to A by simultaneously computing $f(0), f(1), \ldots$ and $g(0), g(1), \ldots$, and stop as soon as one of the computations yields the value n. Since n is either in A or in $\overline{A}$, this will decide if $n \in A$ or not in a finite number of steps.

But let us also give a formal argument not using Church-Turing's Thesis, but instead the fact that both A and $\overline{A}$ are semi-recursive. So suppose there are recursive relations R, S such that $n \in A \Leftrightarrow \exists m R(n,m)$ and $n \in \overline{A} \Leftrightarrow \exists m S(n,m)$. Define

$$f(n) = \mu m(R(n,m) \vee S(n,m))$$

$R \vee S$ is a recursive relation, and since for each n there is m such that $R(n,m) \vee S(n,m)$, f is a total recursive function. Finally, we have

$$n \in A \Leftrightarrow R(n, f(n))$$

which shows that A is recursive. (Recall that substitution of *total* recursive functions in a recursive relation results in a recursive relation; see also Exercise 15.14.33.) The argument for a k-ary relation is completely analogous. □

As a first application, we can as promised prove Theorem 13.1.19, but with Q in place of *PA*. We already know that all recursive relations are representable in Q (Theorem 14.5.11), and hence in every consistent extension of Q; now we must show the converse.

Proof of (the strengthened version of) Theorem 13.1.19. Let T be a consistent recursive extension of Q. Thus, the relation prf_T is recursive. Consider the case of a set A which is representable in T (the case of a k-ary relation is analogous), so there is an arithmetical formula $\psi(x)$ such that $n \in A \Rightarrow T \vdash \psi(\mathbf{n})$ and $n \notin A \Rightarrow T \vdash \neg\psi(\mathbf{n})$. Indeed, since T is consistent, we have

$$n \in A \Leftrightarrow T \vdash \psi(\mathbf{n}) \text{ and } n \notin A \Leftrightarrow T \vdash \neg\psi(\mathbf{n})$$

Now, clearly there are (primitive) recursive functions f_1, f_2 such that $\#(\psi(\mathbf{n})) = f_1(n)$ and $\#(\neg\psi(\mathbf{n})) = f_2(n)$ (cf. the function *sub* from Chapter 11.6). Thus,

$$n \in A \Leftrightarrow \exists m\, prf_T(m, f_1(n)) \text{ and } n \notin A \Leftrightarrow \exists m\, prf_T(m, f_2(n))$$

---

sets, i.e. one that doesn't rely on some notion of computable function (to avoid circularity). Post in fact gave such a definition, in terms of concepts related to derivability in formal systems.

which shows that both A and $\overline{A}$ are semi-recursive. By Theorem 15.2.1, A is recursive, as was to be shown. □

When you think about it, it is quite remarkable that if a relation is representable in some consistent axiomatizable extension of Q, then it is representable (perhaps by another formula) already in Q.

The second application of Post's Lemma is a proof of Lemma 7.2.3: any axiomatizable and complete theory is decidable.

Proof of Lemma 7.2.3. This is almost immediate. When T is axiomatizable, both thm_T and ref_T (the set of Gödel numbers of sentences whose negations are provable in T) are recursively enumerable. Now ref_T is not exactly the complement of thm_T, since there are numbers which are not Gödel numbers of sentences. But the set $sent_{PA}$ of Gödel numbers of sentences in L_{PA} is (primitive) recursive; hence so is its complement, and if T is a complete theory, we have:

$$ref_T \cup \overline{sent_{PA}} = \overline{thm_T}$$

It is easily seen that the union of a recursively enumerable set and a recursive set is recursively enumerable (see Exercise 15.14.1), so the assumptions entail that both thm_T and its complement are recursively enumerable, and hence, by Post's Lemma, thm_T is recursive. □

As we observed in Chapter 7.2.3, this result yields an alternative route to the first incompleteness theorem: if T is a consistent axiomatizable extension of Q, T is incomplete—otherwise T would be decidable, contradicting Theorem 14.5.12(b) (whose proof uses only that all recursive relations are representable in Q). But this proof is less constructive: it gives no concrete example of an undecidable sentence, and it does not lead to the second incompleteness theorem.

15.3. Representability again

According to Theorem 14.5.11, every recursive relation is representable in Q (by a Σ_1 formula). We can use this to give one more characterization of recursive enumerability, analogous to the one we gave for recursivity in Theorem 13.1.19. Recall that a relation R is said to be *weakly representable* in T if there is a formula $\varphi(x_1, \ldots, x_k)$ such that

$$R(n_1, \ldots, n_k) \Leftrightarrow T \vdash \varphi(\mathbf{n}_1, \ldots, \mathbf{n}_k)$$

Lemma 15.3.1

If a relation R is weakly representable in an axiomatizable extension of Q, then R is recursively enumerable.

Proof. Let T be an axiomatizable extension of Q, and suppose the formula $\varphi = \varphi(x_1, \ldots, x_k)$ weakly represents R in T. Let g be a primitive recursive function such that $g(n_1, \ldots, n_k) = \#(\varphi(\mathbf{n}_1, \ldots, \mathbf{n}_k))$. Then:

$$\begin{aligned} R(n_1, \ldots, n_k) &\Leftrightarrow T \vdash \varphi(\mathbf{n}_1, \ldots, \mathbf{n}_k) \\ &\Leftrightarrow \exists m\, \mathit{prf}_T(m, g(n_1, \ldots, n_k)) \end{aligned}$$

The relation $\mathit{prf}_T(m, g(n_1, \ldots, n_k))$ is recursive (since prf_T and g are), so it follows that R is semi-recursive, i.e. recursively enumerable. □

To get a converse of this result we first make an extra assumption. Recall that a theory T is said to be Σ_1*-sound* if all generalized Σ_1 theorems of T are true.

Theorem 15.3.2

(a) *If R is recursively enumerable, then it is weakly representable (by a Σ_1 formula) in every consistent, axiomatizable, and Σ_1-sound extension of Q.*

(b) *If R is recursive, then it is representable (by a Σ_1 formula) in every consistent extension of Q.*

Proof. (b) is already proved (Theorem 14.5.11), and only stated here for comparison. For (a), consider for simplicity the case of a set A. Suppose that A is recursively enumerable, and that T is a consistent, recursive, and Σ_1-sound extension of Q. There is a recursive relation R such that $n \in A \Leftrightarrow \exists m\, R(m, n)$. According to Theorem 14.5.11 there is a Σ_1 formula $\psi(x, y)$ representing R in Q. Thus:

$$\begin{aligned} n \in A &\Rightarrow \exists m\, Q \vdash \psi(\mathbf{m}, \mathbf{n}) \\ &\Rightarrow Q \vdash \exists x \psi(x, \mathbf{n}) \\ &\Rightarrow T \vdash \exists x \psi(x, \mathbf{n}) \end{aligned}$$

Conversely:

$$\begin{aligned} T \vdash \exists x \psi(x, \mathbf{n}) &\Rightarrow \exists x \psi(x, \mathbf{n}) \text{ is true} \quad (\exists x \psi(x, \mathbf{n}) \text{ is generalized } \Sigma_1 \\ &\qquad\qquad \text{and } T \text{ is } \Sigma_1\text{-sound}) \\ &\Rightarrow \exists m \text{ such that } \psi(\mathbf{m}, \mathbf{n}) \text{ is true} \\ &\Rightarrow \exists m\, Q \vdash \psi(\mathbf{m}, \mathbf{n}) \quad (Q \text{ is } \Sigma_1\text{-complete}) \\ &\Rightarrow \exists m\, R(m, n) \\ &\Rightarrow n \in A \end{aligned}$$

□

This proof doesn't work if T is not Σ_1-sound: in that case the assumption that $T \vdash \exists x \psi(x, \mathbf{n})$ does not necessarily imply that there is an m such that $R(m, n)$. But Σ_1-soundness is a rather weak requirement: nothing prevents T from proving lots of false Π_1 sentences.

We have encountered Σ_1-soundness in a similar role before. Exercise 14.8.17 asked the reader to show that the second part of the first incompleteness theorem holds under the assumption that T has the property that all its Σ_1 theorems are true, rather than being ω-consistent, which is stronger.

But we also showed that the assumption of ω-consistency can be replaced by mere consistency, if we instead use Rosser's construction of the self-referential sentence (Chapter 12.3). It turns out that a similar construction works in this case too, giving the following considerable strengthening of Theorem 15.3.2(a):

Theorem 15.3.3
If R is recursively enumerable, then R is weakly representable in every consistent axiomatizable extension of Q.

Proof. See Exercise 15.14.11. □

Corollary 15.3.4
A relation R is recursively enumerable iff it is weakly representable in some (every) consistent axiomatizable extension of Q.

Again, this is a rather remarkable fact, even more so than Theorem 13.1.19: weak representability of a relation R in some bizarre theory that may prove various false statements about numbers (as long as it is consistent, axiomatizable, and extends Q) entails weak representability of R in Q.[7]

By comparison, the corresponding fact about representability and recursivity is straightforward, since representability is *preserved under extensions*, whereas weak representability is not (see below). Accordingly, the proof of Theorem 15.3.3 needs a more complex argument; in fact the weakly representing formula itself is found by an application of the Diagonal Lemma, though in a more general version than the one we used so far.

Summing up, Corollary 15.3.4 gives a new characterization of recursive enumerability, this time in logical terms. As a bonus, we also obtain a new proof of the first incompleteness theorem. To see this, let T be a consistent axiomatizable extension of Q:

Proof that T is incomplete. Let A be a recursively enumerable but nonrecursive set. By Theorem 15.3.3, there is a formula $\varphi(x)$ such that

(a) $\quad n \in A \Leftrightarrow T \vdash \varphi(\mathbf{n})$

But since $\varphi(x)$ does not represent A in T (otherwise A would be recursive), there is $n_0 \notin A$ such that

---

[7]Since $Q \nvdash \forall x\, x' \neq x$ (Exercise 14.8.16), the consistent but Σ_1-unsound theory $Q + \exists x\, x' = x$ is an example.

$$T \nvdash \neg\varphi(\mathbf{n_0})$$

On the other hand, by (a),

$$T \nvdash \varphi(\mathbf{n_0})$$

Thus, $\varphi(\mathbf{n_0})$ is an undecidable sentence in T. □

Note finally that although $\varphi(x)$ weakly represents A in the theory T, the same formula does *not* weakly represent A in the consistent axiomatizable extension $T + \varphi(\mathbf{n_0})$.

15.4. The arithmetical hierarchy

In Chapter 14.5 we met the Δ_0, Σ_1, and Π_1 *formulas*, defined in terms of their syntactic patterns of quantification: Δ_0 formulas have only bounded quantification; Σ_1 (Π_1) formulas have the form $\exists x\psi$ ($\forall x\psi$), where ψ is Δ_0. This can be continued into a formula hierarchy, so that e.g. Σ_2 formulas have the form $\exists x\forall y\psi$ where ψ is Δ_0. In general, a Σ_{n+1} (Π_{n+1}) formula has the form $\exists x\theta$ ($\forall x\theta$), where θ is Π_n (Σ_n).

Now we are interested in the *sets* and relations (and functions) arithmetically defined by such formulas. We could simply say that a set or relation is Δ_0 if it is defined by a Δ_0 formula, and that it is Σ_n (Π_n) if defined by a Σ_n (Π_n) formula. This is sometimes done, but it is more common to start the set/relation hierarchy with the *recursive* sets/relations. We follow that tradition here, in the next definition.

Definition 15.4.1 (arithmetical hierarchy)

(a) A relation R is Σ_0 (also written Π_0 or Δ_0) if it is recursive.

(b) R is Σ_{n+1} (or $R \in \Sigma_{n+1}$) if there is a Π_n relation S such that

$$R(\overline{n}) \Leftrightarrow \exists m\, S(m, \overline{n})$$

R is Π_{n+1} ($R \in \Pi_{n+1}$) if there is a Σ_n relation S such that

$$R(\overline{n}) \Leftrightarrow \forall m\, S(m, \overline{n})$$

(c) R is Δ_n if it is both Σ_n and Π_n. ($\Delta_n = \Sigma_n \cap \Pi_n$)

(d) A function f is Σ_n etc. if its graph G_f is Σ_n etc.

In this definition, we could have allowed sequences of universal or existential quantifiers. For example, a set A defined by

$$n \in A \Leftrightarrow \exists m_1\exists m_2\exists m_3\forall k_1\forall k_2 S(m_1, m_2, m_3, k_1, k_2, n)$$

where S is recursive, is still Σ_2, by *contraction of quantifiers*, as in Exercise 8.9.24, where we observed that

$$\exists m_0 \ldots \exists m_{k-1}\, R(m_0, \ldots, m_{k-1}) \Leftrightarrow \exists m\, R((m)_0, \ldots, (m)_{k-1})$$

and that the 1-ary relation R^* given by $R^*(m) \Leftrightarrow R((m)_0, \ldots, (m)_{k-1})$ is recursive iff R is recursive (similarly for universal quantifiers).

We say that R is *arithmetical* if it is Σ_n or Π_n for some n. The reader may recall that we already said that R is arithmetical if it is arithmetically definable by an arbitrary L_{PA}-formula (Definition 9.8.1). However, there is no conflict, since every L_{PA}-formula φ can be written in *prenex normal form* (Exercise 2.4.28): it is logically equivalent to a formula φ' of the form $Q_1x_1 \ldots Q_mx_m\psi$ with the same free variables, where Q_ix_i is $\forall x_i$ or $\exists x_i$, and ψ is quantifier-free. Since the quantifier-free part defines a (primitive) recursive relation, it follows that φ' mirrors the form of a Σ_n or Π_n relation (allowing sequences of universal or existential quantifiers). Thus, φ defines a Σ_n or Π_n relation.[8]

For the lowest (recursive) level we use Δ_0 or Σ_0. There is a small risk of confusion here, since the set of relations defined by Δ_0 formulas (with only bounded quantification) is a proper subset of the set of recursive relations. Indeed, we have:

Fact 15.4.2
Relations arithmetically definable by Δ_0 formulas are primitive recursive.

Proof. This follows by induction along the build-up of Δ_0 formulas. Atomic formulas define primitive recursive relations, and the set of primitive recursive relations is closed under boolean operations and bounded quantification (Lemma 8.5.2). □

At the next level, however, the differences disappear:

Fact 15.4.3
The following are equivalent:

(a) *R is recursively enumerable.*

(b) *R is Σ_1.*

(c) *R is arithmetically definable by a Σ_1 formula.*

Proof. Consider unary relations (sets) for simplicity. The Σ_1 sets are those we earlier called *semi-recursive*, and Theorem 15.1.2 showed that (a) and (b) are equivalent. To prove that (b) implies (c), suppose A is Σ_1, so there is a recursive relation R such that $n \in A \Leftrightarrow \exists m\, R(m, n)$. By Corollary 14.5.4, R is arithmetically definable by a Σ_1 formula, say $\exists x\, \theta(x, y, z)$. Thus, A is arithmetically definable by $\exists y \exists x\, \theta(x, y, z)$, which, as we have seen, entails that A is definable by a Σ_1 formula.

[8] Σ_n, Π_n, Δ_n are often written Σ^0_n, Π^0_n, Δ^0_n, in contrast with Σ^1_n, Π^1_n, Δ^1_n (the *analytical hierarchy*), which concern sets defined with second-order quantifiers over *sets of numbers* (or functions from numbers to numbers), rather than first-order quantifiers over *numbers*, which is what we consider here. Since we won't discuss second-order quantification, we omit the superscripts.

In the other direction, suppose A is arithmetically defined by a Σ_1 formula $\exists x\psi(x,y)$, where ψ is Δ_0. Then, using Corollary 14.5.8: $n \in A$ iff $\exists x\psi(x,\mathbf{n})$ is true iff $\exists m$ such that $\psi(\mathbf{m},\mathbf{n})$ is true iff $\exists m\ Q \vdash \psi(\mathbf{m},\mathbf{n})$ iff $\exists m\,\exists k\, prf_Q(k,\#(\psi(\mathbf{m},\mathbf{n})))$ iff $\exists m\,\exists k\, S(m,n,k)$, where S is a recursive relation. It follows that A is Σ_1. □

Here are some easy facts about the arithmetical hierarchy.

Fact 15.4.4

(a) *$\Sigma_n \cup \Pi_n \subseteq \Delta_{n+1}$ for all n.*

(b) *R is Σ_n iff $\neg R$ is Π_n.*

(c) *A relation R is Δ_1 iff it is recursive (i.e. Δ_0).*

(d) *A (total) function f is Δ_1 iff it is recursive.*

Proof. For (a), add 'dummy' quantifiers. For example, if a set A is Σ_3, there is a recursive relation S such that

$$n \in A \Leftrightarrow \exists m_1 \forall m_2 \exists m_3\, S(m_1,m_2,m_3,n)$$

Then we also have $n \in A \Leftrightarrow \forall k \exists m_1 \forall m_2 \exists m_3 (S(m_1,m_2,m_3,n \wedge k=k)$, as well as $n \in A \Leftrightarrow \exists m_1 \forall m_2 \exists m_3 \forall k (S(m_1,m_2,m_3,n) \wedge k=k)$, which shows that A is Π_4 as well as Σ_4. (b) follows from the usual logical interaction between $\forall$, $\exists$, and negation. For (c), if R is in $\Sigma_1 \cap \Pi_1$, then both R and $\neg R$ are in Σ_1, hence recursively enumerable, so the result follows from Post's Lemma. For (d), finally, note that it follows from Fact 15.4.3, by taking negations, that a relation is Π_1 iff it is arithmetically definable by a Π_1 formula. And Exercise 14.8.18 showed that a *function* is definable by a Σ_1 formula iff it is definable by a Π_1 formula. Since a function f is Σ_1 (Π_1) iff its graph G_f is Σ_1 (Π_1), (d) follows.[9] □

Now a less obvious, but very useful, result. First, a definition.

Definition 15.4.5

Let Γ be a class of k-ary relations. We say that a $(k+1)$-ary relation S *enumerates* Γ if for every $R \in \Gamma$ there is a number e such that for all $n_1,\ldots,n_k$, $R(n_1,\ldots,n_k) \Leftrightarrow S(e,n_1,\ldots,n_k)$.

Theorem 15.4.6 (arithmetical enumeration theorem)

For all $k,n > 0$, there is a $(k+1)$-ary Σ_n relation S which enumerates the class of k-ary Σ_n relations. Similarly for Π_n.

Proof. For simplicity, take $n = 2$; the general case is similar. If R is a k-ary Π_2 relation, there is a $(k+2)$-ary recursive relation P such that for all $n_1,\ldots,n_k = \overline{n}$, we have

[9] Note that claim (d) is not an immediate consequence of claim (c). For a shorter proof of claim (d), see Exercise 15.14.12.

$$R(\overline{n}) \Leftrightarrow \forall m_1 \exists m_2\, P(m_1, m_2, \overline{n})$$

Let c_P be the characteristic function of P, and recall the T_n predicates from Chapter 13.1.3. Since c_P is total and recursive, there is by the Normal Form Theorem (Theorem 13.1.10) a number e such that

$$\begin{aligned} R(\overline{n}) &\Leftrightarrow \forall m_1 \exists m_2\, c_P(m_1, m_2, \overline{n}) = 1 \\ &\Leftrightarrow \forall m_1 \exists m_2\, \exists s (T_{k+2}(e, m_1, m_2, \overline{n}, s) \wedge U(s) = 1) \\ &\Leftrightarrow \forall m_1 \exists p\, (T_{k+2}(e, m_1, (p)_0, \overline{n}, (p)_1) \wedge U((p)_1) = 1) \\ &\Leftrightarrow S(e, \overline{n}) \end{aligned}$$

So we see that S enumerates the class of k-ary Π_2 relations, and that S itself is Π_2. For the case of k-ary Σ_2 relations, use $\neg S$. □

Now we can show that the arithmetical hierarchy is *proper*:[10]

Theorem 15.4.7 (arithmetical hierarchy theorem)
For every $n > 0$ there is a set A in $\Pi_n - \Sigma_n$, and a set B in $\Sigma_n - \Pi_n$.

Proof. Let S be a binary Π_n relation enumerating the Π_n sets. Such an S exists by the arithmetical enumeration theorem. We use a diagonalization argument, and define the set A by letting, for all k,

(a) $\quad k \in A \Leftrightarrow S(k, k)$

Since S is Π_n, so is A. Furthermore, A is not Σ_n, for otherwise $\overline{A}$ would be Π_n, and then there would be a number e such that for all k,

(b) $\quad k \notin A \Leftrightarrow S(e, k)$.

But with $k = e$, (a) and (b) result in a contradiction. So $A \in \Pi_n - \Sigma_n$, and consequently, $\overline{A} \in \Sigma_n - \Pi_n$. □

It follows that

(a) Δ_n is a proper subset of Σ_n, and a proper subset of Π_n;
(b) Σ_n is a proper subset of Σ_{n+1}, and Π_n is a proper subset of Π_{n+1}.

Now consider the case $n = 1$, when R is a set A. As in the proof of the arithmetical enumeration theorem we get a number d such that

$$n \in A \Leftrightarrow \exists m \exists s (T_2(d, m, n, s) \wedge U(s) = 1)$$

But in this case there is an even simpler description of A, using the fact that A is recursively enumerable, and hence the domain of a partical

[10] Exercise 15.14.16 strengthens this to show that the inclusion in Fact 15.4.4(a) is proper for all n.

recursive function g. If we instead let e be the Gödel number of a Turing machine that computes g, we have,

$$\begin{aligned} n \in A &\Leftrightarrow g \text{ is defined} \\ &\Leftrightarrow \exists s\, T_1(e, n, s) \end{aligned}$$

This relates to the *halting problem* discussed in Chapter 14.7: to decide whether the Turing machine with code number e eventually halts, when started on input n:

$$H(e, n) \Leftrightarrow \exists s T_1(e, n, s)$$

The diagonalization in the proof of the hierarchy theorem now gives a set K such that

(3) $\quad n \in K \Leftrightarrow \exists s T_1(n, n, s)$

And in exactly the same way we see that K is not recursive: otherwise $\overline{K}$ would be recursive, so there would be a number e such that

$$n \notin K \Leftrightarrow \exists m T_1(e, n, m)$$

But with $n = e$ we obtain

$$e \notin K \Leftrightarrow \exists y T_1(e, e, y) \Leftrightarrow e \in K$$

a contradiction. So K is a non-recursive recursively enumerable set, whereas $\overline{K}$ is not even recursively enumerable (by Posts's Lemma). In other words, $K \in \Sigma_1 - \Pi_1$, and $\overline{K} \in \Pi_1 - \Sigma_1$.

From now on we shall identify K with the halting problem, as is usually done in the literature. Some examples of sets higher up in the arithmetical hierarchy are given in Exercise 15.14.18.

15.5. *Hilbert's 10th problem

In this section (which will not be used later on) we pause to look at another famous unsolvable problem, and its connection with the recursively enumerable sets. A *Diophantine equation* has the form

$$p(x_1, \ldots, x_n) = 0$$

where $p(x_1, \ldots, x_n)$ is a *polynomial* in the *unknowns* $x_1, \ldots, x_n$, formed with addition and multiplication with integer (positive or negative) *parameters*. Some examples:

(4) $\quad x - 15y^2 = 0$

(5) $\quad x^2 + y^2 - z^2 = 0$

(6) $\quad x^6 + y^6 - z^6 = 0$

(7) $2x^4 - y^2 - 1 = 0$

Finding the solutions of such equations, or establishing that they have no solutions, has been a central area in mathematics for centuries. In 1900 Hilbert posed as problem number 10 in a list of outstanding mathematical problems, to find a method by which one could decide whether an arbitrary Diophantine equation has a solution or not. By 'method' he meant something like an algorithm.

Equation (4) has infinitely many solutions: for every $y = n$, let $x = 15 \cdot n^2$. Likewise, (5) has infinitely many solutions, as Pythagoras' Theorem shows, it describes the relation between the lengths of the sides of a right triangle. On the other hand, equation (6) has no solutions in the positive integers; this is a consequence of Fermat's Theorem—which as we noted (Chapter 12.9.1) was proved in 1995 with methods far beyond elementary number theory—saying that for no natural number $n > 2$ are there positive numbers x, y, z such that $x^n + y^n = z^n$. Equation (7) has exactly the following two solutions: $x = y = 1$, and $x = 13$, $y = 239$. This was proved in 1942, with complicated number-theoretic reasoning.

Finding solutions to Diophantine equations can be easy or impossibly difficult. Hilbert's 10th problem is not about finding solutions, but about showing whether or not a solution exists. A first observation is that the problem can be restricted to solutions in the natural numbers (Exercise 15.14.13). Next, it is easy to see that the problem is recursively enumerable. This is because each claim of the form

(*) "$x_1 = k_1, \ldots, x_n = k_n$ is a solution to $p(x_1, \ldots, x_n) = 0$"

for given natural numbers $k_1, \ldots, k_n$, is decidable (just calculate). We can effectively enumerate the set of all Diophantine equations, and so we can effectively enumerate the set of all *solvable* Diophantine equations, by enumerating the claims of the form (*) and, at each step, deleting it if the claim is false. So this set (suitably coded) is recursively enumerable. This is of course an informal argument, but it can easily be made precise.

Now, for every Diophantine equation $p(x_1, \ldots, x_n, y) = 0$, the set D_p of numbers m such that $p(x_1, \ldots, x_n, y) = 0$ is solvable with $y = m$ is recursively enumerable: we can generate as before the solvable equations of the form $p(x_1, \ldots, x_n, m) = 0$, and put m in D_p whenever such an equation is found. A set of natural numbers is called *Diophantine* if it is of the form D_p for some equation $p(x_1, \ldots, x_n, y) = 0$. Clearly, Diophantine sets are recursively enumerable.

After 21 years of work by Martin Davis, Julia Robinson, Hilary Putnam, and, for the final step, Yuri Matiyasevič, the remarkable fact, usually called the MRDP Theorem, was proved in 1970 that *every* recursively enumerable set is Diophantine. This is yet another characterization of recursive enumerability:

Theorem 15.5.1 (MRDP Theorem)
A set is recursively enumerable iff it is Diophantine.

This has the immediate consequence that Hilbert's 10th problem is unsolvable: otherwise every recursively enumerable set would be recursive, but we know that is not the case. For another remarkable consequence, see Exercise 15.14.14.

Finally, observe that a Diophantine equation is basically an atomic L_{PA}-formula. Given $p(x_1, \ldots, x_n) = 0$, just move the terms with negative coefficients to the right-hand side. For example,

$$2x^4 - y^2 - 1 = 0$$

becomes

$$2x^4 = y^2 + 1$$

which is the atomic formula $\mathbf{2} \cdot x \cdot x \cdot x \cdot x = y \cdot y + \mathbf{1}$. The existence of a solution thus amounts to the truth of the formula $\exists x \exists y\, \mathbf{2} \cdot x \cdot x \cdot x \cdot x = y \cdot y + \mathbf{1}$. This is a generalized Σ_1 formula, but of a very simple kind. Recall that Σ_1 formulas have the form $\exists x \psi$, where ψ is Δ_0. But Δ_0 formulas may be quite complex, with lots of bounded quantifications. By contrast, the MRDP Theorem shows that the following holds:

(8) *A* is recursively enumerable iff it is defined by a formula of the form $\exists x_1 \ldots \exists x_n \psi$, where ψ is quantifier-free.

This is a much more remarkable characterization of recursive enumerability that the one equating it with being Σ_1. Moreover, n, i.e. the number of variables, in (8) is small; currently it it is known that $n = 9$ is sufficient.

15.6. Universal Turing machines

Chapter 13.2.2 sketched a coding of Turing machines. Let us modify it so that *every* number is the code of some machine: choose a fixed machine, say with code number k_0, and then define a primitive recursive function $\tilde{n}$ such that if n is not the number of a Turing machine (under the old coding), we let $\tilde{n} = k_0$. If we then replace e by $\tilde{e}$ in the definition of the relation *suit* and the function *apply* in Chapter 13.2.2 (the other definitions are as before), all the results will still hold, in particular Kleene's Normal Form Theorem (Theorem 13.1.10), but we no longer need to state the proviso "if e is the Gödel number of a Turing machine, then ... ", since *all* numbers have that property.

Let M_e be the Turing machine with Gödel number e. So

$$M_0, M_1, M_2, \ldots$$

is an enumeration of all Turing machines. Every machine computes, for each $k \geqslant 1$, a k-ary partial function. We shall use the following notation.

Definition 15.6.1 (indices of partial recursive functions)
Let

$$\{e\}^k$$

be the k-ary function computed by M_e. Thus,

(9) $\{0\}^k, \{1\}^k, \{2\}^k, \ldots$

is an enumeration of all k-ary (partial) computable, i.e. recursive, functions. When $F = \{e\}^k$, we say that e is an *index* of F.

We note that every k-ary partial recursive function occurs infinitely often in the list (9). Indeed, for any number e we can effectively generate infinitely many new indices for $\{e\}^k$, that is, infinitely many numbers e' such that $\{e\}^k = \{e'\}^k$. To see this, let k be the largest number such that a state q_k occurs in the instructions of M_e, and then successively add 'dummy' instructions $q_{k+1}11q_{k+1}$, $q_{k+2}11q_{k+2}$, ... So we obtain infinitely many new machines, but the new instructions are never used in computations. This fact is sometimes called the *Padding Lemma*.

The enumeration (9) is effective. In particular, it follows from Theorem 13.1.10 (b) that the partial function F^1 of two variables,

$$F^1(e, n) = \{e\}^1(n)$$

is recursive. So there is a Turing machine, say M, computing F^1. Such a machine is called a *universal Turing machine*. It can compute *all* 1-ary computable (partial) functions. Intuitively, it works as follows: given an input (e, n) it first finds the Turing machine with number e, i.e. M_e, and then runs M_e on input n. So in this sense M acts like a modern programmable computer: given a program it computes the output of that program (if any) for all appropriate inputs.

More generally, there is a $(k+1)$-ary partial recursive universal function F^k that 'simulates' all k-ary partial recursive functions: for all e and all $n_1, \ldots, n_k$,

(10) $F^k(e, n_1, \ldots, n_k) = \{e\}^k(n_1, \ldots, n_k)$

The facts described so far in this section are often summarized as the *Enumeration Theorem*, and go back to work by Post, Turing, and Kleene. They all follow easily from the Normal Form Theorem, due to Kleene in 1938. As we saw in Section 15.4, there are corresponding results for higher levels in the arithmetical hierarchy, but for now we focus on the Σ_1 level.

When F and G are partial functions,[11] we must be clear about what

(11) $F(\overline{n}) = G(\overline{n})$

means. Here we take it to mean that *either* both $F(\overline{n})$ and $G(\overline{n})$ are undefined, *or* both are defined and have the same value. The usual equality between the values of total functions is a special case.[12]

Another special case to note is when one side of the equality is always defined. For example, it is common to *define* a partial function F in the following format, where R is some given relation:

(12) $F(n) = 0 \text{ iff } R(n)$

This means that if $R(n)$ holds, $F(n)$ is defined and has the value 0, but if $R(n)$ does not hold, then $F(n)$ is undefined. (12) could not be taken as a definition of a total function (unless $R(n)$ holds for all n), since we have not specified any value for n such that $\neg R(n)$. But once it is stipulated that (12) is a *definition* of F, it specifies a unique partial function. Moreover, if R is recursively enumerable, F is recursive.[13]

Consider again the function

$$G(n) = \{n\}^1(n) + 1$$

As we have pointed out, this diagonalization does not lead to contradiction. Instead, it follows that if e is an index of G, i.e. $G = \{e\}^1$, then G must be *undefined* for the argument e. (Otherwise, we would have $\{e\}^1(e) = G(e) = \{e\}^1(e) + 1$, which *is* a contradiction.) Thus, G is necessarily a *partial* recursive function.

As a first application, we can prove the result, promised in Chapter 13.1.2, that the class of partial recursive functions is closed under definition by cases (see also Exercise 15.14.7):

Fact 15.6.2
Let $S_1, \ldots, S_k$ be recursive relations s.t. for every $\overline{n}$ there is exactly one i s.t. $S_i(\overline{n})$ holds. If $G_1, \ldots, G_k$ are partial recursive functions, and

$$F(\overline{n}) = \begin{cases} G_1(\overline{n}) & \text{if } \; S_1(\overline{n}) \\ \cdot & \\ \cdot & \\ G_k(\overline{n}) & \text{if } \; S_k(\overline{n}) \end{cases}$$

[11] From now on, we often use capital $F, G, H, \ldots$ to indicate that the functions may be partial, and $f, g, h, \ldots$ for total functions.

[12] The literature sometimes uses a different symbol, such as $\simeq$, for this relation; here we stick to =, understood as just explained. So $F(\overline{n}) \neq G(\overline{n})$, i.e. not $F(\overline{n}) = G(\overline{n})$, means that either one of F, G is defined for the argument $\overline{n}$ and the other is not, or both are defined but the values differ. Note also that the relation $F(\overline{n}) = G(\overline{n})$, understood in this way, is still reflexive, symmetric, and transitive.

[13] This is again a consequence of the Normal Form Theorem; see also Exercise 15.14.6.

then F is a partial recursive function.

Proof. Let $G_i = \{e_i\}^p$ for $1 \leqslant i \leqslant k$ (where F is p-ary), and define

$$h(\overline{n}) = \begin{cases} e_1 & \text{if} \quad S_1(\overline{n}) \\ \cdot & \\ \cdot & \\ e_k & \text{if} \quad S_k(\overline{n}) \end{cases}$$

h is a total recursive function, by Lemma 13.1.8. And we have

$$F(\overline{n}) = \{h(\overline{n})\}^p(\overline{n}) = F^p(h(\overline{n}), \overline{n})$$

where F^p is the universal function from (10). Since F^p and h are recursive, it follows that F is recursive. □

15.7. The s-m-n theorem

The following observation seems trivial, but is in fact extremely useful. Suppose you have a recursive 2-ary function F, possibly partial, and want, for each k, to form the 1-ary function F_k defined by $F_k(p) = F(k, p)$ for all numbers p. That is, you fix the first argument of F. Clearly each F_k is also recursive, and what's more, one can find an index of F_k uniformly from k and the index of F. The general case, given in the next result, is known as the *s-m-n hteorem*:

Theorem 15.7.1 (s-m-n theorem)
For all $m \geqslant 1$ and all n there is a one-one primitive recursive $(n+1)$-ary function S^m_n such that for all $e, k_1, \ldots, k_n, p_1, \ldots, p_m$, we have:[14]

$$\{S^m_n(e, k_1, \ldots, k_n)\}^m(p_1, \ldots, p_m) \quad = \quad \{e\}^{m+n}(k_1, \ldots, k_n, p_1, \ldots, p_m)$$

Proof. As above we look at the case $m = n = 1$; the general case is similar. The proof uses Church-Turing's Thesis, which with some work can be replaced by an explicit construction. We are given a number e, which we decode to find the instructions for Turing machine M_e, and a number k. The task is to describe another machine which for every p computes the value $\{e\}^2(k, p)$, when that value is defined. Clearly, it suffices to represent the pair (k, p) on the tape and then start M_e on this input. This construction is describable in a uniform way, which means that a Gödel number $S^1_1(e, k)$ of the new machine can be computed from e and k; indeed, with the coding machinery for Turing machines described in Chapter 13.2.2 it is easy to see that S^1_1 is

[14]Where an $(n+1)$-ary function f is one-one if $(e, k_1, \ldots, k_n) \neq (e', k'_1, \ldots, k'_n)$ implies that $f(e, k_1, \ldots, k_n) \neq f(e', k'_1, \ldots, k'_n)$.

primitive recursive. In fact, doing this in detail reveals that S_1^1 is also one-one. But we can avoid those details by using the Padding Lemma mentioned after Definition 15.6.1: this effectively generates infinitely many new indices for machines computing the function $\{S_1^1(e,k)\}^1$. So if we enumerate the pairs $\langle e, k\rangle$, say in the one-one fashion given by the *OP* function, we can at each step choose the value $S_1^1(e,k)$ to be distinct from all previous values. □

Here is an easy application of the s-m-n theorem.

Example 15.7.2
We know that the product of two partial recursive function (defined pointwise) is again a partial recursive function. The s-m-n theorem gives us an index of the product $F_1 \cdot F_2$, given indices, say, d and e, for F_1 and F_2, as follows. By the Normal Form Theorem, the function

$$H(d,e,n) = \{d\}^1(n) \cdot \{e\}^1(n)$$

is recursive. So by the s-m-n theorem, there is a primitive recursive function g (namely, $g(d,e) = S_2^1(p,d,e)$, where $H = \{p\}^3$) such that

$$\{g(d,e)\}^1(n) = \{d\}^1(n) \cdot \{e\}^1(n)$$

Here is a slightly more involved application, which we shall need later. Recall the set K from (3).

Fact 15.7.3
There is a primitive recursive function g such that if $n \in K$, then $\{g(n)\}^1$ is a total function, and if $n \notin K$, then $\{g(n)\}^1$ is the everywhere undefined function.

Proof. The trick is to use the 2-ary partial function $H(n,m) = \{n\}^1(n)$, whose value, when defined, does not depend on the second argument m. Thus, if $n \in K$, then $H(n,m)$ is defined for all m, and if $n \notin K$, $H(n,m)$ is undefined for all m. H is a recursive partial function, so it has an index e: $H = \{e\}^2$. By the s-m-n theorem, we have, for all n, m,

$$\{S_1^1(e,n)\}^1(m) = \{e\}^2(n,m) = H(n,m)$$

So g, defined by $g(n) = S_1^1(e,n)$ for all n, is primitive recursive and has the desired property. □

15.8. Enumerating the r.e. sets

Since $\{0\}^1, \{1\}^1, \{2\}^1, \ldots$ is an (effective) enumeration of all 1-ary partial recursive functions, we obtain through Theorem 15.1.2 (c) a corresponding (effective) enumeration of all recursively enumerable sets.

Definition 15.8.1 (indices of r.e. sets)
Define

$$W_e = dom(\{e\}^1) = \{n\colon \exists m\, T_1(e, n, m)\}$$

Then $W_0, W_1, W_2, \ldots$ is an enumeration of all recursively enumerable sets. If $A = W_e$, we say that e is an *index* of A.

For example, there is an index of K, i.e. a number e such that

$$K = W_e = \{n\colon n \in W_n\}$$

but $\overline{K}$ does not occur in the list $W_0, W_1, W_2, \ldots$. As we have seen, the latter claim says that the halting problem is unsolvable. We can now give a maximally short and elegant proof of this fact: Suppose that for some number e_0 we had $\overline{K} = W_{e_0}$. Thus, for all n,

$$n \in W_{e_0} \Leftrightarrow n \notin W_n$$

But this is a contradiction for $n = e_0$! □

There is a similarity between this argument and the argument in Russell's Paradox (Appendix 16.5.2). Russell considered the set of all sets not belonging to themselves, and $\overline{K}$ is the set of numbers that do not belong to the recursively enumerable set they encode. But since $\overline{K}$ is not recursively enumerable, there is no paradox in the latter case.

We have two basic ways of characterizing the r.e. sets: as sets of the form W_n, i.e. *domains* of partial recursive functions, and as *ranges* of total recursive functions (when non-empty). We can now say a bit more about how these two relate. Looking closely at the proof of the basic Theorem 15.1.2, one can see that if we are given a partial recursive function $\{n\}^1$, not only can we write down instructions for a function f that enumerates $dom(\{n\}^1) = W_n$, but we can find an index for f *uniformly* from n. In other words (heavily using the Church-Turing Thesis), there is a total recursive function, say, ρ, such that $f = \{\rho(n)\}^1$. The only snag is that we must *presuppose* that $W_n \neq \varnothing$: as we will see, there is no effective procedure for deciding this.[15]

We state these facts, without further ado, as a corollary (to Theorem 15.1.2):

[15]That is, the set $\{n\colon W_n \neq \varnothing\}$ is (recursively enumerable but) not recursive.

Corollary 15.8.2
There is a total recursive function ρ such that for all n,
(a) $W_n = range(\{\rho(n)\}^1)$,
(b) *if* $W_n \neq \varnothing$, *then* $\{\rho(n)\}^1$ *is total.*

Next, there is a useful version of the s-m-n theorem for recursively enumerable relations worth spelling out:

Theorem 15.8.3 (s-m-n theorem for r.e. relations)
If R is an $(m+1)$-ary recursively enumerable relation, there is a one-one primitive recursive function g such that for all $k_1, \ldots, k_m$,

$$n \in W_{g(k_1,\ldots,k_m)} \text{ iff } R(k_1, \ldots, k_m, n)$$

Proof. Since R is recursively enumerable there is partial recursive function F such that $R = dom(F)$, i.e.

$$R(k_1, \ldots, k_m, n) \text{ iff } F(k_1, \ldots, k_m, n) \text{ is defined}$$

By the s-m-n theorem for functions, with $F = \{e\}^{m+1}$, we have

$$\{S_1^m(e, k_1, \ldots, k_m)\}^1(n) = F(k_1, \ldots, k_m, n)$$

So g defined by $g(k_1, \ldots, k_m) = S_1^m(e, k_1, \ldots, k_m)$ is the function we are looking for. □

We end this section with a technical fact that will be used later.

Lemma 15.8.4
Let F be a partial recursive function of two variables. Then there is a primitive recursive function h s.t. for all e and n, $\{h(e)\}^1$ is total and

$$\text{(a)} \qquad W_{\{h(e)\}^1(n)} = \begin{cases} \{F(e,n)\} & \text{if } F(e,n) \text{ is defined and } n \in K \\ \varnothing & \text{otherwise} \end{cases}$$

Proof. On the right-hand side, $\{F(e,n)\}$ is the singleton set whose only member is the number $F(e,n)$. What we are looking for is a primitive recursive h such that for all m, e, n, $\{h(e)\}^1$ is total and

$$\text{(b)} \qquad m \in W_{\{h(e)\}^1(n)} \text{ iff } m = F(e,n) \text{ and } n \in K$$

(Check that (b) implies (a).) Let $R(e,n,m) \Leftrightarrow m = F(e,n) \wedge n \in K$. Then R is recursively enumerable, so by Theorem 15.8.3 there is a primitive recursive function g such that

$$m \in W_{g(e,n)} \text{ iff } R(e,n,m)$$

By the s-m-n theorem for functions, there is a primitive recursive h such that $\{h(e)\}^1(n) = g(e,n)$. It follows that h is our desired function.
□

15.9. *The Fixed Point Theorem

The natural numbers play a double role in computability theory: on the one hand as the usual objects studied in number theory, and on the other as codes for Turing machines, formulas, proofs, etc. That double role is instrumental for the self-referential or diagonal constructions lying at the heart of this area of logic. For example, we have $n \in K \Leftrightarrow \exists m T_1(n, n, m)$, and here the first argument of T_1 is a code number of a Turing machine, whereas the second is just an element (or not) of a set of numbers. A stark illustration of this phenomenon is the Fixed Point Theorem we prove in this section.

A *fixed point* of a function f is an argument m such that $f(m) = m$. But if we think of numbers as coding partial recursive functions, a fixed point is rather a number e such that e and $f(e)$ code the same partial function, that is, $\{f(e)\}^1 = \{e\}^1$. Let f be a total recursive function. Does it have a fixed point in this sense? That might seem to be a pure accident, perhaps depending on the particular method chosen to code partial recursive functions (i.e. Turing machines). Surprisingly, it is actually a deep fact about recursive functions that (regardless of which coding is used) such a fixed point always exists:

Theorem 15.9.1 (Fixed Point Theorem (Kleene, 1938))
If f is a unary total recursive function, there is a number e such that $\{f(e)\}^1 = \{e\}^1$, and thus $W_{f(e)} = W_e$.

Proof. The Fixed Point Theorem is also called the *Recursion Theorem*. We prove the following slight reformulation (often called *Kleene's Second Recursion Theorem*)

(13) If F is a binary partial recursive function, there is a number e such that for all n, $F(e, n) = \{e\}^1(n)$.

The theorem follows from (13) by letting $F(m, n) = \{f(m)\}^1(n)$. We prove (13) by two diagonalizations. *First diagonalization*: let $G(m, n) = F(S^1_1(m, m), n)$. G is a partial recursive function, so it has an index b, i.e. $G = \{b\}^2$. *Second diagonalization*: let $e = S^1_1(b, b)$. Then we have, using the s-m-n theorem for the second equality:

$$\{e\}^1(n) = \{S^1_1(b, b)\}^1(n) = \{b\}^2(b, n) = F(S^1_1(b, b), n) = F(e, n)$$

□

The proof is short but rather mysterious. The mystery can be unraveled somewhat by describing informally the Turing machine one needs to construct, given f, but we won't try that here. Suffice it to say that the Fixed Point Theorem in a way embodies the central use of diagonalization in computability theory, and that it has many important applications. We give a simple application below, some more in the exercises, and a deeper application in Section 15.11.

A different proof of the Fixed Point Theorem is outlined in Exercise 15.14.21. More general versions of Theorem 15.9.1 are presented in Exercise 15.14.22.

Here is another useful version of the Fixed Point Theorem:

(14) If R is a binary recursively enumerable relation, there is a number e such that for all n, $n \in W_e \Leftrightarrow R(e, n)$.

Proof. By the s-m-n theorem for recursively enumerable relations (Theorem 15.8.3), there is a (primitive) recursive function f such that for all n we have $n \in W_{f(m)} \Leftrightarrow R(m, n)$. Now apply Theorem 15.9.1 to f. □

Consider this question: Is there a number m such that $W_m = \{m\}$, i.e. such that the Turing machine with code m halts exactly on the input m? Again, it may seem totally accidental and dependent on coding if such a number exists or not. But the Fixed Point Theorem shows that this number *must* exist:

(15) There is a number m such that $W_m = \{m\}$.

Proof. Apply (14) to the relation $R(m, n) \Leftrightarrow m = n$. (!) □

For some similar facts, see Exercises 15.14.23 – 15.14.27.

15.10. m-reducibility

A common way of showing that a certain problem is *un*solvable is to *reduce* a known unsolvable problem to it. For example, we showed in Chapter 14.3 that the validity problem for predicate logic—i.e. the set of (Gödel numbers of) logically true sentences—is undecidable by reducing the set of (Gödel numbers of) theorems in a certain theory PA_0 to it: we proved that *if* thm_{FOL} were recursive, *then* the set thm_{PA_0} would also be recursive, and we had already proved that the latter set is *not* recursive.

Similarly, if we can reduce the halting problem, i.e. the set K, to a problem coded as a set A, then we know that A is not recursive. But what exactly does "reduce" mean? Here is one very natural idea:

Definition 15.10.1 (m-reducibility and 1-reducibility (Post, 1944))
A set A is *m-reducible* to a set B, written

$$A \leqslant_m B$$

if there is a total recursive function g s.t. for all n, $n \in A \Leftrightarrow g(n) \in B$. If g is one-one, we say that A is *1-reducible* to B, and write $A \leqslant_1 B$.

Intuitively, thinking of A and B as *problems*, $A \leqslant_m B$ says "B is at least as hard to solve as A". $A \leqslant_1 B$ implies $A \leqslant_m B$, but one can show that the converse fails. We can now observe:

Fact 15.10.2

(a) *If $A \leqslant_m B$ and A is not recursive, then B is not recursive. In particular, if $K \leqslant_m A$, then A is not recursive.*

(b) *If $A \leqslant_m B$ and B is recursively enumerable, so is A.*

Proof. Suppose g is recursive and $n \in A \Leftrightarrow g(n) \in B$. It follows immediately that if B is recursive, then so is A, so (a) holds. As to (b), suppose $B = W_e$ for some e. Then $n \in A \Leftrightarrow g(n) \in W_e \Leftrightarrow \exists m\, T_1(e, g(n), m)$, which shows that A is recursively enumerable. □

Recall the set *Tot* from Chapter 14.7:

$$\mathit{Tot} = \{n\colon \{n\}^1 \text{ is a total function}\} = \{n\colon W_n = \mathbb{N}\}$$

Looking back at the proof of Fact 15.7.3, we see that it in effect says

(16) $K \leqslant_m \mathit{Tot}$

(indeed, $K \leqslant_1 \mathit{Tot}$, since the s-m-n theorem 15.7.1 yields one-one functions). That is, the halting problem is m-reducible to *Tot*, which immediately entails that *Tot* is not recursive (as was proved by a different argument in Chapter 14.7). So even though neither K nor *Tot* are decidable, i.e. recursive, we can still *compare* the difficulty of the corresponding problems. We will see presently that *Tot* is not even recursively enumerable, which entails, by Proposition 15.10.4 below, that $\mathit{Tot} \not\leqslant_m K$. So we now have one precise way of saying that the problem of deciding if a partial recursive function is total, i.e. *Tot*, is *more difficult* than the halting problem, i.e. K.

Actually, for the last statement to make sense we should check that we really obtain an *ordering* of difficulty. We do this next.

(17) $\leqslant_m$ is a *preorder*, i.e. a reflexive and transitive relation between subsets of $\mathbb{N}$. The same holds for $\leqslant_1$.

Proof. Reflexivity: for any set A, $A \leqslant_1 A$ via the identity function. Transitivity: if $n \in A \Leftrightarrow g(n) \in B$, and $m \in B \Leftrightarrow h(m) \in C$, where g and h are recursive, then $n \in A \Leftrightarrow h(g(n)) \in C$, and $h \circ g$ is recursive. And if g and h are 1-1, so is $h \circ g$. □

$\leqslant_m$ is not a partial order since it is not anti-symmetric: it is not the case that $A \leqslant_m B \;\&\; B \leqslant_m A$ implies $A = B$. To see this, we may note:

(18) If A is recursive, and B is any set $\neq \emptyset, \mathbb{N}$, then $A \leqslant_m B$.

Proof. Take $m_0 \in B$ and $m_1 \notin B$, and define the function f by

$$f(n) = \begin{cases} m_0 & \text{if } n \in A \\ m_1 & \text{if } n \notin A \end{cases}$$

Then f is recursive and we have $n \in A \Leftrightarrow f(n) \in B$. □

Now, if we define

$$A \equiv_m B \text{ iff } A \leqslant_m B \text{ and } B \leqslant_m A$$

then $\equiv_m$ is an equivalence relation, whose equivalence classes are called *m-degrees*:

Definition 15.10.3 (m-degrees and 1-degrees)

(i) The *m-degree* of a set A is the equivalence class of A under $\equiv_m$:

$$dg_m(A) = \{B \colon A \equiv_m B\}$$

(ii) An m-degree is called *recursively enumerable* (*recursive*) if it contains a recursively enumerable (recursive) set.

(iii) Define a partial order (also written $\leqslant_m$) between m-degrees of sets by setting

$$dg_m(A) \leqslant_m dg_m(B) \text{ iff } A \leqslant_m B$$

(iv) Similarly for 1-degrees. Clearly, for all A, $dg_1(A) \subseteq dg_m(A)$.

The fact that $\equiv_m$ is an equivalence relation, and that $\leqslant_m$ as specified above is a well-defined partial order (reflexive, transitive, and anti-symmetric) on the equivalence classes of $\equiv_m$, is a general feature of preorders; see Exercise 16.3.11 in the Appendix. Let us use

$$\mathbf{a}, \mathbf{b}, \mathbf{c}, \ldots$$

for m-degrees. It follows from Fact 15.10.2 that if $\mathbf{a}$ is a recursively enumerable (recursive) degree, then all sets in $\mathbf{a}$ are recursively enumerable (recursive). Also, if $\mathbf{a}$ is recursively enumerable and $\mathbf{b} \leqslant \mathbf{a}$, then $\mathbf{b}$ is recursively enumerable.

With respect to m-reducibility, the (recursive) sets $\emptyset$ and $\mathbb{N}$ behave a bit strangely:

(19) $dg_m(\emptyset) = \{\emptyset\}$ and $dg_m(\mathbb{N}) = \{\mathbb{N}\}$.

Proof. If $A \neq \emptyset$ it can never be true that for all n, $n \in A \Leftrightarrow f(n) \in \emptyset$; just take any n in A. So $A \not\leqslant_m \emptyset$, and thus $A \notin dg_m(\emptyset)$. Similarly, if $A \neq \mathbb{N}$, then $A \not\leqslant_m \mathbb{N}$. □

So when looking at m-degrees, it is convenient to disregard the degrees of $\varnothing$ and $\mathbb{N}$. We do that from now on in this section. Thus, we consider the m-degrees partially ordered by $\leqslant_m$, over the set $\mathcal{P}(\mathbb{N})^- = \mathcal{P}(\mathbb{N}) - \{\varnothing, \mathbb{N}\}$. Let

$$\mathbf{0}_m = \{A \in \mathcal{P}(\mathbb{N})^- : A \text{ is recursive}\}$$

Then

(20) $\mathbf{0}_m$ is the m-degree of any recursive set in $\mathcal{P}(\mathbb{N})^-$, and it is the *smallest* m-degree: for all m-degrees $\mathbf{a}$, we have $\mathbf{0}_m \leqslant \mathbf{a}$.

Proof. This is an immediate consequence of (18). □

The ordering $\leqslant_m$ between m-degrees is partial but certainly not total: there are many *incomparable* m-degrees. One example is $dg_m(K)$ and $dg_m(\overline{K})$:

(21) $K \nleqslant_m \overline{K}$ and $\overline{K} \nleqslant_m K$.

Proof. If $\overline{K} \leqslant_m K$, it would follow by Fact 15.10.2(b) that $\overline{K}$ is recursively enumerable (since K is recursively enumerable). But we know that is not the case (since K is not recursive). Next, it is obvious that for all sets A, B,

(22) $A \leqslant_m B$ iff $\overline{A} \leqslant_m \overline{B}$

Thus, since $\overline{K} \nleqslant_m K$, we have $\overline{\overline{K}} \nleqslant_m \overline{K}$, i.e. $K \nleqslant_m \overline{K}$. □

After these preparations we can see that m-reducibility really makes sense as a 'difficulty ordering' among sets of natural numbers. Next comes an important observation:

Proposition 15.10.4 (Post)
Every recursively enumerable set is m-reducible to K.

Proof. Let A be a recursively enumerable set and define the relation R by $R(n, m) \Leftrightarrow n \in A \wedge m = m$. Then R is recursively enumerable, so by the s-m-n theorem there is a primitive recursive function g s.t.

$$m \in W_{g(n)} \Leftrightarrow R(n, m)$$

The we have

$$\begin{aligned} n \in A &\Leftrightarrow n \in A \wedge g(n) = g(n) \\ &\Leftrightarrow R(n, g(n)) \\ &\Leftrightarrow g(n) \in W_{g(n)} \\ &\Leftrightarrow g(n) \in K \end{aligned}$$

So $A \leqslant_m K$ via g. □

This tells us that among recursively enumerable problems (sets), the halting problem (K) is *maximally hard*: *all* other recursively enumerable problems are m-reducible to it. Let

$$\mathbf{0'}_m = dg_m(K)$$

Thus:

(23) $\mathbf{0'}_m$ is the largest recursively enumerable m-degree: if $\mathbf{a}$ is a recursively enumerable m-degree, then $\mathbf{a} \leqslant \mathbf{0'}_m$.

This property of K (the halting problem) has another name:

Definition 15.10.5 (m-completeness)
A set A is *m-complete* if A is r.e. and all r.e. sets are m-reducible to A.

So K is an m-complete set. In other words, among recursively enumerable sets, the halting problem is maximally difficult. And we can give another important example of m-complete sets: recall that Theorem 15.3.3 (which we didn't prove, though a proof is outlined in Exercise 15.14.11) says that *every* recursively enumerable set A is weakly representable in each consistent axiomatizable extension T of Q. That is, there is a formula $\varphi(x)$ such that for all n,

$$n \in A \text{ iff } T \vdash \varphi(\mathbf{n})$$

This clearly means that there is a recursive function f such that

$$n \in A \text{ iff } f(n) \in thm_T$$

We have proved (assuming Theorem 15.3.3):

Fact 15.10.6
If T is a consistent axiomatizable extension of Q, then the set thm_T of (Gödel numbers of) theorems of T is m-complete.

As usual, we write $\mathbf{a} <_m \mathbf{b}$ when $\mathbf{a} \leqslant_m \mathbf{b}$ and $\mathbf{b} \nleqslant_m \mathbf{a}$. Clearly,

(24) $\mathbf{0}_m <_m \mathbf{0'}_m$

And that leads to a very natural question: Are there any recursively enumerable sets whose 'hardness' is *between* that of the recursive sets and K? In other words, is there some recursively enumerable but non-recursive set A such that $K \nleqslant_m A$?

This question is called *Post's Problem* for m-reducibility.[16] The next section presents a solution to this problem. It shows that even though most familiar undecidable problems have been shown to be undecidable by reducing the halting problem to them, there exist undecidable (but semi-decidable) problems whose undecidability does not follow from that of the halting problem.

First, however, we state another useful fact about m-reducibility. To appreciate it, suppose, for example, that for a given number k_0, we want to show that the set $B = \{n : \{n\}^1(k_0) \text{ is defined}\}$ is not recursive, by reducing the halting problem to it. (This set represents a *particularized halting problem*: to decide if an arbitrary Turing machine halts on input k_0.) This can be done as follows. Let

$$f(m,n) = \{n\}^1(n + m \dot{-} k_0)$$

f is a partial and recursive function (Normal Form Theorem), so there is (s-m-n theorem) a primitive recursive function g such that

$$\{g(n)\}^1(m) = f(m,n)$$

It follows that $\{n\}^1(n)$ is defined iff $\{g(n)\}^1(k_0)$ is defined, in other words, we have $n \in K$ iff $g(n) \in B$, so $K \leqslant_m B$.

This construction seems a bit *ad hoc*, and tailored specifically for the problem at hand. The next result allows us to draw the desired conclusion directly, in this and many similar cases.

Definition 15.10.7 (index sets)
A is an *index set* if $W_n = W_m$ implies $n \in A \Leftrightarrow m \in A$.

That is, an index set is characterized by the fact that the only thing that matters for whether a number n belongs to it or not is the recursively enumerable set that n is an index of. For example,

$$\{n \colon W_n = K\}$$

[16]Post also asked the question for the arguably most general notion of reducibility, so-called *Turing reducibility*. Roughly, $A \leqslant_T B$ if there is a Turing machine that computes A *given* that it 'knows' B; such machines, called *oracle machines*, have an extra instruction enabling them to put a correct answer to a question $n \in B$? on the tape, for any n. The machine can thus consult an *oracle* for B, something that always gives the right answer but doesn't tell how. M-reducibility is a special case: you can ask $f(n) \in B$? just once, but in the general case there is no limit to how many times you can consult the oracle or about which numbers. $A \leqslant_m B$ implies $A \leqslant_T B$, but the converse fails. (For example, we have $K \leqslant_T \overline{K}$.) Post saw that this was the real problem, and proved many results about recursively enumerable sets and Turing reducibility. The existence of a recursively enumerable non-recursive set A such that $K \not\leqslant_T A$ was eventually established by Albert Muchnik (1956) and (independently) Richard Friedberg (1957). The proof method introduced by them—the so-called *priority method*—led to an explosion of research in computability theory, in the area of (Turing) *degrees of unsolvability*.

is an index set, and so is the set *Tot*, and the set B defined above. By contrast, K is not an index set (Exercise 15.14.26).

$\varnothing$ and $\mathbb{N}$ are trivially index sets, but we normally exclude these. The following result, known as Rice's Theorem, is obtained by analyzing proofs that various sets, such as *Tot*, are non-recursive by reducing K or $\overline{K}$ to them (e.g. the proof of Fact 15.7.3).

Theorem 15.10.8 (Rice's Theorem)
If A is an index set distinct from $\varnothing$ and $\mathbb{N}$, then either $K \leqslant_1 A$ or $\overline{K} \leqslant_1 A$: if no index of the empty set belongs to A, then $K \leqslant_1 A$. In particular, no non-trivial index set is recursive.

Proof. Suppose first that no index of the empty set belongs to A. Pick $i \in A$. The idea is to find a 1-1 recursive function g such that for all n,

$$\text{(a)} \qquad W_{g(n)} = \begin{cases} W_i & \text{if } n \in K \\ \varnothing & \text{if } n \notin K \end{cases}$$

This gives the result: since A is an index set and contains no index of $\varnothing$, we have $n \in K \Leftrightarrow g(n) \in A$, i.e. $K \leqslant_1 A$. To find g, we first define

$$\text{(b)} \qquad F(n,k) = \begin{cases} \{i\}^1(k) & \text{if } n \in K \\ \text{undefined} & \text{otherwise} \end{cases}$$

This is a definition by so-called positive cases, and Exercise 15.14.7 asserts that it follows that F is a partial recursive function, so $F = \{e\}^2$ for some e. By the s-m-n theorem there is a 1-1 primitive recursive function g (namely, $g(n) = S^1_1(e,n)$) such that $\{g(n)\}^1(k) = F(n,k)$. Let us check that this is the function we are looking for.

Suppose $n \in K$. Then (b) implies that $\{g(n)\}^1 = \{i\}^1$, and so $W_{g(n)} = W_i$. On the other hand, if $n \notin K$, then $\{g(n)\}^1(k)$ is undefined for all k, so $W_{g(n)} = \varnothing$. This shows that (a) holds.

Next, suppose instead that A contains an index for $\varnothing$. But then $\overline{A}$ has no index for $\varnothing$, so the argument just given shows that $K \leqslant_1 \overline{A}$, that is, $\overline{K} \leqslant_1 A$. □

For example, since *Tot* contains no index of the empty set, Rice's Theorem tells us directly what we already know: that $K \leqslant_1 \mathit{Tot}$. Interestingly, we also have:

$$\text{(25)} \qquad \overline{K} \leqslant_1 \mathit{Tot}$$

This shows that, as we claimed earlier, *Tot* is not recursively enumerable (since $\overline{K}$ is not recursively enumerable). (25) is a special case of:

Fact 15.10.9
If A is a Π_2 set, then $A \leqslant_1 \mathit{Tot}$. (Tot is Π_2-complete.)

Proof. If A is Π_2, there is a (primitive) recursive relation R such that $n \in A \Leftrightarrow \forall m \exists k\, R(n,m,k)$. Since $S(n,m) \Leftrightarrow \exists k\, R(n,m,k)$ is recursively enumerable we can find, using the s-m-n theorem for r.e. sets (Theorem 15.8.3), a one-one recursive function h such that

$$m \in W_{h(n)} \Leftrightarrow \exists k\, R(n,m,k)$$

This gives us:

$$\begin{aligned} n \in A &\Leftrightarrow \forall m \exists k\, R(n,m,k) \\ &\Leftrightarrow W_{h(n)} = \mathbb{N} \\ &\Leftrightarrow h(n) \in \mathit{Tot} \end{aligned}$$

so $A \leqslant_1 \mathit{Tot}$ via h. □

This entails that (25) holds, since $\overline{K}$ is Π_2 (indeed it is Π_1).

15.11. Post's Problem, creative and simple sets

Exercise 15.14.5 asks the reader to show that every infinite recursively enumerable set has an infinite recursive subset. Post constructed a recursively enumerable set whose *complement* is infinite and has no infinite recursively enumerable subset. He called such sets *simple*. We will show that the existence of a simple sets solves Post's Problem for m-reducibility. Before that, we present Post's notion of a *creative* set, and note some of its properties.

Definition 15.11.1

1. A set A is *productive* if there is a total recursive function p, called a *productive function* for A, such that for all n, if $W_n \subseteq A$, then $p(n) \in A - W_n$.[17]
2. A set is *creative* if it is r.e. and its complement is productive.

Intuitively, a creative set is a recursively enumerable set with a very *large* complement. By contrast, a simple set is one with a very *small* complement. Here is a prominent creative set:

(26) K is creative.

Proof. $\overline{K}$ is productive via the identity function! □

We next establish the following fact about productive sets.

Lemma 15.11.2

(a) *If A is productive and $A \leqslant_m B$, then B is productive.*

[17]For other equivalent definitions of productivity, see Exercises 15.14.36 – 15.14.38.

(b) *If A is creative, B is r.e. and $A \leqslant_m B$, then B is creative.*

Proof. (b) is an immediate consequence of (a) (since $A \leqslant_m B$ entails $\overline{A} \leqslant_m \overline{B}$ and $\overline{A}$ is productive). For (a), let p be a productive function for A, and g a recursive function such that $n \in A \Leftrightarrow g(n) \in B$. By reasoning that is by now familiar (using the s-m-n theorem), there is a recursive function h such that for all k, n,

$$k \in W_{h(n)} \Leftrightarrow g(k) \in W_n$$

We claim that gph (i.e. $g \circ p \circ h$) is a productive function for B. For suppose $W_n \subseteq B$. It follows that $W_{h(n)} \subseteq A$ (if $k \in W_{h(n)}$, we have $g(k) \in W_n$, so $g(k) \in B$, so $k \in A$). Thus, $p(h(n)) \in A - W_{h(n)}$, from which we can conclude that $g(p(h(n))) \in B - W_n$. □

In the preceding section we showed that $K \leqslant_1$ *Tot* and $\overline{K} \leqslant_1$ *Tot*. So *Tot* is an example of a set such that both it and its complement are productive. Another example is given in Section 15.13.

A productive set cannot be recursively enumerable (otherwise it would have an index e, but no function can find an element in $W_e - W_e$). Therefore, a creative set cannot be recursive (Post's Lemma). Indeed, being creative amounts to being (recursively enumerable and) *effectively non-recursive*: if $\overline{A}$ is productive with productive function p, then for any candidate W_n for $\overline{A}$, $p(n)$ is a counter-example.

Note here the analogy with Gödel's proof of the first incompleteness theorem: the set thm_T of theorems is recursively enumerable, but the proof effectively finds a sentence in its complement. This was precisely why Post called such sets 'creative'; he thought the incompleteness phenomena showed that "mathematical thinking is, and must remain, essentially creative" (Post 1944). Recall that we just showed (Fact 15.10.6) that thm_T is m-complete whenever T is an axiomatizable consistent extension of Q. The next theorem (proved in 1955 by John Myhill) shows that Post had found just the right notion.

Theorem 15.11.3 (Myhill)
A set is m-complete if and only if it is creative.[18]

Proof. If A is m-complete, then it is recursively enumerable and also $K \leqslant_m A$. So by Lemma 15.11.2, A is creative.

In the other direction, suppose A is creative and let p be a productive function for $\overline{A}$. We must show that $K \leqslant_m A$. We shall do this by finding a recursive function g such that

(a) $\quad n \in K \Leftrightarrow p(g(n)) \in A$

[18] The proof of this uses Fixed Point Theorem (Theorem 15.9.1), and can be skipped if you didn't read Section 15.9.

The idea is to define g in such a way that the following holds:

$$\text{(b)} \qquad W_{g(n)} = \begin{cases} \{p(g(n))\} & \text{if } n \in K \\ \varnothing & \text{otherwise} \end{cases}$$

Let us verify that if we manage this, (a) follows, and thus $K \leqslant_m A$. Suppose first that $n \in \overline{K}$. Then $W_{g(n)} = \varnothing \subseteq \overline{A}$, so $p(g(n)) \in \overline{A}$. In the other direction, suppose $p(g(n)) \in \overline{A}$; we must show $n \in \overline{K}$. Suppose to the contrary that $n \in K$. But then $W_{g(n)} = \{p(g(n))\} \subseteq \overline{A}$, so $p(g(n)) \in \overline{A} - W_{g(n)}$, which is a contradiction. This proves that $\overline{K} \leqslant_m \overline{A}$, and so $K \leqslant_m A$, given (b).

Of course, (b) doesn't look like a well-formed definition of g, since it is 'circular'. But the Fixed Point Theorem (Theorem 15.9.1) entails that a recursive function g satisfying (b) must exist!

To see this, we appeal to Lemma 15.8.4, where the partial function F is given by $F(k, n) = p(\{k\}^1(n))$. So there is a primitive recursive function h such that for all k and n, $\{h(k)\}^1$ is total, and

$$\text{(c)} \qquad W_{\{h(k)\}^1(n)} = \begin{cases} \{p(\{k\}^1(n))\} & \text{if } p(\{k\}^1(n)) \text{ is defined } \& \ n \in K \\ \varnothing & \text{otherwise} \end{cases}$$

Now the Fixed Point Theorem says there is a number e such that $\{h(e)\}^1 = \{e\}^1$. So if we let $g = \{e\}^1$, then g is recursive and total (since $\{h(e)\}^1$ is total), and (b) holds (since $p(g(n))$ is always defined). □

Looking closely at the above proof (from right to left), we see (i) that the only property of K used is that it is recursively enumerable, and (ii) that the only property of A used is that $\overline{A}$ is productive. So if K is replaced by any recursively enumerable set B, virtually the same proof yields the following.

Theorem 15.11.4
If $\overline{A}$ is productive and B is recursively enumerable, then $B \leqslant_m A$.

This leads to another characterization of productivity:

Corollary 15.11.5
A is productive if and only if $\overline{K} \leqslant_m A$.

Proof. If $\overline{K} \leqslant_m A$, then, since $\overline{K}$ is productive, it follows by Lemma 15.11.2(a) that A is productive. Conversely, Theorem 15.11.4 tells us (since K is r.e) that if A is productive, then $K \leqslant_m \overline{A}$, i.e. $\overline{K} \leqslant_m A$. □

Now that we understand the role of creative sets, let us get back to Post's problem. We shall need one more fact about productive sets:

Lemma 15.11.6
Every productive set has an infinite recursively enumerable subset.

Proof. Suppose p is a productive function for the set A. With the s-m-n theorem we find a recursive function h s.t. $W_{h(n)} = W_n \cup \{p(n)\}$. Let e be an index of the empty set, so $W_e = \varnothing$. Now define:

$$B = \{p(e), p(h(e)), p(h(h((e))), p(h(h(h(e)))), \ldots\} = \{g(0), g(1), g(2), \ldots\}$$

That is, g is defined as follows: first define f by primitive recursion,

$$\begin{cases} f(0) & = & e \\ f(n+1) & = & h(f(n)) \end{cases}$$

and then let $g(n) = p(f(n))$. Since h is recursive, so is f, and since p is a total recursive function, so is g. Thus, B is recursively enumerable. We claim:

(a) $\quad W_{f(n)} \subseteq A$

for all n. We prove (a) by induction. Since $W_{f(0)} = \varnothing$, the base step is clear. Now suppose $W_{f(n)} \subseteq A$. Then we have $W_{f(n+1)} = W_{h(f(n))} = W_{f(n)} \cup \{p(f(n))\}$, and it follows by productivity that $p(f(n))$ belongs to $A - W_{f(n)}$. This proves (a). In fact, we have proved that for all n,

(b) $\quad g(n+1) \in A - W_{f(n+1)} = A - (W_{f(n)} \cup \{g(n)\})$

It follows that (i) $B \subseteq A$, and (ii) $g(n+1) \neq g(0), \ldots, g(n)$, so B is infinite. □

Now, recall that a recursively enumerable set is simple if its complement is infinite and contains no infinite recursively enumerable subset. At this point we have what we need to conclude that the existence of a simple set solves Post's Problem (for m-reducibility).

Corollary 15.11.7
If A is a simple set, then $K \nleqslant_m A$ (so $dg(A)$ is a recursively enumerable m-degree strictly between $\mathbf{0}_m$ and $\mathbf{0}'_m$).

Proof. We prove the contraposition. If $K \leqslant_m A$, then, by Lemma 15.11.2, $\overline{A}$ is productive. Productive sets are infinite, and, by Lemma 15.11.6, contain an infinite recursively enumerable subset. This means that A is not simple. □

All that remains to prove is that a simple set exists! This is by no means obvious, although by now several kinds of simple sets have been shown to exist. Here we give Post's original example.

Theorem 15.11.8 (Post's simple set)
There is a simple set.

Proof. The idea: We want to effectively build the set S, by successively putting numbers in it, in such a way that it intersects each infinite W_e. Then no such W_e can be a subset of $\overline{S}$. But one cannot effectively enumerate the infinite recursively enumerable sets,[19] so we intersect S with every W_e with enough elements. At the same time we must keep $\overline{S}$ infinite, so when we put a number in S we must ensure another number stays out. Specifically, we put at most half of the numbers $0, 1, \ldots, 2k$ in S, for every k. Then for each k, $\overline{S}$ has at least $k+1$ elements, so it is infinite. This idea can be carried out as follows.

The actual proof: Dovetail an enumeration of all sets W_e: at stage s, perform s steps in each of the computations of $\{0\}^1(0), \ldots, \{0\}^1(s)$, $\{1\}^1(0), \ldots, \{1\}^1(s), \ldots, \{s\}^1(0), \ldots, \{s\}^1(s)$ (if possible). While doing this, put n in S if there is an index e and a stage s such that $n > 2e$ and the computation of $\{e\}^1(n)$ ends at s (so $n \in W_e$ is established at that stage), and n is the *first* number with this property (so for all $m \neq n$, if $m > 2e$ then $m \in W_e$ has not been established at stage $\leqslant s$). This is an effective method to generate S, so S is recursively enumerable. Now we claim:

(a) For every infinite W_e, $S \cap W_e \neq \varnothing$.

For if W_e is infinite it contains some number $n > 2e$, and hence some such n will eventually be put in S. However:

(b) For every k, at most k of the numbers $0, 1, \ldots, 2k$ belong to S.

To see this, note that $n \in \{0, 1, \ldots, 2k\}$ can only enter S if it comes from some W_e with $2e < n$, so $2e < 2k$, i.e. $e < k$. But there are at most k such sets. Hence, for every k, $\overline{S}$ has at least $k+1$ elements. □

Are all recursively enumerable sets either recursive or creative or simple? Exercise 15.14.49 shows that this is not so. In fact, numerous different kinds of recursively enumerable sets 'strictly between' the recursive and the creative sets have been studied, but we shall have to leave this topic here.

15.12. Taking stock

Let us summarize the various characterization of the recursively enumerable sets that we have encountered (some of them in exercises).

[19] The set $\{e : W_e \text{ is infinite}\}$ is not recursively enumerable: it is $\Pi_2 - \Sigma_1$; see Exercise 15.14.34.

For simplicity, we assume $A \neq \varnothing, \mathbb{N}$. Then the statement A *is recursively enumerable* is equivalent to each of the following claims:

1. $A = range(f)$ for some total recursive function f (by definition).
2. $A = range(f)$ for some primitive recursive function f (Cor. 15.1.4).
3. $n \in A \Leftrightarrow \exists m R(m, n)$ for some (primitive) recursive relation R (Thm. 15.1.2), that is, A is Σ_1.
4. $A = dom(F)$ for some partial recursive function F (Thm. 15.1.2).
5. $A = range(F)$ for some partial rec. function F (Exercise 15.14.10).
6. $A = W_e$ for some number e (Enumeration Theorem).
7. A is arithmetically definable by a Σ_1 formula (Thm. 15.4.3).
8. A is arithmetically definable by a formula $\exists x_1 \ldots \exists x_n \psi$, where ψ is quantifier-free (MRDP Theorem).
9. A is weakly representable in some consistent axiomatizable extension of Q (Cor. 15.3.4).
10. $A \leqslant_m K$ (Fact 15.10.2(b) and Proposition 15.10.4).

15.13. Applications to logic

The development of the theory of recursive/computable functions and recursively/computably enumerable sets was largely inspired by issues arising in logic during the early decades of the 19th century. Now, with these tools at our hands, we can go back to logic with a fresh perspective on the incompleteness phenomena.

Given our Gödel numbering of syntactic objects, proofs, Turing machines, etc., we can often ignore the distinction between an object, say a formula, and its Gödel number.[20] Thus we have said, for example, that a *theory* T is recursive, and we can similarly say that a theory is recursively enumerable or creative, meaning that the set thm_T has these properties.

One application was already discussed in the context of Craig's Theorem (Section 15.1.2), which shows that every recursively enumerable theory is equivalent to primitive recursive theory. Recall that we identify a theory by its set of *axioms*, not its set of theorems, and that two theories are equivalent if they have the same set of theorems. Craig's Theorem also means that we can revise our definition of an

[20]Indeed, some modern accounts of arithmetized metalogic simply *identify* formulas and terms with suitable numbers.

axiomatizable theory (Definition 13.1.16): axiomatizability is just that the set of theorems of the theory is recursively enumerable. This is because we have shown that if a theory has a recursive set of axioms, then it is recursively enumerable (for example, Lemma 13.1.15). And the axiomatizable but undecidable theories that we have encountered provide prime examples of recursively enumerable and non-recursive sets, just as the set K is another prime example. In fact, we will see below that there is tight relationship between these theories and K.

The arithmetical language in this book has mostly been the first-order formulas in the vocabulary L_{PA}. If nothing else is stated, this is what we mean by "arithmetical formula" below. But the technique of Gödel numbering applies to any vocabulary L, as long as L is itself recursive. Then it is clear that the sets of terms, formulas, and sentences in L (the sets $term_L$, fml_L, and $sent_L$) are also recursive. When we talk about theories in arbitrary vocabularies below, we always assume that these vocabularies are recursive.

15.13.1. The set of true arithmetical sentences

Let $TRUE = Th(\mathcal{N})$ = the set of true arithmetical sentences, and let $FALSE$ be the set of false arithmetical sentences. We have shown, by various means, that $TRUE$ is undecidable: it is not even recursively enumerable, in fact not even arithmetical. Recall that a relation R is *arithmetically definable* if there is an arithmetical formula $\psi(\overline{x})$ such that

if $R(\overline{n})$, then $\psi(\overline{\mathbf{n}})$ is true, and

if not $R(\overline{n})$, then $\psi(\overline{\mathbf{n}})$ is false.

Also, R is *arithmetical* if it is in the arithmetical hierarchy (Definition 15.4.1). As we pointed out in Section 15.4, these notions are equivalent. So the fact that $TRUE$ is not arithmetical follows from Tarski's Theorem on the undefinability of truth (Theorem 7.2.8), which shows that no L_{PA}-formula can arithmetically define $TRUE$. The decision problem for the set $TRUE$ is quite hard.[21]

Here is another observation about this set. To prepare for it, let R be a (primitive) recursive relation such that

$$n \in K \Leftrightarrow \exists m\, R(m, n)$$

Also, let $\theta(x, y)$ be a Σ_1-formula representing R in Q:

if $R(m, n)$, then $Q \vdash \theta(\mathbf{m}, \mathbf{n})$, and

[21]How hard? Above the arithmetical hierarchy for classifying sets of numbers, there is an *analytical hierarchy*, which considers definability in a second-order arithmetical language, thus allowing quantification over sets (relations, functions) of numbers. $TRUE$ is at the lowest non-arithmetical level in this hierarchy, called the level of Δ^1_1, or *hyperarithmetical*, sets.

if not $R(m,n)$, then $Q \vdash \neg\theta(\mathbf{m},\mathbf{n})$.

Finally, let

$$\psi_K(y) := \exists x \theta(x,y)$$

$\psi_K(y)$ is a generalized Σ_1-formula (Definition 14.5.1). And since Q doesn't prove any false sentences, we have, for all n,

(27) $n \in K \Leftrightarrow \psi_K(\mathbf{n})$ is true

(28) $n \in \overline{K} \Leftrightarrow \neg\psi_K(\mathbf{n})$ is true

Think of $\psi_K(\mathbf{n})$ as 'saying' that n is in K. We can now see that the following holds.

Theorem 15.13.1
TRUE and FALSE are productive sets.

Proof. Define $f_1(n) = \#(\psi_K(\mathbf{n}))$, and $f_2(n) = \#(\neg\psi_K(\mathbf{n}))$. f_1 and f_2 are (primitive) recursive. So if *true* is the set of Gödel numbers of sentences in *TRUE*, and similarly for *false*, we have

(a) $n \in K \Leftrightarrow f_1(n) \in \mathit{true}$

(b) $n \in \overline{K} \Leftrightarrow f_2(n) \in \mathit{true}$

By (b), $\overline{K} \leqslant_m \mathit{true}$, and, since, by (a), $n \in \overline{K} \Leftrightarrow f_1(n) \in \mathit{false}$, it follows from Lemma 15.11.2(a) that *true* and *false* are productive, which is what we mean by saying that *TRUE* and *FALSE* are productive. □

Now we obtain a weak version of the first incompleteness theorem as a corollary.

Corollary 15.13.2
If T is a true and axiomatizable arithmetical theory, there is a true sentence φ which is not provable in T. Consequently, $\neg\varphi$ is not provable in T either.

Proof. Let THM_T be the set of theorems of T. Since T is true and axiomatizable, THM_T is a recursively enumerable subset of *TRUE*. By the productivity of the latter set, we can effectively find a sentence $\varphi \in \mathit{TRUE} - \mathit{THM}_T$. □

This proof effectively produces an undecidable sentence with the recursion-theoretic machinery. Gödel's original proof also produced an undecidable sentence G, by an explicit diagonal construction. In the above proof, the diagonalization occurs in the definition of K. Gödel's proof seems to give more information about exactly what the undecidable sentence 'says' ("I am not provable in T"). The short proof above relies on the unsolvability of the halting problem (K). What does the undecidable sentence in Corollary 15.13.2 'say'?

To answer this question, consider the set

$$\{n : T \vdash \neg\psi_K(\mathbf{n})\}$$

This set is recursively enumerable; let e be an index for it. It follows by (28), and the assumption that all theorems of T are true, that $W_e \subseteq \overline{K}$. Now let φ be the sentence $\neg\psi_K(\mathbf{e})$. Thus, φ 'says' that e is not an element of K. We have:

$$\begin{aligned} e \in \overline{K} & \Leftrightarrow e \notin W_e \\ & \Leftrightarrow T \nvdash \neg\psi_K(\mathbf{e}) \\ & \Leftrightarrow T \nvdash \varphi \end{aligned}$$

So in this sense φ in fact 'says' *about itself* that it is not provable in T, just as the corresponding Gödel sentence G from Chapter 12.2!

In other words, the proof via the set K turns out to be another, more abstract, way to establish the unprovability of the self-referential sentence that Gödel invented. Perhaps surprisingly, the halting problem is seen to be involved in this construction.

15.13.2. Creative theories

We can say more about how recursion-theoretic notions apply to the incompleteness theorems. Fix a consistent axiomatizable extension T of Q. As above, $THM_T = \{\psi : T \vdash \psi\}$, and let $REF_T = \{\psi : T \vdash \neg\psi\}$ be the set of *refutable* sentences in T.

Recall that T is Σ_1-*sound* if T proves no false (generalized) Σ_1 sentences. This is a weaker requirement than ω-consistency, although stronger than mere consistency.

Theorem 15.13.3
If T is Σ_1-sound, the set THM_T is creative.[22]

Proof. THM_T is recursively enumerable by assumption. And since $\psi_K(y)$ is a generalized Σ_1 formula, it follows by Σ_1-soundness that

(29) $\quad n \in K \Leftrightarrow T \vdash \psi_K(\mathbf{n})$

Thus, $K \leqslant_m thm_T$, so by Lemma 15.11.2(b), THM_T is creative. □

Corollary 15.13.4
If T is a Σ_1-sound axiomatizable extension of Q, then T is incomplete.

[22]Usually, one says that the theory T is creative. But, strictly speaking, T is a set of axioms, which is usually recursive and thus not creative, so we should be clear that the creative set here is the set of *theorems* of T, i.e. THM_T.

Proof. From (29), we see that

$$n \in \overline{K} \Leftrightarrow f_1(n) \in \overline{thm_T} \cap sent$$

where *sent* is the set of Gödel numbers of arithmetical sentences. So the set $\overline{thm_T} \cap sent$ is productive. Since T is consistent, we have that $ref_T \subseteq \overline{thm_T} \cap sent$, and ref_T is recursively enumerable, so by productivity we effectively find a sentence φ which does not belong to $THM_T \cup REF_T$. That is, φ is undecidable in T. □

It is straightforward to generalize the above results to theories which may have different vocabularies but are such that all recursive functions are representable in them. We do need to assume, however, that the theories are true, or at least that Σ_1-soundness holds in some suitable sense. In Chapter 12.3 we saw how the assumption of ω-consistency in Gödel's original formulation of the first incompleteness theorem could be replaced by mere consistency. The construction of Rosser sentences there also has an analogue in the current more abstract setting, which can be used to strengthen Theorem 15.13.3, and in particular remove the assumption of Σ_1-soundness. This is presented in Exercises 15.14.50 – 15.14.53.

15.14. Exercises to Chapter 15

The facts stated in the exercises below are common knowledge in computability theory and most of them can be found in standard textbooks. In particular, several of them have been taken or adapted from the classic Rogers 1967.

Exercise 15.14.1
Show that semi-recursive (and hence recursively enumerable) relations have the following properties, where R is semi-recursive:

1. If S is semi-recursive, so are $R \vee S$ and $R \wedge S$.
2. $S(p, n_1, \ldots, n_k,) \Leftrightarrow \forall m_{m<p} R(n_1, \ldots, n_k, m)$ is semi-recursive.
3. The relation $\exists m R(n_1, \ldots, n_k, m)$ is semi-recursive.
4. The result of substituting a total recursive function for a variable in R is a semi-recursive relation.

Exercise 15.14.2
If f is a function and A a set (of numbers), recall that:

$$f(A) = \{f(n) : n \in A\}$$
$$f^{-1}(A) = \{n : f(n) \in A\}$$

Suppose f is a total recursive function, A a recursive set, and B a recursively enumerable set. What about $f(A)$, $f(B)$, $f^{-1}(A)$, and $f^{-1}(B)$?

Exercise 15.14.3
Explain why the everywhere undefined function is a partial recursive function.

Exercise 15.14.4
Show that if A is an infinite recursively enumerable set, there is a *one-one* (injective) recursive function f such that $A = \{f(0), f(1), f(2), \ldots\}$. [Hint: Look at the proof of Theorem 15.1.2.]

Exercise 15.14.5
A (total) function f is *strictly increasing* if $m < n$ implies $f(m) < f(n)$.

1. Show that if f is strictly increasing, then $n \leqslant f(n)$ for all n.
2. Show that if A is infinite and enumerated by a strictly increasing (primitive) recursive function, then A is (primitive) recursive. (Use part 1.)
3. Conversely, show that if A is infinite and recursive, then A can be enumerated by a strictly increasing recursive function. [Hint: Use primitive recursion and the μ-operator.]
4. Conclude from part 2. that every infinite recursively enumerable set has an infinite recursive subset. [Hint: Modify the last part of the proof of Theorem 15.1.2 to define a strictly increasing recursive function enumerating a subset of A.]

Exercise 15.14.6 (Graph Theorem)
The *graph* of a k-ary function f is the $(k+1)$-ary relation G_f defined by

$$G_f(n_1, \ldots, n_k, m) \Leftrightarrow f(n_1, \ldots, n_k) = m$$

Note that the definition of G_f also works when f is partial: if $f(n_1, \ldots, n_k)$ is undefined, then $G_f(n_1, \ldots, n_k, m)$ is false (for every m). The *Graph Theorem* is the following result:

1. A partial function f is recursive iff G_f is recursively enumerable.

   [Hint: *Only if:* use Theorem 13.1.10. *If:* use the μ-operator and that G_f is semi-recursive.]
2. A total function f is recursive iff G_f is recursive.

   [Hint: *Only if:* Show that the characteristic function c_{G_f} is recursive. *If:* Show that f is μ-recursive.]

Exercise 15.14.20 shows that some non-total recursive functions have non-recursive graphs, and others have recursive graphs.

The next four exercises use the Graph Theorem (Exercise 15.14.6).

Exercise 15.14.7 (definition by positive cases)
f is said to be *defined by positive cases* from functions $g_1, \ldots, g_k$ and relations $S_1, \ldots, S_k$ if

$$f(\overline{n}) = \begin{cases} g_1(\overline{n}) & \text{if} \quad S_1(\overline{n}) \\ \cdot & \\ \cdot & \\ g_k(\overline{n}) & \text{if} \quad S_k(\overline{n}) \\ \text{undefined} & \text{otherwise} \end{cases}$$

where for all $\overline{n}$, *at most one* of $S_1(\overline{n}), \ldots S_k(\overline{n})$ holds. Show that if f is defined by positive cases from partial recursive $g_1, \ldots, g_k$ and recursively enumerable $S_1, \ldots, S_k$, then f is recursive.

Exercise 15.14.8
Use Exercise 15.14.7 to give a new proof of Post's Lemma (Lemma 15.2.1). [Hint: Show that c_A is recursive.]

Exercise 15.14.9
A partial function g is said to be an *extension* of a partial function f if (i) $dom(f) \subseteq dom(g)$, and (ii) for all $n \in dom(f)$, $f(n) = g(n)$.

1. Show that g is an extension of f iff $G_f \subseteq G_g$.
2. Show that there is a partial recursive function which has no total recursive extension. [Hint: Consider the function $d(n) = \{n\}^1(n) + 1$.]

Exercise 15.14.10
Show that A is recursively enumerable iff A is the *range* of some partial recursive function.

Exercise 15.14.11 (proof of Theorem 15.3.3)
*Let T be a consistent axiomatizable extension of Q, and A a recursively enumerable set. There is a recursive relation R s.t. $n \in A \Leftrightarrow \exists m\, R(n, m)$. Let $\psi(x, y)$ be a formula representing R in Q. We will need the generalization of the Diagonal Lemma from Exercise 12.10.4 (stated there for *PA*, but the proof works in Q), which entails that there is a formula $\varphi(x)$ such that for all n,

(*) $\quad Q \vdash \varphi(\mathbf{n}) \leftrightarrow \exists y(\psi(\mathbf{n}, y) \wedge \forall z_{z \leqslant y} \neg Prf_T(z, \ulcorner\varphi(\mathbf{n})\urcorner))$

We claim that $\varphi(x)$ weakly represents A in T.

1. Show that if $n \in A$ then $T \vdash \varphi(\mathbf{n})$. (Let $n \in A$, assume $T \nvdash \varphi(\mathbf{n})$ and derive a contradiction.)
2. Suppose $T \vdash \varphi(\mathbf{n})$, so for some number p, $Q \vdash Prf_T(\mathbf{p}, \ulcorner\varphi(\mathbf{n})\urcorner)$. Check that it follows that $T \vdash \exists y(y < \mathbf{p} \wedge \psi(\mathbf{n}, y))$. Conclude that $n \in A$.

Exercise 15.14.12
Use the Graph Theorem to prove claim (d) of Fact 15.4.4.

Exercise 15.14.13
**Lagrange's Square Theorem* states that every natural number n is the sum of four squares: there are natural numbers a, b, c, d such that $n = a^2 + b^2 + c^2 + d^2$. Use this to show that if there is an algorithm for testing if a Diophantine equation has an integer solution, then there is an algorithm for testing if it has solution in the natural numbers.

Exercise 15.14.14
*It turns out that (a formal version of) the MRDP Theorem is actually provable in *PA*. Conclude (with informal reasoning) that there is a Diophantine equation $p(x_1, \ldots, x_n) = 0$ such that

$$PA \vdash Con_{PA} \leftrightarrow \text{`}p(x_1, \ldots, x_n) = 0 \text{ has no solution'}$$

Exercise 15.14.15
Show the following, for all n:

1. Δ_n is closed under negation (i.e. if $R \in \Delta_n$, then $\neg R \in \Delta_n$.
2. Δ_n, Σ_n, and Π_n are closed under conjunction, disjunction, and bounded quantification.

Exercise 15.14.16
By Fact 15.4.4, $\Sigma_n \cup \Pi_n \subseteq \Delta_{n+1}$. Show that the inclusion is proper. [Hint: Using the Arithmetical Hierarchy Thm, take a set $A \in \Sigma_n - \Pi_n$, so $\overline{A} \in \Pi_n - \Sigma_n$. Define $R(k, m) \Leftrightarrow (A(k) \;\&\; m = 1) \vee (\neg A(k) \;\&\; m = 0)$, and show that R is in $\Delta_{n+1} - (\Sigma_n \cup \Pi_n)$.]

Exercise 15.14.17
Formulate and prove a Normal Form Theorem for each Σ_n level in the arithmetical hierarchy. (Define Σ_n-indices for each Σ_n set (relation), using the T_k predicates and the quantifier prefix.) Similarly for Π_n.

Exercise 15.14.18
This exercise uses the Normal Form Theorem, together with quantifier laws such as those given in Chapter 2.3.3 (see also Exercise 2.4.28), as well as contraction of quantifiers as described after Definition 15.4.1. As usual, $|A|$ is the cardinality of the set A. Show the following:

1. The sets $\{n \colon W_n \neq \emptyset\}$ and $\{n \colon 25 \in W_n\}$ are Σ_1 (r.e.).
2. The set $\{n \colon |W_n| \leqslant 15\}$ is Π_1.
3. $Fin = \{n \colon W_n \text{ is finite}\}$ is Σ_2. What about $Inf = \overline{Fin}$? (See also Exercise 15.14.34.)
4. For fixed k, the set $\{n \colon W_n = W_k\}$ is Π_2.
5. The set $\{n \colon |W_n| = 2 \text{ or } |W_n| = 5\}$ is Δ_2.

6. * *Rec* $= \{n: W_n \text{ is recursive}\}$ is Σ_3. [Hint: Use Post's Lemma.]
7. * *Coinf* $= \{n: \mathbf{N} - W_n \text{ is infinite}\}$ is Π_3.

All of these classifications are best possible, but we have not developed the means for showing that (except in a few cases: which ones?).

Exercise 15.14.19
Spell out the proof of the Enumeration Theorem as described in (10).

Exercise 15.14.20

1. Define the function f by $f(n) = 0 \Leftrightarrow n \in K$. That is, $f(n)$ is defined iff $n \in K$, and then takes the value 0. Show that f is a partial recursive function, and that G_f is not recursive.
2. Let e be an index of a recursively enumerable set distinct from $\mathbb{N}$. Define h as follows: $h(n) = \mu p \exists k_{k<p} T_1(e, n, k)$. Show that h is a partial recursive, non-total, function, and that G_h is recursive.

Exercise 15.14.21 (another proof of Theorem 15.9.1)
*Convince yourself using the Church-Turing Thesis that there is a total recursive function g such that for all m, n,

$$\{g(m)\}^1(n) = \begin{cases} \{\{m\}^1(m)\}^1(n) & \text{if } \{m\}^1(m) \text{ is defined} \\ \text{undefined} & \text{otherwise} \end{cases}$$

Since f and g are total and recursive, $f \circ g$ is total and recursive, and so has an index b, i.e. $\{b\}^1(m) = f(g(m))$ for all m. Let $e = g(b)$. Then:

$$\{e\}^1 = \{g(b)\}^1 = \{\{b\}^1(b)\}^1 = \{f(g(b))\}^1 = \{f(e)\}^1$$

as was to be proved. (Explain the second equality.)

Exercise 15.14.22

1. *Show that Theorem 15.9.1 and the version in (13) are equivalent.
2. *The *effective* version of (13) says that the number e can be found effectively from an index for $F = \{d\}^2$; in other words, that there is a (primitive) recursive function h such that for all d, $\{d\}^2(h(d), n) = \{h(d)\}^1(n)$. Prove this version. [Hint: Find an index for G in the proof of Theorem 15.9.1 effectively from d, using the same proof idea].
3. *Prove the following *Fixed Point Theorem with Parameters*:

   If f is a $(k+1)$-ary total recursive function, there is a k-ary total recursive function h such that

   $$\{f(n_1, \ldots, n_k, h(n_1, \ldots, n_k))\}^1 = \{h(n_1, \ldots, n_k)\}^1$$

   [Hint: Generalize the proof of the Fixed Point Theorem in Exercise 15.14.21 by adding k arguments to g.]

4. *Show that the following *Double Fixed Point Theorem* holds:

   If f, g are 2-ary total recursive functions, there are d, e such that

   $$\{d\}^1 = \{f(d,e)\}^1 \text{ and } \{e\}^1 = \{g(d,e)\}^1$$

   [Hint: First use 3. to find a recursive h such that $\{h(n)\}^1 = \{f(h(n),n)\}^1$. Then find e such that $\{e\}^1 = \{g(h(e),e)\}^1$. Let $d = h(e)$.]

The next five exercises use the Fixed Point Theorem and Exercise 15.14.22.

Exercise 15.14.23
Investigate in each of the following cases, using the Fixed Point Theorem, if there are numbers m such that:

1. $W_m = \mathbb{N} - \{m+3\}$
2. $W_m = \{5^m\}$
3. $W_m = \{n : \{m\}^1(n) \text{ is undefined}\}$
4. $W_m = \{n : \exists k(n = 2k \ \&\ k \in W_m)\}$ and $W_m \neq \emptyset$.

   [Hint: Find a recursive f s.t. $\{n : \exists k(n = 2k \ \&\ k \in W_m)\} = W_{f(m)}$. If $W_m = W_{f(m)}$, derive a contradiction from the assumption that W_m is non-empty.]
5. $W_m = \{3\} \cup \{n : \exists k(n = 2k \ \&\ k \in W_m)\}$

   [Hint: Yes. Take m s.t. $W_{g(m)} = \{3\} \cup \{n : \exists k(n = 2k \ \&\ k \in W_m)\} = W_m$ by the recursion theorem. All numbers in W_m are of the form $2^k \cdot 3$ for some $k \geqslant 0$.]

Exercise 15.14.24
Use Exercise 15.14.22:3 to show that there exists a (total) recursive function h such that for all n, $W_{h(n)} = \{n \cdot h(n) + 3\}$.

Exercise 15.14.25
Is there a Turing machine which for all inputs n outputs its own Gödel number? [Hint: Let $F(m,n) = m$ and apply (13).]

Exercise 15.14.26
Show that K is not an index set. [Hint: Consider e s.t. $W_e = \{e\}$.]

Exercise 15.14.27
Show that $A = \{n : W_n \subseteq \overline{K}\}$ is a proper subset of $\overline{K}$. [Hint: Use the Fixed Point Theorem to find e such that $W_e = \overline{\{e\}}$.]

Exercise 15.14.28 (join of two sets)
If $(X, \leqslant)$ is a partially ordered set, and $a, b \in X$, then c is said to be a *least upper bound (l.u.b.)* of a and b if the following holds: (i) $a \leqslant c$ and $b \leqslant c$; (ii) if $a \leqslant d$ and $b \leqslant d$, then $c \leqslant d$.

Given sets $A, B \subseteq N$, define the *join* of A and B:

$$A \oplus B = \{2n \colon n \in A\} \cup \{2n + 1 \colon n \in B\}$$

1. Show that every two m-degrees a and b have a least upper bound in the ordering $\leqslant_m$ of m-degrees. [Hint: Use the join.] This shows that the m-degrees ordered by $\leqslant_m$ form what is called an *upper semi-lattice.*[23] Explain why the proof does *not* show that the same holds in the 1-degree ordering. (In fact, that ordering is not an upper semi-lattice.)
2. Show: if a and b are recursively enumerable, so is their l.u.b.
3. Conclude from the proof of 1. that for all A, B, $A \oplus A \equiv_m A$ and $A \oplus B \equiv_m B \oplus A$.
4. Show that, in fact, $A \oplus A \equiv_1 A$ and $A \oplus B \equiv_1 B \oplus A$. (This does not follow from the proof of 1., but the relevant 1-1 functions can easily be found.)
5. Show that for all A, B we have $\overline{A \oplus B} = \overline{A} \oplus \overline{B}$.

Exercise 15.14.29
Let A be a recursively enumerable set distinct from $\varnothing, \mathbb{N}$. Clearly, if A is recursive, then $A \leqslant_m \overline{A}$. (Why?)

1. Show that the converse holds: if $A \leqslant_m \overline{A}$ then A is recursive.
2. Show that there is a non-recursive set B such that $B \leqslant_m \overline{B}$. [Hint: consider $K \oplus \overline{K}$ (Exercise 15.14.28).]

Exercise 15.14.30
The *symmetric difference* of two sets A, B is the set $(A–B) \cup (B–A)$. Show that if A, B are distinct from $\varnothing$ and $\mathbb{N}$, and their symmetric difference is finite, then $A \equiv_m B$.

Exercise 15.14.31
Let $A = \{n : W_n = \varnothing\}$. Show that $A \equiv_m \overline{K}$. Conclude that $\overline{A}$ is m-complete. [Hint: in one direction, use Rice's Theorem.]

Exercise 15.14.32
The halting problem H that we defined in Chapter 14.7 can be identified with the set

[23] It can be shown that this structure is not a lattice, i.e. that greatest lower bounds need not always exist.

$$K_0 = \{\langle m, n\rangle : m \in W_n\}$$

Show that $K_0 \equiv_m K$.

Exercise 15.14.33
Recall how (11) defined '$F(n) = G(n)$' for F, G partial functions. Let F be the everywhere undefined function and $G(n) = \{n\}^1(n)$.

1. Show that $F(n) = G(n) \Leftrightarrow n \notin K$.
2. Conclude that the class of recursively enumerable relations is not closed under substitution with *partial* recursive functions (cf. Exercise 15.14.1:4).

Exercise 15.14.34

1. Show that *Fin* $= \{n : W_n$ is finite$\}$ is not r.e.
2. *Let *Inf* $= \overline{Fin}$. Show that *Inf* $\equiv_m$ *Tot*.

   [Hint: Check that *Inf* is Π_2. Then use a similar construction as in the proof of Fact 15.10.9 to show that *Inf* is Π_2-complete.]

Exercise 15.14.35
*Show that the set $A = \{n : |W_n| > n\}$ is m-complete.

[Hint: To show that A is recursively enumerable, show that it is generalized Σ_1. To m-reduce K to A, look at Fact 15.7.3.]

Exercise 15.14.36 (alternative definition of productivity 1.1)
*Let A be a set and F a *partial* recursive function such that if $W_n \subseteq A$, then $F(n)$ is defined and $F(n) \in A - W_n$. Show that A is productive, i.e. that here is a *total* recursive function f with the same property.

[First proof (hints): First, show that there is a recursive function g s.t.

$$W_{g(n,m)} = \begin{cases} W_n & \text{if } m \in K \\ \varnothing & \text{otherwise} \end{cases}$$

Let $\{k_0, k_1, \ldots\}$ be an effective (recursive) listing of K. Define $f(n)$ as follows: start computations of each of $F(n), F(g(k_0, n)), F(g(k_1, n)), \ldots$ (dove-tailing, as in the proof of Theorem 15.1.2), and as soon as a value is obtained, let $f(n)$ be that value. Show:

1. f is total. (Assume $f(n)$ is undefined for some n, and show that this would solve the halting problem.)
2. f is a productive function for A.]

Exercise 15.14.37 (alternative definition of productivity 1.2)
*Using the parametric version of the Fixed Point Theorem from Exercise 15.14.22:3, give a shorter and more elegant proof of the result in the preceeding exercise.

[Second proof (hints): Find a recursive function h such that

$$W_{h(n,m)} = \begin{cases} W_m & \text{if } F(n) \text{ is defined} \\ \varnothing & \text{otherwise} \end{cases}$$

By the parametric Fixed Point Thm, there is a recursive function g s.t.

$$W_{g(n)} = W_{h(g(n),n)} = \begin{cases} W_n & \text{if } F(g(n)) \text{ is defined} \\ \varnothing & \text{otherwise} \end{cases}$$

Show that $f = Fg$ is a total productive function for A.]

Exercise 15.14.38 (alternative definition of productivity 2)
Show that A is productive iff A is nonempty and there is a total recursive function f such that if $\varnothing \neq W_n \subseteq A$, then $f(n) \in A - W_n$. [Hint: Take $k_0 \in A$ and find g such that $W_{g(n)} = W_n \cup \{k_0\}$.]

Exercise 15.14.39

1. Show: if A is productive and $B \subseteq A$ is r.e., then $A - B$ is productive. [Hint: Use a recursive function g s.t. $W_{g(n)} = B \cup W_n$.]
2. Conclude that if A is creative and B is finite, $A \cup B$ is creative.

Exercise 15.14.40

1. Show: if B is r.e. and $A \cap B$ is productive, then A is productive.
2. Conclude that if B is r.e. and $A \subseteq B$ is productive, then $A \cup \overline{B}$ is productive.

Exercise 15.14.41
Define:

$$A \times B = \{\langle m, n\rangle : m \in A \wedge n \in B\}$$

where $\langle m, n\rangle$ is the recursive bijection function $OP(m, n)$ from $\mathbb{N}^2$ to $\mathbb{N}$ in Chapter 8.7.3, with its projection functions π_1 and π_2.[24] Show:

1. $A \leqslant_1 A \times \mathbb{N}$ and $A \times \mathbb{N} \leqslant_m A$, so $A \equiv_m A \times \mathbb{N}$

   ($A \times \mathbb{N}$ is called the *cylindrification* of A.)
2. $A \times B \equiv_1 B \times A$.
3. *If A is creative, then $A \equiv_m A \times A$ (so $A \times A$ is also creative). [Hint: use Theorem 15.11.3.]

[24]This is an abuse of notation, since the standard set-theoretic product of any two sets A, B is also written $A \times B$. Here $A, B \subseteq \mathbb{N}$, and $A \times B$ is a set of *code numbers* of pairs of numbers. Hopefully, context will make clear which notion of product we are using.

Exercise 15.14.42 (cylinders)
A is called a *cylinder* if there is a set C such that $A \equiv_1 C \times \mathbb{N}$. Show:

1. A is a cylinder iff for all B, $B \leqslant_m A$ implies $B \leqslant_1 A$. Conclude that A is a cylinder iff $\overline{A}$ is a cylinder.
2. $A \leqslant_m B$ iff $A \times \mathbb{N} \leqslant_1 B \times \mathbb{N}$.
3. A is a cylinder iff $A \equiv_1 A \times \mathbb{N}$.
4. If A or B is a cylinder, then $A \times B$ is a cylinder (use 3.).

Exercise 15.14.43
Consider the sets K, $\overline{K}$, $K \oplus \overline{K}$, and $K \times \overline{K}$. From (21) we know that $K \nleqslant_m \overline{K}$ and $\overline{K} \nleqslant_m K$, and from Exercise 15.14.28:1 we have $K \leqslant_m K \oplus \overline{K}$ as well as $\overline{K} \leqslant_m K \oplus \overline{K}$. Show:

1. $K \leqslant_m K \times \overline{K}$ and $\overline{K} \leqslant_m K \times \overline{K}$. Conclude that $K \oplus \overline{K} \leqslant_m K \times \overline{K}$.
2. $K \oplus \overline{K} \nleqslant_m K$ and $K \oplus \overline{K} \nleqslant_m \overline{K}$.

Exercise 15.14.44

1. *Show that if A, B are recursively enumerable and A is not recursive, then $A \times \overline{A} \nleqslant_m B \oplus \overline{B}$.

   [Hint: (Jockusch) Suppose to the contrary that f is a recursive function s.t. $n \in A \wedge m \in \overline{A} \Leftrightarrow f(\langle n, m \rangle) \in B \oplus \overline{B}$. Then let $C = \{m : \exists n\, f(\langle n, m \rangle) \in B \oplus \varnothing\}$. Show:

   (i) C is recursively enumerable and $C \subseteq \overline{A}$.

   Thus, there is $a \in \overline{A} - C$. Show:

   (ii) $n \in A \Leftrightarrow f(\langle n, a \rangle) \in \varnothing \oplus \overline{B}$.

   (iii) Conclude that $\overline{A}$ is recursively enumerable (contrary to assumption).

2. Conclude from 1. that $K \times \overline{K} \nleqslant_m K \oplus \overline{K}$.

   Thus, all four sets mentioned in the previous exercise have different m-degrees. Still there is a clear sense that if you can decide membership in one of these sets (e.g. K), then you can decide membership in the other three. This indicates that m-reducibility, although very useful (e.g. Theorem 15.11.3), is not an optimal notion of reducing one problem to another. See footnote 16.

Exercise 15.14.45

1. Show that if $A \times \mathbb{N}$ is creative, then A is creative.
2. Show that if A is creative and B is any non-empty recursively enumerable set, then $A \times B$ is creative. [Hint: Use Theorem 15.11.3.]

Exercise 15.14.46
*Show that every infinite recursively enumerable set is the disjoint union of a creative and a productive set. [Hint: Let A be a enumerated by a 1-1 recursive f and consider $f(K)$ and $f(\overline{K})$.]

Exercise 15.14.47
Show that every productive set is the disjoint union of a creative and a productive set. [Hint: Use Lemma 15.11.6, and Exercises 15.14.46 and 15.14.39:1.]

Exercise 15.14.48
Let A and B be simple sets. Show:

1. $A \cap B$ is simple.
2. If C is r.e. and $\overline{A \cup C}$ is infinite, then $A \cup C$ is simple.
3. * $A \oplus B$ is simple. (See exercise 15.14.28.)
4. $A \times B$ is not simple. (See exercise 15.14.41.)

Exercise 15.14.49
Suppose A is a simple set. Show that $A \times \mathbb{N}$ is a recursively enumerable set which is neither recursive, nor creative, nor simple. [Hint: use Exercise 15.14.41:1. Also, show that no set of the form $C \times \mathbb{N}$ is simple.]

Exercise 15.14.50 (recursively and effectively inseparable sets)
Let A, B be disjoint sets. A, B are called *recursively inseparable* if there is no recursive set C separating them, i.e. s.t. $A \subseteq C$ and $B \cap C = \varnothing$. If A, B are recursively enumerable, they are called *effectively inseparable* if there is a recursive function f such that if $A \subseteq W_n$ and $B \subseteq W_m$ and $W_n \cap W_m = \varnothing$, then $f(n, m) \notin W_n \cup W_m$. Show:

1. $A, \overline{A}$ are recursively inseparable iff A is not recursive.
2. If A, B are recursively inseparable then neither A nor B are recursive.
3. Effective inseparability implies recursive inseparability.
4. If A, B are effectively inseparable then both A and B are creative.

Exercise 15.14.51 (example of effectively inseparable sets)
Define

$$K_0 = \{n\colon \{n\}^1(n) = 0\}$$

$$K_1 = \{n\colon \{n\}^1(n) = 1\}$$

1. Show that K_0, K_1 are recursively inseparable.

   [Hint: If D is recursive and separates K_0 and K_1, the characteristic function c_D is recursive and has an index e; derive a contradiction from this.]

2. *Show that K_0, K_1 are effectively inseparable.

   [Hint: Define

$$H(n,m,k) = \begin{cases} 1 & \text{if } \exists p(T_1(n,k,p) \wedge \forall q_{q \leqslant p} \neg T_1(m,k,q)) \\ 0 & \text{if } \exists p(T_1(m,k,p) \wedge \forall q_{q \leqslant p} \neg T_1(n,k,q)) \\ \text{undefined} & \text{otherwise} \end{cases}$$

   (The idea is that we compute $\{n\}^1(k)$ and $\{m\}^1(k)$, and give the value 1 if the computation of $\{n\}^1(k)$ stops first, and 0 if the computation of $\{m\}^1(k)$ stops first.) Show that H is partial recursive (Exercise 15.14.7), and thus that there is a recursive function f such that $\{f(n,m)\}^1(k) = H(m,n,k)$. Conclude that K_0, K_1 are inseparable via f.]

Exercise 15.14.52 (logical version of the example)
Let T be a consistent and axiomatizable extension of Q + the axiom $\forall x \forall y(x \leqslant y \vee y < x)$. With K_0, K_1 as in the preceding exercise, let R_0, R_1 be recursive relations such that

$$n \in K_0 \Leftrightarrow \exists m\, R_0(n,m)$$
$$n \in K_1 \Leftrightarrow \exists m\, R_1(n,m)$$

Let $\theta_0(x,y), \theta_1(x,y)$ be formulas representing R_0, R_1 in T, respectively, and set

$$\psi_0(x) := \exists y(\theta_0(x,y) \wedge \forall z_{z \leqslant y} \neg \theta_1(x,z))$$

$$\psi_1(x) := \exists y(\theta_1(x,y) \wedge \forall z_{z \leqslant y} \neg \theta_0(x,z))$$

Show the following.

1. If $n \in K_i$, then $T \vdash \psi_i(\mathbf{n})$, $i = 0, 1$.
2. If $T \vdash \psi_1(\mathbf{n})$, then $T \vdash \neg\psi_0(\mathbf{n})$.
3. Let $A_0 = \{n : T \vdash \psi_0(\mathbf{n})\}$ and $A_1 = \{n : T \vdash \neg\psi_0(\mathbf{n})\}$, and conclude that $K_0 \subseteq A_0$ and $K_1 \subseteq A_1$.

Exercise 15.14.53 (effectively inseparable theories)
*Continuing the preceding exercise, show that the sets THM_T and REF_T are effectively inseparable (hence both creative), so T is (effectively) incomplete.

[Hint: Let K_0, K_1 be effectively inseparable via f. First note that A_0, A_1 are also effectively inseparable via f. So if $h(n) = \#(\psi_0(\mathbf{n}))$, we have

$$\begin{cases} n \in A_0 & \Leftrightarrow \quad h(n) \in \mathit{thm}_T \\ n \in A_1 & \Leftrightarrow \quad h(n) \in \mathit{ref}_T \end{cases}$$

Take a recursive g such that $W_{g(n)} = \{k \colon h(k) \in W_n\}$, and use it to find a recursive function that separates thm_T and ref_T.]

Exercise 15.14.54 (reduction property)
*Show that if A, B are recursively enumerable, there are recursively enumerable $A' \subseteq A$ and $B' \subseteq B$ such that $A' \cup B' = A \cup B$ and $A' \cap B' = \varnothing$.

[Hint: If $n \in A \Leftrightarrow \exists m R(n, m)$ and $n \in B \Leftrightarrow \exists m S(n, m)$, we define $n \in A' \Leftrightarrow \exists m(R(n, m) \wedge \forall k_{k \leqslant m} \neg S(n, k))$ and $n \in B' \Leftrightarrow \exists m(S(n, m) \wedge \forall k_{k<m} \neg R(n, k))$.]

Part V

Appendix

16 Sets, functions, relations

This appendix presents the basic set-theoretic machinery used in this book. For example, consider the notion of an L-interpretation (Chapter 2.3.2): L is a *set* of non-logical symbosl, and the interpretation (model) is an *ordered pair* (M, I), where M is a *non-empty set*, and I is a *function from L to* (depending on the symbols), *elements, relations,* or *functions* in M. The reader who needs more background on these notions will find it here. We go on to discuss finite, infinite, and countable sets, as well as definitions and proofs by mathematical induction.

16.1. Sets

Intuitively, sets are collections of objects. But the abstract concept of set is primitive and cannot be defined in terms of some even more fundamental concept (though see below on functions). What set theory does is to describe the *properties* of sets as carefully as possible. This can be formulated as an axiomatic theory, where the axioms state the properties we assume (or stipulate) sets to have. We will mention some of the axioms, but the presentation below is informal.

Most of the time we use $A, B, C, \ldots$ for sets and write

$$a \in A$$

which is read "a is an element of A" or "a belongs to A", for the basic *element relation*. Formally, $\in$ is a binary predicate symbol, and the most common axiomatic set theory, *ZF*,[1] is formulated in first-order logic with $\in$ as the only non-logical symbol ($L_{ZF} = \{\in\}$). Thus, every piece of set-theoretic terminology introduced below could in principle be expressed only in terms of $\in$ (and variables and logical symbols).

A fundamental property of sets is that they are determined by their elements, and by nothing else. For example, the *order* in which you present the elements is irrelevant, and *repeating* them has no effect:

$$\{a, b, c\} = \{a, c, b\} = \{b, a, c\} = \{a, b, b, c, a\}$$

[1] Zermelo-Fraenkel set theory, after two of its inventors, Ernst Zermelo (1871–1953) and Abraham Fraenkel (1891-1965).

is the unique set which has a, b, and c as elements. The property is called *extensionality*:

Extensionality Axiom: $A = B$ iff for all a, $a \in A \Leftrightarrow a \in B$.

Another basic way to specify sets is as extensions of properties: you have a certain property P and form the set A of all objects that have property P. Using a notation from first-order logic:

(1) $A = \{x\colon P(x)\}$

There is of course the issue of *which* properties have sets as their extensions. All properties? In that case, for example,

$$V = \{x\colon x = x\}$$

i.e. the set of *everything*, would be a set (since everything is identical to itself). As a special case, we would have

$$V \in V$$

But according to a common intuition about sets, this is impossible: no set can be an element of itself. The intuition is that sets are 'built from below': you need access to the elements before you can form the set of them, so $A \in A$ is impossible. Even more seriously, unrestricted use of (1) leads to contradictions; see Russell's Paradox in Section 16.5.2. The standard solution is to restrict (1) so that you have to start from a given set B, and form the set of all elements *of* B with property P:

(2) $A = \{x\colon x \in B \text{ and } P(x)\} = \{x \in B\colon P(x)\}$

This principle is called the xxiom of Separation:

Separation axiom: If B is a set and P is a property (expressible in the language of set theory), then $\{x \in B\colon P(x)\}$ is also a set.

Digression: set and classes. It is still useful to think of (1) as defining a collection of things; collections defined in this way are called *classes*. Some classes are sets, that is, their existence follows from the axioms of set theory, but others are not; they are *proper classes*. For example, V is a proper class. It's fine to reason about classes, as long as you don't think they are sets. In particular, a proper class cannot be an element of a (set or) class. Classes are best thought of as extensions of properties, and many of the operations we define for sets below work for classes as well, such as union and intersection.[2] *End of digression*

Some simple sets are given on the form (1): we can simply *stipulate* that they are sets. One example is *unordered pairs*: if a and b are given objects, we can form the set

[2]There is also an operation that works for classes but not for sets, namely, *complement*: the complement of $\{x\colon P(x)\}$ is, naturally, the class $\{x\colon \neg P(x)\}$.

(3) $\{x : x = a \text{ or } x = b\} = \{a, b\}$

Note the special case that $a = b$; in this case we have a *unit set* or a *singleton*, i.e. a set $\{a\}$ which has exactly one element. Another example is the *empty set*, which can be defined like this:[3]

(4) $\varnothing = \{x : x \neq x\}$

A third example guarantees the existence of *unions* and *intersections* of sets: given sets A and B, we have (using logical terminology):[4]

(5) a. $A \cup B = \{x : x \in A \vee x \in B\}$
b. $A \cap B = \{x : x \in A \wedge x \in B\}$

Repeating these operations we can get unions and intersections of finitely many sets,

$$A \cup (B \cup C), \text{ etc.}$$

These operations are also defined for infinitely many sets: if, for example, $A_0, A_1, A_2, \ldots$ are sets, then so is

$$\bigcup_n A_n = \{x : \exists k(x \in A_k)\}$$

Since union and intersection are defined in terms of $\vee$ and $\wedge$, some propositional logical laws translate directly to set-theoretic laws:

(6) a. $A \cup A = A \cap A = A$
b. $A \cup B = B \cup A; \ A \cup (B \cup C) = (A \cup B) \cup C$
c. $A \cap B = B \cap A; \ A \cap (B \cap C) = (A \cap B) \cap C$
d. $A \cap (B \cup C) = (A \cap B) \cup (A \cap C)$
$A \cup (B \cap C) = (A \cup B) \cap (A \cup C)$

---

[3]There are many other ways to specify the empty set. But according to Extensionality, there is just one empty set. (Why?) In the early days of set theory there was some confusion about both the empty set and unit sets, i.e. about the difference between a and $\{a\}$. But even if a uniquely determines $\{a\}$, and vice versa, they are two distinct objects: one is a set with exactly one element, the other doesn't have to be a set, but if a is a set it could have arbitrarily many elements.

But is the empty set really a *set*? Well, is the empty bag a bag? (Of course, this is mathematics, so there is just one empty bag ...) In any case, it would be very awkward to exclude the empty set from the realm of sets.

[4]More precisely, we have stated informally some axioms of set theory: the Pair Axiom (that $\{a, b\}$ exists for any a, b), and the Union Axiom (that $A \cup B$ exists for any sets A, B). The existence of the empty set follows from the Axiom of Separation, as soon as any set A exists, since we have $\varnothing = \{x \in A : x \neq x\}$. Likewise, the existence of the intersection $A \cap B$ follows from Separation. (How?) Formally, in *ZF* the Pair and Union Axioms are the sentences:

(Pair) $\forall x \forall y \exists z \forall u(u \in z \leftrightarrow u = x \vee u = y)$

(Union) $\forall x \forall y \exists z \forall u(u \in z \leftrightarrow u \in x \vee u \in y)$

What about negation? If we define $\overline{A} = \{x : x \notin A\}$, we would immediately get back the set of everything, since $V = A \cup \overline{A}$. So here again it is important to restrict to the objects *in a given set* B that are not elements of A:

(7) $B - A = \{x \in B : x \notin A\}$

$B - A$ is the *complement* of A *relative to* B. Often, however, the given set is understood; e.g. the set $\mathbb{N} = \{0, 1, 2, \ldots\}$ of natural numbers, or, more generally, the domain M of an interpretation/model. Then we may write

$$\overline{A}$$

instead of $M - A$, and complement will then correspond to negation in logic, so we have, for example,

(8) a. $\overline{\overline{A}} = A$ (double negation elimination)
b. $A \cap \overline{A} = \varnothing$ (law of contradiction)
c. $A \cup \overline{A} = M$ (excluded middle)
d. $\overline{A \cup B} = \overline{A} \cap \overline{B}$ (de Morgan)
e. $\overline{A \cap B} = \overline{A} \cup \overline{B}$ (de Morgan)

Next, we need the important notion of subset: A is a *subset* of B,

$$A \subseteq B$$

if every element of A is also an element of B. For example, here are all the 8 subsets of the set $\{a, b, c\}$:

$$\varnothing, \{a\}, \{b\}, \{c\}, \{a, b\}, \{a, c\}, \{b, c\}, \{a, b, c\}$$

The *power set* of A, which we write $\mathcal{P}(A)$, is the set of *all* subsets of A:

(9) $\mathcal{P}(A) = \{B : B \subseteq A\}$

For example,

$$\mathcal{P}(\{a, b, c\}) = \{\varnothing, \{a\}, \{b\}, \{c\}, \{a, b\}, \{a, c\}, \{b, c\}, \{a, b, c\}\}$$

So the *Power set Axiom* of *ZF* says that $\mathcal{P}(A)$ exists for every set A.[5]

Here are some 'laws' involving subsets:

(10) a. $\varnothing \subseteq A$; $A \subseteq A$; $A \subseteq M$
b. $A = B$ iff $A \subseteq B$ and $B \subseteq A$
c. $A \subseteq B$ iff $A \cap B = A$ iff $A \cup B = B$

[5]Formally:

(Power set) $\forall x \exists y \forall z (z \in y \leftrightarrow z \subseteq x)$

Finally, we shall need the concept of an *ordered pair*. The ordered pair of a (first) and b (second) is written

$$(a, b)$$

What distinguishes (a, b) from $\{a, b\}$ is precisely that the order matters. This can be expressed as follows:

(11) $(a, b) = (c, d)$ iff $a = c$ and $b = d$

In fact, (11) is the *only* thing we need to know about ordered pairs. We can go on to define

$$(a_1, a_2, a_3) = ((a_1, a_2), a_3)$$
$$\ldots$$
$$(a_1, \ldots, a_n, a_{n+1}) = ((a_1, \ldots, a_n), a_{n+1})$$

The set of all ordered pairs where the first element comes from A and the second from B is called the (cartesian) *product* of A and B, written $A \times B$. Thus:

(12) $A \times B = \{(a, b) \colon a \in A \wedge b \in B\}$

Similarly we have the product of any finite numbers of sets:

(13) $A_1 \times \ldots \times A_n = \{(a_1, \ldots, a_n) \colon a_i \in A_i \text{ for } i = 1, \ldots, n\}$

We can also form the product of a set with itself, in which case we write $A \times A = A^2$, and, more generally,

(14) $A \times \ldots \times A = A^n$

It is often convenient to think of the set-theoretic universe as consisting only of sets.[6] So everything is a set: ordered pairs can be construed as sets (Exercise 16.1.2), and relations and functions can be taken to be sets.

16.1.1. Exercises to Section 16.1

Exercise 16.1.1

1. Verify that (6), (8), and (10) hold.
2. If we think of sets in analogy with statements or sentences, which sentences do $\varnothing$ and M above correspond to?

Exercise 16.1.2 (ordered pairs)
The crucial property of ordered pairs is (11). There are many ways to define special sets with this property; here is the most common one:

[6] Alternatively, it would consist of sets and objects which are not sets, so-called *urelements*; see Example 6.6.6.

$$(a, b) =_{\text{def}} \{\{a\}, \{a, b\}\}$$

Show that under this definition, (11) holds. More generally, show that

$$(a_1, \ldots, a_n) = (b_1, \ldots, b_n) \text{ iff } a_i = b_i \text{ for } i = 1, \ldots, n.$$

Exercise 16.1.3
Verify

1. $\mathcal{P}(A) \cap \mathcal{P}(B) = \mathcal{P}(A \cap B)$
2. $\mathcal{P}(A) \cup \mathcal{P}(B) \subseteq \mathcal{P}(A \cup B)$ (Why doesn't identity hold?)
3. $A \times (B \cup C) = (A \times B) \cup (A \times C)$
4. $A \times (B \cap C) = (A \times B) \cap (A \times C)$

Exercise 16.1.4
If A has n elements and B has m elements, how many elements does $\mathcal{P}(A)$ have? What about $A \times B$? $A \cup B$?

16.2. Functions

Intuitively, a function is a rule or a law f that to every *argument* a assigns a unique *value*, written $f(a)$. Examples:

$f(a)$ = the capital of a (where a is a country)
$f(n) = n^2 + 3$ (where n is a natural number)
$f(x) = \sqrt{x}$ (where x is a real number)
$f(P) = P^{\mathcal{M}}$ (where P is a predicate symbol in L and $\mathcal{M}$ is an L-interpretation)
$f(A) = A \times A$ (where A is a set)
$f(x, y) = 1 \Leftrightarrow x = y = 1$ (where x, y are 0 or 1: the truth function for the connective $\wedge$)

So f has a *domain* of arguments, and a *range* of values. We write

$$f \colon A \to B$$

'f is a function from A to B', where A is the domain and the values are in B.

In set theory, we simply *identify* the function f with the set of ordered pairs $(a, f(a))$ such that a belongs to the domain.[7] More precisely, we say that a *function from A to B* is, by definition, a subset f of $A \times B$ such that

[7] In Chapter 9.8, (30), we called this set G_f, the *graph* of f, but in set theory we identify the two. This doesn't mean that the set-theoretic notion of function is necessarily distinct from the number-theoretic notion used in Chapters 9 – 15. For example, Chapter 9.9.1 distinguished representability of G_f (in a theory T) from representability of f as in Def. 9.9.2. But the latter requirement can also be expressed in terms of G_f; it is just a stronger condition. In computability theory it is convenient to distinguish (partial) functions from their graphs, but the distinction can be seen as merely terminological.

(i) if $(a, b) \in f$ and $(a, b') \in f$, then $b = b'$;
(ii) for every $a \in A$ there is $b \in B$ such that $(a, b) \in f$.[8]

Condition (i) says that the value is uniquely determined by the argument, and instead of $(a, b) \in f$ we write:

$$f(a) = b$$

If $f: A \to B$ then A, the domain of f, can be reconstructed from f:

$$dom(f) = \{x: \exists y\, f(x) = y\} = A$$

The range B, on the other hand, is (by our definition) not determined by f, since we don't require that every element of B is the value of f for some argument. Thus:

$$range(f) = \{y: \exists x\, f(x) = y\} \subseteq B$$

We let

(15) $B^A = \{f: f \text{ is a function from } A \text{ to } B\}$

B^A is sometimes written $[A \to B]$.

Here are some important notions pertaining to functions:

(16) a. f is *surjective* if $range(f) = B$: for every $b \in B$ there is $a \in A$ such that $f(a) = b$. (One also says that f is a function from A *onto* B.)

b. f is *injective* (or *one-one* or *1-1*) if different arguments give different values, i.e. if $a \neq a'$ implies $f(a) \neq f(a')$.

c. f is *bijective* (or a *a one-one correspondence*) if f is both injective and surjective.

If f is bijective, then every element of A corresponds to a unique element of B, *and vice versa*, hence the label 'one-one correspondence'.

Next, we describe how to compose two functions into one:[9]

(17) If $f : A \to B$ and $g : B \to C$ then the function $g \circ f$, the *composition* of f and g is defined as follows: for all $a \in A$,

$$g \circ f(a) = g(f(a))$$

One verifies that $g \circ f$ really is a function from A to C according to our definition (i.e that the value is in C and uniquely determined by the argument, and that the domain is A).

[8]If $A = \varnothing$, we have $A \times B = \varnothing$ for every set B, and (i) and (ii) trivially hold. So $\varnothing$ is a function (from $\varnothing$ to B), the *empty function*, according to our definition. On the other hand, there can be no function from a non-empty set A to $\varnothing$, since condition (ii) cannot then be satisfied.

[9]A more general notion of composition was defined in Chapter 8.2.

If f is an *injective* function from A to B there is a corresponding function in the other direction, called f^{-1}:

(18) $\quad f^{-1}(b) = a \Leftrightarrow f(a) = b$

Since f is injective, $f^{-1}(b)$ is uniquely determined by b, so f^{-1} is a function. Furthermore, it is injective like f: if $b \neq b'$, then $f^{-1}(b) \neq f^{-1}(b')$. But its domain doesn't have to be all of B; we have $dom(f^{-1}) = range(f) \subseteq B$. If the domain is all of B, i.e. if f is surjective, and hence a bijection, we call f^{-1} the *inverse* of f.[10] See also Exercise 16.2.3.

We have construed functions as sets, but conversely, to every set A correspond its *characteristic function* c_A:

(19) $$c_A(a) = \begin{cases} 1 & \text{if } a \in A \\ 0 & \text{if } a \notin A \end{cases}$$

This gives us the possibility to consider sets as functions, which sometimes is convenient.[11] Note however that (19) is not yet a correct definition of c_A: we haven't specified the *domain*. As written, $dom(c_A)$ could be all of V, but V is not a set. Therefore, just as for complements, we must presuppose that there is a given domain M with $A \subseteq M$, so that c_A is a function from M to $\{0, 1\}$.

So far we have talked about functions with one argument, or 1-place functions. Functions can have several arguments, like, for example, truth functions (functions from $\{0, 1\}^n$ to $\{0, 1\}$). Given sets $A_1, \ldots, A_n$ and B we let an *n-place function from $A_1, \ldots, A_n$ to B* simply be a (1-place) function from $A = A_1 \times \ldots \times A_n$ to B. So these n-place functions are special cases of 1-place functions, and everything we said about the latter applies to the former.[12]

In particular, we have the characteristic function of an n-ary relation R, where we as before presuppose a given domain M, that is, $R \subseteq M^n$, so c_R is a function from M^n to $\{0, 1\}$:

$$c_R(a_1, \ldots, a_n) = \begin{cases} 1 & \text{if } R(a_1, \ldots, a_n) \\ 0 & \text{if } \neg R(a_1, \ldots, a_n) \end{cases}$$

So characteristic functions are functions from some set B to the set $\{0, 1\}$, which we may also identify with the number 2 (see Chapter 12.8). The set of all such functions is then

$$2^B$$

[10] One may call f^{-1} the inverse of f even when f is not surjective; terminology varies.

[11] So we have the possibility to let functions be primitive, and sets defined. This is often done when one chooses *type theory*, rather than set theory, as one's framework.

[12] Actually we have defined a special kind of n-place functions, namely, those whose domain is a cartesian product. This is not necessary: the domain can also be a *subset* of such a product, or (equivalently) an arbitrary set of n-tuples.

The latter set is in turn often identified with the power set of B:

$$\mathcal{P}(B)$$

This is because every subset A of B has a unique characteristic function c_A in 2^B, and every function from B to $\{0,1\}$ corresponds to a unique subset of B, namely, $\{a \in B\colon f(a) = 1\}$. More formally:

(20) The function $G : 2^B \to \mathcal{P}(B)$, defined by $G(f) = \{a \in B : f(a) = 1\}$ for $f \in 2^B$, is a bijection, s.t. $G^{-1}(A) = c_A$ for $A \subseteq B$.

Thus G, which can also be defined by $G(c_A) = A$ for all $A \subseteq B$, is not just any bijection between these sets—there are many; see Exercise 16.2.1—but the 'natural' one, which makes it reasonable to sometimes identify sets with characteristic functions (over some domain).

16.2.1. Partial functions

We defined *total* functions from A to B: every argument $a \in A$ gives a value $f(a)$. In some contexts—in particular, in the context of *computable* functions—we needed the notion of a *partial* function from A to B, where the domain $dom(f)$ is a subset of A, not necessarily all of A. For example, f may be given by an algorithm that computes it, but the algorithm need not yield an output for all inputs, and we may not know in advance for which inputs it does.

Thus, a partial function f from A to B is a subset of $A \times B$ satisfying (i) above but not necessarily (ii). If $a \in A - dom(f)$, $f(a)$ is *undefined*.

Any function can be *restricted* to a subset of its domain. If f is a partial or total function f from A to B and $A' \subseteq A$, then the *restriction of f to A'*, denoted $f{\restriction}A'$, is defined, for $a \in A'$, by

(21) $$f{\restriction}A'(a) = \begin{cases} f(a) & \text{if } f(a) \text{ is defined} \\ \text{undefined} & \text{otherwise} \end{cases}$$

Thus, if f is partial, $f{\restriction}dom(f)$ is a total function from $dom(f)$ to B.

Total functions are special cases of partial functions: the special case when $dom(f) = A$. But partial functions can also be seen as special cases of total functions: if f is a partial function from A to B, take any object $*$ outside B, and define, for all $a \in A$:

(22) $$f'(a) = \begin{cases} f(a) & \text{if } f(a) \text{ is defined} \\ * & \text{otherwise} \end{cases}$$

So f' is a total function from A to $B \cup \{*\}$ corresponding to f.[13]

[13]Note that $f = f{\restriction}dom(f)$. Also, with f' as in (22), $f = \{(a,b) \in f' : b \neq *\}$. This indicates why partial functions are mainly useful in circumstances when we may know that f is a partial function from A to B without knowing exactly which set $dom(f)$ is.

16.2.2. Exercises to Section 16.2

Exercise 16.2.1

Suppose A has n elements and B has m elements ($m, n \in \mathbb{N}$).

1. How many elements are there in B^A?
2. Suppose $m \geqslant n$. How many injective functions from A to B are there? How many if $m < n$?
3. What is required of m and n for there to be any bijective functions from A to B? In that case, how many are there?
4. *Suppose $m \leqslant n$. Calculating the number of surjective functions from A to B is more difficult (but can be found in any suitable textbook). Instead, do a simple special case: $n = 5, m = 4$.

Exercise 16.2.2

1. Verify that $h \circ (g \circ f) = (h \circ (g \circ f)$ for all appropriate f, g, h, i.e. that composition of functions is *associative*.
2. If $f\colon A \to B$ and $g\colon B \to C$ and g is surjective, does it follow that $g \circ f$ is surjective? If f and g both are injective (bijective), does it follow that $g \circ f$ is injective (bijective)?

Exercise 16.2.3 (inverses and identity)

1. Let f^{-1} be defined as in (18). Verify that $f^{-1}: B \to A$ iff f is a bijection, and that f^{-1} in that case is also a bijection.
2. The function $id_A : A \to A$ defined by $id_A(a) = a$ for all $a \in A$ is called the *identity function on A*.
   (a) Verify that if $f\colon A \to B$, then $id_B \circ f = f = f \circ id_A$.
   (b) If f is a bijection from A to B, show that $f^{-1} \circ f = id_A$ and $f \circ f^{-1} = id_B$.
   (c) Suppose $f\colon A \to B$ and $g\colon B \to A$. Show that if $g \circ f = id_A$ and $f \circ g = id_B$, then f is bijective and $f^{-1} = g$.
3. Suppose that $f\colon A \to B$ and $g\colon B \to C$ are both bijections. Show that $(g \circ f)^{-1} = f^{-1} \circ g^{-1}$ (cf. Exercise 16.2.2).

Exercise 16.2.4 (images and inverse images)

Every $f\colon A \to B$ induces functions, called (a bit confusingly) f^{-1} and f, from $\mathcal{P}(B)$ to $\mathcal{P}(A)$ and from $\mathcal{P}(A)$ to $\mathcal{P}(B)$: for $X \subseteq A$ and $Y \subseteq B$,

$f^{-1}(Y) = \{a\colon f(a) \in Y\}$ (the *inverse image* of Y under f)

$f(X) = \{f(a)\colon a \in X\}$ (the *image* of X under f)

Prove the following:

1. $X \subseteq f^{-1} \circ f(X)$
2. $f \circ f^{-1}(Y) \subseteq Y$

3. If f is injective, then $f^{-1} \circ f = id_{\mathcal{P}(X)}$.
4. If f is surjective, then $f \circ f^{-1} = id_{\mathcal{P}(Y)}$.

Exercise 16.2.5
Check that (20) is correct.

Exercise 16.2.6
If A has n elements and B has m elements, how many partial functions are there from A to B? [Hint: use (22).]

16.3. Relations

Intuitively, a relation is some kind of connection or link that may hold or not between objects in some domain. A relation has an *arity*, a number n which says how many *arguments* it takes. 1-place (or 1-ary or unary) relations are often called *properties*. We write

(23) $\quad R(a_1, \ldots, a_n)$

when the relation R holds between the objects $a_1, \ldots, a_n$. Each argument might have its own domain. For example, the binary relation 'is born on the' relates people and birth dates, so the domain of the first argument is a set of people, and the second argument's domain is a set of (let's say) dates.

The *extension* of an n-ary relation is the set of n-tuples satisfying it. In set theory we identify relations with their extensions, just as we identified functions with their graphs. We may simply say that an n-ary relation is a subset of $A_1 \times \ldots \times A_n$, for given sets (domains) $A_1, \ldots, A_n$. So in place of (23) we sometimes write

$$(a_1, \ldots, a_n) \in R$$

If $A_1 = \ldots = A_n = A$ we say that R is a *relation over A*, or *on A*, which then means that $R \subseteq A^n$.

So the concept relation is more general than the concept function. We said that a function from A to B is a subset of $A \times B$ such that (i) if $(a, b), (a, b') \in f$ then $b = b'$, and (ii) $dom(f) = A$. In other words, it is a relation over $A \times B$ with these properties.

We shall look briefly at some properties of *binary* relations. In this case we often write

$$aRb$$

instead of Rab or $R(a, b)$. If nothing else is said we assume that R is a relation in some domain M, i.e. $R \subseteq M^2$. There is then an *empty relation* $\varnothing$, and a *universal relation* M^2. $\varnothing$ is the smallest relation on M and M^2 is the largest: for all relations R on M we have $\varnothing \subseteq R \subseteq M^2$.

Another important relation (in M) is the *identity relation* id_M:

$$id_M = \{(a, a) : a \in M\}$$

(This is the same as the *identity function* id_M; see Exercise 16.2.3.)

16.3.1. Operations on binary relations

Since relations are sets, the usual set-theoretic operations apply to them: union, intersection, complement. There is also a natural way to define the *composition* of two relations (also called *relative product*), and the *converse* (also called *inverse*) of a relation. Define:

(24) a. $a(S \circ R)c$ iff there is b such that aRb and bSc

b. $a\check{R}b$ iff bRa

$\check{R}$ is also written R^{-1}. The composition of R and S is sometimes written in reverse order (i.e. $R \circ S$; notations like $S \cdot R$ or R/S are also common). The order chosen here agrees with the one for composition of functions: if $aRb \Leftrightarrow f(a) = b$ and $aSb \Leftrightarrow g(a) = b$, where $f : A \to B$ and $g : B \to C$ ($A, B, C \subseteq M$), then

(25) $a(S \circ R)c$ iff $g \circ f(a) = c$

Just as for functions we can define:

$$dom(R) = \{a : \exists b\, aRb\} \text{ and } range(R) = \{b : \exists a\, aRb\}$$

A relation R is *functional* if aRb and aRb' implies $b = b'$. So a functional relation R is a function from $dom(R)$ to some set B such that $range(R) \subseteq B$. We also say that (an arbitrary relation) R is *injective* if aRb and $a'Rb$ implies $a = a'$. Examples of 'laws' for binary relations are given in the exercises.

Here are some well-known properties of relations:

(26) a. R is *reflexive* if for all $a \in M$, aRa.
b. R is *irreflexive* if for all $a \in M$, $\neg aRa$.

c. R is *symmetric* if for all $a, b \in M$, $aRb \Rightarrow bRa$.
d. R is *asymmetric* if for all $a, b \in M$, $aRb \Rightarrow \neg bRa$.
e. R is *antisymmetric* if for all $a, b \in M$, aRb & $bRa \Rightarrow a = b$.

f. R is *transitive* if for all $a, b, c \in M$, aRb & $bRc \Rightarrow aRc$.
g. R is *intransitive* if for all $a, b, c \in M$, aRb & $bRc \Rightarrow \neg aRc$.

In terms of these and other properties we can classify some common types of binary relations.

16.3.2. Order relations

Order relations of various kinds can be thought of as *strict* ('less than') and *non-strict* ('less than or equal to'). We use the symbol $<$ for the former, and $\leqslant$ for the latter. Starting with the non-strict case:

(27) a. $\leqslant$ is a *preorder* if it is reflexive and transitive.

b. If $\leqslant$ is also antisymmetric, it is called a $\leqslant$ *partial order.*

c. $\leqslant$ is *total* (or *linear*), if it in addition satisfies the condition that any two elements $a, b \in M$ are comparable, i.e.

$$a \leqslant b \text{ or } b \leqslant a$$

Here are corresponding strict variants:

(28) a. $<$ is a *strict partial order* if it is irreflexive and transitive.

b. $<$ is *total* (or *linear*) if in addition, for all $a, b \in M$,

$$a < b \text{ or } a = b \text{ or } b < a$$

Note that if $<$ is irreflexive and transitive, it is also *asymmetric*: if $a < b$ and $b < a$, then $a < a$ by transitivity, which contradicts irreflexivity. Thus: $a < b \Rightarrow \neg b < a$. These definitions concern order relations of different kinds *on* M. Replacing M by A in the definitions we obtain order relations *on* A, for any set $A \subseteq M$. A *partially ordered set*—often called a *poset*—is a set together with a (strict or non-strict) partial order on it. Similarly, an *ordered set* is a set together with a total order (strict or non-strict) on that set.

Power sets, or more generally, any set of subsets of a given set, are typical examples of posets: the relation $\subseteq$ is reflexive, transitive, and antisymmetric.

There is an obvious way to go from from strict to non-strict relations, and vice versa:

(29) a. Given a relation $<$, define: $a \leqslant b$ iff $a < b$ or $a = b$. If $<$ is a strict partial (total) order, $\leqslant$ is a non-strict (total) order.

b. Given a relation $\leqslant$, define: $a < b$ iff $a \leqslant b$ and $a \neq b$. If $\leqslant$ is a partial (total) order, $<$ is a strict partial (total) order.

One way to visualize orders is to let $a < b$ correspond to the relation 'a is to the left of b' in a diagram. For example,

(30) 0 1 2 3 ...

can represent the *ordered set* of natural numbers, i.e. the set $\{0, 1, 2, \ldots\}$ together with the usual order between numbers, while (31) represents a different and partial order of *the same* set: the numbers $\{2, 4, 6, \ldots\}$ have their usual order; and likewise the numbers $\{1, 3, 5, \ldots\}$; whereas the number 0 is smaller than all other numbers; and no even number, except 0, is smaller than or greater than any odd number:

(31)
$$\begin{array}{cl} & 2\ \ 4\ \ 6\ \ \ldots \\ 0 & \\ & 1\ \ 3\ \ 5\ \ \ldots \end{array}$$

There are of course (infinitely) many ways to order the set $\mathbb{N} = \{0, 1, 2, \ldots\}$, even if we restrict attention to total orders. Here are some examples of total orders of $\mathbb{N}$ that differ in important respects (see Exercise 16.3.7):

(32) a. $\ldots\ 3\ \ 2\ \ 1\ \ 0$

b. $0\ \ 2\ \ 4\ \ \ldots\ \ 1\ \ 3\ \ 5\ \ \ldots$

c. $\ldots\ 5\ \ 3\ \ 1\ \ 0\ \ 2\ \ 4\ \ \ldots$

d. $1\ \ 2\ \ 3\ \ \ldots\ \ 0$

e. $1\ \ \ldots\ \ 7\ \ 5\ \ 3\ \ 2\ \ 4\ \ 6\ \ \ldots\ \ 0$

The representations in (32) work for total orders. For partial orders of *finite* sets one can use so-called Hasse diagrams. For example, if we restrict the partial order in (31) to $\{0, 1, \ldots, 6\}$, we draw it as follows:

(33)

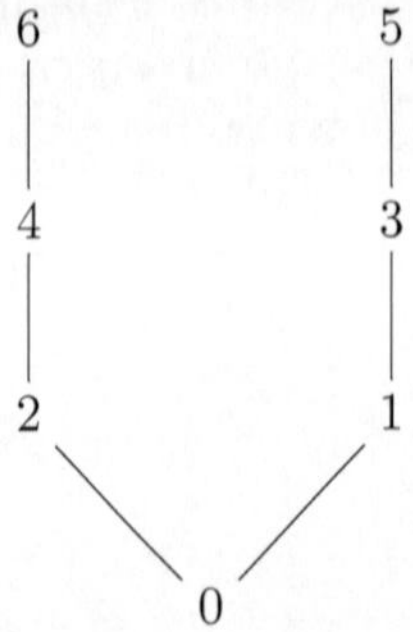

So you draw a line *upwards* from a to b when b is an *immediate successor* of a (i.e. $a < b$ and there is no c such that $a < c < b$), but not otherwise. Thus there is a line from 0 to 2 above, but not from 0 to 4 (even though $0 < 4$, but the transitivity of the order is to be read into the diagram).

In principle, every binary relation R in a finite domain, whether it is an order or not, can be represented by an *arrow diagram* or a (directed) *graph*: you let every individual in the domain be a point in a plane, and draw an arrow from a to b iff aRb. The partial order (33) would be represented as follows:

(34)

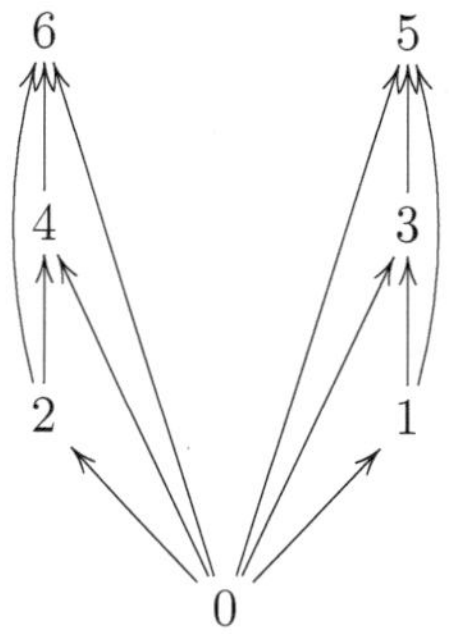

Here the position in the plane is irrelevant: the entire relation is represented by arrows, so we might as well have used, for example, (35).[14]

(35)

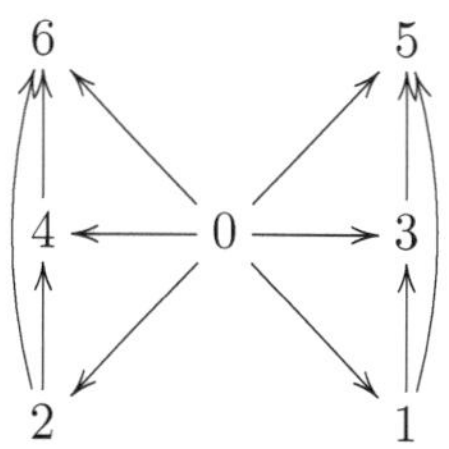

Different representations serve different purposes. The Hasse diagram (33) is certainly simpler for visualizing the relation as a partial order.

16.3.3. Equivalence relations

(36) R is an *equivalence relation* if R is reflexive, symmetric, and transitive.

We use E for equivalence relations. As before, E can be a relation on the whole domain M, or on a subset A of M; the set A can always be recovered from E:

(37) $dom(E) = A = \{a : aEa\}$

The identity relation id_M is an equivalence relation. Likewise, the universal relation is an equivalence relation. These are the *smallest* and *largest* equivalence relations on M, respectively:

(38) If E is an equivalence relation, then $id_M \subseteq E \subseteq M^2$.

[14] *Graph theory* is a mathematical theory studying properties of graphs. In principle, it is thus a general theory about binary relations.

An equivalence relation E partitions the domain into pairwise disjoint non-empty subsets, as follows. For each a, the *equivalence class of* a, which we will write $[a]_E$ (or just $[a]$ if E is understood):

$$[a]_E = \{b\colon bEa\}$$

Formally, a *partition of* M is defined to be a family (a set) of non-empty and pairwise disjoint subsets of M, i.e. a family $\{A_i\}_{i\in I}$ of subsets of M such that:[15]

a. $A_i \neq \varnothing$ for each $i \in I$;
b. if $A_i \neq A_j$, then $A_i \cap A_j = \varnothing$;
c. $\bigcup_{i\in I} A_i = M$

We have the following simple but important fact (Exercise 16.3.10):

(39) a. If E is an equivalence relation in M, then $\{[a]_E\}_{a\in M}$ is a partition of M.

b. If $\{A_i\}_{i\in I}$ is a partition of M, then the relation E defined by $aEb \Leftrightarrow \exists i\ a, b \in A_i$ is an equivalence relation in M, whose equivalence classes are the given partition sets.

Equivalence relations and partitions are really the same thing from different perspectives; we may choose whichever is more convenient in a given context.

Chapter 6 shows how to *classify* equivalence relations/partitions by the number of equivalence classes and the number of elements in each equivalence class.

16.3.4. Exercises to Section 16.3

Exercise 16.3.1
Verify that (25) is correct.

Exercise 16.3.2
Demonstrate the following 'laws' for relations:

1. $(S\circ R)\circ T = S\circ(R\circ T)$
2. $\check{\check{R}} = R$
3. $\widetilde{S\circ R} = \check{R}\circ\check{S}$
4. $\widetilde{R\cup S} = \check{R}\cup\check{S}$ and $\widetilde{R\cap S} = \check{R}\cap\check{S}$
5. $S\circ R \subseteq \overline{T}$ iff $\check{S}\circ T \subseteq \overline{R}$

[15] I is some set used to index the sets in the partition. If M is infinite, I can be an infinite set. Note that we do not require that $A_i \neq A_j$ for $i \neq j$; an example where the same partition set can have different indices is given in (39a).

Exercise 16.3.3
Verify:

1. R is functional iff $R \circ \check{R} \subseteq id_M$
2. R is injective iff $\check{R} \circ R \subseteq id_M$
3. $dom(R) = M$ (R is 'left-total') iff $id_M \subseteq \check{R} \circ R$
4. R is reflexive iff $id_M \subseteq R$

Exercise 16.3.4
Classify the following relations according to the properties in (26) (suitable domains are presupposed):

1. x is a sister of y
2. x is not identical to y
3. x is an ancestor of y
4. $x + y$ is odd (thus: xRy iff $x + y$ is odd, where $x, y \in \mathbb{N}$)
5. $x + y$ is even

Exercise 16.3.5
Express the following properties R by means of inclusions or identities as in Exercise 16.3.3:

1. R is symmetric
2. R is asymmetric
3. R is transitive

Exercise 16.3.6
Verify (29).

Exercise 16.3.7 (properties of order relations)
Consider a total order $\leqslant$ (with corresponding strict version $<$) on some domain. a is a *largest element* if for all b, $b \leqslant a$, and correspondingly for *smallest element*. An (immediate) *successor* of a is a smallest element among those greater than a, i.e. an element b such that $a < b$ and for all b', if $a < b'$ then $b \leqslant b'$. Similarly for *predecessor*. $\leqslant$ is *well-founded* if there is no infinite descending sequence of elements $a_1 > a_2 > a_3 > \ldots$. Finally, $\leqslant$ is *dense* if between two elements there is always a third, i.e. if $a < b$ implies that there is c such that $a < c < b$.

1. Show that a smallest (largest) element, if it exists, is unique.
2. Verify that an element has at most one successor.
3. Examine the orders in (30) and (32) regarding these properties:
   (a) 'has a smallest (largest) element'
   (b) 'every element has a successor (predecessor)'
   (c) 'is well-founded'
   (d) 'is dense' (If you find no example, invent one!)

Exercise 16.3.8
Draw a Hasse-diagram for the set $\mathcal{P}(\{a, b, c\})$, partially ordered by $\subseteq$. (The diagram becomes especially nice if you draw it as a cube.)

Exercise 16.3.9
If R is a relation in M and $A \subseteq M$, let $R{\restriction}A$, *R restricted to A*, be $R \cap A^2$.

1. Verify that if R is a partial (total) order on M then $R{\restriction}A$ a partial (total) order on A.
2. Which of the properties mentioned in Exercise 16.3.7:3 are preserved when you go from M to $A \subseteq M$?
3. *What is the common logical form of the properties that are preserved?

Exercise 16.3.10
Check that (39) is true.

Exercise 16.3.11 (from preorders to partial orders)
Let $\leqslant$ be a preorder, and define: $a \sim b$ iff $a \leqslant b \;\&\; b \leqslant a$.

1. Show that $\sim$ is an equivalence relation.
2. Let $[a]$ be the equivalence class of a, i.e. $[a] = \{a' : a' \sim a\}$. Define a relation $\leqslant'$ between the equivalence classes: $[a] \leqslant' [b]$ iff $a \leqslant b$. Show that $\leqslant'$ is well-defined, i.e. that

   if $a \sim a'$ and $b \sim b'$, then $[a] \leqslant' [b]$ iff $[a'] \leqslant' [b']$.

3. Show that $\leqslant'$ is a partial order.

Exercise 16.3.12
Suppose R and S are equivalence relations on M. Investigate which of the following relations are also equivalence relations (possibly on some subset of M).

1. $\breve{R}$
2. $R \cap S$
3. $R \cup S$
4. $R \circ S$

16.4. Countable sets

A set is called *countable* if it has at most as many elements as the set $\mathbb{N} = \{0, 1, 2, \ldots\}$ of natural numbers. Terminology varies a bit; sometimes A is called countable if it has *exactly* as many elements as $\mathbb{N}$. The difference is that in the former case, also finite sets are classified as countable. We shall follow that terminology here, and say that A is *countably infinite* or *denumerable* if it has as many elements as $\mathbb{N}$.

But we need to explain what it means for two sets to "have the same number of elements", in other words that they are *equinumerous*:

Definition 16.4.1 (equinumerosity)
A is *equinumerous* with B if there is a bijection from A to B.

One may say that modern set theory began when Georg Cantor in 1874 with this definition as point of departure started to compare the number of elements in various sets. The definition builds on the clear intuition that if one can pair each element of A with a unique element of B in such a way that no elements of B remain, then A and B have the same number of elements. This clearly holds for finite sets, but the definition applies to infinite sets as well. And it seems to contradict another intuition, namely, that if you remove some elements from a set, there are fewer elements left. This does not hold for infinite sets, for example, the sets $\mathbb{N}$ and $\mathbb{N} - \{0\}$ are equinumerous,

$$\{0, 1, 2, 3, \ldots\}$$
$$\{1, 2, 3, 4, \ldots\}$$

via the one-one correspondence $f(n) = n+1$. The conclusion, according to Cantor and modern set theory, is that the latter intuition is correct for *finite* sets, but not for infinite sets. Indeed, the intuition comes from thinking about finite sets, and one cannot expect that all such intuitions should transfer to the infinite case. The first intution, on the other hand, about equinumerosity, seems to work fine for infinite sets too. We note (the proof is an exercise):

(40) a. 'Is equinumerous with' is an equivalence relation.

b. If A is equinumerous to $\varnothing$, then $A = \varnothing$. [Cf. footnote 8.]

Now there are several ways to give a precise definition of 'countable'. The following definition relies on the idea of *counting*, i.e. that the elements of the set can be *counted*: first, second, third, etc.

Definition 16.4.2 (countable sets)
A set A is *countable* if either $A = \varnothing$ or there is a *surjective* function from $\mathbb{N}$ to A.

If f is such a function, then $f(0), f(1), f(2), \ldots$ will enumerate the elements of A (provided $A \neq \varnothing$), that is,

$$A = \{f(0), f(1), f(2), \ldots\}$$

So when we write

$$A = \{a_0, a_1, a_2, \ldots\}$$

we mean precisely that there is such a function. Surjectivity guarantees that no elements of A are left out in the enumeration. But we do allow *repetitions* (i.e. we did *not* require that the function is injective).

That's essential in order to treat finite sets as countable—for them the enumeration *must* have (infinitely many) repetitions. To exclude the finite sets, we use the following notion.

Definition 16.4.3 (denumerable sets)
A set A is *denumerable*, or *countably infinite*, if there is a *bijective* function from $\mathbb{N}$ to A, that is, if A is equinumerous with $\mathbb{N}$.

Now we must check that these definitions agree with the one we first sketched:

(41) A is countable iff A is equinumerous with a subset of $\mathbb{N}$.

This seems intuitively obvious. But since we now have precise definitions of 'countable' and 'equinumerous', we must give a *proof* of (41). The proof then confirms that our definitions work as they should.

Proof. Suppose first that A is equinumerous with $N_0 \subseteq \mathbb{N}$. If $N_0 = \varnothing$, then $A = \varnothing$ according to (40b), so A is countable. If $N_0 \neq \varnothing$, then $A \neq \varnothing$, and there is a bijection f from N_0 to A. Fix some $a_0 \in A$, and define the function f^* as follows:

$$f^*(n) = \begin{cases} f(n) & \text{if } n \in N_0 \\ a_0 & \text{if } n \in \mathbb{N} - N_0 \end{cases}$$

Then f^* is a surjective function from $\mathbb{N}$ to A, so A is countable.

In the other direction, suppose A is countable. If $A = \varnothing$, then A is equinumerous with $\varnothing \subseteq \mathbb{N}$. If $A \neq \varnothing$ there is a surjective function f from $\mathbb{N}$ to A, i.e. an enumeration of A. But if we successively delete all numbers n that give repetitions, i.e. all numbers n such that $f(n) = f(m)$ for some $m < n$, then the restriction of f to the set N_0 of the remaining numbers will be both surjective and injective, i.e. a bijection from N_0 to A, so A is equinumerous with N_0. □

16.4.1. *Finite and infinite sets

The set N_0 in the proof above can be finite or infinite, and the same holds for A. But strictly speaking we haven't defined 'finite' or 'infinite'. An intuitive understanding of these concepts suffices for most purposes. But we can also give precise definitions. If the natural numbers are given, there is an easy way:

Definition 16.4.4
A is *finite* if A is equinumerous with $\{0, 1, \ldots, n-1\}$, for some number n.[16] Otherwise, A is *infinite*.

[16]This includes the case $n = 0$; then A is equinumerous with $\varnothing$, i.e. $A = \varnothing$.

So we take $\{0, 1, \ldots, n-1\}$ as the 'canonical' set with n elements. And since it is fairly clear (but can be proved by induction) that $\mathbb{N}$ is not equinumerous with any set $\{0, 1, \ldots, n-1\}$, it follows that $\mathbb{N}$ is an infinite set. Another direct consequence is:

(42) If A is equinumerous with B, then A is finite iff B is finite.[17]

But we would also like to know that (43) holds. Again, this seems obvious, but for the record, we would like to have a proof that it really follows from our definitions.

(43) A is countable iff A is finite or equinumerous with $\mathbb{N}$.

Proof. From right to left this is clear. For if A is equinumerous with $\mathbb{N}$, then A is countable by (41) (since $\mathbb{N} \subseteq \mathbb{N}$), and if A is finite, then A is equinumerous with $\{0, 1, \ldots, n-1\} \subseteq \mathbb{N}$ and thus, again by (41), countable. In the other direction, we can suppose $A \neq \varnothing$. So there is a surjection f from $\mathbb{N}$ to A. Define by induction a new function h by the following procedure:

(a) $h(0) = f(0)$

(b) Suppose $h(0), \ldots, h(n-1)$ have been defined. Let $h(n) = f(k)$, where k is the smallest number s.t. $f(k) \neq h(0), \ldots, h(n-1)$, *if there is* such a number k. If there is no such number, stop the procedure.

By definition, h is one-one, i.e. an injective function. If the above procedure stops for some n, this means that there is no element of A distinct from the already chosen elements, i.e. $h(0), \ldots, h(n-1)$, so h must be a bijection from $\{0, 1, \ldots, n-1\}$ to A, and A is finite.

If the procedure doesn't stop, then for every n there is an element of A distinct from $h(0), \ldots, h(n-1)$, which means h is defined for every n, i.e. $dom(h) = \mathbb{N}$. Moreover, $range(h) = A$. For take any $a \in A$, and let m be the smallest number such that $f(m) = a$ (there is such a number, since f is surjective). Then, by our construction, a will be selected by h no later than at step m, that is, $h(n) = f(m) = a$ for some $n \leqslant m$. Thus, h is a bijection from $\mathbb{N}$ to A, and A is equinumerous with $\mathbb{N}$. □

If you remove elements from a finite set, there are fewer left. We have seen that, for example, $\mathbb{N}$ does not have this property. This can in fact be taken as another definition of infinity (and thus of 'finite'), a definition which is interesting because it doesn't mention the natural numbers at all. The idea was first formulated by the German mathematician Richard Dedekind.

[17] If f is a bijection from A to B, and g is a bijection from $\{0, 1, \ldots, n-1\}$ to A, then $f \circ g$ is a bijection from $\{0, 1, \ldots, n-1\}$ to B (cf. Exercise 16.2.2), and similarly if we start from B instead.

Definition 16.4.5
A is *Dedekind-infinite* if there is $a \in A$ s.t A equinumerous with $A - \{a\}$.

We have the following fact, which again confirms that (some) different intuitions we have about infinite sets agree with each other.

(44) A is infinite iff A is Dedekind-infinite.

Proof. It is easy to see that no finite set can be Dedekind-infinite. In the other direction, suppose first A is countably infinite, so there is bijection f from A to $\mathbb{N}$. Then clearly $A - \{a\}$ is equinumerous with $\mathbb{N} - \{f(a)\}$, which we have already seen is equinumerous with $\mathbb{N}$. In the general case we don't know that A is countable, so, given $a \in A$, we take a countably infinite subset B of A such that $a \in B$.[18] As we just saw, there is a bijection g from B to $B - \{a\}$. Now define h by:

$$h(n) = \begin{cases} g(n) & \text{if } n \in B \\ n & \text{if } n \in A - B \end{cases}$$

Then one checks that h is bijection from A to $A - \{a\}$. □

16.4.2. Examples of countable sets

We give some important examples of countably infinite or denumerable sets. First a simple case:

(45) The set of integers $\mathbb{Z} = \{\ldots, -3, -2, -1, 0, 1, 2, 3, \ldots\}$ is denumerable.

Proof. Map the even numbers on the integers $\geqslant 0$, and the odd numbers on the negative integers. I.e. the following function is a bijection:

$$\begin{cases} f(2n) & = & n \\ f(2n+1) & = & -(n+1) \end{cases}$$

□

(46) The set $\mathbb{N}^2 = \{(m, n) : m, n \in \mathbb{N}\}$ is denumerable.

Proof. We give an intuitive argument. The set $\mathbb{N}^2$ can be represented as an infinite square, and we can enumerate the pairs in this square by 'following diagonals', for example, like this:

[18]It seems intuitively clear that there is a such a set B, but to prove this in set theory, one actually needs (a weak version of) the Axiom of Choice.

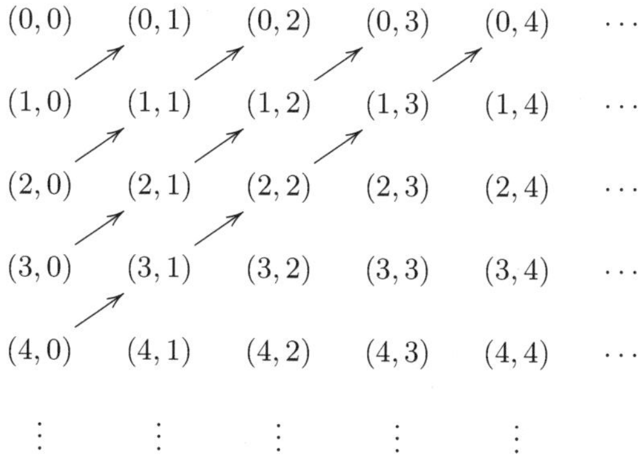

So (0,0) is the 0:th pair, (1,0) the 1:st, (0,1) the 2:nd, (2,0) the 3:rd, etc. It is intuitively clear that every ordered pair in $\mathbb{N}^2$ will appear exactly once in this enumeration, so we have a bijection from $\mathbb{N}$ to $\mathbb{N}^2$. □

With the same method we can also conclude:

(47) The set $\mathbb{Q}^+$ of positive rational numbers is denumerable.

Proof. $\mathbb{Q}^+ = \{m/n\colon m, n > 0\}$. So we can enumerate the expressions m/n 'diagonalwise' just as we enumerated $\mathbb{N}^2$, except that the row $m = 0$ and the column $n = 0$ are excluded. In contrast with the enumeration of $\mathbb{N}^2$, this enumeration is not injective, since the same rational number will occur several times. (In fact, every positive rational number occurs infinitely many times.) But we obtain a *surjective* function from $\mathbb{N}$ to $\mathbb{Q}^+$, i.e. all positive rational numbers will be enumerated. So by Definition 16.4.2, $\mathbb{Q}^+$ is countable. And clearly $\mathbb{Q}^+$ is not finite (every positive natural number is an element of $\mathbb{Q}^+$), so it follows from (43) that $\mathbb{Q}^+$ is equinumerous with $\mathbb{N}$. □

This fact is rather remarkable at first sight. On a 'number line' the natural numbers are scattered but the rational numbers are *dense*: between two rational numbers there is always a third. So between two rational numbers, no matter how close, there are always infinitely many other rational numbers. Nonetheless, there are *as many* rational numbers as natural numbers. The moral is that you *can* enumerate the rational numbers (as we just saw), but *not in order of magnitude*.

(48) If $A_0, A_1, A_2, \ldots$ is a (countable) sequence of countable sets, then $\bigcup_n A_n$ is also countable.

Proof. The assumption is that for every n there is a surjective function f_n from $\mathbb{N}$ to A_n. (The union of finitely many countable sets, say, $A_0, A_1, \ldots, A_k$, can be seen as a special case, by letting $A_n = A_k$ for all $n > k$.) These functions can also be represented in an infinite table:

$$\begin{array}{lllll} A_0: & f_0(0) & f_0(1) & f_0(2) & \cdots \\ A_1: & f_1(0) & f_1(1) & f_1(2) & \cdots \\ A_2: & f_2(0) & f_2(1) & f_2(2) & \cdots \\ \vdots & \vdots & \vdots & \vdots & \end{array}$$

containing all elements of $\bigcup_n A_n$, which can be enumerated just as before. Again there may be repetitions: there may be common elements of different A_n, and the functions f_n may also contain repetitions. But the enumeration is surjective, which is all we need. □

By a similar argument, one shows:

(49) The set of all finite subsets of a countable set is countable.

Finally, an application to logic:

Fact 16.4.6
If L is a countable vocabulary, the set of L-formulas is also countable.

The proofs of (49) and Fact 16.4.6 are left as exercises.

16.4.3. Exercises to Section 16.4

Exercise 16.4.1
Verify that (40) holds.

Exercise 16.4.2
Show that a finite set is not Dedekind-infinite.

Exercise 16.4.3
*Specify explicitly a bijection $f : \mathbb{N}^2 \to \mathbb{N}$ according to the table in the proof of (46). [Hint: The only mathematical fact needed is that, for every n, $1 + 2 + 3 + \ldots + n = n(n + 1)/2$.]

Exercise 16.4.4
Show that for every k, the set $\mathbb{N}^k$ (the set of k-tuples of natural numbers) is countable. [Hint: Recall that we defined $(a_0, \ldots, a_{k+1}) = ((a_0, \ldots, a_k), a_{k+1})$.]

Exercise 16.4.5
Prove (49). [Hint: If A is countable, let $\mathcal{P}^n(A)$ be the set of all subsets of A with exactly n elements, and use (48).]

Exercise 16.4.6
Prove Fact 16.4.6. [Hint: Formulas are finite sequences of symbols.]

16.5. Cantor's Theorem and uncountable sets

We just saw several examples of infinite sets that all turned out to be countable. But the big discovery of Cantor, one which stunned the mathematical world in his time, was that there also has to be infinite sets that, in a precise sense, have *more* elements than $\mathbb{N}$. We call such sets *uncountable*: they cannot be enumerated or 'counted'.

A typical example of an uncountable set is the power set of $\mathbb{N}$, i.e. $\mathcal{P}(\mathbb{N})$. In fact, Cantor showed that for every set A, $\mathcal{P}(A)$ has more elements than A. This is clear for finite sets (if A has n elements, $\mathcal{P}(A)$ has 2^n elements). Cantor generalized this to all sets.

Cantor's proof of this remarkable result also introduced a proof method that has turned out to be enormously fruitful, in various mathematical as well as logical contexts; the so-called *diagonal method*. The incompleteness and undecidability theorems, and much of the work in Chapter 15, rely on this method. We start with Cantor's Theorem for $\mathbb{N}$:

(50) The set $\mathcal{P}(\mathbb{N})$ is (infinite but) not countable.

Proof. That $\mathcal{P}(\mathbb{N})$ is infinite is clear, since $\{n\} \in \mathcal{P}(\mathbb{N})$ for every n. We now show that the set $2^{\mathbb{N}}$ of functions from $\mathbb{N}$ to $\{0, 1\}$ is uncountable. As observed in Section 16.1, $\mathcal{P}(\mathbb{N})$ and $2^{\mathbb{N}}$ are essentially the same mathematical object.

The proof is a *reductio* argument: *Assume* that we have an enumeration $f_0, f_1, f_2, \ldots$ of $2^{\mathbb{N}}$. We derive a contradiction by construing a function in $2^{\mathbb{N}}$ which cannot be in that enumeration.

A function $f \in 2^{\mathbb{N}}$ corresponds to the sequence $f(0), f(1), f(2), \ldots$ of 0's and 1's, and every such sequence of 0's and 1's corresponds to a unique function in $2^{\mathbb{N}}$. So we can represent the assumed enumeration in a table as before:

$$
\begin{array}{llllll}
f_0: & f_0(0) & f_0(1) & f_0(2) & f_0(3) & \cdots \\
f_1: & f_1(0) & f_1(1) & f_1(2) & f_1(3) & \cdots \\
f_2: & f_2(0) & f_2(1) & f_2(2) & f_2(3) & \cdots \\
f_3: & f_3(0) & f_3(1) & f_3(2) & f_3(3) & \cdots \\
\vdots & \vdots & \vdots & \vdots & \vdots &
\end{array}
$$

Now we define a new sequence of 0's and 1's by *changing the diagonal* (marked in the above diagram): if there is a 1 in the diagonal, we change to 0, and vice versa. In other words, we define a function g

from $\mathbb{N}$ to $\{0, 1\}$ by

$$g(n) = \begin{cases} 0 & \text{if } f_n(n) = 1 \\ 1 & \text{if } f_n(n) = 0 \end{cases}$$

Then we have $g \in 2^{\mathbb{N}}$, but

$$g \neq f_n, \text{ for every } n$$

This is because $g(n) \neq f_n(n)$, so the function g differes from each f_n on at least one argument (namely n), and is thus distinct from f_n, for every n. But this contradicts the assumption that $f_0, f_1, f_2, \ldots$ was an enumeration of *all* of $2^{\mathbb{N}}$. Thus, there can be no such enumeration. □

The diagonal method is very general: given an enumeration of countable sequences we can always construct a similar sequence which is not in the given enumeration. It doesn't have to be sequences of 0's and 1's. Here is a striking mathematical application:

(51) The set of real numbers between 0 and 1 is uncountable.

Proof. The proof uses the fact that all such real numbers can be written as infinite decimal expansions:

$$0, a_0 a_1 a_2 a_3 \ldots$$

wher every a_n is a numeral between 0 and 9.[19] Every enumeration of such decimal expansions can be written in an infinite table as before, and we obtain a new infinite decimal expansion by changing in the diagonal. That is, for every enumeration of real numbers between 0 and 1 we can construe a real number between 0 and 1 which is not in the enumeration. Therefore, there is no enumeration of *all* such numbers. □

16.5.1. Cantor's Theorem and cardinal numbers

The proof of Cantor's result for an arbitrary set A builds on the same idea, but has a more elegant proof.

Theorem 16.5.1 (Cantor's Theorem)
If A is any set, there is no surjective function from A to $\mathcal{P}(A)$ (in particular, A and $\mathcal{P}(A)$ are not equinumerous).

Proof. Suppose that $f : A \to \mathcal{P}(A)$. This means that for every $x \in A$ we have $f(x) \subseteq A$. Consider

$$C = \{x \in A : x \notin f(x)\}$$

[19] We write e.g. 1/3 as 0,33333..., and 1/2 as 0,49999...

$C \subseteq A$, so if f is surjective, there is $x_0 \in A$ such that $C = f(x_0)$. That is, for all $x \in A$ we have:

$$x \in f(x_0) \Leftrightarrow x \notin f(x)$$

But this leads to contradiction for $x = x_0$! Thus, f cannot be surjective. □

In the case $A = \mathbb{N}$, diagonalization meant changing in the diagonal of an infinite table. More generally, *diagonalization* is, given a relation $R(x, y)$, to consider $R(x, x)$ (and do something with that). In the above proof, $R(x, y)$ is the relation $x \notin f(y)$. It is remarkable (and a bit of a mystery) that this simple trick has so many applications. Parts III and IV contain several applications.

Cantor's Theorem is the starting point of the theory of *cardinal numbers*. We defined what it means for two sets to have the *same* number of elements, and now we furthermore say that B has *more* elements than A if there is an injection from A to B, but A and B are *not* equinumerous (so there is no *bijection* from A to B). Then Cantor's Theorem says that $\mathcal{P}(A)$ always has more elements than A.

Furthermore, one can introduce *cardinal numbers*, (as special kinds of sets) which represent the number of elements of sets. So if $|A|$ is the cardinal number of A, Cantor's Theorem is that $|A| < |\mathcal{P}(A)|$. The theorem also implies that we have an infinite increasing sequence of cardinal numbers:

$$(52) \qquad |\mathbb{N}| < |\mathcal{P}(\mathbb{N})| < |\mathcal{P}(\mathcal{P}(\mathbb{N}))| < |\mathcal{P}(\mathcal{P}(\mathcal{P}(\mathbb{N})))| < \ldots$$

It is easy to see that the set $\mathbb{R}$ of real numbers (or the set of real numbers between 0 and 1) has the same cardinality as $\mathcal{P}(\mathbb{N})$. The famous *Continuum Problem* is whether there are any (sets with) cardinal numbers *between* $|\mathbb{N}|$ and $|\mathcal{P}(\mathbb{N})|$. The claim that there are none, is the *Continuum Hypothesis* (CH). This is one of the main open problems (or perhaps enigmas) of set theory. Gödel showed in 1940 that CH is *consistent* with ZFC (the negation of CH cannot be proved), and Paul Cohen showed in 1963 that CH is *independent* of ZFC (CH cannot be proved either), and there seem to be no intuitively obvious axioms that decide CH one way or the other.

The theory of cardinal numbers is used all the time in model theory. In this book we only touched on it briefly in Chapter 6 when talking about the *size* of models, and of vocabularies. In particular, in the formulation and proof of Tarski's Theorem (Theorem 6.7.5) we used an uncountable vocabulary to build a model of at least the same size. But this is a very modest use of cardinal numbers: instead of saying, as we did, "let I be of cardinal κ and $\{c_i : i \in I\}$ be a set of κ new individual constants", we could have said "Let I be any uncountable set, and $\{c_i : i \in I\}$ an equinumerous set of individual constants", thus avoiding any mention of cardinal numbers. The main point is that there are uncountable sets of (infinitely) many sizes, and we can construct a model of (at least) any such size of a theory, provided the theory has at least one infinite model.

However, the proof did rely on the fact that the Completeness Theorem (and hence the Compactness Theorem) holds also for uncountable vocabularies. We sketched a proof of this in Exercise 5.6.7. That proof used the theory of *ordinal numbers,* which is a generalization of *counting* to the infinite, just as cardinal numbers generalize the notion of *size* to the infinite. In particular, it used *transfinite induction,* which is a generalization of ordinary induction (over $\mathbb{N}$). The basic theory of ordinal and cardinal numbers can be found in any introduction to set theory, and we will not say more about it here.

16.5.2. Russell's Paradox

There is a striking similarity between Cantor's proof and the reasoning in Russell's Paradox. That paradox arises if one assumes that every property $P(x)$ has a set A as extension: $A = \{x : P(x)\}$. For consider the set R of all sets that are not elements of themselves:

$$R = \{x : x \notin x\}$$

Paradox results when you ask if $R \in R$ or not. For every x, $x \in R \Leftrightarrow x \notin x$, but this leads to contradiction when x is R. What went wrong?

Russell's Paradox is usually taken to show that the class V of all sets is not itself a set, but a proper class (Section 16.1). The Axiom of Separation says that if B is a set and $\varphi(x)$ a formula in the (first-order) language of set theory, then

$$\{x \in B : \varphi(x)\}$$

is also a set (a subset of B). So if V were a set, the definition of R above would be correct, since every set is an element of V, and we have a contradiction.

The reasoning in Russell's Paradox can be seen as a special case of Cantor's argument above. If V is a set, then $\mathcal{P}(V)$ is also a set (by the Power Set Axiom), and since V contains *all* sets, we have in particular

$$\mathcal{P}(V) \subseteq V$$

But this means that the identity function id_V, where $id_V(x) = x$, is a surjective function from V to $\mathcal{P}(V)$,[20] which, as we just saw, leads to contradiction! So Cantor's set C in this case becomes exactly Russell's set R.

[20] If $x \in \mathcal{P}(V)$ then $x \in V$, since V contains all sets, so $id_V : \mathcal{P}(V) \to V$. If we restrict attention to sets whose members are also sets (as one does in *ZF*), then we have that if $x \in V$, all elements of x are also elements of V, that is, $x \subseteq V$, i.e. $x \in \mathcal{P}(V)$, so id_V is surjective. If sets are allowed to have other things than sets as elements, we let V be the class of *everything*, and the same reasoning goes through.

16.6. Mathematical induction

Probably the most commonly used method of proof in the study of logics and their properties is mathematical induction. Such proofs occur in almost every chapter of this book. For the record, we state the principle here, restricted to the natural numbers (which is all we need).

To prove that *every* number n has a property P, it suffices to prove two things: (i) 0 has P; (ii) for every n, if n has P then $n+1$ has P. Besides this formulation, there are a few others:

(Ind) If $P(0)$ and $\forall n(P(n) \Rightarrow P(n+1))$, then $\forall n P(n)$.

(s-Ind) If $\forall n(\forall m(m < n \Rightarrow P(m)) \Rightarrow P(n))$, then $\forall n P(n)$.

(LNP) If $P(n)$ holds for some n, there is a smallest n s.t. $P(n)$ holds.

(Ind) is the principle we just mentioned. (s-Ind) is the principle of *strong induction,* also called *course-of-values induction,* or *well-founded induction.* It says that if, for any number n, the assumption that $P(m)$ holds for all smaller m implies that $P(n)$ holds, then $P(n)$ holds for all n. (LNP) is the *least number principle.* It doesn't look like an induction principle, but in fact all three principles are equivalent:

Fact 16.6.1
(Ind), (s-Ind), *and* (LNP) *are equivalent.*

Proof. In our formal theory of arithmetic *PA*, these equivalences are theorems, provided P is a property that can be expressed by an L_{PA}-formula; see Exercise 9.10.3. But the equivalences don't depend on this assumption about P. We illustrate by showing that (Ind) implies (s-Ind); leaving the other implications as exercises.

Assume that

(*) for all n: $\forall m(m < n \Rightarrow P(m))$ implies $P(n)$.

We must show $\forall n P(n)$. In fact, we use (Ind) to prove something stronger, namely, that every number n has the following property $Q(n)$: for every $m < n$, $P(m)$ holds. $\forall n Q(n)$ implies $\forall n P(n)$: given n, we have $Q(n+1)$ by assumption, and since $n < n+1$, we also have $P(n)$.

The base case, $Q(0)$, holds trivially, since no number is smaller than 0. Suppose $Q(n)$ holds (the induction hypothesis); we must show $Q(n+1)$. Take any $m < n+1$; we must show $P(m)$. Either $m < n$ or $m = n$. If $m < n$, we have $P(m)$ by induction hypothesis. If $m = n$, the induction hypothesis together with (*) entails that $P(m)$ holds. □

This proof illustrates a common situation: in order to prove that every number has some property P, you need to find a stronger property Q and show by induction that every number has property Q: the inductive proof doesn't work directly for P. Finding a suitable Q can be the hardest part of the proof.

Most proofs by induction in this book are not directly about numbers; rather, we do induction 'on formulas' (say). This takes the following form: in order to prove that every FOL-formula φ (in some vocabulary) has property P, you prove:

(53)
a. If φ is atomic, then $P(\varphi)$.
b. If $P(\varphi)$, then $P(\neg\varphi)$.
c. If $P(\varphi)$ and $P(\psi)$, then $P(\varphi \wedge \psi)$, and so on for other connectives.
d. If $P(\varphi)$, then $P(\exists x\varphi)$ and $P(\forall x\varphi)$.

Since the set of formulas is defined inductively with clauses corresponding to the cases above, this will show that $P(\varphi)$ holds for every formula φ. It is possible to extend the induction principles from induction over numbers to induction over suitably defined syntactic objects. But it is not necessary. If we let the *degree* of a formula φ be the number of occurrences of connectives and quantifiers in it, we see that (53) is really an instance of proof by induction over numbers, using (Ind) with the property $Q(n)$: $P(\varphi)$ holds for all formulas φ of degree $\leqslant n$. $Q(0)$ is the base case of atomic formulas, which have degree 0. And if a complex formula has degree $n+1$, then its proper subformulas have degree $\leqslant n$, so the induction hypothesis (that $P(\psi)$ holds for all formulas ψ of degree $\leqslant n$) can be used.

If an inference system is given, we can sometimes prove facts about it by induction on the length of proofs. This is especially clear for Hilbert type system, where the length of a proof is simply the number of (occurrences of) sentences in the proof sequence. In Chapter 3.3.2 we proved the Deduction Theorem in this way; a look at that proof reveals that the relevant property $P(n)$ (which was called (A_n)) is proved by means of (s-Ind).

The property $P(n)$ that we wish to show holds for all n can be any property, also a complex one involving quantification. For example, consider the proof of the Isomorphism Lemma (Chapter 6.4). We are given two models $\mathcal{M}, \mathcal{M}'$ for a vocabulary L, and an isomorphism h from $\mathcal{M}$ to $\mathcal{M}'$. Our proof using (Ind) in effect showed that the following holds for every n:

$P(n)$ For every k and every L-formula $\varphi(x_1, \ldots, x_k)$ of degree $\leqslant n$, and all $a_1, \ldots, a_k \in M$, we have

$$\mathcal{M} \models \varphi[a_1, \ldots, a_n] \text{ iff } \mathcal{M}' \models \varphi[h(a_1), \ldots, h(a_n)]$$

$P(n)$ contains universal quantification over the number k of free variables in the formula, and over k-tuples of objects in M. This is necessary: we cannot let k be a fixed parameter, since when $\varphi(x_1, \ldots, x_k)$ is $\exists y \psi(y, x_1, \ldots, x_k)$, we must use the induction hypothesis on ψ, which may have $k+1$ free variables.

In other cases, fixed parameters may be present. If we want to show that $R(k, m, n)$ holds for all k, m, n by *induction on* n, we fix arbitrary numbers k, m, and prove that $R(k, m, 0)$ holds, and that for all n, if $R(k, m, n)$ holds, then so does $R(k, m, n+1)$. Several examples of such proofs in *PA* appear in Chapter 9.

So far we have talked about *proofs* by induction. These proofs are enabled by *inductive definitions* of the relevant objects. For example, the natural numbers can be taken to be defined by these two clauses:

a. 0 is a natural number.
b. If n is a natural number, then $n+1$ is a natural number.

Likewise, the inductive definitions of terms, formulas, etc. allowed us to prove various properties of these objects by induction. There is a mathematical theory of inductive definitions, but we don't need it here: the examples in the text are clear enough (and we treat the special case of definitions by primitive recursion in detail in Chapter 8).

16.6.1. Exercises to Section 16.6

Exercise 16.6.1
Prove the following facts by induction:

(a) $1 + 2 + \ldots + n \; = \; \frac{n(n+1)}{2}$

(b) $3^0 + 3^1 + 3^2 + \ldots + 3^n \; = \; \frac{3^{n+1}-1}{2}$

(c) $1 + \frac{1}{2^2} + \frac{1}{2^2} + \ldots + \frac{1}{(n+1)^2} \; \leqslant \; 2 - \frac{1}{n+1}$

Exercise 16.6.2
Complete the proof of Fact 16.6.1.

Exercise 16.6.3
Give an inductive definition of the degree of a formula, i.e. define the function $dg(\varphi)$ for every L-formula φ, where L is some vocabulary.

Bibliography

Barwise, J. (1978). "On branching quantifiers in English". *Journal of Philosophical Logic* 8, pp. 47–80.

Barwise, J. and R. Cooper (1981). "Generalized quantifiers and natural language". *Linguistics & Philosophy* 4, pp. 159–219.

Blackburn, P., M. de Rijke, and Y. Venema (2001). *Modal Logic*. Cambridge University Press.

Bolzano, B. (1837). *Wissenschaftslehre*. Sulzbach: J. E. von Seidel. Selections transl. by Jan Berg published by D. Reidel as *Theory of Science*, 1973.

Boolos, G. (1993). *The Logic of Provability*. Cambridge: Cambridge University Press.

Boolos, G. S., J. P. Burgess, and R. C. Jeffrey (2007). *Computability and Logic*. Cambridge: Cambridge University Press.

Copeland, J. (2017). "The Church-Turing Thesis". In: *The Stanford Encyclopedia of Philosophy*. Ed. by E. N. Zalta. Winter 2017. Metaphysics Research Lab, Stanford University. URL: `https://plato.stanford.edu/archives/win2017/entries/church-turing/`.

Dershowitz, N. and Y. Gurevich (2008). "A natural axiomatization of computability and proof of Church's Thesis". *Bulletin of Symbolic Logic* 14, pp. 299–350.

Feferman, S. (1960). "Arithmetization of metamathematics in a general setting". *Fundamenta Mathematica* 49, pp. 35–92.

Feferman, S. et al., eds. (1990). *Kurt Gödel: Collected Works (Volume 2)*. Oxford: Oxford University Press.

Franzén, T. (2004). *Inexhaustibility. A Non-Exhaustive Treatment*. Lecture Notes in Logic 16. Association for Symbolic Logic, CRC Press.

Franzén, T. (2005). *Gödel's Theorem: An Incomplete Guide to its Use and Abuse*. Natick, MA: A. K. Peters, Ltd.

Frege, G. (1879). *Begriffsschrift*. Halle a. S.: Louis Nebert (Transl. as *Concept Script*, by S. Bauer-Mengelberg, in J. van Heijenoort (ed.), *From Frege to Gödel: A Source Book in Mathematical Logic, 1879–1931*, Cambridge MA: Harvard University Press, 1967.)

Gödel, K. (1946). "Remarks before the Princeton Bicentennial Conference". In: *Feferman et al. 1990*. Oxford University Press, pp. 150–153.

Hájek, P. and P. Pudlák (1993). *Metamathematics of First-Order Arithmetic*. Springer.

Halbach, V. and A. Visser (2014a). "Self-reference in arithmetic I". *Review of Symbolic Logic* 7.4, pp. 671–691.

Halbach, V. and A. Visser (2014b). "Self-reference in arithmetic II". *The Review of Symbolic Logic* 7.4, pp. 692–712.

Hella, L., J. Väänänen, and D. Westerståhl (1997). "Definability of polyadic lifts of generalized quantifiers". *Journal of Logic, Language and Information* 6, pp. 305–335.

Hilbert, D. and W. Ackermann (1928). *Grundzüge der theoretischen Logik*. Springer-Verlag. English transl. as *Principles of Mathematical Logic*, AMS Publishing, 1950.

Hodges, W. (1993). *Model Theory*. Vol. 42. Encyclopedia of Mathematics and its Applications. Cambridge University Press.

Hodges, W. (1997). *A Shorter Model Theory*. Cambridge University Press.

Kleene, S. C. (1952). *Introduction to Metamathematics*. North-Holland.

Kripke, S. (2013). "The Church-Turing 'Thesis' as a special corollary of Gödel's Completeness Theorem". In: *Computability: Turing, Gödel, Church and Beyond*. Ed. by B. Copeland, C. Posy, and O. Shagrir. Cambridge MA: MIT Press.

Leitgeb, H. and A. Carus (2021). "Rudolf Carnap". In: *The Stanford Encyclopedia of Philosophy*. Ed. by E. N. Zalta. Metaphysics Research Lab, Stanford University. URL: `https://plato.stanford.edu/archives/sum2021/entries/carnap/`.

Lindström, P. (1966). "First-order predicate logic with generalized quantifiers". *Theoria* 32, pp. 186–195.

Lindström, P. (1969). "On extensions of elementary logic". *Theoria* 35, pp. 1–11.

Lindström, P. (2003). *Aspects of Incompleteness (second edition)*. Lecture Notes in Logic 10. Natick, Massachusetts: Association for Symbolic Logic, A. K. Peters Ltd.

Mendelson, E. (2015). *Introduction to Mathematical Logic*. 6:th. Taylor & Francis Group, CRC Press.

Montague, R. (1974). *Formal Philosophy* (ed. with an introduction by R. Thomason). Yale: New Haven.

Moschovakis, J. (2015). "Intuitionistic Logic". In: *The Stanford Encyclopedia of Philosophy*. Ed. by E. N. Zalta. Spring 2015. Metaphysics Research Lab, Stanford University. URL: `https://plato.stanford.edu/archives/spr2015/entries/logic-intuitionistic/`.

Mostowski, A. (1957). "On a generalization of quantifiers". *Fundamenta Mathematica* 44, pp. 12–36.

Odifreddi, P. (1999). *Classical Recursion Theory*. 2nd. Elsevier.

Peters, S. and D. Westerståhl (2006). *Quantifiers in Language and Logic*. Oxford: Oxford University Press.

Post, E. (1944). "Recursively enumerable sets of positive integers and their decision problems". *Bull. Am. Math. Soc.* 50, pp. 284–316.

Prawitz, D. (1965). *Natural Deduction: A Proof-Theoretical Study*. Vol. 3. Acta Universitatis Stockholmiensis, Stockholm Studies in Philosophy. Almqvist & Wicksell, reprinted 2006 by Dover Publications, New York.

Rogers, J. (1967). *Theory of Recursive Functions and Effective Computability*. McGraw-Hill.

Shoenfield, J. R. (1967). *Mathematical Logic*. Addison-Wesley.

Smith, P. (2007). *An Introduction to Gödel's Theorems*. Cambridge: Cambridge University Press.

Smoryński, C. (1991). *Logical Number Theory 1. An Introduction*. Springer.

Soare, R. I. (2016). *Turing Computability. Theory and Applications*. Springer.

Sundholm, G. (1983). "Systems of deduction". In: *Handbook of Philosophical Logic, vol. I*. Ed. by D. Gabbay and F. Guenthner. D. Reidel, pp. 133–188.

Tarski, A. (1936). "On the concept of logical consequence". In: *Logic, Semantics, Metamathematics*. Oxford: Clarendon Press, pp. 409–420.

Väänänen, J. (2011). *Models and Games*. Cambridge Studies in Advanced Mathematics. Cambridge University Press.

van Benthem, J. (1986). *Essays in Logical Semantics*. Dordrecht: D. Reidel.

van Benthem, J. (2010). *Modal Logic for Open Minds*. Stanford: CSLI Publications.

Visser, A. (2014). *The interpretability of inconsistency, Feferman's theorem and related results*. Logic Group Preprint Series 318. Faculty of Humanities, Philosophy, Utrecht University.

Westerståhl, D. (2019). "Generalized quantifiers". In: *The Stanford Encyclopedia of Philosophy*. Ed. by E. N. Zalta. Winter 2019. Metaphysics Research Lab, Stanford University. URL: `https://plato.stanford.edu/archives/win2019/entries/generalized-quantifiers/`.

Zach, R. (2019). "Hilbert's program". In: *The Stanford Encyclopedia of Philosophy*. Ed. by E. N. Zalta. Fall. Metaphysics Research Lab, Stanford University. URL: `https://plato.stanford.edu/archives/fall2019/entries/hilbert-program/`.

Index